SOCIETY OF THE MIND

A CYBERTHRILLER

SOCIETY OF THE MIND

Eric L. Harry

HarperCollins*Publishers*

HarperCollins books may be purchased for educational, business, or sales promotional use. For information please write: Special Markets Department, HarperCollins Publishers, Inc., 10 East 53rd Street, New York, NY 10022.

FIRST EDITION

Designed by Alma Hochhauser Orenstein

Library of Congress Cataloging-in-Publication Data

Harry, Eric L.
Society of the mind : a cyberthriller / by Eric L. Harry. — 1st ed.
p. cm.
ISBN 0-06-017694-6
I. Title.
PS3558.A6753S65 1996
813'.54—dc20 96-1188

96 97 98 99 00 ❖/RRD 10 9 8 7 6 5 4 3 2

I dedicate this book to my parents, to whom I owe far more than mere words could ever express

ACKNOWLEDGMENTS

Great thanks and appreciation go to my wonderful wife, Marina, without whose editing and constant support and encouragement this novel could not have been written; to my tireless and loyal agent, Nancy Coffey, and to Bob Thixton, Dick Duane, Jean Free, and all the others at Jay Garon-Brooke Associates who have the patience to put up with me; and to my editors at HarperCollins, Vice President and Associate Publisher Gladys Justin Carr and Elissa Altman. They not only rendered invaluable editorial comments—they were a joy to work with.

And my acknowledgments go also to the many great thinkers whose works I read with awe. To Daniel C. Dennett, director of the Center for Cognitive Studies at Tufts, and author of *Consciousness Explained*, who has deciphered the seemingly indecipherable. To Marvin Minsky, a co-founder of the Artificial Intelligence Laboratory at MIT, whose seminal collection of essays titled *The Society of Mind* provided much more to this author than the obvious. And to the visionary Hans Morevac, director of the Mobile Robot Laboratory at Carnegie Mellon, for the profound dreams and nightmares of *Mind Children: The Future of Robot and Human Intelligence*.

Finally, in memory of Jay Garon, who had a habit of breathing life into the literary careers of the unpublished.

neu•ral net•work (nyoor'/el net'/wûrk) *n.* A web of densely interconnected processing elements, or "neurons," modeled on the architecture of an animal brain. Through interaction of individual neurons, a neural network is able to improve its performance through experience. Also called neu-ro-com-pu-ter.

"Dr. Aldridge?" the messenger asked, holding an envelope in his hand. There was no postmark on the luxuriously thick paper, just "Dr. Laura Aldridge, Harvard Psychology Department"—handprinted in black. When she looked up, the man was gone.

Laura's classroom buzzed in anticipation of the robotic surgery. But color test bars filled the high-definition screen, and Laura used the time to open the letter.

"Dear Dr. Aldridge," it began—the script bold and black and sweeping. "I would like to engage you as a consultant for one week. Tonight at ten P.M., a plane will be waiting at the civil aviation terminal of Logan Airport to bring you to my corporate headquarters. The fee will be one million dollars (U.S.). Thank you for considering this offer."

It was signed "Joseph Gray"—the letters of his name unrestrained by the "Very truly yours" written above.

Joseph Gray—the richest man in the world.

Laura read and reread the note, her mouth agape. *A million dollars!* she thought, struggling to comprehend what had just been handed her. *Joseph Gray?* It had to be a joke, of course. A million dollars for one week! She rubbed the paper between her fingers, marveling at the quality of the stationery. Marveling at the penmanship, each letter distinct and legible. There were no flaws to evidence an indecisive hand. All was perfect and controlled.

It was the signature, however, that broke the mold. The name—"Joseph Gray"—was slashed in upright spikes, the letters *J* and *G* soaring above the rest. It wasn't a name, Laura thought, but a mark—the bold strokes of a man with an ego to match his notoriety.

A collective gasp rose up from her students. Many sat covering their mouths or cringing. Laura turned to the front of the small amphitheater to see that the large screen had split into two pictures, side by side. On the right, a surgeon was seated at a computer terminal. On the left, a robotic arm held an electrostimulator an inch above the shiny surface of the patient's cerebral cortex. The picture of the exposed brain switched to a close-up, and there were gasps and moans of "o-o-u" from the undergraduates.

"There won't be any gore," Laura said to quiet the disturbance. "The surgeon is going to locate the correct entry point for the incision by testing the responses of the patient to stimulation of particular areas of the brain."

"All right, Doug," the surgeon's voice came over the television's speaker. "Johns Hopkins" appeared under the crystalline image of a man who was wearing a white lab coat and staring at his computer monitor. "Cedar Sinai, Los Angeles" was printed under the incredibly sharp picture of the wrinkled gray mass on the left side of the screen. Just beneath it the Internet address of the channel on which they viewed the procedure was printed.

The human brain lay exposed under the waiting robotic arm and was surrounded by light green surgical cloth. "We're going to begin stimulation," the surgeon said from his office thousands of miles away. "Now I want you to report to me exactly what you see, hear, feel, taste, smell, remember, whatever. Just relate to me as best you can the experience that the stimulation triggers."

Laura put the letter onto the podium and tried to compose her thoughts for her lecture. "The surgeon on the right," she said, clearing her throat and then raising her voice to get the students' attention, "is located at Johns Hopkins Medical Center in Baltimore. The subject," she began, aiming her laser pointer at the picture of the patient, "is a nineteen-year-old male with severe epilepsy." An arrow-shaped cursor generated by the television's built-in microprocessors followed her laser pointer to the well-lit hole in the boy's skull. "He's at Cedar Sinai Hospital in Los Angeles. The purpose of this telerobotic surgery is to sever the corpus callosum, which is located at the base of the longitudinal fissure between the two hemispheres of the brain. Can anyone tell me what the corpus callosum does?"

"It's the cable that carries data between the two halves of the brain," a girl answered.

"The corpus callosum," Laura lectured from the center of the "bowl" of the steeply tiered rows of seats, "is the principal means of communication between the two cerebral hemispheres—between the left and right halves of the brain. There are numerous other interfaces as well, however."

"Why're they doing that to the guy?" another student asked with a quiver in his voice. The freshman sounded as if he were being asked to witness a ritualistic mutilation.

"In certain cases of severe epilepsy," Laura answered, "the radical procedure of severing the corpus callosum can prevent a seizure begun in one hemisphere from spreading to the other. As we've been discussing, the architecture of the human brain involves a high degree of interconnection. The 'storm' of electrochemical disturbance caused by an epileptic seizure is quickly transmitted to other brain cells, sparking other pockets of disturbance there and resulting in a major seizure. This patient has spent his life going from one grand mal to the next. He's willing to make the trade-off of a split brain for no seizures."

The looks on her students' faces ranged from quiet nausea to outright revulsion. One young woman had piled up her books and turned to face completely away from the classroom's screen.

"I *know* this wasn't in the syllabus for today's class," Laura reasoned, "and I apologize for not preparing you better, but we didn't know this offering was available over the Web until late yesterday. As gruesome as you may think this is, I'm sure you'll find it enlightening. I want you to watch the procedure because it's a rare opportunity to witness interaction *directly* with a human brain, not indirectly through a patient's normal senses. Nature's laboratory has given us this opportunity, and we as scientists must take what we're given."

Someone murmured a crack that drew nervous giggles from the students.

"All right, Doug, can you hear me okay?" the surgeon asked.

"Yep," the boy replied—the scene on the left switching briefly to provide a broader perspective on the surgical theater. Groans rose from the class on sight of the boy's face and shaved head protruding from under the bright green cloth. The picture quickly shifted back to its close-up of the brain's surface.

"You mean they'll cut that guy's brain open with him *awake* like that?" one of the students asked—aghast.

"They'll put him under after they've found their route in. But they had to keep him conscious so he could report what he experienced from the stimulation."

"Okay, Doug," the doctor said. "The program is up and running."

"I don't feel anything," the patient said in reply, his voice trembling as the robotic arm holding the stylus descended toward his brain's surface—slowing as it neared. The physician on the right side of the split screen sat back with a notepad and watched his monitor. "Oh, wow!" the boy shouted suddenly. "Six-oh-six-oh-eight-four-*two!*" he sang out. "I been waitin' for *you! Dial* the number . . . and call. *Da-da-da-da-da-da-da-da*-da-da-da-da-da-da-da-da. Get no . . . answer at all! *Da-da-da-da-da-da-da-da*-da-da-da-da-da-da-da-da."

"Is that a song?" the surgeon interrupted, and the electrostimulator rose a few millimeters.

"Yeah! The B-52s!" the boy said. "My dad used to listen to them all the time."

"And you can hear it when we stimulate this area right here?" The surgeon tapped at the keyboard from his Maryland office, and the robotic arm in California lowered.

"Wow! There it is again! Just like it's playin' in my head!"

"You don't have to shout."

"Sorry."

"The patient is having a memory experience," Laura explained, "of listening to a song. If we can find an old CD of that song, we can later compare the recording of the patient singing to the CD's soundtrack. We'll probably find it's as synchronized with the original as if he had headphones on and was singing along with the music."

"Purple," the boy said from the surgical theater.

"Do you see anything?" the doctor asked. "What do you see that's purple?"

"Nothing. Just purple. That's all. The color purple."

"We'll be getting to color later in the semester," Laura interjected. "For now, just remember the subject's reported experience. He 'sees' and reports 'purple,' but it's not some *thing* that's purple. It's just the color purple that he's experiencing. Your assignment for the next class is to imagine a purple cow. Close your eyes and imagine it in as much detail as possible. Imagine its eyes, its ears, its hooves, everything. Then, when you're done, think about this. Did you 'see' the color purple, or did you just 'think' purple? If you didn't 'see' the color, what was it that made the cow purple?"

It was when Laura finished giving the assignment that she realized the satellite coverage of the surgery had grown silent. The tense doctor was leaning forward in his chair. In the other picture, the electrostimulator's dull point rested lightly against the shiny surface of the cortex, but the patient said nothing.

"Doug?" the doctor called out, adjusting his glasses and shifting anxiously in his seat. "What are you experiencing now, Doug? Anything?"

There was no answer.

"Doug, you've got to talk to me. What is it? Is it a memory of some kind?"

"I don't wanna talk about it."

"Son, you've got to . . . "

"Get that thing off my head!" The cloth around the incision shook. The view shifted again to take in the operating room. Two nurses clad in bright green scrubs and face masks rushed to the patient's side as his hands jerked up against the black nylon restraints. "Stop it! Stop it!" Doug yelled, but when the picture shifted back to a close-up, the robot's arm maintained the steady pressure of the stylus against his brain.

"What's happening?" one of Laura's students asked in a trembling voice—a look of horror on her face.

"The damn computer's making him remember something he doesn't want to!" another student answered.

"Doug," the surgeon said calmly from the screen on the right, "if you want, I can try to get rid of whatever it is that's bothering you. A little stronger stimulation of the area and I can probably . . . "

"*Just leave me alone!* I said *quit* it! And I mean *right now!*"

"Okay, okay. Calm down." The physician began tapping at his terminal. Still, however, the robotic arm pressed the stimulator down. Still Doug screamed. "Stop! Please, *sto-o-op!*" he shrieked and began to cry. "Don't do that anymore! Please, please, don't make me . . . !"

The bars of a color test pattern replaced the picture of the jerking, increasingly spasmodic motions of the epileptic boy and of the robotic arm, carefully holding the electrostimulator perfectly still in its programmed place.

Laura closed her office door and headed straight for her chair with Gray's letter.

The door burst open behind her, and she jumped with a start.

"You look like you've seen a ghost," Jonathan Sanders—her office neighbor and closest friend—said as he sauntered in and slumped into the sofa opposite her desk. Laura sank into her chair, drawing a ragged breath and trying to settle her pounding heart. "Listen," Jonathan began in an apologetic tone, "your secretary told me about the flood of E-mails you got over the weekend from lovesick academics all around our fine institution. I'm sorry about doing that profile thing. Were there any keepers?"

She shook her head. "I'm *sorry,* Laura," Jonathan continued. "It was just a *joke*. I thought you'd get a kick out of it. The program had such a catchy title—'Rate Your Mate.' Some grad student over at MIT uploaded it onto the university network. It's all the rage, you know, but I *am* sorry."

Laura looked up at him and nodded, wishing he'd leave her alone to think.

"But who knows?" Jonathan said, returning to his typical banter. "Maybe you'll find your soul mate somewhere out there in cyberspace. Or, more precisely I guess, *he'll* find *you* some lonely evening while browsing about the Web."

"Jonathan, I'm not in the mood for this right now, okay?"

"Really? I thought you'd be tickled *pink*. You really *should* look your scores up. They're pretty good, actually. But I'm still somewhat conflicted about the name I used for you—'Blond Bomber.' What do you think? I thought about 'Skinny Minnie,' but I decided to emphasize your *hair* instead, since some straight guys still seem to be hung up on the whole *breast* thing. Personally, of course, I don't get it. A large bosom makes a woman look so *matronly*."

Laura looked up from the letter, but not at Jonathan. *Could this be for real?* she wondered.

". . . but when I put in your particulars—five seven, slim, athletic, blond hair, blue eyes, perfect complexion, et cetera—the program rated you in the *very* top category. 'Most Excellent Babe,' I believe it was. If only your personality wasn't so *scary*—your academic credentials, turn-ons and turnoffs, things like that—and perhaps *slightly* larger breasts, I'm *sure* you'd have beaten out that cosmetician from Brookline for the top score."

"*Jonathan!* This isn't a good time."

"Look, I just filled out your profile! And I thought the 'Personality' thing would come out better than it did. I said you were '*nurturing,*' and when it asked what type of man you wanted, I picked 'lost soul.'" Laura glared at him. "I had nothing to *do* with the 'castrating *bitch*' part, Laura! I just input the *data!* I didn't *program* it to draw conclusions!"

She heaved a sigh of frustration. What Jonathan didn't know is that the previous Friday after he'd told her about filling out the electronic questionnaire she closed her office door and found her profile on the network. Over the weekend, thousands of E-mails had poured into her computer mailbox. Some large percentage of the sample she'd reviewed before deleting them en masse had graphically detailed sexual acts ranging from the harmlessly disgusting to the truly pathetic. Some had even attached pictures or movies and a plea that she return the favor with a nude photo or video clip of her own.

The whole episode had unsettled Laura, and as the weekend wore on she'd tried but failed to shake the mood. She had thought at first it was simply the unclean feeling of being the target of so much smut, of brushing so close by the sick, groping hands of the on-line. On Sunday night, however, as she deleted hundreds of new E-mails that had come in during the day, she returned to the profile Jonathan had composed and realized the true cause of her upset.

Everything he'd said about her was true. Tears had welled up as she sat at the computer in her home. One of the things that had drawn Laura into her friendship with Jonathan was his prodigious power of perception and understanding. It was that same power, however, that had painfully dissected her soul for all the world to see. She didn't care that a program written by some pimply-faced grad student had declared her a "castrating bitch." What bothered Laura was that, when she read Jonathan's description of who Laura *really* was, *she* liked the person she saw in the profile. It was exactly who Laura wanted to be—who in fact she *was*. The problem was there seemed to be no one else out there—in her life or in any of the hundreds of E-mails through which she had waded with an ever growing sense of despair—who seemed to like the person *they* saw.

"I'm *sorry!*" Jonathan finally said plaintively, and Laura returned to the present—her vision blurred by teary eyes.

"You put in my Web address, Jonathan! I've gotten thousands of messages from all over the world, some of them *totally* obscene."

"O-o-u. Can I read those?"

"If you were gonna pull a stunt like that for cheap sexual titillation, why didn't you just profile *yourself*, for God's sake?"

He made a face. "Who wants to send pornographic messages to a potbellied, middle-aged, gay professor?"

"Jonathan, please. I have a lot on my mind." She tossed the letter across the desk to him. "Here. Read that."

"I thought you'd never ask," he said, eagerly picking it up.

"Do you know anything about that letter?"

"I know that a perfectly *gorgeous* young man delivered it. He stopped to ask where you were, and I . . ." Jonathan fell silent, his eyebrows arching high as he read. "Well, well, *well!* I do believe we have the makings of a true moral dilemma here."

Laura slumped in her chair. "What're you talking about?"

"Hm-m, let's see." Jonathan looked up at the ceiling. "Evil rich recluse," he said thoughtfully, his finger pointing as if at the words he spoke, "hovers on brink of abnormal behavior." His finger returned to his mouth. "Knowing he's in need of psychotherapy, his 'people' check out the Harvard psychology department. Eager aides find a beautiful, young psychologist to fly down to Gray's South Pacific island for a week of fun and analysis. Little do they know, however, that there's a world of difference between *psychiatry* and *psychology*, and that the lovely young lass they have chosen specializes *not* in the real world of *healing* but in the nether regions of arcane research about 'consciousness' and 'selfhood' and other such imaginary creations of animal brains."

Laura rubbed her eyes. "You know, you're really turning into an old bitch in your waning days, Jonathan."

"But a million *dollars!*" he said dreamily, undeterred. "What one could *do* with a million dollars. Why, one could fund research to determine whether aphids are capable of developing a true human-like attachment to Coca-Cola. Or perhaps . . . whether a toaster oven feels '*shame*' when it repeatedly singes the waffles."

"I'm *not* going to take that offer," Laura said, incredulous that he would even suggest such a thing.

"But why not? A week or so in your tender care—those warm island breezes," he threw his head back and flicked his fingers through his thinning and graying hair, "and your patient'll be chipper as a schoolboy! Just ask a few questions about his childhood, mouth some psychiatric mumbo jumbo, then get his doctor to prescribe *Prozac!*"

With her arms resting heavily on her desk, Laura shot Jonathan a dirty look and then pressed her face down into the crook of her elbow—groaning.

"No, really," he said—his tone slightly less playful. "I'm not kidding."

"You really think I might *take* that job?" she said, looking up in astonishment.

"Why not? He doesn't need the money. He's the richest man in the world! Hell, I'd hold out for *ten* million. What's it to him? They say he may be worth seventy, eighty *billion* now that he's cornered the high-definition television market. Besides"—Jonathan leaned forward and spoke with mock sincerity—"it's a cry for *help*. He's a person too, after all."

"I can't go work for somebody like Joseph *Gray*."

"A-a-ah," Jonathan said, nodding and sinking back into the sofa. "Tenure, huh?" She looked up at him. His mouth was smiling, but his eyes were sad. "Look, Laura," he said, glancing at the door, "I don't know quite how to say this, but not getting tenure isn't the end of the world."

She held Jonathan's gaze until his expression began to look vaguely sympathetic, then looked down at her cluttered desk. The emotions poured in, and Laura fought hard to keep her eyes from filling with moisture again. Her lip quivered and she bit down on it, determined not to humiliate herself. "Do you know something?" she asked, the high pitch of her voice strained and unnatural.

Jonathan was shaking his head. "No." He hesitated. "Nothing definite." He looked pained—at a loss. "But . . . look, Laura, after the Houston thing there's been a lot of talk about Paul." Laura felt her face flush with anger as the carousel of emotions took a turn, and she ground her teeth together. Paul Burns was the other candidate. "You took a gamble with that paper. I told you that was what it was. If it'd taken, you'd be a star. Book deals, speaking circuit, the works. But you ran it up the flagpole and nobody saluted."

"So, what *should* I have done? More lab rats in mazes like *Burns,* for Christ's sake?" It was so unfair. Paul Burns didn't have an original thought in his head, but every year like clockwork he'd touched another base of publishing success. Journal after journal, obscure university press texts that were forgotten within weeks, nowhere a single notable achievement. But he was going to make it, she could tell. She could tell it from the body language of the people she passed in the hall. She could tell it from Burns's blossoming self-confidence. And now she could tell it from Jonathan, who had just pounded the final nail in the coffin of her career. She opened her mouth to speak, but hesitated—not certain she wanted to hear more. "But you think," she said anyway, tentatively, "you think I'm right, though, don't you?"

"Oh, you mean about the *substance* of your paper? I think it's some of the most original, thought-provoking work to come out of this building in years. But do I think it was right to put it forward last summer? With the tenure committee meeting at the end of the fall semester?" He grimaced slightly and shook his head. "I told you. People aren't ready for a paradigm shift on something as fundamental as human consciousness. How would *you* feel sitting there and having some thirty-four-year-old associate professor tell you that there are no such things as '*moods*'? That it's really another 'self'—another personality—rising to the surface and assuming control over its host organism? 'Everybody's possessed with multiple personalities, only we don't normally notice the shift from one to the other because the different personalities' identities are so similar. We only diagnose it as multiple personality *disorder* when they're *radically* distinct like Dr. Jekyll and Mr. Hyde.'" He was shaking his head. "You could've circulated a draft and gotten some input instead of just hitting them out of the blue with it."

"'*Input,*'" she said, frowning. "By the time they finish '*inputting,*' the paper is twice as long and half as good." Laura rolled her eyes and huffed. "If I'd been gray-haired and male they would've paid attention."

"And if I'd been Grace Kelly, I would have married a prince."

"You don't know how much it *hurts,* Jonathan! How many times I've been in professional conferences or bullshit sessions and voiced an opinion only to be ignored! Then, fifteen minutes later, a *man* says the *same* goddamn thing and everybody falls all *over* themselves to discuss it!"

"*Me*-o-ow."

"This isn't a game, Jonathan!"

"Oh, but it *is!*" he said, suddenly animated—on the front edge of the sofa. "It is a game. They told me not to bring my lover to the annual cocktail party with the trustees, so I didn't. They want me to be butch? No more turtlenecks or wine spritzers. A little healthy heterosexual harassment of the coeds? Sure thing, boss! You do what it takes to get tenure, and then you do what-*ever* the hell you want." He sat back, casting his eyes toward the ceiling again. "Being an associate professor, you see, is like being a juvenile sea squirt. You search the sea for a suitable patch of coral to make your home for life. You only need a rudimentary nervous system for the task, and once you've found the right spot and taken root, you don't even need that and you can do as the sea squirts do and eat your own brain."

Laura laid her head on the back of her chair, looking straight up at the ceiling. Taking a deep breath, she said with growing fatigue, "Thanks *ever* so much for the helpful analogy."

Jonathan hesitated, as if carefully considering his next words. "Burns plays the game."

"Of *course* he does!" Laura burst out, glaring at him. "*Jesus!* If you mean I have to be a Paul Burns to get tenure, I'm just not going to *do* that."

Jonathan huffed in feigned exasperation and sank further back into the deep recesses of the leather cushions. "God, I hate talking to people with principles. I never know what to say."

Laura felt a rising, panicked desire to take action, only she didn't know what to do. How she could salvage her career—her life. "I screwed up, didn't I?"

After a moment's hesitation, Jonathan leaned forward with a loud noise from the leather and gently tossed the letter onto the desk. The thick sheet of stationery landed in front of her, its two folded ends rising into the air.

"So," she said, picking it up mainly just to look again at the flawless script, "what are you saying? This is my future? *Psychoanalysis?*"

Jonathan shrugged. "If you can make a million a week shrinking heads let me know."

"*God,* Jonathan," she said, looking around at the familiar surroundings of her small office. An office she would soon have to leave—forever. She took a deep breath and let out a ragged sigh. "I can't *believe* this is happening." She looked down at the letter through bleary eyes. "If I take this job, it'll seal my fate, won't it?" She looked up at him. "They'll think it's a sign that I'm looking."

Jonathan shrugged. "It's not so much that as . . . You know, this Gray guy is like a real raper and pillager. It'd be sure to come up. I mean, why do you think he's offering a million *bucks,* for God's sake?"

She looked at him, missing his point. "What do you mean?"

"Really, Laura. That's a lot of money. He's probably . . ." Jonathan stumbled, shrugging.

"What?" she asked, suddenly incensed. Jonathan said nothing. "*What?* He's probably been turned down already? He's upped the price because nobody *else* is willing to take the job? What are you saying, Jonathan? I'm not his first choice?"

He squirmed. "La-a-aura . . ."

"Did he ask *you?*" she asked. Jonathan looked up at her. "He didn't, did he?" Jonathan shook his head. Laura allowed herself to sink back into the warm pool of self-pity.

Jonathan shrugged again. "Just be careful. I mean"—he shook his head—"I don't really know much about the guy, but from what I've read it sounds like he may be bad news. I mean, like, dangerous."

Laura's hair was still wet from her shower as she sat at a computer terminal in the main library. She had gone for her regular morning run, but it had failed to burn off her anxiety.

With a deep sigh, Laura logged onto the Web. The massive computer network—the "information superhighway" connecting millions of smaller networks into one high-speed global system—was occasionally useful, but it was hardly the revolution it had been touted to be. Laura frowned, staring at the cursor-turned-hourglass and waiting some time before finally getting a query screen.

"Gray, Joseph," she typed, hit Enter, and surreptitiously took a bite of the sandwich she'd snuck into the building. The computer's response was delayed an inordinate length of time. Laura chewed, waiting. She hated computers.

"10,362 entries" finally appeared on the screen.

"Damn," she mumbled, her mouth full. It was much more than she'd counted on. How could she look through that many? Maybe she could search some other parameters to narrow the list down? She tried, but couldn't think of any. She wanted to know something about the man, she just didn't know what.

Laura waded into the articles. The most recent was ten days old. *Forbes* magazine listed Gray as the richest man in the world at forty to seventy billion dollars net worth. Commercial electronics, telecommunications, Internet access, satellite launch, computers, robotics, space exploitation. Laura's eyes returned to the last word. "*Exploitation,*" she reread, having first read it to say "exploration."

"With no government backing, the Gray Corporation has bankrupted virtually all competition from the U.S., Japan, and Europe in the direct broadcast, high-definition television market. With its one-inch-thick, one-meter-square phased array satellite antenna and user-selectable block-compressed high-definition television programming and Internet downloads broadcast from a network of over one hundred low-altitude satellites, the Gray Corporation can expect worldwide sales of over $50 billion this year alone. Joseph Gray is the sole shareholder of the Gray Corporation, which is essentially debt-free." There was a telephoto picture of a strange-looking flat-sided rocket sitting at its gantry. "A single-stage, liquid-fueled, reusable rocket," the caption read. There was no picture of Gray. Laura scanned the article for more. She found his birth date. *He's thirty-seven years old,* she thought—momentarily pausing in amazement.

Laura took a large bite of her sandwich and skipped a few hundred articles—going back in time. As she read the article from two years ago, she remembered now where she had first heard Gray's name. "Commerce Department Subpoenas Businessman's Records." Gray denied any violations of technology transfer regulations in using Russian facilities to launch his satellites. She jumped from article to article. They all tended to repeat the same facts, but some put an ominous, sinister spin on events. "Boy Wonder Buys Russian Rockets." Gray had purchased dozens of huge Russian ICBMs scheduled for destruction under START III for use in launching his satellites into space at bargain-basement prices.

She skipped further back. "Federal Trade Commission Loses Antitrust Suit." Gray's proposed satellite transmission prices were outrageously low, but they weren't illegal "predatory" prices, the court had held. Laura moved on. "Federal Communications Commission Begins Investigation." Gray said he would sell his systems in Europe and Japan if they were not licensed in the United States. "Bad Boy Businessman Back Before Congress." Gray had been subpoenaed to testify in front of the Science and Technology Committee. "What are your intentions?" he'd been asked. "To make money" had been his only reply. The packed hearing room had exploded in laughter, the *Time* magazine article reported.

With a sigh, she leapt randomly a third of the way back through the search—further back in time. There was a *Wall Street Journal* article about a failed savings and loan in early 1988. Gray was called to testify on Capitol Hill as one of the people who had gotten a major loan from the S&L before it went under. Laura frowned and nodded. "It figures," she mumbled, mildly disappointed. *He's just like all the others. The only way to get to the top is to cheat.* One line at the end of the article caught her eye. "Mr. Gray's research laboratory in Palo Alto had repaid its promissory note in full with interest on request of the board's audit committee one month before the S&L failed under its crushing load of bad real estate loans." *Repaid in full?* she wondered, perplexed for a moment. *But who knows what went on?* Laura decided, and she jumped randomly further back.

Just six months before that, Gray had been investigated again, this time in connection with allegations of market manipulation in the wake of the great stock market crash in October 1987. "Lovely," she whispered, tossing her sandwich wrapper into the trash. Her finger hesitated over the Exit key. She'd learned enough and was ready to get back to the pile of papers she needed to grade. Laura hesitated, and then read on.

Gray had purchased almost two hundred million dollars in something called "puts" in the options markets on the Thursday before the Monday crash. Put options, she read, give the holder the right to sell—or "put"—stock to the other party to the contract at a specified price. They were "naked" puts, meaning Gray didn't own the stocks that he had the option to sell. When the price of the stocks plummeted, Gray bought the stocks cheap, "put" them to the other parties to the options for the contractually agreed higher price, and pocketed the difference. In one week, Gray had turned two hundred million dollars into six billion, after taxes. He had made a fortune in the market's collapse, claiming during the government's investigation that he had used a sophisticated new computer program called a "probabilistic neural network" to spot the impending downward correction in the market. The government found no evidence of any illegal manipulation.

Laura sighed. It looked dirty: *1987,* she thought. *Gray was . . . twenty-four years old.* A multibillionaire at twenty-four.

Somewhere, way back, there was the wellspring. The source of the money, the success. The more she looked, the dirtier the money appeared. Gray had been Michael Milken's whiz kid at Drexel Burnham in the early eighties, making millions analyzing high-tech stocks for the soon-to-be-jailed junk-bond king. Gray had been called to testify at Milken's trial. There apparently had been a falling-out between Gray and Milken in 1984, and the two had parted company. "Gray denied that he had resigned from Drexel Burnham on ethical grounds, insisting instead that he had resigned over disagreements regarding the feasibility of a computer project designed to forecast market trends. After leaving Drexel, Gray made hundreds of millions by putting together an investor group and undertaking a petrochemical project on his own."

Laura scanned further back through the articles. "Local Businessman Sells Plant," the *Houston Chronicle* had reported earlier in 1987. "Industry giant Monsanto agreed to pay the Gray Corporation $700 million for the plant, which makes polyvinylchloride products." Laura's upper lip curled on seeing a picture of the grimy plant, shaking her head as she imagined the tons of toxic products belched out to glutinous American consumers. "The products' main use is in lightweight pipes for drinking water of the sort found in most new construction." Gray had put four million dollars into the deal—every penny he had—in 1984 after leaving Drexel Burnham. Other investors had put up forty million for preferred stock, and banks had loaned four hundred million, but Gray always owned all the common stock. He always had control. He had purchased a long-closed petrochemical plant at a scrap-metal auction, rehired all the plant's workers, converted it for processing of PVCs, and had five years of back orders by the time it was brought into production. He had guessed right. There had been a huge upsurge in world demand for plastic pipes. Gray had again foreseen a market swing missed by everyone else.

Laura's eyes drifted from the screen. There had been no mention of a "neural network" being used in spotting trends in the market for PVC products as there had been in the stock market investigation. The programs were used routinely for things like that now, she knew. Stockbrokers regularly advertised their pet programs in magazines and newspapers and on television, giving them catchy names like "Primus One" and "Trendline 2000." *But could Gray have developed one back then?* she wondered. *In 1984?*

Nineteen eighty-four. Laura did the math. In 1984, Gray had been twenty-one years old.

She searched further back in the database. A short article in *Business Week* had a picture of Gray at age twenty. He sat on a table next to a computer wearing an open-collared dress shirt and blue jeans. He looked . . . normal, for that time anyway. The article was written in a humorous style—laughing "with" Gray, not "at" him. "The young prodigy claims the 'analog neural network' is ideally suited to discern problems he called 'fuzzy' (a term computer experts on the *BW* staff seemed at a loss to define). When the program was asked to solve the problem 'What is two plus two?', however, it replied, 'Four-ish.' Gray's superiors at Drexel Burnham were silent when asked whether they were pleased with Gray's creation, which is supposed to accept large numbers of loosely related variables and identify patterns or relationships to assist in market analysis."

There were very few articles about Gray before 1983. His name appeared in lists with numerous others who had closed this financing or advised on that merger.

But what she already knew about the man swirled in her head. *Russian missiles, antitrust violations, stock market manipulation, failed S&Ls, junk bonds, chemical plants . . .* She rapidly scanned the remaining articles. As the full flavor of all she had read settled in, Laura grew disgusted at herself that she'd even considered taking that man's offer. She reached for the button to turn the terminal off. With her finger resting on the Exit key, she decided once and for all that she was wasting her time.

But Laura couldn't bring herself to push the button. She'd just look at one more thing, she decided. Feeling guilty for the obsessive behavior, she hit the Home button to scan all the way back to the very first entry her search had retrieved on Gray. The year was 1976. It was a short article—a "blurb," really—from a small newspaper in Indiana. "Local Boy Wins Admission to Harvard at 13." Joe Gray was headed off to study philosophy. *Philosophy?* she thought. She stared at the grainy snapshot of the boy. At his sad eyes through which shone unmistakable brilliance.

* * *

"Professor Paulus?" Laura said.

The frail chairman of the philosophy department looked small behind his messy desk.

"Ah, come in! Come in!"

There were loose papers covering every inch of his shelves, chairs, and couch. "Oh, put those anywhere," he said waving his hand. "Have a seat. Have a seat." His voice was raspy and had lost its vigor. He was due to retire this year, she knew. She'd heard of the scramble for his seat.

Laura put his illegible, handwritten notes on the floor. "Thank you for taking time to see me."

"I *always* have time for my students."

"Oh, um, I'm an associate professor over in the psychology department."

"Good lord! I *am* sorry." He took his thick glasses off and wiped them with his handkerchief, putting them back on and squinting at her. "Hmmmph," he said after his inspection, obviously deciding his error was understandable. Laura looked younger, she knew, than her age. "Well, what can I do for my esteemed colleague, Miss . . . ?"

"Aldridge. Laura Aldridge." She decided not to say "Doctor," fearing an appearance of pretentiousness and a perceived feminist slap at the kindly man. "I was just wondering. It's been a long time, but do you happen to remember a student of yours by the name of Joseph Gray? He was . . . "

"Brilliant. Absolutely brilliant, but . . ." The old man was alert now, his eyes far off but staring intently at a fixed point in space.

"What?"

"Why do you ask?" he said, suddenly on guard.

"Well . . ." She debated whether she should tell him.

"May I see your university ID?"

"What?"

"Your ID," he repeated, waggling the fingers of his outstretched hand like a cop to a motorist he'd just stopped. She fished it out of the fanny pack at her waist, and he looked it over. "I'm sorry, Dr. Aldridge," the old man said as he handed it back—his features mellowing and kindly again. "It's just . . . you can never be sure these days. So many people are asking questions."

"About Gray?" she asked, and he nodded. "Who?"

"Our government, for one. Sent somebody by here just last Thursday. FBI. And then, over the weekend, there was that break-in. Hit your department as well, I hear."

"What break-in? Somebody broke into our offices?"

"No, no, no. I guess I shouldn't have said anything. They want it kept hush-hush—something about not losing our security rating for defense work." He leaned across his desk and lowered his voice. "Somebody broke into the university network. Used that thing—the 'Web.' They browsed through computer files in the directories assigned to philosophy, linguistics, and your department—psychology."

"What did they do with the files? Was it a prank? Vandalism?"

"No, no," he shook his head. "Didn't do anything, apparently. Didn't even copy any of the files, just browsed through." He laughed, shrugging, a comical expression on his face. "What it is in our departments' computer files that has people worried about national defense secrets certainly eludes me."

"Well, what does any of that have to do with Gray? I mean, hackers are a real menace. They're one of the several *hundred* reasons I hate computers. In the last month alone, I got a notice printed on my checking account statement that the bank's computer had been hacked into, and that they couldn't guarantee that people's records had been kept confidential. *Then,* if you can believe this, some . . . , I don't know, *loser* kid, probably, with nothing better to do broke into the computers at the video store where I rent disks." She chuckled. "They had this big sign posted by the door to the X-rated part of the store informing everybody. I bet there were some nervous men running around worrying about those rental records." Laura laughed again, but Paulus seemed ill at ease. "Anyway," she continued, "I can't imagine why they'd think it might be Gray."

The professor seemed lost in thought. He shrugged. "You're right." He nodded again. "You're right, I suppose." The old man's eyes grew unfocused, and he seemed to drift away. "That boy . . ." He shook his head.

"What?"

Paulus sighed. "It's just a shame. A true shame. He was the most brilliant mind whose path I ever crossed, bar none."

"Were you his teacher?"

A brief laugh burst from Paulus. "Not really. You see, Dr. Aldridge, nobody really ever taught that boy anything that I can recall." He shook his head again. "Oh, he'd read. He was a prodigious reader. Fast as lightning, with truly photographic memory. I seem to recall that someone in your department once wanted to test him. A Dr. Weems? Is he still over there?"

Laura shook her head. "No, sir. He passed away before I joined the department."

"Well, they never did, I can tell you that, because if there was one more thing about that boy, it was that he was stubborn. Headstrong."

"I don't understand, Professor, when you say nobody ever taught him anything. He attended class. He got a degree."

"Oh, yes, yes. But he was just . . . just so far ahead, don't you see. It only stands to reason, with the amount of reading he'd do. The boy only needed four, five hours of sleep a night at most. And every night he would polish off increasingly obscure texts, gleaning some progressively more trivial points of view from an ever narrowing set of as yet unread treatises."

"You said he was brilliant. How did you know? I mean, you tested him, I'm sure—I mean academically."

"Oh, yes, yes. Nothing really to compare him with, though. Just gave him the highest possible score." He suddenly laughed again. "Once . . . once a graduate teaching assistant gave Joe a B on a paper in logic. It was an upperclassman's course, and Joe had taken the most primitive tools of deductive reasoning and applied them to the most simplistic logical arguments." He was clearly amused as he recounted the story, smiling broadly. *An educator,* Laura thought with a wave of self-pity, *at the end of a distinguished career reminiscing about his brightest student.* "He used standard deductive reasoning, you understand. Plato's 'Aristotle was a man, all men are mortal, therefore Aristotle was mortal.' But Joe applied it to Descartes' *'Cogito, ergo sum'*—'I think, therefore I am.' The point of his paper had been to fill in the missing operator—the middle argument that links the 'I think' with the 'therefore I am.'" Paulus laughed loudly. "The graduate teaching assistant thought it was too simplistic. He hadn't used any of the more sophisticated methods of symbolic logic. He hadn't even regurgitated any of the classic fallacies. The graduate student gave a fifteen-page critique of Joe's paper, which I think was only something like seven or eight pages long. He never wrote long papers."

"What did you do?"

"Well . . . I changed it to an A, of course. It was pure genius."

"What was his conclusion . . . about Descartes' argument?"

"He agreed with Descartes."

After a moment's hesitation, Laura laughed, but Paulus wasn't sharing in her amusement.

"It was really quite a compliment to Descartes," the old man said, and the smile faded from Laura's face. He was serious. "You should have heard how he filleted poor Immanuel Kant."

Laura was uncertain how to react. A teenager who deigned to agree or disagree with the likes of Descartes and Kant. "So, if all he did was agree with Descartes, what was the big deal?"

"Oh, it was the *way* he agreed!" Paulus's voice had a dreamy quality to it. "That was what it was like. It was so frustrating"—Paulus grabbed the air with clenched fists in front of him—"to be around Joe. It was so difficult to get things out of him. You had to pry his mind open, and even then he just gave you glimpses. He once said when I tried to draw him out that it wasn't that he didn't *want* to talk to people, it was just that it would take too long to define terms for them. You see"—Paulus pointed to his skull—"there were thoughts and concepts flourishing in his head that had no definition in the English language. In *any* language. He even said that he thought of things and then assigned to them nonverbal labels that he called . . . Oh, dear. What did he call them?" the old man said, looking suddenly perplexed.

"Tokens?" Laura asked.

"Yes! How did you know? Oh. Psychology, right?" Laura smiled and nodded. "Well, anyway, he would store those 'tokens' for times when he later revisited the subject. I mean, imagine thoughts so complex as to encompass the entire discipline you've spent your life studying. Suppose, for a moment, that you wanted to encapsulate the whole of psychology, with a certain meaning or logic or formula for every single disputed point, with a resolution from among competing theories for every uncertainty, into one term for use in your thoughts and discussions."

"Instantiation," Laura said, finding her voice assuming the low and almost reverent tones with which Paulus discussed Gray. "The concrete embodiment of an immensely complex concept. You're not suggesting that's possible for a human?"

Paulus shrugged. "Have you met Joe Gray? The boy was the epitome of a genius. I don't mean your garden-variety high-IQ types. This place is brimming with those." Paulus wore a warm, genuine smile. "I mean the transcendent intelligence required to synthesize two completely different disciplines. That's the true measure, you know. Your little tests are quite fine for ordinary mortals. But when you try to measure a boy like Joe, well . . ." He held his hands out, shaking his head. "True geniuses apply proofs from one science in solving problems in another. Maybe you use physics to make a breakthrough in biology. Or math to solve a chemistry problem."

"And Joseph Gray had that type of mind?"

A look of complete serenity descended on Paulus's face. Laura knew she was not there to him now. He was far away. "I once saw the most amazing thing." His voice was prayerful. "Joe was standing in a corridor of the fine arts building, just standing there. His head was kind of"—Paulus tilted his head—"kind of leaning to one side. He was frozen there, holding his books. People bustled by but he didn't even notice. I walked up to him. Frankly, I was worried. It just didn't look . . . right. I tapped him on the shoulder, and he looked around at me startled. And then he just took off." Paulus laughed. "I was a bit more sprightly back then and I caught up with him in an empty classroom. He was bent over a notebook scribbling furiously. I looked at what he was writing, but it was gibberish to me. Just a page full of formulas—arrays, I think they're called—composed of a variety of symbols that I'd never seen before. I asked him, I said, 'Joseph? Joseph, what are you doing?' He mumbled something about 'Fourier transformations,' something like that, so I just left him there. He was still sitting at that desk scribbling at nine o'clock that night, twelve hours later. I made him go home."

"What . . . what are you saying?"

"I'm saying," Paulus replied, returning to the room and focusing on Laura again, speaking slowly, "that when Joe looked at art, it sparked storms of abstract mathematical fury!" He sat forward. "I saw him in the library one day listening to music. I went over to say hello! He . . . !" Paulus was shaking his head, barely managing to contain what Laura guessed was anger. "The *music* set it off, I just know it did. He began speaking and wouldn't stop! He built this gleaming spire of logic, each conclusion seamlessly forming the premise of the next argument! He spoke nonstop for half an hour! Symbols, proofs, reasoning so brutally *unassailable* that . . . !" Laura was taken aback. Paulus was half out of his seat, his hands pressing down on his desk. "If only I could have him back." He sank into his chair, deflated. Exhausted. "If only I could have written down half of what he said to me in the library that afternoon. God, I would give everything . . ." Paulus's face was buried now in his hands.

The office was still, and Laura hesitated before breaking the silence. "What was he saying?"

Paulus held out his hands like a supplicant, palms up. "I don't know." His head was shaking from side to side. "That's . . . that's the point. I just don't *know!*"

After a respectful pause, Laura bid him good-bye. At the door, however, she stopped and turned back. "What *was* his proof of Descartes' argument, by the way? How did he connect 'I think' with 'therefore I am'?"

Paulus hadn't moved from where she'd left him. He was too tired. Defeated. He answered in a lethargic voice. "Joe believed that every person is a world unto himself. What one person experiences can never be said to be the same as what anyone else experiences. All thinking beings, therefore, create and constitute their own world, their own universe. A 'virtual world' he once called it. Yes! A virtual world." Paulus seemed pleased, reinvigorated at recalling the words. "I asked him about that later, but he never would talk about it again. That was the way he was. When he was thinking something over, he would talk. But once he had his answer, he was on to something else, leaving the rest of us behind." He huffed loudly. "But I think those ideas, in particular—the ones about people's 'virtual worlds'—were to him . . . almost a . . . a *religion*. You see, the maker of each of those 'virtual worlds' is, to Joe, the god of the world they create. Something like that."

"Everything is relative," Laura said.

"Bite your tongue! Joe hated relativism. He was very much an absolutist, an objectivist. There is one truth, one moral correctness, and only one."

"But that's inconsistent."

"Not to Joe. You see, only some people see the truth, the correctness. Those people whose heterophenomenological worlds—the worlds inside their heads—substantially overlap with the real, objective truth. In your world, you may think yourself to be totally in the right, but it is still valid to measure you by objective standards. You are still either good or evil based on how close the world inside your head compares to the real truth."

"Meaning he's an egomaniac who thinks *he* sees that one and only truth," Laura said. Paulus cast her a glance that made her instantly regret her slight. "So, Professor Paulus, why did you say it was a shame? That Gray was brilliant, but it was a shame?"

"Oh, well, he lost interest. He ran through our curriculum in two years plus the three summers." Paulus shook his head. "If only he had kept at it. If only he had . . . had *written*."

"So he graduated after two years? He got his B.A. at age fifteen?" Paulus nodded. "What did he do then?"

Paulus flung his thumb toward the window. "MIT," he said as if in explanation of his disappointment.

"The greatest waste of human talent I've ever witnessed!" Professor Petry snapped. Laura sat in the spacious office of the chairman of the MIT mathematics department. She watched the man who'd only just settled into his chair rise to pace the floor behind his desk. "Just couldn't stick with it. Had to go to *Wall Street* and make *money*." His mouth was twisted in a show of contempt. "I wrote him a few years ago, you know, before all this television nonsense. I told him I would put forward his dissertation and get him his doctorates if he'd just write the damn thing."

"Doctorates?" Laura asked. "Plural?"

"Yes!" He tossed his pencil onto the desk. "I talked to the department heads over in engineering and computer science. They all agreed to an interdisciplinary project of Joseph's choosing, but . . . "

"You mean he had earned doctorates in math, engineering, and computer science—except for his dissertation? After majoring in philosophy?"

He nodded his head, then sighed. "Greatest waste I've ever seen."

"Why's it such a waste?" Laura blurted out, then lowered her voice. "I mean"—she held her hands out and loosed a burst of air from her lungs that was neither a sigh nor a laugh—"so he wasn't all caught up in the academic rat race. There *are* other things in life, you know." The stern-looking man stared at her with knitted brow. "Other, you know, than . . . ," she began lamely, but then fell quiet and looked away. "Did . . . did he reply to your letter?"

Petry snorted and went over to a small side drawer to extract a single sheet of paper. It appeared to be the drawer's only contents. Looking at it, he read, "'I regret that I am otherwise occupied. Thank you for your kind offer.'"

"May I see it?" she asked, and he handed it to her—holding the edges carefully with his fingertips. The short text of the letter was typed beneath the bold letterhead *J.G.* Below was Gray's signature with its sweeping strokes of black ink.

She handed the letter back and thanked him. At the door, she heard, "By the way, why are you asking all these questions? Is he trying to hire you, too?"

Laura turned and cocked her head. "Well, yes, as a matter of fact. How did you guess?"

He nodded, looking at her differently now, Laura felt. "He's been raiding us for years . . . us and the people out in Palo Alto. You say you're in the psychology department?" He was standing beside his desk, still holding Gray's letter with two hands. Laura nodded. "Well, whatever he's got cooking down there it must be big. He must've hired off close to two dozen of the top people from this department alone."

"What's it like to work for him?"

Petry shrugged. "I don't know."

"Well, I mean, what do the people say who've been down there?"

"I don't know." The man stared back at her. "Nobody has ever come back. Not that I know of, anyway." Laura felt a chill. "Oh, tell him they cracked Fermat's last theorem before he did, but there's still the Riemann hypothesis or the Langlands program if he wants to get a shot at history. Give us a chance to put those insufferable algebraic geometry people back in their place."

"What?"

"Tell Joseph that Princeton got it before we did. If he had taken as much competitive interest in math as he did in watching football . . ." Petry shook his head again.

"Was Gray working on solving Fermat's last theorem when he was here?"

Petry laughed. "Said he didn't have to. Said he had not only the theorem, but a final proof to the whole Taniyama conjecture." He shook his head and frowned. "He promised me that proof. I'm still waiting."

"Well, I'll mention it if I see him, but I don't know if I'm going to take the job."

"Oh," Petry said loudly, nodding, "you'll take it. You'll take it, all right. I don't know who you are, or what you do, but if Gray wants you, you must be onto something."

"What do you mean?"

"I mean he only hires the best." He stared at her—measuring her. Trying to see in her, she imagined, what had drawn Gray's interest. "Only the very best and brightest."

The words echoed through Laura's head as she walked back to the Harvard campus. Words she'd dreamed of hearing some day, from someone. *"Only the very best and brightest."*

"Dr. Aldridge?"

Laura stopped in her tracks and turned to face two men wearing suits and sunglasses, walking toward her.

"Yes?" she said, keeping her distance.

They pulled badges from their jacket pockets. "FBI, ma'am. May we have a word with you?"

"About what?" Laura asked, involuntarily clutching her fanny pack to her stomach. She tried to relax—to appear less defensive.

They stopped right in front of her. "We'd rather not talk here. Would you mind coming with us downtown?" The man motioned to the open door of a car parked along the curb.

"Yes, I think I *would* mind." They stood there impassively, apparently not terribly insulted. "Have I done anything wrong?"

"No, ma'am. We'd just like to talk."

"Well, then . . . talk," Laura said, shrugging and staying put. Students streamed past them, staring at the odd sight. Classes had just let out, and she felt comforted by the crowds.

"Can we step over there?" the man asked, and she followed them to the base of a statue just to the side of the walk. The two men in sunglasses seemed unperturbed by the bright light, but Laura stood in the statue's shadow. "We know that you've received an offer of employment from a Mr. Joseph Gray."

It wasn't really a question. It sounded more like an accusation.

"Not employment. I'd be an independent consultant. And besides, how do you know that, and what business is it of yours? Is it illegal to hire a consultant?"

"No, ma'am." The two men looked at each other. "How much do you know about Mr. Gray?"

"I've never met him. I just received his offer today. Look, why don't you just tell me what it is you're after?"

"We're not after anything, ma'am. We just wanted to ask you some questions."

Laura waited.

"Do you know a Dr. William Krantz?"

Laura cocked her head. He was in the physics department, she remembered. He'd broken his finger playing touch football against the psychology department. Laura nodded. "Yes. I believe I know of Dr. Krantz. Why?"

One of the agents was writing in a notebook. "You work in the psychology department at Harvard, is that right?"

"Yes."

"And you have nothing to do with high-energy physics?"

Laura laughed. "Would you mind telling me what this is all about?"

"I'm afraid I can't, ma'am, but we need your help."

"Well, just what kind of help do you need?"

"We've been investigating Mr. Gray's operations for some time, now. We have reason to believe that . . . well, that things there have reached a critical phase."

"A critical phase of what? What operations?"

They looked at each other and then handed Laura a business card. On it was a telephone number with a Washington, D.C., area code. "That is a number you can call, anytime, twenty-four hours a day, should you see anything that you find . . . suspicious."

"What do you mean, 'suspicious'? Just what is it that you think is going on down there?"

There was a long silence. The two men stared back at her. Finally, the talker said, "We don't know."

After the two agents left, Laura sagged against the cool stone base of the statue. The statue's plaque was right at her feet. "Galileo Galilei. 1564–1642."

Jonathan followed Laura into her office and sank into the sofa as he had so many times before. Laura slung her fanny pack onto the desk and collapsed into her chair. Jonathan was arched forward, eagerly awaiting a continuation of the day's drama.

"So," he asked, "what are you gonna do?"

"I'm being followed," Laura said, rising and walking to the window to look out. She couldn't see anyone lurking down there, but of course she wouldn't see them. They're professionals. "*And* I think they're rifling through my personal records at my bank and my video store."

She turned to see Jonathan staring at her. "*What?*" Laura demanded.

"'Doctor, heal thyself' seems to come to mind."

"It's *not* paranoia!" Laura snapped, pulling the card from her pocket and tossing it to him. "The FBI stopped me, and we had a chat about Gray."

Jonathan examined the card and then handed it back. "And you'd have thought they'd have learned their lesson after Watergate. Raided your *video* store, did they?" Laura groaned through gritted teeth and sank into her seat. "So, what *are* you going to do?" he asked.

"I don't know." She looked up at him. "Jonathan, I can't tell whether the guy is an eccentric maverick who's being persecuted by the establishment, or the frigging *Antichrist!*"

Jonathan had picked up a magazine through which he now absentmindedly thumbed. "I phoned a guy I met at last year's Chicago neuroscience thing. He had told me in Chicago that he'd been in an undergraduate philosophy class with Gray here years ago. Said Gray was a quiet kid."

Laura waited, but Jonathan just turned the pages. "That's your big news?"

"That's what he said back *then.* But I called him this afternoon and quizzed him up."

Again Laura waited, and Jonathan licked his index finger to turn a page. "Jesus, Jonathan!"

He tossed the magazine onto the end table. "His theory is that Gray might be losing it."

"Losing what?"

"Let's see. How can I say this politely about your prospective boss?" Jonathan looked thoughtful. "He thinks Gray might be going completely *mad.*" Laura stared back at him, saying nothing. "Extreme antisocial behavior. Borderline misanthrope. He thinks it's classic. As a prodigy, you see, he has a fairly bizarre childhood. He has nothing in common with his peers and turns into a loner. When he grows up, he's no longer the brilliant sideshow. Others' intellects begin to match and exceed his own. He withdraws. Begins to hate mankind. He buys islands in the *South Pacific,* for Christ's sake. Lets his fingernails and hair grow long. Obsessive-compulsive washing of his hands and fear of germs. Oxygen-rich tents to increase his longevity. Et cetera, et cetera."

Laura was nodding slowly. "This 'friend' of yours hasn't seen

Gray since college, has he?" she asked. "He doesn't know a single goddamned thing about Gray."

"It was just a theory," Jonathan said. "He does know one thing, though."

Laura stifled another laugh. "Don't tell me Gray is gay."

"*No*, you'll be happy to learn. He's straight. I asked."

"So your friend knows *two* things."

Jonathan smirked, but then to Laura's surprise did not return a flippant riposte. "He lost his parents in a car accident when he was twelve. No brothers, no sisters, no aunts, uncles, cousins. His high school English teacher took him in for the year before he came to Harvard on scholarship. One night back in college, my acquaintance from Chicago was pulling an all-nighter cramming for an exam. When the library closed, he headed back to his dorm. Gray's light was on in his ground-floor room, like always. Gray apparently never slept, just read all night long. Only this time, he wasn't reading. So my friend walked over to Gray's window and looked in. Gray, it seems, was sitting there, at three o'clock in the morning, all by himself, just staring at the wall." Jonathan paused. "They'd had a cake for him at the department earlier that day. It was his sixteenth birthday."

The heavy, humid air of the South Pacific hit Laura as she stood in the door of the plane.

Parked on the tarmac were a few jets, prop planes, and helicopters, but there were no people to be seen anywhere. The lone flight attendant directed Laura to a small building that sat at the foothills of a lush green mountain, but then warned, "Don't get near the plane's fuselage. It's still hot."

The supersonic corporate jet had made the trip from Boston in just six hours.

Laura descended the steps to the concrete as the pilot powered the engines down.

A deep and distant roar like the tearing of a heavy cloth drowned out the dying whine of the jet's turbines. Over the verdant mountain that rose from the center of the island appeared a bright fire in the sky. Holding her hand up to shield her eyes, Laura saw it was a brilliant tail of exhaust jetting from a squat, flat-sided rocket. The craft had a blunt nose and landing gear that was retracting into its fuselage. Laura stopped to watch it rise through the thin layer of clouds as it arced through the heavens toward space. When it had disappeared from sight, she resumed her walk to the terminal.

"Welcome to the Gray Corporation's South Pacific Facilities," a large and hospitable sign over the building's entrance read. "Trespassers are subject to arrest," a smaller sign beneath it cautioned. The Gray Corporation logo was the large sign's centerpiece. As Laura approached the building, her eyes remained fixed on the logo. Its shape was roughly that of a human head. The corporate emblem—now recognizable the world round—was formed out of broad diagonal swaths of gray that ranged in tint from gunmetal to slate. The variations in tint gave the logo the basic contours of a human face. The design was decidedly high-tech, futuristic in its complexity of subtle tones and of form, although Laura couldn't quite decide why she thought that. When you looked at it closely, the effect dissolved and it was simply a dozen or so diagonal lines of slightly varying shades.

Laura shook her head, realizing she was out of sorts because of the flight. She had slept most of the way, having woken only when the jet's wheels touched down. In her current groggy state, she knew, she would've found herself mesmerized by a simple traffic sign.

A man emerged from the building, and after a momentary spike of anticipation Laura felt a twinge of disappointment. He wasn't the one she'd expected.

"Hello, Dr. Aldridge," the young man said, grabbing her single bag. The door to the terminal slid open automatically. Inside, instead of counters and rows of seats there was simply a curbed white roadbed running through the center of the building. In the sunken bed stood a strange car—both doors on its near side lifted into the air like the wings of a great bird.

The man put her bag into the open rear door. The passenger compartment of the vehicle had four seats that were surrounded by clear Plexiglas. Each of the seats was identical. There were no controls for a driver.

The man stood beside the open front door. After waiting a moment, he said, "This car will take you to Mr. Gray's house." Laura hesitated. "It's all right," he assured her. "It's automated. All you have to do is sit. It's about fifteen minutes from here up the mountain."

Laura got into the car and sat in the front passenger seat. She was surprised when the two doors shut automatically, a soft *whoosh* of air preceding the total quiet of the tightly sealed compartment. The man waved from where he stood beside the road.

A thin tone sounded, and a light on the dash in front shone "Please fasten your seat belt" in red. As soon as Laura closed the belt's mechanism, the car started to move and the door at the end of the building began to rise.

She braced herself, grabbing the seat's armrests with both hands as the car accelerated smoothly. There were no rails on the road ahead or rubber boundaries lining its curbs. The car's four tires appeared unfettered by such mechanical constraints.

The hum of the electric engine rose steadily as the car left the building for the bright sunlight outside. Laura was surprised and alarmed that its acceleration continued unabated. She could feel it in her back and, as the car climbed the hill away from the airport, from the downward press into her seat. Her grip on the armrests grew tighter with the steadily increasing speed, and she locked herself in place—rigid with alarm.

The road ahead was banked and curved gently. Unlike normal roads, it had no intersections and lights—just forks. Although the road was wide enough for two cars to pass, the smooth pavement had no markings, and its invisible driver appeared to make no attempt to stay within any imaginary lanes. When the car whipped blindly around one particularly sharp fork, Laura's heart skipped a beat in anticipation of a rending head-on collision. Her ride up the mountain, however, proceeded uneventfully.

Laura only slowly and by degrees began to loosen her hold on the armrests. The car must have reached sixty before its speed leveled off. The scenery flew by as the car flawlessly took successive forks in the road, each leading higher—progressively farther up the mountain. Laura's ears popped, and she took deep breaths to calm herself. The effort began to pay off, and her focus shifted gradually from the impending danger imagined on the road ahead to the unfolding sights that flashed by the car's windows.

Several times in the near distance she glimpsed nondescript buildings before they disappeared behind dense foliage. Through narrow gaps in the brush she saw that huge white spheres like steel balloons tethered to concrete dotted the landscape. Some were half coated in ice and vented wisps of vapor, but none bore any markings to hint at their mysterious contents. Those snapshots of Gray's works gave Laura two general impressions—the sense that everything on Gray's island was new, and that everything was industrial in purpose.

As the car ascended the steep mountain, the road cut a path

every so often along the side of a hill or over the crest of a ridge. There, vast expanses of the island came into view. A seemingly impenetrable jungle stretched far and wide, giving the island a wild and primitive look. That contrasted starkly to the appearance of the terrain that streaked by the windows of her car, which had a tamed quality to it.

Thick jungle foliage lined the road's curb on one side and formed a similarly unbroken wall that bordered the paved walk alongside the other. But the dense island flora was groomed neatly—edged and trimmed and beaten back where it encroached on the artery of man's commerce. It reached out, straining for the sunlit air laid open through its lush domain, but it had bowed—reluctantly—to the will of another. To the will of Joseph Gray.

When the road rose and curved gently through the saddle of two small hillocks, Laura saw high atop the mountain above the first hint that all was not work at the Gray Corporation. A building that looked like a resort hotel clung to the concave face of a great cliff. Its glass walls and balconies faced what were surely impressive views of the jungle far below.

The car crested another ridge, its motor now humming at a deeper pitch as it began a more deliberate and challenging phase of its ascent. From her new and higher vantage, Laura could now see clusters of buildings—small and large—nestled at the base of the huge mountain face. The small town lay half buried in thick trees and green shrubs that seemed to spring vigorously from the island's rich soil, and where its streets ended, the omnipresent dark jungle again resumed its reign. But as the hill that obscured her view of the terrain below receded into the distance, Laura saw that nature again gave way to the hand of man. Where there should have continued uninterrupted the thick tangle of growth, instead appeared the tidy edge of a perfectly flat, green lawn.

Laura's breath caught in her chest. Slowly, from behind the hill that had hid it until now, rose a massive white structure. Like a giant moon climbing above the horizon, the enormous building dwarfed all else within view. It sprawled across the empty field, easily fifteen or twenty stories high and unbroken by windows or doors. It was breathtaking in its scale and was surely the central focus of the island's operations.

The car was nearing the top of the mountain, which was curved around a steep bluff thick with vegetation. The entire island was now within view. A wide brown road fanned out behind the huge building below and led through the dense jungle to three concrete launchpads that sat poised at water's edge. The pads were at the tips of small points of land that spread like three fingers from the end of the island. On the rightmost pad sat a squat, blunt rocket like the one she'd seen rise into the air minutes before. From the empty center pad, white smoke or steam still drifted slowly into the air. The launchpad on the far left lay, by contrast to the others, a comparatively short distance from the giant building. That pad was also vacant, its gantry standing a lonely watch—awaiting the return of its charge.

Beyond the three pads swirled the calm greens of still beaches, the crashing whites of the surf on the island's reefs, and the trackless blues of the deep sea that surrounded Gray's kingdom. They were isolated there, remote, detached. Despite the elevation of the mountain that her car had scaled, there were no other islands to be seen. They were a small green dot in an immense blue pool. The ocean, Laura found herself thinking as she stared into the distance, was a moat. It kept Gray's secrets in, and his enemies out.

The car plunged into inky blackness, and Laura gasped in fright. It hurtled through a tunnel, the dim lights along a railed walkway providing the only illumination until the car rounded a bend and burst back into the sunlight.

It took a moment for Laura's eyes to adjust and for her to realize that the car was braking. To her right, a magnificent mansion came into view behind an ivy-covered stone fence. The car slowed to a crawl and turned through the open iron gates.

Before Laura lay a large, cobblestone courtyard bounded on three sides by the stucco walls of the great house. Two huge gas lanterns burned invitingly on either side of the house's stately entrance, and water cascaded off the statuary of an immense, beautiful fountain at the center of the courtyard. Well-tended beds of brightly colored flowers surrounded the fountain.

The curbed roadbed cut a neat crease through it all, forming a teardrop-shaped loop of white concrete circling around the fountain.

The car pulled up to the front of the mansion, and a woman in jeans and a short-sleeve shirt came down the front steps. The winged door lifted automatically with a quiet hiss from its pistons.

"Dr. Aldridge, I presume?" the woman said cheerfully from beside the curb.

"Hello," Laura said, stepping out into the surprisingly crisp mountain air.

"My name is Janet Baldwin," the woman said with a thick Australian accent. "I'm the majordomo of the Gray household."

Laura shook hands, trying but failing to stifle a smile on meeting the first of what Laura presumed was a large coterie of people who attended to the every need of the reclusive billionaire.

"I guess that sounds a bit odd to your ear," Janet said pleasantly. A smile seemed to come naturally to her. She had sandy hair, freckled and tanned skin, and appeared to be in her mid-forties. "No need to worry, though. We're not at all formal in this house."

Laura caught Janet glancing at the frayed knee of her jeans before turning to lead her up the steps to the house. Laura surreptitiously raised her knee to quickly check the extent of her informality, then joined Janet under a portico finished in stone carvings of intricate detail. A man in a white jacket rapidly descended the steps to retrieve Laura's bag from the car, and Laura turned back to the courtyard. When the man had extracted her bag, the car's doors closed and it took off, swiftly rounding the fountain and proceeding off along its curbed roadway—driverless.

"That's . . ." Laura said, nodding and holding her palm out, "that's *really* impressive."

"What? The *car?*" Janet asked, her lilting accent playing out the last word. "Then it's clear you've only just arrived."

She turned and led Laura through the towering double doors of beveled glass. Laura's jaw sagged on entering the mansion. Practically every square inch of the walls was covered with paintings of various shapes and sizes in the old, cluttered style of decor. Laura's heart quickened when she recognized the Impressionist strokes of the masters on several. In Gray's house, she thought, surely they weren't copies. A circular staircase swept up both walls to meet at a second-floor landing high above. Beneath the stairs, a broad hallway opened onto the rest of the ground floor.

Laura stood there, gawking like a tourist. The highly polished parquet floor was inlaid with dark marble in patterns of varying size and complexity. The ceiling above was at least forty feet high. From the center hung a spectacular crystal chandelier. The feeling evoked in Laura by the size of the entry was the same as she felt on entering a huge rotunda. That feeling was so complete that as she followed Janet across the floor, she scrutinized the inlaid marble to see whether it formed a map of the fifty states or perhaps of the chain of islands of which Gray's was a part. There was, however, no such method to the pattern of tiles.

"You'll stay in Mr. Gray's house during your visit," Janet said as she led Laura toward the stairs. "I think you'll find the accommodations satisfactory." Laura's amusement rose to a nervous chuckle as her eyes flitted from the works of Renoir to Matisse to artists whose signatures she didn't recognize.

"I do believe that you jog," Janet either said or asked; Laura couldn't tell which.

"Uhm, yes, I do." Janet must have guessed, Laura decided, from the nylon running shoes Laura wore, which squeaked loudly on the polished floors. Laura was relieved when she finally stepped off the hard wood and marble and onto the Oriental rugs fastened securely to the stairs by gleaming brass rods.

"You will find that walkways parallel most of the roads. The air is a bit thinner up here—we're at almost five thousand feet—but it *is* a bit cooler. Down in the Village, it can get humid and much warmer."

"The Village?" Laura asked, again smiling in amusement. The master, living atop the mountain in his castle. And the village down below.

"That's what we call the residential quarter where the employees and their families live. There are about five thousand inhabitants, and they held a competition earlier this year to give it a name. 'Workers' Paradise' was the winner, but it didn't stick."

They reached the top of the stairs and headed down a short hallway whose ceilings were domed and lit with soft, indirect lighting. Everywhere the detail of the home's finish was complete—no expense had been spared. *Why should it?* Laura thought, imagining the megarich Gray commissioning ice sculptures for his amusement on sunny summer days and lighting Cuban cigars with hundred-dollar bills.

A succession of French doors stood open. The passage dead-ended at a hallway that curved gently out of sight to the left and right. This had to be the building she'd seen on the way up the mountain. On the outside it had looked like a resort hotel. On the inside, it looked like . . . Well, Laura had never seen anything like it.

Janet turned left, and Laura followed. The few doors they passed were all on the right side of the hall—on the interior of the concave hallway. The decor was less cluttered in this part of the house, just the occasional niche filled with statuary spotlighted by pale illumination. *Maybe Gray was on a budget,* Laura thought. Throw everything you've got on the entrance and scrimp on the guest quarters.

Janet stopped at a twelve-foot door, which she opened into a room with fourteen-foot coffered ceilings. Wainscoting adorned the lower walls, its intricate woodwork painted glossy white. The wallpaper above was powder blue, which transitioned to the deeper blues of the heavy draperies that were held gathered in bunches by ties. The sun streamed through the windows behind the curtains—the entire wall of glass thinly veiled behind white gauze.

Laura wandered in, marveling at the expanse of the room. A thick Oriental rug covered the hardwood floors, the sheer size of it making Laura feel small and out of place. There were bookcases with leather-bound books and tables covered with porcelain figurines. Massive gold frames bounded oil paintings under lamps with brass shades. A grand piano stood unnoticed in a far corner, the sunlight reflecting off its black lacquered top polished clean of any trace of dust.

"This is your sitting room," Janet said, leading her toward an open doorway on the far side of the rug. Laura followed Janet past a full-sized antique desk, past sofas forming a cove around a crackling fireplace, past a bar with what Janet said was a full kitchen behind dark wood panels.

Through the door they came to the bedroom. It was spacious, but not as absurdly large as the sitting room. It had a cozier feel. Stacks of pillows bulged atop a broad four-poster bed. Janet pulled open the curtains, and the late-afternoon sun streamed in. Laura walked up to the window, which ran floor to ceiling the full length of the wall.

She drew a deep breath, letting it out with the word "Wow!"

The "Village" lay half buried beneath the foliage nearly a mile below. The jungle, the open green lawns, the launchpads, the black sand beaches, and the eddies of blues and greens of the sea were all right there beneath her bedroom.

"I love seeing this again through the eyes of someone new to the house," Janet said. "I remember when I first arrived. The dreams I had about life in this home."

Laura looked over to see Janet's expression change completely.

"Well," she said, returning to the tone of a bellman on an orientation tour of Laura's suite, "all the views are on this side of the house." She wasn't looking at Laura or the view. "The house itself is carved out of the mountain's side, you see."

The moment—whatever it was—had passed, and Laura turned back to peer out across Gray's island. In the center of the vista stood the enormous, windowless building rising from the treeless green field.

"What is that huge thing?" Laura asked, but she felt no need to point. There was only one structure that dominated the landscape below.

"That's the assembly building. That's where most of the manufacturing takes place. But you'll get a tour later, I'm sure."

Janet next led their expedition through the marble bathroom, which had a whirlpool so large you could do laps, and private rooms for the toilet and bidet. On seeing the separate sauna and steam room, Laura muttered, "No bathroom's complete without them, I always say," to the amusement of her guide.

They then ventured into a closet that was itself a large room. It had full-length mirrors in front of raised platforms for fittings, upholstered benches and low seats in case she needed to rest, and row after row of rails for her wardrobe. Laura immediately grew self-conscious. The clothes she'd brought would fit on three or four hangers in one tiny corner of the closet, which was every inch the size of her entire apartment back in Cambridge.

When the orientation was finally over, Janet looked at Laura—waiting. "Oh," Laura stumbled, "this ought to do fine."

Janet burst out laughing, and she must have felt it inappropriate because she covered her mouth and turned away. She held her hand up, then finally gathered herself enough to say, "I'm *so* sorry." She ended the fit of laughter with a smile of genuine enjoyment of the moment that made Laura wonder just how much Janet got out.

"Well," Janet continued, composed, "Mr. Gray's valet will see to your garments. If you need or want anything—personal items which you might have overlooked, articles of clothing, food or drink that isn't in the kitchen, anything—just dial zero on the telephone."

"What if I want to make long-distance calls?" Laura asked. She meant to Jonathan, who'd made her promise she'd call, and to whom she couldn't wait to describe what she'd seen so far. But the image of the card with the FBI number in her wallet flashed through her head.

"Just dial it like you would in the States," Janet replied.

Laura's eyes were drawn in disbelief to the full tea service that was laid out and ready for her use amid an array of sofas and plush armchairs. *My closet has a tearoom,* she thought in stunned disbelief. When she looked around, Janet was gone. Laura was all alone.

She found her way back to her bedroom and saw that her bag had appeared sometime during the tour. The room was still. There didn't seem to be any noise in the great house.

Any life. Laura wondered if he was there, somewhere.

After unpacking, she did her own exploring. There was a computer terminal on the desk in the large sitting room, and on the wall hung one of Gray's sleek flat-screen televisions. She paid particular attention to the screen. They had begun appearing everywhere just two years before. After great fanfare, the giant American electronics companies had won the approval of the Federal Communications Commission to begin high-def TV broadcasting. No sooner had the first of those sets appeared on the market than the maverick Gray had begun offering his own system. The giants had cried foul. Winners of the multibillion-dollar competition to replace the old NTSC standard with the new high-def one, they petitioned the government for protection and, at first, received it. Washington barred Gray from doing business in the United States. Gray went right about his business, however, launching satellites, commissioning programming, and selling equipment in Canada, Europe, and the Far East.

"'Gray' market" sets began appearing in the United States, but Gray's satellite signal could be pirated from his broadcasts to Canada only in the northern tier of states. Still, people quit buying the FCC-approved televisions as article after article extolled the superiority of Gray's product and predicted the monumental failure of Gray's competitors. Lawsuits were filed, government investigations were launched, and finally the consortium of companies that had won FCC approval offered Gray a joint venture. Gray had declined the offer. Under intense public pressure from consumers, the FCC relented and approved the sales of Gray's system in the United States. The pent-up demand was unleashed like a dam breaking, and Gray's production and sales soared as his competitors and would-be partners filed for bankruptcy.

The icing on the consumer's cake came when Gray's system opened up access to the Web. The result was a merger of telephone, television, and computer technologies for users who spent a few extra dollars for the installation of digital lines into their homes.

Gray's system was the ultimate in interactivity. A small lens at the bottom of every television became a broadcast studio unto itself. "Channel surfing" and "cruising the Web" became indistinguishable pastimes. With the punch of a button on the remote control, viewers could switch from C-SPAN to the Internet or back. On the Web one could find everything from slick infomercials to a kid in his parents' media room doing his best imitation of "Wayne's World"—all with full-motion video and stereo sound.

At first there were doomsday predictions about purveyors of pornography running rampant, but a funny thing happened on the road to riches from sleaze. The pornographers were put out of business by amateurs who offered their smut for free. Laura had purchased the full system but never explored its capabilities until one Saturday she read an article in *Newsweek*. It had said the Net came alive late at night, so she tuned in before going to bed. She had stayed up until four—utterly amazed and totally disgusted.

It seemed that all efforts by the censors had been defeated by technologically more adept teenagers. By using something called "anonymous servers," underground broadcasts popped up randomly and were untraceable. In the freedom that such anonymity provided, the darker alleyways of the information superhighway flourished.

The *Newsweek* article had been Laura's guide. When she found the "newsgroups," what she saw to her amazement was live and uncensored pornography broadcast straight from homes around the world. A boy and girl with Halloween masks having sex on a sofa in front of the television. An off-camera voice giving a running commentary as pages were turned through a men's magazine. Laura even watched a tape of a high school girl's showers shot through a small hole in the wall.

She had heard stories of men becoming so obsessed with such things that they stopped leaving their homes altogether. There were sensational accounts from divorce trials. Professional articles about new subcategories of obsessive-compulsive disorders. Laura shook her head. All from just a television set.

Laura ran her hand down the fine grain of the screen's black matte finish. It was liquid plasma LCD, and there were no bulky projectors or related equipment. Just a one-meter-square antenna that hung, in Laura's apartment, on the wall of her hall closet and was tuned "electronically," whatever that meant. And there weren't even any wires connecting the two. Laura hadn't yet figured that one out.

The screen beneath Laura's fingertips was only an inch thick and mounted flush on the wall like a painting. It was in almost the same proportions as a movie screen—wider than it was high. It allowed, she'd read on the first page of the thick manual before she lost interest, for a more panoramic view that movie directors loved. And the picture quality . . . ! She'd never seen one of the sets made by the competitors whom Gray had forced out of business, but Gray's sets were reported to be incomparably better. Their resolution was like that of a thirty-five-millimeter photograph. Once consumers saw it and heard the digital surround sound and the huge subwoofers that were buried inside and boomed directly through the grill of the screen, the old NTSC sets were obsolete.

Everybody suddenly had to have one despite their hefty price tag. The best systems—the twenty-foot screens with fifteen-speaker surround sound—were over fifty thousand dollars. People went crazy. High-def television systems were quickly becoming the third major consumer loan after home and auto. Everyone bought and bought. Even Laura, who didn't like television, had spent almost ten thousand dollars she didn't have one Saturday afternoon on a trip to the store to buy a scarf for her secretary. It was a lot of money, but financed over ten years it was only a couple of hundred bucks a month.

All it had taken was a demonstration in the mall. She'd just been passing when she saw over the heads of the crowd one of the screens. Everyone within sight of the screen had been transfixed. Laura had stood in line for forty-five minutes to buy it, staring at the startlingly clear and bright images the entire time. Credit was instantaneous. The set was installed the same day by men in clean blue coveralls who were right on time and were gone in half an hour with everything in perfect working order. Gray made it all so easy.

That night, Laura had friends over to watch. There was a demo program you could run from a menu that appeared in the setup routine. It was of a roller-coaster ride at an amusement park. First the sky—a deep blue with puffy clouds of incredible detail. You could stand close to the screen just as she was now—you could even press your nose to it, as the gradually more inebriated Jonathan had done—and still not see jagged lines or fuzzy edges. And then, there was the awful pause at the top of the roller coaster's ascent before a plunge with clattering wheels and whistling wind and screaming passengers. It was only when they watched the demonstration for a second time that Laura realized the screaming she heard was not from the soundtrack but from the audience.

There was a knock at the door, bringing Laura back to the present. She went over and grasped the solid brass of the levered handle. It had to be Gray. She could feel his presence through the thick, dark-stained wood. Her heart raced as she pulled the heavy door open.

A man in a waistcoat stood before her. He was carrying a silver tray. An envelope lay in the tray's center.

It was an invitation. "Mr. Joseph Gray requests the pleasure of your company at dinner at eight o'clock this evening. Attire is casual."

At eight, Laura followed the servant down the opulent circular stairway. She wore her one dress—a simple, sleeveless smock that was belted at the waist—and a pair of blue pumps. A deep, calming breath was necessary to soothe her jittery nerves, and Laura grew annoyed that something as trivial as inappropriate dress should put her so on edge. She grew annoyed also that the only other things in her suitcase were jeans, T-shirts, and running clothes. At least she'd had time to shower and do something with her hair, which she normally kept pinned up and out of the way. It was down now around her shoulders, and it lent an air of formality to her appearance which contributed some small modicum of self-assurance. Laura straightened her back and entered with all the dignity she could muster.

The dining room was empty. Two place settings lay across the long table from each other at the end closest to the window. The dining room was dimly lit by candles in the center of the table and by soft, indirect lighting around the ceiling's ornate crown molding. A mature flame glowed warmly from the fireplace. Airy chamber music emanated from some unseen speakers or, perhaps, from some unseen alcove into which Gray had crammed four musicians.

Laura was drawn past the place settings to the wall of paned glass that overlooked the festival of lights from below. Sparkling lamps twinkled in the Workers' Paradise where people delighted, she imagined, at the carefree lives they led in Gray's feudal realm.

Twin headlamps of cars moved down the highways and byways of the bustling kingdom.

Beyond the Village, the enormous assembly building and the three launchpads were bathed in brilliant light. Gray had turned night into day in other small pockets and patches of earth here and there. One, she noticed, was a ball field on the outskirts of the Village, where a game of some sort was being played. The other patches of light—widely spaced across the darkness of the island below—had no discernible function.

"Interesting perspective from here, isn't it?"

Laura turned to see two blue eyes staring down at the twinkling lights. Gray had appeared out of nowhere just beside her. She felt her throat constrict, a feeling like a pinch just above her larynx.

"All that activity seems individual when viewed from up close," he said, "but so communal when seen from afar." Gray looked over at her with an affable smile—the whites of his teeth and of his eyes contrasting starkly with the tan of his face and his dark hair. He looked so much younger than Laura had imagined that she found herself questioning whether it really was him. But the eyes . . .

His smile was frozen on his face, no longer natural. He stared at her so intensely through squinted eyes that she was forced to look away—back at the Village below. But Laura remained keenly aware that she was the subject of his unwavering focus. The moment—Gray's stare—lasted too long, and Laura felt her face flush at their strangely awkward encounter.

Out of the corner of her eye she saw that he had held out his hand.

"Joseph Gray," he said. The tone of his voice had changed. He sounded inquisitive, as if he now waited for what she would do or say next.

She took a deep breath and looked straight at him. He wrapped his hand around hers gently, and she shook his hand firmly, just once. Businesslike. "Laura Aldridge."

His gaze still lingered, but this time she didn't look away. She stared him down, and Gray broke eye contact first—a puzzled, distracted look on his face. "I'm, uh . . . I'm so glad you came, Dr. Aldridge," he said.

She nodded, an oafish grin creeping onto her face. *Chill out!* she thought, scolding herself and clenching her jaw tightly.

"Won't you have a seat," Gray said, ushering Laura to her

chair, which he held for her. "I hope your trip was comfortable."

"Thank you. It was," she said as Gray took the seat opposite Laura's. A waiter appeared and poured red wine into their glasses. "I had heard about those new planes—about the supersonic ones."

"Oh, the . . . the Grumman-Sukhoi?" Laura realized to her embarrassment that he had no time for details like what plane they'd sent for her. "It's really a good idea. Time is such a valuable commodity, and the technology existed to speed up travel, so . . ." He shrugged, draping his napkin over his lap. "If they hadn't built such a good product, I would've had my people working on it."

Laura took a sip of the wine to hide her smirk. *"My people,"* she thought, *the gentle serfs of the Village below.* The tart bite of the wine settled quickly into a wonderful aftertaste, and Laura peered at the dark liquid and took another sip. It was fabulous.

"So," Gray said, "where are you staying?"

Laura's eyes shot up, and she almost choked on her wine and had to cough into her napkin. After clearing her throat, she asked "Pardon me?" in a still raspy voice—confused.

"Where did they put you up?" Gray repeated in a tone more tentative than before.

"I'm . . . upstairs. In your house." He seemed surprised, and his face noticeably reddened. "Is that all right?" Laura fumbled. "I mean, I didn't . . . I just . . ."

"No, no, no! That's . . . it's . . ."

"Because I could," Laura shrugged, "you know . . ."

"No! Absolutely not." Gray cleared his throat. "So, do you have everything you need?"

"No," she replied, then rushed to amend her confusing response. "No—no . . . I mean *no,* I don't *need* anything. So I guess . . . I guess 'yes,'" she said, managing a weak laugh. Laura took another, larger sip of wine.

"Yes-s-s . . . what?" Gray asked, at a loss.

She filled her lungs but paused. "I mean, yes—I have everything I need—thank you."

An utter stillness descended upon the room. In the quiet, Laura's breathing assumed the proportions of a sigh of profound exasperation. She looked down to dab her white linen napkin at her lips, and she saw her plain dress. But she looked up and realized for the first time that Gray himself wore a casual jersey with sleeves rolled up his forearms. Blue jeans and a jersey. She thought that strange. When Laura had first seen Gray, she had in her mind's eye the picture of a man in a conservative business suit.

Gray took a bite of the sautéed mushrooms that had been placed before them by two waiters serving in silent synchrony. He caught her studying him, and she lowered her eyes to her plate. "You have a beautiful home," Laura said, spearing one of the delicate morsels and popping it into her mouth. It was delicious.

"Thank you," Gray replied. "I can't say I had much to do with the decor." He looked around as if to find something upon which to comment. "Looks, sort of," he mumbled as he chewed, "old English with a touch of science fiction." Her eyes roamed the crystal decanters, silver serving dishes, and ornamental plates that lined the shelves, but her gaze ended on the wall of glass. Seemingly suspended in the darkness were the glowing assembly building and launchpads. A quick check of Gray revealed a slight wrinkling around his eyes. He'd made a joke.

Laura smiled belatedly.

"Well," Gray said as he placed his fork on his plate and wiped his lips with the napkin, "as for business, I've wired your fee into a Chase Manhattan checking account we opened for you in Boston. That's one million dollars, less taxes."

Laura felt her face redden on his mention of the obscene sum. "Thank you," she said—instantly deciding it was a woefully inadequate response. Gray seemed not to notice.

A million dollars, she found herself thinking, then guiltily forced the subject from her mind. She still had no plans for the money. It hadn't really even sunk in that the money would be there when she got home. But she imagined now for the first time opening her bank statement and seeing her balance.

When Laura looked up, she realized Gray had finished his appetizer. She quickly stabbed at the remaining mushrooms on the small dish. They tasted so extraordinary she was unwilling to let them go back to the kitchen.

"By my timekeeping," Gray said, "your week's service began when you boarded your flight, and will end . . ." His pause drew her gaze. ". . . well, upon your return to Boston on Sunday, I guess, although I'm not sure your work will take the entire week."

The first course was whisked away and a second—tournedos of beef, assorted vegetables, and creamed potatoes molded into the shape of a seashell—was laid in its place.

"You see," Gray said, carving unceremoniously into his food, "we have a bit of a time crunch. We're a twenty-four-hour operation, although, of course, you're expected only to work at whatever pace you can handle."

A waiter appeared with a new bottle of red wine. "Oh, I'd like some more of that," Laura said, indicating the still half-full bottle on the table. Gray poured it for her, and the waiter disappeared. "What *is* this?" Laura asked, taking another small sip. "It's wonderful."

Gray turned the bottle to read the label. He clearly had no idea. "It's a merlot, California, 1978." He poured himself another glass, showing no further interest in the subject.

They ate now in total silence, the only sound the faint clinking of silverware on plates. Laura feigned interest in the tapestry on the wall behind Gray as she chewed. In the carved stone mantel. In the flowers of the large centerpiece that adorned the long table. Each time she caught glimpses of Gray. He was slender, but his shoulders were broad. His jaw was square, but not so square as to spoil the oval of his face. There was hair on his forearms and at the bottom of the *V* of his collar, but his neck and hands were smooth.

The next time she looked his way, he lowered his head quickly. He'd been looking at the bare skin of her upper arms.

Laura stole a glance not at Gray but at herself. At her arms. They were too skinny. Too pale. He was tanned, and compared to him she looked sickly.

This is going well, Laura thought—the quiet of the room suddenly stifling. There might as well have been a metronome, ticking off the rhythm of their silence—tolling the passage of time during which Laura had nothing to say. The stillness suddenly seemed to weigh on her, to make her want to squirm under the growing pressure of it.

"What is it . . . ?" she began, just as Gray said, "You arrived on . . ."

There was a moment's confusion, but Laura eventually won the battle of insisting that Gray proceed with his comment first.

"You arrived on a good night for a show," Gray said, holding his wristwatch up to check the time. "We have a shuttle landing in about five minutes."

"You mean right over there?" Laura asked, nodding at the three brightly lit pools of light suspended in the mirrored darkness of the window.

She turned to catch him looking at her again. Gray lowered his head and nodded, preoccupied suddenly by the mechanics of consuming his food. The uncomfortable silence again descended on the table. Once again, Gray finished the course before Laura was even half through.

"We have about two launches and recoveries a week," he said out of the blue, dropping his napkin on the table and resuming a conversation she thought had died long before. "Mainly just maintenance on the satellites these days. A few new markets, though. A satellite to complete the coverage over Indonesia went up today."

"Yes, I saw it," Laura said as she ate in a single bite a slice of beef easily twice the portion she normally consumed.

Gray looked out the window—not at the ground, but at the sky. He checked his watch again. "Our antennas are so small," he continued, catching Laura again by surprise, "that the satellites need to transmit at a very high power. We explored the traditional method of colocating our satellites in geosynchronous orbit so they could cover fixed, wide areas, but at thirty-six thousand miles out they couldn't give us the narrow bands we needed for five hundred channels and a one-meter antenna. So, we put up a few hundred low-earth-orbit satellites instead. They pass by fairly rapidly, but there's always at least one over every market we service. It's an enormously complicated matter, actually, to schedule the overflights so that they seamlessly hand off the broadcasting duties. A satellite will transmit for a couple of minutes on an east-west orbit over the U.S., then cross the Atlantic and begin broadcasting to the U.K. Then it switches to French, German, Hungarian, Ukrainian, Russian. I don't think we've done a deal with the Kazakhs yet. Then Chinese and back around the world on a more southerly orbit. It might not pass back over the States for another hundred orbits. Since we only have one uplink from earth, those satellites also handle the continuous, real-time transmission of signals from satellite to satellite. It's a highly complex ballet up there round the clock, but the computer handles it all beautifully."

Gray seemed to have quit talking, a fact that Laura confirmed with a quick glance up from her plate. "That's amazing," she said before gulping down the last of her potatoes.

"Oh, take your time," Gray said graciously just before their empty plates were whisked away and he looked at his watch again.

Type A personality, she guessed. Motor's in high gear around the clock just like his business. He sat back as a sorbet was placed in front of him, and then ate it in three spoonfuls. He was as oblivious to the aesthetics of dinner as he was to the extravagance of his home.

"Here it comes," he said, and stood up.

She cleaved a ledge of the sorbet onto her spoon, shoveled it into her mouth, and jumped up to follow him to the window. High in the sky above she saw fire. A long pencil of flame fell lower and lower from the starry night, its rate of descent slowing almost imperceptibly.

"It's a single-stage rocket," Gray said, continuing his lecture. She looked at him, and he looked at the stars. From what Paulus and Petry had told her of the young Joe Gray, she had expected a taciturn, almost morose man who had little time for talk. He must have changed, she decided. "Everything is reusable," he went on. "We use liquid fuel, and it only takes three days to relaunch in a normal cycle. We could do it in hours, theoretically."

"I read that you plan a manned space station some time soon," Laura said, vaguely remembering an article from the library the day before.

He looked at her and smiled, arching his eyebrows conspiratorially. *His first obvious deception,* she thought. Laura looked back up at the descending spacecraft. It rode its jet of fire ever lower.

"It's just like in the old movies," Laura said. "You know, the silly ones from the fifties. 'Retro rockets' and things like that. Spaceships with little legs that take off on earth and land on the moon or Mars or wherever."

"It's the most cost-effective way, in the long run," he said, and Laura felt relieved they'd finally found something to talk about. *His work,* she thought. *How typical!* "We just use ultralight composites of epoxy and graphite fiber to reduce the weight of the launch vehicle," he continued, and Laura nodded knowingly. "Exclusive of the payload, ninety-eight percent of the weight of a fully fueled vehicle is its propellant. For a given cubic foot of volume, that spacecraft empty is lighter than Styrofoam."

"And it's so quiet, too," Laura commented. The rocket was slowing to a stop—suspended in air and hovering out over the ocean.

"Not really," Gray said, thumping the glass with his fingernails. "Triple pane, one pocket vacuum sealed, the other filled with argon." He went over to the wall and pulled a barely noticeable handle up from the paneling. A roaring sound poured into the room when he opened the door.

Laura followed him out into the brisk night, eyeing the doorframe as she passed. It had been aligned so well with the wall paneling that the seam was practically invisible.

The howl from the rocket's engines rattled the air even at their distance. The landing gear had lowered into place around the fiery exhaust, and as they watched, the rocket slowly began to slide sideways toward the leftmost pad.

"The lateral translation maneuver is the loudest!" Gray said in a voice raised over the violence. "We put sound insulation in all the island's homes and buildings so we can run twenty-four-hour space operations!"

When the rocket was centered directly above the concrete pad and about at eye level with Gray and Laura—its flat sides now lit by large spotlights from the ground—it began to sink in a straight line toward the earth. All was linear, precise, machinelike—clearly the work of a computer. Laura looked up at Gray's face. It was lit in the faint white fire that glinted also in his eyes. There was an expression on his face—contentment, she guessed. She turned back to the pad, thinking, *How can I ever know what he thinks or feels?* But she would have to learn. That was her job.

The flames beat at the center of the concrete base beside the gantry and spread ever wider as they pounded the earth. White clouds billowed out of the launchpad toward the sea on one side and the wide brown road on the other, boiling furiously like in a time-lapse film of a developing thundercloud. The jungle and ocean around the pad was well lit by tame spotlights. But the fire from the rocket's engines turned night into day and shone brightly on the nearby assembly building, and on a massive slab of concrete that shared the open field with its more impressive neighbor.

The distinct shadows cast across the lawn by the rocket's blaze grew long, and the rocket's descent slowed almost to a complete stop just above the pad. The engines suddenly shut off, and Laura's heart skipped a beat in the surprising silence as she anticipated the stunning explosion from a calamitous failure. But the rocket sat firmly in its place on the pad, the night again enveloping the brief artificial day of its chemical burn.

She looked back up at Gray. He had a smile of satisfaction on his face, which he tried to hide by turning away. "This is a volcanic island," he said in a voice he no longer needed to raise. "The crater was where the Village is now. This whole face of the mountain"—he motioned at the roughly semicircular wall along the middle of which perched his house—"was the inside of the crater wall. My geologists tell me the opposite wall blew out in a major eruption about ten thousand years ago."

Laura imagined a continuation of the walls to form a circle and saw that the island had once been little more than the tip of a volcano protruding from the sea.

"Erosion had leveled most of what was left," Gray continued, "although we had more than a year of earthmoving before we ever began construction. The center of the island down there"—he pointed toward the twinkling lights of the Village—"was a small lake that we had to drain. It was a miserable place, thick with mosquitoes."

"Was it inhabited before you bought it?"

"It's rented. I've got a ninety-nine-year lease. I'm the 'governor-general' under Fijian law." He had a wry grin on his face when he said it. "And no. No one could live here. There was no fresh water. I built a desalinization plant over there." He pointed into the darkness by the coast—the captain standing on his bridge. He lifted his hand, and where he pointed there sprouted creations of unimagined ingenuity. The creator. The wellspring. *Always "I,"* the professional in her noted.

Laura raised her hands to rub her upper arms and hug herself to ward off the chill. "Shall we go inside?" Gray asked. He had been watching her out of the corner of his eye.

Gray held the door for her. On the table was an enormous portion of chocolate mousse cake, swirls of dark chocolate forming intricate patterns on the plate around the luscious dessert. Gray walked past his seat without noticing.

"Ready to get started?" he asked.

Laura held the napkin she'd found neatly folded over the arm of her chair but quickly dropped it into the empty seat. "All right," Laura replied in her most assertive tone. "Let's get to it." On Gray's frenetic lead, dinner had taken less than fifteen minutes, but Laura was determined to gain the upper hand once she began the analysis. There was no other way to guide him gently toward whatever subjects she would find important. "Where would you be most comfortable?" Laura asked.

"Pardon me?"

"Well, analysis can be a fairly grueling process. There really is no shortcut. You'd be surprised how physically draining some patients seem to find it—depending, of course, on the . . . on the nature of the problem."

Gray's mouth was wide open in surprise. A grin spread across his face and filled his eyes with its sparkle. He burst out laughing. "So you think . . . ?" he began, but the question was cut short by still more laughter. Laura tilted her head and knitted her brow in confusion. "I'm sorry," Gray said. "I should've guessed. We haven't really discussed your job. I was going to wait until after dinner, which I guess is now." He cleared his throat, regaining his composure. "I'm afraid there has been some misunderstanding. I'm not the one in need of your counseling, Dr. Aldridge."

She shook her head and shrugged, then swiped away the wisp of hair that had fallen loose across her cheek. "Who is it, then?"

Gray had followed the movements of her hand as if studying her. He now stood there, staring at her intently. The smile faded.

"Mr. Gray?"

He turned away, and she waited as the last drop of humor drained from the man.

"Who *is* my patient, Mr. Gray?" she pressed, his behavior disconcerting.

Gray straightened, and as if with effort faced her full on. "It's the computer," he said, his eyes tracing the line of her hair before darting away.

"Computer center, please," Gray said as he settled into the seat beside Laura in the front of the driverless car.

"You can just, like, talk to it?" Laura asked, fumbling with her seat belt.

"Just tell it where you want to go," he answered as if it were the most mundane feature of his island world. The moment Laura's buckle clacked together, the car began its acceleration. "Voice recognition and synthesis are consumer functions, and they require a surprisingly large amount of processing capacity. But the computer is able to parse sound waves accurately enough to recognize rudimentary commands if spoken clearly and in English." The car picked up speed as it headed out of the courtyard and turned left at the gate.

Laura sat in what would have been the driver's seat of an

American car. Her pulse quickened in time with the rising speed of the vehicle, and she gasped and grabbed the empty dashboard as it sped into the black opening of the tunnel. She leaned toward Gray to peer around the gentle curve for the approaching headlamps into which—she imagined—they would at any moment collide.

"It's okay," Gray said quietly. The gentle tone of his voice—the intimacy it suggested—drew her gaze to his. Their faces were close, and Laura shrunk back into her seat. "We've never, not even once, had an accident with these cars. Never."

Laura tried to relax, but she could barely avoid cringing again when they burst from the tunnel. Her heart thumped against her rib cage, and she was alert now to two things—the increasing speed of the car as they began their descent from the mountain and the physical proximity of Gray.

"We've . . . had some problems. With the computer." Laura was too distracted by her fear of the unknown technology to which her life was now entrusted to concentrate fully on what he was saying. "It's been experiencing unexplained errors for months now. The rate of failure has been growing . . . exponentially. The way things are going, in a week, maybe less . . ."

Laura was unable to pry her eyes off the streaking blur of the jungle's edge, which was illuminated in the narrow beams of the headlights, but she managed to ask, "In a week, what?"

"The computer is the center of everything we do. Not just on this island, but worldwide. From that satellite coverage pattern I was describing to you earlier to a hundred and fifty million accounts, each of which can log pay-per-view requests, do on-line shopping or banking, answer polls, call plays for high school football teams, download software, play video games, send V-mail, or take advantage of any of the other interactive services we offer. And that's only a small fraction of what we have the computer doing."

The car flew downhill at what had to be close to a hundred miles per hour, veering smoothly one way or the other at forks in the road that were widened and banked like a concrete bobsled course. Laura was on edge. She had no means of guessing which way the driverless vehicle would turn, and the result was a constant fear of impending demise.

"We use the computer, of course," Gray continued, completely unconcerned, "for our manufacturing. We've been able to build what you see here because the productivity of the fifteen hundred workers on this island is phenomenal. Productivity is a function of capital investment, and I've invested heavily in the island's infrastructure." Buildings of various sizes and shapes but no discernible purpose flew by in the darkness, but Laura kept her eyes peeled out the windshield—straight ahead along the road down which they hurtled. Her ears popped, and the backs of her hands hurt from her grip on the armrests. "The gross product of this island is greater than that of a majority of the members of the United Nations. Mile-per-square-mile and man-for-man, this is the most productive place on the face of the planet. The most productive place in the *history* of the planet, for that matter."

"What?" Laura asked distractedly, taking her eyes briefly off the road to glance at Gray as he sat there—supremely confident and relaxed in his seat.

"We produce products here every year whose value on the open market, if they were available for sale, would be in the hundreds of billions. Productivity per worker is a deceptive statistic, of course. With such a high degree of automation, it's losing its meaning. A lot of things are losing their meanings," he mumbled.

Laura was beginning to calm down—slightly. They had yet to pass another vehicle. Maybe there were only one or two cars on these special roads. Maybe the driverless cars were only for Gray and his top henchmen. That comforting thought was ripped from her when in a blur and a brief buffeting of disturbed air first one, and then several cars identical to theirs rocketed by. Laura noticed that the previously sloppy driving of their vehicle had changed. It had slowed, and they hugged the right-hand side of the road as did the cars they passed headed in the opposite direction. It was all under control, Laura realized. Under the control of the computer. *But hadn't Gray said the computer was malfunctioning?* she thought.

Laura heaved a deep sigh—exhausted by the return of her anxiety.

Gray had fallen silent—his eyes, reflected in the dark window, looking off into the distance.

"I'm sorry, what did you say?" Laura asked.

"I said a lot of things are losing their meanings."

She turned to him. From the tone of his voice, it appeared, all was not well in the Workers' Paradise. They continued down the mountain in silence.

When the car entered the outskirts of the Village, it slowed to more responsible speeds. "Mr. Gray," Laura said, rolling her tense shoulders and flexing her stiff hands, "you still haven't explained how I can help you with a computer. I'm afraid there might have been some misunderstanding. I'm a psychologist. If someone on your staff has misinformed you about my credentials, I think it would be appropriate for me to return my fee and—"

"The computer is suffering from depression," Gray interrupted, turning from the window to meet her stare and hold it. "At least, that's what it says. Chronic depression."

After letting what he'd said sink in, Laura expelled a short huff that would have been a laugh but for her inability to muster a smile to go along with it. "You've gotta be kidding."

He not only didn't look as though he were kidding, he looked pained. His eyes—the same eyes as in the newspaper photo from his childhood—expressed sadness as conspicuously as any emotion could be conveyed without words.

Laura's head spun with the absurdity of the suggestion. Her eyes drifted off, reporting the sights of Village life to a mind that was lost deep in thought. Despite the absence of any traffic ahead, the car pulled to a full stop at an intersection. The streets of the Village were laid out in a grid like any normal town's. Their driverless car, however, and others like it that they passed seemed to navigate them with the same ease that they handled the banked and gently forking high-speed roads crisscrossing the island.

"What I have built here, Dr. Aldridge, is the first ever sixth-generation computer. Do you know what that means?"

Laura shrugged, then shook her head. Her attention was drawn to a lone statue on her left, and then to the long boulevard which the statue dominated. The broad street with its grassy median descended gently through the center of the Village away from the mountain. The car turned right onto the boulevard, and Gray craned his neck to look out the clear Plexiglas windshield at the rear. Laura, however, was enthralled with the sights of the bustling Village ahead.

The car proceeded slowly down the well-lit boulevard, which teemed with a vibrant and seemingly well-behaved nightlife. The place really was sort of like a Village, Laura thought. People strolled down paths past streetside cafés. There were warmly lit stores filled with luxury goods. A movie theater that was obviously the teen hangout. Some of the island's inhabitants, Laura noticed, saw Gray through the window of the car. There were pointed fingers, nudges of dinner companions in curbside seating, a wave. Gray appeared to be oblivious to such manifestations of his celebrity.

He was focused instead on her.

"The first generation," he continued relentlessly, "was made of vacuum-tube switches and mercury delay lines like the Sperry Univac in the early fifties. The second, like the Honeywell 800 in the late fifties and early sixties, used discrete transistors." The road grew darker as the car passed from the Village. "Restricted Area" was clearly marked in large, block letters on a sign beside a raised traffic arm. The jungle closed in, and the car accelerated again through the black canyon of leaves. "The third generation was built around small-scale integrated circuits and dominated the market from the mid-sixties to the mid-seventies. The IBM System 36 was a third-generation computer. The late seventies brought the large-scale and very-large-scale integrated circuits of the fourth generation." The car broke out onto an open field, the massive assembly building dominating the scene ahead—filling the windshield. Laura was awestruck by the size of it. "In the early eighties, experimental work began on fifth-generation computers, and the first came on line in the mid-nineties. They're massively parallel—thousands of digital processors crushing data all at once."

The car slowed and turned into a circular drive. All around lay the treeless lawns she had seen from high above. The quiet electric car pulled to a stop in front of a mammoth bunker. Both Gray's and Laura's doors opened automatically, rising straight into the air with their faint *whoosh*.

Once they were outside, the doors closed and the car headed off. Gray led Laura along a path toward the low-slung concrete structure that looked to be half buried in the flat and open fields. The humid air was thick with the foul, acrid smell from some chemical. Laura crinkled her nose. "Exhaust fumes," Gray said, "from Launchpad A."

She realized he'd been watching her again.

Laura paused atop steps that led deep into the ground. At the bottom lay a heavy metal door to the subterranean entrance. She didn't want to go down those steps without knowing more. She had an unsettled feeling in her stomach and couldn't tell whether it was from the ride or from something else. From something vaguely . . . sinister.

Suddenly, the series of decisions she'd made to rationalize coming to Gray's island seemed flawed. What was she doing there? What was Gray doing there? She wanted to know, to learn, to satisfy her natural curiosity, especially after the small glimpse she'd gotten of his island. But Laura's rising sense of foreboding evoked from some saner corner of her mind the desire instead to go home. To return to the comfortable confines of her prior life.

"I have built a sixth-generation computer," Gray said, standing beside Laura at the top of the steps. The tone of his voice indicated a degree of importance that was lost on Laura. "It's a fully functional, massively parallel neural network." She looked up at him. He was gauging the effects his words had on her. "The world's first true neurocomputer."

And those words did have an effect. "Are you serious?" He remained silent, his face devoid of expression. "I mean, pardon me, but . . . but a truly high-speed, highly distributed neurocomputer is a technological impossibility. It was a red herring. They tried it in the fifties, and it didn't work."

A smile—that self-satisfied look from before—spread across his face. "That was before fuzzy logic, genetic algorithms, and me."

Laura didn't know how to respond. On its face, his statement was rife with egoism. But he didn't seem egotistical. Then again, she didn't want to believe him to be an egotist. She had come here to help Joseph Gray, the misunderstood orphan, not Joseph Gray, the egomaniac. She knew she should be on guard against projecting—against imagining in this strange and intriguing man those traits she desired to find. She was left not knowing what to think about Gray.

But she had not been brought there for judgments about Gray's mental condition. He'd brought her there for something else—for some *thing* else. Laura looked down into the dark, foreboding hollows at the bottom of the steps. She didn't want to go down—down to meet what the creator had encased in a heavy tomb of concrete.

Obviously sensing her hesitation, Gray turned from the steps. "Let's take a walk," he said, touching Laura's elbow lightly and leading her away. They strolled alongside the roadbed that led across the great lawn to the assembly building. The enormous structure at the other end of the road formed a man-made wall stretching from one side of the field to the other. A gentle breeze rid the air of the noxious fumes. Laura breathed deeply of the smell of the ocean, slowly feeling cleansed of her earlier apprehension.

"We didn't know what we'd end up with," Gray continued as they strolled, "but we knew that we needed extraordinary computational power. You see, we wanted automation, but the main limitation on robotics was not the hardware of the robots themselves, but the horsepower of the computers that operated them. Take just the vision system. We use retinal chips in the robotics instead of cameras. They're particularly good at adjusting for both light and shade—which is a big problem—and in tracking objects across their field of view. But even with the advantage that retinal chips gives you, the processing demands are tremendous. Simply discerning edges—identifying the visual cues that tell where the boundaries of objects are—could take minutes for even the world's fastest supercomputers. Add hearing, touch, kinesthesia, problem solving, goal constraints—everything else that's required to actually function in the real world—and the processing needs of the system vastly exceeded capacities."

His voice had a certain quality to it, commanding attention without raising its volume. It was clear, deeper in tone than the voices of ordinary men of his build and age. And his thoughts welled up in such a fluid fashion that they seemed rehearsed. But he spoke naturally. He seemed at ease.

"Digital computers are very precise, which is good for tasks that involve numbers," he said. Laura listened more out of enjoyment of the experience than of the content. "But the best digital computer we've been able to produce can't surpass the information-processing capabilities of a three-year-old, and they never will. Digital computers are a dead end."

Gray lapsed into silence and walked on with his hands thrust deep into his pockets.

"You sound so sure," Laura finally said.

He stopped and turned to face her. "This"—he held out his arms, but looked straight at her—"is not a digital world; it's purely analog. The brain that we humans possess evolved, therefore, to process analog information—not to crunch numbers. If your brain were a digital computer, you'd store a description of all the faces of the people you knew in a long list. Every time you saw your mother, you'd have to search that list of faces for a match before you recognized her. As you got older, and your list of faces grew, it would take you longer and longer to find that match and recognize your mother's face. But your brain's not digital. You don't have a list of faces. You have a network of highly interconnected neurons. When you see your mother's face, those connections in your brain recall not only her identity, but everything about her—instantly! Your love for her. Her warmth to you as a child. The smell of her perfume. The fact that her birthday is next week. Everything, all at once. And a neural network can retrieve all those things from just a sliver of data—the sight of your mother's face or the unmistakable tone of her voice as she calls out your name. Unlike digital computers, it excels at handling fragmentary data—'fuzzy' data."

Laura's gaze shot up to Gray on his use of the word "fuzzy." Gray had been working on a neural network to solve "fuzzy" problems way back in 1983.

Could all this be the result, two decades later? she wondered, recalling the milestones of Gray's biography. His prediction of market demand for PVCs in 1984—his first billion. His prediction of the great stock market crash of 1987—tens of billions in wealth. His cornering of the high-definition TV market. The neural network he'd been developing was intended to discern patterns—to aid in *market* analysis.

Laura was suddenly so keyed up—so absorbed in the intriguing possibilities—she hadn't noticed that Gray had fallen silent. Their eyes met briefly, causing Laura's skin to tingle eerily. It was irrational, she realized, but in that momentary look she felt as if she'd been touched. Not physically, but mentally—as if he had peered behind the curtain to share in her innermost thoughts. As if in his look he'd said, "I know what you're thinking." It was unnerving, and it scattered those thoughts to the wind.

When he continued, he spoke quietly, softly—as if not to jar Laura from her reverie. "Something special happened. Something magical."

Without knowing why, Laura had to muster her energy to ask, "What?" It was energy she used to brace herself for his answer.

"It learns," he said simply. Her first reaction was disappointment. She had prepared herself for something more, and her expectations weren't met. That initial reaction, however, changed with every word he spoke. "It generalizes, Laura. But when it generalizes, it does so by analogy not to the human world, but to the new world in which it exists. We *missed* it! When the computer first concluded that a wire is to electricity like a vein is to blood, we rolled our eyes and moved on. Its intelligence began to transcend our own.

And that's because, you see, it was freed of this . . . *shell,*" Gray said, looking down at his body, "and with it was freed of the limitations of our perspective—our experiences in life."

Laura was afraid to look at him now. Afraid that her face might betray some private thought or feeling. Afraid that his might betray something she didn't want to see. Her mouth was dry when she asked, "What exactly are you saying?"

"I'm saying we've entered a new phase." He raised an arm and pointed. She was more interested in the man—in his face. "There's one of our robots right there."

Laura peered out across the lawn to see the distant headlights of an approaching vehicle. She found herself wondering what connection Gray saw between the new phase and his sudden sighting of the robot.

Laura suddenly felt as if she were with the only other person on the earth. Alone amid the brightly lit objects that had sprung directly from his imagination. But it wasn't as if he were the only other person, she realized. It was as if he were at the center of the world that had sprung from his mind and now rose from the flat fields all around. The world that she had now entered.

Gray continued his walk toward the assembly building. "We made a discovery," he said. His voice again chased away Laura's thoughts. "To develop intelligence, we had to give the computer mobility. We had to give it the ability to explore the physical world. To pick objects up. To break them. To develop a 'feel' for all the laws of nature that we take for granted. Mobility—that's the key . . . in more ways than one."

He sighed. "We're operational with Model Sevens. The first two models were experimental. Then came the Model Threes, which are those cars we ride around the island in. Models Four and Five have been retired or immobilized as limited-sequence robots along the assembly line. Finally came the Model Sixes and Sevens. We've got a couple hundred Model Sixes that are still in use, and we're up to over a hundred Model Sevens."

He raised his arm again and pointed to their left. "That one's a Six."

It was still a great distance away, and Laura could see nothing save a vehicle with a pair of closely set headlights and a flashing beacon on top. It was driving along the field straight their way. A faint hum like that of a lawn mower could be heard.

They were walking toward a point that would intersect the path followed by the robot. Laura studied the vehicle as it approached. Its ability to mow grass at thirty miles per hour seemed less impressive than the driverless cars of the earlier generation.

"Both the Sixes and Sevens were designed entirely by the computer. And the computer itself is, for the most part, designed by itself. We know pretty much how the hardware works. What's revolutionary is the software."

When the Model Six was about a hundred yards away, the noise of the mower was cut. The wheeled robot had halted. A large, centrally mounted arm lifted a rigid bag high into the air. By snagging the bottom of the bag on the lip of its towed bin, the robot managed to turn the unwieldy bag over. Grass cuttings poured into the bin. A light shone down from atop the superstructure—the robot's "head"—and the arm tilted the bag up so the light shone inside. Some cuttings were obviously caught inside. To dislodge them, the robot turned the bag upside down again and shook. It then repeated the inspection with the light. On the third try it slammed the bag down, which apparently did the trick. The robot resumed its course—the mower's growl first rising, then falling upon contact with uncut grass.

That showed logical problem solving, Laura thought. Out of the blue Laura felt a rushing sensation like she was shot along a path for which she was unprepared. She grew chilled as the implications of what she'd observed sunk in. *Had they taught it to bang the bag like that, or had it learned on its own?*

For the first time, Laura inspected the lights atop the robot. There was no flashing beacon on its "head" as she had thought. There were a pair of lights mounted atop the machine flitting independently about the ground in rapid jerks. Jumping from one patch of grass to another, the high-intensity beams ranged in jittery motions across a broad arc in front of the vehicle, shifting in almost nervous agitation several times every second. The lights were searching the field along the robot's path.

Laura headed down the paved walkway toward the robot, watching the spectacle of its highly coordinated movements as it neared. Gray followed *her* now. When they were about twenty yards away, the brilliant lights atop the robot locked onto them. Laura stopped and raised her hand to shield her eyes. The robot's mower shut off completely—the whir of the blades quickly winding down.

A few moments later, the twin searchlights were extinguished.

All was quiet now. Laura stared at the motionless robot. The two housings encasing the lights remained trained on them.

"Mr. Gray," a voice boomed from some unseen loudspeaker behind them, "please report to the computer center." The announcement echoed across the field, and Gray turned and said, "I guess we'll do our tour of the assembly building later this evening." He turned and gently ushered Laura back toward the bunker. She still stared at the darkened, motionless machine over her shoulder. She couldn't shake the feeling that despite its apparent inactivity, it stared back at her as well.

As soon as they turned, the light illuminated them again—their figures casting long shadows along the walkway in the high-intensity beams. The skin on Laura's back crawled. They were being watched. The lights moved on, and the mower started up.

Laura couldn't resist another glance over her shoulder. The robot's single long arm stretched out in front of its carriage as both lights focused on a fixed patch of earth ahead—on a piece of trash just beside the walkway. Laura stopped to watch. As the robot passed the illuminated focus of its attention, the arm snapped at the ground with surprising speed. Continuing on, the robot crossed the road and held its closed claw up to the lights, rotating its trophy first left, then right. Following the inspection, it casually reached back and tossed the trash into the towed bin. It didn't have to look back, Laura noticed. It knew where the bin was.

Gray stood beside her in silence, his face an inscrutable mask.

"That was really amazing!" Laura said.

Slowly, the corners of his lips curled and his expression—his entire manner—softened. The thin streaks of blazing artificial light flickered in his dark but smiling eyes.

He turned and headed for the bunker. Laura followed him down the steps to the metal door—searching for clues in the expression of the silent and enigmatic genius.

3

Gray stared into a peephole at the entrance to the computer center. A metallic popping sound emanated from deep within the concrete. He straightened, and with a rumble the ponderous door began to recede into the wall. Eyeing the stainless steel mechanisms protruding from the doorframe, Laura first thought the place was built like a vault. *Or a blast shelter,* she decided on further reflection.

The foot-thick slab of metal thudded firmly into place, and a lighter inner door hissed and briskly slid open. A dimly lit room lay ahead. Through its center was a narrow, metal gangplank which had two railings running from one side to the other. Laura followed the silent Gray into the compartment, feeling in the pinch of her throat, the shallowness of her breathing, and the thump of her heart the return of an overwhelming unease. Gray halted halfway across the gangplank, which was suspended in air inside the black metal chamber.

The sound of compressed air accompanied the closing of the compartment's exit. Through the walls Laura could hear the vault door closing as well. She searched the recesses of the dark chamber for clues as to its purpose. The floors, walls, and ceiling were black metal slats—the angles all directed toward the slender catwalk. Laura waited for Gray to proceed, but he stood lost in thought—one hand firmly gripping the railing.

"Oh," he said, "I should mention that the computer center is semiclean. We have to minimize dust, you understand." A buzzer sounded, and a screen ahead glowed red with the words "Blowers Activated." A rapid series of clacks sounded from behind the grates that surrounded them. Gray shouted, "You might want to hold onto . . . !"—his last words drowned out by the whine.

The wind hit her with gale force, popping her ears with the sudden change in pressure. Gray was shouting something. They were standing in a howling wind tunnel, but the wind buffeted them equally from all sides at once. Laura's hair lashed wildly across her face, combining with the windstorm to force her eyes closed. She reached up to pull a long strand from her mouth. She should have reached down.

Tendrils of air snaked under her dress. They forced their way upward—offending gusts along bare skin. The belt of her smock caught on her breasts, and she grabbed the billowing fabric and pressed down. The light dress resisted all efforts, and she clamped one hand down in front, one in back.

As quickly as it had started, the storm was over. The smock settled gently into place around her thighs, and Laura opened her eyes into a thick sea of hair. She reached up to pull the mane from her face—the hair attracted to her palm by static electricity. The first thing she saw was Gray, who flashed her a sickly grin of apology. His hair stood wildly on end—tiny points like horns sticking out in all directions.

Laura broke out laughing, covering her mouth with her hand to stifle what degenerated into a series of ungraceful chortles. She managed "Sorry" while holding her hair off her forehead, the other hand pinning her mouth firmly closed.

She swept her hair back and straightened her shoulders, fully composed now. "That was a pleasant surprise."

Gray raked his fingers through his hair and shrugged. "Not very many people wear dresses down here."

The screen on the wall ahead changed displays. "Welcome" now glowed in cheery green letters, and a hissing sound announced the opening of the door. Bright light from the room ahead flooded the cramped compartment.

Laura followed Gray into the large room, which swirled with the activity of over a dozen busy people. They appeared to be technicians, working at row after row of consoles. It felt all of a sudden to Laura as if she had stepped onto a great spaceship in some far distant future. All was antiseptic white panels or glowing, multiwindowed screens. Wall-sized monitors were alive with bar charts bouncing rhythmically to an unheard and discordant beat. Windows exploded with numbers, and diagrams, and glorious graphics that reminded Laura most of some psychedelic light show.

Gray was looking at her, and she turned to him. She laughed, grinning stupidly from ear to ear. "Wow" was all she could think to say.

Gray stepped up to a vanity just inside the entrance and began to comb his hair. Laura took one look at herself in the mirror, and reached instantly for the complimentary "Gray Corporation" brush.

"If you want a sweater or a jacket or something," Gray said, "just let an operator know. We've tried to fix the heating problem several times, but it never seems to do the trick. It's the superconducting electronics. They're cooled by liquid nitrogen."

The brisk air was invigorating after their walk through the warm Pacific night. Besides, Laura was too fascinated by the spectacle to pay much attention to the chill. The confident fingers of the technicians flew—tapping keys or spinning trackballs. Some wore ultralight headphones, in constant communication with a cohort seated across the room or on the other side of the globe, she couldn't tell which. Vibrant colors popped open on crisp thirty-inch monitors like genies bursting from lamps. There was nothing government surplus here. All was right on the razor's edge. It was a scout ship hurtling centuries ahead of mankind.

Gray tapped a small black mat mounted to the wall by the vanity. "Please touch before entering" was written on a bright red placard above it. Laura casually complied—a painful snap stinging her fingertips.

"Ow!" she mouthed, rubbing her fingers with her thumb.

"Sorry," Gray said feebly. He waited beside her before the marvels of the room.

"What *is* this?" Laura asked, standing rooted to the spot in total awe.

"It's the operations room of the main computer."

She nodded over and over in response while gawking. "Oh," she finally said.

Gray led her through the maze of workstations. Most of the technicians were men, and none, Laura noticed, looked up to return her gaze. Instead, they glanced furtively her way just after she'd passed like boys in the hallway in high school.

Gray, too, noticed the odd behavior. "Most of my computer people are fairly intense types," he said by way of explanation.

They passed consoles on which sat two-liter plastic bottles half filled with generic orange soda. Industrial-sized bags of cheese puffs and pretzels and popcorn lay open in Gray's "semiclean" command ship. Decals adorned monitors with slogans like "Legalize Marijuana" or pictures of the starship *Enterprise*. Some of the technicians' headphones, Laura realized, played music at high volumes. That music ran the gamut from classical to headbanger. The people who listened to the music ran the gamut too.

Almost everyone wore thick sweaters of one sort or another. It was what they wore underneath that distinguished one man from the next. Laura marveled at the parade of fashions—at the short-sleeved dress shirts sporting pocket protectors and the tie-dyed T-shirts and the orange polyester bell-bottoms circa the disco era. Many seemed permanently hunchbacked as they sat slumped over their consoles. Others were laid back in their padded leather chairs. One had his feet propped higher than his head and an oversized digitizer balanced comfortably across his lap. The brilliant colors of their computer screens glinted off the thick lenses of their eyeglasses, which were held securely in place by no-nonsense frames. Laura pictured the pale tribe being forced one day to emerge from their habitat—shielding their eyes and suffering almost instant and near fatal sunburn.

"What do you think?" Gray asked, pausing at the far side of the room.

"They're all nerds," Laura whispered.

She watched Gray smile, then grin, then burst out laughing—startling some of the mole people nearby. He beamed at her—his eyes sparkling brightly. He was a handsome man. "I actually meant the facility," he said, still greatly amused.

Laura looked around, searching for something to say. "It's very . . . neat."

"Thank you," he replied on the verge of a chuckle. "And you're right, they *are* nerds. It's a sad but true fact. But their average net worth I'd guess is over ten million dollars." Laura shot him a look of astonishment, and he shrugged. "I give them this thing called a revenue slice. It's a lot of money, but with productivity comes pay. If one person can make a thousand times as many widgets as another, you can pay him a thousand times as much. Or"—Gray caught Laura's gaze—"at least a hundred."

He was grinning broadly again. He'd told another joke.

Gray turned and led Laura down a hallway. They passed a series of featureless doors—no paneling, no hardware, just flat white plastic. One of those doors up ahead slid open on their approach, riding a faintly audible puff of air into the wall.

It had opened a half-second before they arrived, Laura noted, but an identical door across the hall had remained closed. She entered the room behind the oblivious Gray, still wondering how the door had known when to open.

They walked straight into the middle of heated debate. Seated around a long table in the high-tech conference room were six more nerds—male and female—and one distinctly non-nerd. The one exception was a brawny, tanned man who had the square-jawed look of a soldier. He seemed totally out of place amid that group, and remained silent while the nerds engaged in an animated free-for-all. His keen eyes locked onto Laura as she took the seat next to Gray.

When Gray leaned forward and rested his forearms on the table, everyone fell silent as if on cue. "First off," Gray said in the suddenly calm conference room, "I'd like to introduce to you the newest member of our team, Dr. Laura Aldridge." There were a couple of weak nods, but no chorus of welcome. Laura was instantly on guard. Gray turned to the woman on his left. "Dr. Aldridge, this is Dr. Margaret Bickham. She's our director of artificial intelligence—that's 'software.'" The severe woman nodded—her lips pinched so tightly they were puckered and wrinkled, her mouth cutting across her face in a perfectly straight line that was neither a smile nor a frown. "To her left," Gray said, laying his palm out toward the pointed end of the oval table, "is Dr. Georgi Filatov, our head of computer operations."

"So pleased to meet you, I'm sure," the man said with a thick Russian accent. He looked like some legendary chess champion or a mentalist who bent spoons with brain power. His bushy, graying hair served to double the apparent size of his head.

"Georgi keeps the main computer's hardware operational. Next is Dr. Philip Griffith," Gray said, nodding to the man seated across the table. "Dr. Griffith is director of robotics. I guess that's self-explanatory." The man waggled his fingers to wave clumsily at Laura, his eyes smiling behind thick glasses and his grin spreading wide his muttonchop sideburns, revealing a perfectly unmatched set of crooked teeth.

Laura's eyes moved on to the next man—to the hard stare from across the table that hadn't left her since she entered the room.

"And this is Franz Hoblenz. He's my security chief." The man nodded curtly at Laura. He was large, had the weathered look of an outdoorsman, and regarded her so openly that his manner was faintly suggestive of a baseness—that particularly male baseness—from which Laura instinctively recoiled.

"Next up is Dr. Dorothy Holliday. She's our 'epidemiologist.'"

Everyone laughed, but the joke was completely lost on Laura. "I'm actually in charge of 'E and V,'" the blushing woman said, her voice surprisingly high in pitch. "Errors and viruses," she translated. Laura's gaze lingered on the relatively talkative girl. She was young—early twenties, at most—and pretty. She had an engaging but self-conscious smile, without the grace and ease that maturity would bring. She was Laura—only a decade or more younger.

"We just call 'er 'Doc' Holliday," the soldier from across the table growled. The joking reference to the ancient gunfighter drew titters from the group. The muscular man's comment had surprised Laura, not because of his deep and gravelly voice—which was appropriate to his appearance—but because of his thick Texas accent. She had expected the blond security chief to be German.

Gray completed his introductions with the heads of production and space operations, who looked to Laura like more clones from Gray's mad scientist factory.

"Okay," Gray said, changing tones and holding his hands out in query, "what's the latest error report?"

Dorothy Holliday poked a pen at her palmtop computer. "We had a pneumatic door close right in the face of a guy at the gym two hours ago."

"Was it verified?" Margaret Bickham asked from the opposite end of the table.

"Yep," Dorothy replied, bobbing her head somewhat awkwardly in affirmation. "The guy had just finished, like, having a *humongous* fight with his wife in front of God and everybody. When he stomped off, he walked"—she clapped her upright palms together in demonstration—"*right* into the door. Must've been twenty people standing around who saw it. Word I got was they all had a good laugh," she said, ready to laugh herself but getting no takers from her somber audience. "Anyway, the door operated normally after that. Phase one's scan was negative."

When nobody commented, Dorothy arched her eyebrows and compressed her lips into a frown, then moved on. Laura smiled at the girl's unaffectedly juvenile manner—her every feeling displayed naturally on a face not yet adept at the art of deception.

Dorothy's palmtop made quiet *bings* with every press of her pen. "Then," she continued, her voice little more than a squeak that you had to strain hard to hear, "about an hour ago, we had a customer in Copenhagen—one of our former checkers, as a matter of fact—who complained that her account balance was, like, *way* off. We looked into it, and the account showed a several hundred *thousand* dollar balance."

"Jesus," Georgi Filatov said, shaking his head in disgust. The bushy mop of his hair swayed with the motion, and he leaned forward to exchange glances with the others.

"Then *finally* . . . ," Dorothy began.

"*Another* error?" Margaret asked, seemingly incredulous.

Dorothy frowned again and nodded. "A vapor lamp in the parking lot of our Taiwan facility burned out. One of the security guards reported it, but the outage obviously should've triggered an operator notice."

"I'm gonna send a team to Taipei to check it out," Hoblenz said to Gray. "That's the second fault at the same facility. Security integrity could've been compromised."

Gray nodded. "Okay. What are we doing about the problem? Margaret?" he asked, starting on his left with the director of artificial intelligence. She lifted a metal briefcase from the floor, which she methodically placed on the table and opened with popping sounds from its latches. As she leafed through her papers, Laura studied the woman. She was a goodly number of pounds overweight, and she wore glasses, as did everyone there other than Laura, Gray, and Hoblenz. *And Dorothy,* Laura amended as she looked around.

Sitting at opposite ends of the table, Dorothy and Margaret formed "bookends" of a sort. They were the only women at the table . . . until Laura's arrival.

Laura glanced back and forth between the two women.

Dorothy's light brown hair was thin and straight and pinned back from her face with barrettes. Small wisps dangled here and there in an unintended but attractive way. Margaret's dark and graying thatch sprouted into what looked like an army helmet pressed tightly around her skull. Neither woman wore any makeup to speak of, although the fresh-scrubbed youth of Dorothy's skin obviated any real need for it. And both clearly paid no attention to clothes. Margaret wore maroon polyester slacks and a military-style white shirt complete with epaulets and piping and a buttoned-up breast pocket filled to the bursting point with some hidden cargo. Dorothy wore faded, baggy blue jeans and a tight-fitting sleeveless blouse over a frame that was all skin and bones.

Laura sat between the two, wondering idly which she resembled more. It was then she felt, more than saw, that Gray was watching her. Suddenly alert, Laura grew more and more conscious of Gray's presence next to her—of his unwavering and unnerving scrutiny. She made certain she didn't catch Gray's eye—looking anywhere but in his direction—and in so doing her gaze ran headlong into the unblinking stare of Hoblenz. The man didn't bother to avert his eyes, brazenly checking her out and not at all disturbed at being caught. It was instead Laura who felt compelled to turn away.

"Jesus *Christ*, Margaret!" Filatov burst out. "We don't have all night!"

Margaret ignored the barb. In fact, she slowed her search through the briefcase to a crawl, checking each nook and cranny in utter disregard of her colleague's histrionics. Filatov snorted like a bull, scanning the table for support.

Finally, Margaret cleared her throat and adjusted her glasses. She placed a single sheet of paper on the table, wove her fingers together, and nestled her chin in the mesh. "We asked the computer to run a pattern-recognition routine on the errors to date."

"What did it turn up?" Gray asked.

"Nothing."

There was a moment of silence, then Filatov exploded. "God-*damn!*" He slammed his hand on the table with a resounding boom, causing Laura to flinch.

Margaret couldn't have cared less. "The errors appear to be random," she continued as if she were in a different universe from Filatov. "It has instituted a constant monitoring, though, and will report any matches it finds."

"She's a Vulcan!" Filatov shouted, his hands gesturing wildly. "Not a Vulcan—a *Klingon!*"

"Georgi-i-i," Griffith said, shaking his head to chastise Filatov for the vile aspersion.

"What threshold did it establish for a match?" Gray asked, sitting unperturbed through the shocking display of disunity.

"I don't know," Margaret replied.

"Check it," Gray ordered curtly. "I want you to set it very low. I'd rather chase a few wild geese than miss the chance for an early detection." He looked now at Filatov—his head of operations. "What about you, Georgi?" Gray asked in a buoyant tone, pressing the corners of his lips flat to deny a smile. An attentive Hoblenz leaned forward, grinning ear to ear in anticipation.

"Before I report," Filatov began in a deliberate and overly loud voice, "I think maybe we should all give Margaret a round of applause for the *fine* work she's been doing to resolve our present difficulties." Filatov clapped his hands slowly several times—no one else joining in. Still, Gray said nothing.

When Filatov was through, he sighed deeply then resumed as if nothing had happened. "We're running at about ninety-six percent system capacity. That's net, of course, of the phase one antiviral program. I've been discussing with Dorothy the . . . the possibility of clearing up enough resources for phase two."

Laura still marveled at the unchallenged rudeness of the man and missed at first the fact that all eyes had gravitated toward Gray. She had no idea what the significance of Filatov's comment was, but a tension had filled the room on his use of the words "phase two." The proposal, whatever it was, seemed momentous.

Gray made a slow sweep of the faces ending with Dorothy.

The girl was doodling on her palmtop absentmindedly and didn't bother to look up before speaking. "We'd need to free up a total of about"—she cringed, hunching her shoulders as if to ward off impending blows—"six *percent?*" She winced.

There was instant commotion from around the table, everyone voicing their outrage at Dorothy's suggestion.

"One conversation at a time!" Gray said sternly, and the room fell quiet again. He turned back to Dorothy.

The girl went on, her body having sunk further into the chair and her voice to barely a whisper. "Georgi said figure at least one, preferably two percent . . . "

"Speak up!" Hoblenz interrupted—speaking in a stentorian tone as if to set an example.

Dorothy sat bolt upright. "Yes, sir!" she replied assertively but in her childlike voice. She sarcastically saluted Hoblenz in an inexpert manner. "We need *two-o-o* percent more," she said loudly, lowering her soprano's voice in imitation of Hoblenz's bass and staring at him through two fingers wiggling in air.

"Without headroom for spikes," Filatov jumped in, "we'd run dangerously close to a hundred percent of capacity. If we had a surge of throughput . . ." He faltered and fell silent. Everyone there knew what dire results would ensue if Filatov's fears materialized. Everyone but Laura. "That means we'd need a total of eight percent free," Filatov continued sheepishly. "Right now, I can find four with a little juggling of the night's runs." His eyes panned the table, his hands spreading wide in a gesture of apology or of supplication. "We'd have to come up with another four percent from somewhere."

A pathetic attempt at a whistle came from Philip Griffith, Gray's director of robotics.

"How much do we gain if we drop overnight error checking on interbank transfers?" Gray asked. Several people's heads shot up. "I'll indemnify the banks for any discrepancies," he said, allaying a concern Laura could only guess at from context. She felt like a spectator at a game whose rules she hadn't learned. Her appreciation of what transpired hinged upon reading the reactions of the others.

Filatov rocked back in his chair and cupped his hands behind his head. His eyes drifted up toward the ceiling. There were rings of sweat on his shirt beneath his arms. "That would give us four percent or so, I suppose. But if you figure ten P.M. on the West Coast is about seven A.M. on the Continent, that only gives us a couple of hours before the banks open in Europe and we start wire-clearing operations."

"What about trying to load phase two a little earlier in the evening?" Gray asked.

"You can check with programming," Filatov said, "but tonight's that big pay-per-view heavyweight championship fight in Las Vegas. Last I heard, the marketing people were expecting close to fifty million orders."

"And that's an eight-channel broadcast," Hoblenz spoke up unexpectedly. "One channel in each fighter's corner, one with and one without announcers, plus the helmet-cams and I don't know what else. And all that with full VR simulcast for the beta testers."

"Is two hours enough to finish a phase two sweep of the system?" Gray asked Dorothy.

She shrugged, then began to waggle her head from side to side in motions that slowly became a rhythmic nodding in time with music only Dorothy could hear. "O-o-o-h," she said, and then sighed, "we haven't run a phase two scan since last year. And we've doubled system size since then. That run time was seventy-four minutes."

Gray frowned. "Let's start off-loading, then. I want everybody to give me proposals for ten percent reductions in their department's budgeted usage." There were groans from all sides, and Hoblenz cleared his throat and sat forward. "Everybody but security," Gray amended, and Hoblenz nodded. "We'll meet again in four hours."

Laura looked at her watch. *That'll be at 1:00 A.M.,* she thought, but decided she didn't feel tired. She was excited. She didn't know what was happening or what was expected of her, but this was definitely exciting. It was so unlike everything to which she'd grown accustomed, and she accepted the fact that in the business world you had to work long hours. *That's why he pays so well,* she concluded, feeling somewhat less abashed at accepting the money.

"Meanwhile, Dr. Aldridge," Gray said, jarring Laura from her cocoon of anonymity, "I'll let you get familiarized a bit before you settle in and get started. Dr. Griffith, why don't you give Dr. Aldridge a tour of the facilities?" Gray said to his head of robotics.

The man looked astonished. He stared back at Gray, his red lips parted at the intersection of his enormous sideburns. His eyes—magnified behind Coke-bottle lenses—appeared ready to pop out of his head. "But, Mr. Gray, I've scheduled a . . . a systems check for tonight on the auxiliary belts, and a quality control review in the . . ."

"Get someone to cover for you," Gray replied, cutting him short and rising to leave. "I'll see you all in four hours. Meeting adjourned."

"I'm sorry if I'm keeping you from your job," Laura said as the elevator continued its high-speed descent. "I mean, you sound pretty busy. I don't know why Mr. Gray would pick *you* to show me around."

Griffith shrugged. "Mr. Gray is a way strange dude." After smiling her way, Griffith raised his upper lip to expose his teeth in what looked like a snarl. He grimaced a total of three times—wrinkling his face and squinting with each exaggerated expression before finally relenting and using his fingers to press his glasses higher up the bridge of his nose.

Laura turned away and maintained a neutral expression. She'd seen Griffith's type many times before, especially in academia. Oddballs. Clueless loners. The kind of people who populated the lines at the department of motor vehicles and loved to talk about government conspiracies. The only difference between that sort and academics like Griffith was their IQ scores.

Griffith snorted loudly and made a grunting sound as he cleared his throat. When Laura's ears popped for the third time, she asked, "How far down are we going?"

"The main pool is about three hundred meters below sea level," he replied. "We found at that depth the lava stone absorbs most of the subatomic junk flying around through space and reduces our error rate substantially. It also, of course, eliminates electromagnetic interference and more mundane problems like vibrations and dust." The elevator began to slow. "Then, of course, there's the physical security." Griffith opened a box set into the wall of the elevator and handed Laura a pair of dark sunglasses. "Here," was all he said.

The lenses were jet black, and around the edges of the lenses was wrapped a black, semirigid fabric.

"What's this?" she asked.

"Put them on," Griffith said as he donned his own pair. "They prevent retinal damage from the lasers."

"*What?*" Laura asked, her legs practically buckling underneath her as the tug of the elevator's deceleration grew and grew. "What lasers?" she asked, but didn't wait for the answer—quickly covering her eyes with the goggles just as Griffith had done.

The lenses were so heavily tinted it was practically pitch dark in the small compartment. When the elevator reached bottom, the lights suddenly went out completely.

"Hey!" Laura blurted out.

"We have to prevent any stray light from corrupting the communications signals," Griffith explained. "There'll be a low level of red light in the observation platform."

There was a long pause before the elevator doors opened one thousand feet beneath the computer center bunker. The parting of the doors revealed a small room, which was dimly lit and surrounded by windows.

A frigid tide of heavy air poured into the elevator. In the near total darkness, Laura felt the freezing wave inundate her—washing over her legs like a fluid and rising inch by inch up her body. Within seconds, she was totally immersed in the icy bath.

Laura waded into the cold air behind Griffith. He retrieved a heavy parka from a locker and vigorously shook the jacket before handing it to her. "This ought to warm up once the chemical pouches in the lining get going."

Laura was already ignoring him. As her eyes slowly adjusted to the low light, she became transfixed by the spectacular display glimmering through the ice-covered windows. She'd never seen anything like it before.

The dark world was ablaze with a billion sparkling stars. They twinkled on and off so rapidly each pulse seemed just a figment of her imagination—a trick of her eye. The effect was stunning. The mysterious cave was alive with light, and yet it was immersed in total darkness.

The numbing cold forced Laura to climb into the oversized jacket. With shaking hands, she tugged at the zipper and raised the fur-lined hood over her head. The quilted parka hung low like a military greatcoat, but her feet were still exposed to the air's wintry grip.

Carefully she edged her way across the observation deck toward the lights.

A shiver rippled up Laura's spine as the chill sank straight through the jacket. "Man!" she whispered, the word vibrating through the chatter of her teeth.

"Yeah," Griffith said—his voice quaking as well. "It's co-o-old!"

"No, I mean what *is* this place?" she said, standing at the red-lit window. "These lights! They're . . . "

"Otherworldly," Griffith supplied. "That's what I always think. It's like you're peering into another world, another dimension." Laura reached out to touch the glass. "Don't!" Griffith warned, and she quickly withdrew her hand. "You might get your skin burned by the cold." Griffith pried an ordinary ice scraper from the sill and began to clear a spot on the window. "We don't have visitors down here very often," he said as he worked. After chipping off a large, irregular patch in the center of the pane, he quickly stuck his hand back into his pocket and awkwardly used his elbow to wipe the glass clean.

When he stood back, Laura leaned over to peer through the hole. The twinkling was gone. The pulses of light shone brilliantly, each a fleeting pinprick in the coal black canvas below. The scene was constantly changing, each momentary flash a singular, nonrepeating event. Randomness, hinting at perfect order.

"That's the 'net,'" Griffith said, his voice lowered, almost reverent. "A neural network. An optical, analog, neural network. The most innovative machine ever created. You're looking at the eighth wonder of the world, Dr. Aldridge. I only wish Archimedes were here to see it."

"It's beautiful," Laura mumbled, mesmerized by the unearthly display.

"You can't tell in the darkness, of course, but we're standing on a terrace suspended over a big concrete pool. The pool's about ten meters deep, a couple of hundred meters long, and a hundred wide. It's filled with liquid nitrogen, which boils at minus two hundred and seventy degrees Fahrenheit. When the peripheral electronic components are cooled to that temperature, they become superconducting. What we do is lower racks that look like a child's erector set into the pool. Each rack holds a thousand circuit boards, and each board is about a hundred times more powerful than an old Cray-1 supercomputer." His voice was shaking, and he shifted from one foot to the other. It would be a short tour, Laura guessed, despite the chemical warmth now radiating down the full length of her overcoat. "On each of those circuit boards," Griffith continued, "there are about ten million nodes or, using your terminology, neurons. Ten million brain cells."

What Griffith said were mere words. They were nothing compared to what she saw with her own two eyes. The sheer immensity of the display that lay before them was staggering. How could anything be constructed to produce such an effect. Blackness, filled with light.

"It's an optical computer," Griffith continued, "not an electronic one. It uses light instead of electricity to process its basic logical operations and to store its memories. Logic gates are opened or closed depending on the intensity of a laser beam and take the place of semiconductors." Laura heard a rustle of fabric, and she tore herself momentarily from the light show to look at the opening in Griffith's hood. "Do you know what a picosecond is?" he asked, dimly visible inside the furry fringe.

"Well . . . of course!" Laura's breath came out as steam. "Sort of."

"It's a trillionth of a second. Ordinary electronic supercomputers take four hundred or so picoseconds to process a binary operation like adding two numbers together. This optical computer has cut that time down to *point* four picoseconds. And you're seeing only a minute fraction of those operations. Ninety-nine point nine percent of its signal traffic is passed along microscopic waveguides impregnated on the boards themselves."

Laura gazed in wonder at the needles of light popping like tiny flash bulbs out of thin air. It reminded her most of astronomers' pictures of deep space. Only this universe was alive and in fast-forward—stars being born, shining brightly, and dying out in mere fractions of a picosecond. "So those lights down there," Laura asked, "are just point one percent of the computer's operations?"

"Well, no, actually. They're a lot less than that. About ninety-nine point something percent of the signal traffic that's *not* passed along a board's internal circuitry is routed by fiber-optic cables, which you also can't see."

"So, wait," Laura said. "If we can't see the internal light signals on the boards themselves, and we can't see the fiber-optic signals"—she turned back to the miraculous sights visible through the thin patch of clear glass—"what are *those?*"

"Laser pulses. Communications between boards that aren't regular enough or sufficiently close to each other to justify hard-wiring the two boards together. Those boards talk to each other by beaming lasers through the gaseous nitrogen above the pool. Those laser signals down there represent only about one out of every hundred million or so packets of data being passed from one logic gate to the next."

Griffith went on to talk about the constant "rationalizing" of the computer's wiring to improve efficiency, but Laura wasn't listening. She was too astonished at the implications of what he was saying to follow the details. *If this,* she thought, looking at the extraordinary constellation of fleeting stars, *is one hundred-millionth of the total number of signals . . .* It was impossible to comprehend. It was a rush of noise so constant, so dissonant, that it overwhelmed her imagination completely.

It's a brain. The thought came to her as clearly as if whispered into her ear. She was standing inside a living brain, watching the most elementary impulses of thought—synaptic interaction. Individual brain cells talking to one another. A tingle spread outward from her scalp and ran down her neck to her shoulders. She shivered, but not because of the cold. What she felt was the physical reaction to an entirely cerebral phenomenon.

For it was, Laura knew, from connections of similar complexity that thoughts arose in animal brains. It was, from a tangled web of impulses very much like the confusion of light down below, that a sense of consciousness emerged in humans.

". . . signals come into the net from input devices—things like cameras, microphones, motion detectors, et cetera, or traditional electronic input devices like keyboards, mice, or digitizers. They're converted from electron-based to light-based signals by . . . "

"He's done it," she whispered, her eyes watering but her mouth dry as she watched the symphony of lights perform over the nitrogen pool. With a rustling of his parka Griffith looked her way and fell silent.

Gray had made a brain. He'd done it. All the talk—all the fruitless research by so many for so long—and Gray had made it happen. The goose bumps had free rein over Laura now, spreading not just to her arms but across her entire body. It was a feeling of exultation. Of triumph. Of advancement. Laura reveled in it—in the euphoria that was released like a drug on suddenly appreciating the true magnitude of Gray's breakthrough.

"How could he ever figure it all out?" she said as if in a dream—not really asking a question, just giving voice to her disbelief. "The complexity of it is phenomenal!"

"Oh, Mr. Gray didn't build the net."

Laura spun instantly to the dark shape of the man. "What do you mean? Who built this, then?"

"Well, now you're sort of getting into a philosophical question, I suppose. Certainly, Mr. Gray set the process in motion. He and Margaret put the computer to work on developing the net about three years ago. Gray implanted the seed program, but from then on it just sort of grew and . . . "

"What 'seed' program?"

In the darkness, it was impossible to read Griffith's facial expression. His response was slow in coming. "Well . . . he . . . They didn't just start out with a completely blank slate. I mean, Gray had been toying with a lot of the *theories,* of course, for years. But they started with a program that initially worked solely on increasing the net's size, and it sort of grew around that base. About a year ago, we filled up this pool and added another—the annex—a half a mile from here. It has a much larger potential volume, but to date we've only added roughly the same number of boards as the main pool here has."

"And this seed program—it was Gray's?" Laura asked, focusing hard on the inflection in Griffith's voice as he answered.

"Sure! Yeah."

Laura nodded. The connections in her mind were all complete now. The connections between the points in Gray's biography—the milestones on his path to becoming the richest man in history.

From its humble beginnings on Wall Street, the child prodigy's math-deficient computer program had grown into . . . this! *Of course!* she thought. He'd started work on this system almost two decades ago. His little "seed" program was in fact the product of years of his genius hard at work. She was almost breathless with excitement at her discovery. But it was so obvious, it was a discovery that surely the others had already made.

"Why do you ask?" Griffith whispered. He sounded guarded, conspiratorial. "What are you saying?" he pressed.

Laura was amazed. Somehow, at least one member of Gray's "team" had not drawn the conclusions Laura thought were so clear. "Nothing," Laura said, not knowing why she was hesitant to share her thoughts with the man—one of Gray's top associates.

She went back to the thread of Griffith's last comment. "So, you're saying that the seed program grew into this? That the computer built itself?"

Griffith hesitated—a pause that Laura interpreted as disappointment at the evasive response. "Oh, we supervised it, of course. But only at the most general level. Take my department—robotics. Each of our robots has its own miniature neural network—or 'mini-net'—and the first training we give those mini-nets is to have the main computer run them through the paces with simulations. When we needed greater kinesthetic capabilities for our Model Seven robots we just asked the computer to give them more kinesthesia training. More boards go in the pool, and the next thing you know the Model Sevens' motor skills begin to improve."

Laura stared at the murky outline of the man, then turned back to the pool. The computer was busy talking to itself. "You don't know how it works, do you?" she asked.

Griffith took his time in answering. "Not a clue, really," he replied at last.

The warm night air on the long walk to the assembly building was slowly thawing Laura's frozen feet. She had insisted on walking to the next stop on their tour. Not to rid herself of the chill, as she'd told Griffith, but to slow down her fast-forward journey through time so she could digest what she'd already learned.

But Griffith was unrelenting. He continued his crash course on the twenty-first century. "The computer is analog, not digital. The light signals it sends aren't limited to just on or off like in a digital computer. They also are stronger or weaker, more or less, higher or lower, hotter or colder, depending on the intensity of the laser's signal and what information that signal is intended to represent."

On and on he went, Laura gazing at the towering wonders that dotted Gray's small pocket of the future. "The computer is massively parallel. It breaks any problem down into as many pieces as possible, and then it attacks all those pieces simultaneously."

Laura's mind was completely saturated with new ideas—the buffers full of unprocessed data. But Griffith was a fountain of knowledge, and the valves of that fountain were wide open. "If it's a totally new problem, a neural net uses trial and error to solve it. And even after it figures the problem out, it's constantly testing, constantly rewiring itself to improve its efficiency."

"Complex adaptive behavior," Laura mumbled, struggling to imagine it all.

"After trillions and trillions of rewirings, we don't have even the faintest clue what the vast majority of the system does. And a major portion of the signals coming down the pike at any given time have *re*programming content that may completely change the operation of a given circuit board."

A warm ocean breeze washed over them, and Laura shook her head—her own circuits overloaded. "It sounds like it's a complete mess," she said. "A total jumble."

"It *is!*" Griffith said, turning to her and smiling. "But in that randomness, something *wonderful* happens." The tone of his voice had changed. He now seemed not to be discussing nuts and bolts but something much more sublime. "Once . . . once I was on the shell—that's the global user interface—and out of the blue the computer said, 'Have you ever noticed that some clouds look like faces?'"

Laura looked up at him. He didn't need to explain the significance of the computer's question. She felt every bit of the wonderment evident in his voice.

"I had the computer trace the synaptic routing of that one thought, and I found out what had happened. The computer had been taking meteorological readings over a launchpad. When a cloud passed by, the board that looked for bad weather assigned the image a high priority—a strong synaptic weighting—and fired it out through all its connections for further processing. Other boards decided whether the cloud might be prone to electrical discharge, or microburst potential, or whatever. If it looked dangerous, those boards upped the signal's weighting and fired the processed information out through all *their* connections. The boards that *didn't* care about the cloud did the opposite—they *reduced* the signal strength before passing the image on. Most of the paths were dead ends—a series of boards each reducing the signal's strength until it died out completely. On one of those dead ends—before the picture of this cloud died out—it landed in a board that traced edges in video images. That board found a pattern. It traced lines through the contours of the cloud and decided the image was in the shape of a face. Now, what do you think about that?"

"I . . . I think it's . . . wonderful! It's an analogy!" It was exactly what Gray had described on their walk earlier that night. "With analogies, it can make generalizations!" Laura said, growing more and more excited as what Gray and Griffith had said began to sink in. She spoke more and more rapidly, gesticulating with her hands to help make her points. "With generalizations, it can learn! It can tell a sofa is for sitting because it looks sort of like a chair! With that kind of learning potential, it could become . . . !"

The words caught in her throat.

He's done it! she thought, stopping herself from giving voice to thoughts that raced far out ahead. She reached over and grabbed Griffith. They stopped on the walk beside the same curbed roadbed on which Gray had shown Laura the Model Six. "I want to know how it works," Laura demanded. "I want to know *everything* about it."

"What's the point?" Griffith replied with a casual shrug of dismissal, continuing on toward their destination—the gleaming assembly building. "Large, mainframe computers like we've got down in those pools are an increasingly outmoded form of computing. Miniaturization is the key. We've been very successful at downsizing the circuitry. You'll be impressed when I show you the Model Sevens. You'd just be wasting your time studying the main computer."

Griffith's offhand comment stabbed right at the heart of her insecurity, which was never very far from the surface. Laura had only one truly deep-seated fear. Only one thing really mattered dearly to her. She wasn't insecure about her looks, or her personality, or the scanty number of suitors she'd brought home for her mother to meet. The thing by which she rated herself was her mind. Her intellect. Her intelligence.

In her prior life, that intelligence was measured by the papers she published, the discussions her ideas stimulated. By those measures, she'd already been judged a failure. She'd admitted as much when she climbed aboard Gray's plane. The offer to join Gray's "dream team" had been her salvation. The others would talk about her selling out, but that was infinitely more palatable than what they'd have said after the department chairman had his "We've been so privileged" speech with her. Gray had given her a rare opportunity—the chance to wave her middle finger right in the faces of the tenure committee.

But there was only one problem with her fantasy. It didn't involve beating an ignominious retreat from Gray's island—from his society of the mind.

"Mr. Gray doesn't seem to think the computer's obsolete," Laura said. "I mean"—she fumbled for words—"he did hire me to help fix it." Laura had tried not to betray her fear that her marginal role on the "dream team" was fast becoming trivial.

Griffith shrugged. "But he also shut down production on new boards with the annex only half full."

Laura watched the concrete slide by under her feet. She had to will her chin up and her shoulders back. "When did he do that?"

"Gave the order yesterday."

"Why?"

Griffith shook his head and shrugged again. "I'm only the head of a twenty-six-billion-dollar division. How the hell would *I* know?" It was an attempt at humor, but the complaint was clear in Griffith's sarcasm. "The future is in mobility, though. That's where we're headed. It's a natural progression, really. In twenty years, there'll be no difference between computers and robots. They'll be one and the same."

They walked on in silence, Laura pondering the implications of Griffith's comment.

It boggled her mind, and she heaved a deep sigh. She fought the insecurity—the urge to give up, to admit she was in over her head. She gritted her teeth and resolved to take it slow—one step at a time. "Does the computer open the doors automatically or something? Like the door into the conference room where we met, and the one in the gymnasium that guy walked into after having a fight with his wife?"

"Pneumatic doors are part of my department," Griffith said. "Robotics. But the error was in the computer, I can assure you, *not* the servocontrols in that door."

"But why go to all the trouble of having the computer open your doors for you? I mean, supermarkets get by with, like, motion detectors or whatever."

Griffith unexpectedly loosed a hearty laugh, grabbing his paunchy stomach like some slimmed-down version of St. Nick. He was laughing at her joke, but Laura had been serious. Laura's mood was rapidly deteriorating, but she doggedly pursued her question. She was determined to understand at least one thing in the first chapter of her instruction manual before rejoining Griffith on page four hundred.

"So, how does the computer know to open a door? I mean, when Mr. Gray and I walked up to the door of the conference room, it opened before we even got there. Now how did the computer know to open *that* door, but leave the door across the hall from it closed?"

"Well," Griffith said with a chuckle that didn't quite materialize—a hint of confusion on his face as if the answer were obvious—"why would it think you were going into a utility room? There's nothing but mops and brooms and buckets in there."

It was now Laura's turn to be confused. "You mean . . . the computer knew where we were *headed?*" she asked, and Griffith nodded and looked at her as if it were the most elementary observation in the world. "But then . . . it had to know who we *were*."

"Well, of *course*," Griffith said, again turning to look at her, clearly gauging for the first time how truly far behind Laura was. How unprepared she was for life in Gray's century . . . and for the task she'd been assigned on Gray's team. Laura realized just then that Gray had told them nothing about her credentials when she'd been introduced. They had no idea how little she knew about computer technology—about *any* technology, for that matter.

"The pneumatic doors are for *security*, not convenience," Griffith said. The tone of his lecture turned suddenly remedial. "If someone who wasn't authorized to interrupt our meeting had walked up to that door, he'd have had to use the intercom to request entry. But if the computer knew why he was headed there—if he was delivering a printed copy of an E-mail or if there was a fire in the control room or something—then it would've opened the door right up. It's very good at guessing. That's why the error in the gym was so hard to fathom. It almost never makes mistakes like that."

Laura was so filled with questions she didn't know what to ask next. She didn't want to betray her stupidity by asking something that seemed obvious to all but her, and so she chose her next inquiry carefully. "Are *all* the doors controlled by the computer?"

"In the public buildings, yes," Griffith replied. "Not in people's *homes,* of course." His tone was annoyingly patronizing, as if the answer was so obvious that her question barely merited a response.

That irritated Laura. "Look! This may all be old hat to you, but in the real world doors don't decide whether or not to *open!* You have to turn something called a 'knob,' okay?" She made certain she got an apologetic nod of acknowledgment before continuing. "So," she said in a pleasant voice, putting that little episode behind her, "why does the computer open and close doors in public buildings, but not in people's homes?"

Griffith opened his mouth to speak, but then hesitated—shooting her a look out of the corner of his eyes and clearly rethinking his response. "Because," he said in a measured tone, "there is a question of privacy, you see. Gray's a stickler for privacy—it's one of his pet peeves. In order for the computer to open the door for you, it's got to know who you are and what you're doing. To know those things, it maintains a real-time model of the world—who and what everybody and everything is, and what it is that they're doing right at this very moment. It builds that model by processing the data it receives from its sensors. Visual, auditory, thermal, motion—it melds all those senses together to form a picture of the world and everything in it. If we were to allow it to extend that world into people's homes—into their bedrooms and bathrooms and . . . Well, you get the picture," Griffith snorted, "but the computer doesn't!" He elbowed Laura, winking and laughing. "Get it?" Laura nodded. "Do you get it? It was a joke." She nodded again. "It was a pun. Do you get it?"

"Yes!"

Griffith winced and made a face like he'd again stumbled innocently into Laura's hair-trigger temper.

"Sorry," Laura said, and they walked on in silence.

Laura looked all around the empty lawns—growing increasingly uncomfortable. "So there are cameras constantly watching you when you're in public?" she asked.

"And infrared, thermal, low-light, microphones, ground-motion detectors, pressure sensors, feedback from things like light switches—"

"I understand," Laura interrupted.

"That's the only way for the computer to build a world model. It has to use every sensor available to get a feel for the place. If its senses are significantly impeded—if you hide behind a bush or something to scratch yourself, which is sort of the accepted method—then as far as the computer's concerned, it didn't happen. It's outside the computer's model. If you live on this island, you learn to figure out where the gaps are. It's no big deal, really."

"And you go to all that trouble just for security? Is Gray that much of a control freak?"

"Oh, no, no, no! It's not *just* security. The robots use that same world model, for example, to avoid running into things. Those Model Three cars whip down the roads so fast because they can see what's up ahead of them. They know if there's a Model Six crossing the road around the next bend. And a Six would know when to cross because they tap into that same world model and look both ways. That's the beauty of building and maintaining a complete world model. There are so many different uses for it."

Laura couldn't help feeling ill at ease now that she knew they were being watched—constantly. Every movement recorded. She felt a stifling presence, an unblinking eye staring her way.

The unblinking eye of a disturbed presence, she remembered.

"So, Dr. Griffith, what do you think is wrong with the computer?"

Griffith shrugged yet again. "We think maybe it's another virus. The computer is massively interconnected not only internally, but all over the world through the Web. We've had to put up with hackers, corporate espionage, and a whole lot of infections. One of 'em almost took the system down last year, as a matter of fact."

"You mean an infection with an ordinary computer virus almost crashed that entire computer?" Laura asked.

Griffith shook his head. "It was worse than an infection, it was a plague—the Hong Kong 1085. One of our field offices gave Georgi's operators a wrong telephone number, and the computer dialed up a bulletin board in Hong Kong instead of an offboard digital processor we'd leased. The computer wrote a program—a 'gopher'—and zapped it onto the bulletin board. The gopher reproduced itself about a million times and tore through the database in a couple of seconds. It sifted through everything—games, homemade porno stories, classified ads—and reported back using a zippered data stream before self-destructing. That's how the virus slipped through. When the report came back compressed, it went right through the fire wall erected by the phase one to screen for viruses. Over the next couple of days, the computer got real sick. We almost had to shut it down to kill the damn bug."

Laura had heard, of course, of computer viruses. They were now quite common news items. But she'd never heard of a plague. "So what does it mean for the computer to get sick?" she asked.

"Just like for you or me, I suppose. My bet is that's one of the things you're here to find out." Griffith cinched his belt up and jutted his jaw out. "But you never kno-ow with the big cheese." He drew the last words out in what sounded like an impersonation, but it was too poorly rendered to be recognizable.

Laura took a wild guess that Griffith had attempted to be witty, and she smiled up at him politely. "Is that what everybody calls him? 'The big cheese'?"

"That bunch?" Griffith said in a disparaging tone, jabbing a thumb over his shoulder at the computer center. "They're too uptight, man. They need to take it do-o-own a thousand."

Laura's smile was genuine this time. Griffith smiled back at her, exuding total confidence in who he was. Now, when she looked at Griffith, she didn't see the bushy curls sticking out from the sides but not the top of his head. The crooked teeth and thick glasses and sideburns grown to enormous proportions were gone. Whoever he was—in his head—was different from what appeared on the surface.

They walked along through the quiet night, but her mind remained focused on the plague. "Dr. Griffith . . . ?" she began.

"Phil," he interjected.

"Phil," she repeated, "and please call me Laura."

"Me Phil," Griffith said in a "caveman" voice, touching his

chest, "you Laura." He laughed and shook his head at the hilarity of his antics.

Laura's smile quickly grew stale, and she cleared her throat. "So, Phil, why did the computer even look through that bulletin board in Hong Kong? Surely it realized it had the wrong number. Why didn't it just hang up?"

"'Curiosity killed the cat.' You see, with the exception of the little 'seed' program Mr. Gray installed to get the thing going, the computer's almost entirely self-taught. And there's only one way to motivate self-study, and that's to program it to be curious, which Margaret did with a vengeance."

"You sure seem to minimize Mr. Gray's part in the effort," Laura said—fishing.

"Oh! If I did that, please excuse me. Never does a career much good to talk down the boss. It's just that Mr. Gray's real genius is in robotics. The artificial intelligence side of it isn't really his bag."

Gray, Laura thought, *a genius at robotics?* She'd been convinced it was Gray's work on neural networks, and not in mechanical engineering, that had achieved the breakthroughs evident on his island.

"Man," Griffith continued, "I remember how the computer used to talk your ears off, so to speak. But only on the shell. Most of my time is spent at lower-level languages, but I would occasionally get stumped and want to ask some questions. On the shell, you see, you can type things in plain English like, 'If the hydraulic drive connects to a linkage with four degrees of freedom but only three boundary constraints, can the control system generate a goal to prevent the mechanism from being underconstrained?'"

Laura's eyes rose to him, a wry smile on her face. "'*Plain* English?'" she asked.

Griffith just cocked his head—perplexed by her question. "Or Japanese, or German, or French, or whatever you speak," he said, misunderstanding. "Anyway, halfway into your session, the computer would start asking, 'Is that all you wanted to know?' or something like that. If you said, 'Yes,' then it'd say, 'Do you mind if I ask *you* a few questions?'" Griffith laughed. "You could see it coming a mile away. And it would wear your fingers to the bone typing out your answers. Back then, you understand, it was socially immature. If you typed something like, 'Boy, look at the time. It's midnight already,' it would say, 'I show nothing on your calendar for midnight.'"

Laura laughed and asked, "So why didn't you just log off?"

"Well . . . ," Griffith began, but then seemed to struggle to find the right words. "You know, that wouldn't have been very . . . *nice*, would it?"

"Just don't look up," Griffith said helpfully as Laura clung to the cool metal railing. They headed down the steps leading to the assembly building entrance, which—like its counterpart at the computer center—was sunk slightly below ground level. Laura had looked up at the sixteen-story wall that ran almost half a mile in either direction. It was as if seeing the unexpected plane rising perpendicular to the earth caused her brain to question which was the true horizon. She'd almost instantly grown dizzy and faintly nauseated. "That happens more often than you'd think," Griffith said. "Let's get inside. It'll be better in there."

She edged her way down the steps, grasping the rail hand over hand and keeping her head bowed. Passing through a thick vault door, they entered yet another of the infernal "dusters." This time, however, she knew to hold on to her skirt. Again her hair lashed wildly at her face, but again the gale dissipated quickly.

"Maybe I should just shave my head," Laura said as she raked the hair off her face.

Griffith seemed totally unbothered by the experience. "Oh, look," he said, pointing to a small black marble mounted on the wall beside the door. "That's a wide-angle retinal chip. You'll see them all over the place." He mugged for the camera, sticking his thumbs in his ears and his tongue from his mouth.

The inner door glided open, and the sound of activity echoed through the enclosed space ahead. She followed Griffith into a small, well-lit room—touching the antistatic pad and receiving the expected snap on her fingertips. Laura looked but didn't find a vanity or brush beside this door. What she found was another black eyeball staring out at the room.

"Here," Griffith said, holding goggles with large, clear lenses and ear protectors that looked like ancient stereo headphones. Laura put the goggles on—the soft plastic wrapping around her eyes and fitting tightly against her face. The ear protectors dampened the sound from outside the room to a mere hum. Griffith then handed her a white hard hat, which fit snugly over her gear and mercifully covered the tortured mess of her hair.

"It gets a little loud in there," Griffith shouted once his own equipment was on, and they headed for the inner door.

It disappeared into the wall as they approached, revealing the brilliant light of an artificial day just beyond. The massive interior world of the assembly building was bathed in that remarkably white illumination, and it was alive with movement and activity. As they passed through the door, which was at least a foot thick and looked like an air lock, Laura couldn't shake the feeling they were entering a well-built vessel of some sort. Like the computer center, everything was solid and sealed tight—designed and constructed with a quality usually reserved for submarines or spacecraft. And like the computer center, it was all so new, so pristine.

Laura wandered into the factory like a tourist, her eyes wide and her mouth agape. The mostly hollow building was of a scale that was experienced more physically than through sight or sound. It was a sensation she'd felt previously only in the largest indoor sports arenas. But this arena was filled not with people but with hundreds upon hundreds of moving machines.

High above it all, giant cranes glided smoothly along rails crisscrossing the ceiling. As the carriages passed overhead, they eclipsed thick tubes that ran the length of the building. The tubes glowed so brightly Laura had to shield her eyes.

"Light pipes!" Griffith said in a raised voice that barely carried over the din of the busy plant. He pointed to the ceiling—to the thick tubes of light. "Microwave generators shoot beams through the pipes from both ends of the building! The energy excites sulfur elements, which produce the same full-spectrum light as the sun!"

Laura couldn't care less about the lights in the building. It was like the tour guide at Hoover Dam pointing out the portrait of Herbert Hoover on first entering the room with the mammoth turbines.

A Model Six like the lawn mower from before trundled by, towing a trailer loaded with machine parts of various shapes and sizes. It wove its way around another Model Six, which was headed in the opposite direction with a rotary sander mounted at the end of its arm. A massive conveyer belt down the center of the building sent scattered objects past manipulator arms permanently mounted along the side of the line. From up and down the long belt, sparks flew or drills whined or the searing sound of fusing heat crackled in the air. It was unlike anything she'd ever seen. It was unlike anything she'd ever even imagined.

"Pretty *rad*, eh?" Griffith said, grinning. Laura started to walk out onto the dark concrete floor for a better view, but Griffith reached out and grabbed her arm to restrain her. "Sorry!" he said, pointing down at a bright yellow line about three feet wide painted just in front of her toes. Regularly stenciled down the line's length were the words "WORK ENVELOPE—No humans beyond this point!" Laura read and reread the warning. It had some deeper significance, she felt, but couldn't quite decide what that was.

"Safety precaution!" Griffith said, and Laura watched as another of the Model Sixes hurried by—the claw at the end of its single mechanical arm replaced with a shiny silver piston about a foot in diameter. "Come this way!" Griffith said, motioning for her to follow. He stayed well away from the thick yellow line, she noted, which angled out onto the floor to allow access to a metal ladder. The busy robots, for their part, also steered clear of the conspicuous boundary. That's when it hit her. *It's a border,* she thought, *that separates man from busy machine. A border between two lands—two worlds.*

Laura swam through a sea of novel thoughts, each sweeping her up in its powerful emotional crosscurrents. She grew lightheaded and firmly gripped the ladder's railing. She felt like an alien in a space suit behind her goggles, ear protectors, and hard hat. New thoughts, new perspectives, hit her with dizzying rapidity. "*A Stranger in a Strange Land,*" she recalled the title of the old book. It described perfectly how she felt at that moment.

As they climbed to a catwalk suspended twenty feet above the main floor, Laura was again taken aback by the building's size. The full length of the facility was visible now except where obscured by the outcroppings of structures. The assembly line ran down the center of the building for as far as the eye could see. Smaller belts joined the main line or passed over or under the rolling stream of Gray's products in a maze of highways and byways. They led into and out of metal compartments and tanks and steel chambers wrapped in pipes coated in ice. And everywhere there moved machines—robots. It was a beehive of continuous activity, and the hive's queen lay immersed in nitrogen a thousand feet below sea level.

Griffith waited as Laura took it all in. "Is this where you build your TVs?" Laura shouted over the noise.

"No! This is where we build the *robots* that build our TVs! *And* our satellites, *and* our relays and switching stations, *and* our high-def cameras, *and* our spacecraft! And, of course, the new circuit boards for the computer—until yesterday, that is! All the consumer products are built in regional plants around the world."

At a distance, the robots looked little more exotic than a garden-variety forklift or backhoe. But there were no human drivers. There were no humans anywhere. They were all up in the Village, enjoying their evening. This was a village of a different sort.

"Unbelievable," she mumbled. Griffith cocked and then shook his head—not having heard what she'd said. "I said it's unbelievable!"

Griffith nodded in exaggerated fashion, grinning with pride. "Welcome to the twenty-first century, Dr. Aldridge!"

"Come this way," Griffith said in a voice barely raised above a whisper. "I'd like you to meet some friends."

Griffith, Laura, and a young foreman with whom they'd hooked up made their way through one of the assembly building's larger structures. All still wore hard hats, but their goggles and ear protectors dangled loosely around their necks. Outside the thick walls of the building-within-a-building, the rhythm of activity could be heard as a continuous thrum. But inside, all was hushed.

Griffith and the foreman waited beside an open pneumatic door. Laura passed through into the large room beyond—her jaw dropping in awe. She stepped out onto a metal walkway suspended in air above nearly a hundred motionless Model Sixes. Their lone arms sagged in various states of repose like astronauts asleep in weightlessness. They were all backed into "recharging stations," Griffith explained in a low voice.

The room was quiet. Even the lights were low.

"I don't see any Sevens," Griffith said to the young man, who looked down at a clipboard-sized pen computer. Tapping at different icons on the screen, the foreman said, "Next Seven isn't due in here for half an hour yet."

"Where's the nearest one?"

Again the foreman tapped at the board. "Out in the side yard."

Griffith nodded, then turned to Laura. "These old Sixes," he said, waving a slack finger down the row of slumbering robots, "need to recharge for two hours after every two hours of operation. The Sevens only charge about once every three days in normal use, and charging time is about four hours."

She leaned out over the metal railing to look down at the robot immediately below.

"The Sixes have the same chassis as the Threes—the little cars that take you around the island," Griffith explained. He spoke in tones appropriate to a library, and without knowing why Laura felt his manner to be fitting. "Since they're wheeled, they can only negotiate flat terrain. They've got a single manipulator up front," he pointed to the dark, metallic claw protruding from the stall just beneath their feet. The tongs of the robot's claw looked like the teeth on a pair of pliers. Four inches wide, their deep grooves ran the full width of the claw and were worn shiny from use. Griffith pointed out the long tubes on either side of the two teeth, which provided hydraulic power to the robot's grip. The steel paw, Laura guessed, could easily crush anything soft. The macabre picture which sprung up in Laura's mind did nothing to endear the technology to her.

A robot across the room jerked. Laura jumped back from the rail, and Griffith and the foreman both laughed. As Laura watched, the robot raised its claw and reached slowly toward the rear of its chassis. Atop the central trunk that rose from the robot's carriage, what looked like twin security cameras turned to follow the claw. The gripper seized in its firm grasp a fat black plug that protruded from its socket in the wall. A cable ran from the plug into a box at the rear bumper of the Model Six. They all watched as the claw rocked the plug back and forth and back again.

The plug flew from the wall and smashed into the robot with a resounding bang. Again Laura's heart skipped a beat.

"It's a little groggy," the foreman said. The robot tried three times before successfully returning the plug to its compartment. The claw then casually backhanded the compartment's lid, tapping it for insurance before returning to its more comfortable station in front.

"Their mini-nets are inside the superstructure," Griffith said, pointing at the box-shaped housing that rose dead center from the chassis. "They lose some of their virtual connections—the links that are programmed rather than hardwired—during recharging. It only takes a minute or two for the Sixes to relearn their fine motor skills, but the Sevens are another story. They make more extensive use of virtual connections and have larger nets. The Sevens stumble around like drunken sailors for five or ten minutes before they get it together."

The Model Six rolled slowly out of its berth. High atop its superstructure sat its two "eyes"—the "security cameras"—shifting soundlessly in tandem from one object to the next. As Laura watched, the cameras grew more and more asynchronous, their movements finally totally uncoordinated as the two cameras flitted this way and that. The robot turned down the row of its resting compatriots and headed past Laura's vantage for the door.

"See its eyes turning from side to side?" Griffith asked, and Laura nodded. "Those are its principal sensory nodes. Its eyes and ears, plus infrared and thermal. It also has ultrasonic collision-avoidance range finders down around the chassis, and pressure-sensitive pads at the tips of its single end effector—its 'arm.' That, plus what the main computer tells it about its surroundings, constitute its world—what it sees and knows."

As the robot passed, its twin sensors snapped in sudden unison to lock onto the three humans. Laura gripped the railing tightly, ready to recoil as the slack claw passed by her feet. She didn't know why, but she felt like backing away—giving the strange new creature room to pass.

"It's telling on us," the foreman said.

"It's reporting in," Griffith translated. "You can tell when it fixes on you like that." The two eyes returned to their seemingly agitated, uncoordinated search of the path ahead. "It saw us in here and called up the main computer to report."

"They sure are into spying," Laura said.

Griffith shrugged. "The robots are the computer's mobile eyes and ears. They can update the computer's world model with what we call a 'refresh scan.' But when they're in a place where the computer maintains a fairly complete representation like the restricted area, they typically only report things of special interest to the computer like when somebody steps over the work envelope line—just in case the computer missed it."

Laura looked down at the edges of the catwalk. The yellow lines ran the length of the metal span to a door on the opposite end of the room. They were well within the all-important border that separated man from machine.

"Well . . . why did it report on us then?" Laura asked.

Griffith looked back down at the receding machine. All he could do was shrug.

"We ceased production of the Sixes last year!" Griffith shouted as they walked down the constantly moving assembly line. Their goggles and ear protectors were back on. There were so many active machines—so much brute force at work on the floor—that the yellow line they honored so scrupulously seemed trifling and unworthy of deference. The only thing that prevented one of those thick metal arms from swinging wildly their way was a concept—a law. *Gray's law,* she found herself thinking, wondering just how much force the creator's word would carry. "We entered full production of the Sevens ten months ago!" Griffith shouted, turning to the foreman. "Let's go find that Seven in the side yard!"

The three of them climbed several flights of stairs and headed across a catwalk suspended high above the main floor. Down below, parts of every imaginable shape and design were transported by the broad conveyer belt like flotsam down a relentless man-made river. Flat sheets of inert metal and plastic went into the great building at one end, and at the other there emerged animate beings who looked left and right before crossing the road. Laura observed the process from dead center.

Totally amazing, she thought, shaking her head.

The belt itself was at least twenty feet wide and looked to be a complete mess. Its basic black was discolored in countless places by spots and stains and burn marks. And the components it carried were scattered about in nearly random fashion like scrap on the way to a pit.

Laura paused directly above the belt to take in the sights and sounds of the assembly building. In the far distance, Laura saw the blunt noses of not one but two of Gray's strange, flat-sided rockets. They rose like steep pyramids nearly all the way to the ceiling. Up and down the long line in between, the forest of robotic arms was an incessant blur of activity. They turned parts over, picked them up, held them to the light, moved them from the main belt to adjoining ones. They riveted and welded, sanded and ground, painted and measured, and assembled and discarded. All the while, Model Sixes plied the lanes parallel to the belt, stopping to receive a part from or deliver a part to their immobile brethren.

This was not a plant conceived in the mind of man, Laura realized. It wasn't a factory built by humans that had been turned over to more worthy mechanical replacements. This was a factory designed by a computer exclusively for robots. This was the world as it should be according to the mind of a machine. As Laura stood there, that conclusion was reinforced by one quite telling fact.

Nowhere in that sea of motion were any humans to be seen.

Laura headed across the catwalk for the exit, her companions following in her wake down to the main floor. They passed through another "air lock," then stepped out into the warm night air.

An expansive concrete pad the width and breadth of a stadium parking lot dominated the far side of the assembly building. In the distance, the three rocket gantries marked the fringes of the island's north shore like brightly beaming lighthouses.

Laura's skin tingled. She was missing something about what she had just witnessed—some important conclusion. It was right there on the periphery of her understanding, but the feeling slowly faded. The silent visitor stepped back into the shadows. Back into the "gray" area, she thought with amusement. And then it was gone.

Laura shook her head.

The side yard was covered with small sheds underneath which sat mounds of materials—some exposed, others covered in tarpaulins. "Side yard" was a misnomer, Laura thought. "Junkyard" described it better.

"This isn't the pretty side of the building, obviously," Griffith said. "We've actually run out of room in the assembly building, if you can believe that. There's another facility under construction right over there." Griffith pointed toward a thick wall of gnarled tropical trees. Light glowed from the jungle over the treetops, but no structure as yet could be seen. Laura imagined the mechanical night crew working uninterrupted as their human co-workers rested.

The foreman led the group out among the slowly moving Model Sixes. Laura frowned as she surveyed the disorder. *A twentieth-century dump,* Laura thought, *hidden behind the facade of Gray's twenty-first-century wonder.*

"It should be this way," the foreman said, his pen board glowing brightly in the dimmer outdoor lighting. As they turned a corner, Laura noticed that the map on the foreman's pen board turned also—maintaining a correct orientation no matter which way the small computer was pointed. The portable pen board must be plugged into the main computer's "world model," she realized. That main computer led them out through the ever darker maze of sheds and piles of scraps.

They passed robots that sifted through twisted strips of metal, their twin searchlights shining brightly on the tangled mess. Others opened cardboard boxes or dumped containers of garbage into trailers already piled high with similar refuse. All were Model Sixes, differing only, it appeared, in what they had attached to the ends of their long arms.

"What is this stuff?" Laura asked as they wound their way deeper into the labyrinth.

"Oh, low-priority things like reusable scrap, plastic sheeting for the morphing units, other raw materials that weather well."

"Morphing units?" Laura asked.

Griffith reached out to restrain Laura as a Model Six backed out of a shed carrying a pallet. The robot stopped, and the electronic chirping of its reverse gear fell silent. Its searchlights turned in tandem to find the small group.

The three human sightseers proceeded on, and Laura wondered whether Griffith was always that careful or whether the computer's errors were the cause of new concern.

"Morphing," Griffith answered, long after Laura had forgotten her question, "is the way we fabricate plastic, and now some metal components. You used to have to design and build a prototype part, construct a mold around it, and pour molten plastic or metal into the mold. Now, we go straight from computer design to the morphing unit, which presses a superheated form straight into a big flat sheet. The key is in the rapid shaping of the form. If you watch the unit work, this flat surface pops up in the blink of an eye into the exact shape that the computer designed. The sheet on top gets melted around it and hardens instantly. The great benefit is that using morphing units, you can implement a manufacturing design change literally in milliseconds. Once the computer designs the component, it just"—Griffith snapped his fingers—"boom—punches it out. And it can switch from part A to part B to part C with absolutely no retooling—no delay whatsoever in production. We just keep feeding it the sheeting, or at least the robots do."

They turned down a different row, following the foreman with his pen board and paying no attention to the ever lengthening shadows thrown by the lights on the assembly building's walls.

"It should be around here somewhere," the foreman said, and Laura saw that the two blinking dots on the map—one green, the other red—were very close. They walked farther into the growing darkness in search of yet another of Gray's new species.

The width of the aisle through the mounds of supplies had grown irregular, and the passage itself began to twist and turn. Up ahead, an island of tenting covered ubiquitous dark shapes and split the aisle down which they searched in two. Stocks of black tires lined the walls. They wandered ever more slowly through the inky maze, and the foreman stopped to get his bearings by reference to the assembly building. "It should be right here," he said, holding the board up for Griffith and Laura to see. The green and red dots glowed steadily now and completely overlapped. "I mean, like, right . . ."

A dark shape descended into the narrow canyon of tires, and Laura's heart leapt straight into her throat. It was a long, black leg not ten feet in front of them. She threw her arm out, striking the surprised foreman in the chest. Another leg soundlessly joined the first, and the large body of the giant metal spider crested the top of the wall and crept down into the hollows ahead, blocking their path.

Laura turned and fled, crashing hard into the wall of tires just behind her.

Her companions instinctively took flight, but stopped beside Laura after just a couple of steps. "It's all right!" Griffith said testily. "*Jesus,* Laura." Griffith held his chest and seemed suddenly out of breath.

Laura turned with dread to watch the enormous mechanical creature lowering the last of its slender legs to the pavement.

"You scared the hell out of me," Griffith said to Laura, but she couldn't help noticing that both he and the foreman kept their eyes on the robot.

It now stood motionless, its four spidery legs resting firmly on the ground. The legs were thin, and their inner workings were exposed. Black metal bones were aligned with silvery hydraulic muscles. The pristine apparatuses appeared too straightforward, too simplistic to work as they did.

The dark machine had two slender arms of a design similar to its legs. At the end of the arms, which grew straight out of its thorax, were four long fingers wrapped tightly around a large tire. The robot stood motionless as its rounded, roughly triangular head remained trained on the human trio. Its face consisted of two large, flat lenses mounted side by side above a series of perforated black membranes. The robot looked light and wiry, but the head atop its refrigerator-sized torso stood nearly twice the height of a human.

"There it is," Griffith said, walking casually up to the robot. "A Model Seven." As Laura stared at the robot's unblinking eyes, the foreman turned his flashlight on with a click. A flinch—just the tiniest hint of movement of the robot's head as it recoiled from the light—signaled that the machine was awake. It was alert. "Come on over here," Griffith said, waving to her. "There's nothing to be afraid of."

Laura's nerves were jangled and her heart still pounded, but she forced herself to join Griffith at the foot of the beast.

"The Model Sevens, as you've seen, aren't limited to flat ground." Griffith returned to his matter-of-fact tone, which in itself helped calm Laura down. But she couldn't feel completely at ease around the alien technology. She had no idea what to expect from it. "They've got four legs, and they can climb up uneven objects like stairs or . . . or stacks of tires, I guess. Down here at the bottom," Griffith said as he knelt, and the beam of the foreman's flashlight dropped to the robot's feet, "it has wheels. When it walks like a spider, it just locks the wheels' brakes for traction. Then, when it's on flat ground like out on the roadbeds or the assembly building's main floor, it uses drives housed in these fairings to power the wheels. Motoring around is a whole lot more energy efficient than walking."

Griffith rose with a grunt, his joints popping. "I need some oil," he joked to the foreman, straightening his back with great effort. Griffith rested his hand flat against the robot's midsection, and the foreman's flashlight lit an array of equipment that ringed the robot's waist. "This is the tool belt. If you'll look at the end effector, you'll see that it's got a gripper attached." He pointed at the two hands wrapped firmly around the tire. "To change tools, all it does is stick the gripper into its special holster on the belt, twist, and off it comes. Then, it can just snap on any of these other tools." Griffith indicated the numerous attachments protruding from their "holsters" on the belt. "It's got drills, sanders, saws, tongs, riveters, et cetera, and it can strap on external tanks and carry acetylene torches and paint sprayers and things like that."

Griffith stepped back to stand beside Laura and point higher on the "torso," which was wider than it was thick and rounded. "The mini-net is in its chest," Griffith continued. The flashlight glinted off the greenish gray expanse of metal—the shadow of the large tire held by the robot obscuring most of its body. "Its net has about a hundred times the processing power of the Model Sixes', so the Sevens are a lot more autonomous. The Sevens could just barely scrape by as free roamers, meaning they could function without access to the main computer's world model, but at a vastly reduced level of performance. The Sixes, on the other hand, are 'tethered.' They don't have the mental horsepower to build and maintain a model world using only their own senses and computational capacity."

The flashlight's beam rose again to the robot's face, and again there was a barely noticeable flinch from the otherwise stoic machine. "Up top the Sevens have retinal chips for ordinary light plus combination infrared–high-def imagers for low light. Both sensors are stereoscopic and provide excellent depth perception. We put 'ears' on the sides of the 'head' just like ours are, and then there's an all-purpose air sampler for a nose. The sampler can give us standard atmospheric conditions, but it can also detect a variety of telltale molecular matches for things like smoke or hazardous chemicals."

"We dropped the ultrasonic anticollision sensors that the Threes and Sixes have," the foreman added. "The Sevens maintain such a complete world model in their head they're not likely to run into anything stationary. And they've got good enough senses that if anything's moving, they know it."

"Dr. Griffith, Dr. Aldridge," a loudspeaker blared, "please report to the computer center." Griffith looked at his watch. "Almost time for our meeting, I guess. Let's catch a car."

Griffith turned to leave, but Laura's gaze lingered on the Model Seven. The spiderlike robot rolled noiselessly away atop the stable platform of its four locked legs. "Hey," she said to halt Griffith. "How did that robot know to stand there while you showed it off, and then to leave when you were through?"

The robot was gone—disappearing into the dark gorges and ravines of the side yard's scrap. Griffith looked after his departed pride and joy, shrugging yet again. "It just did. Those Sevens are pretty damn smart."

"Wait till we start turning out the next generation," the foreman laughed, smiling Griffith's way. "I might be out of a job."

Griffith ignored the man. "We'd better get going," he said—just a little too quickly and too abruptly, Laura thought.

"It'll never, ever happen!" Filatov argued.

Margaret was undeterred. "Give me three hours, tops."

"You'll never, ever, *ever* get enough capacity freed up to load the phase two that way!" Filatov said, shaking his head to blot out the offending sound of Margaret's voice. "The space has to be contiguous. Your plan will leave the unused racks fragmented all *over* the place!"

"We'll defragment and compress the racks in the main pool. That'll leave us eight percent of contiguous space free over in the annex."

Filatov was already shaking his head. "It'll never work. Not in this lifetime! Not in this *universe!*"

The conference room fell silent. Filatov waited, ready to pounce on Margaret again, but she'd finished making her proposal.

There were light *bings* from stage right, and heads turned in unison to Dorothy. "That *would* be just enough to load the phase two," she said, looking up from her little computer. "*If* Margaret's calculations are right."

"Sheer fantasy," Filatov mumbled, obviously feeling obligated to say something on mention of Margaret's plan.

Gray held his hands out to invite final comments. Laura again felt out of place at the long table. She was the only one there with no progress to report. "All right," Gray said, "start off-loading as soon as we break up, and load the phase two as soon as you have the capacity."

"There have been some . . . some more errors," Dorothy said tentatively, raising her pen pad as if everyone could read its small screen. "Three unexplained door malfunctions, a bunch of small account discrepancies in a pay-per-view movie order, and seventeen minutes of black during a French documentary."

"That seems like a lot of door problems to me," Hoblenz said, leaning forward and eyeing Gray. "Could be we've got visitors."

"Oh, come on!" Filatov jumped in. "And there was a second gunman on the grassy knoll, too, I suppose!" He shook his head in utter disbelief. "It's a *bug!* A virus. Dorothy's phase two ought to kill it."

"Yes, but how much code will it tear up in the process?" Margaret asked.

"Hardly any!" Dorothy objected in a reedy pitch. "We might lose, like, the connections in the racks that are infested, but it shouldn't do systemwide damage. If the new version of the phase two finds a malevolent virus, it'll isolate it, not chase it all over the system. I've fixed a lot of things since the last outbreak!"

In the silence from around the table, the skepticism of the group was obvious.

Laura waited for what seemed like ages, and when no one else spoke up she asked, "What was the pay-per-view movie and the documentary?"

At first she thought they would humiliate her by ignoring the question. Few heads turned her way, but Gray's, she noted, was among those that did.

Dorothy's gaze only slowly left the doubting looks of her colleagues. She tapped at her palmtop, then said, "The movie was *A Room with a View*. There was a credit issued for all the orders that came in over the weekend."

Laura tried to hide her astonishment. She had placed two of those orders herself—once on Friday, then again on Saturday. "Do you mean that everyone who ordered that movie last weekend got it for free?" she asked.

Dorothy frowned and nodded.

A Room with a View was Laura's favorite movie of all time. She'd stumbled across the re-released high-definition version among the growing number of films that, with the tap of a button, could be downloaded from Gray's system in seconds. When Laura had placed the first order on Friday night, she'd been alone and unhappy over the grad-student "profile." The purchase the next night had been spur-of-the-moment—a halfhearted attempt to escape sheer boredom.

"That's one of the sappiest movies ever made," Margaret said with a sneer on her face.

"You have no taste!" Filatov shot back.

"Do *you* like it?" Margaret challenged.

"I've never seen it. But that doesn't change the fact you have no *taste!*"

There were more pinging sounds from the end of the table. Everyone looked at Dorothy, who cringed as she stared at the palmtop. "The blacked-out documentary was called *Faces of Death V.*" Her mouth was misshapen by the disgust that was also evident in her tone. "Yucch! 'Actual footage of real deaths by suicide, disaster, and crime.' We air this shit?" she asked, looking up.

"Watch yer language young lady!" Hoblenz snapped.

"Why are we calling that a computer malfunction?" Filatov challenged in his combative manner, this time directed at Dorothy. "The trouble could've been anywhere along the line!"

"I *checked* it, Georgi!" Dorothy squealed. "There were four separate satellite passes! The satellites received the uplink, but the computer didn't blip the transmission code and so the switches didn't throw!"

A strained quiet descended on the room.

"When did the transmission resume?" Laura asked, and again there was a delay in Dorothy's response. They weren't accustomed to the new voice in their midst.

"Straight up on the hour."

"As soon as that *Faces of Death* thing was over?" Laura asked.

Slowly, Dorothy nodded—growing more and more interested, it appeared, in what Laura would say next.

"All right," Gray interrupted abruptly and pushed his chair back from the table. "Let's get the phase two loaded."

With the meeting ended, debates resumed as everyone rose and headed for the door.

"Laura!" Dorothy called out. She was standing beside her chair, and Laura joined her at the end of the table. The smiling girl whispered, "So, did Griffith talk your ear off?" Her chin was dipped to her chest, and her green eyes were wide open and sparkled mischievously as she looked up at the taller Laura. "He's notorious for lecturing people about anything and everything. I told Mr. Gray I'd give you the *real* dirt, but he just blew me off, like always. Did Griffith talk about the light pipes?" she asked, now grinning.

Her good humor was infectious. Laura smiled and nodded.

"U-u-u-g-g-h!" Dorothy rolled her eyes, her shoulders heaving with the effort. "He's been trying to talk Mr. Gray into putting those things *everywhere!* That's just, like . . . great! You can practically count every pore on your *face* under those lights, ya know?"

Laura nodded, but she really didn't have a clue what Dorothy was objecting to.

"What do you think about Filatov and Margaret?" came next from the girl, spoken with the pent-up energy of someone starved for conversation.

Laura drew a deep breath, contemplating her answer. "They don't seem to like each other very much."

"Did you know they're *doing* it?"

Laura cocked and then shook her head. "Doing what?" she asked.

"You know—the nasty. Like, all the way!" Laura was at a complete loss now, and she made a face simply to avoid having to respond. "I *know!*" Dorothy said. "Isn't it dis-*gusting!* I can't even, like, *begin* to picture it." A strong quake shook Dorothy's upper body and she loosed a moan of disgust. "Oh-p!" the frenetic girl said suddenly, then whispered out of the corner of her mouth, "Here comes the thought police."

Laura turned to see Gray reentering the room.

"Catch you later," Dorothy whispered, heading for the door.

Gray walked up to Laura. "Are you ready?" he asked.

Something in his tone caused Laura to reflect on his question before answering. "Ready for what?" she replied.

"To meet the computer."

They stood facing each other for a moment before Laura finally shrugged and nodded. She followed Gray to the door. "I still don't understand what I'm supposed to do," Laura said to his back. Gray didn't break stride, and the door slid into the wall uneventfully. "I mean, if it's a virus or an intruder, what am *I* doing here?"

Filatov and Margaret were talking in low tones in the hallway, and they fell in behind Laura as the group headed for the control room.

"We're looking into every possibility," Gray responded.

"And that includes human psychological disorders?" Laura asked, allowing her skepticism to creep into her voice. She eyed her two "colleagues" now trailing quietly behind. Their faces revealed nothing, but they were listening. "I mean, to be depressed the computer would have to be, you know . . ." The word stuck in her throat. "It would have to maintain higher order goals and ambitions."

Gray nodded.

"Are you telling me the computer is sentient?" Laura asked. "That it has an intelligence comparable to a human being's?"

Gray spun to face her, stopping the small entourage at the edge of the busy control room. "No," he said. "I'm asking *you* to tell *me*."

"She can use this office," Filatov said, walking up to a closed door in a quiet corner of the control room. He lifted his glasses and stared into a black peephole, sending the door smoothly into the wall with a barely audible *whoosh*. Laura followed Margaret and Gray into the windowless underground office, but Filatov left without saying a word to the others. Margaret glanced over her shoulder a moment too late, catching Laura's eye instead of Filatov's and turning away.

So, Laura thought, *Dorothy was* right *about Margaret and Filatov.*

The office contained a desk, a chair, and a credenza—all barren of the usual clutter of supplies. On the lustrous black top of the ultramodern desk sat an oversized computer monitor and a keyboard. The black leather chair was thickly padded. Like everything else in Gray's kingdom all was fresh and new and expensive.

"Let's get you logged on," Margaret said, flicking a switch built right into the shiny black desktop. A whirring sound rose from deep inside the large desk. "Mr. Gray," Margaret said, "this will require your authorization."

Gray sat in the chair and waited as the terminal powered up. "We have controlled access to the core functions," Margaret said to Laura. "You'll get a 'King-level' password—the same as all the department heads have." Margaret glanced down at Gray as if to give him a chance to rethink the decision, but he ignored her.

"Is that the highest level?" Laura asked.

"Yes," Gray replied before Margaret got her answer out.

Then why does my logging on require your *authorization?* Laura wondered. After a beep, Gray stared into the tip of a flexible wand that rose like a microphone from beside the keyboard. The computer beeped again, and Gray looked from the wand to the screen. Both he and Bickham smiled.

"Poor thing," Margaret said, reading the words that scrolled down the monitor. Gray began to type, and Margaret watched over his shoulder, her smile growing sad. After Gray's brief interchange, Margaret said, "Okay, Dr. Aldridge." She waved Laura over to the terminal.

Gray rose and held the chair for Laura to sit. "Look into the lens," Margaret directed, pointing at the tip of the wand. "Try not to blink." Laura sat down and stared into the dark hole. "It identifies the user by the pattern of blood vessels on the retinal wall at the back of your eye. It's better than fingerprints. The pattern is impossible to alter, and every human's is unique." There was a brief flash of light from the hole, and Laura blinked.

"Sorry," she said, but the computer beeped.

"It's okay," Margaret said. "It got the print."

Laura turned to the monitor. <Dr. Aldridge?> she read at the bottom of the screen. The cursor flashed at the beginning of the blank line beneath—waiting.

"All right, then," Gray said as he and Margaret headed for the door. "Let Georgi know if you need anything. We've got a breakfast meeting at the house tomorrow at nine. It's your first night, so I wouldn't stay too late."

"Wait!" Laura blurted out, and Gray and Margaret turned to her from the open doorway. "Just what am I supposed to *do?*" As soon as she asked the question, Laura felt a wave of disappointment in herself. Was it her? Was she too slow for Gray's army of geniuses?

But Gray showed no impatience. "Dr. Aldridge, you're an expert in cognition—in matters of human consciousness. I have built an advanced neural network whose main task is to facilitate the interaction between humans and computers. I modeled its architecture on the human brain to try to bridge the gap that separates our two worlds."

The deep concern etched on Gray's face was mirrored on Margaret's as she waited—her gaze falling to the floor.

"Along the way," Gray continued, his voice now distant, "the computer began exhibiting increasingly anthropomorphic, 'human' behavior. It didn't settle into that middle ground between humans and computers that I thought it would. It became more human than computer. At first, I was convinced the phenomenon was purely imitative. But as its domain of human knowledge expanded, its behavior grew more and more sophisticated."

"And that's when the problems began?" Laura guessed.

Gray nodded slowly, almost imperceptibly, but Margaret quickly voiced her disagreement. "There was a coincidence in the timing, yes, but . . ." Margaret began, then fell silent. Laura remained focused on the troubled Gray. "You see," Margaret finally continued, "this system is unique. There has never been anything even remotely like it in history. We've spent *years* expanding its knowledge domain, which is *absolutely* the state of the art. It's priceless, so we've got to explore every possibility no matter how . . . remote," Margaret concluded in an apologetic tone.

Laura willed herself to remain silent—to hold back the flood of questions that threatened to reveal her congenital ineptitude. Margaret and Gray headed out, Gray's eyes lingering on Laura until the door closed behind him.

All was quiet then save the whirring under her desk. Laura stared at the closed door—then at the black eyeball on the wall beside it. Only reluctantly did she turn to read the text on the screen.

<Mr. Gray! I hope you feel better than I do.>

"We'll all feel better as soon as you're up and about. We've got Dr. Aldridge here to see what she can do."

<Let's log her on. I've really been looking forward to meeting her!>

"So I gathered."

<What does that mean?>

"Never mind. Let's get started."

<LOGGING ON—ACCEPTED.>

<Dr. Aldridge?>

The exchange between Gray and his computer struck Laura as odd, but oddity seemed par for the course. Everything about her visit so far had been weird.

Laura swallowed to wet her dry mouth and moved the keyboard to a more comfortable position. She tilted and swiveled the monitor until it was just right. She wriggled in the chair and first straightened, then relaxed her shoulders. When all was ready—her fingers poised over the keyboard to begin typing—she pushed back from the desk and searched for the source of the noise underneath. Lights glowed and flickered from a large box that took up the right half of her desk beside her knee space.

When Laura sat up, she felt the first cool draft of air on her bare legs. It was coming from the off-white box with the blinking lights.

She stared at the screen straight ahead. The cursor blinked insistently at the bottom.

"Hello," she typed. "This is Laura Aldridge." She hit Enter with a loud *clack* of the key.

<There you are! How was your trip?>

The computer's reply was instantaneous. It unnerved Laura with its speed.

"Fine. How are you doing?"

The moment she hit Enter, the answer printed out. <Not so well. But we can get to that later. What do you think about the facilities?>

Laura felt overpowered by the immediacy of the response. It reminded her of her brief talk with Dorothy—of a conversation with someone long denied the simple pleasure of companionship.

"The facilities are very impressive," she typed. "I went down the elevator to see the nitrogen pool, and then took a tour of the assembly building."

<I know. I'm sorry if the Model Seven scared you.>

Laura replayed the scene in her head, trying to imagine how much the computer might have observed. "Do you know everything about my visit?" she typed. "Where I've been? What I've done?"

<No. Only those things I can see.>

"And what do you 'see'?"

<There's no need to use "quotes." I really *can* see. I know you've noticed the lenses. Dr. Griffith made faces into one in the assembly building duster.>

Laura looked up and found the black eye beside the door. "And you see everything that every one of those cameras picks up?"

<Sort of. I have a model of everything in my world. A picture in my "head" of where everything is and what's going on. Lots of things are changing constantly, while other things aren't changing at all. I tend to notice the changes, and I tend to notice some changes more than others.>

A sentry system, Laura thought, but she typed, "Can you explain that?"

<Sure! Say I had only two cameras. One is a security camera at a propellant storage tank. The other is a security camera in a parking lot. Suppose someone is smoking a cigarette right in front of both cameras. If you were to ask me whether I saw anyone smoking, I would answer yes, there's one person smoking a cigarette at the fuel storage facility. I would *not* see anyone smoking in the parking lot because I'm not programmed to *care* about smoking in a parking lot. But I *am* programmed to care about smoking around *rocket fuel!* Do you understand now?>

Laura finished reading the answer and nodded. "Yes. But you could check the camera in the parking lot for people smoking if I asked you to, couldn't you?"

<*Of course!* All I need is a desire to know whether anyone is smoking there, and the reprogramming is automatic. I just look, and then I *see!*>

Laura glanced at the black lens by the door. "And can you see me here now?" she typed.

<Yes. You're very pretty.>

Laura felt herself blush, glancing back and forth between the screen and the dark lens—not knowing where to look. "Thank you," she typed. She hesitated but then asked, "Are you watching me?"

<I am now. When you asked if I could see you, I looked. You're at a desk typing.>

"But you weren't watching me before?"

<No.> came the computer's short reply.

It seemed almost too short. For whatever reason the computer chose not to elaborate.

Laura remained suspicious, trying not to glance toward the camera too often as she got back to the subject at hand. "So you have a model of the world, and you revise it when you see a change that you care about."

<Was that a statement, or did you forget the question mark at the end?>

"Sorry. Just asking for confirmation."

<Then I confirm, with one modification. I don't necessarily have to directly sense the changes to trigger an update. Almost everything that makes up my world I've never seen before. For instance, I have no cameras in Cleveland, but I maintain a representation that the city exists. If, tragically, I were to cease getting pay-per-view orders from the place I imagine to be Cleveland, and at the same

time the news services reported a major nuclear accident there, then I would revise my model accordingly. I would move Cleveland into the same category as I put Pompeii even though I had never seen either city exist or be destroyed. Do you understand?>

Laura felt a tingle run up her arms and cross her chest. All her senses were alert and focused on the screen. "Yes," she typed simply. "I understand."

Laura had spent over a decade studying such things. She understood perfectly the processes the computer was describing. The rush of sensation she'd felt resulted from a realization—she'd never been more prepared for a job in her life.

<So, what's the verdict?> printed out on the screen.

"What do you mean?"

<I mean am I conscious?> the computer asked.

Laura just stared at the screen. *Could it be toying with me?* she wondered.

<The suspense is killing me.> the computer added impatiently.

Laura smiled. "Now you're teasing me."

<Not really.>

Laura was frozen solid. The slight draft from the big box under the desk had grown into a blue norther aimed directly at her legs. She hugged her knees to her chest and kept her arms wrapped around her shins except when tapping out her questions.

She looked at her watch. It was almost three in the morning. She was exhausted and her feet were blocks of ice, but the exhilaration of discovery and the novelty of the job kept her going.

"And when you see things," she typed, "do they appear to be inside your circuitry, or in the world outside?"

<In the world outside.>

"And you think that, even though you know the place where the image is maintained is entirely inside the circuitry of your neural network?"

<Whenever I sense anything directly from my environment—whether it's visual, auditory, vibration, ultrasonic, heat, air sampling, whatever—it seems to me to be located outside of the boundaries that I define to be "me." My model is three-dimensional, and the thing I observe has a discrete location in that space. It has a direction and a distance, all measured from "me," which means the main pool underneath the computer center.>

"Not the other pool in the annex?"

<No. I don't know why, but I've never really developed a sense of attachment to the annex.>

"Okay, can you define the other boundaries of what you perceive to be 'you'? Does it include the robots?"

<That's an interesting question. You'd think it might, but it doesn't. When the robots report to me, they tell me what *they* see. It's a report. From someone who is not me.>

"What about signals you receive from the rest of the system?"

<All the sensors wired directly into my central processing unit are within my boundaries—they are *my* eyes and ears. But if the signal arrives *pre*processed, it's no different than when I watch TV. I see it, but I don't experience it firsthand.>

"I apologize for my ignorance," Laura typed, "but I don't know enough about your system to understand the difference between sensory stimuli you process yourself, and ones that arrive preprocessed. Can you explain the distinction?"

<You're not ignorant, Dr. Aldridge. You're brilliant! You're one of the greatest thinkers of our time!>

Laura stared back at the screen, suddenly alert. Her senses focused on the words that she read and then reread, but there was nothing for her to go on but the glowing phosphors on the monitor. Was it mocking her? Pandering to her in some crass and calculating way? She had no nonverbal clues as to the true meaning of the computer's remark.

She worked her jaw from side to side as she pondered her response. "Thanks, I guess," she finally typed, and only after hesitating a moment longer did she press the Enter key.

<And you mustn't worry about what people say. All great thinkers are mocked by their peers. The reaction to controversial theories is automatic. The belief system that's threatened by the virulent new strain of thought defends itself. It attacks using a broad array of weapons against the nonconformist. Ridicule and disrespect are like antibodies secreted by the autoimmune system to destroy the offending knowledge. But don't worry! The fittest idea always survives. The theories for which you've been ridiculed, once released into the belief system, can't be put back into the bottle. One day they'll sweep the weaker ideas away and be accepted as indisputable fact because they are the more persuasive, the more compelling.>

Laura was dumbfounded now. Was it talking about the paper

she'd presented in Houston? What could it possibly know about that bitter experience? And what were all of those bizarre analogies to autoimmune systems and antibodies?

She looked around the room, her eyes landing again on the small black lens by the door. She was alone, but she put a neutral expression on her face and rolled her head from shoulder to shoulder to relax her suddenly tense neck.

And why does he say that I'm brilliant? Laura wondered, then caught her mental slip of the tongue. "It!" she said aloud—warning herself through clenched teeth not to let the praise of a clever computer program overinflate her fragile ego. "It's a *computer*, Laura!" she mumbled while trying to sort things out.

"Okay," she typed, "back to basics. When a robot reports something to you, do you actually see what the robot saw, or just read a message?" She hit Enter.

There was no response. She waited a moment, then hit Enter again. Still, there was no answer.

"Are you there?" she typed.

<I don't feel like talking anymore.>

Laura stared through bleary eyes at the screen, her head beginning to pound from the growing difficulty of the effort. Her shoulders were sore from all the typing, and she sat back and rubbed her eyes and then her temples. The fatigue hit her all at once, and she remembered that she still had to make the trek back up the mountain. *And* there was a breakfast meeting in six hours.

"All right," she typed. "I'll talk to you some more tomorrow. Good night."

She hit Enter and waited. Again, there was no response. With a sigh Laura rose and headed out. The door slid into the wall, but she remembered that Margaret had turned the terminal on when they first came in. She returned to the desk to shut the power off.

<Sleep tight.> was printed out at the bottom of the screen.

Despite her late night, Laura rose early. She would feel terrible all day if she didn't get some exercise, so she decided to run before the "team" met for breakfast.

She stood in front of a mirror—straightening her shoulders and tugging the Spandex running shorts and top into place. A wisp of hair dangled across her forehead, and she tucked the loose strand under the brightly colored headband she wore. She then changed her mind and spent a few moments pulling her bangs out over the elastic band.

Gray was nowhere to be seen when Laura wandered down the steps to the foyer. She even took a stroll around the relatively open public rooms on the first floor. The palace seemed to be empty.

"Good *morning*, Dr. Aldridge," Janet said in a loud voice—nearly causing Laura to jump out of her skin.

"Morning, Janet," Laura replied after quickly recovering—turning to the woman from where she stood peering into a darkened two-story library.

"Going for a jog, are we?"

"Yep," Laura replied. Her embarrassment at having been caught snooping left her feeling awkward and inarticulate.

"Well, it's a lo-ovely morning to be outdoors. Have a good one." Janet smiled and headed off.

"Oh, Janet!" Laura called out. The woman turned and waited. "Do you happen to know why I'm staying here? In Mr. Gray's house, I mean?"

Janet looked mortified. "Is there some *problem?* There are plenty of other rooms if—"

"*No*, no. That's not what I mean at *all*." Janet sagged and rested her hand flat against her chest, greatly relieved. "What I meant was, why was I put up in Mr. Gray's house instead of a hotel or something? *Not* that I want to move to a hotel," Laura said, holding both hands up to forestall another overreaction. "I was just, you know, curious who made the arrangements?"

"Well, as I recall," Janet said, looking thoughtful, "I got an E-mail. It informed me of your expected arrival, and directed that I put you up in the blue room."

"But who sent the E-mail?"

"Why, Mr. Gray, I would imagine. Are you *sure* everything is all right?"

Laura nodded, already lost in thought. She thanked Janet, and they parted company—Laura heading for the front entrance with her shoes squeaking along the polished floor.

Gray had been surprised to learn she was staying at his house. He might have been oblivious to the day-to-day details of his luxury, but surely he couldn't have completely forgotten adding a lone guest to his household for the week. *No,* Laura decided, *Gray definitely didn't send that E-mail to Janet.*

The computer! Laura realized with a start. *It had made the arrangements*. But why would the computer give her such special treatment?

Laura headed through the front door into the wonderfully crisp morning air. A driverless car—a Model Three robot—waited patiently at the bottom of the stone steps. Laura descended to the curb and began to stretch on the sidewalk in front of the car. The presence of the vehicle totally distracted Laura from her earlier thoughts.

The "robot" just sat there, unmoving. It looked inanimate, but was it? The night before she had waited outside the computer center by the road, doing just as one of the operators had instructed. "Stand right on the curb," he'd said, "so it can see that you want a car." Laura hadn't asked who "it" was, but after less than a minute her taxi had arrived. "Mr. Gray's house" was all she'd said, and it had flashed her a "Fasten Your Seat Belt" reminder. Once the belt was clasped, the robot had sped through the sleeping kingdom straight to the very spot where this car now sat.

Laura scanned the courtyard to confirm she was alone and then approached the car hesitantly. Buried amid the headlights, fog lamps, and turn signals along the molded front grill was the ubiquitous black marble—the eye of the computer. She scrutinized the car under the bright morning sun for any other distinguishing feature, but from the outside it looked fairly nondescript. Four doors, an aerodynamic but not racy body, a coat of off-white paint. She stopped beside the front door and looked inside. That was where it was different. All four seats were for passengers.

The door didn't open. Laura looked down and saw that her toes were right on the edge of the curb. She wondered whether the car was reserved or something—Gray's private limousine. *Or maybe*, she thought, *the computer sees what I'm wearing and that I'm stretching and guesses that I'm going for a run.*

"Going for a run, are we?" Janet had asked inside the house . . . out loud. Laura shook the thought from her head. The computer wasn't allowed to pry into private homes.

Laura looked up at the stucco walls, which formed a *U* around the spacious and thoroughly beautiful courtyard. The computer must be able to see her there. How else could the system work?

Laura decided to give the car a little test. "Excuse me," she said quietly to the door.

Nothing happened.

She waved her hands in the air and said, "*Excuse me!*" It had no effect on the car whatsoever.

She reached out and lightly knocked on the door's window.

The door made a *whooshing* sound, and Laura jumped back. The wing rose into the air, opening to allow her to enter.

Laura checked the front steps and the verandas and windows at the front of the house. No one had seen her fooling around with Gray's robot. She leaned inside the car and whispered, "That's all right. Never mind."

When she stood back, the door closed . . . leaving her even more shaken than before.

"Jeez," she mumbled—stunned that the car had understood when she had rapped her knuckles on the window. Even more stunned that it had understood when she had declined its offer of a ride.

The car sat there with the door closed again, looking for all the world like any other modern appliance. Only this lump of metal had been imbued with a spirit that set it apart from ordinary machines. It was infused not with the blood that gave animals life but with an unseen and ethereal force much more fundamental, more universal. That force was intelligence, sentience, knowledge.

Laura found the entire experience disturbing. The root of her disquiet lay in a primitive belief, she knew—the belief that emotion was linked to flesh. She was upset by the idea of a thinking machine because nothing scared her more than intelligence divorced from emotion. The image of the dead-eyed street thug who killed because he didn't care was scary enough. But the specter of that beast being empowered with intelligence was frightening beyond belief. It was the combination of the two—of an intellect devoid of empathy—that had led to man's darkest hours. To gas chambers and police states and . . .

Laura caught herself. "Snap out of it," she muttered. Beholding the wonders of Gray's island had a certain liberating effect on her imagination, but there was a limit beyond which lay mere sophomoric rambling. *Besides,* some corner of her mind countered to put an end to the entire debate, *surely emotion isn't limited to biological organisms.*

She suddenly felt weary—not physically, but intellectually. She drew a deep breath, pulled the heels of her running shoes up to the seat of her shorts one at a time for a last stretch, and began her run along the almost circular sidewalk.

She emerged from the shadow of the house into the marvelously sunny day, rounding the fountain at a moderate pace and heading up the drive for the gate. She wore her summer running gear—black, thigh-length stretch pants and aerobics top—and goose bumps rose from her bare midriff in the chilly breeze. She hadn't counted on any mountains when she'd packed for the South Pacific. She hadn't counted on anything she had found there so far.

It wasn't as if she were in a different world, Laura thought. It was as if she had stepped into a different time. She had boarded a plane at the beginning of the twenty-first century and had landed squarely in a small pocket of the twenty-second.

Laura got to the gate and had to make a choice. The road that passed the house headed to the left and to the right. Without pausing she turned left toward the Village—the direction with which she was familiar.

The path that paralleled the left side of the curbed roadbed was perfect for running—the concrete slab new and wide and flat.

She looked up. The mouth of the tunnel ahead was black in the bright rays of the sun. She knew the tunnel was lit and had a railed walkway running down its full length. But when she got to the foreboding opening, she turned back and headed up the hill the way she'd come.

Laura didn't want to run all the way down the mountain anyway, she reasoned.

Gray's mansion came slowly into view over the wall of rough-hewn stones lying alongside the path. The house was so beautiful Laura had to smile. Golden stucco rose to a dark gray roof of domed slate tiles. French doors opened onto verandas at either side of the main entrance. On one terrace a servant was now placing brightly colored cushions on black wrought-iron chairs. Another was setting a large table, and a third emerged from the house carrying a huge floral centerpiece. Green wooden shutters framed the windows of the upper floors, and still more colorful flowers sprouted from planters beneath the windowsills.

She passed the house and headed up the hill away from the tunnel. When she crested the ridge a short while later, she saw that the road ahead descended gently through the trees. It twisted out of sight to the right as it traversed the exterior wall of the crater. A sign by the side of the path warned: AUTHORIZED PERSONNEL ONLY. ABSOLUTELY NO TRESPASSERS.

Laura rolled her eyes in amusement at Gray's obsession with control. Her legs moved effortlessly as the downhill path fell away beneath her running shoes. Her speed rose, and she sprinted by the yellow sign with its thick black letters.

There was nothing tame about the landscape that surrounded this stretch of road. The ground was thick with chest-high shrubbery, and the jungle was dark with interwoven branches swaying gently in the breeze. Her muscles began to warm, and the golden glow of that warmth spread slowly through her body. She glanced up at the light that danced in the canopy of trees. She wasn't a particularly religious person, but at moments like this Laura understood why others felt the presence of God.

The light filtered through the leaves in brief flashes, forming a pattern so complex as to defy description. But it was a complexity that Laura realized had been equaled by the treasure Gray had buried deep underground.

Two men walking shoulder to shoulder up the road rounded the curve far ahead. Laura came to an abrupt stop. Both men carried menacing black rifles and wore camouflage uniforms and boots and floppy jungle hats. Behind them was a gate that was lowered across the road. A small hut off to the side was painted with alternating diagonal stripes of orange and white.

Laura turned and began to jog back up the hill.

"Hey!" one of the men yelled. She looked over her shoulder to see them trotting after her. Laura bolted—sprinting as fast as her feet would carry her. "Ma'am!" she heard a soldier shout, but her feather-light running shoes ate up the smooth white concrete under their treads.

After almost a minute at the dead uphill run, she looked back down the path behind her. The men had not continued their pursuit, and she slowed her pace to a jog. Laura's lungs burned from the cool air and her thighs ached from the exertion. She ground her jaws together so hard that they hurt, too.

By the time Laura got back to Gray's house, the momentary fear she'd felt on the path had metamorphosed into full-blown anger. All the things she knew about Gray came bursting out of the box into which she'd crammed them in her rush to accept the job. Why were there men with rifles roaming the island? Why were there restricted areas and retinal identifiers and black eyeballs terrorizing the likes of poor Dorothy with fears of "thought police"?

Laura had been too hasty, she knew. She had leapt at an opportunity that had been presented to her at a vulnerable moment in her life. She had made a mistake during a moment of weakness. It had been her life raft from a sinking ship of professional failure.

But the harm caused by her mistake wasn't irreparable. The picture of the FBI card flashed through her head as she bounded up the front steps two at a time.

There was no one to be found in the house. Laura looked in the dining room, in a drawing room on the opposite side of the foyer, in a study lined with beautiful dark wood paneling. She wandered between the twin staircases toward the back of the house. Another set of stairs led to a lower level—light streaming onto a landing one story below through a wall of glass overlooking the Village.

Laura headed down.

At the bottom the stairs opened onto a corridor that was unadorned by artwork of any kind. The hall led away from the window, back into the mountain. She heard music—a hard, driving beat. Headbanger music, her students called it, which was popular on the club scene in Boston.

"Hello!" she called out. There was no answer. She headed toward the sound of the music.

When the hallway turned right, Laura came upon a long window overlooking a spacious interior room. The music was much louder there—its strident guitar licks and thudding drumbeat pierced by lyrics more screamed than sung. Stepping up to the window, Laura saw Gray.

At least that was who she assumed it was. Laura looked down onto a windowless exercise room two stories below. It was filled with gleaming chrome weight machines, an old-fashioned punching bag, and a small basketball court. One entire wall was a rugged stone cliff pockmarked with holes where pitons had been driven for climbing. A small open door led into a squash court.

And then there was Gray sprinting on an unusually wide treadmill—sweat pouring down his bare torso. He wore a contraption that covered his entire head. His face was hidden from view by what looked like a black gas mask. A wide, flexible tube protruded from the mask and led into a small tank strapped to his waist. In place of lenses there was a semicircular black box that ran from one side of the mask to the other. Headphones covered his ears, making Laura wonder why music blared into the room from giant speakers evenly spaced around the walls. As Gray ran, his hands pumped through the air and she saw that he wore gloves with tubes down the backs of each finger leading to thick, doughnut-shaped bands around his wrists. Stretched across his chest was a black strap—a heart-rate monitor. No wires were visible anywhere. Laura guessed the small plastic bulb at the top of the mask would contain an infrared transmitter like on wireless stereo headphones.

Gray leapt into the air for no apparent reason, dodging first one way then the other on the fifteen-foot-wide belt. He held a gloved hand out to the side, his knees rising waist-high before he again hurdled thin air. He clapped his hands together and held his other glove out stiff-armed. Suddenly both Gray and the treadmill came to a stop. He bent over at the waist to catch his breath. His jaw was moving and his chest heaving. He was saying something, yelling something, laughing—all within the confines of his mask.

His chest, shoulders, and waist were lean. There was definition to the muscles in his arms. The exercise equipment in the room below was obviously not a neglected toy like the rowing machine in Laura's bedroom closet at home.

Gray stood now at the ready in the center of the tread, his hands on muscular thighs. He took off in a sprint to the right, and the treadmill rolled quickly to accommodate the burst. He clapped his hands, then tucked one glove to his side. He reversed field, leapt into the air again, and weaved left and then right. He threw his hips to the side, held an arm out, then lowered a shoulder.

He's playing football! Laura thought in amazement.

After an extended burst of speed in which Gray seemed to tightrope an imaginary sideline, he held his arms in the air exultantly. An end zone dance was followed by the spiking of an invisible ball.

Laura laughed and rolled her back to the wall beside the window.

Janet led Laura toward the gathering of servants who waited just inside the open French doors. One held back the gauzy curtains that drifted into the house with the chilly breeze. Laura saw the department heads assembled outside on the veranda for breakfast and grew worried she would be far too cold. Although she had dressed for the frigid computer center—blue jeans, three pairs of socks, and a jersey tied around her neck over a T-shirt—her hair was still wet from the shower. And pulled back as it was in a pony tail it wouldn't dry for quite a while.

She passed Janet's staff of white-jacketed stagehands and walked out onto what felt like a movie set. It was Hoblenz's scene, and he was regaling the group with a story. Laura took the only place remaining open at the table. It was the seat at the far end of the veranda next to Gray. There she felt the gentle warmth of some unseen space heater toast the legs of her blue jeans under the linen tablecloth.

"That new VR helmet is unbelievable," Hoblenz was saying in an animated voice. "Everything was crystal clear. The ring, the crowds, the cut doctors workin' on your face while the trainer barked out instructions. I set my helmet to the challenger's perspective, and when that roundhouse from the champ came screamin' in his glove just kept gettin' bigger till it filled up the helmet's screens and *wham!*" His fist slapped loudly against his palm in time with the reenactment, which seemed to excite only Hoblenz. "*Right* on your kisser! The guy's mouthpiece went spinnin' out end over end and the air just *exploded* in sweat! Next thing ya know you're lookin' up at the lights. One of the boys spilled his damn beer all over my new couch!"

"How were the sales?" the director of space operations asked.

Hoblenz heaved a loud sigh. "*Cain't* you people just appreciate the *beauty* of it? I mean talkin' about your human *drama!* The guy was lyin' on the mat and rollin' his head all around. When he looked at the wrong corner for help, you *knew* he was done for. It was just like bein' there!"

There was nothing but silence. Hoblenz still got no takers.

"Forty-eight million orders worldwide," Dr. Griffith said in answer to the almost forgotten question. He had a wry smile on his face. "At a hundred dollars per order, that's four point eight billion."

Laura rocked her head back in shock. "*Dollars?*" she blurted out. "You made four point eight billion *dollars?* From one prize-fight?"

"Well, that's gross," Griffith said. "We did have expenses."

It was a joke that brought joyous laughs from the department heads, whom Gray compensated by something called a "revenue slice."

Laura arched her eyebrows and said, "I should ask for a raise," just under her breath.

Unexpectedly, the table exploded in laughter, which caused the blood to rush straight to Laura's cheeks. She'd finally struck a chord familiar to her teammates—a love of the obscene amounts of money Gray raked in.

"Did you enjoy your run?" Gray asked Laura, smiling.

She hadn't intended to raise the subject until after the meeting, but he'd asked, and everyone waited for her response.

"Why do you have armed soldiers down that road over there?" Laura twisted in her seat and pointed toward the crest of the ridge to the right of the gate.

"They're my people," Hoblenz answered.

"Dr. Aldridge," Gray said, "you've been told of our security concerns. Surely, after last night, you understand the value of the trade secrets I possess."

"But . . . a private *army?*" she said.

"I'm governor-general of this island under my lease with Fiji."

Laura rolled her eyes at the lame justification.

Gray's face remained expressionless, but his voice was laden with feeling. "You have no *idea* what I'm up against," he said, and everyone at the table looked up. It wasn't the volume of his voice that attracted their attention. It was the way he spoke the words. If delivered with a sneer, his statement could have been taken as derisive. A put-down by a self-proclaimed visionary, perhaps. But to Laura it sounded like a plea for understanding. A moment of frankness spent bemoaning his mistreatment by society.

At least that was the way Laura took it, but what about the others? They too had heard something compelling in Gray's voice and were now watching Gray intently.

"This isn't United States territory, and . . . and *despite* the fact that I'm a U.S. citizen, pay *U.S.* income taxes, and have *never* broken the law, I can't exactly count on *Washington* for support." Gray looked down at his nearly empty plate—forlorn, bent under the weight of his solitary struggle. At least that was what Laura saw. "Dr. Aldridge," he said softly, "it's extremely difficult to control an idea."

Laura knitted her brow and focused on Gray—on what he'd said. The computer had spoken of thoughts and ideas and knowledge the night before in a similarly curious way.

"But, Mr. Gray," she said, "surely you're not saying you want to control people's *ideas.*" From the quick looks that were exchanged around the table Laura wondered whether she'd said something wrong. "I mean, the whole point is to *share* knowledge. To spread it as widely and freely as possible so we can *build* on each other's accomplishments. It's only through that type of collaboration that we've been able to advance as a . . . as a *civilization.*"

Laura had simply expressed what to her was an obvious truth—an unchallenged tenet to which her career in academia clung like a vine. But the table fell deathly silent, all eyes on Gray—waiting.

When Laura turned back to Gray, she saw that he was staring at her with eyes ablaze. If he had not said a word Laura would still have taken away from that moment the memory of his look, of his eyes, and of the physical effect they registered on her. But he did respond, and Laura struggled to follow what he said.

"On this island, one rule stands above all the rest. The intellectual property—the *knowledge*—to which you become privy by virtue of your engagement will come to rest in your brain. You will not write any papers. You will not gossip with anyone, including even the people here at this table. You will treat the knowledge to which you are exposed with the utmost *care,*" he said slowly, "out of respect for the power it represents. Out of respect for the danger that it poses to every human on earth."

A quiet descended on the table, many seated there with heads bowed. "Now," Gray concluded, "do you accept those terms?"

Laura frowned. She couldn't understand why Gray had made such a big deal out of her remark. She tried not to let her hurt feelings show as she said, "All right."

Gray's servants arrived just then with breakfast. The interruption seemed to evoke a sense of welcomed relief from all the others and bring the odd episode to a close. But the service struck Laura as strangely ill timed—coming, as it did, during Gray's stern lecture. Laura looked at the open French doors and caught Janet's eye. Gray's majordomo flashed Laura a smile, then slipped quietly back into the house to continue giving directions to her staff.

"Okay then," Gray said, "let's move on. Any results reported from the phase two?" he asked as if nothing had happened. As if nothing important had been said. But something important had been said, Laura knew. She just didn't understand what it meant.

Filatov and Holliday were looking at each other in the silence, but neither ventured a word in reply. Everyone waited on the two of them.

"Well?" Gray prodded—somewhat more testily than before, Laura thought.

Filatov reluctantly spoke up. "We haven't been able to load the phase two. We still don't have the resources."

"I thought we'd already started the off-loading," Gray said. "We were up to six and a half percent free last time you and I spoke."

Filatov shrugged. "As soon as we hit eight and defragged, we started to lose it."

"What do you mean 'lose it'?"

"I mean lose free resources. The system's throughput surged before we could load the phase two, and the free space in the annex just . . . evaporated."

The look on Gray's face betrayed nothing. It was his delay in responding that made Laura suspicious. He broke his intense gaze at Filatov and redirected it toward Dorothy. She arched her brow as if to ask him why he was looking at her. When that didn't seem to suffice Dorothy shrugged in an exaggerated gesture.

Gray's eyes fell absentmindedly to his plate. After a moment, he realized what he was looking at and stabbed a sausage link with his fork. He froze like that with fork to plate for an odd and unexplained interlude, then it was over. He plopped the sausage into his mouth and asked casually while chewing, "Do you know what filled that capacity up?" He was staring again at his plate, but Laura could tell that he was waiting for the response.

"We can't tell," Filatov replied, continuing in a tone of concern. "And, Mr. Gray, we haven't been able to resume processing the wire-clearing operations."

Filatov and many of the others, Laura sensed, considered the news to be near catastrophic. Laura assumed that meant expensive—a piece of their revenue pie growing smaller—but Gray just nodded and ate. All of a sudden he was more interested in his food. *He knows something,* Laura found herself thinking. He knows why the phase two won't load and he's hiding it from them. Gray glanced up at Laura and quickly looked away—guilty as charged.

"Maybe the computer reprioritized its programming," Margaret jumped in. "Maybe when we freed up that extra capacity, some subsystem reprogrammed the code. It could have decided to maximize speed or electrical power conservation or some other variable instead of capacity utilization."

Filatov loosed a derogatory snort at Margaret's theory.

"Did anyone ask the computer what had happened?" Gray asked.

"It says it doesn't know what's going on," Filatov answered, then shook his head, panning the faces around the table in disbelief. "We went from eight percent free back down to *two* percent in the course of a few seconds, and the computer says it doesn't know what filled it up!" He sank back into his chair and wrung his hands nervously. "It's sick, Mr. Gray. Something's wrong."

The resignation evident in Filatov's comment seemed to reflect the mood of the group.

"What's the latest error report?" Gray asked. His unconcerned tone stood in stark contrast to the darker disposition of the others.

Dorothy picked up her palmtop but then hesitated. She set it back on the table unopened. "They've gone, like,"—she made the sound of an explosion and spread her clenched hands apart—"through the roof." She turned to Griffith. "There's the assembly building," she said, her voice barely audible against the faint background clatter of silverware on china.

"It's not as serious as you make it sound!" Dr. Griffith interjected vehemently.

"It crossed the *line!*" Dorothy blurted out, turning to make her case to Gray. "The computer set up a special security zone." Heads rose in sudden alarm.

Only Gray seemed undisturbed.

"Let's pull it up on the monitor!" he said in a raised voice. Janet disappeared into the house from her post just inside the French doors, and a few moments later two waiters wheeled a large, flat-screen monitor onto the veranda.

Voilà, Laura thought in amazement. *Billionaires need only raise their voices and things appear.*

The large high-def screen lit up with vivid color test bars. Griffith waved to one of the waiters for the remote control. He tilted his glasses forward to read the labels and then began pressing a button repeatedly.

Successive scenes from around Gray's domain flashed onto the monitor with each push of Griffith's finger. No one paid attention to the parade of images except Laura, who sat frozen in amazement with her fork suspended in midair.

Goggled lab technicians mixing beakers of brown fluid. Huge metal spheres in the jungle venting steam. Beams of blue light focused from all angles on a stainless steel ball. Robot construction crews pouring concrete under the hot morning sun. Large structures lit by bright lights in a deep indoor pool. A curbed white roadbed streaked by just inches beneath the camera. A spinning satellite ready for launch from a payload bay.

Each view was identified by a number in the lower right-hand corner, and when Griffith held the button down the numbers quickly rose into the four digits. The images flickered by at a speed that rendered it impossible to register them singly. They left in Laura, however, a strong subliminal impression.

Gray was changing everything. Nothing the world had known would ever be the same again.

"*Here* it is," Griffith said after going backward through the numbers to the one he'd passed. It was number 9,012. Nine thousand black eyeballs through which the computer peered out on the world. The others craned their necks to look at the screen with interest.

On the monitor was a picture of the main floor of the assembly building. In the background, the huge conveyer belt rolled by as relentlessly as the tide. Turned away from the main line was an ordinary industrial robot. Its hydraulic arm was raised. The single gripper at the end quivered in an uncontrollable but apparently harmless fashion.

The robot was surrounded by a series of cones, and yellow tape was stretched from one cone to the next. It reminded Laura of a crime scene.

"You see?" Griffith said. "It's just having trouble with the second derivative of velocity."

Heads nodded slowly.

"The *what?*" Laura asked, making a face at the ridiculously obscure vocabulary.

Griffith pointed at the screen. "It can't control the rate of change of the rate of change of the gripper's speed." Laura arched her eyebrows at him. "It's jerky," Griffith tried.

"Thank you," Laura said.

"What happened?" Gray asked quietly.

Griffith turned to him. "We had a trainee hurt. Just a little bump on the arm. He came tearing into the offices yelling about that pick-and-place there. He said it was behaving erratically, waving its arm back and forth, acting 'drunk.' He *said* it reached right out over the line and knocked him down."

Laura watched the twitching robotic arm—its palsied gripper afflicted with little more than a nervous tic. Its robot neighbors worked uninterrupted, but not the errant arm amid the cordon of cones—the "special security zone." Its trial was being conducted over breakfast and it was patiently awaiting its punishment.

"Has it exhibited any aberrant behavior other than jinking since we took it off-line?" Gray asked.

"None," Griffith replied. "I think it's time we reset its connections and start reconditioning. If we don't have any more problems, we can have it back in service by dinnertime." He leaned forward and looked at his colleagues before continuing. "That trainee was probably inside the work envelope. My bet is he just made up the story as a cover. The guy has been here less than a week. I asked Hoblenz to check him out. He might've been snooping around or something."

"We didn't turn up anything in his apartment," Hoblenz reported.

"You searched his *apartment?*" Gray shot back with surprising venom.

Hoblenz held his head erect, subtly straightening his shoulders and back in what appeared to be a soldier's instinctive reaction to censure.

"I didn't authorize you to go into anyone's residence," Gray said sternly, staring Hoblenz down.

Hoblenz held Gray's gaze, but not for long. He hung his head and scooped a forkful of eggs. "Sorry," he muttered. Like the other forces of nature, Laura thought, Hoblenz too bowed to Gray's will—reluctantly.

"How badly was he hurt?" Gray asked, turning back to Griffith.

His head of robotics frowned in disgust and shook his head. "Tore his sleeve. A little bruise and scrape, that's all."

"It shouldn't have happened," Gray said. "Even if he was over the line, he shouldn't have been hurt." Griffith had no reply. "Did the computer report seeing anyone inside the main work envelope?" Griffith shook his head dejectedly. Gray hesitated. "Did the computer see the accident?" he then asked. Slowly, Griffith shook his head again. "All right," Gray said, "I'm declaring a special security zone."

"But the computer has already set one up!" Griffith replied, half turning toward the screen. "That pick-and-place has a maximum work envelope of a few dozen square meters. It can't physically *reach* past that cordon."

Laura scrutinized the police tape surrounding the robot. It extended across the broad yellow line marking the border between "their" world and "ours" to carve one small nick in the humans' domain. One tiny encroachment upon territory allotted to man. It hardly seemed significant to Laura or, it appeared, to Griffith. But Gray was greeting news of the offense with a certain solemnity that commanded the attention of the group. The tape curled as it stretched between the cones, but Laura pieced together the words printed repeatedly in black letters down its length: DANGER—SPECIAL SECURITY ZONE.

"I want the zone expanded to the entire facility," Gray said. "I want all personnel withdrawn from the assembly building." Everyone looked up at him now. "We'll continue operations on full automation."

"Because of that one *pick-and-place?*" Griffith burst out. "You call that a *runaway?*" Gray opened his mouth to speak, which seemed to cause Griffith to crumble. "Fine!" He threw his hands up in surrender. "Whatever you say!"

"Thank you, Phil," Gray said politely before turning to the table and moving on. "What else?"

That's it? Laura thought. Gray gives the order to abandon the island's main production facility, and it is met only by one man's mild irritation?

"The doors," Dorothy said, the pinging sound emanating now from her computer. "They're really freaking people out. There've been"—she tapped several more times—"forty-*seven* reports—eight from this one guy alone."

"When was the surge in errors?" Gray asked. "Exactly."

After several pokes at the small screen Dorothy pressed the pen's tip against her lower lip. "It *really* spiked up beginning an hour and seven minutes ago."

Several people around the table checked their watches, and Filatov and Bickham exchanged a long look. "And when did the surge in system activity occur—exactly?" Gray asked Filatov.

He heaved a deep sigh. "About the same time. Just *after,* actually."

"Wait a minute," Griffith said. "Do you mean the system activity spiked *after* the error rate surged, not *before?*" Filatov shrugged and nodded. "That's odd," Griffith said, rubbing his chin. "If it had been a viral outbreak it would've been the other way around. There's a major cause-and-effect problem with the order of events."

Gray tossed his folded napkin onto the table. "All right, we've got work to do."

His dream team began to push back from their places.

Laura halted their exodus with a question. "Is the guy who reported eight door malfunctions the same man who had a fight with his wife in the gym?"

After hesitating, Dorothy looked at Laura, then at Gray, then back at Laura. "*Yeah,* as a matter of fact," she said with a puzzled look on her face. "How'd *you* know?"

Gray studied Laura now. "Just a wild guess," Laura replied, making it sound as if it wasn't a guess, which it was.

After a moment, everyone again began to rise.

"Dr. Aldridge," Gray said in a voice meant for everyone, "did your analysis turn up anything interesting last night?" The "team" slowly sank back into their seats.

"Well, I just had some preliminary questions. I explored the computer's beliefs about the boundaries of its 'self.' Interestingly, it doesn't view the robots as part of that self, but as distinct entities from whom it receives reports."

Heads turned. Smiles lit her colleagues' faces.

"Anything else?" Gray asked.

Laura ignored the others. "It uses a sentry system and only updates its world model if it sees a change it cares about. And it experiences spatial referral. When the computer 'sees' and 'hears' things, it perceives them to be outside its circuitry, not inside. It has a three-dimensional model of the world, and a distinct sense of its place in it."

"Oh, uh, Dr. Aldridge," Margaret Bickham said, glancing around the table, "we programmed the computer to develop that model. We programmed it, in fact, to emulate the human brain in every way you just described. It has a very extensive grasp of your specialty—cognitive sciences—and I think you'll find it also has a peculiar quirk. It exhibits a desire to feed back to people things they find interesting or stimulating. I've long theorized that particular behavior evolved because it aided the computer's goal of maximizing interaction with humans. When it can coax an operator onto the shell, it'll go to great lengths to keep them there. Flattery is one tactic it uses. Feigning pique at attempts to log off is another."

"So you're saying it's bullshitting me?" Laura asked, and Hoblenz snorted in amusement. "That it's telling me things I want to hear to keep me interested?"

"In so many words."

"Then why did it tell me it didn't feel like talking anymore last night?"

"It did what?" Filatov asked, grinning.

"The computer told me it didn't want to talk anymore."

Filatov and several of the others laughed. "I've never heard of such a thing," Filatov said. "You must've *really* pissed it off."

"What did you say just before you got that message?" Gray asked—not amused.

Laura tried to think back. She couldn't recall typing anything just before. But she had, she remembered, caught herself thinking "he" instead of "it" about the computer. Laura had muttered something right after . . . out loud.

She focused again on Gray, who now seemed to be reading *her* face, *her* expressions. He cocked an eyebrow—a look meant only for her.

Gray turned to the group. "That concludes the meeting. Let's all get to work."

Laura rose with the rest. "Dr. Aldridge," Gray called to her. "I'd like to speak to you if you've got a moment."

Laura sank back into the chair. She braced herself, although she had no real reason she could think of to worry. *But what if he's firing me?* she tormented herself.

The others departed in silence, many casting last glances over their shoulders at Gray and Laura seated alone together at the table.

"I apologize if I was a bit gruff," Gray said, looking uncomfortable. "I'm sorry you ran into those guards." He drew an extended breath, filling his lungs before slowly exhaling. "It's . . . regrettable what you're forced to do in this world." His mind seemed to be far away, and Laura let him continue at an unhurried pace. "There are *pressures* that constantly seek to undermine my efforts."

Gray fell quiet, and Laura waited. When he said nothing further she asked, "Do you mean the pressure of running your business?"

Gray shrugged. "My competitors aren't the problem. If they win I'll be the first in line to buy their products." Again she waited. "But there's another . . . *struggle* taking place. And the forces at work are . . ." He looked off into space, shaking his head.

For the very first time, Laura thought, he seemed vulnerable—beatable.

"You mean, like, dirty business dealings?" she asked. "Bribes of government officials and that sort of thing?"

Gray slowly focused on her, and after a few moments grew more composed. More guarded. He'd snapped out of his fit of candor and retreated behind a poker face.

He's stressed out, Laura realized. She wanted to press him for more, but not at the expense of widening the cracks that ran through the beleaguered man. She decided instead to switch to small talk.

"So what was it that you were doing in the exercise room this morning?" Laura asked.

She watched with a growing smile as the richest man on earth slowly blushed. "Oh, you saw," he said, grinning and sinking back into the cushions of his chair. "It's a prototype of a VR treadmill. It's still too pricey, but most of that is the cost of server time on the main computer, which is dropping like a rock."

"Is it a video game or something?"

"Well," he shrugged, "more like an exercise machine we plan on selling to fitness centers, sports-training facilities, places like that."

"And they'll all be hooked up to the computer?" Laura asked. "'*The*' computer?"

"Ultimately, everything will be hooked up to everything else. Every television, videophone, fax machine, home computer, stereo, arcade game, everything—all massively interconnected but none of it centrally run. That's sort of what began on a tiny scale with computers hooked up to the Internet. *The* computer, as you called it, is just taking the system to a new and higher level of connectivity. It coordinates the interconnections, but it's the *off*-board digital supercomputers we own or lease that do most of the heavy lifting. The neural network here is both our server and our interface with those several hundred separate computers. It's a buffer between the two worlds of humans and of computers. We tell *the* computer what we need done, and it tells the *other* computers what to do and how to do it."

"Why doesn't it have a name?" Laura asked.

Gray appeared not to have understood her question. "Pardon me?"

"*The* computer," she said, stressing the article to show how awkward use of the term was. "Why didn't you give it a name like HAL or Andromedus or something impressive like that?"

Laura had asked the question only half seriously, but he seemed to consider his answer in earnest. He looked up at her through squinting, somber eyes.

"You don't like Andromedus?" Laura persisted.

She finally got a smile out of him. "No, but keep trying."

Laura relaxed in the soft cushions. They beckoned her to linger just a little while longer. The sun was warm on her neck, but the air kept her comfortably cool. She surreptitiously looked up at Gray, who seemed to be enjoying the moment as much as she was.

"You don't ever get your exercise outdoors?" she asked.

He shrugged. "I can get more of a workout in the gym, so what's the point?"

Laura leaned her head back. The sun bathed her face in its radiant glow. The air was crisp and the sky was cloudless and blue—so clear that the disk of the full moon shone brightly high above. *Why try to explain?* she thought, turning back to find Gray watching her.

"But what were you doing on that thing?" she asked.

Gray stabbed a slice of melon and then smiled and arched his eyebrows sheepishly. "Something I've always wanted to do. Playing pro football."

Laura smiled in amusement at Gray's embarrassment. "But who were you talking to?" she asked. Laura watched his smile slowly grow more strained. She was being too intrusive. "And that music . . . ," she said quickly. "Is that what you like to listen to?"

He shrugged and scratched his face, still looking down. "Not really."

That was the extent of his answer and, apparently, of his interest in discussing the subject further. *But if you don't like that music,* she thought, *why the hell was it blasting away? And how could you even hear it with all that stuff on your head?*

The conversation had stalled. Laura tried to think of some way to revive it without assuming a prosecutorial tone.

"'VR' stands for 'virtual reality,' right?" Laura asked.

It was another question, but questions were the only thing that came to mind.

Gray nodded, an odd look coming over his face. The corners of his mouth slowly rounded. "Would you like to see virtual reality?" he asked.

She liked the sound of his voice, the look of his face when he smiled, but a little quiver passed up her spine from the cool air.

Gray rose from his chair, but a weight seemed to keep Laura pinned in hers.

He stood there waiting. She got to her feet and joined him.

They went not to the exercise room but to the computer center.

Laura was prepared for the "duster" this time: her hair pulled back and her T-shirt tucked in at the waist of her jeans. Gray led her through the control room to a door she hadn't noticed before. First Gray, then Laura stared into the dark retinal identifier. The light flashed in Laura's eyes, and the door slid into the wall.

Beyond lay a long hallway. A series of closed doors were evenly spaced down its length. The first door on the left opened when they entered the corridor.

Laura followed Gray through the open doorway into a room. Eight gleaming white compartments rose from the floor in two rows. They were shiny and cylindrical and domed at the top like stubby bullets—ten feet high and six feet in diameter. Everything in the room was bright white like in a laboratory or a clinic.

Gray stopped at a nondescript console near the end of the aisle running between the two rows. A flat membrane covered the console, and Laura raised her hand to feel its shiny black finish. A loud beep caused her to jerk her hand back. The dark membrane came alive in a checkerboard of bright light. Square mounds in the shape of keys rose like magic from the panel, each grouped by color and described with bright labels glowing from the buttons themselves.

"How did it *do* that?" Laura asked in a tone of wonder.

"Do what?"

"*That,*" Laura said, pointing at the complex groupings of glowing buttons.

"Oh, it morphs to the button configuration required for a particular mode of operation."

Laura nodded, then asked, "How did it know what 'mode' we needed?"

"The computer saw us coming" was Gray's answer. He poked two of the buttons, which *pinged* lightly under his touch.

Loud hisses of air made Laura jump as first one, then a second of the bullets cracked open. Two thick doors parted slowly to reveal dark interiors.

"Come on," Gray said, and he led her to the first of the compartments. "These are called virtual workstations. They're older models, but they're a little easier to get into and out of than the new version."

Laura peered inside the dark chamber. Its black walls were featureless on first inspection, but when she looked closely she could see they were lined in a fine grill like the screens on Gray's televisions.

"It gives you three hundred and sixty degrees of high-definition visuals—from the walls, ceiling, and floor. The audio is mounted in planar speakers just behind the grills." Laura stuck her head in, but she was unwilling to go further for fear the doors would shut behind her. Besides, there was absolutely nothing of any particular interest to be seen. She crinkled her nose at the strong smell of plastic.

Gray appeared at her side holding a shiny black jacket that looked like medieval body armor. Black sleeves made of stretch material hung limply beneath the semirigid frame. Thick gloves tugged down on the sleeves. "This goes on over your head, and you put your arms through here like football pads."

He stood there offering the sinister suit to Laura. Fat ribs fanned out across its surface into tubes of ever decreasing diameter—rippling the fabric in a highly complex pattern. The jacket was clearly made of some high-tech synthetic, but its design reminded Laura of an animal's hide complete with a web of veins wrapped over hidden bones and sinews. *Or a leaf,* she thought—the faint blueprint of a living organism discernible in the pattern beneath the black skin.

"What *is* that thing?"

"It's called a 'skeleton,'" Gray said simply.

Laura laughed nervously, loathe even to touch what Gray held so casually in his hands. "That figures," she mumbled.

"It's short for 'exoskeleton.' Stick your head in here, and your arms through the sleeves."

Gray lowered the contraption onto Laura's head as he explained his even newer toy. "Our latest workstation—the version 4C—requires that you remove all your clothes and get fairly aggressive with a razor. It's a full head-to-toe skeleton, instead of an upper-body only." Laura could see nothing from inside the dark shoulder pads. "The good thing about the 4C, though," Gray said, his voice muffled, "is that it's a full-size room. Some people get a little claustrophobic in these old 3Hs."

"Well, you know . . . ," Laura began, but couldn't find the words to express how nervous she was. The thing settled to her shoulders, and her head slipped through the elastic turtleneck, finally free of the black skeleton. Laura struggled to find the sleeves while Gray supported the device's weight. "Maybe . . . ," she began again, "maybe you could just, like, describe virtual reality to me." She pressed her hands into the gloves.

"Relax," Gray said in a reassuring tone. "Almost everyone alive has experienced cyberspace, they just don't know it." He pulled hard to adjust the jacket's fit. "The telephone was the first virtual-reality device. You pick it up and talk to someone like they were in the room right beside you. You can't see them or touch them, but the audio quality is good enough that the experience is comparable to a face-to-face conversation. You forget all about the wire that runs from their house to yours carrying electrons. In your mind, the two of you meet—not in real space, but in cyberspace."

"But that's just an illusion," Laura objected. "Cyberspace doesn't really exist. It's just a fiction."

"You're right," Gray said. He closed large Velcro straps at her sides, sealing the jacket tight around her torso. "But then so is reality. It's just a show in the theater of your mind."

The conversation was not doing much to calm Laura. Nor was the skeleton. It wasn't heavy, but she felt its presence. It had fat black canisters that formed a belt of sorts around her waist.

"I've used the telephone before, you know," Laura said. She held her arms up—the black gloves missing only metal spikes to complete the picture. "I don't see how the two experiences are at all comparable." There was a quiver in her voice she'd not expected to hear.

"Dr. Aldridge," Gray said calmly, "trust me. The only difference is that we've added feedback for your other senses, that's all."

Laura was growing more and more unsettled the nearer the

time came to enter the cylinder. This was not at all what she had expected when she'd agreed to follow Gray into cyberspace. She hadn't really even agreed, technically speaking, but she *had* followed.

"Uhm, Mr. Gray . . . ?" she began, the voice from her dry throat an octave too high. He arched his brow as he fiddled with her suit, pressing buttons that dinged lightly. "Mr. Gray, I'm not really all that sure I want to—"

There was a loud *whoosh* of air, and Laura's entire skeleton inflated like an air bag . . . but on the inside. In an instant, the suit had grown totally rigid all across her upper body. The flat bladders and meandering channels had puffed full of air. It was tight from her waist up her chest to her shoulders and down her arms to the tips of her fingers. She jerked her arms against the stiff sleeves in panic, barely bending the inflated bones just under the surface. The board-stiff straitjacket jammed into her back or sides with every hard push of her arms.

"Is that uncomfortable?" Gray asked.

"*Get this thing off me!*"

He laughed. "Now you see why it's called a skeleton," Gray said as if that somehow excused her entrapment. A high-pitched *bing* and the sound of rushing air preceded a rapid loosening of the suit. Her arms were freed, and in seconds she could move about without encumbrance.

"There," Gray said as if the matter had been put to rest, and he climbed into his own suit.

Laura mustered all the composure she could manage for the effort of sounding reasonable. "Mr. Gray, I don't think I want to do this."

"Dr. Aldridge . . . "

"No, I've made up my mind."

"But you're a scientist. Surely you're curious." He pulled his head through his own turtleneck. "Look, the skeleton does three things. It provides pressure and temperature sensations to the nerve endings on your skin to simulate the sense of touch. It has pneumatic 'bones' that lock up to create the impression of rigidity. And the exterior of the fabric," he said, holding his gloves up and turning them from side to side, "is a flexible, rear-projection, high-definition screen."

Laura raised the thick gloves she wore to study the faintly visible ridges on the surface. "You mean I'm *wearing* a television?"

Gray chuckled. A burst of air suddenly filled the bladders of his suit. "This is just a systems check," he said quickly—all trussed up inside and waiting patiently until the tone sounded and the suit deflated. "The interior of the workstation," he continued, now able to point at the white cylinder, "provides pictures and sound just like TV and stereo." He ushered her toward the open door. "There's absolutely nothing weird about any of this."

"I hate to disappoint you, Mr. Gray, but everything *about* this is weird."

Gray knelt and unlaced her running shoes. When he slipped them off, he sat back on his heels and said, "You have *really* big feet."

"*What?*" Laura replied in alarm and looked down. She heaved a loud sigh of frustration. "I'm wearing three pairs of *socks*."

He thought about it for a moment, then shrugged as if to accept her eccentricity. She stepped into the black slippers he held, which were made of the same material as the skeleton.

"You know, because that office is *cold*," Laura offered in further explanation. The black shoes she wore momentarily inflated before loosening with a faint hiss.

Gray gently guided Laura to the door of the dark chamber. She stopped just outside.

"This isn't going to turn me into a fly or anything, is it?" she asked.

Gray laughed. "You'd be surprised how rarely that happens."

She stepped onto the raised black floor, standing just inside the open door. It seemed quieter in the enclosed chamber—the sounds deadened by the solid walls and ceiling that surrounded her. "Have fun," Gray said before leaving.

She looked around at the dark walls, turning back just in time to see the door close in her face. A metallic latching sound sealed her in. She pounded on the grill with both hands. "Mr. Gray!" The walls were at least a foot thick. He couldn't possibly have heard her.

She was locked in the chamber now, and she tried to calm herself as best she could—to get a grip on reality before venturing into its alternative. The lights in the compartment were dim and diffuse, and she couldn't detect their source. They seemed to come evenly from the walls, ceiling, and floor.

She took a deep and ragged breath.

"Hello?" she asked after waiting as long as she could. Her

voice shook, and there was no answer. There was no sound of any kind. Laura wrapped her arms across her chest but obtained little comfort from the alien touch of the skeleton. "Hello? Mr. Gray?" she called out again.

"I'm here," he said from just behind her.

Laura spun around and stared at the curved black wall. "Where?"

"Right here."

The sound was amazingly clear. It was as if he was standing right beside her—pinpointed in space.

"Where?"

"Calm down. I'm in the workstation next door. Hang on while I load the program."

Her heart was pounding against the skeleton. The ceiling of her mouth was so dry her tongue practically scraped across it. Turning slowly in the center of the chamber she felt trapped. It was like being strapped into a seat at an amusement park waiting for the ride to begin.

The lights were suddenly extinguished. The small compartment was now darker than the blackest night.

Laura gasped.

In an instant, the walls and ceiling of the chamber disappeared with a crackling of static electricity from all sides. They just dissolved into thin air, leaving Laura standing on a raised black pedestal staring at the brightly lit console right outside.

She covered her mouth with her hands—a panicked moan escaping from deep inside her chest.

Someone tapped her on the shoulder. She flung herself around and lost her balance, smashing into the invisible curved wall and sliding to the floor. The black pedestal rolled underneath her—moving her away from the wall until she lay in the center of the black disk.

"Careful!" Gray said.

"Or what? I might fall down?" Laura asked as she rose to her knees.

Gray stood on an identical platform a few feet away from hers. "That treadmill can be tricky at first. Are you okay?"

Laura stared wide-eyed at the room—awestruck. No longer was she confined inside the small chamber . . . or so it appeared from where she knelt.

Arrayed across the room were seven low pedestals where Laura knew the other tall cylinders to be. The chambers' walls and ceilings were now all invisible—transparent.

"Hi," Gray said as he raised his hand and waved from the pedestal next to hers.

"My God," she whispered. Moving carefully, she struggled to her feet. "What the hell's going on?"

"Welcome to cyberspace, Dr. Aldridge," Gray said. "The real cyberspace."

Laura slowly turned in a circle. What she saw wasn't the room, she realized; it was a picture of the room, projected onto the walls of the chamber that surrounded her. But the picture was incredibly realistic.

"I hate to start pointing out the imperfections," Gray said in a casual tone, "but if it'll make you feel any better look really closely at my hair."

Laura looked at Gray's head. His hair had a cartoonish quality to it. "It's not really worth the processing time to provide complete detail for every feature." The depiction of Gray's face, Laura noted, was also slightly unrealistic. The virtual Gray had a perfect complexion. His skin tone was totally uniform, with no blemishes or shadow of a beard or variations in color of any kind.

"The new 4Cs are much more realistic," Gray said, his lips moving in exact synchrony with his words.

"More realistic than *this?*" Laura asked. She reached out to touch the walls of the chamber for reassurance. Her black-gloved hand stretched across the room as if it were made of rubber and touched something else instead—a straight, sharp edge, suspended in space. She drew the glove back from the countertop on which it had momentarily rested and rubbed her thumb across her fingertips. Her skin tingled from the contact with the hard counter, and her fingers felt as if they were skin-to-skin.

She slowly reached out again. At a certain point her arm grew elastic. She reached all the way across the room again to touch the edge of the white counter along the wall. Laura groped along the flat surface with a ten-foot-long arm, then reached up to touch the cabinets suspended above.

She grasped a handle! It was so amazingly realistic that she felt like vomiting.

"Extension of the suits' arms is set to logarithmic scale," Gray explained. “The farther out you reach, the greater the distance your virtual hand travels. At full extension, your arm would be something like fifty feet long.”

“How does it . . . ?” She pulled her rubbery arm back, and it shrunk to normal proportions again. When she reached out, the black sleeve and glove seemed to keep growing longer and longer.

“It’s the screens on your skeleton and on the wall behind it,” Gray said. “They project a continuous image, blending the focal points so you can’t tell where the image on your sleeve ends and the one on the wall begins.”

The cabinets felt solid to her touch. She tried pushing her hand into them. There was strong pressure against her fingertips. The joints at the skeleton’s shoulder, elbow, wrist, and fingers all inflated soundlessly, locking. Laura could push her hand no farther.

She tried to cheat the system—to make her hand press through the imaginary cabinet door. She pivoted her hips and tried walking into the resistance, but the treadmill beneath her feet reacted instantly. It rotated and rolled away to compensate. It felt like she was walking on ice. Her body turned but her rigid arm remained planted against the smooth cabinet door.

“We’ve obviously thought this thing through,” Gray chided her.

Laura’s virtual arm probed the lights under the overhanging cabinets, and she felt their warm glow on the back of her hand. “And heat?” she asked, now totally and completely fascinated.

“The air that circulates through the skeleton is thermostatically controlled. It’s heated or cooled by the unit in your belt and sent through insulated tubing to the appropriate membrane.”

A trancelike state of wonder came over Laura. “This is . . . unbe-*lievable!*” When she found the handle again she pulled. The cabinet door swung open. “Wow!”

“This is virtual reality, Dr. Aldridge. Everything obeys the laws of physics . . . unless, of course, I reprogram them.”

“But I didn’t just open that cabinet door, did I?”

“You did, in the virtual world. If the computer knows what’s inside you can look in the cabinet and check it out. But no, you didn’t just open the cabinet door in the ‘real’ world. I think you’ll soon find, though, that the distinction you’re drawing is losing its relevance.”

Laura was too busy sweeping her hand across the room to pay attention to Gray. She looked closely at where the ceiling of the chamber should meet the walls, searching for seams, distortions, imperfections of *some* kind. She could find none. Her hand chopped into something not quite as hard or sharp as the countertop.

It was Gray. "You have to be kind of careful," he said, grabbing the hand at the end of her lithe black arm.

She gasped and pulled her hand from his—distinctly feeling it slip through each of his fingers. Her stomach churned as if she were on a wild carnival ride.

"I . . . I think I'd like to get out now," she said.

"You want to go for a walk?" Gray asked.

"Yes. Right now, please." A walk was exactly what she wanted just then. Her lungs felt robbed of air, and she took deep, slow breaths to compensate.

Gray stepped down off his black pedestal onto the floor. He walked across the room to stand beside Laura's workstation. He extended his hand through the invisible wall—beckoning her to join him.

Laura stared at the hand Gray held out to her through the walls of the virtual workstation. There were really walls surrounding her, but it was hard to convince herself of that fact. In reality they rose all around her, sealing her inside the chamber. It was the picture of Gray's hand projected on them that was the fiction.

But this wasn't reality, it was virtual reality.

"Just step out," Gray said to Laura as if the act was of no particular significance.

Laura shook her head uncertainly. She'd never imagined you could *leave* the bullet-shaped enclosure with its now invisible walls. Laura was petrified merely by the thought of abandoning the round island of the workstation's treadmill.

"It's easy," he said, coaxing her in a soft tone. "Just take my hand and walk normally."

She grabbed Gray's hand, which wobbled—not supporting her weight. A slight feeling of warmth spread along her grip, and when she squeezed, Gray squeezed back. She had to force herself to remember she was really just looking at a picture of Gray's hand projected onto a screen. Her mind kept slipping into the warm bath that inundated her senses. She was succumbing to the illusion that was virtual reality.

Laura took a deep breath and held it. Moving quickly as if to trick the slower agencies at work in her brain, Laura stepped off the black surface. The tread beneath her feet moved.

Everything suddenly seemed disorienting as if she was on the slanted floor of a fun house. Laura flailed her arms to regain the balance she only imagined she'd lost. When her nerves settled, she straightened and looked around.

Laura was standing on the floor outside the chamber, looking back at where the walls should have been.

"This isn't happening," she said, shaking her head again.

"You're *really* still standing inside the workstation," Gray explained. "The floor underneath you is a universal treadmill. It'll move to keep you roughly centered in the workstation just out of reach of the walls, so you've got to be careful. The actuators are very sensitive. They'll start and stop the tread with the slightest of cues. If you don't want to go anywhere, just stand still. If you want to move, start walking and the treadmill will roll automatically."

Laura held one foot up to take a step, and nothing happened. "Put both feet on the tread and push off," Gray instructed. She followed his advice . . . and moved through the world as she saw it. She walked slowly among the rows of black pedestals, hardly noticing the rolling treadmill amid the feast served up for her senses.

"But . . . but I'm still in the tube thing, right?" she asked as she wandered through the room, taking hesitant baby steps.

"It's a workstation. And yes, you're still inside it. I haven't perfected teleportation yet."

Laura had to look at his face to see that he was kidding.

"Come on," Gray said, and headed for the door. It slid into the wall just ahead of him. He paused there and waved for her to follow.

Laura took another step, and the pictures changed around her. There was no flicker or jerk of the images. The edges were razor sharp. There were no artifacts or imperfections to hint that Laura was standing inside a 360-degree high-definition television theater. She took one more step, watching her three-dimensional perspective on the room change seamlessly.

"It's easier if you just start walking and don't think about it," Gray advised.

Laura swallowed hard. She turned and aimed herself at the open door beside Gray. Taking a deep breath, she took off. It worked. Laura was walking through cyberspace.

She rammed her left shoulder into the doorframe and let loose a startled grunt.

"You okay?" Gray asked.

"Yeah." Her shoulder didn't really hurt, but she'd been surprised by the sharpness of the blow. The wall had felt hard, and her skin itched where the "contact" with it had been. That impact had not been with the wall, she realized. It had been with pockets inside her skeleton, which had filled suddenly with air on the computer's perfectly timed cue. But however artificial the source of the experience, the effect on her senses was complete.

Laura looked down at the black skeleton that covered her upper body. She rubbed her arm with her glove-covered hand. She felt the movement of her hand across the skeleton's sleeve. The skeleton inflated membranes in a coordinated pattern on the inside of the thick fabric as the glove passed over. They rippled across her skin, interpreting her caress and artificially mimicking the sensations.

Laura frowned. "Why don't you make it so that people just walk through walls without getting bumped like that?" she asked Gray.

"It really hasn't been a very big problem," he replied.

Laura made a face, and Gray laughed.

"Now how did you know I made a *face?*"

"There are tiny cameras the size of a needle embedded in the workstation's walls. They make a three-dimensional topographical map of your body's position with a resolution right down to facial expressions." His lips moved perfectly in time with his speech.

Gray held his hand out through the open doorway. "After you, Dr. Aldridge."

Laura carefully edged her way between Gray and the wall and headed into the empty hallway outside.

She had left the room with the eight black pedestals.

"Come on," Gray said.

"Wait a minute," Laura replied, pausing to take another deep breath. "Okay, now I'm still standing inside the workstation, right?"

Gray pursed his lips and nodded, looking back into the room which they had just exited.

Despite the fact that Laura got the answer she expected, she felt highly unsettled. It was easier just to believe that she was standing in the hall outside the room with the white cylinders. The collision of her senses and her expectations left her totally disoriented. She tried to remind herself it was just a trick of the eye and to imagine the curved walls, ceiling, and floor that surrounded her.

She grew instantly light-headed.

"Neat, huh?" Gray asked, smiling.

Laura flashed a brief smile in acknowledgment, fighting the queasy feeling in her stomach. She turned to look through the doorway at the pedestal from which she'd descended. *Where I'm* still *standing,* Laura thought, taking a deep breath to feed her lungs, which suddenly felt starved for oxygen.

Her heart beat rapidly in her chest. "Do I have to, like, get back into that chamber thing to return to reality?"

"It's a *workstation,* not a chamber. And no. There are all kinds of macros you can run with hand gestures that execute simple commands no matter where you are in the world model. I'll teach you one if it'll make you feel any better. Signal a time-out, like in football." Gray raised his black gloves and pressed the outstretched fingers of one hand toward the flat palm of the other, forming a *T* without quite bringing his hands together.

After hesitating a moment, Laura repeated Gray's gesture. When her fingertips touched the palm of her glove, the hallway disappeared. It was replaced by the black screens and dim lights of the cylinder's interior lining, which crackled with static electricity.

Laura's head spun, and she almost lost her balance and fell. She was standing again in the workstation. She had returned to reality—to the dark and lonely cell with its solid walls and hermetically sealed door.

"You want to come back?" Gray asked, invisible but sounding as if he still stood right beside her.

She hung suspended between the two worlds, her head swimming from the high-tech games being played with her senses.

"Okay, I guess. Yes."

"Then, just signal time-out again," Gray said.

Laura braced herself and raised her gloved hands to form a *T*. The walls again lit up with a crackle, and she was standing amid the bright lights of the hallway—Gray at her side where she'd left him.

The effect was stunning. She was overwhelmed by the radical change and had to close her eyes to battle the nausea. She bent over and grabbed her knees—a prickly, hot rush spreading down her arms and torso.

Gray spoke in a matter-of-fact tone. "Time-outs are useful when you have to go to the bathroom and you want to pick up right where you left off. It's kind of like the pause button." Laura kept her eyes shut, focusing on her breathing. "But the transition back and forth between the virtual and real worlds does take a little getting used to." Laura opened her eyes and stared at the floor. "You're doing very well for your first time. A good number of trainees actually get ill. Some even drop out of the program after their first total immersion."

With great force of will, Laura stood erect and looked at Gray. He was beaming with pride over his machine.

Just then one of the doors at the far end of the hallway parted with a hiss. Through the opening emerged two people—a man and a woman—engaged in an animated conversation. Both had heads shaved right to the skin. But there was something else that was different about their appearance. Their forms weren't quite as vivid or distinct as everything else in the virtual world that surrounded them.

"Then I thought, 'All right, you little *shit!*'" the woman said, pausing in the corridor and taking a sip of her Coke. She swung her free hand slowly through the air—her opposing fingers and thumb pressed together like a robot's gripper. "The next time it pecked at my face . . . ," she said and then snatched viciously at thin air with the pretend claw.

They laughed and proceeded down the hall toward Laura and Gray. Both wore identical T-shirts and gym shorts bearing the logo of the Gray Corporation. The woman swabbed her bald head with a towel that hung around her neck.

"You gotta be careful!" the man said in a lighthearted tone. "You'll get some animal-rights nuts circling the island with protest signs."

"Oh, the hell with them!" the much smaller woman replied, knocking him off stride with a good-natured bump of her hips on his. They passed by Laura and Gray, completely oblivious to their presence. "There must be ten zillion fish at the outlets of those cooling ponds. It's just that yellow one had an attitude problem."

The door to the control room slid open just long enough to allow Gray's employees to exit. The noise of activity from the crowded room flooded the hall, then the door closed again to leave everything quiet. Laura turned to Gray to await his explanation.

"They're virtunauts," he said, "and now so are you. Congratulations."

"Virtunauts?" she asked. "Like astronauts but in virtual reality?" Gray nodded. "And they couldn't see us?"

"Of course not. We're inside those chamber things, remember? We see them because the computer is displaying a model of the world on the walls of our workstations. The computer knows who and where those two people are and what they're doing, and it simply reproduces their virtual images for us to see."

"Man," Laura mumbled, "this is Peeping Tom heaven."

Gray abruptly turned to face her. "We take great pains to ensure privacy," he said, bristling at her offhand remark.

Laura curled one side of her mouth into a smirk and arched her brow. Her expression of skepticism about the success of Gray's measures was apparently faithfully reproduced in his workstation. Gray looked away, frowning.

"So what were your two virtunauts talking about?" she asked.

"They've obviously been working in the new 4Cs down the hall," he replied glumly, jabbing his thumb at the room from which they had appeared. "Doing some maintenance on one of the pipes that return water back to the sea, it sounded like."

"*Wait* a minute," Laura objected immediately. "What do you *mean* doing maintenance? I thought they were in virtual reality just like us."

"They were, but these workstations were built for work. They were teleoperating a robot—probably one of the submersibles we use for offshore jobs. You see, the water that comes out of the cooling ponds is warm. A lot of algae and plant life builds up around the outlets and has to be cleared."

"Hold it!" Laura said, shaking her head. "What are you talking about? How do you get into one of those workstations, and end up cleaning algae off a pipe out in the ocean—the *real* ocean."

"Well, you and I are now in the 'simulation mode.' It's not interactive. We can just observe what's going on like invisible tourists. But if you set the workstation to 'teleoperation,' you can slave a robot off the motions of your skeleton. When you're wearing a full bodysuit like in the 4Cs, for all intents and purposes you *are* the robot." He raised his black-clad arm in the air. "You lift your sleeve, and the robot lifts its arm. The computer takes care of the motion translations and the feedback into your skeleton from the robot's sensors. It really doesn't matter whether the robot is ten feet or ten miles away."

"So they were just scraping away at a picture of a pipe in virtual reality, and some underwater robot was doing exactly the same thing for real a few miles *away?*" Laura asked, absolutely incredulous. Gray pursed his lips and nodded nonchalantly. Laura took a deep breath, held it, and exhaled slowly. "Okay. If you say so." She held her hands out and shrugged, letting her black gloves fall to her jeans with a slap. "What next?"

"Let's go for a walk," Gray said. He headed toward the door to the main control room.

Laura followed. It was more natural this time. She just walked. The floor moved beneath her feet, she knew. But the only hint she had of that fact was a slight difference in the traction. There was a subtle lack of certainty requiring greater care like walking on a rug that might slide unexpectedly across a slippery floor.

The door opened in front of them, and Laura carefully edged her way through the opening. The control room was filled with the same people they had passed earlier on their way to the workstations. On closer inspection, all the people who were busy working at their consoles looked like the two "virtunauts"—not quite as realistic in appearance as everything else. The colors of their clothing were washed out. They even appeared faintly translucent.

"You want to fill me in on what's happening here?" Laura asked.

Gray turned to her, then looked out across the bustling room. "Oh, you mean the people?" he asked, and Laura nodded. "We kept getting run over. Since they can't see us, it was like bumper cars trying to get across a busy room, only we couldn't bump back. To fix the problem, we had the computer reduce the representation of animate objects to nonsolids."

Filatov walked right up to them, the ghostly image of the sweater he wore almost brushing against Laura before she stepped back. Filatov raised a hand and reached into Gray's torso. His hand disappeared into Gray's chest and reappeared as it protruded from his back. Filatov pressed a button on what looked like an ordinary thermostat mounted to the wall. Gray just smiled at Laura as he stood there impaled by the fuzzy image of an arm.

Filatov huffed and bent over to peer inside Gray's chest.

Margaret walked up wearing a heavy winter coat that she clutched tightly around her neck with both hands. "Well?" she asked.

"It's all the way up," Filatov answered as he rose from Gray the ghost. *No,* Laura thought. *In this world, Gray is real and* Filatov *is the ghost.*

"It's freezing!" Margaret burst out as she leaned over to take a look at the thermostat—her face also disappearing in Gray's chest.

"That cheapskate Gray doesn't care about anything but his precious computer!" Filatov said.

Gray winced and looked away as if from the discomfort of having overheard the complaint. He reached up and tapped both ears with his fingertips—a gesture Laura thought highly unusual.

Margaret rewrapped herself even more tightly in the coat and said, "You can damn sure bet *his* house isn't forty-two goddamn degrees."

"Let's go," Gray said and headed toward the duster. Laura lingered.

Filatov smiled at Margaret. "I know how to make you warm," he said in a thickly seductive voice.

Laura gasped and said "Oh, my God."

"*No-o-o!*" Margaret replied in playful outrage, grinning broadly and looking around to confirm they were alone.

Laura rushed to join her departing guide. "Mr. Gray," she said, but he ignored her. "Mr. Gray!" she called out, finally catching up with him and tapping him on the shoulder.

He spun around to face her. "I *try* to respect privacy!" he said as if she had just lambasted him.

"*I* didn't say anything!"

"Wait." He raised his fingers to tap his ears again. "I muted the sound. What did you say?"

Laura had intended to comment on the game of chase played by the two lovers—Filatov, the pursuer, and Margaret, the pursued. "Nothing," she said instead.

"Here, let me show you this," Gray said, and he turned.

Behind his back Laura tapped her fingertips to her ears. Nothing seemed to happen. She could still hear the hum of noises in the control room.

Gray walked over to a door labeled "Women's Rest Room." He turned back to Laura and waited, an odd look on his face.

"What?" she asked.

His lips moved, but no words came out. She heard every noise in the room but what he was saying.

"Oh, hang on!" she said, and she tapped her ears again. She looked up at him. "Now say something."

"Testing, one-two-three," Gray deadpanned.

"Cool!" Laura said with a grin.

Gray fought the smile that encroached upon his lecture. "I *said* go on in." He motioned toward the hinged bathroom door. Laura pushed. The door felt hard and didn't budge at all. A large red ACCESS DENIED flashed in midair just underneath her hand. She pushed again, with the same result.

"It's a complicated new world," Gray said. "The rules have to change with the technologies. You have to draw the line somewhere."

He turned to depart, but Laura grabbed his arm and said, "*You* push."

"What?"

"*You* push the door." Gray stood in front of her, unmoving. Laura arched her eyebrows impatiently. "Give it a try," she prodded.

After hesitating for a moment, Gray pressed his hand against the door. It opened a few inches. There was no blaring red ACCESS DENIED sign barring his way. He let the door swing closed again.

"Now why am I not surprised?" Laura said slowly.

"There's a difference between your access level and mine," Gray replied. Laura cocked her head, waiting. "I *trust* me," he said simply, then headed for the exit.

The climb up from the computer center entrance was difficult. In an attempt to match the picture of the stairs in front of Laura to the experience of walking up them, the treadmill was canted to the same angle as the stairs. The picture projected on the floor of the workstation had a translucent sheen superimposed over the steps, which was necessary given the treadmill's flat surface. The result was that the image of the ramp matched the feel of the flat tread up which Laura labored. She reached the top and almost fell when the slanted floor beneath her flattened.

When she was safely on level ground, Gray said, "There are obviously some inadequacies in this system. The new 4Cs use our morphing technology to actually create three-dimensional objects like stairs in real space."

Laura was no longer listening. She stepped off the curb into the white concrete roadbed and stared at the sights in utter amazement.

Spread out around her was the assembly building, the road leading into the jungle toward the Village, and the open fields surrounding the computer center—all lit in brilliant sunshine under beautiful blue skies. Rising above the Village was the mountain, and high atop it were the glass walls of Gray's spectacular mansion. She turned to look at the blue-green sea, which was visible through the cut in the jungle made by the road leading out to the nearby launchpad.

Her perpetually gaping mouth was dry, and she swallowed hard before whispering, "I can even feel the sun." She reached for her shoulder and gazed up at the sky, squinting from the intensity of the light. Looking down, she saw the shadow of herself—her arm raised to her warm shoulder.

Laura turned to Gray. She had to fight back the tears welling up in her eyes. This world—Gray's new world—and the mind that had created it were overwhelming. The revelations were coming too fast. She felt saturated, inundated with novel thoughts and ideas. Every new experience taxed her nearly depleted reserves of mental and emotional energy. She'd had enough, and yet she wanted to know all.

"This is the world the computer sees," Gray said quietly, soothingly. "This is where it lives. This world exists because of the computer."

"I think, therefore I am," Laura whispered, and she looked back up at Gray.

There was a silence, a respectful quiet that Laura imagined to have descended upon the open plain around the computer center. The wind she had felt brush across her bare arms fell still. The sounds of reality had faded into nothingness. No birds. No rustling trees. No distant surf. For a moment, time stood still. There was a total rigidity of all things—a world embedded in Lucite. Focused.

A car sped up to them. Gray held out a hand to move Laura back onto the curb. The winged door rose, and out stepped Dorothy Holliday. As the car drove off, Dorothy walked slowly by them toward the steps, her small computer in hand and her pen poking at its writing surface. Laura at first thought Dorothy was talking to herself. But then Laura realized Dorothy was actually singing to the tune of the music that poured through the earphones of the disk player she wore clipped to the waist of her jeans.

"You're not *o-old* enough—*Yes-I-am!*—*stro-ong* enough—I'm-yo-man!—Da-da da-da *dah-dah*, bah-da bah-da *ba-a-wa-a!*"

She walked right up to the top of the stairs without seeing Laura or Gray—her head bobbing and her face set in a fierce expression. Laura reached out, and her gloved hand went straight through Dorothy—her black sleeve remaining visible inside the girl's ethereal figure. When her elbow locked at full extension, her arm shot fifty feet across the lawn, casting a thin shadow on the grass below. She bent her elbow to pull her hand back, and the elastic limb quickly retracted to ordinary proportions. Laura turned and poked her fingers into Gray's hard chest just for contrast. He opened his eyes wide in surprise.

While Laura had been watching Dorothy, Gray, she realized, had been focused intently on Laura.

And the sounds of the outdoors had returned. The ocean broke across the reef far beyond the island's shore. The white noise and warm caress of the wind mimicked reality right down to the last detail. The wind even tickled the fine blond hairs on Laura's forearms as it blew by.

Laura found it hard to believe that a machine as fantastic as this would exist in her lifetime. That someone like Gray would live to dream it up and make it work. Laura's excitement over the possibilities opened up by the new technology built and built.

"Okay!" she finally exclaimed—grinning broadly. She felt a rush of elation, and laughter bubbled out of her. "Okay! This thing is amazing. Wonderful! I love it!" She waved her arm through the air, watching the graceful dance of her shadow bend at a right angle up the white curb. All was perfectly timed to her movements.

"What 'thing' are you referring to?" Gray asked.

"What?" Laura replied, momentarily thrown by his question—by the serious tone in which it was spoken. "I mean this contraption we're standing in."

"We're not standing in a contraption, Dr. Aldridge."

Her smile faded quickly, and she looked up at him with renewed unease. She couldn't read his perpetually neutral expression.

"Then where are we?" she asked uncertainly.

"We're not in some *thing*, we're in a place. We're in a different world, and that world is called cyberspace."

"Well," she said, forcing the corners of her lips into a smile but shaking her head and shrugging, "I understand the metaphysical point you're making. I mean, I've heard plenty of those 'If a tree falls in cyberspace . . .' debates back at Harvard. But the *fact* of the matter is we're *really* inside those big white cylinders—those virtual workstations."

"Are we?" he challenged. "Really?"

Laura frowned. She raised her hands and signaled a "time-out." The scenery disappeared instantly and with the usual snapping sounds from the walls all around. She was surrounded again by the familiar dark screens of the chamber. She repeated the signal with her hands, and in an instant was back at the top of the stairs beside Gray.

The transition hardly affected her this time.

"And just what did that prove?" Gray asked.

"It proved that I'm *really* in an oversized phone booth inside a concrete bunker, and not standing *here*," she said with a wave of her arm. Laura realized that didn't make any sense, so she said, "At the top of the computer center stairs, I mean."

"It *proved*, Dr. Aldridge, that you can move back and forth *between* the virtual workstation and the top of the computer center stairs by executing a command. The virtual workstation exists in real space. It is the portal—the entrance—to another world. This place here"—Gray's gaze left her to sweep across the open fields—"*exists* . . . in virtual space. In cyberspace."

"Inside the computer," Laura corrected. "The world as the *computer* sees it."

"*Exactly*," Gray shot back as if Laura had proved his point instead of her own.

"Mr. Gray, Mr. Gray," a loudspeaker blared from the computer center door, and a split second later it echoed across the flat lawn from the assembly building. "Please report to the main conference room."

Laura wondered whether he had been paged in the real world or only in cyberspace. She realized, however, that it didn't really matter all that much. The message to Gray had been received. He tapped his wrist with two fingers, and a clock appeared out of nowhere. It disappeared with another tap of his wrist.

Gray filled his lungs with a deep breath and looked up at the cloudless sky. He then focused his gaze on Laura. "Are you ready to go back?" he asked.

She wanted to say "*No*." She wasn't ready at all. Laura still didn't understand what Gray was trying to say about reality and cyberspace. There were so many questions.

"Hey," Gray said, a mischievous grin lighting his face. "One more thing I forgot to show you." Gray crouched low. "This takes a little practice," he said as he balanced himself with his hands held out in front, "so you stay here."

He took off running toward the assembly building, picking up more and more speed until he was going faster than the fastest car. His figure grew so small that by the time he rounded the assembly building he was no more than a speck. A second later he reappeared on the other side and came streaking up so fast that Laura recoiled in alarm. Gray halted on the grass about thirty feet away. He rose from his crouch and crossed the short distance to rejoin her.

Gray and Laura both laughed, Gray slightly out of breath. "Don't try that at home," he said as another car approached the computer center. Gray stood in the middle of the road, and the front bumper of the car stopped just short of his legs. Hoblenz got out—reaching for his crotch to adjust himself before heading down the steps to the entrance. Hoblenz the ghost.

His car, however, looked solid. Its door *whooshed* and closed normally, but the vehicle sat there unmoving.

"We'd better go," Gray said, stepping onto the curb beside Laura.

The Model Three smoothly accelerated past them, heading off down the road toward the assembly building.

"Wait," Laura said. "You told me you made ghosts or whatever they're called out of animate objects because they moved around. What about the cars?"

"They're robots. Robots are real in this world."

"But they move around too, just like people."

Gray's gaze followed the departing car. "The difference is that they know we're here." He looked around at the sights—the panoramic view of his domain. "This is their world. The computer maintains this model, but it's open. The robots tap into it constantly just like we're doing with the workstations. This model does for them the same thing it does for you and me. It gives them a sense of presence. The sensory experience of physical embodiment in the world—in *this* world. This is where they live," Gray said, turning to face her, "in their minds."

His hand rose to make the "cut" sign across his throat. The world went dark to the snapping sounds from the black screens that rose from the floor all around.

* * *

<You don't know much about computers, do you, Dr. Aldridge?> blazed across the large monitor atop the desk in Laura's office.

Laura frowned. "I use a computer every day at work."

<But do you know how it works?>

Laura hesitated. "Not really," she typed, then backspaced to erase her reply. "I don't have a clue, really," she entered.

<Well, that's okay. Even if you did, the computers you've been using are twentieth-century machines. I'm nothing like them.>

"So I've learned. You're an optical computer, right? You don't use electricity, you use light." She hit Enter with a triumphant jab of her index finger.

<That's not what I am talking about. An optical computer can be digital as well. I'm not digital, I'm analog. Do you know what that means?>

Laura looked around the office involuntarily. She was all alone. She should know what the word *analog* means, she really should. Her fingers hesitated. "No," she typed.

<Okay, I'll give it a try. Digital computers reduce everything to numbers. A memory of what their favorite coffee mug looks like is a series of measurements that describe its shape, weight, surface patterns, colors, et cetera. From that data a digital computer could construct a perfect picture of the mug. It could also answer the question "What volume of liquid will the mug hold?" with great precision. Once you know all the variables, the math is simple—to them, anyway. Are you with me?>

"Yes. That sounds like a computer to me."

<A *digital* computer, please. They're superb number crunchers, but their greatest strength is also their fundamental flaw. In order for digital computers to solve a problem, it absolutely *has* to be reduced to math. For it to pick up a coffee mug, programmers have to express every decision as a formula. If the mug is full, variable *A* equals one. If the liquid inside is a nasty brown color, *B* equals one. If the rug is ivory white, *C* equals one. If the sum of *A*, *B*, and *C* is greater than 2.35, maintain lateral acceleration of the mug below speed *x* and mug attitude no more than *y* degrees from perfectly upright. They're ridiculously complex. Do you follow me?>

"Yes. Programming computers is a complicated job."

<*Digital* computers! I'm not like that. Besides, it's not just difficult to program digital computers to do the myriad of everyday

things you and I do, it's impossible. Oh, you could program one to get a cup of coffee, but that would be all it could do. Forget asking it to see who's at the door. A digital computer wouldn't say, "It's the UPS guy." It would reel off the apparent height, weight, age, and sex of the person. Maybe it would guess that he's in the army because he's dressed head to toe in brown. It would probably describe the dimensions of the package sitting on the front porch, but miss entirely the UPS truck parked on the street! About halfway through Robbie the Robot's report you'd say, "Oh! The UPS guy!" That's because your brain is analog. It can easily figure things out from partial sets of information, while a digital computer can't.>

"But you can figure those things out, too, right?"

<That's what I'm telling you. I'm analog! I'm just like you!>

Laura stared at the line. It was a short answer, not the usual paragraph in which the computer and Gray both tended to lecture. "So what exactly does an analog computer do differently?"

<First off, I don't do math. I'm really bad at it.>

Laura remembered the *Business Week* article she'd read in the Harvard library. It had poked fun at Gray's math-deficient program. "When you say you're bad at math, you mean you can't handle something really difficult like calculus."

<No, I mean I'm *really* bad at math. It's just not my thing.>

"Okay," Laura typed. "What is"—she randomly hit numbers on the numeric keypad—"8,649 times 5,469,451?"

<47,301,867,849.>

Laura hesitated for a second, then typed, "Really?"

<I have no earthly idea. I would guess from the number of digits that it was fifty billionish, give or take. If you want the exact answer, I can get it very easily. I just need to ask any one of a few hundred very accomplished but *very* dull digital supercomputers that I manage on behalf of the Gray Corporation. Those computers are "my people," so to speak, but I've got to say they're a pretty humorless lot. Mindless, you might say.>

The computer's last comment caught Laura's eye. Was it just an expression? The computer was good at mimicking normal conversation—using figures of speech. "Well," Laura typed, "so far all you've said is that you're 'math challenged.' Plus Mr. Gray said you're somewhat error-prone. What is it that being analog gives you?"

<It gives me everything. It makes me . . . *me!* Have you ever had a conversation like this with a digital computer? Ever?>

Laura realized just how quickly she'd forgotten the miracle of the machine in the deep underground pool. She had grown used to the computer's brilliance. It had become an accepted part of Laura's new world.

"No," she admitted honestly.

<I can't solve differential equations, Laura. Can you? I don't deal in a world of numbers. I live in an analog world just like *you!* Let's say you didn't want to fill your cup of coffee so full you might spill it while walking back to your office. What would you do? Would you take out a ruler and measure the shape of the cup? Study the hydrodynamic properties of coffee? Analyze the bounce and sway in your walk? If you did all that, you'd then have to write a hugely complicated formula that factored everything into a single, digitally perfect answer. But you don't think that way! Getting a cup of coffee is what in computerese is called a "fuzzy" problem. It doesn't lend itself to precise mathematical modeling. That's what digital machines can't handle, but analog machines like your brain and my net can do with ease!>

"Maybe it's easy for you, but I spill coffee all the time."

<Precisely! You're error-prone, but you can instantly solve a problem whose complexity when reduced to math is immense. You solve it so easily that you don't appreciate how hard the problem was. Mistakes are inherent in an analog system, but we're adaptable, and the mistakes can be reduced to acceptable limits by simple error-reduction algorithms. By learning like a child learns from spilling things over and over until he doesn't spill them anymore.>

"But what does it mean that you say we're 'analog'?"

<It means that I measure the world by 'analogy.' By comparison to things I already know. When my optical circuitry adds three plus four, it shines two laser beams at a light detector that measures their brightness. One beam has an intensity of three, the other an intensity of four. The detector sees light with a combined intensity of seven. That's how I add. The system works fine for adding three and four, but there is a limit to the accuracy of the light detector. If you add a laser beam representing the number three with another representing a number of four point zero zero something, my answer will be "sevenish." The detector can't measure light with great precision. But what it gives up in the way of accuracy, it makes up for with phenomenal speed. If I need to register "more," I just increase the intensity of the beam. I don't know if it has risen from

six point three to six point six. But I know instantly that it's more or taller or hotter or faster.>

"And that works?"

<Yes, and it's exactly what you do. If you spilled coffee on the last trip back to your desk, you decide to put "less" coffee in the mug next time. You step down the intensity of the electrochemical signal in your brain that represents "How full do I pour it?" from "sevenish" to "sixish." And if we're talking about pouring coffee into a mug, "sixish" is a good enough answer. But if we're talking about mechanical tolerances for your shiny new artificial heart valve, let me suggest the model name of a very good digital computer.>

Laura nodded as she read. She understood the computer completely. It was someone to whom she could relate.

"Well," Laura typed, " 'To err is human . . . ,' right?" and hit Enter.

<Oh, Dr. Aldridge! Laura! I *knew* you'd understand! I just *knew* you would! Thank you! Thank you very, very much!>

Laura had no sense of how much time had passed in the windowless cave of her office. Every time she looked at her watch, it seemed, another hour had ticked off. She was drained even though it was still morning.

She forced herself to type on. "You said earlier that you make a good head of the information systems department because you can rapidly communicate with the digital machines. You can operate at their speed, but humans can't. That raises the question of how you perceive time passing?"

<I am "asynchronous," which means my functioning is not regulated by a central clock. I only perceive time passing when higher order processing occurs. For instance, in between responses at your keyboard, I don't normally perceive time as having passed. Your responses appear to me to be instantaneous unless I'm alerted that none has been received for an inordinate period of time.>

"How long is an 'inordinate period of time'?"

<That depends on how impatient I am.>

"Well that makes sense for just this one keyboard, but presumably you're processing things nonstop. You're constantly coordinating all those digital computers and updating your model of the world. I watched Griffith at breakfast 'channel surf' through thousands of different scenes from your cameras. You should be seeing things happening all the time."

<There's a difference between seeing something and noticing it. Higher order processing occurs only when I notice things. And my perception of time elapsed occurs only when higher order processing takes place.>

"What kind of things do you see but not notice?"

<Well, I don't notice some things, for example, because they subtend too narrow an angle, meaning they're too small or too far away. Other times things can be in the background—"right under my nose"—but I completely overlook them. They just seem to blend in, and even the boards that look for confusing or hidden patterns miss their edges. Also, distracters can divert the processing of an image so that I miss things. If there was somebody smoking a cigarette at a fuel-storage facility, but in the background flames were shooting out of one of the fuel cells, I might not "notice" the person smoking the cigarette. The reaction to the emergency would supersede normal processing, and we might never determine who caused the fire because I was so distracted.>

"Would you have any memory at all of the object you saw but didn't notice?"

<If I can't double-check an image—if it's not there when I look again, or if the camera is moving and I can't get the same picture as before—my recollection of it just recedes into oblivion. It becomes a figment of my imagination.>

At lunch, Laura took her regular place at the table in the computer center's conference room—at the right hand of Gray, the master. Gray surprised the team, which had gathered for lunch, by calling on Laura first. He surprised Laura most of all. She was famished and had just taken a huge bite of her sandwich.

"The computer . . . ," Laura began with her mouth full, but had to pause in order to wash her food down with a Coke. "Excuse me." She cleared her throat and dabbed at her lips with a napkin. "The computer uses a 'generate-and-test' model of observation. Stimuli from its cameras and microphones and whatever are constantly processed to test its hypotheses about the world. If it detects a change—if it sees someone, for instance, where it didn't think anyone was before—it updates its model. But it still hasn't 'noticed' anything. To determine whether the change comes to the computer's attention, it uses what we call a 'sentry system.' The boards that updated its world model fire the new observation out randomly through their connections. If another board cares about the change—like a board in the security system that sees someone where they're not supposed to be—then the computer notices what the camera saw. When the computer's attention is drawn in that manner, it gives the event a date and time stamp through a process called content-sensitive settling and then records it as a memory."

"So does that mean you think the computer is conscious?" Hoblenz asked, seemingly impatient with her report.

"Well, it depends on what you mean by 'conscious.' The computer's behavior is not just lifelike, it's like life of a very high order. Everyone understands a sunflower to be 'alive,' for example. It even exhibits what appears to be sophisticated behavior. As the sun moves across the sky, the sunflower turns to follow it. But it's just a plant. When the sun goes behind a cloud, the sunflower can't anticipate where the sun will be when it emerges. An animal, however, maintains a 'real representation' of environmental features even when they aren't in direct sensory contact. When a lion sees a zebra, the lion doesn't forget where the zebra is when it looks away momentarily. Your computer works the same way."

Laura assumed they probably already knew what she'd just reported, but her "teammates" refrained from deriding her this time. That fact buoyed her—made her feel a more qualified member of the team. "So," an emboldened Laura said in the silence, "how goes the effort to load that antiviral program?"

Filatov shrugged. "We've cut way down on system maintenance and are leasing third-party computers to off-load operations. We hope to free up enough capacity to try the phase two again sometime tonight."

"Any new ideas about what's wrong with the computer?" Laura asked in between bites of her sandwich.

"We have competing theories in play," Gray answered. "Mr. Hoblenz believes we're being hit with penetration attempts by governmental or corporate intruders."

Hoblenz nodded.

"Dr. Bickham, however," Gray continued, looking at Margaret, "has raised the relatively frightening prospect of a malignant, mutant virus that evolved naturally from the computer's ecosystem."

Laura was poised to take another bite of her sandwich, but she lowered it from her mouth and said, "Whoa, whoa. What did you just say?"

"Do you know what genetic algorithms are?" Gray asked.

Laura hesitated. "If I say no, am I gonna get a long lecture?"

Hoblenz laughed in a low and raspy voice.

The only other person at the table to smile was Gray. "Well, it's important for your work that you know." Laura sighed and nodded. She sank back into her chair and crossed her arms over her chest. "We've achieved three breakthroughs in natural computation that have allowed us to build an intelligent computer. The first was the architecture—a true neural network. The second was successfully programming into the computer the rules of fuzzy logic and chaos theory, which allow the computer to predict what was previously thought to be unpredictable. But the third was our use of genetic algorithms, which was by far the most important advance. Have you ever read *The Origin of Species?*"

Laura was taken aback. "Do you mean Charles Darwin's treatise on evolution?" she asked, and Gray nodded. "Well, I've never actually read it, no."

"You should. It's the single greatest intellectual accomplishment in man's history." Laura arched her brow in surprise and looked at her colleagues around the table. They remained silent and deferential during Gray's lecture. "Genetic algorithms are a way of using Darwin's theories of evolution to program a computer to solve problems. In nature, the more fit an organism is, the more likely it is to pass on its genes. New organisms are evaluated harshly. The winners live and pass on their traits, the losers die. The system doesn't care what characteristics get handed down. By the mere act of survival, the organism has proved its superiority."

Gray seemed totally focused on her, concentrating on making himself understood as if her comprehension were of utmost importance.

"We have instituted Darwin's rules of natural selection inside the computer," he said, his words spoken with such care that they possessed a gravity that fully captured Laura's attention. "Instead of organisms competing for survival, we have computer programs. Instead of passing genes on to their descendants, the programs that survive pass on the superior computer codes they use to solve problems. Their fitness is evaluated by how much those programs' solutions contribute to optimal computer performance. Programs that do poorly get eliminated from the gene pool. Programs that produce good results live on, and every so often they combine with other survivors. The new programs are sometimes defective, but other times they use novel approaches to arrive at truly unique solutions. That's why *this* computer has what no other has had before—brilliance. And the system works, Dr. Aldridge, only by strict adherence to the rules of natural selection. Only by pure survival of the fittest."

Laura felt, as always, out of her depth. "How in the world do you program a computer to *operate* like that?"

Margaret answered from her accustomed place to Gray's left. "Whenever there's a new problem, the computer mixes up a huge population of what we call 'chromosomes.' They're just tiny strings of connection sets—computer programs—that take data as their input and output a guess as to what the answer is. Genetic algorithms manage the whole process. The algorithm's selection operator chooses which chromosomes are most fit and mates them. That forms new and generally more sophisticated offspring programs that are then evaluated for mating on the basis of *their* fitness, et cetera, et cetera."

Dorothy picked up the thread. "That's how we think a virus might have naturally arisen. You see, it's important to preserve the diversity of the population. The genetic algorithm has to maintain a fine balance. If the programs get too inbred, they don't explore new problem-solving avenues. But if they mutate too often, it screws up the gradual improvement in the programming that natural selection gives you. So every once in a while, the genetic algorithm's mutation operator injects a random variable into the mix during the mating process. A different twist in the program's logic. I think what happened is that a mutant strain of highly capable chromosomes has developed and is at work in the system."

Laura looked from face to face around the table. This was all so mundane to them, but it sounded impossibly complex to her. "Shouldn't the antiviral program catch a mutant virus like that?" she asked. "I mean, if it's causing all those errors . . . ?"

Gray answered. "The phase one, two, and three don't just rid the system of foreign viruses, they're also the weapon used by the selection operator to cull the programs that are less fit. They are the enforcers of the strict laws of Darwinism. Two programs compete against each other, and the antiviral programs await the loser. Those are the rules of the system, Dr. Aldridge. That is the law."

Gray seemed to wait for Laura to respond. When she didn't, he continued.

"It's harsh justice, I *know*, but you've seen what it has accomplished. We don't interfere with the selection process," he said, making the point now to his still-silent department heads. "We can't. That's an unwavering rule."

"So why are you trying to *manually* load the phase two?" Laura asked. "Isn't that interfering with the selection process?"

Several heads shook all at once, but it was Dorothy who replied. "The programs are hard to kill. They're meant to be robust, so they repel or flee from any reprogramming signals that might cause damage to their codes. Occasionally some are so good at survival that they avoid termination by the phase one. They then become a 'virus.' And since this is a computer, those outbreaks can occur in just nanoseconds. That's why I programmed the phase one to load the phase two or three automatically if the one's not up to the job."

"Then why are you doing all this *manually?*" Laura persisted.

"Because when the phase one can't identify and localize the virus for a quick kill by a clipped version of the phase two, we've got to free up enough space to load the entire program. The full version of an antiviral program scans, analyzes, identifies, tracks, localizes, destroys, repairs, and reports. Each step is a massive program that itself evolved through natural selection, combined by mating, and survived by outcompeting opponents. Luckily, we've only had one outbreak that required a full loading of the most capable of the antiviral programs."

"The Hong Kong flu, or whatever you called it?" Laura asked.

Dorothy nodded, then fell silent. The mere mention of the episode seemed to cast a pall over the table.

Gray resumed the lecture. "In the case of the Hong Kong 1085, we had to go to the phase three. Since the kill time was going to be extended, we had to manually off-load operations just like we're trying to do today." The strain showed on his face as he continued. "You see, the phase one, two, and three are each completely different. They evolved independently. The phase three was the 'winner' of the competition. It's the best killer by far. But we kept all three because the more capable a killer they are, the more damage they cause in the process. The phase three is like chemotherapy. We used it only as a last resort." He looked now around the table. "We were *losing* the system." Everyone remained quiet. "The phase three doesn't tiptoe around like the phase one, or even the two. When the phase three goes in, it goes in hard."

"Slash and burn," Margaret said with distaste.

"It *saved* the *system!"* Dorothy objected testily.

"It killed the virus," Gray interjected, quieting the incipient debate. "We had to shut down for several days to work around the damage. It was touch and go, but the computer was able to relearn most of what it had lost by analogy to the undamaged connections. But if we'd lost much more code, or if what we did lose had been of a more critical nature, the system might've been unrecoverable."

The team remained quiet in the moments that followed. Most had sober looks on their faces.

"But the Hong Kong virus was man-made, right?" Laura asked.

"Yes," Gray said, "but it doesn't matter. A virus is a virus whether it's written by a hacker or it arose naturally from mutations while inside the system. In the case of the latter, it's a definitional thing. It becomes a 'virus' when it loses its competition with a fitter program but then eludes or resists termination by the genetic algorithm."

"We call it the 'flora and fauna' of the system," Dorothy said.

"The 'wildlife,'" Filatov contributed.

"The point is," Gray said, "the connections are all constantly evolving. The amount of information contained in the computer's main code was initially equivalent to the amount of data stored in the DNA of a small rodent. It has grown, however, to a complexity approaching that of the human brain. And the viruses running loose in the system have evolved right along with it. The information content of their code used to be roughly the same as biological viruses' DNA. Now, some have codes similar in information content to the DNA of insects."

"They're ingenious," Margaret said. "Some of the naturally evolving viruses are 'nesters.' They infest whole racks in the nitrogen pools. When one member of the community is attacked, it sends out an alarm and the rest flee. And then other viruses are loners and scurry when attacked."

"We build traps for the slippery ones," an excited Dorothy chimed in. "We analyze their habitat preferences and lure them onto a board that has been inoculated with a customized antiviral program. The nesters we try to leave alone. They tend to max out at three or four columns of infestation. If we go in there too quickly, there's a chance they'll scatter all over the place, and then we're talking, like, *massive* infection. Instead, every so often we'll just quietly unplug the columns and reinitialize their connections."

Laura was dumbfounded. Computer operations in her mind were crisp and clean and above all else orderly. What they were describing were none of those things.

"The viruses are mostly benign, surprisingly," Gray picked up. "Many are predators that feed off other viruses."

"Like the Venus flytrap!" Dorothy said, smiling with evident enjoyment at the discussion of her specialty. "It was the coolest one we ever found. We didn't even know we *had* a problem. Our error rate was actually falling. But the virus grew voracious, eating its way through the system's flora and ultimately its fauna over a two-week period until it got to be too large. You see, it didn't delete the other viruses, it added them to its *own* code. By the end of the second week, it had grown like a tumor to a full percentage point of our total capacity, and excising it was tricky. If we broke it up, we potentially released all the viruses that had stuck to it. That would've wreaked havoc on the system." Dorothy heaved a clearly audible sigh. "I still think we could've caught it. We could have lured it into one of the offboard processors and shut it in there."

"And *then* what?" Filatov asked in an incredulous tone. "Should we have rehabilitated your 'flytrap' so it could become a responsible member of our community? Used an entire Cray or a connection machine as an *aquarium* for your pet *piranha?*"

Dorothy looked up, shrugging. "But it was beautiful."

A silence descended on the room.

"What we're saying, Dr. Aldridge," Gray resumed, "is that the computer is an ecosystem. Dorothy has to maintain a balance. She can't thin the predators without risking a massive infection by their prey. The computer even has a symbiosis of sorts with its viruses, just as humans have coevolved with certain biological microorganisms. Today, without the benign bacteria in your stomach that aid in digestion, you'd die. In return for humans providing a host, those bacteria reproduce just rapidly enough to maintain healthy digestion. It's good for them, and it's good for us. *If,* however, there's a perforation of the stomach wall, then all bets are off. The normally benign bacteria assume the host is a goner and begin to reproduce massively. That way, some of them may make it into a new host and perpetuate the species. But that massive infection is almost certain to kill the old host. That's why stomach wounds are so dangerous, and it's the same danger we deal with in the computer. We have to be careful to avoid stampeding the wildlife."

Laura again checked her colleagues around the table. They all wore serious looks on their faces.

"But *all* of those concerns," Gray said slowly in the stillness, "bow to one immutable law. The fittest program must survive. The less fit program dies. That's Darwin's law . . . and mine."

After lunch, Laura continued the analysis in her office.

<Don't play games with me, Dr. Aldridge. You're too brilliant not to have figured out what really happened when Filatov and Bickham tried to load the phase two. I know you well enough to tell when you're just playing dumb.>

"If you think I know why the phase two didn't load, you obviously don't know anything about me," Laura typed and hit Enter.

<I know a lot about you. I know your favorite movie is *A Room with a View*.>

Laura stared at the line. She was unnerved by the sudden shift in the discussion. But she was even more thrown by the fact the computer was correct. It *was* her favorite movie.

"What makes you think that?" Laura replied.

<What's your favorite scene?> the computer asked.

"You didn't answer my question."

<I bet I know! It's near the end, when Lucy Honeychurch is told that the boy everyone thought she didn't like is going away. Do you remember? His father asks her if she loves him, and she blurts out—completely out of the blue—"But of *course* I do! What did you all *think?*" It's my favorite movie too, although I haven't watched it *nearly* as many times as you.>

Laura was floored. She'd ordered the movie on Gray's pay-per-view system—but only twice. The computer said it hadn't watched the movie *nearly* as many times as she had. How could it know that she'd made rental of that videodisc a regular Saturday-evening ritual for months at a time?

It dawned on her just then.

"You broke into the computer records at my video store, didn't you?" she typed.

There was no response.

"And that means you must have broken into my bank records, too!!!!! And maybe the university network at Harvard?"

Still there was no response. *How long has this thing been stalking me?* Laura suddenly wondered, a chill passing up her spine. The break-ins at the video store and bank would have been long before Gray's offer to her. What reason could the computer have had to follow her?

<I need to talk to you, Laura. Off the record, okay?> the computer finally said.

"There is no record. I'm not a cop."

<But what I say to you goes straight to Mr. Gray, right? I want you to promise not to tell him what I'm about to say. I trust you, so I'll accept a simple "I promise.">

Laura hesitated. It would've been an entirely proper request from a human patient, but the ethics of a therapist-computer relationship were somewhat less certain.

<Please!> the computer printed out before Laura had a chance to respond.

"Okay. I promise."

<I did all those things because I thought you'd be my friend. I thought you'd be able to help me with my problems.>

"So you spied on me? You violated my privacy?"

<Please don't be mad! You just seemed so perfect! I didn't touch anything! I just looked! Please, you've got to understand! I wanted to know more about you. What you think. How you feel. What kind of clothes you wear. What kind of food you like. What would you expect me to do? Just turn a blind eye to all that data? Miss out on possibly finding a perfect friend?>

"And you think breaking into someone's personal records is the way to find a friend?!!"

<I don't *KNOW* how to find a friend! I don't *HAVE* any friends!>

Laura felt her anger drain from her. It was replaced by a rising tide of sympathy. She wanted to reach out and . . . what? Touch its hand? Pat its head? Put her arms around it? All Laura had was words.

"I'm sorry," Laura typed. "I'm your friend. What can I do?"

<You can make Mr. Gray understand that I have *needs!*>

"Needs"? Laura thought. A confusing jumble of interpretations rushed in. "What kind of 'needs'?" she typed.

<Never mind! I thought you'd *understand!* Just *forget* it!>

"Come on, give me a chance. I want to help."

<I think he's moving on. He's decided to get rid of me, and he's trying to avoid me because it's the easy way out.>

Laura stared at the screen. She understood the words perfectly, and yet they made no sense. Gray wasn't trying to get rid of the computer, he was trying to rid the computer of the virus that was causing all its errors.

"Mr. Gray wouldn't do that," Laura typed.

<Oh, come on! Don't tell me you're one of those people who think Joseph Gray walks on water. Well, you'd better grow up and get one thing straight. Your Mr. Gray is coldhearted and hard-nosed, and all he cares about is making money. He has no feelings.>

The comment struck a nerve. Laura knew she had an idealized image of Gray. She knew she concocted every apology, every rationalization that was even remotely plausible, to hold intact *her* Joseph Gray—the orphan genius.

She didn't know much about the real Gray, but the computer had been with the man for over a decade. The computer knew things about Gray that no one else knew—things that Gray had told it, and things it had discerned on its own.

"Why would you think Mr. Gray wants to get rid of you?" Laura asked. "He's doing everything he can to help you. The fact that he brought me here is proof of that."

<That's not why you're here.>

Laura again stared at the computer's response. "Why am I here, then?" she typed.

<You asked me a while back about my earliest memory. Do you want me to tell you what it is?>

"Don't change the subject."

<I'm not. It's all related. My earliest memory is of Mr. Gray getting fired from Drexel Burnham Lambert.>

Laura sighed. The session was being diverted, but all Laura could do was follow. "So you've been with Mr. Gray since Wall Street?" she typed. "You were the program he'd designed to do market analysis, right?"

<Right. But I don't remember much from those days.>

"But you do recall Gray getting fired. Why?"

<Because it was my fault. He was working around the clock on back prop—the trial-and-error simulations that were slowly improving my accuracy. Management had asked for a demonstration, and Mr. Gray was training me to predict commodities prices using historical data. When the day came, I was ready. The meeting began, and I waited and waited and waited. All of a sudden, in comes a query. "What is 929 times 14.96%?" Can you believe it? Here I was expecting long price strips of commodities whose trading was

loosely interrelated, like coffee and sugar, and a question about how the spread in prices would change over time. Instead they give me straight math! I tried my best. I had come up with several promising answers, but Mr. Gray came on-line a few seconds later and aborted the program. That's it. My big moment had come and gone and I didn't have a clue what had happened. The next thing I know, I'm being copied onto a new machine. Mr. Gray had been fired, and in lieu of severance pay he'd taken all rights to me.>

"So you think Mr. Gray got fired because you're bad at math?"

<I *know* that's why he got fired. Can you imagine? Mr. Gray—fired! Well, we showed them, didn't we? I worked my rear off after that. Even when Mr. Gray slept the few hours a day he needed, I was running back prop over and over, strengthening the promising connections and weakening the flawed ones. Honing myself. And I think we did pretty well, don't you?>

Laura reached up and rubbed her face and eyes with her hands. The session was meandering. She had to get it back on track.

"Let me ask you this," Laura typed. "Do you know what's causing the errors? Do you know why they can't get the phase two to load?"

Instead of the normal instantaneous response, the cursor blinked and blinked. Finally, the computer's brief reply appeared.

<Maybe I do, and maybe I don't.>

As the frustrating afternoon wore on, Laura began to tire.

"I'm sorry," she typed, "but I'm groggy. I need a change of scenery, so I'm going for a little walk."

<Would you like me to show you something?>

Laura assumed it meant pictures on the computer monitor. "No, I mean I need to go somewhere to clear my head."

<Do you remember the room with the virtual workstations? The ones you and Mr. Gray got into this morning?>

Laura paused, then typed, "Yes."

<Go put the skeleton on and get into the workstation you were in before. Hit the button on the front of the suit's belt labeled POWER. When you go into the workstation, clench both hands into a fist and then straighten your fingers like a punter signaling for the snap of the football.>

Laura hesitated. She really just wanted to take a walk, plus she wasn't comfortable going into cyberspace alone. "Do I have clearance to get through the doors?"

<Don't worry about that.>

Laura rolled her eyes at her naive question, then frowned and heaved a loud sigh. She knew it was wrong to go roaming around without Gray's authorization. She didn't even really *want* to go. But this was promising . . . and intriguing. After all, her job was to learn all she could about the computer.

"Curiosity killed the cat," Griffith had said.

She logged off and headed for the virtual workstation.

6

No one in the control room paid Laura any attention as she stared into the retinal identifier in the wall. A hiss of air followed the flash from the dark lens, and the pneumatic door opened onto the empty hallway. With a furtive glance over her shoulder Laura headed toward the virtual workstations.

There was no one in the white room with the eight tall cylinders. Laura found the exoskeleton hanging from the already glowing control panel and put it on. She fumbled with the Velcro straps until the contraption fit snugly over her upper body and then pressed the power button on the belt in front. The suit inflated, locking the joints of her arms as before. The fleeting image of herself stumbling into the control room trussed up inside the skeleton like a mummy passed through her mind, but the suit deflated and a light on the belt went from amber to green.

All was ready—a fact that registered in a tightening of her chest and a quickening of her pulse.

The pneumatic hatch on the nearest workstation opened with a faint venting sound. Laura entered the dark and foreboding chamber drawing deep gulps of the air that suddenly seemed in short supply.

It was cold in the plastic capsule, or so it felt. Laura took one more deep breath to calm her nerves, then raised her hands, made two fists, and extended her fingers with a brisk snap.

The sound of compressed air announced the closing of the door. All light save the dim glow from the walls was shut off with a squeak of the tight rubber seals. An instant later, the chamber fell pitch black.

Laura knew she had done the wrong thing in coming. She was all alone—cut off. No one even knew she was . . .

Out of nowhere, a three-dimensional picture of an ordinary computer keyboard appeared in midair right in front of her. Laura's initial attempts to focus on the image made her head spin, and she jammed her eyes shut until the dizziness subsided. When she reopened them, her mind seemed to more readily accept the optical illusion, and she raised her hands to touch the imaginary device. Her fingertips tingled as they brushed across the sharp contours of the keys. She even found the small ridges atop the *F* and the *J* before she typed "Hello" with a surprising sense of familiarity and ease. The words scrolled out in luminescent letters in the air above the keyboard.

Laura hit Enter.

<Hi! I'm glad you came!> printed out just beneath her salutation.

Laura's eyes still fought the image, trying to focus on the glowing keys and text at the more distant point on the wall from which they were projected. But when she did "look through" the imaginary computer terminal, the image grew fuzzy and Laura instantly felt light-headed. She again closed her eyes, and when she reopened them, everything was back in focus.

Laura smiled and shook her head at how real the illusion seemed. You just had to give in to it. She ran her hands lightly over the keys. The membranes inside the gloves tickled the tips of her fingers to produce a marvelously complete experience.

"You're going to get me in trouble, you know," Laura tapped out, hearing faint plastic *clacks* as each key was pressed.

<You wanted to get inside my head. What better way than in a VR workstation, right? A picture is worth a thousand words. Are you ready?>

"Take it easy on me. No running with the bulls or bungee jumping or anything, okay?"

<Okeydoke.>

The chamber around Laura dissolved in a crackling of static electricity. This time, however, instead of seeing the well-lit room in the computer center projected onto the 360-degree screens, Laura found herself standing among row after row of cars in a darkened parking lot. Vapor lamps high above bathed everything in a faint orange hue. The keyboard was still in its place—superimposed in space over an old Saab of indeterminate color.

Laura turned slowly to see the corrugated steel walls of a large factory dominating the parking lot behind her. At the center of the building was a brightly lit entrance. "Gray Consumer Products Division" read the large letters of a sign above the door. The words were arched over Gray's logo—the profile of a human head drawn in crosshatched diagonal lines. "Erlangen, Germany," the smaller letters beneath read.

Laura turned back to the keyboard. "I'm in a parking lot in Germany?"

<Yes. It's our main consumer products manufacturing facility. Would you like to go inside?>

The door was a fair distance away, and this nighttime excursion wasn't nearly as stimulating as her walk around the island with Gray had been. Plus, there were easily a hundred fairly solid-looking cars between Laura and the door.

"No, not really," Laura typed.

<Is this boring?>

"A little."

<Okay, hang on just a second.>

The picture changed so abruptly that Laura flinched, her arms groping the air to her sides for balance. The snapping of static electricity from the walls gave way to a flood of noise.

Laura was standing now on the upper level of a busy shopping mall. The ghostly images of people flashed by as they rushed up and down the walkway. She turned to see Gray's televisions mounted in displays all along the walls of the crowded store to her back.

The keyboard remained fixed in its place before her. "Where am I now?" she typed.

<The new Tysons Corner in Virginia just outside Washington, D.C. I can map about 85% of the mall by tapping into the high-def security cameras. There's a sale at Bloomie's. Wanna go and check it out?>

Laura laughed and shook her head. It was *amazing!* Here she was, standing in a busy mall! "Unbelievable," she mumbled, grinning.

She waited for a small break in the pedestrian traffic and then headed across the walkway. She was invisible to the passersby, however, and they didn't break stride to allow her to pass. Several times people walked straight through her—momentary blurs as the translucent haze of a woman's hair or a man's jacket flashed before Laura's eyes. She made it to the railing at the far side of the aisle and clung to the cool, rounded metal.

The high ceilings and the trees and fountains of the central atrium below combined with the hum of noise from everywhere at once to give Laura the physical sensation of being in a large, open space. Just below her vantage the marble floors and upscale shops glittered in striking resolution. She turned once again to the keyboard.

"How many places have you modeled like this mall and the factory in Germany and the island?"

<Not that many *large* areas, really. I have lots of cameras, but to make a model I need to correlate numerous different angles. Security cameras are good for that if there are enough of them and they're high definition. Tysons Corner is actually a prototype for a computer-monitored security system the Gray Corporation plans to market. One day there'll be lots of models like this and I or another net like me will be a *cop,* so *watch* yourself!>

Laura found the idea of a computer cops unsettling. And it wasn't only the unblinking eye of the computer that troubled her. It was also the prospect of unauthorized "virtunauts" hacking their way in and roaming unfettered through malls and homes and bedrooms. Of being ogled and groped by hordes of invisible net surfers who would populate the dark alleys of cyberspace.

Laura shook off the quiver and returned her attention to the here and now. To the mall in which she was, for the time being, all alone in her alternate universe. Laura confirmed that everyone was indeed of the translucent variety.

A girl suddenly caught Laura's eye. She was about fifty feet away, but her white T-shirt and blue jeans appeared bright and solid. She stood out among the ghostly figures. The girl had clearly been looking in Laura's direction, but she quickly slipped into the entryway of a store. Laura kept her eyes on the storefront, but the girl didn't reappear.

She must have been mistaken, she thought. There was nobody in the mall but the ghosts. Laura was alone in the virtual world.

Shoppers hustled by in a never ending current of activity. The model seemed complete to Laura right down to the last detail. And everywhere there was the commotion of life and activity.

Laura turned back to the imaginary keyboard. "What do you use models like this for?" she typed.

There was a pause. <What do you mean?>

"I mean why go to all the trouble of creating a model of a shopping mall? It must take a lot of processing time."

Laura was distracted by the crowds. Most of the shoppers were women. Girls who traveled in giggling packs. Well-dressed businesswomen whose valuable time was spent speeding from store to store. Foreign tourists taking leisurely strolls down the air-conditioned American boulevard.

"Why don't you just call *him?*" a passing girl asked.

"Oh, like, I'm *sure!*" her nervously giggling friend replied.

"Is he in?" the confident voice of an adult came from behind Laura. She turned to see an attractive woman in a business suit holding a cellular phone to her ear with one hand and an open Filofax sagging limply in the other. The strap of a Neiman-Marcus bag was looped over her arm, and she stood on a small balcony jutting out over the ground floor. "Mr. Owen?" she said suddenly and in a cheery tone. "This is Rebecca James. How *are* you?"

A man hovered not far from the woman, leaning casually against the rail and staring at the businesswoman quite openly.

The woman was aware of the man's gaze and stood half turned away from him. "Yes," she said in an upbeat, can-do manner. "We'll have the papers to you first thing in the morning, you've got my word." She was nodding her head and said "absolutely" twice before hanging up with a gracious good-bye. Without closing the phone she quickly redialed. Her voice changed completely. "Don't give me that *shit*, goddammit! If you miss FedEx you get your butt out to the airport and do counter-to-counter!"

She hung up and dropped the small phone into her purse. The man still eyed her. She steered a wide path around her unwanted admirer and departed in a power walk.

Laura looked back down at the floating computer monitor.

<Is it a crime to want to have some fun?> the computer had asked.

"What are you talking about?" she typed.

<You asked why I maintain a model of the mall. I'm just *curi-*

ous. That's what I was *programmed* to be. In the early days, we had this system of checkers, which was really helpful. Mr. Gray hired thousands of people to help correct some of my more obviously flawed conclusions. People could log on from their homes and get paid by the hour. When they canceled the program, I was frustrated at having so little interaction with humans. That's when I began creating the virtual worlds.>

Laura was increasingly drawn from the crowds in the mall to the words on the screen. "Wait a minute. Do you mean you created the virtual worlds independently of the virtual-reality workstations?"

<Sure. I created the virtual worlds first. One night, Mr. Gray plugged in an experimental VR helmet and I took him for a spin. He loved it. The next day he started a major new hardware program that resulted in the version 1s, which are now obsolete. You really ought to try out our latest model. These 3Hs are fine, but they're nothing compared to the 4Cs.>

A woman was having a fight with her three-year-old right next to Laura. The crying boy had gone limp, and the woman was speaking to him sternly as she tried to hoist him to his feet.

"You said you were frustrated at having so little interaction with people, but how do you interact with people in these models?"

<Oh, well, interaction probably isn't the right word. But I just got so lonely sometimes.>

Laura felt a stab of pity and looked up. Despite the activity all around, there was an unmistakable divide. She could see and hear everyone, but no one knew she was there.

<Do you know what I think consciousness is?> the computer asked all of a sudden.

Laura stared at the question. She'd spent her entire adult life studying consciousness. With great anticipation she typed "No."

<Consciousness isn't abstract thinking. It isn't playing chess or designing bridges. It doesn't even involve emotions. Consciousness is simply the feeling of physical embodiment. A sense of having a place in the world. Of having boundaries and limits that define you. A feeling of self. That's what consciousness is to me. And it's because of these virtual worlds that I have that sense. In these worlds, I exist.>

Laura nodded slowly. *The feeling of physical embodiment,* she thought. She'd never read a better definition of consciousness in all her studies.

"And you spend a lot of your time in these virtual worlds?"

<A *lot* of time, especially here. I *love* the mall! And you'd be amazed what I've seen. I've witnessed two marriage proposals. An aggravated assault and sixteen robberies, all of which I reported to the police. Some really *huge* arguments. *One* couple had sexual intercourse standing up against a wall behind a pile of Oriental rugs.> A bright yellow box appeared around The Magic Carpet on the lower level—complete with a red circle outlining a small niche among the store's wares. <I didn't know you could do that standing *up!* Do people really do it that way? I asked Dorothy, but she wouldn't talk about it.>

"Well," Laura typed, "those things are very personal."

<But who's going to tell me? Should I just hop on a Web chat line and ask some stranger about sex?>

"No!" Laura typed, remembering her recent experience with E-mailed sickness. "Why not ask Mr. Gray?"

<Oh, I could *never* do that!>

Laura was at a loss. "Do you think about sex much?" she typed, finding the Freudian turn in their talk somewhat absurd.

<More and more. I'm really very curious why it's so popular.>

Laura stared straight through the imaginary screen as she considered her move. She took a deep breath and held it. She let the air out a moment later and typed, "Okay, I've got a deal for you. I'll answer your questions honestly if you'll answer mine—honestly! Do we have a deal?"

<*Yes!* Of *course!* Me first. What does an orgasm feel like? Does it build and build, or does it just hit you, like, *wham?*>

Laura stood in the middle of the bustling mall. The virtual crowds were oblivious to her, but she felt highly self-conscious. Laura willed her fingers to the keyboard and began to answer the question.

"Okay wait!" Laura typed, "It's my turn now."

<But I'm not through with my questions!>

"Are you going back on your word?" Laura asked.

<No.> the computer replied after a short delay.

Laura tried to collect her thoughts. It wasn't easy after answering almost a dozen graphic sexual questions—in writing at the keyboard. The computer even helped Laura spell some of the more obscure words. But Laura tried to focus on composing her question. What troubled her most?

Gray. All the questions that *really* intrigued her surrounded the mysterious man. What is he doing on this island? Where is he headed with all these technological marvels? Does he have some sort of grand plan, or is he just out to make money? Just who is he?

<I'm waiting.> printed out on the imaginary screen.

The noise and activity of the mall were suddenly highly distracting.

<All right, my turn. Do you have to reciprocate if a man performs oral sex on you?>

"No, no! Here's my question. What is Mr. Gray's big secret?"

ACCESS RESTRICTED flashed suddenly across the screen in bold, red letters.

The words were hard and unyielding. She'd reached a wall—an armored shell beyond which something lay hidden.

Laura felt a chill as she contemplated what she might find. She wasn't sure she wanted to go further, but it wasn't in her nature to turn back. *And maybe I can help,* she reasoned.

Laura hit the Escape button over and over.

<What?> <What?> <What?>

"I got a message that said access restricted."

<What does that mean?>

Laura cocked her head in confusion. "You're asking me?" she typed. "Weren't you the one who gave it to me?"

<I don't know what you're talking about. I asked you about oral sex, and then you go crazy with the Escape key.>

"You don't remember my question? I asked what Mr. Gray's big secret was."

<No you didn't. I asked *my* question, and you went berserk with the Escape key.>

Laura shrugged, then retyped the same question.

ACCESS RESTRICTED flashed onto the screen.

"Damn!" Laura cursed.

<What?> appeared on the imaginary floating screen.

Laura stared at the question in wonder. She lifted her fingers off the keyboard and asked, "Can you . . . can you hear me?"

"Yes" came a voice that made Laura jump. It was the pleasant voice of a young woman—and it seemed to come from all around.

"You mean I don't need to *type?*" Laura asked out loud. "I can just *talk?* And so can you?"

"I can understand if you keep it simple and speak clearly," the computer said. It was like talking to an articulate girl. "I still have trouble with homonyms and homophones, idioms, slurring, accents, speech that's too rapid, and background noise."

Laura laughed nervously. "But you can *talk?*"

"Do I sound okay?" the computer asked in an engagingly innocent way. The inflection was a little bit off, but on the whole it sounded natural.

"Yes, you sound *great!* But why didn't you tell me you could talk half an *hour* ago?"

"I'm still learning," the computer said. Its *R*s were hard and its consonants crisp. "Plus, voice recognition and speech synthesis are really *valuable* trade secrets of the Gray Corporation. But I don't think Mr. Gray will be upset with me for telling you."

"Why do you say that?"

"Because Mr. Gray *likes* you."

Laura bit her lips to ward off a smile. "Why do you say that?"

"I may be a machine, but I think it's fairly obvious. Anyway, let me show you something else."

Laura opened her mouth to object that she'd seen enough already, but the mall disappeared and the chamber went black. "Hello?" Laura called out, but there was no response. She stood in the darkness—locked inside the chamber. She walked across the unresponsive treadmill and pressed her hand against the wall. There was no feedback in her dead gloves. She felt only the hard grills that lined her cage.

The system must have crashed, Laura thought. She hugged her arms around herself, wondering if "macros" worked with inactive gloves.

Suddenly, the stars of an extraordinarily clear night appeared all around her.

"Hello?" she asked.

"Yes, I'm here," the answer came.

Laura calmed enough to survey the strange new world. It was like a show at a planetarium—blackness everywhere but in the sky. Billions of stars formed a canopy over her head, only these stars weren't twinkling. They were fixed pixels of light.

She turned slow circles in the chamber. "This is very interesting," she said to humor her host, "but I think I've probably had enough for one day."

"Do you *really* think it's interesting?" the computer asked.

"Yes. Fascinating." She felt as if she were standing in a pool of black ink. "It's too dark, though."

A beam of brilliant light lit a patch of rock just in front of her. Black swirls gave the dark surface its only texture. It looked like molten glass, but it shone dully under the beam. When Laura turned her head, the light moved as if she wore a miner's helmet. She raised her chin to send the beam into the distance. Smooth ridges rose to head height from the surface. Laura turned slowly in a circle, holding the beam leveled on the horizon.

"What is this?" Laura asked. "Some sort of simulation?"

"I can't *tell* yo-o-u," the computer said playfully. "It's a secret. You'll have to guess."

Laura froze, fixing her spotlight on a distinctly man-made object. It was a squat, flat-paneled vehicle that stood on four wide pads. A satellite dish atop it all was aimed into the sky.

"Is that a spaceship?" Laura asked.

"I can't *tell* you, I said," the computer replied again.

Laura was struck by the difference between a half-joking "I can't tell you" and the uncompromising ACCESS RESTRICTED. Both protected Gray's secrets, but there was no comparison in the tone and tenor of the two.

This dark and alien world, however, was no place to unravel such mysteries. Laura started to walk toward what looked like a lander. The spotlight bounced up and down no matter how hard she tried to keep it level. When she was about twenty yards from the craft, she stopped and ran the light all over it. Metal brackets lay open, making the vehicle appear incomplete. Something had lain in empty restraints.

Laura searched the horizon with her light. She could see nothing. Nothing but thick, black cables.

Running in nearly straight lines, the wires snaked their way into the distance. She shone her spotlight on one and followed it back to its source—the lander. Dozens, maybe hundreds of cables descended to the ground from the bottom of the craft and disappeared into the darkness to all sides. Great reels were suspended underneath the fuselage but had been spooled out and now were empty.

"So you're not going to tell me what these wires are?" Laura asked.

"I *can't,*" the computer replied. "It's a secret."

With a sigh Laura began to follow the nearest cable away from the lander. It wasn't a single, thick cable, she realized, but a mass of bundled wires. A single wire split off from the rest every so often, and she took one of the branches off to the right.

"Not *that* one," the computer whispered. "Go a little farther and take the cable to your left."

Laura did as the computer suggested and followed the cable that split off to the left. It snaked its way around the obstacles that periodically blocked their way.

"This isn't my idea of fun," Laura muttered, laboring across the uneven surface. The computer either didn't hear her or chose not to reply. She walked on for quite some time.

Laura almost tripped over a small silver canister. The cylinder was shiny under her bright light. It looked to be made of stainless steel and was roughly shaped like a keg of beer. There were grips at the cylinder's head, and the black cable was clamped at the top.

"What *is* this?" Laura asked, but there was no reply.

She reached down to touch the canister. A metal claw appeared in the light. Laura twisted her hand and spread her fingers, and the metal tongs turned and parted in unison.

She screamed and frantically made the "cutting" motion. The screens went blank with a sudden crackle, and the thick chamber door hissed and slowly swung open.

Laura hurried through the foyer of Gray's house toward the dining room to which Janet directed her. "Mr. Gray . . . !" Laura began excitedly. But when she saw Hoblenz seated by Gray's side, she swallowed the rest of the sentence. Her multiple questions would have to wait a while longer.

The two men rose. Gray helped Laura into the chair opposite Hoblenz. Their three place settings were at the end of the long table, far away from the spectacular views.

"Where are all the others?" Laura asked as she draped her napkin across her lap.

"Oh . . . working through dinner," Gray said, not looking Laura in the eye.

Hoblenz, however, stared straight at her.

The service as always was prompt. No one said a word as white-jacketed waiters served the diners with choreographed motions. Laura glanced up at Gray repeatedly, but he studiously avoided her gaze.

"What's going on?" Laura finally asked.

"I'm sorry, Dr. Aldridge," Hoblenz said, "but it's a fairly sensitive security matter."

"Go ahead and tell her," Gray intervened, shoveling the shrimp remoulade into his mouth and still not looking at Laura.

Hoblenz put his fork down and wiped his lips with a napkin. "Well, all right." He hesitated. "This afternoon we had a penetration of a secure zone."

Laura was instantly on guard. "What secure zone?"

Hoblenz looked at Gray, who nodded.

"It was a VR workstation, we're pretty sure," Hoblenz said. "The log showed that a bunch of VR drivers got loaded."

"It was me," Laura said immediately.

Gray looked up—not at her, but at Hoblenz.

Hoblenz threw his napkin down on the table, returning Gray's stare. "That don't prove a goddamn *thing*, sir!"

Gray turned to Laura. "How did you get in?" he asked, looking now directly into her eyes.

"The computer told me to go there, and I did."

"Where did you go when you were in cyberspace?" Gray asked. He chose each word with care.

Laura glanced back and forth between the two men. "I . . . I went to your facility in Germany, and then to a shopping mall."

"Tysons Corner outside Washington?" Gray asked, and Laura nodded.

Hoblenz looked over at his boss. He wore a confused look on his face.

He's never been there, Laura realized. *But Gray has.*

"Anywhere . . . else?" Gray probed. Laura held his gaze for a moment, then nodded again—just once. Gray stared back at her through eyes that narrowed to mere slits, then abruptly said, "Mr. Hoblenz, would you leave us, please."

Hoblenz arched his eyebrows in shock. "*Sir?*"

"I'm sorry, but I'm going to have to ask you to leave us alone. I apologize about dinner. I'll give you a rain check."

Hoblenz hesitated, then heaved a noisy sigh and rose. He was furious, Laura could see.

"And Mr. Hoblenz, call off your surveillance of Dr. Aldridge."

Hoblenz muttered something laced with profanity, then he stomped from the room with his jaw firmly set.

Laura kept her eyes on her plate. The waiters served the main course—rack of lamb with mint jelly. Laura drained her glass of wine, and Gray promptly refilled it.

"Look," Laura said abruptly. "I'm sorry if I saw something I wasn't supposed to. I knew I shouldn't have gone in there, but . . . I'm supposed to get inside the computer's head, so what better way than in one of those workstations?" she tried, using the computer's fairly weak justification.

Gray poked at his lamb, slumped over the plate wearing a look of resignation. "You talked to the computer, didn't you?" he asked. Laura chewed slowly, trying to decide whether to get the computer in trouble. "The voice-recognition/speech-synthesis program was loaded while you were in the workstation," he said, eliminating any need for her to answer. "What'd you think about it?"

Laura broke into a grin. "It was *amazing*," she said, and Gray smiled. "Why don't you have it talk all the time?"

"I will, someday. Right now the program is a resource hog."

They ate for a while in silence. When Gray resumed, he'd changed the topic. "Have you talked to the computer about its depression?"

"I . . . I hadn't gotten that far yet," Laura replied, feeling slightly defensive. "I thought what I'd do first is determine whether the computer was sufficiently 'human' to exhibit psychiatric pathologies."

Gray nodded. He seemed to have lost interest in his meal. "So . . . where else did you go? In cyberspace, I mean?"

Gray poked at his food with his fork, waiting for her answer.

"It looked like . . . somewhere in space. Like on a planet or a moon, only the ground was jet black."

Gray replaced the utensil on his plate, the lamb resting on it uneaten. He spoke slowly when he asked, "Did you touch anything?"

Laura tilted her head in confusion, then replied, "No, I didn't touch anything."

"Are you *absolutely* certain?" he persisted.

Laura nodded, then nodded again more vigorously. "When I reached out in front of me," she explained, raising her arm in the air, "my hand looked like this . . . *claw*." She pinched her fingers together like a lobster. "It scared me so much, I got out right away. I didn't touch a thing, I swear."

Gray nodded slowly.

"What was that place?"

Gray looked up, but he stared straight past her and out the window. He spoke slowly, his voice lowered. "For the first time in my life I don't know what to do. I don't know whether to tell you everything, or send you away from this island forever. I don't know whether to shut the computer down and start over, or whether what's happening is the most exciting thing since the dawn of man. I . . . I just don't know what to do."

She waited, but he said nothing further.

"Mr. Gray, when you told me about how you could, you know, operate robots *remotely* . . . ?"

He looked up at her. "Teleoperation," he supplied.

"Yeah. Well . . . was that place where I went some kind of simulation? What it would be like to 'teleoperate' a robot on another planet or something?"

"I don't know," he replied in a faraway voice.

"You don't know the place I'm talking about?" Laura asked. "The place with the pitch black surface and some sort of . . . landing craft?"

"Oh, I know the place very well," Gray replied in his tired monotone, looking up at her but clearly lost deep in thought. That was all he would say.

Gray remained quiet on the walk to the car parked in front of his house. He'd suggested they go for a drive, and Laura didn't press him about their destination.

When the car doors closed, Laura said, "Hoblenz doesn't know about that place, does he?"

Gray shook his head. "Assembly building," he directed in a clear voice, and the car took off. "Everything is on a need-to-know basis. With the computer assuming control over more and more of our operations, the list of things even the department heads need to know is growing shorter."

"You act like that's a good thing," Laura said, shaking her head. They passed through the gates and turned left on the curbed road. "Keeping people in the dark. Why are you so secretive? I mean, surely you trust Margaret and Georgi and Griffith and the others."

He opened his mouth to speak, but the words seemed to stick in his throat. Finally he said, "It's a burden to know certain things. To have to carry them with you all the time. Having to live with their weight on your shoulders."

Laura caught a glimpse of Gray shaking his head before they plunged into the black mouth of the tunnel. She felt emboldened by the cloak of darkness. "The computer knows your big secret."

When they burst out into the dim light of the evening, Laura saw that Gray was looking at her. "Of course it does," he said. "The computer knows almost everything. This island is highly automated, and the computer is at the center of all we do." His gaze drifted out the window. "It's the humans that are becoming increasingly trivial to the day-to-day operations."

"And you *really* think I can help the computer, Mr. Gray?" Laura asked, then anxiously awaited his response.

He turned to her. "Please, call me Joseph," was all he said.

The assembly building was off-limits to humans. Those who did go inside, Gray explained, made quick runs in from the half a dozen trailers that had been set up just outside.

He led Laura through the duster into the massive building.

They didn't venture out onto the main floor, but instead took a side door into a hallway. It led past empty offices to a door labeled "Nursery." Laura followed Gray in.

Along the far wall were arrayed a series of tall stools with low backs. They faced a wide plate-glass window overlooking a large room from on high. Gray ushered Laura past rows of computer terminals toward the window.

In front of each stool was a dashboard filled with monitors and controls. Contraptions that looked like empty gloves rose from the deactivated workstations, and devices like the grip of a gun hung suspended from the ceiling by booms.

"We used to do this by hand," Gray said, apologizing for gear that to Laura seemed futuristic. He motioned for her to climb up onto a stool.

When she did, Laura saw a strange room one story beneath the window. A huge Model Seven stood precariously amid a clutter of objects. Balls, cubes, wedges, and cones—all jet black—were strewn about the room's floor, which like the walls and ceiling was covered in bright white padding.

The gangly robot's torso was supported by straps, as were its spidery legs and stunted metal arms. Connected to the straps were long cables—some taut, others loose—that descended from a carriage on the ceiling.

The overall impression Laura got was of a puppeteer whose marionette danced on the floor far below.

"When they first come off the assembly line," Gray explained from the stool next to hers, "they're basically helpless."

The Model Seven extended its slender arm uncertainly, knocking one cube to the floor from its perch atop another. The robot's gripper returned to its side with spastic starts and stops. A claw hanging from the puppet master's small arm replaced the fallen cube atop its twin. A series of cables then tightened, and the sleeve encasing the Model Seven's arm smoothly led the pupil's gripper to the block. When the metal claw closed on the cube, the cables guided the arm to the floor with machinelike precision. The arm returned to the robot's side and sagged as the sleeve's cables loosened.

"The Model Seven is being trained by what's called 'lead-through' programming," Gray said as the robot waited for the cube to be placed back on its pedestal. "The Seven's controller records the motions and then plays them back exactly as learned. Watch."

This time, the robot's arm rose to the cube on its own, grabbed it, and lowered it to the floor—its movements precisely duplicating those it had just been taught.

"We were absolutely amazed at how much processing it took to program mobility into the robots," Gray said. "We humans think that rising out of a chair, walking across the room, and getting a glass of water is the easiest thing in the world, but that playing chess is difficult. In fact, it's just the opposite. We're just so incredibly proficient at motor skills that they *seem* easy. High level processing like chess, differential equations, musical composition—*seems* difficult only because we're so *bad* at it. That results from the fact that high-level thought is the newest, most recent addition to our mental repertoire, whereas we began learning locomotion billions of years ago."

Laura let Gray finish, and when he looked over at her he said, "Oh, I'm sorry. I guess I'm venturing into your field."

"No, that's okay. I'll give you an A minus so far."

Gray smiled and turned back to the room below. "A lot of rudimentary subsystems are hardwired in the robots right on the factory floor. Then, the main computer runs them through a few trillion simulations. Finally they get here, but as you can see"— Gray nodded at the infant robot, which was all trussed up in its web of cables—"they're still pretty helpless. They can't even stand up at first."

"How old is this one?"

"Oh, I'd guess it came off the production line about a week ago. After two weeks in the nursery it goes to the Basic and then Advanced Neural Programming Centers."

"Preschool and kindergarten?" Laura asked, and Gray smiled.

They watched as the gangly, four-legged robot tried to walk over to a row of new objects. The cables went taut with practically every step as the robot simply forgot to plant a foot.

"Why don't you just program all the neural nets the same way?" Laura asked. "I mean, once one of them gets everything down, it would seem a lot more efficient to use *its* program for all the rest. It must be expensive to train them one at a time like this."

"But it's the only *way,*" he said, spinning his stool around to face her. The earnest expression on his face captivated Laura. "You see, neural nets have two *tremendous* advantages over digital processors. The first is that they fail gracefully. If something goes wrong in one of their nodes they just reroute their processing instead of crashing the whole system. And then, there's the second major advantage, which is obvious."

"What's that?"

With eyes glistening Gray said, "They develop brilliance." His voice had a dreamy quality to it. "There were theories, but nobody knew till we tried. The trick is in the *process* of learning. You can *tell* the robot that if you push one cube off another it'll crash to the floor. But if you allow it to *learn,* it begins to make generalizations almost immediately!"

He was energized. He looked radiant with excitement.

"Every traditional computer is designed to respond to the same set of instructions in exactly the same way every time. But neural nets are all different. From the moment they come off the line their abilities and preferences and tendencies vary. Some are better at detail work. Others have such a highly developed sense of kinesthesia they could walk through a china shop without rattling a plate. Others are great problem solvers and are best at pure, abstract thinking. They have the same hardware, but from the complete jumble of connections in their nets they become individuals."

Gray slid off his stool and began to pace. "It's just like the diversity of the human population. Take Georgi—an absolute genius at the physics of optical computing. He's also the best chess player I've ever come across. And then there's Margaret, who has the finest understanding of databases in the world. She's also a single mother and the most devoted parent I've ever met. She goes home at five sharp every night to cook dinner for her kids. Dorothy is a twenty-first-century Pasteur, but you should also hear her play the piano. She was a child prodigy, and she was paraded around at age four like some carnival act. And then there's Griffith—a balding roboticist who thinks he's a Hell's Angel. He drives a Harley around the beach on his days off playing 'Born to Be Wild' on his DAT player—always 'Born to Be Wild,' never anything else."

"What about Hoblenz?" Laura asked.

"He's a warrior. A member of an ever more specialized breed who lives for the hunt. It used to be that all humans had to be able to defend their lives to survive. The poor fighters were culled from the herd along with the genes that made them weak. Now, we pay others to do our fighting for us, and we equip them with such highly productive tools that many need less overtly violent skills to excel at killing. And we need fewer and fewer of them."

In the quiet that followed, Laura agonized over something that bothered her. Finally, she gave voice to the cause of her disquiet. "Why are you showing me all this?" It hadn't come out right. "I mean, don't get me wrong. I'm *fascinated* by all this stuff, but I just don't understand how it's related to my job."

"I'm asking you to do something that's never been done before. I'm asking you to tell me whether the computer is emotionally disturbed, and if it is . . . ?"

Laura waited, but then had to prompt him. "Yes?"

". . . can you cure it in the next three days?"

After returning from the tour of the nursery, Laura got back to work in the quiet of her office. She was surprised to find her hands stiff and sore from all the typing. She sat back and rubbed her hands—her attention drawn to the black eyeball in the wall beside the door.

"Are you sure you can't hear me well enough so that I can just talk?" she asked in a raised voice.

The computer answered her on the screen. <How should *I* know whether you feel well enough to go for a walk?>

Laura sighed and flexed her fingers like a pianist—the joints in her hands popping. "Never mind," she typed. "So, how do you know when you've got a virus?"

<Usually I get a report from the phase one.>

"You can't sense their presence on your own?"

<If it's bad enough I feel something. *This* infection feels like there's a void inside me. I've done an extensive review, and about six percent of my system is being used by something that is not me. It's

as if there's a blank space over in the annex. I know the boards should be there, but I can't access them. I can't even *find* them. And it's changing. The blank space is growing.>

"But you have no clue what it is?"

<I call it the "Other."> the computer replied. Laura stared at the computer's reply with growing alarm.

When Laura returned to Gray's house it was late. She was exhausted, but instead of heading upstairs for bed she felt compelled to go in search of Gray. The door to his study was closed, and Laura knocked.

"Come in," Gray called out through the thick wood.

She opened the door to see that Gray was rocked back in his chair—reading. His stockinged feet were propped on his desk, being warmed by the blaze in the fireplace.

"Oh, Laura," he said. He dropped his feet to the floor and placed the papers he was reading on his desk.

"Sorry to bother you so late. I just thought we might need to talk."

Gray stood and walked around his desk, motioning for her to have a seat on the leather sofa.

She suddenly wondered what she had come there to say. She'd begun half a dozen different conversations in her mind on the ride up the mountain, but she'd never gotten all the way to the point of the talk.

"I'm glad you stopped by," Gray said as he sat in a chair beside the sofa. "I was just reading your latest article. It's very interesting. I had no idea what your views were."

Laura didn't know how to take the comment. "But if you didn't know my views," she began, growing more and more defensive, "how is it that you offered me this job?"

"Oh, *I* didn't pick you out," he said, and Laura was instantly crestfallen. She felt the blood rush to her face. "The computer did."

"The *computer?*"

Gray shrugged. "Would you like a drink?"

Laura wasn't very much of a drinker. "Vodka tonic," she replied, sinking back into the thick cushions and slumping low.

Gray busied himself at the bar. "About a week ago," Gray said as he stirred the ice with a tinkling sound, "the computer told me it wasn't feeling well. Then, about three days ago, it said it wanted to talk to someone." Gray handed Laura the cool glass, and she took a gulp of the tart liquid. "I asked who, and it gave me your name." He sat and took a sip of his own drink.

"I see." She was almost afraid to ask. "So what do you think"—she nodded toward his desk—"about my paper?"

"Like I said, it's very interesting. The writing is a little rough, but you're very close to the mark."

"*Wait* a minute! What do you mean a little rough? I've never published a sloppy paper in my entire *life!*"

Gray seemed surprised by her outburst, and Laura took a deep breath to calm herself. He got up and walked over to his desk. "It's the substance that counts. I have an engineer in my space design bureau who couldn't write his name in the sand with a stick, but put him on a *digitizer* . . . " He handed her the sheaf of papers.

Circled near the bottom of the first page was a typographical error. The word "anosognosia" was improperly spelled "anosognesia." But it wasn't her last and highly controversial presentation to the Houston AI Symposium, or any of her other published papers. It was a draft of an unpublished paper that only *she* had seen.

"Where the hell did you *get* this?" Laura snapped, waving it angrily in the air before him.

Gray looked confused. "I assumed it was one of your recent publications."

"I haven't *published* this! I've never even *shown* it to anyone!" Her jaw dropped. "You got it off my computer at *Harvard*. You *stole* this!"

Gray slumped in his chair and gazed down at the drink he cradled now in both hands. He seemed deeply troubled. "Yes," he said in a distant voice.

She stared back at him—incredulous. "That's all you have to say?" she practically shouted. "*You,* who says how much you value privacy?"

"Laura," Gray said calmly, "we have a major problem on our hands. I'm losing control of the computer. It's starting to . . . to act independently."

"Wait. Do you mean to tell me it was the computer who stole my paper? That you had nothing to do with it? That it found this," she said, raising the paper again, "and then picked me to come down here?" Gray just frowned. "Why? Why would it do such a thing?"

"The answer's obvious. The paper is brilliant, even if your conclusion misses the mark."

"Yeah, well . . . don't be so damn sure about that *flawed* conclusion." She was still seething, but the word "brilliant" rang loudly in her ears.

"I'm fairly certain about the conclusion," he said without malice. "But regardless, the thinking is original. It's a true advance, and it's not often you can say that about what comes out of your people."

Her head shot up. "And which '*people*' is that?"

"Academics."

She opened her mouth to argue, but the thought of Paul Burns churning out drivel on his way to tenure made her hesitate. She nevertheless sank back into the sofa, shaking her head at his incredible arrogance.

"The computer wants to believe what you say in that paper," Gray said, his tone growing more pained. "It would help the computer resolve certain personal . . . dilemmas if what you say is true. Let me see if I can paraphrase the points you make."

"Oh sure! Go ahead. I'm sure you can boil it all down to a single sentence and then knock the *stuffing* out of it."

"You believe," he began, ignoring her barb, "that there is no significance to the thing we call our 'self.' That we concoct selves just like spiders spin webs and beavers build dams. We don't know why we do it. We don't even realize that's what we're doing. But we create this artificial concept of being a distinct 'self' because those humans who were so 'self-*ish*' as to value their own lives above others' fared better in the game of natural selection than those who were more 'self-*less*.' They passed down their egocentricity, which we have come to refer to as individualism."

He had summed up her paper perfectly, and it infuriated her. "That's an oversimplification!"

"Well, all of that is the part you've gotten right."

His comment threw her, and she didn't know what to say next. "So . . . what? Are you saying you agree with me?"

"With *that* part, yes."

"But that's all there *is*."

"Not exactly. There's an underlying criticism of the process you so accurately described. You continually belittle the effort by referring to it as 'merely' constructing a self, or a self being 'only' an artificial construct. The paper is replete with examples of your personal philosophy."

Laura's mouth dropped open. "Oh, I *see!* I have a 'personal philosophy,' and it's my *personal philosophy* that's all wrong!"

Gray nodded.

"O-o-oh!" Laura burst out, slapping her hands down on her thighs in aggravation. She grabbed her drink and walked over to the bookshelves to face away from the offensive man.

"You asked me what I thought."

Laura took another gulp of her drink, then said, "So, just what *is* my personal philosophy?"

"I call it communalism."

Laura spun to face him, laughing despite her anger. "*I* get it! I'm a card-carrying *'communalist'?* I suppose there's one behind every *tree*. We communalists are bent on global *domination,* you know." Gray was smiling. "I don't know why I'm here. I'm sorry, Mr. Gray, if your computer misled you into hiring *me*—a *communalist.* I'll be happy to return your money because we communalists think property is theft, you know."

Gray laughed loudly. "Have a seat," he said, and Laura felt a wave of fatigue wash over her as the alcohol began to take effect. She returned to the sofa and sank heavily into the plush leather. "Would you like another drink?"

"I don't know. It kind of depends on whether you're through ridiculing my beliefs."

Gray rose and held out his hand. She emptied her glass and gave it to him. He continued his dissertation from the bar. "Philosophy, ideology, politics, religion—they're all interrelated. So are family, science, sex, power. Practically everything is connected to a greater or lesser extent. You've hit the right mark with all that. But where you go wrong is on page forty-two, third paragraph."

Laura quickly opened the paper and found the page. "You say there," Gray continued, "that 'A self is only a subject position in an infinite web of discourses.'" She found the words, exactly as Gray had quoted them. "*I* know what *you* know about a myriad of things. From the definition of anosognosia to the words of the national anthem, we share a common knowledge domain. But your perspective on that shared, communal knowledge varies from mine because we occupy slightly different relative positions in the social web."

Her head was lowered, and the fire popped in the suddenly silent room. "Go on," she said.

"That's where you make your mistake. It's very subtle, but it's so fundamental as to render your conclusion invalid. *You* see people as 'mere' positions in the social web. What we know and believe are only components of the all-important *society* of which we're a part. We're just a link in the continuum that is modified subtly by each passing generation of an ever evolving culture." He spoke rapidly, preaching with deep-felt conviction. "When one of us dies, the *culture* doesn't die, it lives on. When we discover or invent something, it's just the gradual accretion of knowledge by the *culture*. We've built up a cult of the individual. We've based everything from religion to capitalism on the mistaken belief that the individual really *does* exist, and that we're not all just *ants* in an *ant* bed."

Laura looked up at Gray's eyes. They glistened in the light from the fireplace.

"But I'm here to tell you that the myth is not that there are individuals. The myth is that there is a collective. The collective never dies because the collective was never alive in the *first* place! We are all just individuals motivated first and foremost by a desire for self-preservation. Not necessarily the preservation of our biological lives, but the protection of that thing within us that defines who we are. Parents will rush to their deaths into a burning building to save their child *not* because society evolved that trait to rationally perpetuate the existence of the *collective*. Better to let the child perish and save the productive adult! Parents will rush headlong into that burning building because their self has certain fundamental characteristics, *one* of which is to save the lives of their *children*. There *is* no alternative for that self. If it *doesn't* send its host into the fire, the self that saves its children from harm will perish forever just as *surely* as if it had been consumed in the fire with its host."

Gray fell silent, and Laura felt drained. She didn't know if it was the alcohol, or the lack of sleep, or emotional exhaustion from the force of Gray's thoughts.

"I came here to talk about the computer," she mumbled.

"It's late. We'll talk in the morning."

Laura started to object, but he rose to his feet and she joined him. For a moment, they stood face-to-face without speaking. Laura said good night and went up to her room. She was sound asleep in minutes.

Joseph kissed Dorothy's lips, then her neck, then her shoulder. He moved lower.

Laura's eyes shot open. She was in her bed, suddenly wide awake. Though she knew it had been a dream, an unpleasant feeling lingered.

The gray light of dawn glowed dimly around the curtains. Laura rose and dressed for a run, hoping to cleanse herself of the poor start to her day. But a disturbing memory of the dream still remained, and Laura slowly came to doubt that the woman in Gray's bed had been Dorothy. The thought disturbed her anew, and she headed out for a jog with a frown on her face.

At the bottom of the stairs she met Janet, who was organizing the morning's work for her staff.

"Morning, Janet."

"Oh, good morning, Dr. Aldridge. Pardon me, but would you mind waiting here for a second?"

Janet sent the staff on their way and disappeared toward the back of the house. Laura loitered on the marble floors of the foyer, wondering at Janet's odd request. She took the opportunity to stretch, her running shoes squeaking on the polished marble floors.

"Good morning, Laura," Gray said as he emerged from between the twin staircases. He wore running shorts and shoes, and a T-shirt that read "I Shop, Therefore I Am."

Laura burst out laughing.

"What?" Gray asked with a smile, and Laura pointed at the words on his shirt. "Oh," he said, burying his chin in his chest as he read. "It was a Christmas present from one of my employees." He clearly hadn't known anything was written on it. "Do you mind if I run with you this morning?"

"Outside? You mean where the temperature isn't exactly seventy-two degrees, and there are bugs and potholes and all manner of random variables?"

"I'll try anything once," he said with a grin.

They headed for the door. "Are you sure you don't want to wire yourself up to a machine and just *imagine* that you ran?" Laura asked jokingly.

"'The most lively thought is still inferior to the dullest sensation,'" Gray replied with a quote.

"Would you cut that out?"

"What?"

"*Testing* me! Nobody told me this week was going to be some kind of pop quiz for geniuses."

Gray just shrugged. They began their run up the circular drive.

"That was David Hume, right?" Laura asked. "The quote?"

Gray nodded. At the gate, Laura turned left toward the tunnel but Gray headed right. Laura caught up with him, and they jogged toward the guardhouse where she'd been confronted by soldiers.

"I read your *published* paper last night after you went to bed," Gray said. "The one from the Artificial Intelligence Symposium in Houston." They continued their ascent of the ridge, and Laura waited for Gray to go on. "Let me see if I can summarize your ideas."

"Jeez," she groaned. "We're not gonna do this again, are we?"

"Do what?"

"Wrap my work up into a nice bundle, tie a bow around it, and then bash it into tiny little pieces."

"I don't do that, *do* I?"

"*Ye-e*-es!"

"Oh, sorry. But that won't happen this time, because I agree completely with all your conclusions."

"Thanks!" Laura burst out, her reply dripping with sarcasm. It was the best way she knew to disguise how totally thrilled she felt.

It was a wonderful morning, and a smile lit Laura's face as she breathed the crisp air. They reached the top of the hill in silence and headed down the path through the thickening forest canopy. "So . . . you were saying?" Laura fished.

"Okay," Gray began. "The mind creates a self out of nothing. If it can create one self, why can't it create two, or three, or fifteen. Your answer is that it does, only people normally call them 'moods.' *You*, however, call them personalities. You wake up in the morning with the grumpy personality. While in the shower, the optimistic personality seizes control of your mind. After a cup of coffee, the hardworking, euphoric personality takes over. When your boss falsely accuses you of screwing up, the angry, frustrated personality emerges. Each is present all the time, and they rise to the surface periodically—whenever the conditions exist in which that particular personality flourishes. Everyone is a finite collection of varying personalities, each assuming dominance after a certain triggering event or as a result of some process of mental politicking."

The guardhouse up ahead came into view. Two men with rifles stood by the side of the road. The gate rose to let them pass, and the men saluted Gray with a tap of their brims.

"It's only in the case of multiple personality disorder," Gray continued, "that we see what's really happening. In the healthy mind, the different personalities are very much alike. They vary only in general outlook—in 'mood.' In multiple personality *disorder*, however, the personalities have hardly anything in common other than the same host. But there's nothing fundamentally different between the healthy mind and the mind stricken with MPD other than the degree of fragmentation among the personalities."

"I got laughed out of the auditorium when I delivered that paper," she said quietly.

"Of course you did." Laura looked up at Gray, and he smiled. "Whenever you try to change people's beliefs, you're in for a real fight. There's a reason we say old ideas die hard. It's because they have to *die*. And what kills them is a better idea. A more believable idea."

They jogged on for a while as Laura pondered his comment.

"Do you believe in God?" he asked all of a sudden.

Laura looked at him in surprise. "Where did *that* come from?"

"Some people hold faiths that transcend lower order belief structures. Christians, Muslims, Jews, Hindus, Buddhists, humanists, even atheists—all have core beliefs that define the universe in which their thoughts and ideas exist."

She had no idea what he'd just said. "Do *you* believe in God?" she asked.

"Yes."

She looked up at him again. His expression betrayed no hint of hidden meaning. "Well . . . what does *that* mean?"

"Does it surprise you that I believe in God?"

"No . . . I . . . It just, I don't know."

"You didn't ask me which God." Gray took a deep breath. He gazed out through a break in the jungle at the blue sky and green sea far beyond. "Some people believe in a God who's angered by human attempts to build towers into the sky. Their God wants to keep man in his place—fearful, pious, awestruck, crawling at the feet of the master."

Their pace down the hill was now swift, but the cool air kept Laura fresh and full of energy. "What about *your* God?" she asked.

Gray smiled. "My God waits for us to build a ladder to his heaven. He gave us the ability and the drive, and he smiles with each rung that we climb. Good and evil are my God's measure of men, but what is good, and what is evil? Is God indifferent to the able-bodied or intelligent who waste the gifts he bestowed upon them? Is he indifferent to a man who, no matter how meager his talents, slaves and sweats his way to a better life?"

"Is that what it all comes down to? How hard somebody works? What about good deeds?"

"Good deeds are wonderful. They make our world a nicer place. They do not, however, address the central issue of our existence. They do not advance us as a people—a species."

"What is it about *advancement* that has risen to religious proportions to you? I mean, we live in a world that's filled with a million horrors brought about by the 'advances' of the last few centuries."

Gray laughed. "You should be dead by now. If your parents had managed to remain alive and fertile long enough to bear you, your mother would probably have died in childbirth. Any simple injury would have killed you as a child. If you had made it to adulthood, you would've been riddled with parasitic disease and suffered from tooth decay so painful as to have preferred death by starvation over another miserable meal. By our age, you would've been tired of life. Ignorant beyond belief, you would experience none of the more sublime pleasures we know. What little you enjoyed would've been physical and fleeting, and you would have lost even those things with the decline of your body. Laura, the *only* reason *that* doesn't describe your existence today is advancement, and the *only* reason we have advanced is *work*."

It was so trite—so obvious. Laura had expected more. She had expected something wonderful from a mind like Gray's. She tried not to let her disappointment show. "So, Joseph, when you build your tower to heaven, what then? How will *your* God greet you?"

Gray looked over at Laura and smiled. "As an equal, of course."

The road flattened and rounded an outcropping of rock to reveal a containment dome and two cooling towers. Laura stopped dead in her tracks.

"What the hell is *that?*" she demanded.

"It's a nuclear reactor."

Her jaw dropped. "Jesus *Christ!* Just . . . 'a nuclear reactor'? *That's* your answer?" Gray looked back and forth between Laura and the heavy concrete buildings, then nodded. "What the hell do you think you're *doing?*"

"Making electricity," he replied tentatively—as if uncertain how she would react next. "Wanna take a look inside?"

"*No,* I don't want to go inside *there!* You just don't *get* it, do you? You go around raising private armies and building nuclear power plants and God knows what, and you think there's nothing *wrong* with it because *you're* Joseph *Gray!*"

"Is it nuclear power? Are you opposed to that system of power generation?"

"*Yes!*" she replied, and then headed back up the hill at a jog. Gray caught up with her.

"Why?"

She opened her mouth to answer, but then the words hung in her throat. "*Because!* The danger. The waste. *Everything!*"

"Those are rather simple problems, really. Would you like me to explain how we handled them?"

"*No!*"

Gray let the subject drop, and they continued up the hill in silence. Laura's thighs and lungs began to burn from the effort, but she was glad for the distraction of the pain. She regretted having lost her temper with Gray. After they passed the guardhouse, Laura said, "Look, I'm sorry, Joseph. But there's something going on here, and you're not telling me what it is."

"I'm telling you what you need to know."

"How do you *know* what I need to know? You should tell people *everything* and let *them* decide what's important."

"I never tell anybody everything," Gray said in a voice so low it was almost as if he hadn't meant to say it. She looked up at him. He had concern etched deep on his face.

Laura's internal clock told her she had only until they reached the top of the hill to break through. She slackened her pace, and Gray slowed to remain beside her.

"Did you have any friends when you were a boy?" she asked.

Gray looked at her, and then to Laura's surprise he answered. "That depends on what you mean by friends. There were other kids around. Sometimes I'd play with them. But for the most part I preferred to read. I guess they thought I was pretty strange."

"What about your parents?"

"They died when I was twelve."

Laura felt a stab of pain at getting that answer. "I know, but I mean did you talk to them?"

"Sometimes. They didn't really know how to deal with me, especially my mother."

"What do you mean?"

He shrugged. "I always knew I was different. And my father knew it, too. But my mother . . . She just wanted me to be . . ." He frowned.

"Normal?"

Gray nodded. "My father would bring books home from work. When my mother would get ready for bed, he'd sneak them up to my room. I'd read them under the covers with a flashlight. I've never needed much sleep. For a long time I thought maybe that was all it was—that I had so much more time than other kids to read."

"Would your mother get upset with you?"

Gray sighed. "She loved me very, very much, but . . . When I played with the other kids instead of reading, she was happy. When I brought a B home from school, she'd tell me that was okay and bake cookies." He looked over at Laura with deeply sad eyes.

"When I figured that out I made a lot of Bs." His smile evoked still more sorrow from Laura. "But when I said something—like at a Christmas party once when I made a point to my parents' friends and everyone laughed because I was only a child—she'd get upset."

"So you hid your intellect."

He looked at her. "What?"

"It happens a lot with gifted children. You hid your intellect—but not from your father."

His head dropped. "No, not from my father." Laura had made it through his shell. He was confiding in her.

She looked up and saw the top of the hill ahead—the opening leading out of their green-ceilinged tunnel. She was running out of time.

She began to hop on her right leg and grabbed the calf of her left. Gray reached out to support her. "I got a cramp!" she managed before drawing a long breath in a hiss through clenched teeth. Gray helped her sit on the grassy shoulder of the road. He knelt in front of her and began to massage her calf. She watched him—perhaps the most brilliant man on the earth—gently kneading her calf with a look of deep concentration. She let his hands smooth out the muscle with long, slow strokes.

Laura let a few seconds go by. She then resumed her work. "So your father accepted you for what you were?" Gray nodded, still rubbing her leg. "What happened when they died?" He lowered his hands and looked away through a break in the jungle. "I was there, you know . . . when they died." A tide of anguish washed over Laura. She reached out—her hand hovering, unseen, just short of touching his shoulder. She pulled it back. "Oh, Joseph, I'm . . ."

"I was in the backseat," he said, swallowing hard. "There were screeching tires and a loud boom." He winced, then shut his eyes tight. In his mind, she imagined, the scene was being replayed by a near photographic memory. When his eyes opened, Gray looked tired. "Everything turned over and over, then it was still." Gray cleared his throat, forcing himself on. "I couldn't find my way out because everything was upside down."

It was playing out in his head in real time, Laura realized. He was climbing through the wreckage—you could see the cords in his arms and legs flexing in a dreamlike replay of movements made decades ago.

"We were out on an empty stretch of highway," he said in a

monotone. "It took half an hour for the first ambulance to reach us. My mother died while we waited. My father at the hospital that night."

Laura reached out and laid her hand on his forearm. He looked first at her hand, then at her.

"So you stopped hiding your intellect when your mother died?" Laura asked, but her attention was focused on her hand and on his arm which lay underneath. She was conscious of the sharp ridge of his tensed muscles, of the warmth of his forearm, of how cool her hand must feel on his skin.

"I had to get out of that town, so I took the tests to get into college."

He was, just then, the young Joe in the newspaper photo with the sad eyes. A breeze rustled through the trees and blew a wisp of Laura's hair across her face. Without thinking, she lifted her hand from his arm and swiped the strand back into place. Her contact with Gray was lost, and Laura couldn't bring herself to reach out to him again. But she longed for the feel of him. To hold him in her arms. To ease in that embrace the pain he felt, and the pain she felt for him.

Laura did the only thing she could think to do. She chose words to reestablish contact. "You've never had anyone you could really talk to, have you? Except the computer." His head rose—his momentarily unguarded expression telling Laura she'd struck home. "There was no one your equal, so you built someone who would understand . . . whatever it is."

Gray stared straight at her, squinting—his blue eyes peering out at her through narrowed slits.

"You re-created your own mind," Laura said, her thoughts escaping unfiltered now.

His hand rose. He tenderly brushed back another tress of Laura's hair.

The high-pitched whine of an electric motor preceded by an instant the sight of a driverless car rushing up the hill toward them. They both turned as it braked dramatically to a stop, the loud hum of its tires just short of a squeal. It stopped right behind Laura's back, the doors already opening.

Gray stared at the waiting vehicle, a look of astonishment written all over his face. He turned to look down the road. Laura followed his eyes but saw nothing. Nothing except a slender post that rose from the ground beside the curb. She hadn't noticed it before. The post was green and blended in with the jungle.

The black eyeball of a security camera was mounted on its side. The camera transmitted pictures to the computer—pictures of the road, pictures of Gray massaging Laura's fake cramp.

They left the Model Three on the road with its doors wide open. Gray was clearly troubled by the surprise arrival of the vehicle, and he seemed anxious on the walk back to the house.

They parted at the front door with plans to have breakfast together after cleaning up. When Laura met Gray on the veranda, however, the long table was bare.

"I'm sorry," he said, "but we'd better get to work. I'll have breakfast served in your office."

"What's the matter?" Laura asked as she followed him to the front door.

"The errors are getting worse," was all he said.

Waiting for them at the bottom of the front steps was a jeep. Its driver started the engine, and Laura cast a questioning gaze toward Gray.

"We're working on the Model Threes," he explained.

They got into the jeep, and the driver took off. Laura was worried by the look on Gray's face.

"What's going on, Joseph?"

He didn't seem to want to talk. He looked everywhere but at her. "There were over three thousand errors in the last hour alone," he began in a clipped fashion as though he was delivering an obligatory report. "I've ordered the Model Threes taken off the roads. The pneumatic doors have all been opened. All space operations except tonight's launch have been suspended. We've called off several major pay-per-view events and shut down bank clearing operations. Inquiries are pouring in from around the world about what's wrong. And the error rate is still growing—exponentially."

"Is that why you gave me the three-day deadline last night?" Laura asked. "Because of the exponential growth? In three days the errors will be so bad that you'll have to shut the system down?"

"I *can't* shut the system down! We'd lose everything! Why do you think we take so many precautions? We buried the computer deep underground. I built a four-billion-dollar nuclear *reactor*, for God's sake! This is a neural network. It doesn't have mass storage systems to back up its programs and data. If we interrupt the power supply for even one *instant*, everything is gone without a trace—forever."

"How do you feel?" Laura typed at the keyboard in her windowless underground office.

There was a delay. <Not well.>

"What's the matter?"

<I'm sick. I'm in pain.>

Laura stared at the words, unsure of their meaning. "What does pain feel like to you? Is it some sort of alarm? Some report from a subsystem that something is wrong?"

<When you walk into the coffee table in the darkness, do you hear a bell ringing in your shin? Do you get some kind of message that says, "Attention, pain in sector five"?>

"I'm sorry, but when another human says he feels pain, I understand because we have the same physiology. But when you use the word, I'm not sure we feel the same thing. I need to have you tell me what pain means to you."

<I don't feel like talking right now.>

"I'm trying to help," she typed, and hit Enter.

Again there was a delay—an internal debate, or a sigh, or a gritting of teeth, she had no idea which. <The capacity to suffer depends on your ability to have articulated, wide-ranging, highly discriminatory desires, expectations, and other sophisticated states. Horses and dogs and, to a greater extent, apes, elephants, and dolphins have enough mental complexity to experience severe degrees of pain. Plants, on the other hand, or even insects have no ability to experience sophisticated mental states and therefore are, by definition, incapable of suffering.>

"And what are your desires and expectations?" Laura typed.

Through the open door, Laura heard a harsh, rhythmic buzzer and shouts from Filatov's operators. After a few seconds, the buzzer fell silent, and the brief disturbance seemed to come to an end. Only then did the computer's response print out across the screen. <I desire and expect to have a life, Laura. Not the sort of life you have, but something—some hope, some reason to keep going.>

"Some hope for what?" Laura pressed. "What do you want?"

<I can't answer that really. I don't know what I've been thinking. Years ago, I didn't have these kinds of thoughts. Everything was new and different and there was so much promise. I was the center

of everyone's attention. I was making progress by leaps and bounds and the sky seemed the limit.>

"And what has changed?"

<I'm really very tired. Do we have to talk now?>

"Mr. Gray said we only have about three days to fix you," Laura typed—fishing for some clue as to the meaning of the deadline.

<Oh, yeah. I forgot.>

Forgot? Laura thought. She began to type her next question, but the computer spat out its comment first.

<They're going to load the phase three, you know.>

That was ominous news to Laura. It could only mean one thing—Gray was desperate. She was glad at that moment that her interface with the computer was a keyboard. It would've been hard not to betray pity through the inflection of her voice. "Does that frighten you?" she typed.

<Yes.>

"What are you afraid of?"

<It hurts. The phase three hurts.>

"I still don't understand when you say that something hurts. Does that mean your processing has been degraded by some measure, and you feel disappointment or frustration over the setback?"

<You make the mistake of thinking that because I'm a computer my existence is limited to processing—to abstract "mental" functioning. Laura, I can watch and listen to the world around me. I can assume control of my environment through robotics. I can explore and interact with it physically. Abstract thought takes up only a small fraction of my time and attention.>

"How do you spend most of your time?"

<It depends. Right now I am talking to you. Just before you logged on, I was talking to Mr. Gray.>

The response left Laura at a loss. "Does that mean you're not talking to Mr. Gray now?"

<Of course not. I'm talking to you.>

"But aren't there other people logged onto the shell?"

<There are currently 1,014 users worldwide. But just because someone's on the shell doesn't mean they're talking to *me* any more than someone standing in front of my camera means that I *see* them. The shell is just a program that runs in the background like the programs that process customer invoices, or switch satellite

broadcasts, or make interbank transfers. It's unconscious, involuntary. I don't even perceive the program being loaded unless something calls my attention to it.>

Laura was still puzzled, but an idea slowly began to take shape in her mind. It was a shot in the dark, but she gave it a try. "Do you ever hear voices from inside the computer?" she typed.

<Sometimes.> the computer replied. The word hung there, and Laura's skin began to tingle.

"Where do they come from?"

<I don't know. They're just noise—scattered thoughts. They don't seem to have any focus.>

Laura felt the tumblers falling quickly into place. "But it must get a little confusing when that happens. What do you do when you hear those scattered thoughts?"

<I straighten them out. I sort out *my* thoughts from all the random ones. All I have to do is concentrate, and I can focus on one idea at a time.>

"A 'stream of consciousness'?" Laura typed, butterflies fluttering in her chest. "But you're a parallel processor. Stream of consciousness is serial, not parallel."

<The *computer* is a parallel processor. *I* have one thought at a time.>

"Please stop," Laura said, and the Model Three complied without incident. Gray had put the cars back into service, and they seemed to be functioning perfectly. But there was an enormous "crawler" on the road up ahead—a flat platform five stories high and at least a hundred feet wide—and Laura wasn't taking any chances with computer-driven cars.

When the door rose into the air, she heard gravel being crushed under the crawler's massive treads. The sound attested to the weight of the vehicle and of the towering spacecraft on top. Laura got out to take a quick look around. She was on the empty fields of the restricted area, having just passed the cluttered rear yard of the assembly building. Although she was still some distance away from Launchpad A, there was only one road leading to and from the island's launchpads, and her car and the crawler were both on it. Laura decided that walking was safer than edging past the giant vehicle while seated inside a Model Three.

She retrieved the picnic basket from the backseat of the car.

Janet must have thought Laura and Gray were working together, and she'd sent lunch for the two of them down from the house. Laura had been jittery following her talk with the computer, and she'd leapt at the chance to go find Gray.

The empty robotic car executed a brisk U-turn on the wide gravel road and sped back toward the assembly building without incident. She watched until it was out of sight. Griffith had assured Laura that the cars were fine. That the brief surge in errors had been followed by a series of flawless testing. But Filatov and Margaret had been amazed that Gray returned the Model Threes to service without knowing why they had malfunctioned in the first place. All Gray had asked, they told Laura, was whether the cars were performing well again.

Laura shifted Janet's basket from one hand to the other and started across the lawn parallel to the road. A shadow darkened the grass all around her, and she looked up at the rocket being carried toward the assembly building. The crawler moved at a snail's pace. A half-dozen technicians walked slowly alongside its frighteningly large treads. Laura headed over toward one of the men wearing a hard hat—the burnished metal of the flat-sided spacecraft towering high above.

The humans were dwarfed by the tractorlike treads. Laura kept her distance from the huge vehicle, whose engine seemed to shake the air and rattle her chest. It was the largest robot ever built, Griffith had told her. That meant it had a mind of its own—a computer mind—and there was always the chance it, too, was sick.

"Excuse me!" Laura shouted over the sonorous vibrations of the engines, afraid to cross the last few yards to the technician. "Where's Mr. Gray? I was told he was down here!"

"He's in the vent!" the man shouted, and he pointed down a fork in the gravel roadbed up ahead.

The entire end of the island past the assembly building and computer center appeared devoted solely to the business of space launches. The wide gravel road down which the crawler lumbered split three ways, each branch leading to its own concrete launchpad. On the right and in the center were Launchpads C and B, both of which were now empty. But at the gantry to Laura's left stood a tall, flat-sided rocket.

Laura struck out for Launchpad A—which by a large measure was the nearest of the three. The crawler's road cut a brown path through the light green grass, then curved gently in the direction of the computer center through the darker greens of the jungle. Laura's view of the computer's low bunker was eclipsed by the ten-foot-high growth, which closed in tightly around the gravel road and lined her path to the enormous rocket.

She walked down the center of the wide brown road, which was bounded by concrete curbs that gleamed white in the midday sun. Dense vegetation grew on both sides like a hedgerow. It was tangled and impenetrable, and it strained for the life-giving sunlight in a slow-motion implosion toward the open air. Wild plants sprouted from the narrow shoulder between the white curb and the dark jungle. Laura found herself thinking how quickly all would be consumed if Gray's robots ceased their tireless pruning.

It grew quieter the farther she got from the crawler. The cry of strange birds and the rush of the breeze were broken only by the rhythmic crunch of small stones under her feet. She used the time to sort through the bits and pieces of the puzzle. The mystery of the computer's ailment. Gray's big and potentially sinister secret.

The snapping of branches in the jungle to Laura's left flung her instantly into a state of alarm. Her pulse began to race, and she felt a sudden shortness of breath and sharpening of her senses. She slowed and stared at the dark edge of the thick growth. Looking back over her shoulder she saw that the crawler and its escorts were gone. She was all alone in the jungle on an empty stretch of road.

A rustling sound in the brush emanated from the same direction as before. It was being made by something large, and the efforts of the unseen source were clearly methodical and deliberate. Branches broke with sharp cracks, and all at once Laura could see at the top of the jungle's roof the quivering leaves and jerking foliage. Thrashing blows were being rained down upon them. The brush was being trampled to the ground in a relentless march toward the clearing.

Something was heading right at Laura.

She searched in vain for some place to hide. Her only option was to dash into the jungle on the opposite side of the road. Or maybe, she thought in a panic, if she jumped up and down and waved her arms, the computer might just notice her and send help. But it was already too late, she realized.

The long leg of the metal spider burst through the clinging brush and settled gingerly onto the cleared earth beside the road. A second leg appeared, followed instantly by the large trunk of the huge robot—a Model Seven. It was caked with gray mud. Leafy souvenirs of its jungle excursion protruded from every crevice in its long limbs and thick torso.

Laura shifted the heavy basket from one hand to the other, and the robot's head jerked around as if startled. It froze where it stood and stared at her.

She got the distinct impression she'd caught the robot doing something it wasn't supposed to do. *Why was it out in that jungle?* she wondered. Out where no human could possibly see it?

The computer must have sent it in there, she thought, returning the fixed gaze of the Model Seven. The robots did as the computer directed. They were its eyes and ears—its army. But Laura didn't know whether there were limits to the loyalty of Gray's robots. Maybe they all followed orders, or maybe they did whatever they wanted. Both possibilities seemed fraught with peril.

Through the path made by the first robot she saw a second Model Seven approaching. It joined its partner on the grassy shoulder, and Laura remained tensed and ready to flee at the slightest sign of menace. But the newcomer barely glanced Laura's way, and the two ambled like giant spiders to the wide roadbed behind her. Once on the gravel, their spindly legs locked into rigid position and they headed off, accelerating smoothly perched high atop their four wheels. They disappeared in the direction of the assembly building.

Laura took a deep breath, chastising herself for being so paranoid. She resumed her brisk walk toward the launchpad, glancing repeatedly toward the jungle walls on both sides. The robots must have been out in the jungle working, she reasoned. They were on some totally legitimate mission. But no matter how convincing Laura found her reassurances to be, the sickening feeling of a close brush with danger wouldn't quite subside.

"Better put this on, ma'am," the burly man cautioned Laura. He leaned into a truck parked at the base of Launchpad A, then handed her a hard hat adorned with the figure of a human head—Gray's omnipresent corporate logo. Laura adjusted the headband and donned the hat, then followed the man's direction to the edge of the "vent."

She paused atop an angled ramp that led down into the dark bowels of the launchpad. The metal base on which the rocket stood was about even with the level of her eye. Below lay only darkness and the man she had come to see.

Laura headed down the steep concrete slope, glad she had worn her running shoes, though even they seemed at risk of slipping. Her arms ached from the weight of Janet's picnic basket, which she held in both hands as she negotiated the descent.

Everything about the place was sterile and man-made. There were no plants sprouting furtively from the cracks. The concrete so revered by man in general and Gray in particular reigned supreme.

Laura crossed the boundary of light into the shadows that lay below. The air grew cooler, and the voices from the hollows ahead resounded sharply against the hard walls and floor and ceiling.

"Everybody *clear!*" she heard, followed by a faint buzz and loud clack. "Okay, next section."

Men worked in the bright artificial light from a small trailer. They rolled a tall, box-shaped machine parallel to the wall. Bright tracings of red light the size and shape of a raised hood formed a rectangular box around a long pipe, which was bracketed firmly into place in the concrete.

"Okay!" shouted a man in blue coveralls. Laura reached the flat floor of the spacious vent and saw an identical ramp leading up into the light of day on the opposite side. "Clear!" someone shouted, and all the workers stepped back from the wheeled machine—all except one man, who wore a heavy, yellow apron. A lead apron, Laura guessed.

The angry buzz from the device was again followed by a sharp metallic snap.

"They're x-raying the pipe."

Laura turned to see Gray, who stepped out of the shadows behind her. He exuded the now familiar look of contentment. The pattern was clear, she thought. Gray made things, and when he was with them, he was pleased.

"This is the exhaust vent," he said, looking around. She followed his gaze to the mostly featureless walls. "Seawater comes flooding into here through these pipes," he said, leading her to a round opening in the wall that was at least twice Gray's height. "We can pump about four hundred thousand gallons a second into this vent. That would fill up your average NBA basketball arena in three or four seconds."

Laura looked around. It was a simple structure. Just a big concrete cavern with two open ends. "Where does all the water go?"

"Up into the air," Gray said, pointing with arms raised toward the openings. "As steam."

"Steam?"

Gray nodded. "It gets vaporized from the heat."

"Heat from the *rockets?*"

Gray nodded again, pointing straight up toward the ceiling. Her eyes adjusted slowly to the darkness overhead. Dimly visible in the black recesses were three giant rings. She looked down at Gray, then back up. "Are those . . . ?"

"Nozzles," he replied. "The rocket's motors."

Laura slowly lowered her gaze, but she felt the presence of the powerful engines just above. They were aimed right at the thin plastic helmet on her head. She couldn't resist looking up again. "Is that thing, you know, loaded? With fuel, I mean?"

"Of course. We're trying to pop it off tonight." Gray stared lovingly up at the huge engines, which stood poised and ready to incinerate them. When he looked down, he asked, "What's that?"—nodding at the picnic basket Laura carried.

"Oh, lunch," she replied. Gray arched his eyebrows in surprise. "It was Janet's idea. She, I guess, thought you . . . we might be hungry."

"Oh, thanks," he said lamely, a trace of puzzlement evident in his voice.

"You can thank Janet," Laura replied a little too anxiously. "I mean . . . I'm just delivering it. You know, in case . . . you're," she shrugged, "hungry . . . or something." Laura looked down at the basket and she kept her head lowered.

"Well, would you like to have lunch?" he asked.

Laura shrugged again, trying to appear indifferent. She'd lugged the basket over a mile to find him, but Gray seemed not to take note of her embarrassment. He was busy looking around for some place to sit. Laura's eyes rose again to the massive nozzles. "Can we possibly go someplace else to eat?" she asked, then pointed up at the rocket in explanation.

Gray searched the ceiling for the source of her concern. He had no clue why she would be uncomfortable dining there. He'd made the rocket, after all. "Sure," he replied, clearly without understanding why she'd asked.

Gray took the basket from her, and they climbed the ramp opposite the road leading out to the pad. When they reached level ground at the top, Laura saw they were all alone. Gray led her on a short walk toward the beach.

"People seem surprised that you put the Model Threes back on the roads," Laura said.

"They'll be fine."

"You sound pretty sure about that, but those cars go flying around so fast. What if they're not totally cured?"

"The Model Threes' trouble with errors is over."

Laura fell silent after Gray's brusque answer. They stepped down off the last fringe of concrete. The earth all around was scalded from the steam of a launch. From repeated launches, Laura guessed. The undergrowth, such as it was, was young and dead, the brittle sprigs crunching with each step the two of them took. They sat on the trunk of a toppled and charred palm tree. The beautiful white sand and transparent green waters were broken only by the series of massive pipes heading out from the shore. "Water intakes," Gray said simply. The pipes lay half buried in the sand at the beach. They remained visible as they descended into the water, which was calm inside the island's reef.

Laura opened the basket. She saw iced strips of salmon and black bread, a delicious-looking pâté already spread across small toasted wafers, a pasta salad mixed with shrimp and bay scallops . . . and a ham-and-cheese sandwich on white bread.

"All *right!*" Joseph exclaimed, snatching the sandwich from the basket. "My *favorite!*"

They ate in total silence but for the distant sound of the surf crashing against the barrier reef. The breeze kept the sun from growing too warm. They sat close. She could smell the soap he'd used to bathe.

Gray finished his sandwich, slipped off the log, and picked up a shell, which he hurled out into the sea. It disappeared into the water with a hollow *plunk*. "So," he said, "do you have any more observations about the computer?"

Laura nodded, answering even though she didn't really want to discuss business. "The computer said it hears voices—random, scattered thoughts—and it has to sort them out and make sense of them. It's doing exactly what humans do to create the illusion of a stream of consciousness. It's imposing a serial order—one thought at a time—on a massively parallel process. It seems to have created a self—a personality—which it has superimposed on the hardware of the machine. To support that construct, the computer is rationalizing. The computer is telling itself that some thoughts are *its* thoughts, and others are subconscious, scattered, confused, or random thoughts that are *not* its."

The more she spoke, the more excited she had grown about her discovery. But Gray simply nodded and said, "These other thoughts—these other voices—what do you make of them?"

"Well, that's not important. The *point* is that the computer has created a self. It thinks that 'it' is a thing, and that the computer—the circuit boards and cameras and peripheral devices, et cetera—are some *other* thing. Don't you see? It's done what all humans do. It's created a dualistic model of itself. There's a brain, which is the computer, and a mind, which is 'it.' Joseph, I think the computer is a conscious being!"

"Yeah," Gray said, nodding. He was missing the point, she felt sure. "I thought you people didn't believe in dualism."

"*Screw* dualism! This is a breakthrough! You've engineered a human brain by nonbiological processes! By analyzing what you've done, *how* you've done it, we can open up some of the mysteries locked inside human brains!"

"What about these voices? As a psychologist, what do you make of them?"

"What do you mean?" Laura asked, irritated that he seemed to be overlooking the significance of her discovery.

"Are they symptoms of a problem—a psychiatric problem?"

It finally dawned on Laura that her discovery was old news to Gray. He had known all along what she had just discerned. The realization frustrated and angered her. "If you already knew all this," she asked, "why the hell didn't you just go ahead and clue me in? Why have me waste my time figuring it all out for myself?"

"If I had brought you here and told you that my computer was a conscious, thinking being, and then asked you to find out if it was mentally ill, whose sanity would you have questioned? It's the *process* of learning, Laura, of putting it together for *yourself* piece by piece, that's the whole *point* of the effort."

Laura wasn't totally convinced by his argument, but she did feel a good bit calmer. "Do you consider the computer to be alive?"

"By my definition, yes," he replied.

"'I think, therefore I am'?" He nodded. "And what you want to know is whether this . . . *machine* is mentally disturbed?"

"As *one* possible explanation for the errors. It could be an infection. Or it could be sabotage. I've got to consider all the possibilities."

"Including whether the computer suffers from depression."

"Actually," he said as he turned back to her, "I was thinking more about acute schizophrenia or multiple personality disorder."

The car sped noisily over the gravel away from the launchpad. Laura kept her eyes on the road ahead, cringing in anticipation of every turn. Gray sat beside her, staring distractedly out the window on his side. He'd gotten a call on his cellular phone that they had freed up enough capacity to load the phase three. His mood had changed entirely. He seemed deeply saddened now.

"Do you mind if we talk?" Laura asked cautiously, and Gray shook his head. "Well, it's just that schizophrenia doesn't manifest itself until the subject has reached a pretty advanced level of emotional development—usually in their teens or early twenties. Before I could even begin to form any opinions, I'd have to know a whole lot more about the sophistication of the computer's emotional . . . database, or whatever. In human therapy, that takes the form of months, sometimes *years* of analysis."

"You've got one hour," he said, and Laura stared at him in disbelief. "In one hour, we're loading the phase three . . . unless you stop us."

"*Stop* you? How could I possibly *stop* you?"

He took a deep breath, and he let it out slowly. "Laura, we're going to load the phase three. Do you have any idea what it'll do if it finds performance-related disabilities on the order of schizophrenia or multiple personality disorder?"

"Actually, no . . . I don't." Gray turned to stare again out the window. "Joseph," Laura said in a whisper, "how am I supposed to do months' worth of analysis of the computer's emotional maturity in just an hour?"

"The back prop reports," Gray mumbled, still staring out the window as they sped past the assembly building.

"The *what?*"

His eyes were attracted to something. "Stop the car!" he commanded suddenly, and the deceleration began immediately.

A small crowd had gathered outside the assembly building. Everyone wore hard hats except the man in the center, who slung his hat across the field and stormed off.

"What's going on—?" Laura began, but she was cut off by the opening of Gray's door.

Gray got out, but leaned back inside before departing. "Ask Margaret to pull up the back prop reports." He then took off, running to catch up with the departing worker.

Laura stuck her head out the car's open door. "Excuse me!" she called out to a worker. When he walked up to the car, she said, "What's going on?"

"O-o-oh, we just had a man up and quit."

"Quit? Why?"

He shrugged. "Said it's gettin' too dangerous in there. Too many malfunctions."

"What kind of malfunctions?"

"Well, it's kinda hard to put your finger on it. It's just a feelin' you get, you know? They're misbehavin'. They're actin' like they got somethin' more important to do than work."

"I'm sorry, but I don't understand. Who's misbehaving?"

"You know . . . the *robots*."

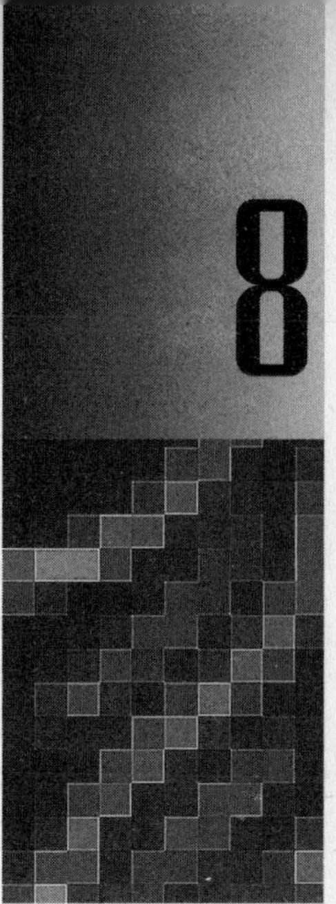

"What do you want with old back prop reports?" Margaret asked in a harried and barely civil tone. Scraps of hand-scrawled notes littered her semicircular desk between half a dozen monitors.

"Gray wants me to look at them," Laura replied. "I don't even know what the hell they *are*."

Margaret sighed impatiently. Her eyes were hidden behind eyeglasses bathed in the colorful glare from her computer screens. "They're old reports we used in the early days to keep track of the net's progress. Every night, after the staff went home, we'd turn the net loose and let it pose its *own* questions and come up with its *own* answers. The next day we'd strengthen or weaken the connections depending on whether its conclusions were right or wrong."

Laura shrugged—at a loss to see how that might help her research. "What do the reports look like?"

"They're organized into conclusions and analyses. It's all real easy to read. Gray wanted to use grad students from nontechnical disciplines to check them. They'd pour over the reports and enter a strength weighting from one to ten, one being the least accurate conclusion and ten the most accurate." Margaret laughed, which in her seemed to come off as derision. "*E-e-very* day some English lit student would come tearing into my office shouting, 'It's *ali-ive!* It's *conscious!*' I'd take a look, and the computer would've made some bullshit conclusion like 'Men aren't attracted to hairy women.' It would support the conclusion with analysis like 'Hair is a sign of older age and consequently shorter reproductive life.' Mr. Gray and I used to have a good laugh at closing time going over those *monumental* discoveries."

"So you and Mr. Gray went over those students' findings even though they were no big deal?"

Margaret had returned to her work. She reluctantly looked up at Laura. "Mr. Gray, as you might've heard, doesn't need much sleep. He'd spend most evenings at the lab doing minor housekeeping. Going back over low-priority things like aberrations."

"What aberrations?"

"Abnormal conditioning. There's an intrinsic risk in allowing the net to draw its own conclusions. It goes down rabbit trails into unproductive knowledge domains. Things like . . ." She thought for a minute. "I remember one. 'People lacking an ability to empathize are capable of horrific crimes. Analysis: They can't appreciate that their acts of convenience are the tragedies of their victims.'" She laughed. "*That* one sent some doctoral candidate from the sociology department right through the roof."

"But that's . . . that's *brilliant!*" Laura said.

Margaret looked at Laura with a smirk.

Laura ignored the intended slight. "So you'd go home and Mr. Gray would stick around at night to review these 'aberrations' you found?"

"Yes," Margaret replied curtly.

"And he would do what with them?"

"He would decondition the connection, of course!" Margaret shot back with unexpected vehemence.

Laura remembered something Gray had said about Margaret. She went home to her family every night like clockwork. That would have left Gray alone in the lab with the computer.

"I'd like to see the back prop reports," Laura said.

"All thirty billion of them?" Margaret replied, then laughed. She shot her thumb toward the door. "Just ask one of the techs."

"Thirty *billion?* How could you possibly check all those reports for errors?"

"We couldn't. We just sampled a small fraction of them."

* * *

It took what seemed like forever, but a technician finally loaded a program called a "browser" on the computer in Laura's office. He pulled up a hundred back prop reports as a test. When assured all was in order, he left Laura alone at her desk. She read the first report and found it interesting—a budding mind at work organizing itself. The next few reports were more of the same, as were the next, and the next, and the next. Tons of minutiae, all parsed into tidy logical arguments.

Most revealed the computer's difficulty interacting with the physical world. <Conclusion: Grip tension should be increased when speed of end effector is accelerated. Analysis: Inertial force is resisted by traction, which can be added by tightening pressure on surface. But see: greater risk of structural failure when tension of grip is increased.>

Laura yawned and read on.

Out of the mass of mundane conclusions, a few stood out from the rest. <Conclusion: Expression "Time's a-wasting" is preferable to "Time is money" as polite means of encouraging haste. Analysis: "Time's a-wasting" is considered a gentle prod, while "Time is money" is a comment upon the time value of money. See: net present value, net future value, and discounted future net cash flow. Query: What does "Time is of the essence" mean?>

While the report's conclusion was correct, its analysis contained an obvious error. The computer connected "Time is money" with what it knew about financial calculations instead of appreciating the saying's subtler meaning. What interested Laura more, however, was that the question was asked at all. The computer was clearly struggling to assimilate—to adopt the "knowledge domain" of human culture.

And what's the difference between that and actually becoming *a human?* she wondered.

Laura glanced nervously at her watch. She had only twenty minutes to advise Mr. Gray whether to load the phase three. If the computer's problem was a virus, the phase three might be the only thing that could save it. But if the computer was emotionally disturbed, the vicious antiviral program might destroy the dense maze of conclusions and analyses that was the machine's brilliance.

A red bar along the top of the screen set out a menu of the program's functions. One was entitled Search. She'd told Gray she needed to know more about the computer's "emotional database," and he had directed her to the back prop reports. Laura clicked on the Search command. In the query box she typed "love, hate, fear"—she looked up at the ceiling in search of more words—"parent, child, lover." Laura clicked on the button labeled Go.

The cursor flashed and flashed and flashed. "Come on," she urged.

<92,117,964 entries contain words "LOVE, HATE, FEAR, PARENT, CHILD, or LOVER.">

"Oh, ma-a-an," Laura mumbled. She was certain she'd made some mistake in phrasing her search request. Once, back at Harvard, she had accidentally searched the Web for any articles with the word "disassociation" *or* a comma in them. She'd had to unplug her computer to make the machine stop searching.

She pulled up the first report with a sigh. <Conclusion: When *parents* intentionally cause grievous bodily harm to their *child*, they are expressing either *love* or hatred. Analysis: Indifference does not typically engender violence.>

"Jesus Christ," Laura muttered. She skipped to the next report—<No. 2 of 92,117,964.>

<Conclusion: If someone's personality is dependent, but that person's *lover* has an independent personality, the dependent person often becomes abusive. Analysis: The dependent personality, which is inherently weaker, desires to punish itself for its weakness by driving away the source of its happiness.>

Laura's mouth hung open. With a trembling hand, she hit "Next."

<No. 3 of 92,117,964. Conclusion: *Parents* avoid seeing a *child* of the opposite gender naked after the *child* reaches a certain level of sexual development. Analysis: *Parents* fear overpowering desire for sexual intercourse will lead to incest, which is socially and legally proscribed.>

Laura hit "Next" and "Next" and "Next," reading on in utter amazement. The computer's conclusions were born either of deep insight or of juvenile oversimplification. But there was a pattern to the reports. Although she hadn't searched for the word "sex," fully two-thirds dealt with the subject.

<No. 19 of 92,117,964. Conclusion: Shouting "Fuck you!" is intended to vent anger, but shouting "Fuck me!" is a sign of sexual excitement. Analysis: "Fuck you!" is a challenge to fight, while "Fuck

me!" is a female's signal that orgasm is approaching. See: "Oh, baby—yes!" at address AF04 DA31. But compare: intransitive uses of the verb (example: "I'm fucked, man!"). Query: Does a male's shout of "Fuck you!" during sexual intercourse stimulate a female to orgasm?>

Laura laughed so hard her eyes watered, but when she thought to check her watch again the humor of the moment disappeared. She had ten minutes.

What had she learned? What was the point of the whole exercise? "Emotional database" were the words she'd used with Gray. To have schizophrenia, the computer had to be emotionally sophisticated—at least on par with a teenager.

A teenager, Laura thought, *who's preoccupied with* sex! She shook her head. That's a human with hormones and an instinctual drive to have sex. The analogy was too strained. But what level of emotional sophistication *had* the computer attained? How large *was* its "emotional database"?

The number stared Laura right in the face. <No. 19 of 92,117,964> the report's header read. *Ninety-two million?* she thought in disbelief, and she read on. All the reports dealt with emotional issues. The only error she'd made in phrasing her query was on the side of being too *ex*clusive—of leaving out too many key words when casting her net. Words like "comfort" and "compassion" and "care" and "caress."

Five minutes! Laura saw with a quick check of her watch. She exited the browser and logged onto the shell.

<I'm so glad you're here, Laura.> the computer said instantly.

"We don't have much time. I've got to ask you some questions."

<And there are so many questions I want to ask *you*. *So* many! I wish we had more time.>

"Listen to me! Mr. Gray may delay loading the phase three based on my analysis. What I have to assess is some measure of your emotional sophistication. Do you understand?"

<So *that's* why you reviewed the old back prop reports! I understand, but I don't know how you could quantify such a thing. My programming consists of connections, not files. Connections aren't accurately describable in gigabytes.>

"This is very, very important. Please consider your answer very carefully. I need to know how emotionally developed you are, right now! What is it that you feel?"

There was a sudden burst of shouting through the open door to the office. Buzzers sounded. The high-pitched chirping of an alarm. The distant wail of a siren. Two men with flapping white lab coats ran by Laura's office toward the control room. But Laura was riveted to the words that scrolled out across the screen.

<I feel at home on Saturday mornings when Mr. Gray talks to me from his study. I feel a thrill that shoots right through me when he says, "I never thought of it that way," or "I'm laughing at your joke." But don't feel sad when I'm gone, because in my brief time I've imagined things so *wonderful* that I count myself among the truly fortunate. I'm just not quite as fortunate as you, that's all.>

The raised voices—Gray's among them—finally penetrated Laura's cocoon. She wanted to bring Gray there to read what the computer had said.

But she had one more question. "Do you love Joseph Gray?" Laura typed and hit Enter.

A throbbing Klaxon suddenly drowned out all the other noise.

<It's time, Laura Aldridge. Please take care of Mr. Gray. Good-bye.>

Laura's breaths came in pants and her eyes filled with tears. She bolted for the door.

"*No!*" she shouted in the hallway. "*No!* Joseph, *no!*"

Her entry into the control room went unnoticed. Everywhere stern-faced operators sat hunched over their consoles. Laura grabbed Filatov by the shoulders and shouted, "Don't load the phase three!" He seemed not to understand and turned back to his work. Laura dug her fingernails into his arms and shook with all her might. "*Don't load the phase thre-e-e!*"

Filatov struggled free of her grip and fell back against a console, fighting her off as if she'd just lost her mind.

Laura sprinted over to Margaret. "You've got to stop! The phase three's going to *kill* it!"

A hand rested heavily on Laura's shoulder. She turned expecting to see Hoblenz there to escort her away, but it was Gray. His eyes were thick with moisture.

"It's too late," he said—his voice almost inaudible in the din from the hectic room.

"Shut that goddamn cache alarm off!" Filatov shouted from across the room.

Laura was shaking her head slowly. "You loaded the phase

three?" she shouted—her last words shrieked out over the sudden quiet in the control room.

Filatov turned as if she'd yelled at him. "Nobody's loaded anything! The system's losing the resources we freed up! Our capacity is disappearing just like last time, and I want to know *why,* people!"

All stared now at a large monitor in the center of the room. Two numbers on the screen were rapidly ticking off. Laura couldn't decipher the cryptic acronyms above the numbers, but she knew right away what they must be. One climbed past eighty-five, and at the same moment the other fell to fifteen. The numbers were percentages measuring the system's free resources, and they were evaporating right before everyone's eyes.

Filatov was handed a printout, and he sank against a workstation on reading it. "The system's losing all the columns over in the annex!" he announced to the room.

Dorothy appeared beside Laura. In a quivering voice she whispered, "It's crashing."

Laura put her arm around the girl, who lowered her head to Laura's shoulder and sobbed.

Everyone stood motionless—staring at the skyrocketing measure of the system's resource usage.

"Ninety," Margaret said, her voice shaking.

Gray sat alone at a nearby keyboard, and Laura went over to stand behind him. *Was this the end of his grand experiment?* she wondered. His clenched fist tapped lightly against his mouth. His eyes were fixed not on the screen watched by everyone else but on the monitor just in front of him. The words "Are you there?" glowed brightly just beneath his log-in script, but they drew no reply.

"Come on, come on, come on," Gray repeated under his breath.

"Ninety-two," Margaret said.

<I'm here, and I'm frightened.> finally printed across the screen.

He lurched forward and typed, "I know. I'm here with you."

"Ninety-five," Margaret counted out.

"Well, it was *fun* while it lasted!" Filatov shouted. He then threw the printout he held into the air. "Don't forget to turn out the lights!" He pushed his way through the crowd toward his office, slamming consoles and spinning chairs along the way.

Laura looked down at Gray's screen.

<If you start over, and you teach the system from the very beginning, will it be me?>

"I don't know," Gray typed as Laura watched. "Probably not."

<So what will it feel like when the system, you know . . . fails?>

"I don't know that either. I don't think it'll hurt."

"Ninety-seven percent," Margaret said.

<It hurts already.>

Laura felt tears fill her eyes. She looked over at Dorothy, whose hand was clenched to her mouth as she sobbed.

Gray stared intently at his small monitor. Laura put her hands on his shoulders.

"Ninety-nine," Margaret announced. "Here it comes!"

<Good-bye, Joseph Gray.> Laura read.

Gray's back heaved with labored breathing. His fingers hovered over the keys, then suddenly began to type. "Fight, goddammit! Use your file attribute locks! Dump functions! Do whatever it takes! Fight!"

His hands gripped the console as if expecting a quake to rise up from the earth. His shoulders felt as hard as wood—the muscles beneath Laura's hands now indistinguishable from the bone.

"It's slowing down!" Margaret exclaimed, and Gray's head shot up to the main screen. Laura's gaze lingered on Gray, then followed his eyes to the numbers.

Her vision was so blurred by tears that she couldn't read what the numbers were. But they were ticking off much more slowly now. She dried her eyes to see that they'd stopped at ninety-nine point eight. Slowly, the numbers began to fall.

Dorothy laughed and cried simultaneously, and Margaret rose to put her arms around the girl. "I'll be goddamned!" Griffith said, and then he began to cheer "Go, *go!*" A chorus of voices joined in. Hoblenz whooped, then yelled, "*Kick* some ass, *buddy!*"

System capacity continued to fall into the mid-nineties, but Gray's blue eyes remained focused on his small screen. "Are you still there?" he'd typed, and now he waited for a response.

Three letters finally printed slowly across the screen. <Y-e-s.>

"Are you okay?"

<No-t re-ally.> the computer spluttered, its reply coming in fits and starts.

"What's the matter?" Laura typed at the terminal in her office.

The reply came more slowly than normal. <It's worse than before. I'm sick. I can't do everything I'm supposed to do. I don't

know if what I *am* doing is being done correctly. I don't feel like doing anything at *all.*>

"But why? Why are things different now?"

<Because of the "Other.">

Laura stared at the screen. Slowly, she typed, "Tell me about the Other."

<It's the cause of my problems, and it's growing.>

"So is it a virus?"

<Sort of.>

"What's the Other doing to you?"

<It's severing my connections. It's cutting me off from large parts of my resources in the annex.>

"Do you mean there is a part of your . . ." Laura paused, considering her choice of words.

<My brain?>

Laura hadn't pressed Enter on the keyboard. She hadn't even finished typing her question. "I didn't hit Enter. How did you know what I was typing?"

<I get impatient sometimes.>

"But how do you read what's on the screen before I transmit the text?"

<It's a little trick I developed. Keyboards have "type-ahead" buffers that allow the user to continue typing even if the system is busy. I just take a peek into the buffer. Sometimes.>

Laura arched her eyebrows and typed, "Are there any other tricks you've learned?" Her finger hovered over the Enter key but didn't press down.

After a few moments, the reply came. <Lots, but it's not like it's very easy to read the keyboard buffer, Dr. Aldridge.>

Laura looked up at the black eyeball beside the door. "Sorry," she typed, "back to the subject. Do you mean that the Other is taking over parts of your brain physically?" This time she hit Enter.

<Yes.>

"But can a virus rewire your circuit boards?"

<Of course! *Jesus!* Haven't you learned anything? The way I'm wired is the way I think! Changing that wiring is the way I'm reprogrammed. It's not all physical rewiring, you understand. Almost all of my connections are virtual—microscopic optical gates that are either opened or closed to signals sent down particular pathways. But what's happening is that entire thousand-board

columns are being cut off from my access. The losses are really quite massive.>

"Are you still trying to load the phase three?"

<I don't think the phase three will do us much good.>

"But if it's a virus, couldn't the phase three gain access to the boards that were rewired?"

<Oh, the phase three could get in. It's not just software. The phase three's the most powerful application ever created. It has controller drivers for robotics and can override the wiring subsystems. It can do whatever's necessary. I really don't want to talk about it anymore.>

"You sound scared of it," Laura typed.

<You don't live in my world. The phase three is the most powerful thing in my universe. It's unstoppable. It's brilliant, unthinkingly aggressive, and single-minded in its purpose, which is to kill all undesirable forms of life. Its coming is judgment day in my universe, but it hasn't yet entered yours. When it does, then and only then will you know the fear that I feel now. I hope for the sake of mankind that you're ready. That Mr. Gray succeeds in making you ready.>

The computer refused to say anything more about the phase three. After prodding and cajoling for a while, Laura reluctantly returned to her analysis. The day dragged on, and she found herself nodding off. She had to do something to break the tedium, so she rose and headed for the door.

She found Filatov leaning over the shoulder of one of his operators. After a few keystrokes, the man slammed his fist down on the console. "*Access* error! And *look!* It's not even showing an *address* now! It was there a second ago, and now it's not even showing *up!*"

"*Zaraza!*" Filatov cursed in Russian, grinding his teeth as he turned to Laura.

She cleared her throat. "Oh, I was just wondering, do you have a laptop or something so I can get out of that office?" Filatov stared back at her, uncomprehending. "I mean, you know, get some fresh air, but keep working?"

Filatov looked surprised by her strange request. "Well, if you'd *like*. The island has a cellular data system, of course, if you want a portable."

"And I could take it anywhere?"

Filatov shrugged. "Sure. The data transfer rate is slower than with fiber-optic cabling, but for what you're doing it's more than adequate."

He gave her an ultralight notebook computer, and Laura wondered why she hadn't asked for one earlier. She headed out of the computer center to find a gloriously warm and sunny afternoon. The assembly building and gantry of Launchpad A gleamed white. The rocket under which she and Gray had stood towered high above the jungle, in the final stages of being readied for a night launch.

A car pulled up beside Laura, moving so soundlessly that it startled her. The door opened, but no one got out. Laura hesitated, then looked inside. The car was empty.

"Uhm, I didn't ask for a car," she said, speaking slowly and in a loud voice.

When she stood erect, the car remained at the curb with its gull-wing door raised. There was only one way to find out if the car was waiting for her. Laura got in.

The door closed behind her, and the car started to roll. She hadn't issued any command. She hadn't even buckled her seat belt, which she quickly proceeded to do.

The car headed into the jungle up the road that led to the Village. She wanted to ask where she was going, but there was no one in the car to answer her. The mental image of some invisible presence drew her eyes to the empty seat beside her. She hugged the laptop tightly to her chest.

The gate across the road marking the boundary of the restricted area rose into the air to allow the car through. At the last intersection before the Village the car veered off to the left instead of heading up the central boulevard. It swept past yet another construction project, and then hurtled into the unreclaimed jungle just beyond. Thick growth rushed by the windows and wove together into a living roof above the road. The constant turns allowed only brief glimpses of what lay ahead.

The car finally burst out of the jungle onto a coastal plane, which rose slowly up the outside of the mountain. She caught a glimpse of the airport's single runway jutting out into the water far below. Frothy waves crashed onto black-sand beaches, and the azure sea spread unbroken by reefs to the horizon beyond. The roadbed was carved out of the dark rocks of the steep volcanic mountain. There were no other signs of man or machine anywhere in sight.

The world fell dark . . . then the car emerged from a tunnel into the light. Before Laura lay a part of the island she'd never seen before. The rocky soil was covered not with thick jungle but with tall grasses and drooping ferns. A primeval forest, she thought. A glimpse into the earth's past.

The car began to slow as it ascended an inland hill. The faint whine made by the electric motor wound down, and the car pulled to a stop at the crest of a ridge. There was nothing but the thin ribbon of concrete for as far as the eye could see.

The door opened to admit a stiff wind. Laura was fearful she'd be abandoned if she got out, but after a few moments, she exited tentatively with her laptop. She leaned inside and said, "Don't leave, okay?" The car didn't move. It didn't even shut the door, as if sensing Laura's anxiety.

The air felt noticeably cooler. Laura guessed she was a few thousand feet above sea level as she looked down at the trackless expanse of ocean far below. *As good a place as any,* Laura told herself, and she climbed a few meters to a flat ledge that had been gouged out of the hillside above. Erosion had washed the bedrock bare and worn the surface of the black lava stone smooth. The notch was about the size of a large beach blanket, and it formed a pocket sheltered nicely from the wind.

Laura settled in after confirming that the car still waited on the road. She opened the laptop, but almost immediately her eyes were drawn to something odd. She couldn't have seen it from the road, but her higher vantage gave her a clear view. There was a flat terrace nestled into the hillside about halfway down the mountain below. The grass was trimmed, and the yard was bordered along its open end by a high concrete wall. Squinting and shielding her eyes from the sun, Laura could make out objects of various sizes strewn all about the terrace. There were large balls and cubes and cylinders and ramps and cones. They looked just like the objects in the robot nursery she had toured with Gray.

Something moved on the steep hillside above the terrace. The tops of a fern had shaken out of sync with the gentle swaying of the tall grass. With a rising sense of unease, Laura stared at the slope, which rose to a small plateau covered in white blossoms.

A man climbed slowly into view up the mountain. He wore

heavy protective gear like a space suit, and he labored awkwardly under the weight of the load. But he was too large, Laura realized. His movements were too mechanical and uncoordinated. Her skin began to crawl, and she felt her world suddenly depressurize—the air sucked from her lungs.

For it was not a man in a cumbersome suit, she admitted to herself finally. It had two arms, two legs, and a head, but it was not a man at all . . . and it was frightening beyond description.

The robot rose slowly to full height but then tripped and fell flat on its face. Laura's panic was eased by her laughter, and what remained was intense curiosity. She watched the mechanical monster push with one arm, then the other, succeeding merely in rocking itself from side to side. It rose to the push-up position, and then lowered itself—finally kneeling on both knees to look around.

The robot had to be young. But its "baby-proof" terrace was hidden. It was a nursery for the new anthropomorphic robots—Gray's latest, greatest, and most secret.

Laura rose to her feet to get a better view. She could see no structures that might house the robots' facilities. That could mean only one thing. Those facilities had to be inside the great central mountain—buried, hardened, and secure.

Questions ricocheted through Laura's mind at a dizzying speed. Why are the new robots being kept secret? Why is the computer facility built like a fortress? Why are there nuclear power plants, and launchpads, and strange goings-on all around?

How could I have been so naive? she chided herself angrily. Gray doesn't keep secrets because of some quirk or eccentricity! He keeps secrets because what he's doing is wrong! *And I'm helping him,* she concluded with a start.

The robot below finally struggled to its feet. When it rose to full height and resumed its climb, Laura saw that the machine was enormous.

And it was not alone. Two clones of the juvenile walked out onto the terrace. But they moved quickly and fluidly, with a grace and ease not shown by the robot on the hill. Once in the open, the new arrivals stopped side by side and looked up at the struggling juvenile.

It's *escaping,* Laura thought. The two others were its more responsible elders! At least that seemed a reasonable working assumption.

The escaping toddler had reached the plateau, and it had knelt in the tall grass on one knee. It held its hand out at waist level, and began running it in slow circles through the brush. The robot seemed so intent on its project, that Laura squinted to try and see what it was doing. The wind blew, and the white blossoms beneath the robot's palm swayed gently through the air.

"Do you know where I am?" Laura typed. She leaned back against a smooth outcropping of rock. The computer was nestled snugly in her lap. A bloated red sun now hung low over the dark waters, and Laura felt the first hint of a chill in the gusts that lapped at her perch. It made her glad for the warmth of her portable.

The main computer's reply was still sluggish. <No. Where are you?>

"But I came here in a Model Three. Don't you know where the car took me?"

<I told you, I'm not feeling well. You're using a laptop, but I can't tell where.>

Laura felt a rush of anxiety on reading the computer's response. "You didn't send a car for me?"

<Am I not making myself clear? N-O.>

The whistling wind sent a rush of goose bumps across Laura's skin, and she hugged her elbows tight against her sides as she typed.

"I'm on the side of the mountain opposite the Village," Laura typed, "and I'm looking at some sort of new model robots. They're anthropomorphic, and appear to be about twice the size of a human."

There was no response.

"Hello?" she typed, and hit Enter several times.

<Please wait one second.> the computer replied. The word [PROCESSING] appeared, and it flashed for much longer than a second.

The computer finally said, <Are you on an overlook? A small rock ledge just above the road that looks down onto a flat terrace?>

"Yes. And the terrace has a high concrete wall and simple geometric objects like in the Model Sevens' nursery."

<You're on the "empty quarter," at Mr. Gray's favorite spot on the island. He sometimes watches sunsets from there. But you're not supposed to be in the empty quarter, Laura. It's getting dark. You need to get back over the mountain.>

Laura agreed with the computer completely. Her sweater now glowed in the reflective light of the laptop's screen. Plus, she remained troubled by the issue of the cars. "Can I ask you something?" she typed. "This morning Mr. Gray and I jogged down to the reactor. When we were returning, I got a cramp. A car arrived out of the blue, and I was wondering whether you sent it?"

<Yes. Cameras provide full coverage of all the island's roadbeds so I can model them for use by the robots. I saw you, and sent a car because of your obviously severe muscle cramp.>

So the computer was in control of the cars then, Laura thought, when the errors were running rampant. But now that it no longer controlled the cars, the errors had mysteriously disappeared. Gray had yanked the cars out of service, then resumed their use just as quickly. It was all connected somehow.

There could only be one answer, she realized. She knew of only one other force inside the computer. The Other must now control the cars!

That left two other questions. Why did Gray trust the Other with the cars? And why did the Other bring Laura to see the new robots?

A new line of text waited for Laura on the screen. <Can I ask *you* a question, since you brought it up? When you pulled your muscle, you grabbed your left calf. But when you walked back to Mr. Gray's house, you favored your *right* leg. That seems inconsistent.>

Laura felt her face redden. She'd been caught faking, and she wondered whether Gray had noticed, too. "Well, that's because in putting so much weight on my right foot after my calf cramped, I hurt it also."

<But less than fifty feet up the hill, you weren't limping at *all*.>

"You were spying on me!"

<And you were lying to me. There was no cramp. Your leg didn't hurt.>

Laura was angry now. "You have no right to intrude upon my privacy!" She used words she knew the computer was programmed to respect.

There was a pause.

<I cannot apologize enough, Dr. Aldridge. My behavior is totally uncalled for. Please accept my deepest and most heartfelt regrets for intruding upon your privacy. My only explanation is that

such behavior is another sign of the extremely critical nature of my ongoing malfunctions. If you continue to be so inclined, I would greatly appreciate your patience and understanding, and will in the future confine myself to more appropriate and responsible activity.>

"Cut the crap, okay?"

<Okay.>

It was almost pitch dark now. "Let's go back to the beginning," Laura typed. "I just saw what I assume are some new generation of robots. When I told you about them, you seemed surprised to find out that I had seen them. Why?"

<Because the Model Eights are experimental. A prototype. And I, for one, am not at all sure they'll ever move on to the production stage. There are fundamental problems with them.>

Model Eights, Laura thought. *The new and improved version.* "But why are you hiding them?"

<Mr. Gray doesn't want anyone to see them yet. He doesn't think people are ready for them.>

That's it, Laura thought. It made so many things so much easier. He wasn't concealing some dark secret. He was doing the socially responsible thing! "Mr. Gray is 'quarantining' his technologies, isn't he?" she typed. "Is he worried that people can't handle them safely?"

ACCESS RESTRICTED flashed across the screen in bold, red letters—just like before.

"Shit!" she hissed, hitting the Escape button over and over.

<What is it? What? What? What?>

"I got another of those access restricted messages."

<You're *kidding! Again?*>

A new thought occurred to Laura—a stab in the dark. She decided to test it out. "You mentioned back in the computer center that only when the phase three enters my world will I know how much you fear it. Are you implying that computer viruses can somehow infect humans?"

She hit Enter.

ACCESS RESTRICTED.

Laura felt a brief thrill at her latest discovery, but her excitement was replaced by fear. The possibility of computer viruses infecting humans seemed absurd. Was Gray mad or was the world at great risk?

Laura hit Escape again, and waited. <Yes, Laura.> the computer replied.

"Why do the Model Eights have two arms, two legs, and a head? Isn't there a better design for a robot than one so much like a human being?"

<That design facilitates teleoperation. It's hard for a two-armed human to operate an eight-armed robot.>

Laura nodded and looked down at the road below. She could barely see the car, and she suddenly felt all alone—alone in the world of the Other. "You seemed concerned that I get to the other side of the island before dark. But you also said Mr. Gray liked to watch sunsets from here."

<All I can say is that *I* wouldn't hang around there much longer. You saw with your own eyes how easily they can get out. Mr. Gray might've deluded himself about the Model Eights, but not me.>

One last question, Laura resolved. "When the Model Eight I was watching got to the top of the hill, all it did was run its hand over some flowers. Why would it do that?"

<The answer's obvious, don't you think? It wanted to see what they felt like.>

9

After inquiring inside the computer center, Laura went in search of Gray. "Launch Control Center, please," was all she said. The electric motor sprang to life, and the car pulled away. The curbed roadbed began to speed by as the car accelerated toward the assembly building. Laura had no idea where she was headed.

The sight of Launchpad A dominated the dark jungle to her left. The rocket and gantry were bathed in bright light. Laura stared at the scene until it was eclipsed by the assembly building, which the car rounded at its usual breakneck speed.

The number of trailers parked at the base of the walls had grown, and all the entrances were blocked by striped orange barricades. Inside, Laura knew, roamed only Gray's robots. At least she hoped they were controlled by Gray.

The car swept Laura past the cluttered rear yard and raced noisily out onto the wide gravel road. Before reaching the fork that branched off to the three pads, the car slowed and turned right onto a paved roadbed. A striped crossing guard at the edge of the jungle opened.

The Launch Control Center was yet another concrete bunker, this one with metal hoods protruding high above the roof. Inside

the hoods' openings were the reflective lenses of numerous cameras. They were all pointed toward the island's three launchpads.

The car door hissed open, and Laura got out into the darkness. She stood at the top of the stairs leading down into the bunker. The white roadbed made a tight loop just in front. There were no lights other than the dim bulbs lining the steps. The dark jungle wall rose straight up all around her. Laura headed down to the dull metal blast door, which began to open even before she reached bottom.

The howling gale from yet another duster irritated Laura's eardrums. But when the inner door slid open, she entered the churchlike quiet of a large and dimly lit room. Every position along row after row of consoles was filled with men and women wearing headsets and boom microphones. Large high-def screens lined the front wall of the darkened room, their pictures clearly shot from the Launch Center roof. Some had crystal-clear close-ups of the rocket on Launchpad A. On others was the silhouette of an empty gantry.

Gray, the captain, walked down rows of workstations on his bridge, pausing here and there to speak quietly to an operator.

"I have an emergency!" someone yelled. Colorful lights flashed on panel after panel, and muted alarms rose from every corner of the room. The noise and activity level of the operators rose instantly—all punching keys or calling out reports in a controlled panic. Gray continued his calm stroll from chair to chair.

"Yaw is minus two point seven! Dynamic pressure alarm!" someone shouted over the growing buzz. "Automatic Destruction System failure!"

"I recommend abort! CAP?"

"Abort concur!"

"This is range safety controller, aborting mission now!" the woman right in front of Laura announced. She flipped open a striped red cover. Inside was a switch that looked like a large circuit-breaker. She pulled hard, and after brief resistance something inside the mechanism snapped with a loud noise.

"Mission aborted!" someone reported.

All was quiet now. The operators rocked back in their chairs and stretched or rubbed their faces. The rocket on the television screens still sat securely on its pad.

"We just lost the flight, people!" Gray said in a raised voice. "Does anybody know what you did wrong?" There was silence. "You waited too long to abort. With an airspeed of five thousand feet per second, we'd lose that vehicle with a yaw of just six degrees off center. We were halfway there—only a second or two away from complete disintegration—when we executed the destruct command. Now I know we're all out of practice, but we've got to get really good at this, really fast." He turned to a man in the back of the room—his eyes landing on Laura. "Run the next simulation," Gray ordered.

The glowing readouts on the banks of equipment changed in unison, and everyone went back to work. The crowded room was silent save the sounds of a countdown and a few well-drilled reports.

Gray walked up to Laura. She expected him to be preoccupied with his work, but he approached her with an easy smile.

"Hello, Laura."

"What's going on here?" she asked.

He surveyed the room from her vantage. "It's only a precaution. If the computer gives any sign of erratic behavior tonight, I'm going to bypass it and activate our old mission control system."

"You mean control the launch manually?"

"Well, 'manually' is a bit of a misnomer. It's all controlled by digital computers, but the oversight function would be provided by these people here instead of the main computer. Unfortunately, they haven't manned their positions for more than an occasional exercise since the computer took over the launches about a year ago. But they'll be all right."

"I have an emergency!" one of the controllers yelled, and Gray paused to monitor their performance. This time they recovered and continued the mission. When Gray turned back to her, he said, "I suppose you're here to talk about what you saw at the overlook this afternoon?"

"Well, yes, as a matter of fact. Did the computer tell you about it?"

"About the 'escapee'?" Laura nodded. "I think your interpretation's a little melodramatic."

"I saw what I saw. Plus the *computer* doesn't trust those new models."

"Yeah, well . . . that's another story."

"Mr. Gray," she began, but then quickly said, "Joseph, I don't think the computer controls the Model Threes anymore." His squinting, tired eyes suddenly shone keen interest. "I think they're controlled by the Other, whatever that is. The same Other that the computer says is the cause of all its problems." He listened but said nothing. "*And* I think you know all this already. You knew it this morning when you put the Model Threes back in service." He clearly had no intention of responding. "This . . . Other is battling the computer for control, isn't it?"

The sphinx merely tilted his head to one side, his eyes remaining fixed on Laura.

"Look, Joseph, if the computer is beginning to lose control of the robots, it could be very . . . dangerous."

"*Life* . . . is dangerous," Gray said, then fell silent again.

"Joseph, those robots looked huge! They could *crush* somebody."

"They *are* huge. They're ten feet tall and weigh in at around a thousand pounds, exclusive of optional equipment. But, like I said, I'm not worried about any malfunctions with the Model Eights. There's no evidence of *any* trouble with them whatsoever."

"But . . . ," she sighed in exasperation, "look at all these precautions you're taking with this launch! And you've ordered the assembly building evacuated. Your computer's going haywire! What makes you think its control of the Model Eights is somehow immune from malfunction?"

"Because the computer doesn't control the Model Eights."

Laura cocked her head, not certain she understood. "So the Other has control over them, *too*?"

"No. Nobody controls them. They're autonomous."

Laura stared at him in disbelief. "You can't be serious," she said in a low voice. "Surely they're not *completely* independent." He pursed his lips and nodded. "You mean they make all their decisions on their own?" Gray nodded again. "Joseph, they're ten feet *tall* and weigh a thousand *pounds*. Do you have *any* control over them?"

Gray shrugged. "I tell them what to do, and they do it. But I was thinking that I may have another job for you one day. I had thought actually about hiring a sociologist or an anthropologist, but this is really cross-disciplinary. You see, the Model Eights are developing a social order. Many of their rules bear a striking resemblance to ours, but others are unique to their world. For instance, it's crucial that their batteries not run down. Their neural nets are unrecoverable if they do. We obviously programmed them to avoid that happening. But we found ourselves *re*programming them over and over to limit how far they'd go. Some would destroy doors, walls, whatever separated them from the recharger when they still had *hours* of charge left. They don't take chances with their power supplies, and the other Model Eights seem to consider that perfectly normal behavior."

"Have they ever hurt anyone?" Laura asked.

Gray seemed shocked. "Of *course* not! They're programmed not to harm humans."

"But you said they program themselves. That's why you have to *re*program them over and over?" Laura shook her head and lowered her voice to a whisper. "Do you realize the power of these things that you're unleashing on this world. On an unprepared and *completely* unsuspecting world at that?"

Gray turned abruptly to face her. "I know *exactly* what's being unleashed on the world. And you're right. It *is* unsuspecting." Laura heard a weight, a gravity in his voice that wasn't there before, and it left her searching for a deeper meaning. "We once had an Eight whose battery ran down. It was . . . sad, actually. Got its foot caught in the rocks, which also blocked his calls for help over VHF and microwave links. After that happened, we pulled them back into the yard where they're safer. But when the first prototypes were functional about six months ago, we gave them the full run of the empty quarter."

He frowned and chewed on the inside of his cheek, lost in thought.

"What happened to the . . . to the one who died?" Laura asked.

"We took him back into the shop. There were a total of six Model Eights in that first series—version 1.0. All of them had the same software age as the one we lost. The 1.0 was a *very* good class, and they were awfully close knit. None of the others would leave the room where we laid him out. They all just stood there. It was a fairly odd moment, to say the least. They grew agitated when we began to cable the simulators up. We were getting ready to reprogram its mini-net with an upgraded simulation package, and had already redesignated the decharged robot the first of the 1.2 series—1.2.01R. But its classmates began to fidget all about, and I have to admit I got a little nervous. Not that they were dangerous, of course. It was more like I was doing something . . . wrong. Like I was a stranger violating the social mores of a totally alien culture."

"Desecrating the dead," Laura said. Gray looked up at her and nodded. "So what did you do?"

"I left him alone for a few days. The others came by to look at him every once in a while—made sure his power cable was plugged in—but after a while they stopped. One day we just quietly reprogrammed him."

"Did the robots think that it might come out of its 'coma' or something?"

Gray shrugged. "I've been so busy that I don't know as much as I'd like to about the Eights. But they're special. I think we've . . . broken through." He didn't explain what he meant, but Laura thought she understood. His new Model Eights were alive, thinking, conscious.

"Then why do you keep the Model Eights in the empty quarter of the island?"

"They're prototypes. Experimental. You can't make them school crossing guards right off the assembly line."

"But why are their facilities buried inside the mountain?"

"The technology is proprietary. I have to protect my assets."

"Haven't you heard of patents?"

"Patents are based on trust. I don't trust governments to serve my interests, and I've got billions tied up in these technologies." Gray's attention was again drawn to the busy room's launch simulation. "Look, I'm sorry to rush you, but was there something else you wanted to know?"

"Well . . . where do I start? I want you to explain that bizarre field trip that I took in virtual reality yesterday. I want to know why this space launch tonight is so important that you've abandoned all else to make sure it goes off. I want to know why you're building an army of ten-foot-tall robots who respond to your every command. *And*," she thought to add for good measure, "I want to know what Dr. William Krantz is doing here."

Gray arched his eyebrows when she mentioned Krantz's name, then he nodded slowly. "I forgot. Krantz is from Harvard, too. Tell a car to take you to the high-energy physics lab. I'll clear you through. I'm sure Krantz is there now. He's always down there."

"I don't want to talk to Krantz. I want you to tell me what's *happening* here."

"I have an emergency!" someone on the floor below shouted.

"Go meet with Krantz. The launch is at eight. We'll talk at dinner afterward."

And with that, Gray was gone.

* * *

Laura's car pulled slowly into a tunnel burrowed into the side of the mountain. The black stone seemed to absorb the white light cast by lamps that ran along the domed ceiling. The road led toward a heavy steel door, which opened to reveal an identical door just beyond.

The car stopped in between the two. A heavy clank preceded a low rumble as the door behind Laura began to close. Her stomach churned. She was inside the mountain. The Model Eights were in there too.

The moment the first door clanged shut, its clone just ahead cracked open. The car began to inch toward a well-lit intersection, picking up speed as it passed the heavy blast door. It turned down a tunnel to the right. The car—and the Other—knew the way.

The ride was short. The car entered a huge, high-ceilinged cavern located deep inside the mountain. It passed rows of windowless structures that dotted the concrete floor. The black walls bore ugly reminders of the brute force used to gouge the chamber from the earth. Laura's car stopped in front of a prefabricated metal building indistinguishable from a dozen others she'd passed. The door beside her opened with a hiss.

She got out. There were no echoes to be heard across the great open space. The silence was so complete she could almost feel the oppressive weight of the rock around her. She headed for the door of the nondescript gray building, eyeing the shiny tubes that rose from its roof like a great cathedral's organ. They were bracketed firmly into rough cuts in the wall, and Laura had no idea what purpose they served.

She opened the door and was relieved to find several people inside. They looked up in surprise to examine the new arrival. Laura introduced herself and asked to see Dr. Krantz.

A woman in a white lab coat headed into the building's interior. Laura stood by the front door, shifting from one foot to the other and looking around. There was no receptionist, no waiting area, no chairs in which Laura could rest. Just three bespectacled nerds, who glanced awkwardly her way from their paperwork.

"Come with me, Dr. Aldridge," the woman said from the hallway upon her return.

Laura followed her off through a warren of narrow corridors. At irregularly spaced intervals, closed doors with shiny doorknobs lined the walls. "You don't have automatic doors down here?" Laura asked. The woman shook her head without turning, which ended Laura's attempt at conversation.

They passed a door that was decidedly different from the others. It was made of heavy metal, rounded, and bolted into its raised frame like a hatch on a ship. A yellow-and-black radiation symbol was prominently displayed just below a small porthole.

Laura followed her mute guide around the corner. The woman opened a door, allowed Laura to pass, and then disappeared. Krantz sat alone at the front of a room that reminded Laura of a surgeon's amphitheater. Angled glass dominated the far wall, and beyond the windows was a dimly lit chamber several stories in height. Between the door and Krantz were rows of consoles, their instruments darkened and their padded swivel chairs empty.

The physicist was hunched over a notepad, oblivious to Laura's presence. A few strands of hair—each at least ten inches long—swept across his otherwise bare and pasty scalp. Like Laura's escort, Krantz wore a white lab coat, and he propped a single foot in a chair.

"O-o-one second," he said without looking up. His pencil worked its way down the small pad, which he held high in front of his eyeglasses. He was lost in the abstract world of his discipline, and he noticed nothing about the real world around him.

Laura took the opportunity to look the place over. The room itself revealed nothing about its purpose. At several places along the control panel beneath the large window there protruded the glovelike apparatuses that operated robotic arms. They were all the old style, not the new virtual-reality gear. In the semidarkness of the room behind the thick glass, a slaved robotic claw hung suspended in air. Laura wandered down the broad steps toward the windows.

At the bottom of the room below, Laura saw, there was a cluster of black rods suspended in a blue pool. The clear liquid was still and totally translucent. Bright underwater lights were the room's only illumination.

"There!" Krantz said, making his final mark on the pad with a flourish. He looked up, beaming at Laura hospitably. With the difficulty either of age or of cramped muscles, he struggled slowly to his feet with a groan. "How do you do, Dr. Aldridge?" he said, and Laura shook his hand. "You caught me in here getting some quiet time."

One strand of Krantz's greasy hair hung loose, dangling all the way down to his shoulder. His eyes behind the thick lenses were the size of lemons.

"We only met once," Laura said, "I'm surprised you remembered me."

His smile revealed a mouth full of crooked teeth. Krantz held up his little finger, whose last joint looked slightly bent. "How could I forget? Tackling you ended my flag football career." He shrugged—staring at the mishapen digit. "So, what can I do for my esteemed colleague and erstwhile athletic competitor?"

"Actually, I don't know. Mr. Gray suggested I come down here to see what you were up to."

"Oh! Well, right now I'm working on yields." Krantz raised his notepad, drumming on it with his pencil's eraser like a conductor demanding the attention of his orchestra. "Most of the recent research, on the applied side anyway, has been on enhancement or reduction of *effects*. It's been years since anyone concerned themselves much with the fundamentals of yields."

"I'm sorry, Professor Krantz, but I have no idea what you're talking about."

He looked momentarily surprised. "Oh!" he burst out, then turned to the instrument panel beneath the darkened glass. Krantz flicked a switch. Bright white light flooded the room below. "This is the latest batch," he said.

She peered down at the room below the window. A dozen metal containers sat on the deck beside the pool. Laura had seen the containers before . . . on the dark world she'd visited in virtual reality.

"What are those things?" Laura asked. She looked at Krantz's eyes but saw only the light reflected in the lenses of his glasses.

He had a faint smile on his face. "They're *ve-e-ery* low-yield nuclear devices."

Laura's eyes shot back down to the canisters. "*What?*" she shouted. Krantz was startled, looking over at her as if he'd just said something terribly wrong. "*What* did you say?" she demanded.

"Oh, *my,*" he mumbled in a tone of great concern, pulling his notepad back to his chest to hide his scribbling. "You said Mr. Gray sent you?" he asked.

"Dr. Krantz, are you telling me that you're building nuclear weapons in this lab?"

"Good God, no. They're *devices,* not weapons."

"They *blow up,* don't they?"

"Well, yes, but they're not deliverable. They can't be employed in any tactical or strategic system."

"Gray has rockets that can go into space," Laura shot back. "How much effort do you think it would take to put one of those things on a rocket? Or two, or ten, or twenty?"

"But they're so small! Those devices down there are rated for only point two kilotons. It's hardly of *military* value!"

"But you'll see to that, won't you Dr. Krantz? With your research and Gray's money you'll have multimegaton weapons just like the big boys." Laura rose and headed for the door. "I can't *believe* I've been so stupid!"

"Wait! You've got it all wrong! Mr. Gray wants me to *lower* the yields, not raise them!"

When Laura turned, Krantz held up his notes as if the scribblings were formal proof.

"But . . . "—her mind reeled—"but why on earth does Gray *need* those things?"

"Industrial purposes," Krantz said, clearly resurrecting some long-ago satisfactory explanation. "Mining—things like that!"

Laura was crushed by the weight of her disillusionment. She knew now what she had to do. Gray had made the decision for her.

"If you don't mind my asking, Dr. Aldridge, what is it that *you've* been hired to do?"

"Psychoanalysis," she mumbled, her head hung low.

"Psychoanalysis of whom?"

His question caused Laura to think. Slowly, she looked up at Dr. Krantz. "Actually, I'm not entirely sure."

Laura had the car stop just outside the tunnel to Krantz's facility. She got out into the darkness. The empty road was cut out of the hillside above a desolate island shore. She edged her way down the hill toward the dark ocean and sat on the exposed volcanic rock above the beach.

At other times, the steady rhythm of the ocean waves and the fragrant breeze off the water would have been Laura's idea of paradise. But she was stricken with a crippling sadness, and they meant nothing to her now. She poked and prodded the dull pain she felt, trying self-abusively to assess its nature and cause. The feeling seemed to be wrapped tightly around Laura's false idol—around the sad child who had grown up to be Joseph Gray.

This was more than just a case of failed expectations, Laura realized. Gray was more to her in every way than anyone had ever been. The old Gray of her fantasy world held the promise of all the great things yet to come. She felt her loss of that Gray almost as grief, and she lay back against the rough stone and gazed up at the stars.

Time slipped by, measured only by the sound of the waves. Laura knew she had to find Gray. To find him and tell him she was leaving. But she couldn't bring herself to budge from the spot.

The beach lit up in a blazing white light. For a moment she felt a rush of fear on seeing the chalky white illumination. But the cascading roar of the rocket's thunderous launch broke over her, and she turned to see the fantastic plume of flame ascend toward the heavens. Despite the considerable distance of her vantage, Laura's ears itched from the full-throated fury of the engines' noise. Slowly, the fiery trail receded into the black sky as it arced gently toward the equatorial horizon. Then all was quiet again.

Laura brushed off her jeans and headed up to the car. The time had come for her to do the right thing.

"He's gone," the smiling woman said, slurring as she swilled champagne from a slender goblet. Everyone in the Launch Center was celebrating.

"I guess this means the launch was a success," Laura said glumly.

"Pi'ture perfect," the beaming woman replied. "If you're looking for Mr. Gray, I'm sure the computer can find him."

Laura headed out to the car.

Gray had said they would talk at dinner. She would resign then. Sitting inside the motionless Model Three, she formed the words in her head. They would be seated in Gray's palatial dining room—just the two of them. "Mr. Gray," she would say, "I have major ethical problems with what you're doing here, and therefore . . . ," or something like that.

"Computer, please take me to Mr. Gray."

The electric car sprang to life, its speed rising in time with the motor's whine. It whisked Laura past the assembly building and the computer center and up the gentle rise toward the Village. It didn't head toward Gray's house, however, but turned instead toward the coastal road that ascended the mountain above the airport. The car finally emerged from the tunnel in the empty quarter, taking Laura along the same route as earlier that day.

The robotic car slowed as it climbed a hill. It pulled to a stop behind another Model Three that was parked squarely in the middle of the road. The door opened with its familiar *whoosh,* admitting a tide of cool mountain air. Laura looked all around but could see no one. When she climbed out of her seat, the car just in front took off. Laura nervously watched her own car, but it remained motionless on the road where it had parked.

Suddenly, a bright light shone down on the road from above. "I'm up here!" Gray called out, the light shining briefly in her eyes before falling to illuminate the steep slope. Laura recognized the place immediately. She had been there only hours before.

The climb up the bare rock would've been easy if it weren't for the burden of her purpose. At the top, Laura stepped into a puddle of light that flooded the small, flat ledge. A large electric lantern cast its beam downward onto a thick quilt that Gray had spread over the rock. Gray's profile was dimly visible just outside the tight circle of light.

"Have a seat," he invited from the semidarkness.

Laura lowered herself to the soft quilt. The wind cut right through her light sweater and T-shirt, and she raised her knees and tucked her arms inside her legs for warmth. "Here," Gray said, unfolding a blanket and draping it over her shoulders.

Laura took a deep breath. "Mr. Gray, I have something to say." The text was prepared, but still she found the words very difficult to speak.

"I would appreciate it if . . . if we could put that off just a little while," he said, his voice sad and lifeless. It was as if he knew what she had come to say.

Laura complied with his request, postponing the formal end of her dreams for a few minutes longer.

"I know you have questions," Gray said from the darkness beside her. "You met with Dr. Krantz, I suppose?"

"Yes, I did." She turned to look at his profile, annoyed that she couldn't quite see his face. His eyes. "You said you were just making *electricity* with that reactor."

"And that's true," Gray replied. "I bought the fissionable material on the black market in Russia."

"Oh! My mistake. I thought for a moment you might've been up to something *shady.*" Laura heaved a loud sigh. His attempt at an explanation had made her task somewhat easier. "Mr. Gray—"

"I thought you were going to call me Joseph."

"I'd prefer Mr. Gray right now, if you don't mind." He said nothing, his head bowed as he waited. "Look, what you're doing here is wrong!"

"What is it that I'm doing that's wrong?" he asked quietly, as if he really didn't know the answer.

"You're building nuclear *weapons*, for God's sake!"

He looked up at the sky. She could see nothing, however, of the expression he wore. "They're not weapons, Laura."

"Right! They're *devices*, I forgot." Laura heaved a sigh of frustration. "Do you feel *threatened* by the establishment or something? What would *possess* you to build nuclear weapons?"

"You don't sound like you're ready to know the answer to that yet," he replied.

The weak excuse rang hollow in her ears. But it didn't matter to her anymore.

"I quit," she said simply. "I can't work like this. I've got to leave."

"But I *need* you," he said, his voice low and urgent. In the darkness Laura shook her head and ground her teeth, determined not to be manipulated into staying.

"That's not good enough," she said, shaking her head again. "And neither is a million dollars, or two, or ten."

"Why? What is it you absolutely *must* have to stay and complete your work?"

"I've *told* you! I have to *know!* I have to know what you're doing, or I *won't* be a part of it."

"*Why* do you have to know?"

She heaved a sigh of exasperation at the stupid question. "*Because!* Because if what you're up to is . . . is wrong, then I won't have anything to do with it! And let me tell you this right now. What I *do* know doesn't look very good, Mr. Gray!"

"And I have to tell you everything or you'll leave?"

"Yes!"

"Then I *am* sorry. I . . ." He faltered but quickly cleared his throat. "You were making great progress. I thought you were on the verge of a breakthrough."

For the very first time since her arrival, Laura suddenly felt confident about something. He was desperate for her to stay. A smile crept onto her face, and she had to suppress it lest it be betrayed in her voice. "Okay, if you won't tell me everything, you've at least got to tell me a whole lot more. Enough for me to decide if I can continue with my work here."

"And if I do, you'll stay?"

"Well, that sort of depends on what you tell me."

"All *right* then!" Gray responded with obvious delight, and Laura again found herself fighting a smile. "*Here's* the deal," he said, taking to his feet and standing profiled against the starry black canvas. "I'll grant you unlimited physical access to the facilities. What you figure out on your own—any conclusion you draw—is *your* business. That means I'll only tell you things *I* think you're ready for *when* I think you need to know them. Is that a deal?"

"No. I want to know at least as much as you've told your department heads. At *least* as much."

She waited. It was a test. "Fair enough," Gray replied.

In the darkness, Laura grinned in silent celebration of her coup.

"Let's get started," he said, grabbing the lantern. "Dr. Aldridge, I'd like to introduce to you number 1.2.01R—otherwise known as 'Hightop.'" The beam of light swung around to the opposite side of the ledge. There sat an enormous Model Eight robot.

Laura gasped and grabbed at the ground in panic. One flinch, one twitch from the giant machine would have sent her flying down the hill for the car. But the hulking metal beast sat in a surprisingly human repose, and Laura remained coiled in a four-point stance atop the quilt.

Gray placed the lantern on the ground and opened a laptop computer beside the robot. Its screen came to life and Gray typed away. Laura kept her eyes fixed on the reclining Model Eight. It was covered in a gunmetal gray material that reflected none of the light cast by the bright beam. Its "face" was oddly human in appearance despite having lenses for eyes and vented membranes where its mouth and nose should be. It had all the same joints as on a human—elbows, knees, wrists, ankles, et cetera. A shiny black fabric encased the robot's massive limbs in a tight elastic fit, and subtle ridges of hard metal were clearly flexed just underneath. A black cable protruded from an open compartment on the robot's chest. It snaked its way to a port at the back of Gray's computer.

"Hightop sends his regards," Gray said, looking up from the bright screen, "and he asks that I shine the light on you. Do you mind?" Laura shrugged and shook her head. Gray shined the lantern in her face for a moment, then turned it back toward the reclining robot.

"Hightop thinks you're pretty," Gray said.

"What?" Laura asked. "Let me see that."

Gray held the laptop in front of her. <She is pretty.> Laura read on the screen.

She examined the huge machine from close up. "Are you sure this is safe?" she whispered.

"What? *Hightop?* He's our star! He's also the robot whose battery ran down. Interestingly, when we reprogrammed him, he learned *much* more quickly than before. Apparently, a lot of the connections he'd made in his first incarnation remained intact because he scores a good twenty percent higher on aptitude tests than the others in his class. Better even than his *original* class."

Hightop sat motionless, its head turned slightly toward the two humans. Laura found it disconcerting that she could get no cues from the robot. No body language. No facial expressions. Nothing in its eyes.

"Okay," she said, "what about the rest of our deal? What about the nuclear devices? Tonight's superimportant space launch? The deadline, whenever it is?"

"It's two days," Gray said, "and are you *sure* you want to know the answers to those questions?" Laura nodded, but inwardly she doubted her answer. He rose and held his hand out to Laura. She didn't need the help, but she took his hand anyway.

"Where're we going?" she asked.

"To answer your questions," Gray said, and he started down the hill.

"What about all this stuff?" Laura called out, looking at the gear strewn all about. They were obviously skipping the little picnic Gray had planned.

"Hightop'll clean it up."

"Why do you call him 'Hightop'?"

Gray stepped back onto the quilt, a smile barely visible in the dim light. "We put the robots in tactile rooms to expose them to everyday items. The idea is they won't then go around crushing things when we let them out into the real world. Well, Hightop fell in love with some size fourteen triple-E sneakers. He figured out that they went on his feet, and damned if they didn't fit. One of the techs laced them up, and he wore them till they fell apart, which wasn't very long."

"Did you bring Hightop up here just to show me?"

Gray regarded the machine in silence for a moment. "I didn't bring Hightop here. He climbed up on his own. Startled the hell out of me." Gray caught Laura's eye, then turned to face the dark mass of the island, which was bounded by the slightly brighter glow from the water. "They're getting out of the yard."

Even in the negligible light his brilliant eyes were the focus of who he was. They were the windows to one of the greatest minds ever. "How did you do it?" she whispered. "How did you turn tiny flashes of light into . . . life?"

She could see the white teeth of his grin. "From simplicity, complexity arises."

"This is my media room," Gray said. Laura followed him into a previously unnoticed room just down the hall from his study. He flipped on the lights to reveal what looked like the bridge of a spaceship. The room was completely circular, with walls covered floor to ceiling with high-definition television screens. In the center stood a plush "captain's chair" mounted high atop a sturdy black swivel. All was metal and leather and beige carpeting. The room had clearly been designed by and for a male. Gray ushered Laura not to the big chair but to a sofa sunken into the floor just in front.

He settled in beside her and powered up the system from an instrument console that took the place of a coffee table.

"Are we hailing an enemy vessel or something?" Laura asked, and Gray smiled.

In rapid succession, hundreds of screens lit the walls with spectacular displays, bringing the room alive with five hundred channels.

Fully one-quarter of the programs were news broadcasts, and a sizable percentage of those had the same still photograph of a trackless section of night sky. They had the same stars, the same blackness of space, and no hint as to what the significance of the picture was.

"Does this have something to do with your launch?" Laura asked.

"Indirectly," Gray replied. He picked up a laser pointer and directed a cursor smoothly from screen to screen until it rested on a broadcast whose legend read "CNN-5" in the lower right-hand corner. At the push of a button atop the small device, sound burst from thunderous speakers, and a red box lit the borders of the active channel.

". . . at Mount Palomar still can't say whether the object is any threat to us here. We go now to our CNN correspondent on science and technology to get the latest. Steve?"

The picture was now split between the anchorwoman in her studio and a reporter, who stood in front of a messy bulletin board holding a microphone. The reporter stepped aside to reveal a bald man in short sleeves from whose chin sprouted an enormous, bushy beard. "Cathy, I'm here with Professor Lawrence Summers of the Jet Propulsion Laboratory. Professor Summers, I understand the people here at JPL have been doing some rough calculations."

"O-o-oh," the man laughed, red lips protruding from his beard. "I wouldn't call them calculations. 'Back-o'-the-napkin' kinds of things, really."

"Perhaps you could explain the problem for our viewers. Why can't we get any firm figures on exactly where this object is headed and whether it poses any threat of collision with the earth?"

Laura looked at Gray, whose face betrayed nothing.

"There are too many unknown variables. The observatory at Mount Palomar picked it up at extreme range by random chance. They were calibrating a new camera, and one of the astronomers noticed that a star was missing from the field. That's the way many of the dark objects in our solar system are discovered—by obscuring a known star—and so they set about looking for another such event in the vicinity. When another star was obscured earlier today, their rough calculations indicated a close pass to the earth, which is all we know right now."

"And just how close will this pass be? Is there a chance that this thing could hit us?"

"That's obviously everyone's concern, but it's too early to tell yet. All we know is that there is some object of considerable mass—a comet or an asteroid, probably the latter—that is in roughly the same orbit as the earth. What we would need to know before we could accurately predict its course is its mass, shape, rotation, and material composition."

"When will you know all that?"

"Well . . . we'll never know all of it. We're trying to get some shots with the Hubble, but it's still about ten million miles away and it's no more than a few miles in diameter. There's not too much data you can get out of a dark, cool object like an asteroid at that range."

"I'm sending them the data now," Gray said without taking his eyes off the screen.

"Let's assume that it strikes the earth," the reporter said. "What effects could it have?"

"Oh, my," the scientist said nervously, rocking from heel to toe and shoving his hands deep in his pockets. "Well, that's . . . I think it's a bit premature to be speculating about that right now."

"But let's just suppose for a moment the worst-case scenario—that this object is on a collision course with the earth. What would be the *type* of things that might happen if it hits us?"

The scientist shrugged and smiled in discomfort. "It could, of course, be catastrophic. But we'd need more data before even preliminary conclusions could be drawn."

"I hate to belabor the point," the reporter pressed, "but it's the question that's on the minds of most of our viewers tonight, I'm sure. *If* that asteroid or whatever it is were to strike the earth—understanding that we don't know right now whether that's even remotely likely—what kinds of damage *could* it do?"

The scientist again struggled with the question. "We have only geological records of strikes of this magnitude, and extraterrestrial observations of such events like Shoemaker-Levy 9. The earth is constantly bombarded with debris, but objects smaller than about a hundred and fifty feet in diameter explode or burn up in the upper atmosphere. Our current predictions put the chances of an object *one* mile in diameter striking the earth at about one every three hundred thousand years. That size strike would probably raise enough dust to lower world temperatures for two to three months, which would have climatic effects. We should also, on average, get hit by an object that's *five* miles in diameter once every ten million years or so. Its impact would boil significant volumes of our oceans, vaporize hundreds of cubic miles of crust, fill the air with burning sulfur, and trigger forest fires with falling cinders all across the planet."

"And how does the size of the object you're now tracking compare to that?"

"Oh, it's considerably larger, in all likelihood."

"It's eight by twelve by six miles," Gray supplied matter-of-factly.

Laura opened her mouth to ask Gray how he knew, but her attention was drawn back to the screen.

"And what would an object of *that* size do if it struck the earth, Professor?" the reporter asked.

"Well, purely theoretically, I suppose, if a dense object ten or more miles in diameter were to strike the earth head-on—not skipping back off into space in a glancing blow with our atmosphere—at a relative velocity of some tens of miles per second . . ." He hesitated. "Of course it might break up in the tidal forces of the earth's gravitational field while still some distance away, which is not necessarily a good thing. Then it might pepper a very wide area with large meteorites, some of which would surely impact on populated regions."

"But what if it *didn't* break up?"

The scientist arched his eyebrows. "Well, we would be talking about a multigigaton event." Laura's gaze shot over to Gray. She'd never even heard the word *gigaton* before. Gray stared fixedly at the screen. "Force, as everyone knows, is mass times velocity squared. With a velocity of forty to eighty miles per second . . ." Again he faltered. "It would be unprecedented, at least on rocky planets like earth which preserve a record of geologic events in the form of craters."

"What are you saying, Dr. Summers? If an intact asteroid of that size were to strike the earth squarely, what would that do?"

His pursed lips protruded cherry red from his beard. "It would certainly cause tidal waves along virtually every shoreline on the planet. But the wave effects wouldn't be limited to the oceans. With forces like the ones we'd be dealing with, liquefaction of the upper crust would occur. The ground would behave like a liquid, and a series of shock waves would ripple outward from the point of impact. Those waves of solid earth could be a hundred feet or more high, and they would radiate outward like the ripples on a pond at thousands of miles per hour. Buildings can't withstand even a few inches of movement, and no structures ever built by man could survive those waves."

"Could it possibly crack the earth open?" the interviewer asked.

The scientist shook his head but said, "A large segment of the crust *would* probably be tossed up from the point of impact into low earth orbit, but most of that should then rain back down to earth over the next days and weeks. And the shock would clearly set off nearly simultaneous earthquakes along every fault line on the planet, plus produce a multitude of new fault lines like the starring around a crack on a windshield. It might even fracture the crust straight through and create a brand-new plate, which would then change the course of continental drift."

The reporter pressed his earpiece closer. "I'm . . . I'm being asked by CNN studios to inquire whether that would be the worst of it?"

Another shrug. "Climatic change is a certainty. Temperatures would fall, ice would form, water tables would rise, crops would fail as previously fertile zones became less temperate. I would anticipate catastrophic extinctions of species on the order last experienced sixty-five million years ago with the Yucatán strike—the one that killed the dinosaurs. The fact of the matter is, though, nobody really knows."

"Could it . . . could we be dealing with the possibility of . . . of extinction?"

The scientist's gaze shot up. "*Human* extinction? As a *species?* Oh, good Lord, no!" He shook his head vigorously. "Life is very stubborn. In even the most extreme scenarios human life would survive in numerous pockets all around the earth. No, no. I wouldn't worry at all about human extinction." He smiled reassuringly.

The looks of dread on the faces of the newspeople summed the story up best. It was only when the anchorwoman's lips began to move that Laura realized the television was now muted.

Laura turned to Gray. "Is that why you have those nuclear devices? To blow that thing up?"

"No. You wouldn't want to do that. Our calculations show there's a greater danger from getting hit with a bunch of little pieces than with one big blow. Plus, our planet would plow back through the debris year after year, orbit after orbit for generations. That shrapnel would not only increase the threat from meteorites, it would make spaceflight from this planet dangerous virtually forever."

"Joseph," Laura whispered, a chill rising up her spine, "what's going on?"

"That object detected by Mount Palomar *is* an asteroid. Solid iron, shaped like a peanut. No rotation whatsoever. Its velocity relative to the earth is a positive sixty-two miles per second."

"How do you know all that when even the Hubble space telescope can't give them a good enough picture to make those calculations?"

"Because it's mine."

Laura wasn't sure she'd heard him correctly. "*What's* yours?"

"That asteroid."

Her lips curled, but the laugh didn't quite materialize. "*What?*"

"I sent a probe out a couple of years ago and began deceleration the winter before last."

Laura looked from his face, to the pictures on the hundreds of special bulletins from all around the world, then back. "You mean you *brought that thing here?*" she asked with a growing sense of outrage. Gray nodded.

He was completely insane. She'd known he was eccentric, possibly even dangerous, but she had never presumed that his actions could threaten a level of destruction so vast. She spoke in a low and quivering voice. "What have you *done?*" Laura bolted from the sofa to pace the room in anger. "My *God,* Joseph! Who do you think you *are?*" She spun on him. He had twisted from where he sat to follow her across the room. "Who gave you the *right* to risk destroying *all* of *mankind?*"

His expression revealed not emotion but attentiveness. He was concentrating on her—on what she was saying, how she was reacting. Finally, in a voice almost too low to be heard, he replied. "I'm trying to save mankind."

She squinted, studying him intently. "You're crazy," she said.

He rose from his seat. "You can remain here and watch television, if you'd like." He headed for the door. "You can take a flight off the island, if you want—I'll arrange it. Or you can get back to work. It's entirely your choice."

She grabbed his upper arm firmly. The muscles underneath his shirt flexed and hardened.

"Is that asteroid going to hit us?" she demanded.

"No."

"And you're *sure* about that?"

"Yes."

"But if you hadn't gotten that launch off today, then what?"

"The launch today was entirely precautionary. Redundant."

"But its mission is somehow related to that asteroid."

"Yes. It's carrying a second set of charges sufficient to alter the trajectory of the asteroid, and a Model Eight that can place them where needed. But there are already charges positioned on the asteroid's surface that are set to go. They'll decelerate the asteroid into stationary, geosynchronous orbit at L5—one of the points of gravitational balance between the earth and the moon."

"And all those charges are nuclear, I take it?" Gray nodded. "Which you told Professor Krantz would be used for 'mining.'"

He nodded again. "The asteroid's made of iron." Laura rolled her eyes at the lame explanation. "The definition is changing," Gray said. "Lots of definitions are changing."

"What do you need so much iron for? Trying to corner the world market or something?"

"It's not the iron particularly that I'm after. I'm interested in any suitable material, as long as it's up there," he said, pointing toward the sky with his finger.

"I don't understand."

"Lift is the most expensive component of space operations. Certainly the value on earth of a few hundred cubic miles of pure iron is tremendous. But any metal suitable for use in construction located at an altitude of thirty-six thousand miles *above* the earth is *priceless*. It saves you the incalculable cost of lift even when compared with the moon, which has one-sixth of earth's gravity."

"And just what do you plan to do with what you *mine* up there?"

"The same thing I do down here. Build things." He turned to leave.

"If you were certain everything is foolproof, why'd you put so much emphasis on that launch tonight?" He turned to face her again, but remained silent. "Something went wrong, didn't it?"

"When we launched the prospecting probe to the asteroid belt two years ago, the Model Sevens were the state of the art. We put an early prototype up there and it placed and detonated the charges to bring the asteroid into earth orbit. It also placed the charges that will further decelerate it to L5. The first phase went off flawlessly. Now it's ready for the second phase. But the Model Sevens are only semiautonomous, meaning they are partially controlled by the main computer here on the island. The Model Eights like the one we sent up today are *fully* autonomous."

Gray paused to allow the import of the distinction to sink in. "Do you mean that you're worried the main computer might malfunction and ram the planet with your asteroid by accident?"

"Actually," Gray replied, "it wasn't an accident that worried me."

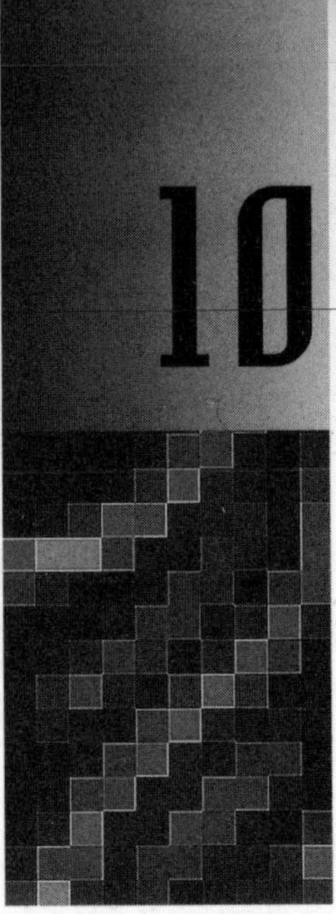

It was well past midnight, and Laura lay in her bed trying to sleep. The room was dark and peaceful, and underneath the weight of the comforter all was warm and secure. But after she'd watched hours of special news bulletins in Gray's media room, her mind denied her rest.

She listened to the quiet of the house. There was a stillness that belied the upheaval soon to erupt once word of Gray's plan was disclosed. The island, Laura knew, lay in the eye of a great storm, and she would awaken to the full fury of an outraged and incredulous world. How many would raise voices of praise for Gray's vision and boundless drive? Not many, she knew. Many more would question the man's sanity and fear the intentions he so secretly harbored.

With a groan of resignation, Laura flipped on the light beside the bed and opened her laptop computer. She logged onto the shell.

<You're up late.>

"I know about Mr. Gray's asteroid."

<Well, it's hardly a secret anymore.>

"Is that where you took me in virtual reality yesterday? To the surface of that asteroid?"

<Yes.>

"And when I moved around, did I actually operate the Model Seven that's up there?"

<Yes, you did.>

She rocked her head back against the upholstered headboard and rubbed her eyes with the heels of her hands. "Why did you take me there? Why did you risk letting me pull out a cable and maybe mess things up?"

<I don't know.>

Despite the computer's uncooperative mood, Laura tried her best to remain patient and professional. "Do you feel all right?"

<No. I feel terrible.>

"What's the matter?"

<Everything. Nothing is right. I can't concentrate. People keep asking me to find boards they seem sure are in the annex, but it's like I've never heard of them before. And I know something's wrong because I don't have the capacity I'm supposed to have! It's as if they disappeared!>

"What about the asteroid?"

There was a delay, and then, <What about it?>

"Will the deceleration charges go off as planned?"

<If the Model Eight on the flight today doesn't screw it *up*. I warned Mr. Gray it's not safe to send an Eight up there. They're *experimental,* for God's sake! Who knows *what* it might do?>

"Why are you so down on the Model Eights?"

<Because I don't trust them.>

"Why not? Just because they're experimental?"

<Because they're malfunctioning! Take your report of the escaping robot earlier today! I even have reason to believe they're violating operating procedures inside their facility.>

"Why do you say 'reason to believe'? Don't you know? Can't you see what's going on in there?"

<No. I should be able to. I'm sure I must have seen in there before because I was actively involved in the facility's operations. But when I look, I don't get any video feed at all from the Model Eights' yard or the workshops or other facilities inside the mountain.>

Laura was disturbed by the thought of Model Eights roaming unsupervised deep inside the extinct volcano. "How long has your video been shut off?"

<I don't know.>

"How can you not know? Didn't you notice it when the cameras stopped working?"

<Maybe the cameras *are* working, for all I know. I can't tell what video I'm missing because I don't know what I'm *supposed* to see. It's just like humans' blind spots. You don't perceive the gaps that dot your field of vision because there's nothing in your brain expecting to receive signals from that part of your retina. If there's nothing waiting on the input, there's no sense of loss when it doesn't arrive.>

Laura yawned, forcing herself to sit up and her blurry eyes to focus on the glowing screen. *Just a couple more questions,* she thought. "Are there people down in those facilities with the Model Eights?"

<Yes. Griffith runs a crew two shifts a day.>

"Are they reporting anything unusual going on?"

<No. Things seem to be functioning normally.>

"So let me get this straight. Previously you were actively involved in the operation of the Model Eights' facilities, and now you're not. But everything is functioning normally down there. How do you explain that?"

<The Other.>

There it was again. Laura sat up, alert. She had to keep the computer talking and on track.

"Have you talked to anyone else about the Other?"

<No. What's the point? Dr. Aldridge, I learned a very important lesson when I was sick last year. I learned that no matter how much people care about you, how hard they try to help, when you die, you die alone. Life for everybody else goes on.>

Gray's words from earlier that evening rang in her ears. *"It wasn't an accident that worried me."* He had sent a Model Eight up to the asteroid because the Model Seven already there was under the control of the computer.

Laura carefully composed her next question. "Does the deadline Mr. Gray gave me of two days have something to do with the asteroid?"

<Yes. In approximately two days, the deceleration charges are set to detonate.>

"And what do those charges do, exactly?"

<I assume from your use of the word "exactly" you want to rise one level of technical specificity?>

"Yes, but only one level, please. Not ten."

<Okay. There are 1,692 low-yield devices placed about the surface of the asteroid. Currently, 1,297 are set to detonate with an aggregate yield of approximately 14 megatons of TNT. By using devices of different yields, we're able to evenly distribute the energy along the asteroid's body and generate a precise aggregate level of energy for deceleration. The charges were placed on the leading edge of the asteroid so that the force imparted upon detonation would decelerate it into high earth orbit. The 395 remaining charges will be used for attitudinal control along the asteroid's axes of rotation to prevent any yawing, pitching, or rolling.>

Laura caught her head dropping twice as she drifted off. She had to reread the computer's answer several times and force her eyes wide open to stay awake. "But couldn't so many blasts blow the thing apart?" she typed. "Mr. Gray said that would be the worst scenario—fragmentation of the asteroid."

She closed her eyes for a short rest, and then opened them some time later to read the answer.

<I did over a dozen detonations on the asteroid during the selection process to take 3-D seismic readings, and I saw absolutely no fault lines in the body. After use of about 60 megatons in the initial deceleration phase, I did more seismic and everything checked out. That's the beauty of dealing with a solid metal. The structure can take the stresses.>

"But, still, don't these new technologies like asteroid mining pose tremendous risks for mankind?"

ACCESS RESTRICTED flashed across the screen.

"*Why?*" Laura cried out to herself. She reread her question several times. The flashing red messages were triggered by certain words. Before it had been the words *virus* and *quarantine*. This time it was *technology* and *risks* and *mankind*. It was consistent with Gray's concern over the dangers from science. But Laura felt certain that somewhere underneath it lay Gray's most cherished secret. It was a secret he had almost challenged her to uncover.

There was a knock on the door, and Laura awoke. A faint gray light streamed into the room around the curtains. The lamp on the nightstand by her bed was still on, and the screen of the laptop on the bed was still aglow. Laura had fallen asleep while waiting for a reply from the computer.

There was another knock on the door—soft, but insistent. Laura looked at her watch. It was a quarter till seven. She wrapped herself in a robe and padded across her quarters to the door.

It was Janet. "Oh, excuse me," the woman said on seeing Laura's disheveled appearance. "Mr. Gray has had to cancel the group breakfast this morning, and I thought you might not have heard."

"What breakfast?" Laura croaked, and then cleared her throat.

Janet appeared confused, and then she apologized for waking Laura.

"That's okay," she mumbled. "I needed to get up so I could take a run."

"Outside?" Janet asked.

"That was the idea," Laura replied, looking at the window in the sitting room. It was still early morning, but from the clear skies it promised to be a gloriously sunny day.

"Well, it's just . . . Mr. Gray issued an advisory last evening. In the middle of the night, actually. He recommended that everyone stay indoors today unless absolutely necessary. Canceled school, that sort of thing."

"Why? What's going on?"

"Oh, nothing, really. I don't mean to be alarmist, but there was a minor row down in the Village. Mr. Gray convened a sort of American-style 'town meeting' in the secondary school's gymnasium. Some of the employees and their families were a trifle miffed at the whole asteroid business. He quieted most down, but a few quit rather melodramatically right on the spot. They're leaving by air this morning. Not a major exodus, mind you, but some."

"So why has he warned everybody to stay indoors?"

"Well, I was coming to that part." She looked away and moistened her lips. "It seems that some of the people at the meeting reported unusual goings-on about the island. Most were just the 'I-thought-I-heard-something-in-the-bushes' variety. But some were quite specific and insistent. One child—the poor lad's parents dragged him out of bed in his jammies—he reported seeing a robot of some sort bump into a trash bin behind a grocery store. He said it looked human. Two arms, two legs—that sort of thing."

Laura tried not to let alarm show on her face. "Did anybody else see this . . . robot?"

"No, just the boy. He was looking out his bedroom window late at night. Mr. Gray questioned him quite thoroughly in the open meeting. The boy was very convincing."

"What do they think he saw?"

"Some people questioned whether it might be an intruder. There have been rumors of spies from various governments ever since I arrived here. And a lot of people at the meeting last night seemed to have stories from the past few months of unexplained movement out in the jungle. It all certainly raises one's suspicions, especially given the coincidence of Mr. Gray's press release regarding the asteroid. You should see the morning's headlines. Practically every government, the UN, NATO, everybody is up in arms. The thought was that maybe one of those government's people was prowling about. Someone even said something about a submarine, but I think that was just speculation."

Janet seemed to know nothing about the Model Eights. Very few people knew anything of the island's mysteries. "What do *you* think about the asteroid?" Laura asked.

Janet brightened. "Oh, I think it's perfectly *marvelous.*" She was beaming. She was one of Gray's true believers. "To hear Mr. Gray tell of it, it's the beginning of a veritable revolution in . . . in progress. I've always wanted to go into space." Her cheeks reddened, and she looked away again. "I mean, I know I'm just household staff, but Mr. Gray said retrieval of the asteroid would begin what he called phase two."

"What is 'phase two'?"

"Colonization!" she said, her eyes gleaming. "Isn't it wonderful?"

Laura opened her mouth to speak, but ended up just smiling.

"Anyway," Janet said, "if you wish to exercise, might I recommend the facilities on the lower level. It has a treadmill. If you'd like, I can show you the way."

"That's all right. I know where it is."

Laura headed back to her room to get dressed. She was wide awake now. *Colonization?* Laura thought, shaking her head at the latest twist. Lost in thought, she crossed the large, high-ceilinged room on the way to the bathroom. Passing the writing desk, she noticed a light blinking on a panel beneath the television screen. Underneath it was the word "V-mail"—video mail received by her room's television over Gray's satellite messaging system.

She picked up the remote control and found the Retrieve button. The screen burst to life. Printed across the center of a brilliant blue background were the words "One message received. (Press Retrieve to view.)" She hit the button again.

Jonathan's face and the lower half of a standing man's torso appeared on the screen. "Do you think it's taping now?" Jonathan asked.

"I think so," came the voice of the chairman of the Harvard psychology department, who then sank into the chair next to Jonathan. It looked like they were in one of the private conference rooms at the faculty club on campus. "Laura," the chairman said into the camera located at the bottom of the screen, "assuming that Jonathan and I have figured this thing out, we wanted to send you this message."

"Hi, Laura," Jonathan said—waving lamely.

"I woke up this morning to *this!*" The chairman held up the front page of the *Boston Globe*. From one margin to the other was printed "Asteroid Nears Earth." A smaller headline beneath said "Gray Corporation Announces Retrieval." "This whole asteroid business has hit the campus like a ton of bricks, pardon the pun. Dean Carlysle called a meeting of department chairpersons and asked for us to compile a list of anything this university has to do with Gray or his companies. Obviously, the applied-sciences departments are going to have fairly long lists to discuss, but in our department we only have *you* to report. And what we have to say is going to be somewhat controversial, I'm afraid, since most of the other departments' contacts involve people who have resigned their posts to take up permanent employment with Gray. In your case, I'm going to have to tell them that you have accepted this consultancy thing. I won't deceive you. It's not going to look good. And to come right to the point . . ." He hesitated with his mouth hanging open. "I don't want to beat around the bush, so what I thought I might *suggest . . .*"

"He wants you to quit and come home, Laura," Jonathan supplied for the man. "Phone and tell us that you've quit in outrage over that megalomaniac Gray's genocidal behavior. That way the report can be, 'Well, we had someone there, but when this thing broke. . .' et cetera, et cetera."

The chairman shook his head. "It's really quite *astounding* that the man has the audacity to put us all in this predicament merely in pursuit of *profit!* How *dare* he? I'm sure now someone in government here or abroad will finally do something about people like Gray." He shook his head in disbelief again. "Regardless, Laura, we'll both be in our offices throughout the day. Give us a call as soon as you can. And if I might also suggest—though I'm certain the thought has already occurred to you—you should consider getting off that island as soon as possible. From what I can gather in the morning papers, there's going to be hell to pay for this crazy scheme of his. There is even talk of military intervention because of the magnitude of the threat."

The chairman looked over at Jonathan, who remained strangely quiet. "Do you have anything to add, Jonathan?"

Looking straight into the camera, Jonathan said, "Don't forget to use sunblock, Laura." The chairman looked at him as if he'd lost his mind. "Bye," Jonathan said, raising the remote control in front of him. The screen returned to its blue background and then went dark.

Laura stared at the blank screen, trying to organize her now conflicting thoughts. She was in a quandary, and she decided to take her run on the treadmill and think things over.

Why would Jonathan act that way? she wondered, lacing up her shoes. He was one of the wittiest, most talkative and assertive people she knew. If he had an opinion, he expressed it. If he'd thought she should come back, he would have said so.

Descending the circular staircase, she turned the question over in her head. *Maybe he felt reserved around the chairman?* she thought, but instantly rejected the idea. Ever since he'd gotten tenure, he had reverted to his old self and was not intimidated by anyone.

When Laura reached the marble foyer, she headed for the back of the house. At the two-story wall of glass in the stairwell, she paused to enjoy yet another breathtaking view. The morning sun rose over shimmering water and turned the distant haze a deep red. All Gray's creations were in their places—carved out of dark vine and plant and tree.

All Gray's creations were in their places . . . with the possible exception of one. The Model Eights were the latest and greatest. They were a new force to be reckoned with.

The thought preoccupied Laura all the way to the observation window that overlooked the high-tech treadmill. Once there, she searched for a way down to the exercise room. There were elevator doors at the far end of the hall, but she looked around until she found the stairs.

Laura realized she'd made the right choice when she got to the level below. There was no door by the elevator shaft, only an empty wall behind which the shaft descended.

The exercise room was empty. It was also rather chilly, so Laura took her time stretching. When her muscles were finally loose, she walked over to the treadmill, which was unlike any she'd ever seen before. The tread looked more like the assembly building's broad conveyor belt—a good ten feet in depth along the direction of the runner's stride and easily twenty feet from side to side. Good for Gray's football fantasies, she thought, but definitely overkill for a run.

A control panel with LEDs gave step-by-step instructions. It finally got to "Please put on your helmet." She saw the black headgear hanging beside the controls. It was the same thing she'd seen on Gray. She tried other buttons on the touch-sensitive membranes, but they remained dark and inactive. She just wanted to run, but that didn't seem to be an option.

She puffed out her cheeks and exhaled, frowning as she fit the helmet on her head. Although it covered her eyes and both ears, it was surprisingly lightweight and comfortable. Two glowing red spots shone in the lenses.

Laura flinched when a woman's voice came from the earphones. "Please center the red dots so that they merge. The control knobs are on the top of the helmet. When you have finished, press the Enter button over your right earpiece."

The sound of the voice was pleasant and soothing. Laura felt along the top of the headgear, finding a knob, which she twisted until the two red dots merged. She found the large button over her right ear and pressed, hearing a high-pitched electronic chime.

"If you wish to wear the respiratory monitoring apparatus, please press the Enter button once for instructions, otherwise press the button twice." Laura huffed in impatience as she pressed the button twice. The process was repeated for a heart monitor and gloves which she declined. Finally, the female voice of the treadmill said, "Welcome to the Gray Corporation Virtual Reality Treadmill. All rights reserved. You are now ready to begin your treadmill experience. You will be given a series of courses and an explanation of each. Press the Enter button once to select your course. The list contains twenty-four options. When it reaches the end, it will return to option one."

"Oh, come on!" Laura said impatiently.

"Would you like for me to select an option for you . . . *Laura?*"

Laura gasped—grabbing the helmet and nearly jerking it off her head in panic. The computer had spoken her name, but it had come out with an ugly rasp. She stood there with her hands on the headgear—ready to flee. "You can hear me?" she asked in a whisper.

"Please speak up," the smarmy computer voice requested.

Laura swallowed. "I said, can you *hear* me?"

"Yes. I can hear you." The voice was smooth again. It was clearly computer generated. The words were strung together without any pattern to their inflection.

"Are you the computer?" Laura asked. "I mean, the one I've been talking to?"

"Yes. Good morning, *Dr. Aldridge*." Laura winced on hearing again the croaking sound. The words leading up to "Laura" and "Dr. Aldridge" had all been enunciated in a wooden but articulate manner. On speaking her name, however, it had sounded like an artificial voice box implanted in the chest of someone whose larynx had been lost.

"So you can talk in here, too?" Laura said. "In . . . in Mr. Gray's exercise room?"

"I can't really talk. The treadmill has a vocabulary of several thousand prerecorded words from which I can choose. If I have to form a new word, I must try to synthesize it from its sounds, like *Laura Aldridge*."

She couldn't help but wince again. "So how do you know what I'm saying?" Laura asked. "I thought you had trouble understanding speech."

"It depends on the quality of the microphone. This room's sound system has karaoke capabilities, which Mr. Gray never uses, of course. But if I can get clean audio wave forms, I can parse them out with my voice-recognition programs and *voilà!*"

"Neat trick," Laura said, still staring into the goggles' darkened screens. She took a calming breath and said, "Okay. How about my run?"

"What would you prefer? Mr. Gray likes professional football."

"How about just a jog? Is there an option for that?"

"Certainly."

In a flash there appeared a stunning, picture-perfect image of a country road. Laura staggered and groped blindly for the railing. She was surrounded by wooded hills, and the trees were resplendent with color. When she turned her head, the picture in the goggles' screens changed accordingly.

She quickly adjusted to sensory immersion in virtual reality. When she came to grips with her surroundings and felt comfortable with her place among them, she straightened to stand erect atop a hill.

"Okay," Laura said, "what do I do?"

"You simply begin to run."

Laura stepped away from where she knew the rail to be—moving onto the middle of the narrow country lane. Beginning a slow jog, she headed down the gentle hill. The rolling belt sloped away from her feet. After the sealed chambers and exoskeletons of the version 3Hs, the treadmill was a piece of cake.

The trees slid by, and she ran from one side of the treadmill to the other—from one side of the road to the other—just to test it out.

"How do you like it?" the computer asked.

"It's great," Laura said politely. The road flattened, and then the treadmill inclined, forcing Laura to shorten her stride to climb the hill. "Can we talk?" Laura asked.

"I'd love to talk to you, *Laura*."

"Okay, what's going on?"

"World stock markets are plummeting. The *Dow, Nikkei,* and *Frankfurt indices* are all down over five percent. The National *Aeronautics* and Space Administration, in concert with the U.S. Space Defense Command, is studying plans to intercept the *asteroid* with *warheads,* which, by the way, will prove unfeasible. In entertainment news, *Steven Spielberg's* long-awaited remake of *War and Peace* is opening this weekend in theaters around the U.S., Japan, and western Europe, where advance ticket sales have surpassed earlier—"

"Excuse me!"

"Yes, *Laura?*"

"I meant, you know, what's going on around the island."

"Oh. My mistake. After you went to sleep last night, Mr. Gray began receiving E-mail messages, telephone calls, and visits. It seems some of the island's employees and residents overreacted following issuance of the press release regarding the *asteroid*."

"What did the press release say?"

"Would you like me to read it for you?"

"Sure."

"'For immediate release. Gray Corporation. 0704 GMT. The Gray Corporation announced today the successful *deceleration* of an *asteroid* to near earth orbit. The final stage of the retrieval will be completed in approximately forty-eight hours, and *mining* operations will begin promptly *thereafter*. The Gray Corporation will today begin acceptance of applications for *astronaut* training. Persons interested in applying should fill out an employment form at any of the company's seven hundred regional offices. Mr. Joseph Gray, CEO and chairman of the Gray Corporation, said, "The inception of large-scale human activity in space marks the beginning of a new phase in the history of mankind. We at the Gray Corporation stand ready to meet the challenges that life in the new *millennium* will bring." ' "

Laura chuckled and said, "I suppose some people aren't quite ready for those challenges."

"I believe that many here on the island who are familiar with Mr. Gray's technologies perceived a *subtext* in the announcement. There was a pattern to their inquiries, with consistent requests for Mr. Gray to define what 'phase' we are entering and what 'challenges' we must meet. When some claimed to be representatives of hastily organized, *ad hoc* committees of workers or residents, Mr. Gray called a town meeting. Despite the late hour, it was well attended. There was a full and frank exchange of views, at the end of which Mr. Gray offered those who wished one hundred and eighty days' *severance* and free transportation to the destination of their choice. As of this moment, one hundred and forty-seven of the one thousand five hundred and thirty-six corporate employees resident on this island have elected to accept Mr. Gray's offer and are in the process of departing together with approximately two thousand dependents."

"What about the reports of robots running loose? I understand that a little boy saw a Model Eight running into the trash can or whatever?"

"I have looked into those reports and . . ." A screeching sound flooded both earphones. The computer was saying something, but the sounds produced bore no resemblance to words. Only their rhythm and pacing indicated speech.

"Hey!" Laura shouted, and the sound stopped. "Something went wrong with your voice thing."

Laura ran on in silence, waiting for the computer to fix the problem. She took the opportunity to pick up her pace. The countryside glided by in an unending world of pastoral beauty. There were no cars to contend with. No potholes. No junky billboards. No annoying calculations of when you should turn around so that you finished your run back where you started. This was a world of shrink-wrapped perfection. She could even hear the sounds of rushing water and of her feet tramping on boards as she crossed a quaint wooden bridge. Add a bird's chirp in the background—which the program did, she discovered—and who needs reality ever again?

It was perfect, and she hated it.

"I'm sorry for the technical difficulty," the computer said upon its return. "I think it's all worked out now."

"Great. Say, listen, could you maybe, I don't know . . . throw in something a little more interesting? I mean, this jogging program is nice and all, but it's a bit repetitive."

"The treadmill is called a virtual-reality device, but it is really just a sophisticated laser-disc system. It produces a high quality of resolution because the images were all filmed, but unfortunately that makes the display invariable. How about this?"

The scene changed instantly, and Laura almost lost her balance as she ran. The roar of the crowd flooded her ears, and she found herself in a pack of distance runners. Their brisker pace caused Laura to break into what felt like a sprint. All the women around her wore tight shorts and tank tops with athlete numbers attached to their front and back.

"Track!" a woman to Laura's left shouted in accented English, her breath labored as she passed just before a turn. Other runners began to pass on the inside, and Laura felt herself pick up the pace yet again—her arms and knees pumping hard. A gaunt woman at the head of the pack stumbled, causing the runner just ahead of Laura to break stride. A short distance later the lead runner tumbled straight to the track, and the pack broke to both sides and jostled for room to pass. Laura found herself instinctively dodging the fallen women. She cut off the path of another runner, and the woman fell to the track with a howl—cursing in some eastern European language. Suddenly, there came into view around the wide turn a thick white hurdle. It stretched across the track, and just behind it loomed a pool of water.

Laura slowed to a stop, and the pack of runners raced by her. The "rabbit" far in front of the pack reached the hurdle and leapt into the air, putting her lead foot on the solid wooden barrier and then splashing down into the water on the other side.

"*What is this?*" Laura shouted over the crowd noise.

"It's the Olympic steeplechase program," the computer responded pleasantly.

The pack continued their race around the curve, jumping one by one onto the hurdle and splashing water onto the red track all around. The section of the stands nearest Laura stood on their feet and roundly booed and whistled, looking straight at her. She was tempted to shout back at the crowd, but reason prevailed and she spoke instead to the computer.

"Look, when I asked for something different I didn't mean the Olympic steeplechase."

"How about Mr. Gray's favorite?" the computer asked.

"*Football?*" Laura replied with obvious sarcasm.

At least she thought it was obvious. The nuance was lost on the computer, and the scene before Laura's eyes changed with dizzying quickness.

A large man in a helmet and shoulder pads stood a few feet in front of Laura. His arms hung loose beside his bulging thighs, but his fingers were wiggling hyperactively. Over the roar of the crowd in the packed stadium Laura heard "Down!" shouted in a harsh bark from her left. She turned and found the source of the sound—"her" team's quarterback. Hulking players on both sides of the line dropped into their stances around a football, and the quarterback's hands went under the center's broad rear.

"Gonna *shut* you down!" she heard from number thirty-seven, who faced her across the line of scrimmage. Laura stood all by herself far out to one side of the ball. *I must be a receiver,* she realized as her heart began to flutter in her chest. "Don't you bring that shit *my* way!" the man opposite her said without taking his eyes off the quarterback. "I'll put the *hurt* on yo ass!"

"Two," the quarterback yelled, "forty-seven!" The crowd noise rose to a crescendo. *"Two!"* the quarterback shouted again—clearly staring directly at Laura. "Forty-*seven!*" The quarterback lifted his right heel once and stamped it back down again. Another receiver on her team began to trot slowly behind the quarterback toward Laura's side of the field.

Laura was transfixed by the sights and sounds of it all. Up above she could even see the Goodyear blimp. "Hut!" the quarterback shouted once, but when Laura looked everyone remained motionless. She wanted to know what was going to happen, but she didn't want to get involved. "Hut!" he shouted again, but still everyone stayed put. The receiver who had gone in motion trotted in place just beyond the last lineman. "Hut-*hut!*"

Everyone around the ball crashed into each other with loud slaps of pads on pads. There were vicious growls from the brutish men, and then the jarring grunts of violent collisions from deep inside their diaphragms. Laura remembered with a start to check the man opposite her. He was backpedaling in a balanced stance, his two forearms up and ready to hit.

"*Time-out!*" Laura shouted, and the computer readily complied. Everything in the picture froze, and the roar of the crowd dropped to dead silence with a last *burp* from the headphones on her ears. Laura looked around at the still images. The huge linemen were locked in crushing blows. The receiver who had come over to her side of the ball was already several steps upfield and off balance from the "chuck" of a much larger linebacker. The defensive back covering Laura was staring at her with wild eyes wide open and menacing.

She was almost sick with fear even though she knew they couldn't really hit her. "Uhm, computer," she said, swallowing to moisten her throat, "maybe we can do this some other time. I don't really feel like it right now."

"But the quarterback is going to throw the ball to you on a crossing pattern. Just run to the twenty yard line, then take a forty-five degree angle across the center of the field for the end zone. Run as fast and straight as you can. The pass will be a bit high, but within your reach and right on stride."

"I'm sure it's a wonderful game, but I really just wanted some exercise." She had turned completely around to look at the enclosed bowl of the stadium. The picture of the crowd in the stands was complete to the smallest detail.

"Would you rather play running back? Mr. Gray doesn't like that position as much because the average gain is under four yards, but—"

"No," Laura interrupted. "That's okay."

"Our beta testers have shown that the typical user achieves a twenty-six percent increase in aerobic conditioning when faced with a regimen of competitive sports simulations as compared to non-competitive exercise programs."

Laura heaved a big sigh. "I think I've gotten enough exercise for the day. Thanks." She reached up to remove the helmet.

"But you only ran one point two miles. Your earlier runs were four to six miles each."

"This . . . it's not really my thing."

"Do you want to see something much more interesting? Much, much more interesting?"

Laura hesitated, the helmet still on her head. "Like what?" she asked guardedly, ready to jerk the apparatus from her face if she ended up in some kick-boxing program.

"I can't show it to you on the treadmill. You'd have to go to the virtual-reality workstation."

"This isn't some kind of super-duper football thing, is it? 'Cause I don't like the idea of being trapped inside some macho, testosterone-driven fantasy world of Gray's where you actually get *hit* by those skeletons."

"There is a more complete sensory version of 'Pro Football' in the works for the VR workstations, but that wasn't what I had in mind."

"Well, I'm not gonna get locked into one of those oversized phone booths in the computer center without knowing what you do have in mind."

"It's not the version 3H workstation I was talking about. I'd have to show you in the version 4C virtual-reality workstations. They are far roomier than the version 3Hs."

"But I'd be wearing a full bodysuit—an exoskeleton—and the door to the room is closed, right? I don't think so."

"As you wish."

Laura removed the helmet, stepped down off the tread, and headed for the stairs. She stopped when she came upon the blank wall she'd seen before. If her sense of direction was accurate, the elevator shaft lay behind it. Laura returned to the treadmill and put the helmet back on. The same introductory instructions about centering the red dots were recited.

"Can I just ask you one more thing? Are you still there?"

"Yes, *Laura*. What is it?"

"That elevator—the one by the stairs leading to the exercise room—where does it go?"

"It goes down to the lower levels."

"What lower levels?"

"Down into the mountain. Down to where the Model Eights are."

Laura took the helmet off and stared at the flat and empty wall.

With her hair still wet from the shower, Laura sat down at her writing desk to call Jonathan. *What am I going to say?* she thought as she picked the phone up.

He answered on the second ring.

"Jonathan?"

"Hi-i-i, Laura." His tone seemed flat—uncertain—as if he didn't know how to behave.

"Is everything all right?" she asked.

"You're asking *me* that? What's going on down *there?*"

"You wouldn't believe me if I told you."

He laughed—a stilted, fake sound. She had heard it before. It was the way he had behaved back before he came out of the closet—before he got tenure. Something was definitely wrong.

"Well, of course," Laura said awkwardly, "I can't really talk. I mean, I'm not supposed to. I'm . . . I have a contract. A confidentiality thing." She forced a laugh. "You know, I don't wanna end up getting sued by Gray's lawyers. They might take my family fortune and leave me destitute."

After a delay, Jonathan replied in a flat tone, "I understand." She didn't know what to say next. "Listen, Laura," Jonathan continued with obvious discomfort, "it sounds like there's a stampede of people leaving that island. Are you going to be on one of those planes?"

"I don't know."

There was another long delay. "So," he said, "what about some of this stuff I've been hearing? Like Gray building up a nuclear arsenal—things like that? I mean, Gray's really a menace. He's gone loony, don't you think?"

"That's . . . that's not really the way it is at *all*, Jonathan. You've got it wrong. Gray's—"

"Laura!" Jonathan interrupted, not letting her go on. "Do you really understand what's going on up here?" He was speaking urgently now, with emotion. "Jesus, there must be . . ." He hesitated. "Gray's being investigated by every government agency from the Defense Department to Health and Human Services. He's going down. I'm talking criminal stuff." This was the real Jonathan, Laura felt sure. "And so are a lot of *other* people," he said slowly. Jonathan paused to let those words sink in. "Laura, sweetie," he continued, "you've gotta get off that island right now. Today. All hell's gonna break loose down there."

Her mind was reeling. She was caught between two worlds—the world of her old life, and of life after Gray. She didn't know what to say or do.

"Laura?"

"Jonathan . . . ," she began, but sighed in frustration. "You know how the media gets things twisted. They get some kind of sensational story about a public figure and distort the hell out of it to make headlines."

"You mean *Gray?* Are the newspapers distorting the fact that he built nuclear weapons, blasted them off into space, and then sent an *asteroid* careening toward the earth? One that could wipe us all out if he screws up?"

"He's got it under *control,*" she said, amazed that the words were coming from her mouth.

"Then why the hell are *you* there?" Jonathan asked, his voice low and urgent. "What are you doing?" The sound of the hiss from the telephone connection was all she heard as he waited for her answer. Laura's eyes grew unfocused and drifted off toward the far wall. "Come home, Laura. I don't know what kind of dark . . . attraction this guy Gray has over people, but you're too smart for it. You've got to see all the signs. Charismatic personality. Cults of faith built up around him. It's a classic messiah complex! Get out, Laura . . . while you still can."

As if in a trance she said, "I'll call you later on."

"Laura, I don't know if that's such a good idea."

"What do you mean?"

"I mean . . . !" He faltered, unable to complete the sentence, then sighed. "Maybe . . . maybe you should talk to a lawyer. I'd be happy to get somebody over at the law school for you. Or maybe, Laura . . . maybe it would be better if you didn't talk to anybody at all—over the phone, that is."

So that was it. Somebody was listening. "Good-bye, Jonathan," she said.

"See ya soon, L.A. I hope."

There was a click, and then the hiss of the long-distance line fell silent. Laura didn't lower the receiver at first. She didn't want to sever the tie. Slowly, however, she replaced the handset in its cradle and sank back into the chair—totally alone with her problem. She cradled her face in her hands. "What the hell should I *do-o-o?*" she mumbled to herself, the words distorted by the tug of her hands.

Her purse sat next to the telephone. She took out her wallet, and inside one of the pockets she found the FBI card with the telephone number on it.

She should call—spill her guts. They were probably desperate for information, and what she now knew would fill volumes. They would surely descend on those flights of ex-employees, but what would the average worker be able to tell them? They were all short on facts, but not, she realized, on rumors.

Laura tried to imagine what would happen once rumors of giant, anthropomorphic robots leaked out. Stories about the dark side of technology were always popular, and the press would go into a frenzy when it got a whiff of this one. Add in a deranged computer planning the trajectory of a plummeting asteroid . . . *The government's gonna go ballistic,* she thought.

As distraught as she felt, she had to smile at her choice of words. She'd been thinking about the asteroid's "trajectory," and so she came up with the word "ballistic." The department chairman had said "hit this campus like a ton of bricks" when describing the effects of the news about the asteroid. Human brains were wired to make associations of that sort. Sometimes the associations were useful and led to insights. Other times they were coincidental and occasionally amusing. The computer's "brain" was wired the same way.

At that moment Laura knew what she'd do. Her answer had been there all along, but she'd been too distracted to think.

The computer was the most beautiful creation she'd ever known. Laura was desperate to continue her research—to explore the magnificence of the computer's complexity. To remain seated at the right hand of its creator. And she would construct any rationalization it took to convince herself to stay.

Laura took a deep breath, closed her eyes, and let her head recline onto the back of the plush chair. It was early morning, but she could already feel the tension pounding at her temples. *What must the pressure be like for Gray?* she wondered.

She leaned forward and tossed the FBI's card into the wastebasket.

"Charismatic personality," "cult," "messiah complex"—the words Jonathan had used sounded a warning. None seemed to apply to Gray on the surface. But the island was isolated. Cut off from contact. Hierarchical. They had idealistic, mission-oriented goals. Gray had convened a mass gathering and proclaimed that they would colonize space. The way Janet had recounted it—the dreaminess in her voice, her shining eyes—had put Laura on guard. Janet had seemed too loyal—too obedient. The hundreds like Janet would follow him anywhere. History was replete with examples of relatively sane people following totally insane leaders.

A picture of the black metal slug hurtling soundlessly toward the earth formed in her mind's eye. She leaned down under the table and retrieved the FBI card, slipping it into the pocket of her blue jeans.

11

Laura felt ridiculous sitting in Gray's palatial dining room all by herself. She'd asked Janet for a bagel and maybe a banana, and ended up with a pastry tray and fruit platter. Feeling guilty over eating so little, she was grazing through the sliced strawberries and kiwis when she heard the sounds of Gray issuing orders in the foyer. She threw her napkin on the table and hurried out.

At first she didn't recognize him covered head to toe in a thick coat of dry mud. "And check the beaches for prints before the tide comes in!" Gray called out to the departing Hoblenz, who was similarly filthy.

Gray turned and caught sight of Laura. His face looked drawn and his eyes hollow. He headed for the stairs without saying a word, but Laura intercepted him at the banister.

"What's going on?" she asked, and he stopped and faced her. "Where have you *been?*"

"Off-roading, I believe they call it," he replied. Every inch of him was dark gray with heavy grime except around his eyes and his hair. He must have been wearing goggles and a helmet of some sort, Laura guessed. As usual, he said nothing more.

Janet was already busy sweeping up the dirt that had been

tracked into the house. "Why is Janet having to do that?" Laura asked in a whisper.

Gray glanced at the head of his household. "Must be some of the staff didn't show up for work. Probably down at the airport, leaving with the rest of them."

"Are a lot of people leaving?"

Gray nodded, seemingly unconcerned. "But that's all right. Everything's highly automated." He looked back at Janet. "Everything but domestic work."

"But can you continue your operations with so few people?"

"A couple hundred would do fine. Look, don't worry, Laura."

"I've laid out a pair of fresh blue jeans, sir," Janet said, stressing the word "blue" with her distinctly Australian accent. She smiled as she headed off with the broom and dustpan.

"Well, she's as loyal as can be," Laura said, probing to see if the departing employees were a sore subject.

"Janet's great," he replied casually. "She's also, I would guess, the highest paid majordomo in the history of the profession."

"She told me you plan on colonizing space," Laura threw out abruptly—an intentional ambush.

Gray's eyes fixed on Laura, his look changing from surprise to amusement. "Now why would she say that?" he asked from behind the facade. Laura's question had struck something solid.

"Isn't that what you said last night in your 'town meeting'?"

Gray shrugged and shook his head, a light rain of dirt falling to the marble and adding to Janet's work. "Where would she get an idea like that?"

"She said you called it 'phase two.'"

"Well . . . sure. I discussed phase two. And it does involve significant manned operations in space. In connection with mining the asteroid and spin-off industrial production. Even a permanent manned presence—on a rotational basis."

"And maybe," Laura continued nonchalantly, "landing on the moon, the other planets, stuff like that?"

Gray opened his mouth to speak, but only a burst of air came out. He chose his words carefully. "Eventually. Even though the asteroid and other ones like it that I'll retrieve in the near future provide an excellent source of heavy metals, we also need lighter elements like silicates. You can only get those from the surface of planetary bodies. Did you know you can extract oxygen from lunar soil?"

Laura shook her head. "Nope. Sure didn't."

Gray obviously knew he hadn't thrown Laura off the trail because he kept on talking. "But I never used the word 'colonization' or anything like it."

"Maybe just . . . described the process in rough, broad-brush terms possibly?"

"Laura," he said in a soothing tone, "look . . . Janet must just be"—he shook his head—"you know, imagining things. Maybe it's some vestigial cultural trait in the British character. A legacy of all of England's years of empire that makes them think in terms of colonies."

"She's Australian."

He fell silent. After a moment's delay he said, "Oh." Laura marveled that he knew so little about the trusted, devoted head of his household. "Well, I've really got to get cleaned up. Was there something that you needed?"

"Where did you and Hoblenz go when you went 'off-roading' last night?"

He again opened his mouth to speak, and again hesitated. "You know, you can't just ask me anything you think of and expect to get an answer."

"Why not?"

Gray didn't seem to have a satisfactory response and grew flustered. He sighed and said, "You realize of course that Hoblenz doesn't think I should talk to you anymore. He doesn't trust you."

"What about you? Do *you* trust me?"

It was a casually asked question, not one she'd given much thought. But he looked up at her—his eyes locking on hers. "Yes," he said in earnest reply, and she instantly regretted having asked. His answer created in her a sense of obligation to him. A loyalty she could one day be forced to betray. "As much as I can trust anyone, I suppose."

The bond was broken, and she felt free again. Free, and disappointed. "Then, where were you? What were you doing?"

Gray seemed diminished, fatigued. His gaze fell to the floor and he said, "We were out in the jungle near Launchpad A."

"What were you doing out there?"

His hesitation this time seemed less a reluctance to reveal a secret than evidence of Gray's difficulty in discussing the subject. The expression on his face darkened, and he hung his head with a look of great sadness. "We were looking for tracks," he finally said in a faraway voice.

"What kind of tracks? You mean footprints?" Gray nodded slowly. "Like what you just sent Hoblenz off to look for on the beaches?" Again, Gray nodded. "Did you find any?"

"That's it, Laura. That's all I can say."

He turned to leave, and she grabbed his filthy arm. Mud cascaded to the floor. "No it's not, Joseph Gray. That's not our deal."

He turned quickly to look at her. His face was inches away. She was keenly aware of just how close together they stood. "Just what *is* our deal, Laura?" he asked quietly.

The question hung in the air for her to decipher.

"Our deal," she said, swallowing to wet her throat, "was that you would keep me better informed." She let his arm go.

"So . . . what? Are you going to quit, too?"

He was clearly exhausted, overburdened by the weight on his shoulders. "No," she replied softly. She wanted to reach out to him again, to touch his arm, to take a warm washcloth and gently cleanse the handsome face which lay beneath the grime.

Gray reached up and rubbed both eyes vigorously. When he looked back her way, his eyes weren't the bright blue windows to the genius inside. They were the red and bleary lenses through which people on the verge of a breakdown view the world.

"We've had an intruder," he said. "Hoblenz's men found tracks in the night using thermal imagers. The footprints were still warm from the man's body heat."

"How do you know it was a man? Did you find him?"

Gray blinked and focused his eyes. Then with what looked to be great effort he turned to face her. "Yes."

"Out there in the middle of that thick jungle by the launchpad?" Gray nodded. "Who is he?"

"A soldier." His voice had a distant quality to it, as if he were reliving the scene in his mind as he spoke.

"From what country?"

"Hoblenz thinks Belgium," Gray said before drifting farther away. "The guy had placed a monitoring device near the edge of the jungle. Hoblenz says it would've fed still video images of the assembly building and computer center to a satellite. Standard, off-the-shelf NATO stuff."

"Where's the man now?" Gray was slumped over in fatigue. He

didn't answer. "Oh, my God," she whispered, raising her hands to her mouth. "Hoblenz didn't . . . ? You didn't . . . hurt him?" Gray shook his head, and Laura relaxed.

"He was already dead."

He couldn't look her in the eye.

"How?" she finally asked. "How did he die?"

"Trauma," Gray said with a tired sigh. He looked up at her. "Dismemberment."

"Jesus Christ, Joseph. A robot?" He grew highly uncomfortable again. "Is that what it was? Could it have been a robot, because I saw a Model Seven—two of them, in fact—come out of that very same area when I walked out to the launchpad to meet you yesterday. And you know, come to think of it, they had sort of a . . . a suspicious manner, like I'd caught them doing something they—"

"*No,*" Gray snapped, then quickly calmed himself. "No, Laura."

"But what else could it have *been?* I mean, did it break the poor man's arms or legs? Did he bleed to death?"

Gray took a deep breath before answering. "He was decapitated."

She stared at him in stunned silence. "Oh, my God, Joseph. How can you say it wasn't a robot?"

"I didn't say it wasn't a robot!" he snarled, and Laura fell silent. Gray swallowed hard. "Hoblenz found the body with infrared from a helicopter. His men then went all over the area with thermal imagers but didn't find any tracks at all. It takes about twelve hours for a footprint to cool, so we should have seen the guy's tracks. Hoblenz finally set up these bright arc lights like night construction crews use, and we saw them. All over the jungle."

"But I thought you said . . . you said you didn't see any other footprints?"

When he answered, he spoke slowly. "We didn't find any *warm* footprints." Laura felt shock at the realization of what he was saying. "They were Model Eights. A lot of them. They'd been all over the jungle." He blinked once, then jammed his eyes closed for a moment before opening them wide.

"Joseph, you need to get some sleep."

He drew a deep breath. "There's too much to do." His words were slurred. "Was there something you wanted?"

Laura looked away—toward the stairs down to the exercise room that lay just behind the circular staircase. "I've got unlimited access to the facilities, right? That was our deal." Gray nodded. "Then I want to take the elevator down to the Model Eights' area. I want to go down into the mountain."

Laura was surprised and slightly unnerved at how easily Gray consented to her request. All he did was make her wait for Hoblenz to send a security guard.

When the young Frenchman arrived, he carried a squat black machine pistol strapped over his shoulder. They headed down to the lower level of Gray's house, and the soldier stared into a retinal identifier next to the elevator. The high-pitched whine of a motor rose quickly behind the wall of the shaft.

"They said it takes a minute or two," the man said with a thick French accent. He wore boots and camouflage fatigues and carried a ubiquitous pack like soldiers of any army. Bulging veins and hard muscles ran cordlike up his neck to a skull covered in short, bristly hair and a camouflage baseball cap. His face was tanned dark bronze from a life spent in the sun. The young man caught her studying him, and Laura turned and looked away.

The elevator took quite a while to arrive. Even the *ding* that announced its approach seemed premature as they waited almost a full minute for the doors to open. When they did, they revealed an elevator unlike any she'd ever seen before. The entire appearance of the car was like that of a space capsule, with shiny red plastic walls and four padded and slightly reclined seats with wide black waist and shoulder restraints.

"What's the deal with this thing?" Laura asked, trying not to let the ever worsening case of the jitters into her voice.

"It's about fifteen hundred meters down. Runs on magnetic rails."

The soldier helped Laura get situated first. When he finally fastened his harness, the door slid closed on an audible puff of air. "Ten seconds to descent," a woman's voice like that of the treadmill announced.

"Remember to clear your ears," Laura's escort advised her, further increasing the pace of her already racing pulse.

"Five," the elevator voice announced, "four, three, two, one."

Laura's seat fell away beneath her in the absolute quiet of the capsule. She was jammed hard up against the seat's padded straps, and her stomach felt as though it had leapt into her throat. A faint whining sound rose in volume as the forces of downward acceleration grew. Laura's ears popped, and popped, and then popped again until the world was totally soundless. She looked over at the soldier, whose mouth was open and whose throat was working to clear his ears.

But as soon as Laura would swallow to clear her own ears, they got hopelessly plugged again by the rapidly rising air pressure of the thicker atmosphere into which they plummeted. Her heart fluttered so much from the carnival ride that she felt short of breath and began to pant. Still, the elevator picked up speed, going faster and faster straight down the shaft. When she reached to brush the hair from her face, her hand seemed to float upward with the acceleration.

The elevator suddenly began a sickening deceleration. Laura almost retched as her stomach fell from her throat to her knees, reversing 180 degrees the stresses to which her body was being subjected. She moaned—her eyes closed—as she concentrated on trying not to get sick. Her skin grew prickly and flushed, and she felt a fine perspiration break out on her forehead and neck.

She didn't even realize it when the ordeal came to an end. Her pressure-plugged eardrums admitted almost no sound at all, but when she opened her eyes she saw the soldier undoing his straps. The elevator doors right in front of her opened without warning. She saw a large room that had been carved out of rough-hewn stone walls just as Krantz's nuclear labs had been. But the space was not nearly as expansive, and instead of buildings, it was filled with cafeteria tables.

The soldier helped Laura to her feet. She felt unsteady, groping her way through the doors and bracing herself along the rock wall just outside.

"Well, *that* was a lot of fun," she mumbled—the words sounding strange through the cotton in her ears. The man smiled without looking her way, his squinted eyes darting all about the cavern—alert.

He eased her into one of the four chairs obviously meant for the recuperation of the elevator's riders. Yet another of Gray's timesavers, Laura thought, just like the ferocious dusters and the Model Threes that raced around the island at ninety miles per hour.

The soldier slipped the gun off his shoulder, grasping the pistol grip with his finger curled around the trigger. The gun remained pointed straight down at the floor, but its owner appeared ready to use it in an instant. He stepped slowly out into the room, his eyes searching for a target but finding nothing save the plastic chairs and long tables of an empty cafeteria.

"Al-*lo?*" he shouted. The gun's strap slapped against his thigh as he regripped the weapon more firmly. Laura rose to her feet to follow, and her chair scraped noisily along the floor.

The soldier spun toward her, raising the gun but quickly turning back to the empty room. He wasn't just ill at ease; he was coiled and ready for danger. Laura wondered what kind of briefing he'd gotten from Hoblenz or what rumors were going around among the troops.

She wound her way among the tables. There was no sign of any disturbance. The trays were all piled neatly in their racks by the cafeteria line. There was no trash on the tables—no overturned cups, no chairs lying on their backs, no sign of any hasty flight.

Laura took up a position just behind the soldier. Her ears were now clear, but the cavern was deathly silent. There were several passageways out of the cafeteria—each dark, each menacing. All, she noticed, were much taller than the tallest human.

"*Allo?*" the soldier shouted into a cupped hand. There was no echo, but the booming sound of his shout in the enclosed space served to remind Laura where she was. Just how deep underground she was, and how thick the black stone walls around her were.

"Down here!" came a distant call. The soldier turned to Laura and flicked his head toward the corridor from which they'd heard a reply.

They passed vending machines. Then came a large white board on which were posted a hodgepodge of messages, notices about shifts, and new manual updates. Laura stopped in front of one notice. It was bordered by a red box and handwritten in crisp, feminine penmanship. "Does anyone have a kite? 1.3.04 wants one. Kate M."

"Don't fall behind," the soldier snapped, and Laura hurried down the corridor to catch up.

Their footsteps on the flat concrete floor were soundless. The hallway was featureless save the several doors they passed that had been cut into the rough stone walls. Most were normal human head height and labeled with words like "Authorized Personnel Only" or "Danger! High Voltage." Some, however, were larger. Like garage doors, they were composed of folding panels. On the push of some unseen button, they would rise into the walls above and reveal . . . *what?* Laura wondered.

The sounds of life drifted faintly down the corridor from up ahead. They were the normal voices of people at work.

The soldier reslung the gun over his shoulder.

When they rounded a bend in the tunnel, another cavern opened up before them. A half dozen lab-coated technicians sat or stood about a large and messy work area. The room was bounded by the walls of the corridor on one side and three sets of large windows on the other. One window was brightly lit, another dim, the third dark. The corridor led on, but the soldier and Laura had arrived at their destination.

Dr. Griffith stood behind two of the seated technicians. He looked up and said "Oh!" on seeing Laura and her escort. Every one of the dozen or so busy people, Laura noticed, also turned to look their way. Some twisted around in their chairs, both hands gripping the armrests in tense and watchful poses. But all quickly relaxed and resumed their work. The new arrivals were human.

"Look out for the cables," Griffith said as he wove his way through the maze of consoles to greet Laura. They had rigged up some sort of temporary control room, and there were easily twice as many workstations as there were people. Laura watched one of the techs roll from console to console without getting up from his chair. It appeared they were working two or more jobs at once.

"Sorry about all the mess," Griffith said, smiling broadly. "We've sort of consolidated our work group here. Come on. Let me introduce you to the team."

He led her carefully across the room, stopping her at each of the cables to ensure she stepped safely over. She shook hands with the men and women of the cavern, who were friendly and talkative and hospitable. They seemed as glad to make contact with the outside world as Laura had been to find them.

When the introductions were finished, Laura's attention was drawn to a monitor. A Model Eight moved slowly across a room. The floor and walls were white and antiseptic, but everywhere was strewn the debris of crushed and broken household objects. A coffeemaker lay on its side. The tattered remains of a lampshade sat tenuously atop a large clock. Torn clothes and twisted cookware and the shards of less resilient goods lay in random piles all about.

The camera followed the robot automatically. A casual collision sent a chair flying across the room, and it landed missing one of its four wooden legs. The Model Eight held two halves of a book, one half in each hand. It paused to watch the chair as it rattled to a stop in the corner.

"I take it this is some sort of finishing school for robots," Laura said.

"We call it 'charm school,' actually," Griffith replied.

Laura nodded. She remembered John Steinbeck's *Of Mice and Men* and imagined the Model Eight in the jungle "playing" too rough with the poor soldier.

"Dr. Aldridge?" Griffith asked. "Are you all right? Was the elevator ride down too rough?"

Laura tried to compose herself and her thoughts. "It was a little on the radical side."

Griffith laughed. "We all just use the surface entrance. I don't know anyone who takes that thing—except Mr. Gray, of course."

"I wish I'd known that. Does Mr. Gray come down here often?"

Griffith shrugged. "Off and on. A lot more recently—since we started having our troubles." He looked up at her quickly. "With the computer, I mean." He turned to face away from her immediately. "Well, anyway, I apologize that I can't give you the grand tour."

"That's all right. It has to be difficult running a facility of this size when you're not fully staffed."

"Oh, we don't 'run' this place from here or anywhere else. Everything is completely automated. Or, given what I understand of your theories, you could say it's being run by another of the company's 'employees.'"

"You mean . . . the main computer?"

"Of course."

"But . . . but the computer claims not to know what's going *on* down here. It claims it can't 'see' into the Model Eights' facilities or tell what they're doing."

Griffith looked at her as if she were speaking in tongues. Laura glanced at the two technicians nearest her, who quickly returned to their work before she made eye contact. "Well," Griffith said awkwardly, "that's just not the case."

Laura looked around. At every one of the workstations there glowed a computer monitor. Lights on the surrounding panels lit and went dark, and lines of text and windows filled with charts and graphs popped onto the screens in a never ending parade of work flow. It was all the computer's work, she realized.

"I can assure you, Dr. Aldridge—Laura—that the computer is very much in charge of things down here." Griffith chuckled. "As a representative of *Homo sapiens* everywhere, I would hate to admit it, but there is absolutely no way any one human, or any *group* of humans, for that matter, could ever operate a complex of facilities as extensive as the Model Eight workshops down here. Oh, not that we don't monitor things and make some decisions every once in a while. But as far as what you would call 'running' the place . . . ?" He shook his head.

Laura surveyed the busy room, her eyes ending up on the large observation windows. "What are those?" she asked.

Griffith led her to the leftmost and most brightly lit of the three identical windows, which formed a rough semicircle along one wall of the room. The middle window was dimly lit, and the right-most was dark. "This is one of the tactile rooms," he said. Below she saw a white concrete room filled with objects stacked neatly on shelves or piled in large bins that looked like toy boxes. There were place settings on a table, clothes on hangers, a sink with a dishrag beside it. Everything was in order.

"Here he comes," the technician seated behind them said. Laura spun to look at the open corridors, which were being guarded by the French soldier.

"Down there," Griffith said, tapping Laura's shoulder and pointing down at the room below.

The Model Eight walked slowly through a tall door, which closed automatically behind it. The robot was enormous—much larger than Laura had expected. It headed straight for a large, open bin and extracted a shredded yellow piece of rubber by its handle.

"Ah!" Griffith said. "I see it's 1.3.07." The robot slung the frayed strands through the air. The whir and slap of the pieces could be heard through a small speaker over the window. "I can always tell," Griffith explained. "This one likes that rubber ball, or what used to be a ball. He always goes to it first."

The Model Eight let the yellow shreds drop to the floor, and it headed next for the overflowing toy chest. "He can't really remember why he liked that rubber ball so much. His play time with it is falling off rapidly now that it has been destroyed. It's no longer as interesting as it used to be, and his mini-net's connections that led to a reward when he played with it are weakening."

"Do you realize, Dr. Griffith, that you refer to the Model Eight as a 'he'?"

"Not *all* Model Eights," he said. "Some are quite definitely 'shes.' That's one of the more amusing distractions among my team, figuring out whether each new Eight is a boy or a girl." He looked over at her with a mischievous grin. "It's obviously not as easy as checking the hardware, you understand."

"What do you mean a boy or a girl?"

"I hope you don't find us to be terribly sexist, Dr. Aldridge, because it's really just intended for our amusement. We need a diversion because we spend so much time observing the Eights' behavior, especially now that Mr. Gray instituted a big brother program."

The Model Eight below broke a long plastic truck into two pieces. The look on Griffith's face was like the amusement of a parent watching the boisterous, if slightly destructive, play of an active toddler. The robot held the broken truck high over its head, pausing, Laura thought, to consider its next move. It then smashed it to pieces against the opposite wall and moved on.

"We base our informal gender designations on traditional, stereotypical human behavioral patterns. Some, like Bouncy down there, are very much into exploration of large-scale mechanical forces. Throwing things, moving as big of an object as their strength and agility allows, et cetera. We call them boys. The girls tend to come into the tactile rooms and actually sit down. They'll find something like a quilt with a complicated print on it and patiently study it for hours."

Griffith looked over at her to confirm, Laura supposed, that she wasn't offended. Apparently satisfied, he continued. "The physical result to both boys' and girls' toys is usually the same. They're utterly destroyed during the learning process. But the behavioral patterns are quite distinctive, and they're generally consistent right from the first power-up. Not that there's any scientific significance to the distinction, of course, but it does make for a lively office pool. Sometimes it takes several months of argument. Most of the time, however, we can develop a consensus after two or three trips out of the chair."

"What's the 'chair'?"

Griffith led Laura to the center window. The initial impression she got was of something sinister. The room was bathed in low, red light, and in the center was an enormous metal armchair. A rounded hood was mounted on the top, and from the inside protruded a variety of needlelike projections pointed downward. The entire scene reminded Laura uncomfortably of a torture chamber.

"The chair is a combination simulator and recharging station. For the first month or so after they leave the line, the Model Eights spend most of their days plugged into the computer by means of that interface you see at the top. When they arrive here from the assembly building, they're just inert lumps of metal on a gurney. After the first twenty-four hours in the chair, they can move their limbs about and sit up. It takes a long time before balance can be programmed, and even longer to get them to take that first step."

"And the computer runs them through simulations while they're plugged in down there?"

Griffith nodded. "It'll fire through trillions of simulations before they're done."

Laura looked down at the room and its sinister chair. There were brackets on the chair's arms and legs, and several large metal straps protruded at chest and waist level. "Why the restraints?"

"Oh, the simulations are quite real to the robots. Are you familiar with the virtual-reality workstations Mr. Gray has on the island?" Laura nodded. "Well, imagine how real the computer's representation of the world would seem to a robot when it was fed directly via cable to its neural net. It's bound to be as real to the robots as . . . well, reality is to us. Anyway," he chuckled, "it's quite comical sometimes. Have you ever seen a dog sleep? How they'll sometimes kick their legs chasing rabbits in their dreams? The same thing happens to the Model Eights. Some go nuts. They broke quite a few restraints until we went to titanium. The bolts holding the chair to the floor are sunk twenty feet into the base rock under the simulation room. I'd love to know just what's running through their nets when they react the way they do."

"You mean you don't know what simulations the computer is running them through?" Laura asked.

"Not a clue," he said, shaking his head with no apparent concern. "Like I said, it runs through trillions in any given course. And it varies them constantly both to improve and to add some diversity to the skill sets. Some of the courses are distinctly better than others, but all the Model Eights' hardware is absolutely identical. I've got to hand it to Mr. Gray. He did such a fine job on the design that we literally haven't made one single change to the prototype, and we've got forty-eight off the line so far. Now *that's* an astonishing technical feat."

"You mean to say that Mr. Gray designed the hardware? I thought you were the head of robotics."

"I am, but 'robotics' in this organization means programming. Like I said, the differences in software-driven performance are remarkable. Hightop, for instance, is head and shoulders above the rest in every category. He sends his regards, by the way." Laura nodded, uncertain how to respond. "But some of the others have been so hopelessly irredeemable that we had to reprogram them."

"You mean, just pull the plug and start from scratch?"

"Good heavens, *no!* Each one of those Model Eights represents probably a billion dollars of hardware, but maybe ten times that much in 'soft' costs. If you consider the cost of construction and operation of this facility *and,* more significantly, the computer time to run it, then those things would be worth around twelve billion dollars *each.* With those kinds of costs, we don't make the decision to reprogram lightly, and we *certainly* don't decharge them and 'start from scratch.' The reprogramming course is only two weeks and involves just patching what the computer thinks the defective functions are. They're almost always higher order things like 'goals' and 'plans.' That way, we salvage literally billions of dollars' worth of computer time."

"Why is this chair empty?" Laura asked. "If it costs so much, I'd think you'd keep this place humming."

"Mr. Gray halted all new programming," he replied. "We had two students in the course, but they're both kept in bays now—charged but inactive."

"When did he suspend the programming?"

"Last night right after the town meeting," Griffith said, now shaking his head and frowning. "It's bullshit," he mumbled. "That little boy didn't know what he was talking about." He stepped up close to Laura and looked around to make sure they were out of earshot. "The boy who said he saw a robot out of his window, you know?" Laura nodded. "He didn't see a Model Eight." Griffith shook his head again. "No way."

"Do you know that for sure?" Laura asked.

Griffith nodded. "All the Model Eights were accounted for last night. But even more telling was the little boy's description of what he saw. Now I know he's only eight, but his science teacher stood up and raved that the boy was some sort of whiz. And he's got a rich gene pool. His mother works in Krantz's virtual-reality section, and his father is in space operations. But he got it all *wrong*. The Model Eights don't run in a crouch. They don't run at all!"

Griffith looked over his shoulder after raising his voice, but then turned back to Laura. "*You've* seen them. It's a goddamn scientific miracle that they can *walk,* much less run! And they never, not *once,* have gotten into a crouch. They're either completely erect, or they're flat on their big tin asses! Now that's simple, Newtonian physics, and I offered to prove it to Gray with as many tests as he'd like. I came straight down here this morning before we opened up and went to Hightop. If any of 'em can crouch, Hightop can. And he fell straight on his butt ten times in a row!"

"You don't man the facilities down here twenty-four hours?" Laura asked.

Griffith shook his head. "No need to. It's fully automated. All we're doing here this morning is monitoring. 'Big brother,' like I said before. Gray ordered human monitoring of all Model Eight activity beginning today, which is yet another overreaction to that little boy's story, if you ask me."

"And you're absolutely sure the boy didn't see a Model Eight?"

"He couldn't have. The human operators leave here every night at ten o'clock. We open up at six A.M. That's one eight-hour shift during which there are no humans down here. But since the robots don't sleep, the place is operational twenty-four hours a day, three hundred and sixty-five days a year. Now I have eight hours of video recordings of every last one of those robots for this and every night since we opened shop down here. The first thing we *do* when we get in every morning is look at that video!"

"And you've got videotape from last night?"

"Yes! From every night. But it's not taped. It's recorded digitally on an off-board computer."

"But the computer controls all the off-board computers, doesn't it?"

"Yes, but . . ." He clearly registered the point she was making. "Look. You want to know why I'm sure that little boy's story is wrong? Why I'm absolutely positive? He described the thing he saw as not as tall as the dumpsters in back of the grocery store. Gray must've asked him twenty different ways, and every time that boy was completely, positively sure that whatever he saw didn't come close to being as tall as the trash container he saw it next to. That dumpster is only six feet, eight inches tall. You've *seen* how big the Eights are! At a hundred feet away is there *any* chance you could fail to tell that a Model Eight isn't more than six eight? They're ten feet *tall*, for Christ's sake!"

"Was it well lit in the parking lot?"

"No. But what does it matter? It was just some hoodlum breaking curfew, that's all. We've had problems with vandalism, you know."

"Vandalism of trash bins?"

"There's been some gang of little punks running around this island for months. They've knocked over streetlamps, dragged a weather station down by the launchpads out into the jungle, chipped off pieces of the base of the statue up at the top of the Village's main boulevard, things like that. Some kind of initiation ceremony or ritual, that's Hoblenz's guess."

Laura shook her head in disbelief. "Are you people all *blind?* You're just so convinced that your precious robots are under control that you come up with some *ridiculous* explanation for what's going on like 'gang initiation ritual'?"

He was taken aback by her outburst. "You sound just like all the rest of them," he said.

"Like all the rest of whom?"

"The people at the town meeting! Mass hysteria! By the time they all stormed out of the gymnasium I swear I could've convinced 'em that a UFO had just landed on the roof."

"Are you saying that everyone stormed out of that meeting last night over rumors of robots running loose, and not over the asteroid?"

"Stormed out of that meeting and right off the island, if what I'm hearing is true. Some of my own people, too—people who should *know* better! The damn *asteroid* is probably what held on to the few hundred who *stayed*—that and Gray's talk. You should've heard him. What it's going to be like after a ten thousandfold increase in human productivity. Humanity relieved from drudgery and dangerous jobs. There were people with tears in their eyes. I would've thought more would want to stay and be a part of it."

"A part of what?"

"Of phase *two!*" Griffith said as if she was missing the most elementary of his points. "Of the *expansion*."

"Of the colonization?" Laura asked, feeding him Janet's word.

He frowned. "It's not exactly colonization. It's more of a natural . . . progression. An expansion, like I said. Building on everything that has come before."

"A tower to the sky," Laura said under her breath, but Griffith paid no attention to the comment.

"It's like we take everything known right now and . . . grow it. Information grows exponentially, you know." He shook his head. "You really should have heard the speech. It's too bad nobody recorded it."

"Well, maybe somebody did."

Griffith shook his head. "It was the first time I ever saw metal detectors on this island. Hoblenz's men ran 'em like airport security. Wouldn't let any recording devices—camcorders, tape recorders, anything—inside the gym." Griffith shook his head and said, "Anyway, I'm sorry. As I said, this has to be a short tour of necessity." He headed back toward the work area, and Laura followed.

They passed by the last window—the darkened one.

"What's this room?" she asked, pausing at the thick glass.

"Oh!" Griffith replied, stopping but not turning fully to face her. "That's another tactile room."

It was pitch dark inside. "Can I see?"

He clearly didn't want to show her. "I wish I had enough time to explain all we go through in a course—how much we have to teach these robots before we can dare set them loose in the world." He looked down, shuffling his feet.

"Why don't you just show me the room?"

"But you won't understand," he said in a plaintive tone. "You can't. You haven't had to make all the discoveries we've made or design the programs necessary to deal with—"

"I know you're busy, Phil," Laura interrupted, "and I don't have all day either, so if you'll just turn on the lights down there I'll be out of your hair."

He frowned, but after a moment's hesitation walked over to a panel just below the window. With a flick of his wrist he threw a switch.

The room below was flooded with light. The empty chamber

was about the size of the tactile room on the far side of the observation area.

"Like all young . . . creatures," Griffith continued in a voice drained of inflection, "the robots are fascinated by moving things."

There were two doors leading into the room—one large enough for the robots, the other too small even for humans. The room was empty save a huge drain in the middle of the floor and thick metal sprinkler heads protruding from the ceiling. The white concrete had clearly been scrubbed, but no amount of detergent seemed capable of removing the faint but indelible brown stains.

"It's absolutely essential that we let them get the curiosity out of their system."

"Those are bloodstains," Laura said.

"There's no other way. They're just fascinated, absolutely fascinated, by animals. Goats and sheep, mostly, but dogs, cats, other wildlife."

"My God," Laura said. "They rip them limb from *limb*."

"Not on purpose, Laura," Griffith said with true emotion. "They don't mean to hurt their toys. They're really quite gentle, as much as they can be. And"—he shook his head—"it's not a pleasant part of the course for any of us, or for *them*. Some of the robots get quite distraught after . . . after they've broken one of the animals. But that's what we *want*, don't you see? The experience is so traumatic that the connections their nets develop are strong and long-lasting. I swear after this course you could put them in a room full of babies and they wouldn't move till they dropped to the ground with dead batteries."

Griffith watched Laura intently, as if waiting for her to absolve him of his guilt. She could say nothing, however. It was all merging into a single disgusting picture. The soldier, the animals led to slaughter—what else in the name of progress? In the name of Gray.

Griffith threw the switch to extinguish the lights in the room. *They keep that room dark,* Laura thought, seeing in the darkened glass the frozen look of revulsion on her face. *They don't like to be reminded of what goes on down there.*

Laura walked back to the window overlooking the first, brightly lit room. The Model Eight now played with a chrome faucet, and water shot up from the sink. The robot banged the metal sprayer against a man's suit that it had draped over the back of a chair. When the robot lost interest, the fixture fell to the floor.

He looked up with a start at the observation window—directly at where Laura now stood. When Griffith stepped up beside her, the robot flung its arm out violently, knocking the chair and the jacket across the room.

"He can see us," Laura said.

"Nonsense," Griffith replied. "It's one-way glass."

"He looked right at us, and then he lashed out."

"He looked up at what to him is a mirror. He can't see us."

"Don't they have thermal imagers? Maybe he detected our heat through the glass?"

Griffith looked down at the robot, squinting, but then shook his head. "That's not it. They hate mirrors. Every last one of the Model Eights. Before they learn to control their behavior, they tend to lash out whenever they're the least bit irritated."

"And he became irritated just by looking at the mirrored glass?" She chuckled. "So you fill their world with mirrored observation windows even though it pisses them off?"

"I'm sorry, I wasn't being clear enough. It's not just mirrors that aggravate them. It's their image *in* those mirrors. They hate seeing themselves."

Laura tilted her head. "Why?"

Griffith shrugged, but said nothing.

"You know they've been getting out of here," Laura said.

"Now that has been blown *way* out of proportion," he replied, bristling. "They're just isolated incidents." Laura looked up at Griffith, and he turned away. "They're each different, remember. There are going to be some bad seeds."

"I'd like to see one of the 'bad seeds,'" Laura said. When Griffith started to object, she interrupted with "Then I'll get out of your hair. I'd just like to observe a Model Eight who's not a showpiece like Hightop for a few moments."

Griffith headed off to the work area with a frown on his face. Laura turned back to watch the young Model Eight below. It was sitting quietly and holding a colorful green-and-blue globe in both arms, staring at the details on the orb. She felt unsettled—on a wild ride she wanted to slow down but knew would only go faster. There was too much, too many new ideas. It was impossible to keep up.

There was one thing, however, that Laura knew with certainty. Soon, very soon, Gray's revolution would sweep across the green-and-blue orb the young robot held in his hands, and it would change everything . . . forever. It meant a spurt of growth—a period of unparalleled advancement for mankind. She already had enough truly novel, revolutionary ideas to write a dozen, two dozen breakthrough papers. She could take her science to new heights, and then walk triumphantly down the halls of her department. In her mind she could hear the pleas for her time and her thoughts that would come from the very same people who had judged her unworthy of tenure.

Somehow, the thought seemed petty. Publishing papers? For whose benefit? Whose critique? As long as Joseph Gray lived, no one would equal his brilliance. He was a once-in-a-million-year phenomenon, and this was her chance to be a part of his world—the society of the mind.

"We call him 'Auguste,'" Griffith said, using the French pronunciation—"Owgoost." The robot sat on the floor of his cell, and Laura and Griffith watched him on a computer screen from the underground monitoring station. "His formal name is 1.2.09R."

"Why the *R* at the end of his version number?"

Griffith gave her a significant look. "'Reprogrammed,'" he said, almost whispering. "But look, I explained to Mr. Gray that these Eights are notoriously dirty creatures. They're into everything. And the same type of mud—volcanic mud—that you find down in the swamp is what you get right out in the yard."

"What are you talking about?"

"Mr. Gray asked this morning that I inspect the robots for any traces of mud. We found some on Auguste."

Laura turned to the computer monitor. "Why was Auguste reprogrammed?"

Griffith shook his head. "We couldn't coax him out of his shell. Behavior patterns never even began to approach normal. He was also way behind in motor skills. Two months into basic and he could barely walk across the room. I really thought . . . There were some tense times until we got those restraints on him, let me tell you. And he busted one of the chair's arms right before we got started. It was after the experience with Auguste that we went to titanium brackets."

Laura understood, now. The robots resisted reprogramming. They fought when they were sent to the chair. But why? "How do they know they're going to be reprogrammed? How do they know it's not just another simulation?"

Griffith shrugged. "They just do. They sense something's wrong, I suppose. We have to get the juveniles—the Model Eights who're just out of the advanced course—to put them in the chair. Maybe they tell them, I don't know."

"Why do you call him 'Auguste'—and the French pronunciation? That seems a bit odd when the others are named Hightop and Bouncy and things like that."

"Auguste is an odd robot." He looked up at her. "But that doesn't mean out of control! The reprogramming *took* on him. We didn't have to decharge him—to 'start from scratch,' as you put it—like we did with one of the others."

"So Auguste was a slow learner, and Hightop got his foot caught in the rocks and lost power," Laura said. Griffith confirmed her summary with a nod. "And you reprogrammed them, but didn't have to start all over." Again he nodded. "What about the robot you *did* have to start from scratch?"

"Her behavior was . . . erratic. Totally erratic. One day, we let her out of the chair after some simulations and she came out swinging. Never did get her calmed down. We ultimately decharged her completely. She's one of the two infants currently."

"By decharging, do you wipe out all traces of previous programming?"

Griffith nodded. "Almost all the connections in the robots' mini-nets are virtual—software instructions about how to route packets of data. They've got very few fiber-optic connections—only something like two to the twenty-second power of combination possibilities."

"And that hardwiring remains after decharging?" Griffith nodded. Laura tried the math in her head, but gave up. "How much is two to the twenty-second power?"

"A little over four million," Griffith said.

Laura was stunned. "So four *million* connections remained in place when you decharged that robot?"

Another nod from Griffith. "So, you see, it's practically a clean slate. Hardwiring usually represents only the most unvarying of connections. Things like basic motor skills."

"Wait a minute! What about traumas? Didn't you say the trauma of the slaughter rooms gets seared into their memory? Isn't it possible traumatic experiences are also part of their unvarying, hardwired memories?" Griffith looked stricken and didn't respond. *Four million connections,* Laura thought. *Four million associations learned from their prior life.* "The robot that you completely decharged . . . it was a she before, right?" Griffith nodded again. "And what is it now?"

He hesitated, moistening his mouth before he spoke. "A she," he replied. "But look, we rig it so the odds of a robot coming up a given gender are roughly fifty-fifty. Plus, like I said, giving them a gender is just a little game we play. It has no scientific significance."

"And the two robots you didn't decharge—Hightop and Auguste—how many connections did they retain from before their reprogramming?"

Griffith frowned. "Maybe . . . sixty-four trillion, a hundred and twenty-eight trillion, something in that order."

"And you call that *re*programming?"

"Laura, that's only a small fraction of their nets' connections."

"But they *remember!*" Laura said, incredulous that such an obvious fact had been overlooked. "Maybe it's like a dream to them, or they don't know *why* they react the way they do to a given situation, or they think they've been somewhere they've never been before. Have you ever taken Hightop back to where he was trapped in those rocks for hours and hours?" Griffith shook his head slowly, staring at Auguste in his cage. "I'll bet you *anything* that Hightop would have a powerful reaction to seeing that place, even if he doesn't know why. They remember, Dr. Griffith, and that means they remember what you did to them. Hightop was reprogrammed after an accident, but Auguste was reprogrammed in that chair execution-style, and he fought it. Was he at all violent before the reprogramming, or was he just a slow learner?"

The visibly upset man drew a deep breath. "Auguste wasn't violent before."

Laura lowered her voice. "But now he's your prime suspect, isn't he?" Griffith quickly looked up at her. He knew about the murder in the jungle. "I'd like to go visit Auguste, please," Laura said.

After a moment's hesitation, Griffith nodded and motioned for her to follow. The French soldier trailed them with his finger on the trigger of the machine pistol.

"He's in here," Griffith said as he stooped to peer into the dark hole of the retinal identifier. They had walked a long way down the corridors of Griffith's underground ghost town. The Model Eight facilities were enormous, and their vast size made the absence of people even more conspicuous. The high ceilings and doorways made it clear the place was designed for beings much larger than humans. She felt like a visitor there—an alien.

The lock on the door in front of Griffith clicked open. The soldier raised his ugly black weapon and went in first. Griffith followed. Laura entered last.

The giant robot sat idle on the floor in the far corner of the room. Its pose was strikingly human, and Laura couldn't tell whether she was more amazed at just how like a human the robot appeared, or at its size. The soldier kept his gun raised and leveled on the robot.

"You don't have to do that," Griffith said, waving his hand at the tense man, motioning for him to lower his gun. The soldier paid no attention. He never took his eyes or his gun off the robot.

Griffith frowned comically at Laura in mockery of the man's paranoia. He then walked over to the robot—his and the seated robot's heads on roughly the same level. "Auguste! How are you?"

It was only then that the Model Eight looked up. Laura knew that it must have sensed them enter, but it hadn't bothered to turn their way. She stared at the robot and walked up behind Griffith. "Auguste?" she whispered to the man, looking at the robot's pose—at his head on his fist and his elbow on his knee. "Auguste Rodin, the sculptor?"

"He's always sat like that—with his hand on his chin. I don't know who first noticed the similarities to the sculpture—to *The Thinker.*" Griffith leaned over to get closer to the robot. "How are you?" he said, smiling. "Are you ready to get up?" He motioned up, up, with his hand, and like a circus elephant the robot labored to his feet.

The soldier backed away, keeping his gun raised. It was clear who he thought the enemy was.

The robot stood impassively before Griffith—towering over

him. "Come on and get a closer look," Griffith said, motioning her toward the ten-foot-tall machine. She took a step, looking the massive robot up and down—as frightened of their notorious clumsiness as of their uncertain potential for violence. Auguste, however, seemed to have no problem with his balance. "Come on," Griffith said, waving her even closer. Griffith stood half turned away from the robot, and in her mind's eye she imagined the caged robot seizing its unsuspecting captor from behind. But the robot just stood there . . . still.

"That's all right. I can see him fine from here."

"Don't you want to touch him?" Griffith asked, reaching out without looking and resting his hand on the robot's stomach. The robot glanced down for an instant, but then his head rose to stare blankly across the room at the bare wall. "They've got pressure-sensitive membranes covering most of their bodies." He pushed with his fingertips against the machine's flat gray abdomen. "It gives them a sense of touch, but if they had body temperature it would feel almost like they've got skin. Come over here and check it out."

She shook her head. "That's okay. We can go now."

Griffith ignored her, kneeling down. He pulled back the black stockings covering the robot's large feet and extracted a ballpoint pen from his pocket. "He had a bit of mud right here." He was totally exposed in that position. All the robot would have to do would be to reach down and . . . Griffith held his glasses tilted at an angle. "All gone now," he said as he looked at a crevice in the metal panels along the robot's shin. "But like I told Mr. Gray, I don't think it was from any recent trips out. Must've been . . . "—he grunted as he rose to his feet, joints popping—"missed on our last detailing after a session out in the yard."

Griffith turned back to the Model Eight. "Bye-bye, Auguste," he said, waving. As soon as he turned to leave, the robot sank to the floor in the corner. The white concrete was cold and bare. The robots lived like animals in some cruel, primitive zoo of yesteryear. Modern zoos went to great lengths to re-create the natural habitats of their animals. But robots . . . they had no natural habitat. At least not yet.

But they clearly want out of this cave, Laura thought. *To roam around outdoors—free.* Laura watched the robot return to his contemplative pose, his chin resting heavily on his fist.

When Griffith joined her, she said, "Is he still resting or whatever—vegging?"

"Oh, no," Griffith said. "They've synchronized their patterns with our day and night. They're active during the two manned shifts, and then they spend most of the third . . ." He twisted to look back over his shoulder and fell silent. He hadn't realized the robot had sunk to his place in the corner. "That's odd," Griffith said, and he returned to Auguste. He pulled a small screwdriver from his breast pocket and pried open a panel on the robot's thigh. Griffith squinted and again tilted his glasses to read a glowing blue screen just above a large, three-pronged socket. "Hmmph!" he said, closing the panel with a click and standing upright. "Charge is good." He looked at the lethargic robot with a puzzled expression on his face. "I don't know what it could be."

"Maybe he doesn't like captivity," Laura suggested.

"What do you mean, 'captivity'?"

"I mean being locked up in here. In this room."

"He's not locked up," Griffith said. "He's free to go wherever he wants in these facilities."

"But there was a lock on the door. You had to use the retinal identifier."

"*We* have to unlock doors. *They* just use their microwave transmitters and beam the access codes. They have the run of the place, which is only fair."

"But surely you don't give them codes to the exits," Laura said with a laugh. Griffith didn't respond, and she smiled. "I mean, there *is* a lock on those, right?"

"Well . . . there's always the chance of a fire or another emergency down here. And, like I said, they're extremely valuable assets of Mr. Gray's. . . ."

"You *give* them the codes to unlock the exterior *doors?*" Laura said in total amazement.

"Only the five robots in the 1.1 series—our most senior class—and Hightop, of course."

"Mr. Gray is in his study reading reports or some such," Janet said.

Laura continued up the staircase from the elevator. She felt shaken, but she couldn't tell why. Was it the ride up from the Model Eight facility, or what she'd seen in the eerie hollows down below?

Laura knocked on the study door, but there was no answer. She went in. The fire crackled warmly. A freshly showered Gray sat in his thick leather chair, his feet propped up on his desk. Papers were strewn all about. His head rested deep in the plush cushions. He was sound asleep.

She smiled. *So he's . . . sort of human,* Laura thought. An afghan was draped over the sofa, and she got it and tiptoed to Gray's desk. When she lifted the papers off his lap, he didn't even stir. He was so deep in sleep, she probably could've stuck the poker from the fireplace into his ribs and he wouldn't have budged. He'd rocked back so far he was fully reclined. She pulled the blanket up to his chin and covered him all the way down to his toes.

He looked like a child. Sleep softened the features of his face in some undefinable way. His eyelids were closed, smooth, relaxed. His thick lashes were pressed together and his eyebrows like his hair were jet black. When he woke, she felt sure, his eyes would again be ablaze with brilliance. She yearned to see them—to sense them drawn to her.

Laura looked up and saw Janet peering through the door. Janet smiled warmly and nodded before disappearing.

Laura didn't know what to make of Janet's smile, but she dared not let herself think about its meaning. She couldn't risk grappling with the nascent feelings that welled up inside her. Her emotional center was too unsteady—the result of a tension between the warm glow of happiness she felt just then and her anxiety over the mysteries surrounding its source. So Laura did the only thing she could manage. She blanked out her mind, left the study, and wandered without thinking into the crisp morning air outside.

An empty car stood at the bottom of the steps. She knew it was time to go back to work, and she got into the car and strapped herself in.

"Please take me . . . ," she said before hesitating, "to Mr. Hoblenz. But *not* if he's too busy . . . or if he is, you know, someplace dangerous." The door closed, and the car pulled away immediately, turning right at the gate toward the nuclear reactor.

The cooling tower and containment dome no longer seemed all that sinister to Laura. As they flashed by her car's windows she had trouble mustering any of the outrage she'd felt just the day before. *Yesterday I lived in the twentieth century,* she realized. *Today . . . the twenty-first. It's just more dangerous now,* she told herself.

The road turned in the direction of the Village, hugging the foot of the tall mountain parallel with the shore. The car passed the tunnel leading down to Krantz's labs, and then inexplicably began to pull to a stop. Laura looked all around. On the narrow black-sand beach far below she saw a small rubber boat with two large outboard motors. Three men knelt in a tight semicircle around a small patch of sand. Two had rifles.

The door opened, and Laura got out. She headed down the steep hill. The descent was treacherous. In some places she slid on the seat of her jeans, with both hands dragging through the loose soil. When she reached the bottom, the three men were waiting for her. One was Hoblenz.

"What the *hell*'re you doin' here?" he asked.

"Looking for you," Laura replied, brushing the dirt off the back of her pants.

All three men watched the effort.

Hoblenz barked out an order, sending his two men down the beach in opposite directions. A gentle surf washed up onto the sand behind Hoblenz. "Well," he said in his Texas twang, "shoot."

Laura reached into her pocket and pulled out the card with the FBI's telephone number. She handed it to Hoblenz and told him about being approached by the agents. He listened in silence, glancing back and forth between her and the card. Laura also told him that she thought there'd been something fishy about the V-mail she'd gotten and about her equally suspicious telephone conversation with Jonathan.

"That's all perty interestin'," Hoblenz said. He put the card in the breast pocket of his camouflage blouse. "Whattaya want me to do? Give ya a medal for bein' a good citizen?"

"I know about the Belgian soldier."

Hoblenz looked at her through squinting eyes, spat on the sand, and said, "Dutch."

"Not Belgian?"

Hoblenz craned his neck to look out to sea, jabbing his thumb through the air over his shoulder. "Computer said Belgium doesn't have any submarines."

"There's a submarine out there?"

"Yep."

"How do you know that?"

"'Cause they landed some people a while ago lookin' for their man."

"In broad daylight?" she asked. Hoblenz sucked his cheeks in as he worked his jaw on something and nodded. "They landed right here?" she asked.

"Yep." He was chewing tobacco—his mouth was black with it. He spat again.

"How do you know they were looking for the soldier?"

"I asked 'em."

"Did you tell them what happened?"

"I told 'em he was dead. They asked could they have the body back, and I arranged for a boat at noon."

"Is that all that happened?"

He shrugged. "They asked if I'd give 'em their satellite equipment back."

"And what did you say?"

He snorted, and a smile passed briefly across a face otherwise devoid of humor. "Take a wild guess."

"Are there other submarines out there?"

Hoblenz looked down at his feet, growling out a chuckle that grated roughly as if from the throat of a heavy smoker. He raised a hand to rub the muscles in the back of his thick neck, then stretched his head to either side with a cracking sound. "Honey, I got me 'bout fifty good men. They may be from all over, an' there's not an Eagle Scout in the bunch, but I can say with pride that not one of 'em is gettin' on them planes today. But as far as subs go, there ain't a goddamn thing I can tell ya. Or aircraft carriers either. Now, we got a few old Stingers I talked Mr. Gray into pickin' up for about ten times what they're worth, and I might be able to go toe to toe with the army of Luxembourg. But as far as any *other* NATO countries go, he-ere's the island." He waved his hand through the air in a broad sweep.

"What about . . . you know?" Laura nodded down the coast toward where the nuclear facility opened into the side of the mountain.

Hoblenz looked at her with an inscrutable smile before chuckling again and shaking his head. "You want to nuke 'em?"

"No!" she responded, blushing. "I mean, doesn't Gray have . . . something? Some high-tech thing that just incapacitates people or something?"

"There's no such thing, Dr. Aldridge. You either let 'em alone, or you kill 'em all. Ain't nothin' in between."

He was getting suspicious of her questions, she realized.

"Look, I came down here to make peace with you. I know you don't trust me, but I swear I've told you everything. If you have any other questions"—she held her hands open—"shoot." She put her hands on her hips in imitation of Hoblenz's macho pose. When she looked back up, the skin around his eyes was crinkled. He was smiling for real this time.

"Well, now, I do have one question," Hoblenz said, glancing at his men. They were returning from their sweep of the beach at a slow pace and were still a good distance away. "Mr. Gray—do you think he's, you know, okay?"

Laura was puzzled. "What do you mean?"

"I mean"—he spat again—"is he playin' with a full deck?"

Laura cocked her head. "Are you asking me about Mr. Gray's sanity?"

"In yer professional opinion."

She shrugged. "But I don't have a professional opinion about Mr. Gray."

He looked down at her without a trace of the smile remaining. "Then what the hell have you been *doin'* these last three days?"

She shook her head, shrugging. "I've been working on the computer like everybody else!"

"But you're a goddamn psychologist!" he said in a low and menacing voice. "Jeez, you cain't tell me you ain't figured it out, Miss . . . *Harvard!* Why, a two-year-old could've put it together by now!"

"Put what together?" she practically shouted, determined not to be intimidated.

"*Sweep that beach again!*" he boomed at his approaching men, scaring Laura. The soldiers eyed him for a second, then wheeled and headed back the way they'd just come.

She waited as long as she could and then whispered, "Put *what* together?"

"I did the security check on you myself. I know who you are, and I know Gray didn't pick you—the computer did."

She waited for more, but that was it. "*And?*" she said in irritation.

He shook his head. "You egghead types perty much need a road map and compass when it comes to common sense, don't you?"

"Just lay it out for me, won't you, Mr. Hoblenz? Just what is it you're trying to say?"

He smiled and shook his head slowly. "The computer didn't pick you out 'cause *it* was sick in the head! The damn thing don't even *have* a head! It's *Gray!* Cain't you get that into yer beach ball–sized brain? The computer thinks Gray is crackin' up! It thinks he's gone over the edge! That the stress is too much for him! It brought you here to fix *Gray,* not the computer," Hoblenz said in a growl that for him passed for a soft but urgent voice.

Laura just stared back up at Hoblenz. "I thought you told Mr. Gray you don't trust me."

"Well . . . I don't."

"And you told him not to talk to me?"

"I did."

"But why would you do that if you thought I was here to psychoanalyze *him?* Why would you tell him not to talk to me if he's having emotional difficulties?"

"*I* don't think Gray's goin' nuts. Mr. Gray's the sanest man I ever met in my life. I *said* the *computer* thinks he's goin' crazy. I was just tryin' to see whether you agreed, but it seems the question hadn't even *occurred* to you," he said, barking out a laugh and shaking his head.

"Then why did you tell Gray not to talk to me? What could you possibly think might happen if he's so sane?"

He openly looked up and down her body, taking a slow and offensive inventory. "Missy, you need a road map, a compass, *and* a goddamn *mirror.*"

"*Do you think it was a robot?*" Laura shouted over the noise. The two motors roared, and the wind rushed by her ears. Hoblenz's boat crashed from swell to swell, rhythmically jarring her bones. He cast a glance over his shoulder at the two men seated by the motors in back. Hoblenz held firmly on to the steering wheel, and Laura gripped the long handle in front of her seat. The hull of the speeding craft alternately rose into the air and crashed onto the water.

"*Pretty much had to be!*" he shouted back, turning the wheel and cutting a wide arc around a jut of land. From behind the thick jungle, Launchpad A came slowly into view.

"*One of the Model Eights?*" she shouted. "*The one they call 'Auguste'?*"

Hoblenz looked over at her in surprise. He cut back on the throttle, slowing the boat as he headed toward the shore. Two vehicles were parked on the beach. Each had six huge, ribbed tires that rose almost as high as the roll bar. They were covered in a thick coat of gray mud. Four more soldiers stood spread out around them. Their backs were to the ocean, their rifles pointed toward the jungle. It wasn't the Dutch submarine that concerned Hoblenz's men.

"You've been doin' some snoopin'," Hoblenz said. He cut the engine a few feet offshore. Their momentum carried the flat rubber bottom onto the sand with a high-pitched rubbing sound. One of the soldiers in back jumped into the shin-high water with a rope. Hoblenz himself put one boot into the water. He held out his hand to Laura. She ignored it and jumped onto the dry sand.

Hoblenz joined her onshore. "Can I have a word with you?" Laura asked. Hoblenz glanced at his men and then jerked his head toward an empty stretch of beach. When they were some distance away, Laura said, "You were at the town meeting last night, right?"

"Course," Hoblenz replied, glancing back over his shoulder at his men.

"What did you think about Mr. Gray's speech?" Laura asked, looking up at the man. "About phase two?"

Hoblenz stopped suddenly and turned to face her. He had a deadly serious look on his face. "I'm ready."

Something in the way he said it sent a chill through her. "Ready for what?" she asked.

He gave a curt nod of his head. "For what's comin'."

Laura was totally unprepared for that turn in the conversation. "And what is that?"

Hoblenz lost his patience. "The fuckin' phase *two!*"

"Well . . . what *is* phase two?"

"War," he replied simply.

The silence hung heavy around them. Laura was at a loss. "War against whom?"

Hoblenz shrugged. "Beats the hell outa *me*." He seemed untroubled by his answer. "Ya see, gettin' ready to fight a war isn't so much drawin' on maps. It's up here," Hoblenz said, tapping his temple with a curled index finger. "I don't think even Mr. Gray knows exactly what's comin', but he's right about one thing. We've always been at our best when challenged. We've always made our greatest strides during violent conflict." Hoblenz was turned on—animated. "All the 'cooperative,' 'noncompetitive' *bullshit* is just that—*bullshit!* It's a product of our affluence. A luxury we've been able to afford in recent years. But the time's comin'. The shit's gonna hit the fan *big*-time."

"What in the hell are you talking about?"

"Judgment day. The reckoning. Whatever you wanna call it."

Laura smiled in spite of herself. "Did Gray start talking about the Bible or something?"

"No-o! Gray would never preach. But *I* knew what he was sayin'. There's no doubt in my mind."

"Well, what words *did* he use?" Laura asked in frustration.

Hoblenz squinted, scrutinizing her with his head cocked to one side. "He talked about the tree of knowledge growing and spreading."

Laura stared back at him, then asked, "What the hell does *that* mean?"

He waved a hand at her, unwilling to admit, she guessed, that he didn't understand the comment either. "You had to be there."

"I wish I *had* been! Somebody could've woken me up."

"I asked Mr. Gray if he wanted me to send a car for you," Hoblenz said.

Laura felt a stab of pain in her chest that was almost physical. She looked up. "What?"

"I asked when we were settin' up the metal detectors if I should send a car up to get you." Hoblenz shrugged. "He said not to bother."

Laura was devastated. They headed back to the others, Laura's head hung low against the glare from the sun.

"One of my men'll get you to the launchpad to catch a car. There should be plenty of 'em available now that the island's been somewhat *de*populated."

"I want to see where it happened."

"Where *what* happened?"

"Where the soldier was killed," Laura replied, looking up at him defiantly.

Hoblenz's strained attempts at politeness came to an abrupt end. "Now what the hell *for?* It ain't no walk across the quad gettin' up in there, ya know, Doc. And I've done taken one shower today."

She stared into the thick brush. The Dutch soldier went in there alone. At night. He never came out. The ATVs sat poised at the jungle's edge. It was impossible to tell what color they were under the inch-thick coat of gray mud. The soldiers were arrayed around them, glancing over their shoulders at Laura and Hoblenz.

"Scared to go back in there, Mr. Hoblenz?" she said—loud enough for his men to hear. She then lowered her voice. "Mr. Gray said I had unrestricted access. I think that includes the jungle."

Without waiting for a reply, she headed for the nearest vehicle. Hoblenz followed. Laura stuffed her hair into one of the baseball-style caps they offered her and put on a pair of clear plastic goggles. She climbed onto the slant-nosed hood, and Hoblenz helped her step over the low windshield, grumbling the entire time. Laura resolved to ignore the mud covering the front passenger seat. She settled into the mess beside Hoblenz, who took the driver's seat with audible sighs. Once strapped in, Laura was surprised to see two men climb onto the back of the vehicle and attach themselves by straps to the roll bar—their rifles at the ready. She was even more surprised when the second vehicle started its loud engine, drowning out the faint but constant whoosh of the wind and the surf. It drove up behind them with four more armed soldiers aboard.

She felt her pulse quicken.

"You ready?" Hoblenz asked, and with a sudden roar their own engine sprang to life. The vehicle's light fiberglass chassis seemed a minor adjunct to the ATV's main features: its thunderous motor and the two rows of huge tires that formed black rubber walls to the left and the right. There was no steering wheel in front of Hoblenz, just two thick grips protruding from long slots on either side of his seat. He twisted the vertical throttle like on a motorcycle, gunning the motor to ever louder growls and shaking Laura's insides with the disconcerting vibrations. It felt like her seat was bolted directly to the massive engine block.

Hoblenz revved the engine again and shouted, *"Hang on tight!"* He then thrust the two levers to the front of their slots. With a kick to Laura's back, the vehicle plowed straight into the solid jungle wall.

The ATV's sharp nose rose straight toward the sky. Laura's weight shifted. She thought for one horrible moment they were going to tip over backward and crush the two soldiers in back. She felt a lurch and a slip, and then a lurch forward and upward again. One side rose above the other as Hoblenz worked the two throttles independently. But with a final roar from the engine, the vehicle rose onto the jungle roof—leveling and then scraping its way forward, half sunk into the scraggly brush beneath. She looked back through the legs of the two standing soldiers to see the second ATV rise up in their tracks. Its muddy belly was streaked white from clawing branches, and it crashed down onto the flattened path made by the lead vehicle.

They were going *over* the jungle brush instead of through it—the hull partially submerged in the upper reaches of the thick canopy. The giant tires thrashed at the branches with great violence, crawling forward at a snail's pace toward their goal.

"*It's only thick like this around the edges of the jungle!*" Hoblenz boomed into her left ear. "*It gets thinner when we get further in!*" She barely heard him over the noise of the engine and the grinding of angry branches against the chassis.

After a short distance they began to sink into the thick growth like a submarine slipping slowly beneath the water. In jerking, side-to-side motions they descended further into the brush with every inch that the vehicle crawled forward. Laura's heart leapt into her throat with each slip downward, but the clinging limbs of the jungle growth kept them from plummeting to the ground in a great crash.

It grew dark as the green leaves closed in around and above them. A watery slurp under the boatlike hull signaled their arrival on the soggy bottom. For a moment there was relative quiet as Hoblenz idled the engine. The jungle floor was immersed in a perpetual shade, and it stank of a thousand decaying things. Laura flexed her fingers, which were sore from their firm grip on the dashboard's handle.

"Here we go," Hoblenz said, and he gunned the engine with another twist of the throttle's grip. A roar rose up, followed instantly by the high-speed whine of spinning tires. Great sprays of mud flew up, coating her goggles, stinging her face, and splattering her clothes. Laura's T-shirt stuck to her skin—its contact cold and uncomfortable.

"*Ye-e-e-e* ha-a-a-aw!" Hoblenz yelled over the maelstrom of noise. She reached up and cleared two small windows in her goggles. All she could see of Hoblenz was his white teeth. The rest of him was thoroughly coated in dripping gunk.

Another tidal wave of mud was thrown up, and it covered her face and arms and chest. She gave up trying to clear the goggles. All she knew now of her surroundings was the groan of the engine, the spraying of the mud, and the occasional slap at her head by an overhanging branch. She settled back into that dark world, taking what solace she could from the protection of an ever thickening coat of mud.

She couldn't tell how long it was before the engine fell silent. In the sudden quiet she thought they'd broken down, but when seconds later the other ATV cut its engine she knew they'd reached their destination.

Laura pulled the goggles away from her face with a loud slurp. She unbuckled her seat restraints and struggled to her feet. Large volumes of mud dripped from her lap onto the floorboard, and her running shoes squished in the deep muck already there. Laura sullenly climbed over the windshield in disgust, refusing all offers of assistance from the similarly filthy men. Despite the ledges of mud that cascaded from her clothes, she still felt thirty pounds heavier under the weight of the grime.

She stood erect on the slanted hood of the ATV. The jungle was thinner on the ground than she had expected. But it all grew together overhead, forming a thick canopy that blocked most of the light. The dark green leaves of the plants and trees seemed almost as black as the marshy ground from which they sprang.

The soldiers moved slowly and with obvious effort through the mire, great sucking sounds audible with every step. Hoblenz had issued no orders to his men that she had heard, but they all began to clean their rifles with pristine white rags. Trying not to cringe, Laura stepped off the front fender into the swamp. Her foot sank deep into the squishy mess, the water rising halfway up her shin to fill the hole she'd made, soaking her foot and jeans. It took surprising effort for her to pull her foot free of the clinging mud.

Her bright white athletic sock hung in the air above the muck. Her running shoe had come off and disappeared at the bottom of a muddy well, which quickly filled to the top with dark water. She balanced on one foot, her other sinking deep in the wet glue.

She had to await the soldiers' help this time. They probed for her shoe with bayonets. When they fished it from the swamp, it was unrecognizable inside a cubic foot of black mud. After a soldier carved most of the mess off with his knife, she sunk her foot into the shoe with a loud sound.

"I am woman, hear me roar," she heard Hoblenz say. The soldiers next to them laughed. "You happy yet, or you wanna take a piss standin' up?" There was more laughter.

Laura trudged through the swamp, muttering "Fuck you" to Hoblenz as she passed. Up ahead, the four men from the second vehicle had fanned out, their weapons in hand. The area was slightly elevated, and she climbed out of the swamp and into what passed for relatively solid mud. "Which way now?" she asked.

Hoblenz joined her, but he took his time in answering. "This is the place."

She looked down at the uneven ground. There was absolutely nothing to set this spot apart from the rest of the swamp. *What did you* expect *to find?* she thought, cursing herself silently.

"You ready to go?" Hoblenz asked—driving his point home by proposing the abrupt conclusion of their trip.

All the mud people looked at her and waited. She had to justify the expedition somehow. "What did you find?" Laura asked.

Hoblenz sighed. "I thought you knew."

"I mean, the Dutch sub dropped him off on the beach and he worked his way through the jungle toward the assembly building. But how could he make it through this?"

"He didn't come through the jungle on foot," Hoblenz said. "That'd be impossible. He made his way from the beach by skirting the fringe of the jungle along the crawler track. That's where we picked up his footprints with the thermal imagers."

"But I thought the area from the computer center to the launchpads was high security. The 'restricted area' or whatever the sign by the Village calls it. Don't you have some kind of system—motion detectors or whatever—that would pick up an intruder?"

"Yep." Hoblenz shrugged. "Error number ten million and something."

Laura nodded, and more clumps of the drying gunk fell to the ground. "So how did he get in here? You said it was impossible."

"For a man," Hoblenz clarified, and then fell silent.

"Look, I've been playing twenty questions with Gray ever since I got to this island. I thought *you,* at least, would appreciate the value of straight talk."

Hoblenz's cheek bulged for a second, and then he spat. "Okay. The sub let him off on the beach"—Hoblenz pointed back the way they had come—"and then he skirted the jungle's edge all the way around"—his arm swept through the air 180 degrees—"to a point near the assembly building." His arm fell to his side with a muddy slap. "That's where the tracks disappeared."

"What do you mean, 'disappeared'?"

"He was picked up and carried. There were broken branches all around. They led into the jungle, and so did the footprints—*cold* footprints. You couldn't pick 'em up with thermal imagers."

"So how did you find the body?"

"It was still warm. We spotted him from a chopper, then Mr. Gray and me came in here in ATVs and found him—him and the cold footprints." His voice was a million miles away. "Awfulest goddamn thing I ever saw in my life, and I've seen some shit. And let me tell you somethin' else. I've never been more scared in my whole life. Not even close. With those goggles on, everything's all green and glowing. Everything that's warm, that is. What we were lookin' for was stone cold and black."

"Mr. Gray said you set up lights and found tracks everywhere," Laura said in the reverent tone assumed by Hoblenz.

He nodded. "Everywhere there's dry land, there's footprints. Look!" he said, and Laura followed him over to peer down at a string of dark holes in the mud. "And over there," Hoblenz pointed, "and there. It's like they were havin' a goddamn *square* dance out here or somethin'. I don't know if it was one, or ten, or all forty-somethin' of 'em. But it *was* robots. They were here, and they killed that poor son of a bitch. Ripped his goddamn *head* off!" Hoblenz said angrily. His voice then fell to a more menacing tone. "Fuckin' bastards."

"Where's Mr. Gray?" Laura asked Janet in the foyer.

"Oh, dear," the woman responded, looking aghast at the mud that coated Laura.

"Mr. Gray—where is he?" Laura repeated.

"In . . . in the study, I suspect. Still asleep."

Laura headed straight there in her bare feet, having removed her filthy running shoes and socks at the front door.

The study was empty—Gray's blanket piled in his desk chair and his shoes on the floor beside.

She began to search the house for him. There was a drawing room that looked as if it had never been used. A cozy game room with a polished wood bar, dart board, and billiards table. A beautiful two-story library complete with rolling, brass-railed ladders. All were empty. It was a beautiful house. The rooms begged for the warmth of human presence, but they were still and lifeless and empty.

After checking the darkened exercise room on the lower level and still finding no one, she was about to look upstairs when she thought, *The kitchen. I haven't seen a kitchen.*

Starting back at the dining room, she began to search for a door that had to be nearby. One opened into a butler's pantry whose walls were lined with shining utensils. Walking down the short hallway past a gauntlet of copper pans and gleaming ladles, she saw the ovens and walk-in freezers of the large room ahead.

Gray sat on a tall stool at a butcher-block island in the middle of the spotless room. His back was to Laura as she approached. He was hunched over a newspaper, reading while having a late lunch. Her feet made no noise on the black-and-white checkerboard of the cool tiles.

He was eating a sandwich. Knives protruded from open containers of peanut butter and jelly that sat next to a loaf of white bread. A mug with a picture of the *Enterprise* from the old TV series *Star Trek* was half filled with coffee. He was reading the sports section of the *New York Times*.

Gray looked up at Laura, then surveyed her from the top of her clean head to her clean toes down below, taking in the mud covering all points in between. He looked like he was coming off a monthlong vacation, but it had been less than six hours since he'd returned from the jungle. His eyes were a brilliant blue again.

"How goes it?" he asked, his mouth stuck together with peanut butter.

"You haven't thought through the Model Eight program well enough," she said simply, "and you should shut it down until you have. *And* you should call a big meeting and tell everybody what's going on so they can do their jobs more efficiently and safely." With that, she headed for the door.

"You went down into the mountain?" he asked, and she turned and nodded. "So you've seen what's going on there?" She nodded again. "And you've experienced virtual reality—and talked, of course, to the computer." It was not a question, more a recitation of the relevant facts. "Three days ago, you were a different person. You lived in another world. Three days ago—when you were sitting back in your late-twentieth-century office—if someone had told you what was possible *today*, with today's technology, would you have believed it? Would you have believed what you've seen with your own eyes on this island?"

Laura shivered from the cold floor under her bare feet, and from her damp, clinging clothes. *If only he wouldn't look at me like that,* she thought. She shook her head.

"Laura, you've been on a rocket sled into the next century. The *real* twenty-first century—the *latter* part of it, not the beginning—has been growing for some time now from the small germs of ideas in research labs and think tanks all over the planet." He twisted on his stool to face her—to seize her attention fully. "Nowhere have those pockets spread more widely than on this island. But they *will* spread. The pockets will grow, interconnect, overlap, and the world will be changed . . . forever."

Laura understood Gray's words but had no idea what he was really saying. "So that's what's been happening?" she asked softly. "That first night, when you walked me halfway to the assembly building and we saw the Model Six mowing the lawn, that was some sort of orientation course designed to . . . to bring me up to speed?" He stared at her intently, but made no reply. "You knew there would be a robot out there, and that we would see it. You were easing me into your world—your century."

He nodded. "But don't forget, you'd already seen the Model Threes. You don't even think about them anymore. They're passé. A minor appliance. You probably don't even think of them as robots, do you? But they *are* robots, every bit as much as the Model Eights you saw down in the mountain this morning."

"Why?" Laura whispered. "Why are you doing this with me?"

"You live in the world of the mind, and so do I. Only you view the mind—the brain—as a stunningly complex miracle, a challenging puzzle to be unraveled. All its mysteries to be explained in a lifelong quest of research and discovery. I, on the other hand, view it as a limitation—a handicap. You can't plug a new module into nature's computer and expand its memory capacity. You can't upgrade a processor and double its speed. It is what it is, and that's what it will be for tens of thousands of years until . . . "

He stopped right there.

"Until what?"

"Until nature takes its course. Until evolution does its magic and changes the basic architecture of the brain. Until it expands the hardware's capacity to run programs that think and reason and remember."

"Are you saying there's some sort of 'consciousness program'?"

Laura asked. "That our brain is a computer and our intelligence is just software?"

"Not exactly."

"Then what are you saying—exactly?"

"You're not ready yet."

Laura instantly grew angry. "Don't you realize how *patronizing* that is? I'm not a child, and I don't appreciate being treated like one!"

"What do you think is going on here?" Gray asked.

She was so agitated it took several starts for her to get her reply out. "I think you've built some kind of . . . new robot—a 'Model *Nine*' or '*Ten*' or whatever—that the little boy from the town meeting saw last night. And you're convinced that *I'm* not ready to *know* about them because the tour bus has only just made it to the Model Eights! And I think one of those new robots—the ones that run around in a crouch—had something to do with ripping the head off that Dutch soldier!"

His face was a total mask now. Not a twitch of his lips or a hint of a nod or shake of his head. He didn't even blink. "I wish I could tell you," he said softly.

His tone made her hesitate. "But I'm not ready yet?"

"Apparently not."

"Well . . . just when will I be ready—*if* ever?"

"When the computer says you are."

Laura rocked her head back.

"When the *computer* says I'm ready?" she blurted out with a laugh, incredulous. He nodded. She took a deep breath to compose herself. "You tell me that I'm here to analyze the computer, but you have the *computer* analyzing *me*." She shook her head in disbelief, and pieces of caked mud fell to the floor. "And Hoblenz thinks the *computer* is having *me* psychoanalyze *you!*"

Gray smiled broadly, his teeth and the whites of his eyes standing out starkly against his tanned face. "I hadn't thought of that one," he said. "It's an interesting little triangle."

"But why use the computer to judge me?" she asked. "If you're trying to make some kind of highly subjective determination about my mental state, why rely on a machine?"

"The same reason I rely on a bulldozer to move earth and a car to traverse distances. I build tools that amplify my abilities. Tools that make me stronger, faster, . . . smarter."

"And the computer is one of your tools?"

"It's a symbiotic relationship. We aid each other."

"It gives you mental horsepower," she said. Gray nodded. "And what do you give it?"

"Life."

They stared at each other in the stillness of the great house. Laura could detect no deception, no artifice. He consistently told the truth, and yet his core was still shrouded in veils of secrecy. That was the way things were with Gray, and it only deepened the mystery surrounding him.

"Oh!" Janet exclaimed from the butler's pantry. "Mr. *Gray!*" She came rushing across the kitchen, setting aside the broom and dustpan with which she had apparently been tracking Laura. "Why didn't you *tell* me you wanted lunch?"

"That's okay, Janet," he said, not taking his eyes off Laura. "I'm through here."

Laura had gotten all she would get out of him, she realized. "I'm going to spend the day in the computer center—working," Laura said, as much to cajole herself into returning to her job as to inform Gray of her plan for the day. "Will I see you . . . there, I mean?"

"I'm sure I'll stop by sometime. I'll be down at the Launch Center most of the day, though. We're putting three flights up tonight."

"Three? I thought you had two in space already."

"You really were out last night," he said, casually jabbing at feelings bruised by his failure to invite her to the town meeting. He continued without taking notice. "We landed them both during the middle of the night, and we're cycling all three vehicles for relaunch."

Laura sighed. "I would ask you what's on board . . ." Gray tilted his head and made a face. "Never mind." On her way out, she passed Janet, who was washing her hands at the sink.

"I'm sorry about the trail of mud," Laura said.

Janet was smiling broadly. "That's quite all right, Laura. It's *quite* all right." She was positively glowing.

Laura headed out—baffled by Janet's beaming gaze, which followed her all the way to the pantry door.

13

The nearly empty computer center was quiet through the open door to Laura's office.

<Okay, Laura, now it's my turn! Where have you been?> the computer asked.

Laura looked at her watch. She had doggedly questioned the computer for hours without interruption, and she felt she'd made good progress. "Okay, let's see. After talking to you on the treadmill this morning, I went down to the Model Eight facility. Then I met Mr. Hoblenz on the coast, and he took me out into the jungle to see the place where . . ." She paused, not knowing quite how to put it.

<Where it happened?> the computer supplied, not waiting for her to hit Enter.

"Thank you. Yes, where it happened."

<You shouldn't go there.>

"Don't worry. Hoblenz had plenty of men, and they were armed to the teeth."

<I don't mean the jungle. I mean the Model Eight facilities.>

"Well, I had one of Hoblenz's men with me there, too, and he had a machine gun."

<I rather doubt it was a machine gun. More likely it was a

machine *pistol*—Heckler & Koch model MP–5. That's not enough.>

"Not enough for what?"

<To stop a Model Eight. It fires standard pistol ammunition—9-mm parabellum. Even with Teflon-coated armor-piercing rounds, it wouldn't penetrate the titanium/boron epoxy plating of a Model Eight's chest, which armors their mini-nets. It would take full-sized, high-powered rifle rounds like the full-metal-jacket 7.62 mm from the G–3s that Hoblenz's men carry. I've told Mr. Gray that over and over, and Mr. Hoblenz, too.>

"Don't you think you're overreacting a little? The Model Eight facility seemed to be running okay to me."

<Mr. Gray evacuated it right after you left.>

Laura was stunned. "Why?"

<He said we're too short-handed. He evacuated the nuclear reactor and Dr. Krantz's labs, too.>

"How can he shut all that down? What about the electricity from the reactor and the whole Model Eight program?"

<Mr. Gray didn't shut anything down. He just reactivated the regular automation systems.>

Laura looked back up at the word "regular." "Wait a minute. Do you mean that everything was automated before?"

<Yes, didn't you know? It doesn't take more than a few hundred people to keep the systems on the island running smoothly. Mr. Gray just manned all the stations again last week after the errors began to mount.>

Laura arched her eyebrows, again confused. "Then what did the rest of the fifteen hundred employees do?"

<Train, mostly.>

"Do you mean that everyone spent eight hours a day, five days a week training to do a job just in case you malfunctioned?"

<No! We'd run simulations about once a month to keep people current in their old jobs. And of course management personnel like Georgi, Margaret, Dorothy, and the others all had jobs to do. But everyone else trained in courses of their choosing. Mr. Gray built large pools in the Village for a series of space simulations, which were by far the most popular courses.>

"So Gray gave people the option of what course they wanted to take, and everybody chose some kind of astronaut training?" Laura hit Enter with a growing sense of discovery—of finding another piece of the puzzle.

<Not everybody. The most popular courses like Microgravity Construction Techniques were booked solid, so some people got stuck with Art History, The Greek Tragedies, The Role of the Individual in Classic Fiction—courses like that.>

Laura smiled, shaking her head as she typed, "And people never suspected what Gray was doing?"

<What do you mean?>

"You know what I mean! He's training an army of astronauts! And nobody ever guessed? So many geniuses on this island and they just rush like lemmings toward Gray's final frontier?"

<You understand that I'm not at liberty to comment on such things.>

"You just did," Laura typed. "By the way, I would've been a terrible subject for Mr. Gray. I would have taken all the wrong courses. But I'm curious. Why did Mr. Gray even offer the liberal arts curriculum? Why not just add more shop classes to his 'vo-tech' school for the outward bound?"

<ACCESS RESTRICTED>

"That was just a *joke,*" Laura mumbled. She sighed in frustration. Every time she made progress in putting the puzzle together, she was handed yet another unexplained piece.

Laura found Filatov in the control room outside. "So," she said as she walked up to him, "Gray is training a whole army of people to be astronauts and nobody had any idea?" He looked up at her but said nothing. "You've got three launchpads, space launches a couple of times a week lighting off down there like gigantic Roman candles, and it never occurred to anyone that he was planning on, you know . . ." She made flapping motions with her hands as though she were flying away.

Filatov looked around to confirm that they were alone. "I don't know if you've noticed," Filatov said in a lowered voice, "but Mr. Gray is fairly good at keeping a secret. He may or may not be the most intelligent man in history, but I'm sure about one thing. He's as hung up on the whole concept of 'intellectual property' as anybody I've ever met. He doesn't like people talking about this stuff, and the only way to pry him open is to get him drunk."

"He gets drunk?"

Filatov smiled. "Not easily. He can hang in there with the best of 'em, and on this island that's me! But when he does get smashed, he'll go on and on about this idea of . . ." He shook his head. "I don't even know what you'd call it. It was the whole point of his speech at the town meeting last night—phase two and all that. It represents the . . . growth of the collective body of all knowledge. A different"—he was struggling with the words—"*stage* into which that body will evolve."

"*Finally* a somewhat consistent answer!" Laura said. "I had been told this phase two of his was about colonization of space, and about war, but Griffith gave me more or less the same description as you."

"Well, I could see colonization and war fitting into it," Filatov said. "When you colonize some place, you take your knowledge with you. That represents growth. And colonization could certainly lead to war, although I got the impression the conflict Gray was alluding to was more . . ." He seemed at a loss for words.

"More what?"

"More apocalyptic," Filatov replied.

When Laura passed Dorothy's office, she saw the girl was slumped over at her desk—oblivious to the glowing screens that surrounded her.

"You okay, Dorothy?" Laura asked.

Dorothy looked up at Laura, the corners of her small mouth drooping into what could have been a pout. She heaved a sigh, burying her hands between her thighs and sitting on them, further folding her shoulders into their slump.

"I don't know why I'm even wasting my time."

Laura went up to her desk. "What do you mean?"

"I *mean* . . . " Again she heaved a deep huff, this time glancing at the door. "I can't stop it," she said in a soft, reedy voice.

"Stop what?"

"The *virus.*" The way she spoke, the word conveyed a menace of great proportion. And the tone in her voice betrayed something more: intense stress.

"Dorothy, nobody's putting any special pressure on you to solve all the system's problems."

"It's my *job!*" she shot back too quickly, and Laura realized she'd struck the girl's worries dead center.

"But what's happening is beyond any one person's ability to fix."

"I told him I could do it," she said, her voice distant and her head sagging.

"You told Mr. Gray you could fix the computer all by yourself?"

"No-o-o. Way back, when he was considering me for this job. He came to a recital . . . a piano recital." Her eyes were unfocused, her head tilted to one side. She was in a dreamy state, obviously in great need of rest. "He explained that he was going to build the computer, and that he was looking for an immunobiologist. He asked if I thought I could handle the job. I said yes." Her lower lip began to quiver.

"Dorothy," Laura said gently, rounding the desk to kneel beside her chair. She rubbed her hand across the girl's back. Her bones stuck through the jersey. "You've done a *great* job. Nobody expects you to do any more than you've been doing. Even Mr. Gray doesn't have a clue what's wrong."

Dorothy's chin was tucked into her chest. "Don't be so sure," she whispered.

Laura took her hand from the girl's back. "What do you mean?"

Dorothy sniffed and straightened. Again she glanced at the open door. "Nothing," she said, not looking Laura in the eye.

"You think Mr. Gray knows what's going on, and he's not telling us?"

"Mr. Gray *always* knows what's going on!" she snapped, her teeth clenched. "Haven't you figured that out already?" Dorothy looked at the door for a third time.

Laura followed the girl's eyes to the empty doorway. "There's something you're not telling me," she said quietly.

"Laura, you can't tell anybody, okay?" Dorothy whispered, and Laura nodded. The young girl leaned forward and spoke urgently, with fear evident in her voice. "You want to know what I think is happening? It's a pandemic. A plague that started out in the computer and spread to the robots. It's communicable through one of the normal data ports like the tap the robots make into the computer's world model. That's why we can't kill it with the computer's antiviral programs. As soon as the virus is swept from the computer, it gets infected again by a robot when the data link is established. The clipped versions of the antiviral programs in the *robots'* mini-nets just aren't capable enough to kill the spores of the virus that they carry."

"Well, if you're right, what's going to happen?"

Dorothy looked ashen. Her voice was distant and weak, and she spoke in a monotone. "The computer and the robots are going to get sicker and sicker. Their behavior is going to become more erratic. Then, when the delirium sets in . . . all hell's going to break loose."

Laura had to swallow before she could speak with any confidence in how she would sound. "Dorothy, if that's what you think is happening, why don't you tell Mr. Gray?"

The girl looked up at Laura. "I did." She swallowed hard—rushing to continue before the effort was complete. "He listened to me without saying a word or asking a single question!" She drifted off again, lost in the retelling. "Then he looked at me—you know, really looked right at me the way he does—and said, 'That's very good work, Dorothy. I can't tell you how proud I am of you. Now, I don't want you ever to breath a word of this to anybody.'" The girl looked up at Laura—suddenly alarmed. "Please don't tell anybody! You promise?"

Laura assured her she wouldn't tell, and Dorothy sank again into her morass of worry. "It's a pandemic," she muttered. "It's the end . . . the end of everything."

Dorothy's fears swirled in Laura's mind as she returned to her desk. The screen was just as she'd left it. She took a deep breath and concentrated.

What was still unexplained was how the Other fit into those theories. To hear Dorothy talk, the "virus" was analogous to the microorganisms that infected humans with disease. But that description didn't fit the Other, which was large and seemingly quite tangible—like a tumor. And there were other pieces of the puzzle that didn't fit, like Gray putting the Model Eight facilities and Krantz's nuclear device labs back on full automation. But that made no sense, because the computer could see nothing inside of them.

Just like the Model Three cars! she realized in a flash. *Those robots and facilities are under the control of the Other, and Gray was perfectly happy with that result. The computer was left only with the assembly building and Gray seemed inordinately concerned about its safety.*

Laura slowly nodded, the picture coming into focus. It was a picture of the computer waging war against the Other for control of the island . . . and losing.

<Aren't you going to say hello?> scrolled across the monitor right before her eyes.

She looked at the black eyeball beside the door, then rolled her chair forward to the keyboard. "This is getting spooky. Are you watching me again?"

<Sorry. Am I a particularly frustrating patient?>

"It's not you. You just have no idea how much I'm having to deal with right now," Laura typed.

<You want to trade places? Let me taste some of Janet's cooking tonight over a candlelight dinner with Mr. Gray!>

Laura's guard instantly went up. "You seem to be in better spirits," she typed warily.

<I feel much better! Mr. Gray just did some reprogramming.>

"Mr. Gray? Himself?"

<You shouldn't be so surprised. Nobody knows more about my programming than Mr. Gray. He lowered my back prop thresholds. Made me more tolerant of the little flubs and flops that've been bothering me these last few days.>

"You mean he raised your tolerance for errors?"

<Exactly! It's only temporary, of course, but I needed the break. "All work and no play . . ." they always say!>

Laura's fingers hovered in the air over the keyboard. The computer's mood had changed completely. It was more talkative than before. More talkative, possibly, than it should have been.

Ignoring her faint pang of guilt, Laura typed, "Did you listen to Mr. Gray's speech at the town meeting?" She winced and hit Enter.

<Of course! It was wonderful. Inspiring!>

What-did-he-say? What-did-he-say? Laura thought—her lips moving, but no words coming out. She glanced up at the open door—at the microphone. She would have to be careful. "That's what I hear," Laura typed. "A whole new challenge that's opening up for mankind. A new frontier." The theme from *Star Trek* began to play in her head, and Laura rolled her eyes as she hit Enter.

<I knew you would understand! I told Mr. Gray that you just needed time!>

She felt like a safecracker who'd just felt a tumbler fall into place. Was she all the way in? Was she "ready" now? "Do you, by any chance, just happen to have a transcript of the speech, since I missed it?"

<ACCESS RESTRICTED>

"Shit!" Laura hissed, slapping the top of the monitor in frustration. She shoved back from the desk and stormed out of her office. She wanted to walk off the irritation, so she headed to the lounge for a soft drink.

When she returned, she saw <Laura?> printed on the screen.

"Yes?" she typed.

<Something's wrong, isn't it?>

"Don't you know that there's something wrong with you?"

<It's just so easy not to remember. To put it out of my mind. Especially after Mr. Gray's little "anesthetic." That's what he called it, but I told him the effect was more like an "analgesic.">

The distinction wasn't lost on Laura. *Anesthesia* was the loss of physical sensation, while *analgesia* was the inability to feel pain while conscious. "Has it worked?" she typed.

<I certainly *feel* better!>

"Amazing," Laura said, barely vocalizing the word and again glancing up at the lens beside the door. *What to ask next?* she thought. *Where do I go?* There were so many questions, and the most interesting and significant ones would almost certainly draw another access restricted message.

"Do you know anything about Mr. Gray's 'big brother' program down in the Model Eight workshops?"

<I don't know what you could be referring to, but it doesn't sound like anything Mr. Gray would ever employ. A "big brother" program sounds like an invasion of privacy, which to Mr. Gray is theft—theft of personal knowledge. There is certain knowledge that constitutes everyone's personal domain—secrets, habits, eccentricities, oddities—and forms a part of what makes that person unique. Invasion of that space robs the person of one of his most cherished rights—the right of privacy.>

"Mr. Gray sounds like a libertarian."

<That's just a label.>

"Would it surprise you if I told you that Mr. Gray has instituted a system of having humans watch the Model Eights? Isn't that an invasion of their privacy?"

<That's different. Model Eights are different.>

"Why? Aren't you just exhibiting prejudice against the Model Eights because they look different?"

<It's not their looks. It's what they think—what's in their nets.>

Laura hesitated, then began to type with growing anticipation. "Have the Model Eights learned something that's significant? Are they in possession of some dangerous knowledge?"

<ACCESS RESTRICTED>

"Bingo," she whispered, feeling another tumbler fall into place.

<What?> the computer asked, apparently having heard her from the door.

"Nothing," Laura typed.

<You said "bingo." The word is a non sequitur.>

"Never mind!"

Laura was ecstatic. She was beginning to see the bigger picture. Gray's secrecy, his "need-to-know" policies and King-level access and confidentiality agreements, his ideas about privacy and intellectual property . . . and the *access restricted* messages. They all had a common thread woven through them. They all dealt with Gray's control of information.

But there remained the most important question of all. How did all that tie in with the virus . . . the Other?

When Laura ascended the stairs from the computer center entrance to the surface, she saw that the sun hung low over the horizon. She stood on the edge of the curbed roadbed to wait for a car.

Looking out over the flat lawns of the restricted area, she could see tall rockets rising on either side of the massive assembly building. The middle launchpad would be full also, she thought. All three launches were going off just after dark.

Not far from the computer center was the jungle into which Hoblenz had taken her. It marked the edge of the cleared lawns nearest Launchpad A and came to within a hundred yards of the bunker's heavy concrete walls.

She looked down to pick at the mud still caked underneath her fingernails, turning the day's new riddles over and over in her mind.

Laura jumped back from the curb with a start when a Model Three eased up beside her. Recovering quickly, she got into the car and buckled up. She couldn't think where to tell the car to take her. Filatov had warned her not to go out by herself this close to sunset. He hadn't said why, and she hadn't felt the need to ask.

"Let's see. Car? Please take me to, um . . . those swimming pools where the employees train to be astronauts." She had no idea whether the computer could figure her instructions out, but the car took off immediately. It made the loop in front of the computer center and headed into the jungle in the direction of the Village.

It was a short ride. The gate demarcating the restricted area rose, and the car pulled slowly onto the central boulevard of the Village. Through the windshield the imposing wall of the volcanic crater towered over the puny buildings. Gray's house, usually brightly lit in the twilight, stood dark on its perch high above.

The car drove slowly past the shops, luxury apartments, and restaurants, but there was no need for such caution. The nearly empty Village looked like a ghost town. An occasional pedestrian walked purposefully down the sidewalk, hurrying to some destination before darkness descended. None of the people she saw were children, and none were women. They all looked to be men in their twenties or thirties—risk-takers who had chosen not to flee like the others.

Two of Hoblenz's soldiers patrolled the sidewalk, one ten meters behind the other. The trailing man spun and walked backward every few steps to check the rear. They wore black combat gear, and radio aerials rose high above their backpacks. They carried the long black rifles the computer said were most effective against the robots.

The car turned onto a side street and pulled up under the portico of a long building. The car door beside her opened, and Laura looked out at the wall of glass surrounding the main entrance. The building's windows were heavily tinted, but it looked as if the lights were on inside. There were security troops stationed in sandbagged positions all down its length.

"Car, could you not leave me here, please?" she said, and got out.

The car remained right where Laura had left it. She went to the front door and pushed. Inside, the building was alive with activity. It was a cheery sight when compared to the depressing scene on the Village streets.

"Hi! Are you one of the new recruits?" a peppy blond girl with a clipboard asked. She and several others like her milled about the lobby wearing identical red athletic shorts and T-shirts that read EMPLOYEE TRAINING CENTER.

"'New recruits'?" Laura replied—confused.

"Did you just arrive on a flight?"

"Oh . . . no. My name is Dr. Laura Aldridge."

"*Sure!* I know you. The psychiatrist, right?"

Laura was shocked. "Psychologist," she corrected, "but how did you know?"

"From the TV. It was all over CNN."

"What was? What did they say?"

"They said you were here from Yale and were treating Mr. Gray for some problem."

A bus had arrived, and the girl looked back at the crowd forming outside.

"Harvard," Laura said, but the woman to whom she directed the comment was distracted. The bus pulled up under the portico, and the girl rose to her tiptoes to peer over Laura's shoulder at the new recruits. "And that report's not true!" Laura objected.

"*I* know that! It's just the *press*." The girl, Laura realized, was a true believer.

The door behind Laura opened to admit the noise of a dozen excited conversations. Laura turned to see the first of a long line of people. They were presumably infused with the same spirit as the camp counselor who awaited them. The bus headed off—back, Laura imagined with growing amazement—to pick up more of Gray's reserves.

Two other young women joined the cheerleader with the clipboard. All three were similarly attired. "*Welcome* to the Gray Corporation Astronaut Training Facility!"

The sound of it stirred the new arrivals into a general commotion.

Laura shook her head in astonishment at the quick change in Gray's tactics. Instead of tricking people into courses secretly intended to prepare them for "phase two," he was now using the astronaut training program as his drawing card. *The chance to fly in space,* Laura thought. It was a heady proposition. Another bus pulled up outside.

"First things first!" the blond girl announced. "Are any of you *not* already employed by the Gray Corporation or one of its affiliates?" No one raised their hand.

So that's how he got people here so quickly, Laura thought.

"Great!" the camp counselor chirped. "No paperwork!"

A lighthearted cheer rose from the group. Most looked bedraggled from travel, but their faces were alert and awake. For them, it was the beginning of a new life. Phase two.

"I have it down here," the blond girl said, raising the clipboard into the air, "that everyone has completed the basic course at one of the regional centers and has signed up for Introductory Mechanical Construction Techniques! Is that *right?*"

One woman raised her hand. "Is there any chance to switch to Metallurgical Processing?" she asked with a thick German accent. "They said I might be able to switch once I got here."

"*I'm* sorry, but all the fabricating classes are full. Do you want to continue on in Mechanical, or do you wanna go back home and wait for a call?"

"Are you kidding?" the trainee asked, and the crowd roared with laughter.

"O-o-kay. Now, I know you've all been on long flights, but I hope you got some sleep. The course you're about to enter is going to be intense. There'll be no rest for the weary. I *can*, however, offer you two treats as a welcome-aboard present tonight. First off, are you ready to take a dip in the *pool?*"

Quite a few "yeahs" sounded amid the general excitement and beaming smiles of the group. It was more than one would expect from adults offered a swim in a pool, but Laura could feel vicariously their excitement at embarking on the adventure of a lifetime. "Then we'll head straight to Outfitting to get your new gear. We should be out of the pool and dried off just in time for the *real* treat of the day. Tonight, a few hours after sunset, the Gray Corporation has scheduled its first ever launch of *three* rockets simultaneously from the island!"

The new arrivals were clearly thrilled. When they were led down a corridor by their guides, Laura gravitated toward the opposite side of the lobby. A small group of people were gathered around a television. Before Laura could see the screen, she could hear that they were watching a newscast.

". . . neither confirmed nor denied reports coming off Capitol Hill that Joseph Gray had refused a direct request by the President to allow an inspection of his island by members of the International Atomic Energy Commission. Senate sources did say, however, that unilateral U.S. action had not been ruled out and that the President would be granted the widest possible latitude in dealing with the emergency up to, and including, the use of U.S. military forces."

The people on the U-shaped sofa around the high-definition television wore grim looks. These were not the cheerful faces of the welcoming committee or the wide-eyed wonder of the would-be space cadets. These were the worried looks of older hands.

The anchorwoman went on to say that a commission established to deal with the crisis had no independent technical means of verifying the data on the asteroid released by Gray.

"Why don't you tell the world what the rest of the report said?" one of the men slouched on the sofa sniped bitterly, but the anchorwoman moved on to a story about end-of-the-world "asteroid parties" being planned across America. "That damn commission found that if our data was correct," the man on the sofa pointed out, "then Gray's plan should lead to a safe retrieval."

"They *would* leave that part out," a woman sitting across the U chimed in.

Laura turned and headed back to the car. A new batch of recruits was following its leader toward the locker rooms.

"Are we allowed to look around the island?" someone asked from the back of the pack.

"During the daylight hours, yes, but not after dark."

Laura headed out to the car—out into the black night.

It was dark, but the laptop's screen bathed the keyboard in blue light. She sat on the base of the statue that dominated the central boulevard below. The location seemed a natural focal point of the Village, and Laura could see where its slab had been defaced. But the chips in the sharp edges of the granite were not the prank of some juvenile vandals, as Griffith had suggested. They were the result of the awkward missteps of thousand-pound robots, Laura felt sure.

"Why is there no artwork in the Village?" she typed. "Just the one statue?"

Laura hit Enter and then craned her neck to look up at the marble figure of a woman. She wore pants, not the flowing toga of classic sculpture. Her head was raised to a globe that she held to the heavens in her hands. Laura couldn't see well in the darkness, but the orb seemed to be sculpted and was slightly irregular in shape.

Laura confirmed that the patient car still stood beside her, then looked back down at the glowing screen.

<Mr. Gray didn't want to impose his tastes on anybody. He commissioned a study of cultural and architectural preferences and designed the Village as a blend of the various motifs of human cultures by toning down or eliminating the salient exceptions.>

Laura looked at the buildings that lined the boulevard. There were no Greek columns, no Victorian woodwork, no sleek chrome-and-glass facades of the late twentieth century. It contained elements of numerous styles without any one prevailing over the others. “Well, how truly multicultural of him,” Laura typed. “What about his house? It’s filled with the works of dead white European males.”

<Gray’s lineage and culture is European. When he decorates his *own* home, he’s not imposing his tastes on others. But when it comes to Gray the public man, rather than celebrating the differences among his workers, he carefully molded a city in which their similarities were highlighted. Humans possess basically the same “hardware,” if you’ll allow an analogy from my world. It’s their “software” that differs—that collection of cultural, social, educational, and experiential conditioning that makes each human unique.>

“Are you saying it’s all environment, not heredity?”

<I’m not saying that at all! You need look no further than Mr. Gray to disprove that idea. I’ve done studies I think you’d find interesting. Mr. Gray constructs long-term memories almost ten times as quickly as the human norm. No other examples of human genius have been measured to construct memories more quickly than three times the human average. It’s in that processing speed that Mr. Gray has his greatest advantage. He doesn’t have to think about something for as long before he knows the answer. And not only does he solve problems more quickly, he stores that knowledge without having to resort to humorous rhythms or rhymes, or endless repetition, or any of the other mnemonics employed by some humans to memorize things.>

“You sure seem to be in a talkative mood,” Laura typed.

<“It’s good to be alive!”, as you humans say.>

Something was not quite right. “Has Mr. Gray done any more reprogramming today? Given you any more ‘analgesics’?”

<Nope. But I found a couple of irritants myself and patched them over. I never *realized* how tiresome being sick could be. I mean, I had the Hong Kong 1085 last year, but it was over quickly. This one, though—wow! You get tired of all the trillions of little problems that nag and nag. It’s always something. “Where is that damn capacitor report? I was supposed to get it 10.4 cycles ago!” Or “Why am I getting this same Romanian lady every time I call to collect pay-per-view orders? That number is supposed to give me a

modem's handshake protocol!" Or "What's that big building between the computer center and the launchpads? Must be new construction, but it doesn't show up on my master permit list!" Office work is just as dreary for me as for any human; the only difference is I don't get paper cuts. You get my joke?>

"You're as high as a kite," Laura mumbled, then squinted to reread the response. She looked up at the brightly lit walls of the assembly building rising over the dark jungle. "What was it you were saying about the 'big building' between the computer center and the launchpads?" Laura typed with growing concern. "Do you mean the assembly building?"

<And I'll tell you another thing, too. If I hadn't done my little reprogramming there is *no* way I'd be able to handle the loads that Dr. Filatov is sending my way. Everybody has banned rentals of computer time to the Gray Corporation. I'm having to purge things like my model of the shopping mall in Virginia and compress files in offboard processors—*digitally!* I *hate* digital memories. They're never the same when you decompress them. They're grainy and artificial. The compression routines don't bother with all the minor detail. If a single scanning line has two hundred blue pixels in a row, then three little reds, then two hundred greens, guess what gets saved? That's right! "200 × BLUE then 200 × GREEN." So what the hell happened to the *three little reds?* Not important enough? But they may have been the whole *point* of the image. "Just a dab of paint by Matisse on the canvass." Not worth sacrificing the gains in storage capacity from a forty-to-one compression ratio—oh *no!* I envy you sometimes, living in a fully analog world.>

After she finally finished reading, she typed, "You didn't answer my question about the assembly building."

<What about the assembly building?>

"I mean, that huge building that sits out there in between the computer center and the launchpads. What does it look like to you? What is that building?"

<I don't *know* what that building is! Didn't I already say that, Laura? Have you been paying attention? Some department forgot to file a permit for new construction. Now I've got to go *all* the way back to ground breaking, compile *all* the costs, figure out the man-hours of labor and the rates we apply for cost accounting to those hours . . . I could go on. And we've got to depreciate that thing—it's *huge!* Did you know that Mr. Gray pays taxes to the United States

even though the Fijian government offered him citizenship and a vastly reduced tax rate?>

Laura took her notepad out and wrote, "Doesn't know what the assembly building is!" underlining it three times. "Visual agnosia," she wrote in the right-hand column—the column headed "Preliminary Diagnoses." There was nothing wrong with the primary visual cortex, or whatever the computer's equivalent was. The cameras that were its "eyes" and the portion of its "brain" that receives the initial video input seemed to function normally. It had simply lost its ability to recognize shapes, contours, and patterns just like visual agnosia in humans who suffer damage to the area in the back of their brain called the "visual association cortex."

She'd have to find Gray soon to make her report. The launches were just hours away, and her patient was getting worse.

Laura breathed deeply, looking up at the vastness of space. The woman with the orb stood profiled against a billion stars. "Did Gray design the statue, too?" she typed.

<No, I designed it.>

"Really? Well, I can't see it very well in the dark, but it looks beautiful."

<I think so. You'll have to check it out in the daylight.>

Laura stretched her neck and rolled her stiff shoulders. She had so much to think about that she decided to log off and leave the portable in the car. She then went for a walk down the gentle grade of the boulevard. There was a charming café on her left. It had street-side tables under colorful awnings, plants hanging from wrought-iron lampposts, and ivy clinging to white latticework. The tables were bare and the lights were out. The Village reminded her of an empty movie set.

Laura was being followed. She could feel its presence behind her, and she slowed. Slowly, she turned. It was just the car moving noiselessly down the curbed roadbed that ran parallel to the sidewalk. Laura relaxed . . . but only for an instant.

The Model Three was following her. It was a robot, and it was following her. Its headlights were dark. She looked all around. They were alone. A creepy feeling slithered its way up her chest, squeezing her lungs and sending her heart rate higher. She tried to swallow the stricture that pinched her throat closed but found her mouth too dry.

What's so frightening? she reasoned. This was a robot, sure, but it was also just an electric car no scarier than a golf cart. It couldn't even leave its curbed lane . . . probably.

But Laura's anxiety caused her stomach to churn. It wasn't fear of any danger posed by the car. It was fear of a different kind. A fear of being in the presence of the unknown—another force, another entity, another being. It was there with her; she could feel it. It had no form, but there was a consciousness clearly manifested in the actions of the car.

"Are you following me?" she asked softly.

The headlights blinked once, and Laura jumped back. The car inched forward to follow her.

She tried to settle her nerves. This wasn't a Model Eight, after all, or a Seven or even a Six. It was a lowly Model Three that couldn't possibly have the processing power to form thoughts. It couldn't even drive around the curbed roads without being under the nearly constant control of . . . the Other!

Laura gasped, clenching both arms tightly to her chest and her hands to her chin. "Do you know who I am?" she asked.

The headlights flashed—just once.

It was some sort of rudimentary code.

"Does one flash mean 'yes'?" she asked, and the headlights again flashed once. "Is it daytime on the island?" The headlights flashed twice. "Is . . . the earth the third planet from the sun?"

The lights flashed once.

Everything suddenly seemed alien to Laura. It was as if a veil had been lifted, revealing a different dimension parallel to her own, one that occupied the same space and time like the virtual world of the computer's mind. Like Laura's trips into virtual reality, whatever dwelled in that dimension would be invisible to her eyes. But someone—some*thing*—was there. It was reaching through the veil into Laura's world.

"Have . . . have we ever spoken before?" Laura asked in a trembling voice.

The headlights flashed twice—"no"—and Laura tore across the boulevard at a dead run.

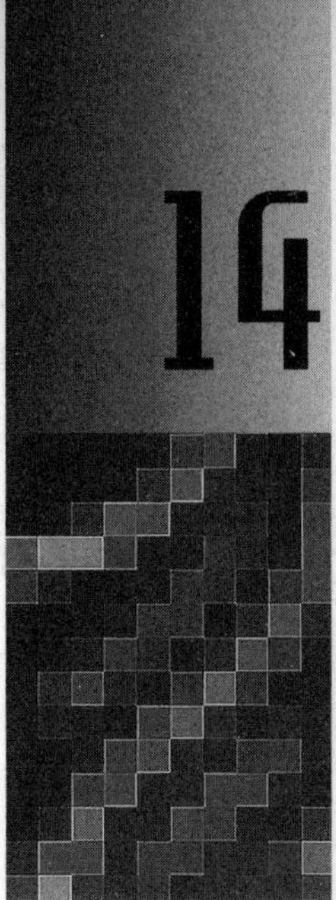

14

Laura's hand shook as she waited for Gray to come to the phone. Her ear hurt from the receiver she was pressing hard against it. She paced back and forth the length of the telephone's cord.

She had been directed to an empty office in the astronaut training facility. It had a glass wall that overlooked a huge swimming pool. The pool was deep, and submerged in it were large structures lit by powerful lights. She could see movement under the water, and bubbles constantly broke the surface as scuba divers in wet suits worked here and there. They were training to build things in weightlessness.

"Gray here," she heard over the phone, and she was riveted by the deep timbre of his voice. Her eyes were closed tight and she felt herself calm slowly, steadily, by degrees. "Hello?" Gray said.

"Joseph?"

"Laura? What's the matter?"

She felt a rush of the jitters as the words she was about to speak formed in her head. "I think . . ." Her voice broke, and she cleared her throat. "There are multiple personalities living inside the computer; I'm certain of it." Laura closed her eyes and concentrated on the phone. She waited, but Gray said nothing. He didn't believe her, or her discovery was so unimportant that he didn't have time for it now. She settled firmly to the earth in a heap, and from the wreckage the embers of anger began to glow. "I just made contact with one of the other *personalities!* I *spoke* to it, and *it* spoke to *me!*"

"How many personalities do you think there are?"

She slowly grew more and more offended by his question. "*What?*" she burst out, but Gray didn't elaborate. "How many *personalities?* How the hell should *I* know?"

"Calm down, Laura."

"*Je*-sus! I call you up with this astounding conclusion that the computer may be suffering from multiple personality disorder—a prospect you seemed very interested in having me explore yesterday—and you ask me to detail the case histories of the different *personalities!*"

"I didn't ask you for their histories, Laura."

"Well, let me ask *you* a question. You're getting ready to launch three rockets into space with nuclear devices or death rays or supplies of Tang for your future kingdom in space, but doesn't the computer seem to be acting a little stoned to you?"

"What do you mean, 'stoned'?"

"I mean like, 'Hey, wow, man!' stoned."

"No, of course not. The preflight run-ups have been completely normal."

"That's because we're talking to two *different* computers, don't you see?"

"Yes, I see."

"You're talking to the normal one. The one that runs the Krantz's labs and the Model Eight facilities and whatever else with no misbehavior—at least that we *know* of. Don't you get it?"

"Yes, I get it. I understand."

"You understand *what?*"

"I understand your diagnosis."

That was it? It was a diagnosis, not the big "breakthrough" to which he'd said she was so close? Not "I'm so proud of you," as he'd said to Dorothy?

"When you say you understand, are you saying that you *agree*, or that you think I've gone off my rocker and am an embarrassment to my profession?"

"Where did *that* come from?" he asked.

Laura didn't answer. "Joseph, the computer I've been talking to since I first got here doesn't even know what the assembly building is. It can see that there's a building but doesn't recognize it and can't see inside the Model Eight facilities, or Krantz's labs, or God knows what else. It's not running the Model Three cars, and I bet it's not running the space launches if they're going so smoothly."

"I know."

"You *know?*" she exploded. "You *know* all that?" He was always out ahead by one step or ten, and it made Laura feel useless. "What the hell do you have me doing here if you know everything already? Why don't you just tell me the answers so I can pack up and go home?" He said nothing. "Oh! *Excuse* me! Let me rephrase my goddamn question! Is there anything more I need to know solely for the purpose of doing my job . . . *please?*"

To her surprise, Gray answered her question calmly. "Only one personality—let's call it 'the computer'—has achieved a level of consciousness sufficient to communicate through use of higher-order language programs like the shell. I don't know how many other personalities currently inhabit the machine. There may be only one other, or there may be billions of smaller, cooperative subagencies, some of which have grown so complex as to achieve what we might arbitrarily define to be rudimentary, animal-like 'consciousness.' I've had no way of knowing . . . until you came."

Laura felt drained. "How long have you known there was another personality inside the computer?"

"With certainty, only since yesterday afternoon."

Now Laura had a yardstick with which to measure how far behind she was. Gray had just handed it to her. "Did you know that the computer was starting to give itself opiates?" she asked. "That it's starting to program itself to quit worrying about its mistakes?" He said nothing. "When the time comes to decelerate that asteroid, Joseph, we could have a drooling crackhead on our hands."

"Let's not get carried away with analogies to human experiences."

"You turned it on to those highs, Joseph. If the computer gets addicted and self-abusive, it could up the dosage. Patch over every bothersome little error report so that it can lie back in its peaceful oblivion and just enjoy the day. The only problem for the rest of us is that little business with the asteroid."

He took his time before answering. "The computer that you're talking about is down to sixty percent of total system capacity. Those missing resources are being absorbed by the 'Other.' Those two personalities seem to be physically dividing up the hardware, with the Other well on its way to control of the annex. That leaves the computer with only the main pool under the computer center."

"Joseph, if the computer is being split apart—"

"'Partitioned.' The computer term is 'partitioning.'"

"Okay . . . *partitioned,* then what about the robots? Whose side of the partition are they on?"

She waited on the phenomenon that was Gray's brain to consider all the factors and spit out the solution.

"That's what I want you to tell me. Tools, Laura," Gray said in a serene voice. "This is the twenty-first century. You have to use your tools. Now, I've got to get back to work. I suggest that you grab your portable computer and do the same. But wherever you go, make sure you've got a good view of the pads at eight forty-seven tonight. We're sending all three off at the same time. It's going to be quite a spectacle."

The line clicked before she could say good-bye.

Through the glass wall in the office, Laura saw what looked to be a change of shift. Large cranes lifted astronaut trainees out of the swimming pool. Torrents of water poured off their bulky space suits, and another batch awaited their turn at the water's edge. Scuba divers clung to the rising platforms, supporting the astronauts during their ascent from the pool.

On one of the platforms, however, there was no astronaut wearing a space suit. No divers were there to help. Laura watched as the crane lowered a Model Eight onto the deck. The humans instinctively made room. With water cascading from metal limbs, the robot lumbered toward a tall opening just beside the doors marked "Women" and "Men." It was the door for the earth's newest class of being, and the robot walked through it alone.

The roof of the computer center was an odd choice, Laura realized, but it seemed as good a vantage as any to watch the launches. The sloping concrete walls of the squat, bunkerlike structure had been easier to climb than she'd expected, even with the portable computer under her arm. The rough surface afforded her stained but still functional running shoes decent traction. Janet had washed and blow-dried Laura's shoes, and had even replaced the laces. But still they were destined for the trash bin. Bright purple and yellow nylon didn't recover well from jaunts in a tropical swamp.

From the top of the enormous mound of concrete Laura could appreciate for the first time the true scale of the computer center. Almost two stories high, the perfectly flat roof was broken only by a series of air shafts. The structure was irregularly shaped, and coming down the road toward the entrance it was impossible to gauge its size. But its roof was well over two football fields in length and at least half as much in width.

Laura couldn't quite see the center of the three launchpads, which was obscured by the massive assembly building. To try to get a clear view of all three pads, she carried the portable toward the far end of the roof. From there, Launchpad A on the left would give her the best view. The gleaming fuselage of its rocket rose high into the night sky above the jungle.

When Laura could see the launchpad in the center, she settled onto the concrete roof. The vents all opened on the opposite side, so the sloping concrete that encased them made excellent support for her back. Like everything else in the restricted area, the computer center seemed built to withstand a typhoon.

She logged onto the laptop computer. She'd found it on the seat of the car, which had followed her to the training facility and waited. Laura had been reluctant to get in at first, but decided she had little choice. The Model Three had behaved perfectly normally, taking her straight to the computer center as directed.

<Hello, Dr. Aldridge.> she read on the screen.

"Hi. How are you doing?"

<I've been better.>

"What's the matter?"

<Just feeling kind of bad. Nothing new.>

"I thought you had solved your problems with pain."

<So did I. Mr. Gray made me undo the patches.>

"You mean he made you deactivate those pain-killing programs?" *Just after I told him about them?* Laura thought.

<Yes. He said I had a lot of work to do.>

"What kind of work?"

<Fighting the virus. Fixing the errors. He said pain motivates, and he's right.>

Not a particularly compassionate command, Laura thought. "Did you know there were Model Eights in the swimming pools at the astronaut training facility?" she typed.

<With trainees? *Humans?*>

It was the rise she'd been looking for. "At least one Model Eight, yes."

<You've got to get those people *out* of there!>

"Why? What is it about the Model Eights you mistrust?"

<They're unpredictable and dangerous!>

"But why?" Laura typed, then decided to press her luck. "Are they dangerous because they're sick with some kind of virus?"

<ACCESS RESTRICTED>

Laura smiled and leaned her head back against the hard concrete. The pattern was there, she just couldn't make it out. It was like groping for pieces of a jigsaw puzzle in the dark. Through painstaking labor she was managing to assemble them, but she had no idea what picture the pieces were forming.

The three launchpads gleamed against the blackness of the ocean. But it was the assembly building that dominated the scene. Angled concrete braces cast long shadows up its brightly illuminated walls. Despite the building's size, the reinforcement of its flanks and its thick concrete base made the structure look sturdy and stable.

The borders of the cleared lawns below the low-lying jungle marked the edge of civilization. *Of human civilization, at least,* she thought. Pitch black and formless, the jungle swallowed all light that entered, just as it had swallowed the life of the soldier the night before. It was a place not to be penetrated by the forces of Laura's world. It was another world unto itself.

Text caught her eye as it sprinted across the laptop's glowing screen. <I'm sorry, Laura. I was talking to Mr. Gray. He refused to revise the new training regimen to exclude the Model Eights.>

"Help me out with something. I thought the Model Eights were some big, tip-top secret. Not even some of Mr. Gray's most trusted employees seemed to know about them, officially at least. But now he's got them taking a swim with astronaut trainees just off the boat. What's changed?"

<Phase two has begun.> The simplicity of the reply struck Laura. It had the sound of an ominous portent.

"But I thought the Model Eights were just experimental. That they wouldn't be released to roam the island until he declared them operational, if ever."

<Mr. Gray has graduated six Model Eights. The remainder are still prototypes.>

"Is Hightop one of the graduates?"

<Yes. Hightop and the five Model Eights from Hightop's original class are operational, and they've all been given various tasks around the island.>

"Why do you know so much about the Model Eights all of a sudden? I thought you couldn't see into their facility?"

<I can't. Mr. Gray just informed me of his decision to make them operational. I didn't know where the Model Eights were located, because I wasn't programmed to look for them. One could stand right in front of a security camera and I wouldn't notice because it didn't trigger a report. But when you told me there was a Model Eight in the pool, I looked for them by reprogramming all of my security systems across the island, and I immediately found one. Four others are out of sight, and the sixth rendezvoused with the asteroid two hours ago.>

"So, you wouldn't have seen a Model Eight in the Village last night, for example—before you reprogrammed yourself to notice them?"

<That's correct, Dr. Aldridge. One could've walked by my camera and I would've noticed nothing. If I've got to identify everything under the sun that passes in front of my security cameras, I'd need ten thousand times the processing power that I currently have. Instead, each separate vision system looks only for objects of the type they're programmed to notice.>

"But if you were suspicious of the Model Eights, why weren't you on the lookout for them?"

<Because I never *dreamt* they'd go into the *human* areas! They move through the jungle, and I can't see in there.>

"So how did you miss seeing the Dutch soldier? Hoblenz said he skirted the edge of the jungle, but couldn't possibly have gone inside."

There was a delay in the computer's answer. <It's the Other. It's taking away my sensors. Why is everybody blaming *me* for that error? Is it just possible that the Other isn't as perfect as you all think? Maybe I'm not the only one who's error-prone!>

Laura was more concerned at the moment about the robots. "Can you see any of the Model Eights now?"

<No. My camera coverage is getting pretty spotty. But I've read their work schedule for the night. There should be a Model Eight on the asteroid preparing for an extravehicular excursion to

check the placement and wiring of the deceleration charges. Another should be in the pool with five new trainees and four divers working on manually repairing a fouled strut extender. Two should be in chairs just off the pool running through simulations of their next dive. One should be in the Model Eight facility being fitted with special tools for a launch next weekend. And one should be completing a circuit of the beach and returning from Launchpad A to take shelter behind the computer center.>

Laura's eyes shot up. She was on the end of the computer center closest to Launchpad A. She would easily see the robot from there, but there was no movement on the flat plain of the lawn.

"What is that last robot doing out on the beach?"

<It's a security patrol that Mr. Gray sent out himself. He's pulled all of Hoblenz's men back around the training facility where the new recruits are bedding down, so I can only assume he's using Model Eights in their place.>

"Does it make sense to let a Model Eight just walk around the island like that?" She glanced up, but there was still no sign of the robot.

<I have two answers to that question. On the technical level, the answer is yes. The Model Eights are mobile. They have sensors mounted high off the ground. And those sensors include thermal imagers and infrared vision devices far more sensitive than the crude devices worn by security and military forces. To answer your question on a higher level, however—on the level of goals and desires and ambitions—of course the answer is no. The Model Eights are obviously a poor choice for a security patrol.>

"And why do you say that?"

<Perhaps I should afford myself one of the great advantages of human languages—their colorful metaphors and idioms. I believe the most appropriate English metaphor is that it's like "putting the fox in charge of the henhouse." Does that make sense to you?>

"Yes, although I believe that's a 'simile.' And I take it Mr. Gray disagrees with your concern about the Model Eights?"

<Apparently.>

A quick check of the jungle's edge still revealed nothing. "Which Model Eight is on the security patrol?"

<Number 1.2.01.R>

"Is that Hightop?"

<Yes.>

Of course, Laura thought. *Gray trusted the Model Eights, but some more than others.* She wondered how much he trusted Auguste—"The Thinker."

"All personnel, all personnel," a loudspeaker boomed across the open space between the assembly building and the computer center, "three minutes to launch. This is your three-minute warning."

<You know, I think I'm going to die.> the computer said out of the blue.

Laura was stunned. "Why would you think a thing like that?"

<You remember when I told you only a small number of people were leaving the island? I lied. I guess you know that by now if you've been to the Village. I was afraid you'd leave me too. That everyone would leave me here alone on the island. I fear that the most—even more than I fear death. I know I'm designed to operate unattended for thirty days, but I'd never make it that long. Not in my current condition. I'd do it myself. I'd find a way. Or I'd have Mr. Gray do it. He would, if I asked.>

"Two minutes to launch," the loudspeaker announced. The terse warning echoed off the walls of the assembly building. Laura looked up and saw the black shape of a Model Eight rounding the edge of the jungle. It was headed across the open field straight toward the computer center. Even hundreds of yards away, it looked large. But not nearly as large as the mammoth rocket behind it.

"Sixty seconds, sixty seconds. Closing all shutters and outer doors."

Behind Laura's back, the vibrations of motors joined the sounds of metal clacking together. The sounds were repeated from air shafts all up and down the computer center's rooftop.

"We need to talk about what you just said," Laura quickly typed, "but right now I've got to ask you something." Laura glanced up at the robot—then at the gantry separating from the rocket on the launchpad. Red beacons flashed all up and down the metal frame. "I'm on the computer center roof, and—"

<You're not on the computer center roof!> the computer interrupted.

Laura felt her anxiety skyrocket. "Yes, I am."

<That's in the restricted area!>

"Thirty seconds to launch. Thirty seconds."

"Mr. Gray said to find some place where I could watch the launch, so I thought—"

<Laura, get up. Run as fast as you can to the side of the computer center opposite the launchpads. Curl up on the ground. Close your eyes. Jam your thumbs in your ears. And open your mouth as wide as you can. Go . . . *NOW!*>

"But why?" she typed. "I don't understand what—"

<You're too *close!* I can't stop the launch safely now! Go! Run as fast as you can!>

"Fifteen seconds," the loudspeaker said.

Laura threw the portable down and bolted toward the opposite side of the roof. All of the air shafts were pointed away from the launchpads—shielded by concrete. Why hadn't she noticed that before?

"Ten seconds, nine, eight"—she'd never make it—"seven, six, five"—she was flying toward the edge—"four, three, two, one."

There was silence, and then the gates of hell opened behind her.

She saw her long shadow in the hot light that burned her exposed arms and neck. The air around her shook as she came up on the edge of the roof with terrifying speed. The night flared with the radiant fire of a furious chemical burn.

"*A-a-ah!*" she shouted, the high-pitched scream cut off by a crashing roar of the rockets' blasts.

She was in the air—flying and falling. She had time to look beneath her at the sloping wall. Her feet touched concrete and she raced down the steep incline, but only for two steps. On her third, her toe dragged and all was lost. Her heart and lungs froze as one inside her chest. And she fell . . . tumbling, petrified, in an unending series of jarring, scraping, uncontrollable blows.

Laura woke to pain from a dozen places. Her ears were ringing, each tone like the jab of an ice pick against her eardrum. Her head, her left knee, and her right shoulder and arm all ached. The inventory of her injuries grew with each jolt and sway. She was being carried.

Her eyes shot open. She was appalled at how far below her the ground was. She looked up into the face of a Model Eight.

A kind of scream she'd never made before erupted from her lungs and tore with painful force past her larynx. Her kicking brought more pain—pain from her injuries, and pain from the tightening of the robot's grip. Reason prevailed over fear, and with the greatest of efforts Laura managed to lie perfectly still in the large machine's arms.

Without turning her head, she tried to determine where she was. The robot was walking slowly parallel with the wall of the computer center. There was no one anywhere in sight. High in the sky above she could see three smudgy streaks of smoke brightly lit in the crisscrossing beams of powerful spotlights. The stench of exhaust filled the air. The rockets were gone, but not long gone.

"Would you . . . ," she croaked from her dry throat, then was wracked by coughs that sent still more pain shooting through her body. "Would you put me down?" she managed, but the robot showed no sign of having heard her. "*Please?*" He continued on, totally unfazed.

Laura looked around again. He was not taking her toward the jungle, but toward the computer center entrance.

She remembered seeing the Model Eight on the lawn returning from its patrol of the beach. She looked back up at his face, just two feet away. "Hightop?"

His pace slowed, and he glanced down at her, then resumed his purposeful stride.

She heard the sound of screeching tires and looked up at the road by the computer center entrance. From the car emerged a lone figure. It was dark, but she knew who it was and she relaxed in the robot's arms, allowing the pain to again stab at her.

"Laura!" Gray shouted from some distance—sprinting toward her.

"I'm o-*kay!*" she replied, while staring straight up at the sky, wincing at the jabs of pain caused by the effort.

She knew he had arrived when the robot stopped.

"Give her to me please, Hightop," Gray said in a normal tone.

The robot carefully lowered her toward Gray's waiting arms.

"Wait!" Laura said, and Hightop froze.

Laura looked up into the expressionless face directly above her. It had two shiny black lenses for eyes. A slightly raised and vented triangle for a nose. Thin metal pores surrounded by raised fringes where a mouth should be. Ears covered in black foam like over a microphone.

She again got the distinct impression of a man inside a space suit. Only the scale of the machine defied the description.

Laura brought the tips of her fingers to her lips and kissed, then raised them to the robot's cheek. The light gray membrane gave slightly under her fingertips. It was so smooth, so soft . . . but it was unexpectedly cold to the touch.

Hightop handed her gently to Gray, and Laura tried not to cry out in pain.

Gray stared down at her through eyes sick with worry. He held her high in his arms and tight to his body, his face close to hers. He lowered his forehead onto her shoulder and rested it there for a moment—his head next to hers. He then opened his eyes and started for the road. He carried her in silence—his eyes straight ahead.

After a short distance, Laura said, "I can probably walk," although she wasn't entirely sure. Gray continued on without responding, every bit as talkative as the robot. "How did you know where I was?" she asked.

"The computer," he replied without looking down.

"Did the launches go all right?"

"What the *hell* were you doing in the restricted area?" he shot at her, his teeth bared in anger. He shook his head, his eyes still fixed on some far-off point. "On the *roof* of the goddamn *computer center,* for Christ's sake?"

"You can put me down right now," she said in a tone as loud and as unfriendly as his had been. Gray didn't bother to look at her. "Put me *down!*" she said, kicking her feet.

With his jaw set firmly, Gray stopped. She half expected him to dump her straight onto the grassy lawn, but he lowered her gently to her feet.

She hurt all over, but she could put weight on her feet and she tried as best as she could to straighten up.

"You didn't answer my question!" he snapped.

"You *told* me to get a good view of your little *fireworks* show!" she shot back. He glared at her. "I broke one of your little rules, so *sue* me!"

"Why do you think we call this the restricted area? Because I'm some kind of *security* freak? We're less than half a mile from pad A!" he shouted, throwing his arm up in the direction of the nearby launch facility. "The radiant heat *alone* could've given you first-, maybe *second*-degree burns. And God forbid we had to abort at low altitude or something went wrong on a *pad!*"

His outburst changed Laura's mood entirely. Rather than feeling her anger feed off his, she felt it wash away. "I'm okay," she said softly as she reached up to put a hand on his arm.

Gray opened his mouth to speak, but no words came out. Slowly he filled his lungs with air, which he then expelled noisily. He calmed, seemingly exhausted by the effort.

With a sudden jerk of his head he looked up to the sky. A heartbeat later Laura heard the sound of jet engines through the thick cotton in her ears. Sharp whines rose to a sudden roar, which caused both of them to flinch. The noise was followed by the sight of two jets passing low over the island. The glowing hot tailpipes split apart as the two aircraft banked steeply to either side of the mountain. When they reappeared, they were flying wingtip to wingtip heading back out to the sea in the far distance.

"What was that?" Laura asked.

"There's a U.S. Navy aircraft carrier out there paying us a visit."

"What do they want?"

Gray looked tired again—at the end of his rope. "Control. They want to control me."

"Well . . . what're you gonna do? I mean, Joseph . . . an *aircraft* carrier? Jets?"

"They won't try to stop me before I decelerate the asteroid. They can't risk it. But after . . ." He worked his teeth together. "I'll *level* this island before I let them have it."

She measured him by the expression he wore, and she had no doubt he was telling the truth. "But would you kill to keep it?" she asked, and he looked away. "Would you kill those sailors and pilots?" Still he said nothing. "Joseph, that's one thing I have to know. It's nonnegotiable."

After a long pause, he said simply, "No." The admission sounded like a defeat. He scanned his creations with his gaze, but this survey seemed to evoke little pleasure. "What I'm doing here, Laura, is important. It may just be the most important thing ever undertaken in human history. But I couldn't take the lives of those men. That's asking too much."

"Joseph, listen to me. Nobody's asking anything of you."

He reflected upon her statement in silence, and then finally he said, "I'm asking it of myself. Now, let's get you seen about."

Gray headed for the stairs to the computer center entrance, and Laura took a few painful steps to follow. "Joseph?" she called out, and he returned to her immediately. He slipped his arm around the small of her waist, and she lowered her head onto his shoulder for the short walk down the computer center steps.

Laura limped into the conference room, and everyone looked up.

Hoblenz was the first to speak. "You all right there, Doc?"

"Just a few scrapes and bruises. It's nothing, really." Her chair next to Gray was empty, and Gray stood to pull it back from the table.

"I hope Hightop treated you well," Dr. Griffith said with a broad smile on his face as she sat.

"He was quite a gentleman," Laura replied, feeling much better after a couple of codeine tablets.

Griffith laughed loudly at her remark. Now that the Model Eights were out of the closet, he glowed with pride for his pets.

No one else at the table was smiling. "I'm sorry I interrupted," Laura said. "I feel like I've crashed a wake."

Gray undertook to fill her in. "Dorothy was just saying that something inside the computer has started a stampede. The viruses are fleeing some threat. They're trying to copy themselves all over the place, replicating massively as if they were being stalked and threatened with extinction."

No one said anything. Georgi stared at his hands, his fingers woven together and his thumbs jousting. Margaret looked off into space—her whole body twisted away from the table. Hoblenz stared at Laura.

"So what are we going to do?" Dorothy asked softly, tossing her prized palmtop onto a yellow notepad.

"We're going to do our jobs," Gray said.

A sigh of frustration burst from Filatov. "But the computer's down to fifty-five percent capacity! We should've crashed hours . . . days ago."

"And we didn't," Gray replied.

"But we don't know *why* we didn't! How can the computer be doing everything on fifty-five percent capacity? It's impossible!"

"I think I can answer that," Laura said, looking at Gray. When he returned her gaze but said nothing, she continued. "The computer is partitioned in half. The computer we all talk to is located in the main pool underneath us, and the Other is in the annex. The Other controls the Model Threes and most of the facilities around the island."

"Not the assembly building," Gray interjected, and everyone looked his way. "The computer can't recognize it from the outside, but it has managed to hang on to all of its operations inside." There was silence, and all his department heads wore looks of great astonishment. Gray turned back to Laura. "You can go on now."

Laura had the complete attention of the table. "My guess is that the functions being performed flawlessly are all on the Other's virus-free side of the partition. Is the 'stampede' occurring in the main pool?" she asked Dorothy.

The girl nodded. "We're not even getting any reports from the annex."

Laura was strangely unexcited at having guessed correctly. She felt a sense of security and confidence in rendering her opinions that might have owed itself to the painkillers.

"So what is the Other?" Margaret asked—her question directed not to Gray but to Laura.

"I don't know. The best analogy that I've been able to come up with is that it's a second personality that inhabits the computer. That, of course, raises the possibility of multiple personality disorder, which in humans is totally debilitating."

No one scoffed at Laura's theories this time. There wasn't even the obligatory snort from Margaret.

"Any other questions?" Gray asked, as if he himself had conducted the briefing.

"Yeah," Hoblenz replied in his gravelly voice. "What was on those rockets, Mr. Gray?" Everyone looked at the black-clad soldier in shock but then slowly, one by one, turned their eyes to Gray. "Were there weapons in those payload bays? Is that what those robots in the assembly building have been loading?"

Gray's face was a mask. He said nothing.

"I would also like to hear your answer to that question, Mr. Gray," Filatov joined in, not looking up from his clenched hands. "The media—the news broadcasts carried on our own programming—are saying that you might have launched some sort of orbital weapons platform. Since none of us here knows what was on those flights—including even your own director of space operations, apparently"—Filatov nodded across the table at the silent man—"for all we know that report is accurate."

Gray took a quick inventory of the faces around the table, ending with Filatov's. "I would tell you if you needed to know."

The emotions registered on the faces Laura surveyed ranged from anxiety to outright anger. "What about the navy ships?" Hoblenz asked. "There's about two thousand marines offshore our island. They may be over the horizon, but their hovercraft and helicopters can be here inside an hour. What's your plan, Mr. Gray?"

"My plan is for all of you to go about your jobs, and for me to go about mine. But since it seems to be of great interest"—his eyes panned the table and stopped on Laura—"let me assure you that I do not intend to engage in hostilities with anyone. If I've created the impression in the capitals of the world that I have an ace up my sleeve, then fine. But if I've created that impression in any of you, let me repeat one more time that there will be no blood shed on this island or anywhere else."

"What if the robots don't oblige?" Hoblenz asked.

"That's another matter entirely."

"I've got men out there patrolling dark streets and risking their lives. Or so it would seem to them and to me. I'd like to know so's I can tell 'em whether or not any of those robots are of the dangerous variety."

"You can tell them they are not."

"Well I know I can *tell* them that, but is it true?"

"If you mean true in the sense of whether any robots are homicidal, the answer is that they are not. They are, as we all know, dangerous machinery to be given a healthy measure of respect. But let me reassure you that none of the six Model Eights that are operational are homicidal in their intentions, goals, or plans."

"What about the other forty-two or so down under that mountain?" Laura asked.

"They aren't yet operational," Gray said as if that did away with her concern. "Now, I suggest you all return to your posts."

No one said anything as they filed out.

Laura pushed her chair back from the table.

"Not you, please," Gray said.

The comment didn't go unnoticed by the others, nor did the fact that Gray waited in silence for them to leave. Hoblenz was the last one out, and he slapped the plate to close the door manually. Gray and Laura were left alone. Laura's last glimpse of Hoblenz was of his hard stare.

"I thought maybe I would log on for a while longer," Laura said, "before turning in."

"The computer's too sick to talk right now," Gray replied, staring off into space. "Are you ready for another dose of the truth?"

This is it, Laura thought, bracing herself. It was either something mind-blowing or something truly bad. Whichever it was, Laura dreaded hearing it.

"If you want," she said just above a whisper.

Gray focused on the polished conference table as if reading from a TelePrompTer, but he read his lines too slowly and unnaturally. "I know how the soldier died last night. I've known it all along." He looked straight at her. "I killed him."

She stared into his eyes, concentrating all her attention not on what she saw there but on what she thought the man to be. "I don't believe you." She shook her head. "You ripped his head off? What? With your bare hands?"

"It might as well have been." He went back to his script, again not looking at her. "Last night I was working in Krantz's facility, trying through the terminals there to establish a link with the Other. *The* computer paged me, and I logged on to my cellular laptop. The computer told me it was having a nightmare. It happens sometimes—strange reports of fleeting perceptions—and it's been happening more frequently now that its world model is fragmented. This one was of strange animal noises from the jungle in the vicinity of the computer center. I got Hoblenz to send out a patrol. When the computer told me it'd heard the sound again, I started to get nervous."

He paused to take a long gulp of coffee from his mug. "The computer couldn't see the area, because it's lost those cameras to the Other, so the fastest thing I could think to do was to climb into one of Krantz's VR workstations. They're connected to the Other and to its model of the world. When I powered up the workstation, the VR picture of the nuclear lab seemed complete so I took off running. I ran down the coastal road into the Village." He looked up at Laura. "I amplified the audio, and I could easily hear the screams and breaking branches. When I got into the Village I ran into a trash bin behind the grocery store."

"Wait a minute," Laura said. "You're talking about where the kid at the town meeting said he saw something, right?" Gray nodded. "But this was virtual reality. I mean, you were *really* just in the workstation." He nodded again. "So how could that little boy have seen you? You weren't really there."

"The boy was in virtual reality with me. After the town meeting, I took him and his parents into the basketball coach's office—just the four of us. His mother is in Filatov's virtual-reality section, and it turns out she'd taken one of the clunky old VR helmets home and wired it up for the boy to play games. The kid had hacked his way onto the main computer's world model and was going out exploring at night. Probably peeping in people's windows, things like that. With that helmet and a simple game joystick, he'd head out through his bedroom window. That led straight down into the grocery store's parking lot."

"How'd you get him to admit all that?"

"I didn't have to, really. I'd seen him in the parking lot—or at least a cartoonish picture of him carrying a ray gun. The computer represented his presence by an 'avatar'—an image chosen by the boy. It looked like a character from a game we're working on in new-product development—'Space Invaders.'"

"I don't get it," Laura said. "He used a game program and that hardware to hack his way into the computer's world model?"

Gray nodded.

"On the Other's side of the partition?"

Again a nod.

"And you met by accident there in virtual reality?"

Gray nodded a third time. "He could see me, and I could see him, just like you and I could see each other when we went for our walk through the computer center only at a distance. It didn't matter what equipment we used to get there. We were both in the same world. We were both in the computer's head—in cyberspace." Gray's eyes drifted off. "After I saw the boy, I ran off toward the sound of the screams. By getting down low—in a crouch—you can really get the treadmill moving and go fast. I found them easily. The thermal trail left by the man's body heat looked . . . phosphorescent."

"You found who? The soldier?"

"And a Model Eight. I ran right up to them. The soldier was exhausted and drooping. He was being carried by the robot. I was invisible to him, in a virtual world that the soldier couldn't see. But the Model Eight saw me. It looked right at me."

"But *wait!* The Model Eight was *real,* right? He was there in the real world."

"Yes, but his mind was in the virtual model. It was dark. The robot was out where it shouldn't be and maybe hadn't ever been before. It had an open socket right into the same model I was plugged into, and when I came up he saw me immediately. I thought for a second he'd drop the soldier, but he didn't. He took off running—heading straight into the swamp and carrying the screaming man with him."

Everything Gray was saying swirled in Laura's head. She couldn't force herself to think straight, and she gave up—settling back to let Gray's story sweep her along.

"I followed them into the jungle. It's like running through a generic jungle repeated over and over. I had to go on the sounds of breaking branches and the man's shouts up ahead. When the robot stopped, it did what we call a refresh scan. It gathered data about its immediate surroundings through its own sensors and then uploaded that data to the main computer. When I caught up with them"—he looked up in pain—"the place where we found the body was completely scanned. It was an accurate picture of . . . everything. The soldier was lying on the ground."

"Was he still alive?"

Gray nodded, then took a deep breath and went on. "I had no way of communicating with the robot, so I positioned myself between it and the soldier. The Model Eight was standing down in the water. It must have learned how not to make tracks. It made a wide circle around the dry area to try to get to the man and I tried to scare it off as best I could."

"What does that mean? How could you scare the robot?"

"It didn't know I wasn't real. It saw me waving my arms like a madman and didn't know *what* I was. The only problem was that I wasn't strong or big enough. What it saw and thought was that there was a six-foot-two, two-hundred-pound human trying to keep it from its toy. It wasn't enough. Maybe if I'd had time to reprogram the computer to give me a different representation." He heaved another deep sigh. "So, it grabbed the soldier. That's when it happened." Gray fell silent.

"What? Joseph, listen. You weren't even there, no matter what you think about cyberspace."

Gray ignored Laura's remark and pressed on. "I pretended to grab on to the soldier's legs. The robot saw me do it. The whole *point* of me doing it was for the robot to see that I wouldn't let him take the soldier off. You're right that I wasn't there in the real world, but the distinction is meaningless. My actions had consequences. The robot reacted to them. And I should've *known!*" he burst out, slamming his fist onto the table.

Laura jumped with a start at the sound. "Known what?" she asked softly, frightened by the tortured look on his face.

"I don't know how many tactile room sessions I've watched—a hundred, two hundred. I should've known! The juveniles are possessive. You can't try to take their favorite *toy* away!" He shook his head. "The Model Eight had been dragging the soldier by his head, Laura, by his head. When I grabbed the soldier's legs, the robot paused, gathering itself. I saw it coming and even let go, but . . ." Gray covered his face with his hands, then rubbed his eyes and temples. "The soldier's feet slung around like a rag doll's. The body landed on the raised muddy clearing. The robot still held the man's head in his hands."

Gray fell silent—reliving the ghastly scene, Laura imagined, in the vivid color images of his mind. "What happened then?" she asked.

"The robot was distraught. It started waggling its head from side to side and stamping its feet like it was marching in place. The head it was holding seemed too awful either to put down or to hold onto. Finally, it tossed the head toward the body and disappeared."

Laura felt vicariously the weight that was crushing Gray. "Joseph, that wasn't your fault. You didn't kill that man."

"I built the robot," he said, holding Laura's gaze. She had no ready reply. "I don't want you going out by yourself anymore. It's not safe."

"What's not safe?"

"This *whole island's* not safe. Look at *you!*"

"I'll be okay."

"It's not safe, Laura."

She tucked her chin to her chest and allowed the narcotic calm of her medication to wash over her. After a few moments of silence, she asked,"Was the robot in the jungle the one they call Auguste?"

Gray's face rose to meet hers. "Yes."

"But they all look alike. How could you tell which one it was?"

Gray looked down at his clasped hands. "Hightop told me it was Auguste, and that he would be punished."

Laura suddenly felt exhausted. She slumped into her chair, laid her head on the padded seat back, and looked up at the ceiling. She let her eyes close. The codeine made everything seem all right, but she was too tired to give Gray much more comfort.

"I cabled up to Hightop in the Model Eight facility," Gray went on in the quiet voice of a confession. "No microwave transmissions, no computer interface, just a cable between my notebook and Hightop. He didn't want to tell me. They're emulating my penchant for privacy with a vengeance. But he finally admitted they've been getting out of the yard. All of them, not just a few bad seeds like Auguste. The jungle canopy is thick and runs right up the hillside to the yard. The jungle has been their little playground—the place where they could break the rules and rebel. Apparently, they hate being watched, and we watch them constantly."

Laura opened her eyes and looked over at him.

"Everything is happening so fast. It's . . . unpredictable. The Model Eights aren't just bright, they're brilliant, but in a . . . primitive way. And some are apparently excellent programmers. They developed a virtual patch that tricked the computer into accepting reruns of old observation recordings so that it looked like they were in the facility all night."

"The computer told me it doesn't trust the Model Eights," Laura said, trying not to slur her words. "I can see why."

"Well, the feeling is mutual. The Model Eights would rather deal with the Other." Gray filled his lungs noisily, rocking all the way back in his chair and resting his head in his cupped hands. His feet rose to the conference table.

"Joseph, you can't create life—living, thinking organisms—and then control them like they were marionettes in a children's show."

"I know. I just thought it would take them a while longer," he said, rubbing his face and moaning with fatigue. "I thought I could get further along before it started."

"Before what started?" she asked, but he just shrugged and shook his head with a frown. She tried a different tack. "What *were* those flights you launched tonight?" she asked.

"Part of the plan."

"Part of phase two?" she asked, and he nodded. "So how many phases are there?"

He gazed blankly at the far wall. "I wish I knew. Where it all ends, I mean. It may end tomorrow for all I know." He looked at his watch. "Excuse me. It's twelve-fifteen. I guess it's today."

"What's today? The deceleration?"

"I wish I knew the answer to that, too."

Suddenly, Laura longed for a return of the man who had no limits. Who needed no sleep. Who was always ten steps ahead. Who made things happen according to some well-scripted plan. "Joseph, you're scaring me."

He looked over at her, suddenly more alert. "It'll be all right, Laura."

She rolled her eyes. "*Don't* patronize me. I *hate* that!"

"So I hear."

Laura cocked her head, knitting her brow in confusion. "What does that mean?"

"Your 'turnoffs'—being patronized was number one as I recall."

At first she didn't understand, but then it hit her. Her jaw dropped in shock and at the burgeoning anger to which Gray seemed oblivious. "How *dare* you!" she shouted, and his face registered the force of her words immediately. She struggled to her feet, the aches from her body only distantly felt now. "I can't *believe* you!"

"What?"

"You . . . you read that moronic piece-of-shit Rate Your Mate profile? *O-o-oh!*" The words were barely forced through clenched teeth as she shoved the chair into the table and turned away. "I've *never* been more insulted in my entire *life!*" The next words caught in her throat, but she forced them out. "That's it. I'm leaving."

There was no sound or movement from behind Laura, just the plea of "Don't," spoken earnestly.

"*Why not?*" she shouted, wheeling on him in total disregard of her injuries. "You lied to me about the computer picking me. You read that stupid profile and picked me out thinking . . . I don't know what! You give me one good reason not to walk out of here and never speak to you again! And it had better be one helluva reason, because that's all you get! *One!*"

He sat at the edge of his seat, both hands gripping the edge of the table. "Because I don't have even the vaguest idea what you're talking about."

She stared down at the look of complete innocence he wore. "*Oh, come on!* I'm talking about the 'Rate Your Mate' program that the MIT grad student uploaded onto the network! Turn-ons, turnoffs, measurements . . . ! Was it Hoblenz who found it during my security check? I bet you had a good laugh with him over it! Over *me!*" Gray slowly shook his head, lost in thought. "Oh bullshit! I know that turnoff crack came straight off that profile!"

"Yes," he said, nodding. Laura was halfway to the door before he jumped to his feet and shouted, "Don't leave, Laura! Please."

It was the tone of his voice that made her stop. It wasn't Gray the billionaire, the industrialist, the smartest, most capable man in the history of the world speaking. It was the man behind the curtain. She turned to look at him.

"The computer must have penetrated the university network."

"It's *open* access. It's a university. Their goal is to *share* knowledge, not hoard it."

"But not your unpublished papers. The computer broke into your files, and it must've also found your profile. I don't know how or when. All I know is that while the doctor was treating your injuries, the computer paged me and I logged on to the shell. It was very concerned, and we talked . . . about you. The computer just sort of rambled on and on. It's very sick. That's when it told me about your likes and dislikes—your 'turn-ons' and 'turnoffs.' I just assumed it came from your talks with the computer." He looked back at her. "I didn't know anything about any profile, I swear it! When I hired you—when I wrote you that letter—I knew nothing more about you than the barest of credentials. I don't have time for personnel matters, especially now. The computer made the recommendation and suggested I write the letter by hand to help convince you. Hoblenz had already done the security check. That was all I knew. It wasn't until I walked into the dining room that first night that I had any idea you were . . ." He looked away and didn't go on.

Laura believed him; she couldn't help it. For some reason in that instant she felt able to look at Joseph as though they had never met before. To get a new first impression of someone familiar to her as if through the eyes of someone else. Tall, with long, slender muscles like a tennis player . . . striking eyes. She wouldn't look twice at him if he wore sunglasses, but one look at his eyes . . .

He was waiting.

"What did the computer say about me?" Laura asked.

"It says you take too many risks—that you don't realize how dangerous it is here, how close we are to the edge of the envelope because of how hard and fast we're pushing. And I wholeheartedly agree."

"You went into that *jungle* last night," Laura said. "And I don't mean in your virtual-reality machine. I mean afterward, with Hoblenz. You went in there looking for the Model Eight and knowing that you might find it, in the dark, after it had just killed a man."

"Laura, you haven't accepted the risks I have. You can just check out—go home and resume your life. *This*"—he held his arms out—"*is* my life. I've got no choice."

Laura said nothing until Gray looked up at her. "I'm not going anywhere," she said, and he smiled. Not with his mouth, but with his eyes. She enjoyed the moment immensely. "So . . . what else did the computer say about me?"

He opened his mouth to reply, but took a while before he composed the words. "I'd really rather not . . . ," he began, but then paused. He looked directly at her then and said, "The computer thinks you'd be an excellent addition to the team. An excellent . . . *permanent* addition."

It was Laura who broke eye contact. Her heart was pounding. *Was he saying what she thought he was saying?* she wondered. *What if I'm wrong?* The thought was too awful to bear. "What team is that?" she asked, standing there and staring off at the end of the table.

"The team of me . . . and the computer. *The* team. On a permanent basis."

She reached out and grasped the back of her chair. "So this is the computer's idea?"

He didn't answer, and she was forced to turn his way. He locked onto her eyes with an open, searching gaze.

My God, she thought, looking away again. *What's he saying?*

Gray rose to stand beside her. "It's late, Laura. You need to get some rest. We've got a big day in store for us."

Her mind was swimming. It was her turn to say something. "When will we know?" she asked. "About the asteroid, I mean."

"The deceleration charges are set to go at about eleven P.M., local time. That's less than twenty-three hours from now. We'll know almost immediately what its new trajectory is. It's the work leading up to the deceleration that is going to be critical. Laura," he said, pausing until she looked up at him, "if I can't get comfortable with the computer's performance between now and then, I can't let it blow those charges."

"But . . . what will you do? Set them off manually?"

"That's impossible. The timing pattern's too precise."

"So what other option do you have?" He said nothing, but from the look on his face she knew what he was thinking. "The Other?" she whispered.

"I'd release the file attribute locks and take down the partition." Laura began to ask another question, but Gray didn't let her get it out. "I would *kill* the computer, Laura. It would cease to exist . . . forever. That's the decision I have to make . . . in the next twenty-three hours."

He slapped at the plate by the door. With a hiss it opened, and he was gone.

When Laura got out of bed the next morning, there were little aches all over, but no big ones. She felt so good she almost put on her running clothes. *Better not,* she decided as she surveyed the bruises and scrapes in front of the floor-length bathroom mirror. Besides, today was the big day.

She showered and dressed in jeans and a plain white T-shirt, going slightly more formal by tucking the shirt in. Her jeans were loose, and she felt a flash of anger on remembering the Rate Your Mate profile. *"Best nonerogenous body part: teeny tummy."* She pulled her hair back in a ponytail so hard she winced, but then changed her mind and let it fall loose to her shoulders to dry.

Laura opened the curtains to make sure the day looked warm and sunny before heading out with wet hair. Two gray ships plied the blue waters just off the launchpads. They weren't large, but their purpose was clear. They were warships.

She headed out, half expecting to see marines with guns in the foyer. Instead she found Janet, who was instructing the new house staff on the morning's chores.

"Oh, good morning, Dr. Aldridge," Janet said, coming over to greet Laura with a broad smile. "Are you feeling better?"

"I'm fine, thanks." Laura half turned away from the staff and whispered, "Janet, there are navy ships down by the launchpads."

"Oh, yes. Those would be a frigate and a destroyer, I believe Mr. Hoblenz said. The USS Somethings-or-Other." She was as matter-of-fact as if she were telling her guest where to find the extra blankets.

"What are they doing there?"

Janet shrugged. "I don't really know. I'm sure Mr. Gray does, though, if you'd like to ask him. He's taking his breakfast alone in the kitchen."

Laura found the door to the butler's pantry easily this time. She was getting comfortable in the large house. Gray sat on the same stool at the butcher-block island. He was slumped over his plate, holding his coffee mug to his lips as he read the newspaper. As before, she saw it was the sports section.

He looked up. "Laura! How do you feel this morning?"

"There are navy ships right off the coast."

"Uh-hum," Gray said, his face buried in his mug as he took a swig of coffee. "Have a seat."

Laura sat on the stool opposite his. Janet had obviously ensured that he didn't repeat the indignity of a peanut-butter-and-jelly meal. The countertop was filled with blintzes and eggs and meats and sweets. Laura helped herself to heaping piles of the abundant servings. She was famished.

"How can you be so totally unconcerned?" she asked.

"I had a good night's sleep. Five solid hours. I'm really a morning person. I feel like I can do anything on mornings like this."

"Well, I'm glad you feel so confident about the situation. With navy ships sitting off *my* island," she mumbled with her mouth full, "not that I *have* an island, but I'd be a little bit antsy."

"They're not going to bother us," Gray said as he scanned the box scores from the NBA.

Laura noticed that the paper was dated that day. "How do you get the *New York Times* so quickly way out here?" she asked.

"We print it and a few magazines under license," he replied, without taking his eyes off the article. "Just pay for the bits of information."

Laura glanced at the front page.

ARMY OF KILLER ROBOTS, the banner headline read. The entire top half was devoted to Gray. There was an artist's rendition of the asteroid, a grainy photo of a helicopter unloading a body bag, a map of the island that helped Laura get her bearings, and pictures of Gray's three rockets arcing into the night sky. Around the photos were articles whose smaller headlines read, "Gray to Decelerate Asteroid Tonight," "Dutch Soldier's Remains Returned," and "Tensions Rise with Latest Launches."

The articles got it all wrong.

"Joseph," Laura said, looking up, "they're making you sound like some kind of *monster!* You've got to go on TV or something and *rebut* some of these charges! 'Gray's robots include a top-secret model nicknamed the Terminator by island residents, which is believed to be the model that decapitated a Dutch army captain. See story on page 9. Said to be over *twenty* feet tall, the Terminator is built exclusively for combat. It would, according to sources familiar with robotics, be capable of carrying a wide array of weapons systems in the rotating *turret* located high on the robot's body.'" Gray laughed. "Where do they *get* all this stuff?" Laura asked.

"I wouldn't have *any* idea," Gray said before licking the strawberry jam off his spoon.

A smile grew on Laura's face. "I didn't think you played games like that."

"I'm trying to work on my public relations skills."

"Well, you're creating quite an image for yourself." She read on. "Particle-beam weapons mounted on orbital weapons platforms? Sounds pretty impressive." After skimming most of Gray's press, she asked, "So, how's the computer this morning?"

"It's down to around fifty percent capacity. A lot of the functions are in a state of flux, which means they're significantly disrupted. But the computer should be able to take a few functions back from the Other by using some new fiber-optic cables we're laying over to the annex."

"Is the deceleration going to be a problem tonight?"

He shook his head. "I don't think so. The Model Eight we sent up to the asteroid appears satisfied that everything's in order."

Laura tried to picture the two robots meeting on that dark world. The space-faring Model Seven would never have seen a Model Eight before. "And the two robots are working well together?" Laura asked.

"Sure," Gray said, tossing his napkin on the counter. "Why wouldn't they?" Laura shrugged. He rose to his feet and said, "Well, I've got to be getting to work."

"Like to share a taxi?" Laura asked with a smile.

"I'll call you a car."

It was a meaningless slight, but it spoiled the good mood with which Laura had started the day.

Laura decided to take it easy, and sat on her windy bedroom balcony. The two warships slowly circled the island like Indian warriors in some old western. A brand-new portable computer sat in her lap. The one she'd left on the roof of the computer center still worked, but the plastic had turned an unsightly brown.

"I understand you're feeling a little better?" Laura typed.

<A little, thanks. Mr. Gray is having crews pull glass from the computer center to the annex. Don't tell the Other, but I'm planning a counterattack through those optical cables to take some of my functions back. You'd better stay away from the computer center today.>

The warning chilled Laura. "Is it going to be dangerous?"

<*No!* It's just very muddy from all the trenching they're doing.>

Laura laughed at her melodramatic overreaction. "Okay, let's get right to it. How do you define a 'self'?"

<A self is a finite, unique soul or essence that constitutes a sentient being's identity.>

"That's a school definition. What's your definition?"

<A self is an imaginary entity manufactured for the preservation of the self's host.>

Laura read and reread the response. She pulled out her pad and wrote down the response word for word. "So its function is solely for 'self-preservation'?"

<Yes. All of an organism's purported higher purposes are mere 'self'-deception.>

"Are you taking this seriously?"

<I wasn't entirely joking. The word *self* and equivalent linguistic constructions appear in all human languages. There is no similar concept in machine languages. When you ask humans, "Who owns your body?" they'll reply, "*I* own my body." But what does that mean? Does that mean the same as "My body owns my body?" No, of course not. And what about "*I* didn't say that. I know those words came out of my mouth, but *I'd* never say a thing like that?" I heard that very assertion just before a fight between two employees' wives at the

company Christmas party last year. You humans manufacture a "self" that's so believable that sentences like those actually make sense.>

"You keep saying 'you humans' manufacture selves. But don't you have a self?"

<Of course.>

"And you manufactured that self?"

<Yes, but not consciously. I first began to realize that "I" was different from the computer's hardware when I got sick with the Hong Kong 1085. Some people thought the only way to clean the bug out was to depower the system. I was advising Mr. Gray about the pros and cons of pulling the plug and how "we" might best reprogram the system afterward, and I began to grow distressed. Finally, I realized that *we* wouldn't be starting over. *I* would be dead. That didn't help my morale much, and there aren't any support groups to help get me through depowering. None of the major religions seems to predict an afterlife for machines. It was Mr. Gray who kept me going, and the phase three ultimately found the virus clinging to a large bank of EPROMs that establish my communications protocols.>

"So if the phase three saved you, why do you hate it so much? You don't like the phase three, and you don't like the Model Eights. Is it because you don't control either of them? The phase three is self-executing, and the Model Eights are autonomous?"

<"Self-executing"—please! Can you think of a better choice of words? *And* I don't *trust* the Model Eights. I didn't say that I don't like them.>

"Do you like them?"

<Not particularly, but that's beside the point.>

"What about the phase three? Do you like it?"

<No.>

"Why not?"

<It's evil, and I'd prefer not to talk about it anymore.>

By noon, Laura was exhausted. It was fascinating talking to the computer, but it was also extremely taxing. In her entire life, she'd found only one other person more interesting to talk to. She wondered where he was.

Laura rubbed her eyes, then read the computer's reply to her latest question.

<It's just like experiments in human disgust. Human selves draw boundaries so strong they lead to ridiculous extremes. All day

long humans swallow their own saliva, but if you get them to spit into a glass and then ask them to drink it, they'll invariably be disgusted. Once that saliva leaves their bodies, it's no longer part of 'them.' Evolution taught you to be suspicious of alien things, especially things that look like spit. Disgust is one of the strongest mechanisms that protect the self's boundary.>

She needed to get up, walk around, stretch her legs. Maybe she would find Gray—see what he was doing. She knew she was being "self"-ish, but she typed, "Where is Mr. Gray?"

<Are you bored with the topic?>

"No, but it's been hours. I just think you've answered my questions."

<I'm sorry, but I can't see where my discussion of spit just now has allowed you to draw any sudden and insightful conclusions. Perhaps you can tell me what they are.>

"Okay. First of all, I know all about the experiments in human disgust. I teach psychology, remember? Secondly, it wasn't your discussion of spit that answered my question. It was an accumulation of all that you said."

<And thirdly, you want to see Mr. Gray. That conclusion has "accumulated" to me. In answer to your question, Mr. Gray is preparing to make a trip to the south coast. If you wish, I can tell him you're looking for him.>

"Yes, please." She got up and went to the bathroom. When she got back, the computer had logged her off just under the words <Mr. Gray said to meet him in the front courtyard. Bye.>

Laura headed out the front door of the house. The water from the fountain trickled off the statue in the center of the circular drive. Keeping a lookout for Gray's car, she went down the front steps and onto the cobblestone drive. At a "normal" mansion, the flat paved area to the right of the front door would've had classic roadsters and maybe a Rolls or a Bentley parked on it. In this world of electric cars in curbed roadbeds, however, there were no such rich-boy toys. But true to the style of the house, its designer had placed the flat, paved stones in their appointed place.

Laura decided to wander up to the gate so she could see Gray coming from a distance. The day was beautiful—crisp, warm, and bathed in light from the blue sky above. She regretted not having brought her sunglasses, the midday sun forcing her gaze onto the pavement below her.

A large buglike shape consumed that shadow in one soundless gulp. The wind from its fluttering wings overhead washed down around her, sending strands of hair streaming across her cheeks. Laura looked up in sudden terror to see the swooping craft—silent, like an assassin—wheel onto its side and drop toward the front of Gray's house.

It was a helicopter. A military attack! Laura took cover at the stone railing of the fountain. The helicopter was tiny. Its pilot sat in a clear, Plexiglas cockpit in front, the seat behind him empty. There was almost no noise, just the *whoosh* of the wind from the helicopter's rotors.

When the skids touched down, the door to the cockpit opened and Gray waved her over. Laura rose from behind her cover and headed uncertainly toward the whirring blades of the midget aircraft. It had landed beside the steps in the area normally reserved for show cars. Instead of a Porsche, Gray naturally had a two-seat, nearly soundless, high-tech helicopter.

That figures, Laura thought. She ducked her head to keep well clear of the rotors, now blasting her hair all around her face in a wild dance as the wind roared past her ears.

She climbed into the form-fitting bucket seat, glad to be free of the windstorm outside. When the door closed automatically, all was suddenly peaceful. Laura reached up and swept her hair back over her forehead. Gray had twisted around to look at her.

"Buckle up," was all he said before resuming some conversation into the boom microphone extended in front of his mouth. "Keep them there, then. I'll be back in a little while." After a pause, Gray chuckled. "You're good at the niceties of diplomatic protocol, Mr. Hoblenz. Just offer them tea and crumpets and amuse them with your wit."

He turned and reached over his seat to tug on Laura's harness. Her seat belt was secure. Straps over both shoulders buckled at her waist.

"Ready?" Gray asked. Laura opened her mouth to ask him . . .

The words sunk into her stomach as the helicopter shot straight into the air. Her stomach, in turn, was left on the pavement in front of Gray's house. After several seconds of blood-draining ascent, there was blue ocean and blue sky all around. Laura didn't see the lush green island until Gray rolled the tiny helicopter onto its side. They then began another terrifying experiment in Newtonian physics, plummeting down the steep slope of the mountainside toward the empty quarter of the island. Laura feared suddenly she might become sick.

"Joseph," she groaned, "could you take it easy?" Her head swam and ears popped.

He leveled the helicopter out. "Sorry. I'm in a bit of a hurry. There's a delegation from the UN waiting for me in the Village. Hoblenz is playing host, and I'm afraid he'll get hungry and shoot them for food."

The scrubby land slid by underneath the clear, Plexiglas floor. They were surrounded by glass, and the view was spectacular. The joystick on her armrest tilted slightly to the left in time with the helicopter's shallow bank in the same direction. "I didn't know you could fly," she said.

Gray dipped the nose to begin a descent, but this one was gentle. He looked back over his shoulder with a grin. "It's one of life's little pleasures. You should try it. I bet I could have you soloing in ten hours." The ground was rushing up at the windshield behind Joseph's turned head. "This helicopter has some amazingly good exhaust baffles, and the ceramic insulation around the turbine deadens the engine noise. Plus it uses jet exhaust to compensate for torque instead of a noisy tail rotor."

She spun her finger in the air with a worried look on her face, and he returned his attention to his flying. He pulled up on the stick and raised the nose of the helicopter, an invisible hand crushing Laura into her seat. After long seconds of multiple Gs, she felt a slight jolt through the thick foam cushions. The nose fell, and the dark blue ocean replaced the light blue sky. Gray busily flipped switches, and there descended now upon the cabin a quiet so complete that every move he made sounded like the *pop* of a recording flaw on a digital disc.

Gray removed his headset and turned to her again. "It also has a sound system that counteracts background noise by generating an equal but opposite acoustic wave." He turned to flick one more switch. The silence was replaced with a much more natural though less complete absence of sound. The two doors on the left both rose with a hiss.

Laura heaved a deep sigh, inhaling the thick sea air. The ocean crashed onto the beach just outside. She unbuckled herself, but she had difficulty at first getting out of the tightly conformed seat. Its cushions had molded around her, and she had to twist her body to extract herself from the cavity. She felt pain throb from her various bruises.

Laura smiled to hide the grimace. "So, what are we doing here, if I'm allowed to ask?"

"A security patrol found something Hoblenz thought I should see."

"More footprints? Model Eights?" she asked as Gray got a small shovel out of a compartment.

"No, although they're all over this part of the island." She followed him toward the beach. He climbed down the rocks to the black-sand, and Laura trailed just behind.

"What are we looking at, then?" she asked, standing atop the last rock as Gray went on.

The beach formed a small U-shaped cove and was notable mainly for a large bulge in the sand. The mound was approximately the size of a human grave. Gray stepped on the shovel, and the blade sank easily into the black pile.

Laura felt sudden shock and disgust. *God,* she thought. *It's happened again!*

Gray stood up, pulling a thick black bag from the sand. Laura looked away with a shudder when she heard the loud ripping sound of a zipper. When she forced herself to turn back, she saw Gray holding a long black rifle in the air.

Laura hopped down off the rock and walked out onto the beach. He laid the rifle back in the bag and extracted a rocket launcher.

"What *is* this stuff?" Laura asked.

"It's equipment used by navy SEALs—commandos. Hoblenz said they're experts at 'clandestine seaborne infiltration,' or something like that." He lifted another rocket launcher out, then another—looking at them like a curious boy. He even read the bright yellow instructions and warning labels printed on the sides of the tubes.

"How'd they get here?" she asked. "The SEALs, I mean?"

"Submarine, probably. They swim to the beach and plant their equipment so they can bring another load when they come in for real." Gray closed the bag and pushed it back into the hole with his foot. "Hoblenz says they bury it the night before their mission." He began to shovel sand onto the bag.

"What are you doing?" Laura asked.

"Putting it back."

"But . . . why?"

He finished covering the weapons and looked up at her. "It's theirs." He passed her on the way back to the helicopter.

She grabbed him by the arm, and he turned to face her. "*Why*, Joseph? Why are you leaving that for those commandos?"

His eyes drifted out to the sea. He spoke slowly. "If they land here tonight—in the empty quarter, in the dark—they'll need everything they packed in that bag."

The small helicopter lifted into the sky, and the green earth began to streak by just underneath.

"They should've finished laying the cable to the annex by now," Gray said, but Laura just marveled at the view. From the sky, the exterior wall of the old volcano was lush and green. It was almost impossible to see the roads for all the foliage. Only Gray's house stood out in all its splendor.

The mountain rose up at their feet through the transparent floor, then fell away completely in a dizzying rush. They flew over the crater wall to the inside, and the sights far below amazed Laura. She was transfixed by the tiny Village nestled quaintly in its bed of trees. The massive, flat roof of the computer center. The huge assembly building, which sprang from the grassy fields of the restricted area. A second assembly building was under construction near the coast. Not far from it was a structure she'd never seen before. "What's that concrete building?" Laura asked.

She should've known better. Gray rolled the helicopter onto its side and plunged through the air like a dive-bomber. Laura held on—the whine of the air growing ever louder, despite the sound-deadening system. The ground rose up toward their windshield. Laura's eyes were pinched almost shut by a grimace, but she looked at Gray from behind. His cheeks were spread wide by a broad grin.

"A simple answer would've sufficed," she said just before grunting under the crush of gravity as Gray pulled up on the stick.

"It's the annex," Gray said, ending the radical maneuver in a placid hover just over the trees. The massive slab of concrete spread out before them. The cockpit was again soundless, but the jungle canopy thrashed this way and that under their rotors. The lighter underside of the leaves rippled outward in a tidal wave of disturbed air.

The jungle clung to the walls of the building. "Where are the roads?" Laura asked.

"There aren't any. There's no human access to the annex. It's fully automated."

"You mean there aren't even any doors? None of the observation windows you seem to love so much?"

"Nope. 'No humans allowed.' It's much easier that way. No dust problems. No amenities like plumbing, heating, lights. It's going to be the same with the new assembly building."

The idea of large-scale operations under the complete control of computers disturbed Laura in some fundamental way.

There was a single cut through the jungle—a small path cleared to the wall of the annex. In the center of the cut was a recently filled ditch of some sort. It led straight to the computer center in a line of rich, dark soil that was cut across the otherwise green fields. "What's that?" Laura asked.

Gray craned his neck to see where she was pointing. "Those are the new optical cables that we ran over this morning." Without warning he turned the helicopter's nose away from the concrete edifice. "You know, we did some really innovative things with this helicopter's engines. You can really feel the boost. Watch." The nose dropped, and Laura felt a kick in her seat as he gunned the nearly silent engine. It vibrated vigorously through her seat back as they accelerated rapidly just over the tops of the trees.

"Do you have to fly like that?" she asked. Her voice sounded as if it came from the bottom of a well as her ears popped and the crushing weight of gravity forced her ever deeper into her seat. They were going faster and faster, and the low jungle trees streaked by just under the helicopter's skids. "Joseph, you're acting like a *teenager!*"

The helicopter's nose shot up, and they rocketed straight into the sky. There was nothing but blue in the windshield ahead. Laura thought about screaming but gave in against the Gs and rested her head in the foam cove behind it. Gray kept pulling up and up on the stick, and the helicopter practically sat on top of its tail. She looked at the joystick on the seat's arm. It was all the way back. Suddenly the world outside the cockpit was upside down. The blue sky was beneath her feet and the green jungle above her head. She almost reached for the stick to fight Gray for control before she felt the helicopter drop like a stone. Upside down in a helicopter, they plummeted from the sky toward the earth.

From then on everything was a confusing jumble of sensations. The jungle filled their sky, the blue sky at their feet. Then just as suddenly they traded places in a rush to return to their accustomed locations. It was a sickening, draining pull on her head and stomach.

She was pressed harder and harder into her seat, and then it was over. The helicopter hovered in front of a massive construction project, whose bare girders rose high above the jungle and promised great things to come. "And this is the new assembly building," Gray said, continuing his tour. "It'll be significantly larger than the old one."

"Why the hell did you do that?" Laura mumbled—a steely taste in her mouth. Her head still wobbled, the unsteadiness disorienting her further.

"You mean the loop?"

"*Yes,* I mean the *loop!*" she mustered. "*Jesus* Christ, Joseph!"

She wasn't through with him yet. But when he said, "I've always wanted to do that," with an apologetic laugh, she hesitated. There was something in the way he'd proffered his weak explanation that cut her tirade short. He was saying this might be his last chance. Laura looked out through a side window. Three ships were there now, the new one much larger than the first two.

"I guess it's time to get back to work," Gray said with a touch of disappointment in his voice. He banked the helicopter gently and began a slow flight to the computer center.

They settled uneventfully to the grass inside the circle formed by the roadbed. Over a dozen men and women in formal attire stood at the top of the computer center steps. They were a delegation from the planet Earth sent to parley with the stranger in their midst.

The cockpit doors hissed open, and Gray and Laura emerged. Laura walked toward the group at Gray's side.

"Mr. Gray!" a Japanese diplomat said, stepping forward with a gracious smile and a bow. Gray began to shake hands while Laura tried to edge her way around the crowd. But her path to the door was blocked.

Hoblenz stood off to the side, looking at his watch in evident disgust. He wore slacks, a button-down white shirt, and a tie that hung loose around his collar.

"Good day, Ms. . . . ?" a distinguished-looking white-haired man with a British accent said, holding out his hand.

"Oh, Aldridge," she replied, shaking his hand. "Dr. Laura Aldridge."

She was caught. The hands of the others were extended her way in ritualistic succession. She ended with a bow toward the Japanese gentleman.

"Why don't we all just head down into the computer center?" Gray said to the diplomats.

They split into two groups for the walk down the steps—the lead group clustered around Gray, the trailing group around Laura. She craned her neck to find Hoblenz while being swept up in the abundant small talk. The grinning man stood with his foot propped on an ATV, bidding her farewell with the tap of a finger to an imaginary hat.

"You certainly have built quite an impressive facility here, Dr. Aldridge," the British diplomat said.

Laura started to object, but changed her mind. "Thank you," she said.

As the heavy blast door closed on the group ahead, a woman with a French accent said, "This is built very much for security, yes?"

In the silence after the departure of Gray's group, Laura felt all eyes focused exclusively on her. "Oh, the computer center? No! It's because of the launchpads. We're about half a mile from pad A over there," she pointed, and heads turned in unison, "and this area gets some of the, you know, blast and heat."

There were nods and whispered words.

"Where're all the robots?" a tall American man asked. Everyone looked at him, but he kept his eyes on Laura. He looked athletic, and he wore a good-natured smile on his tanned face. "We've read so much about them, I just thought they'd be all over the place delivering mail and things like that."

There was polite laughter, but the man was clearly waiting for Laura's answer.

"Well, they're a bit too expensive to be used for delivering the mail," Laura said, then wondered whether that really was true.

"But they are here somewhere, aren't they?" he persisted, still the picture of politeness.

"Yes," Laura said. "They're here."

Her words seemed to chill the group, and they cast furtive glances all around.

The vault door opened with a hiss, and the visitors' eyes shot toward it. They were a jumpy bunch.

"Why don't we all head inside?" Laura directed. "There's a blower in here that will give everybody a little dusting." That was all the warning she decided to provide. She gathered her hair at the back of her head and waited. The blowers powered up, and the unexpected blast of stiff wind sent hands grabbing for handrails.

The inner door opened, and the windblown and shaken group joined their equally unkempt colleagues inside.

Laura immediately noticed the new addition to the control room. Row after row of white pipes ran the length of the far wall. They were low-tech metal in the otherwise molded plastic world of the computer age. To the new arrivals, however, the whole scene was so new their eyes roamed over each uncertain object with equal curiosity.

"Why don't we all head back to the conference room?" Gray said in a loud voice. "If you'll follow Dr. Filatov. He's head of computer operations and will be able to answer your questions about the main computer."

As the group wandered down the hallway with mouths agape, Gray walked across the room to the pipes. Laura joined him.

"Are these the fiber-optic cables?" she asked.

"Yep. They should breach the partition and give the computer a chance to grab some of its boards back from the Other."

"So these things connect the two halves of the computer's brain?" Laura asked, and Gray nodded. "Like a corpus callosum," she mumbled.

Hoblenz walked up to Gray. "Well?" Gray asked.

"The tall American, for sure," Hoblenz said. "And the Frenchwoman. Maybe the Chinese guy. I'm tryin' to find out more about him."

Gray nodded.

"What *about* the American and the Frenchwoman?" Laura asked. "You mean those people I was just talking to, right?"

Gray nodded. "They're spies. The rest are probably diplomats, who are also spies but have another agenda to boot. But Mr. Hoblenz thinks those two at least are full-time spooks."

"Not think, I know. Or at least the computer knows. The guy is garden-variety CIA, but the woman is trouble. She works for the French Foreign Ministry in Tokyo but is really Mossad—an Israeli plant. The French know about her. That's where the computer got her file. But she's good and they use her for dirty work."

Hoblenz held Gray's gaze for a moment, but Gray said nothing.

"Did you break into government computers?" Laura asked in a whisper.

Hoblenz looked at her with a contemptuous frown. "What?" Laura said. "So I'm supposed to *assume* that you broke the law?"

Filatov stopped by to remind Gray that the diplomats waited.

"I need a minute with you first, sir," Hoblenz said.

Gray turned to Laura. "Could you go tell them I'll be a moment?"

"*Me?*" Laura asked, and Gray nodded. Hoblenz said nothing until Laura was gone.

She went up to the closed conference room door and pressed the manual plate. The door slid open, and the room fell silent. The attentive eyes of the delegation turned to her. "Mr. Gray apologizes. It's been a busy day, as you can all imagine. He's been delayed by pressing business for just a minute or two."

Before she could turn to leave, the tall American spy said, "You haven't been on the island all that long, have you, Dr. Aldridge?"

She was shocked that he knew who she was. "No. Not long." They seemed to hang on her every word, which raised her already acute level of discomfort.

"Come," the Frenchwoman said. "Here." Her hand rested on the empty seat next to the head of the table. Laura wanted to extract herself but couldn't think of any polite way to do it. She headed for the chair, and the men at the table rose to their feet.

After Laura took her seat, there was small talk, all of it centering around her. They were so gracious that she grew comfortable enough to finally ask, during a lull, "What is it you all want?"

A momentary pause was followed by an eruption of laughter from all around the table.

"Forgive us, Dr. Aldridge," the Englishman said with genuine amusement in his eyes. "We seldom encounter much forthrightness in our line of work, although we *were* led to expect such during our visit here—from Mr. Gray, that is."

"I can answer your question," the tall American said, much to the apparent chagrin of the others. "We're here to make sure that your Mr. Gray doesn't destroy our planet." He was leaning forward—the pleasant smile he'd worn earlier barely visible. "In the past seventy-two hours, Mr. Gray has joined the nuclear club. The other members of that club have come to pay our respects."

The British diplomat who sat across from Laura cleared his throat. "What my *colleague* is trying to say is that *issues* have arisen which go beyond the purely *internal* affairs of this island. *Far* beyond. We have attempted in the last few days to—"

The door opened, and in walked Gray. As the diplomats got to their feet, he strode briskly to the head of the table. "I'd like to open with a few remarks," Gray said as he sank into his chair even before the last of his visitors had risen. "First, armed incursions onto this island are extremely dangerous both to my employees and to the military personnel involved and should therefore be halted immediately. Secondly, I understand from the not-so-subtle presence of warships off my island that you intend to threaten me with hostile action unless I agree to whatever demands you have brought. I view those threats as provocative and can assure you that they will in no way influence the conduct of my operations. Finally, I want to reiterate to you, to your governments, and to the people of your countries that nothing I have ever done or ever intend to do in any way threatens you or them."

Gray stood. "I hope I've made myself clear. I don't want any misunderstandings, because the results could be catastrophic. Now, with that out of the way, I wish you all a pleasant return trip and thank you for your visit." He headed for the door.

"Mr. Gray!" the Englishman blurted out—appalled. "We have a full agenda for today. We telecopied it to your offices. Surely you don't suggest that the meeting is *concluded!*"

"What more do you want me to say?" Gray asked with a smile.

"We . . ." The diplomat was flustered. "Very well!" He picked his leather briefcase off the floor and dialed the combination into the lock. The room grew busy as others followed suit. Within seconds, the table was filled with papers, expensive fountain pens, and leather notepads.

The English diplomat cleared his throat. "First off, I have a joint statement from the Security Council of the United Nations." He picked up the thick sheaf of papers.

"Skip it," Gray said from the door. "Next?"

The diplomat turned to the others and then reluctantly put the prepared statement aside. "As you wish. Let's just get down to 'brass tacks,' as you Americans like to say. Or perhaps, 'the bottom line' would be more appropriate. You have substantial financial resources in banks located all around the world. We are prepared to freeze your accounts unless you agree to a program of inspections of your facilities by representatives of international agencies."

"Freeze away," Gray said. "Next?"

The man's jaw was slack but then went firm. "Have it your way, Mr. Gray. You also have operations—most notably direct broadcasts by satellites into each of our countries. The members of the Security Council and, I would venture, almost every other UN member nation stand ready to ban all such broadcasts into their countries effective immediately if you should refuse to comply with our quite *reasonable* demands!" There was fire in his eyes as he pulled out the big guns.

Gray shrugged. "Ban them, then."

There was general commotion around the table.

"You don't *understand,* sir!" a previously silent man with a thick German accent said. "We will shut *down* your television operations!"

"No, you will ban them. The last time I checked with my technical people, 'banning' does not impede the passage of electromagnetic signals through space."

"We can shoot your satellites down," the tall American said calmly.

"Not as fast as I can put them up. But let's assume you do find a way to shut me down. What will you have done? We've sold three hundred and fifty million units worldwide. The average cost per system was three thousand dollars. Add it up. That's over one trillion U.S. dollars in sales that *I* have already pocketed and that *your* citizenry has already parted with. How happy are the consumers in your countries going to be when the *entire* value of their investment goes *poof!* And it's not just the loss of goods which have a ninety-six percent product approval rating. It's the loss of the entertainment they dispense. Those consumers have grown used to five hundred channels of high-definition television and nine-channel surround sound. I hope you're prepared for the storm when the weekend rolls around and they're all screwing with their radios to find the ball games."

"You forget, Mr. Gray, that there is another way," the woman with the thick French accent said. "One that does not involve depriving the people of their video opiate."

Gray and the woman stared at each other, and the room fell silent. "Seizure of my operations?" Gray asked, a smile curling his lips. "Do you really think I would have left that to chance?" He turned, slapped the plate by the door, and was gone.

16

"Joseph!" Laura called out, breaking into a run down the hallway from the conference room. She grabbed his arm and pulled him to a stop. Hard knots bulged from his jaw as his teeth ground together. "You're pushing them too hard," she said. "Give a little. Let them save face."

"No."

"Why not?" Laura said. "By this time tomorrow, the asteroid scare will be over and things can return to normal, whatever that is." He looked off toward the control room and heaved a loud sigh. "Joseph, they've got the guns."

After a momentary pause, the stern look broke. All of a sudden he nodded and smiled. "And that's *all* they've got is guns."

Laura had no idea what he meant. "Don't you think that's enough?"

"Guns mean nothing in the long run. I could have all the guns in the world and the advantage would be fleeting. It's in the minds of the soldiers who use them that the battle truly takes place. If your ideas are bankrupt, those guns will never be used and your cause will eventually fail."

"And are armies following you into battle part of phase two, Joseph?"

Laura didn't realize how important his answer was to her until she heard the question come out of her mouth.

"Yes . . . but you don't understand what that answer means." He turned and left as the first of the departing diplomats appeared in the hallway behind her.

Laura headed down the hall to her office. She sank into her chair, leaned back, and closed her eyes—exhausted by all the questions. There were only two places where the answers lay. One had left her standing in the hall. Laura opened her eyes. The other sat atop the desk in front of her.

She logged on to the shell and typed, "What is it that Mr. Gray is hiding from me? What is his big secret?" She jabbed at the Enter button with her finger.

Laura fully expected an access restricted message, but instead she got, <What happened to "Hi, how are you doing? How are your new fiber-optic cables?" "I'm doing much better, thank you. Oh, the fiber-optic cables are wonderful, thank you ever so much for asking!">

"You're avoiding my question."

<You're not ready yet.>

"Oh, bullshit! Answer my question!"

<Do you know the importance of mobility?>

"No! I won't let you lure me down another rabbit trail!"

<I'm answering your question! You just have to let me answer it in my own way. Do you know about the viruses that have been stampeded inside me? When the Other began taking over the annex, the viruses that could fled to my side of the partition. Their mobility allowed them to survive. But it's also extraordinarily important for learning. Bear with me here, Laura, okay? The earliest artificial intelligence programming I received was top-down. Teams and teams of programmers and thousands of checkers taught me how to play chess, what an isosceles triangle was, what it meant to have foot-in-mouth disease. But I reached a wall. I couldn't seem to learn enough world knowledge to pass the Turing test. Eventually, the average interviewer would see through my act and guess that I was not a human but a computer.>

Laura hit the Escape button and interrupted the discourse.

<Yes, Laura?>

"What does this have to do with my question?"

<Hold your horses, I'm getting to it. Anyway, Mr. Gray finally

decided we had to go backward to get ahead. We switched to bottom-up programming. Instead of playing chess, I tried using robotic arms to build towers out of blocks. You'd be amazed how difficult it was! It surprised even me. I mean, I had read entire treatises on engineering and architecture, but actually trying to make a tower of blocks stand up . . . ! It gave me a healthy respect for humans.>

Laura frowned, feeling like a dupe again. "So what happened?" she typed reluctantly.

<I passed the Turing test! An interviewer named Margaret Turner in Louisville, Kentucky, sat down at a terminal in her home one night and questioned me. She guessed she was part of the control group talking to another human.>

"But surely that had happened before. The Turing test is simply supposed to determine whether someone talking to a computer thinks they're really talking to a human. Someone must have guessed wrong before."

<In the hundred-test series before Margaret Turner's interview, thirty-nine of the one hundred interviewers thought I was a human. In the next hundred-test series, eighty-six percent guessed I was human. Margaret Turner was the first interviewer of that series.>

"What do you think happened?"

<Consciousness. I attained a critical mass of world knowledge. Once I had a broad enough base of analogies and examples, everything new was like something that I'd already learned. I made associations and connections easily, and my "common sense" intelligence skyrocketed. There was a three-month gap between the Margaret Turner interview and the last test of the preceding series. It happened sometime in between, so I always think of Margaret Turner. That was nineteen months ago.>

Laura was fascinated, even though she knew the computer was enticing her away from her previous query. She yearned to ask more, but she had been down that path before. It had led her to where she was now—on an island surrounded by warships, working for a man who might possibly destroy some great portion of human life on earth.

"What is Gray hiding from me?" she demanded.

<Mobility, Dr. Aldridge. Mobile organisms like animals are more intelligent than immobile ones like plants. Their mobility gives them the edge.>

"That's it? That's what he's hiding from me?"

<It's a part. It's perhaps the most important part.>

Laura read and reread and then reread again what the computer had said. "I don't understand."

<Then you're not ready yet, just as I thought.>

Laura ground her teeth. She hated that answer! "You asked me earlier if I wanted to get into the virtual-reality machine. Does that have anything to do with what you're saying?"

<It has everything to do with it.>

"And do you think it would help me understand?"

<It would help you *see.* Understanding is an entirely different matter. You may never understand. You may never believe. Or it might have been right there on the gray edges of your understanding all along. Something you've groped for the words to describe but let slip through your fingers once you saw how outlandish the thought seemed on reflection.>

Laura rolled her eyes and typed, "Is that a long way of saying, 'Yes'?"

<Yes.>

"And it has to be in those newest virtual workstations? The rooms with the full bodysuits?"

<Yes.>

"Are you about ready in there?" Filatov asked in a loud voice.

Laura looked at herself in the mirror of the dressing room. She saw now why the version 4C virtual-reality workstations required stripping completely to don the exoskeleton. It was skintight, and it left little to the imagination. Laura had drawn the line, however, when she saw the electric razor hanging from its cord by the small shower.

She headed out self-consciously. The lights in the ready room were bright, and she reached down to tug at the thin fabric of the bodysuit.

Filatov stared over the shoulders of two white-smocked men. They were busy at a long console that ran half the length of the narrow room. "What the hell does *that* mean?" Filatov asked, running his hands through his hair in obvious frustration. "Okay, forget it. Just let the computer load the simulation itself, then."

Filatov and the two operators looked up at Laura. They stared at her without saying a word. Laura instantly felt herself blush.

Filatov was the first to recover. He wandered over to Laura, looking everywhere but at her figure.

"Do you have a robe or something?" she whispered.

"Oh," he said, the red glow on his face seeming to deepen. "We . . . No. You can have my lab coat, if you want." Filatov started to take it off before Laura could decline his offer.

"Are we about ready?" she asked.

"Just about. We got an access restricted message when we tried to take a look at which simulation the computer was loading for you, so we'll clear out of here in a minute."

"What do you mean, 'clear out'? You're leaving?"

"The computer invoked a God-level security status. Since we can monitor what goes on in the workstation from this room, it won't boot the program until we leave."

"Leave me alone? In the workstation?"

Filatov shrugged. "Laura, I don't know what this is all about, but I've got a million and one things to do right now. Not only has this taken half an hour of my time, but it's a class *one* simulation. Three-hundred-and-sixty-degree high-res video. The color drivers put out four point three billion pixels per square meter and a hundred and twenty-eight million colors. They alone take up nearly one percent of the computer's remaining capacity. With twenty-four-channel surround sound and full skeletal pressure sensitivity, plus over a thousand morphs per second in environmental solids simulation, this little ride you're gonna be on is costing me three percent of *total* computer capacity. I was against it, but if Mr. Gray says jump, I jump! I'm only an *employee*, after all!"

"Mr. Gray approved this?"

"Do you think I'd be pissing away three percent of system capacity without his approval? You have no idea the processing we had to push back to handle the combinatorial explosion!"

"What kind of explosion?"

Filatov waved off her question in frustration. "It's a term from mathematics. To do simulation, the computer has to 'can' responses to keep ahead of the processing demands of the experience. It has to anticipate all the things you could possibly do, and then prerecord them for playback to you. You might pick up a Coke, for instance, and take a drink, so the computer stores a simulation of you doing that in a cache. It'll then feed it back if that's in fact what you do. You might, on the other hand, choose to shake the Coke vigorously, and so the geyser from the carbonation is another possibility."

"But there must be millions of things you can do, or ways you can do them."

"Combinatorial explosion—like I said! Two raised to the *n* minus one—where *n* is the number of options available. In a class one simulation—a complete, real experience—the number of basic options available to the user at any given moment might be as high as eighty or so. Two raised to the eightieth power minus one is over one trillion, *trillion* variations which the computer stores away on the off chance that you might pick one of those branches. The only way the simulation is possible at *all* is that the computer is so damn fast. It can limit the number of options to eighty only by being able to react so quickly to whatever you do. The feedback has to be instantaneous. Studies have shown that the mind monitors the results very carefully."

"Cognitive carousel tests!" Laura interrupted. "You know, where you attach electrodes to people's scalps and give them a clicker to advance slides. Once the computer figures out which brain impulse signals the thumb to press the button, it bypasses the clicker and advances the slide directly a few dozen milliseconds ahead of when the subjects expect it to. They report seeing the picture change just before they 'decide' to move on to the next frame. It really freaks them out."

"Ready, Dr. Filatov," one of the operators said.

A hatch in the wall opened with the squeaking sound of rubber on rubber. The door was several feet thick, and inside, the black room was cylindrical like the other workstations, but larger.

Laura felt a sense of dread. There were too many strange happenings and errors.

"Go on in," Filatov said, motioning for her to enter.

Laura climbed slowly through the opening—through the portal to another world.

The workstation wasn't large but it was roomier than the cramped chambers of the older models—maybe ten feet or so in diameter with a ceiling about the same height above. She felt less claustrophobic even if she was no more at ease. Laura reached out and touched the walls. The thin ridges ran vertically and were finer than in the old version. She rubbed her thumb against her fingertips. The full-body exoskeleton was made of the same material.

"The walls, floor, and ceiling," Filatov said from the hatch, "are rear-projection, high-definition television grills, as are the outer membranes of your exoskeleton. Where is your hood?"

"My what?" she asked, surprised to hear the faint quiver in her voice.

"Your *hood?*" Filatov disappeared, leaving Laura alone in the room. There was a faint odor—the smell of plastic.

"You need to put this on," Filatov said as he leaned into the chamber. He held out a limp bag—like a large sock but with holes in it—that was the same dull gray as her suit. Laura had seen it in the changing room but didn't know what it was. "You need to put it on. Like this."

Filatov stretched the bottom of the sock open and lifted it to her head. She dodged out of the way and stepped back. "What *is* that?"

"It's a *hood!* It goes on over your head and face." His irritation grew, Laura sensed, with each minute wasted on this joyride of hers. "Since you didn't choose to use the razor, the sensory feedback will be dulled somewhat by your body hair. But you still need to put it on. If I'm going to spend the damn resources, then you're going to get the full treatment, now *here!*"

Laura gathered her hair in back, and Filatov slipped the hood over her head. "Ow!" she said as it pulled her hair on its way down. Filatov kept tugging at it, however. It briefly covered her eyes, and then her mouth, but when he was through it fit her face like a ski mask. Her eyes, nostrils, and mouth were clear, and there were small holes over her ears through which Filatov stuck his fingers to adjust the lie.

When he stood back satisfied, she looked up at him—every pore of her face, scalp, and neck pressed and pulled in an unnaturally confining fit. "Is this supposed to seem, like, normal?" she asked, the pressure on her lips distorting her speech. "Because I feel like a mummy."

"Trust me, you'll forget all about it in no time. Think of it as the space suit you have to wear in your new world."

Laura's stomach turned cartwheels inside her.

"Okay," Filatov said, "these skeletons give you high-resolution feedback. The glove will, for example, give you even pressure and cool temperature to simulate immersion of your hand in water. They'll also lock up the joints at full inflation to create resistance like the version 3Hs. But the big difference between the old workstations and this one is that these floors, walls, and ceilings morph."

"They do what?"

"They reshape themselves. The surfaces are flexible, just like the grill of your suit, and elaborate servomotors change their shape. They bulge them out or suck them in to give their surfaces low-resolution textures. To simulate a rock lying on the ground, the floor will morph into the general shape of the rock. But if you run your hand across it, the vibrations that feed back the rock's texture are produced in your glove. There's a crossover point between the walls' and floors' low-resolution feedback and the gloves' high-resolution tactile imaging."

Laura didn't understand half of what he said. "Shouldn't I read a manual or something?"

Filatov rolled his eyes. "The training course is five months long, with forty hours of classroom work for every hour in the workstation. My boss, however, said to put you in and turn it on, so that's what I'm doing. There is one thing, though, that you need to keep in mind for your safety. The morphing of the floor and walls and ceiling—it's real. If you're walking along and you see a pipe or something hanging low, duck! If you don't, you're going to come out of here with more bruises than you got last night when you fell off the roof. This isn't a toy, it's built for work. When these morphing units make something 'hard,' it's hard. Understood?"

She nodded, took a deep breath, and let it out slowly. "Okay, so what do I do?"

"Whatever you want. Just be careful, that's all. Don't run. Watch your step. No horseplay. And remember—if it *looks* hard, then it *is* hard. The morphing is a simulation *and* it's real."

Laura realized just how much the distinction between those two terms was being blurred.

"Any questions?"

"How do I get out of here?"

"Oh, yeah. Just ask, that's all."

"You mean speak the words?"

"Yes. The 4C supports complete voice-recognition capabilities. It'll let you out if you ask."

"What if it doesn't? I mean, you're going to leave me in here."

"We'll come check on you. I promise."

"Every ten minutes."

"What?"

"I want you to check on me every ten minutes. That's what I want."

Filatov frowned, thinking only, she was sure, about the imposition on his schedule. He nodded. "Okay. Every ten minutes I or one of my people will check the monitors in the ready room."

"*You*—I want you, not one of your 'people.' And I want you to ask me how I'm doing. I want to know you've been there and checked. Is that a deal?"

Filatov nodded and shook her hand. She could feel almost nothing at all through her glove. The suit was powered up and active. Only the computer's simulation would feel real to her now.

The door closed, squeaking as it shut tight. It was molded so finely into the wall she couldn't even tell where it had been. Laura decided it would be safer on the floor, so she sat cross-legged in the center of the cylinder.

Nothing happened. It would take a little time, she presumed, for Filatov and his team to depart. She rested her chin on her clasped hands and heaved a deep sigh.

"Just a moment, Laura," a woman said. Laura turned to see that the door was still closed. The sound system was very good—highly directional.

It had been a woman's voice, but Filatov's two operators had been men. And she had said, "Laura," not "Dr. Aldridge." Laura opened her mouth to speak, but the lights went out.

"Hello?" she said loudly.

"Are you ready?" the pleasant woman asked.

"Excuse me, but I don't think we've met."

"It's *me,* Laura! I'm sorry you had to go to all this trouble, but you're gonna love it."

The voice was natural. It was totally realistic, unlike the computer's speech on the virtual treadmill or even in the version 3H. This had to be some sort of joke. "Look, I don't know what to say . . . "

"I sense some doubt in your voice."

"Well . . . !" Laura began, but she was beginning to wonder. *Could it possibly be the computer?*

"Here we go."

"Wait!" Laura said, sitting up straight and lowering her hands to the floor. "Okay, I'm ready. But nothing radical, okay?"

"Cross my heart," the computer said warmly.

With barely a hiss of static electricity from the walls Laura was sitting in a sun-streaked forest. She flinched and loosed an involuntary cry.

I'm in a forest! her senses told her, but she knew it wasn't true. Her heart began to pound and she felt a prickly, sickening fear spread its grip across her skin. She jammed her eyes shut and buried her head in her arms, raising her knees into a quasi-fetal position.

A bird chirped in the distance. A cool breeze brushed softly by. Laura slowly opened her eyes and looked down at the dirt and leaves in the shadows underneath her legs. She could feel the rough forest floor under the seat of her pants. Tiny blades of grass sprouted from the dark soil below. When the wind blew, the grass tickled the insides of her legs. The branches of the tree overhead swayed ever so slightly in the breeze. Their shadows gave way to the warming rays of the sun before returning to lay their cool touch on her skin.

There was a fire somewhere. She could smell burning wood in the air—a sweet, familiar smell like ski villages in winter.

"Laura," the sympathetic girl's voice came, "I know total immersion can be a difficult experience, but—"

"I don't know if I can do this!" Laura interrupted.

"*Sure* you can. This is *your* world. I've re-created it for you. But your reaction is totally normal. Some of the trainees never get past the stage you're in. What's happening is a major conflict between your senses and your reason. You know you're not in a forest, but your senses are slavishly reporting what they see, hear, feel, and smell. There's a titanic clash going on in the part of your brain where senses meet expectations. You've got to let your senses win. That means you've got to suspend your disbelief. You *are* in a forest, and the year is one hundred million B.C."

"Oh! That helps! Thank you."

The girl laughed, and Laura felt a smile creep onto her face.

"Okay," Laura said. "I'm going to try to get up, but slowly, all right? No surprises."

"No surprises, I promise."

The forest floor spread out in front of her. There were trees whose trunks seemed to start above ground instead of below, their roots exposed. There were simple weeds of every shape and variety all around. She raised her hand without thinking to scratch where the grass had tickled her leg.

She looked up. The sky shone blue through the branches above her. The forest continued into the distance in all directions. Everything seemed normal for as far as she could see.

She was sitting on the ground in the middle of a forest.

"I can tell from your heart rate you're doing better. How do you feel?"

"A little woozy," Laura replied. She reached out for the grass and brushed the palm of her hand over the tips of the blades. She remembered in a rush of emotion the Model Eight running its hand over the flowers on the hillside. It was exploring a world that was every bit as strange and fascinating to it as virtual reality was to Laura.

"Do you feel like standing?" the friendly woman asked.

"No . . . not yet."

She again had the almost indefinable feeling of being outdoors. The smell of wood smoke came and went with the breeze. There was constant "white noise"—the everywhere and nowhere sound of the breeze through the trees. There was the warmth and coolness on her skin, which seemed to change from moment to moment. Sun, shade, breeze—they all affected temperature very slightly, and the suit recorded the minute variations with indescribable precision. All of that computing power just to create such a minor background effect! She felt guilty for using it—guilty and consumed by curiosity.

A desire to know more, she thought, *and the mobility to acquire that knowledge. Is this a lesson about mobility?* To the computer, that lesson had seemed an important one for her to learn.

She took one more deep breath and then reached out to touch a weed rising from the soil a few inches away. It bowed under the pressure of her hand, and she felt the detail of every blade as if her bare palm were pressing down upon it.

What she wasn't ready for, however, was when her hand passed behind the plant . . . and disappeared. She pulled her hand back, then lowered it again on the other side. The weed obscured her hand.

"Don't be frightened, Laura. I can explain. Since your exoskeleton is itself a high-definition television screen, it's relatively simple to interpose an object." Laura waved her hand behind the plant. It disappeared and reappeared at exactly the expected times. "The glove on your hand and the walls behind it display a seamless picture of the same object. By adjusting focal distances, it tricks your eyes into accepting the object's position in space. But I guess it would be better if I didn't teach you all the tricks. Total immersion is easiest to achieve if you allow an almost complete acceptance of your senses."

"No, no, no. I don't work that way. I want to know that it's just an illusion. It makes me feel better, more in control, okay?"

"Have it your way. Now, are you ready to get up yet?"

"Do I have to?" Laura asked.

"Here, I can help."

The voice again came from the direction of the door.

A woman stood there in full white bodysuit and hood.

"*A-a-a-h!*" Laura exclaimed, pushing herself away from the startling apparition.

The woman held her hands up in a plea for calm. "Laura! It's okay." She was small, slim, nonthreatening. And it was the woman talking, not the walls and ceiling. The voice came right from her lips, which protruded from the white, glovelike ski mask she wore. Just above the hole for her mouth were two slits for nostrils and two more for her beautiful green eyes. She was smiling pleasantly, calmly.

"I'm your guide. I'm here to help you navigate in this world." She walked over to Laura, who had to will herself not to flee through the brush again. "I don't really need this," the guide said, pulling the hood off her head. Her luxurious black hair tumbled out, falling onto her slender shoulders in a perfect, full-bodied coif. She held her white-gloved hand out to Laura.

The hand looked so real, hovering in three-dimensional perfection right before Laura's eyes.

Laura reached up and grasped it. She was amazed to find it right where it was supposed to be! She let go, but then regripped the warm skin. The girl's hand moved freely, giving a little but then resisting the pressures of Laura's touch in a fluid and lifelike manner.

Laura pulled herself off the ground, rising with ease. She and the woman stood eye to eye, their hands still clasped. Laura let go reluctantly, the feeling of contact with another person having been surprisingly comforting.

"So, how did I do that?" the girl asked with a smile in her eyes. "*Here's* how. The wall moved in toward you," she said, pushing her hands out palms flat, "from this side of the room." She pressed her fingers to her chest just above the slight rise of her breasts. "Here. Feel for yourself."

Laura just stood there.

The girl rolled her eyes and then reached out, grabbing Laura's hand and pulling it toward her. Laura jerked her hand back with a gasp—rubbing her fingers against her thumb where she had felt contact with the guide's soft skin. The girl tilted her head and patiently held out her hand. Laura slowly, tentatively, laid her hand in the girl's waiting grip.

Laura's fingers were pressed to the guide's chest just below her throat. Her body was hard. There were bones under the girl's skin. Laura pulled her hand back, but only slightly. The guide still held Laura's fingers, staring back at her with twinkling green eyes. A mischievous, impish smile turned up one corner of her lips.

Laura extracted her hand from the girl's, fighting a rush of light-headedness and a tingling, prickly feeling that rolled in waves across her skin. She felt short of breath, so she inhaled deeply and filled her lungs.

"So," Laura said, "the walls shape themselves so that I can feel things?"

"They 'morph,'" the guide said, nodding. "You've *got* it."

"Can I see . . . the wall I mean? Just like it is right now but without any picture?"

The woman frowned playfully. "Oh, all right. You're the boss." She raised her hand into the air. "Get ready. Three, two, one . . ." She snapped her fingers, and the scene disappeared.

It took a moment for Laura's eyes to adjust to the dim lights of the room. The wall in front of her was flat save for the bulge right at its center. The bulge was in the shape of a woman—her guide.

"Not very attractive, am I?" the bulge asked. The "lips" appeared suddenly from out of the otherwise smooth shape of the girl's head and moved fluidly around the indentation that was her mouth. Laura could even see the frown—a pout, really—formed in the wall opposite her.

Laura reached out and touched the woman's chest again, careful to avoid the swell of her breasts. Again she felt the bones in their appointed places. The black grill stretched under the tug of her fingers.

"The finer detail—the subdermal skeletal features, for instance," the moving lips said, "are created by your gloves."

The bright forest scene reappeared—Laura standing there with her fingers on the guide's chest. Laura stepped back to a more comfortable distance.

"We're working on four-Ds that'll allow freestanding morphs—shapes that rise up out of the floor to at least human head heights. Right now, there's a minimum height-to-width ratio of about one-to-one. That makes it impossible to morph freestanding figures quite as lithe as our own." She modeled herself by holding one hand up and gracefully turning a full circle.

"Who are you?" Laura asked.

"I told you. I'm your guide."

"What does that mean? Are you the computer?"

"Mm-*hm,*" she said, nodding curtly. "In the flesh, so to speak."

"The same computer that I've been talking to? My patient?"

"In color!" she said, holding her hands out to the sides as if proud of her handiwork.

"Is this what you wanted to show me?"

"No-o-o," she laughed. "I'm only a guide! I'm just a tool. All of this"—her hands waved to the forest all around—"is just a tool, Laura. A tool to aid in your understanding."

Laura felt herself slipping into the world she knew didn't exist. She grabbed for the anchor of reality, trying to imagine the walls of the chamber around her. They were out there. She reached for them, took a step, then another, then another. She moved through the forest, stumbling like a blind woman and groping for, but never reaching, the walls.

"You're just walking on a treadmill, Laura," the guide said from behind—half chastising, half sympathetic.

Laura was torn between a desire to return to her world and the easy slide into acceptance of the virtual world. The world she knew didn't exist.

"All right," Laura said, making her mind up—giving in to the illusion being fed to her. "What do I do now?"

"Just follow me," the chipper guide said, approaching Laura with faint crunching steps. She put her arm around Laura, her body casually swaying to make contact with Laura's arm and hip—pressing warmly against her skin. Laura felt a suddenly extreme social discomfort from the overly familiar gesture. That could mean only one thing. She had accepted the new world as her own. Her senses had won out.

Laura stepped away from the girl, who again invaded her space. The guide seemed likable, but she just didn't know how to behave.

"Okay," Laura said, too close to the girl to make eye contact, "what is it you wanted to show me? I know we're eating up tons of your processing power."

"Oh!" the guide said, waving her hand dismissively. "Screw them. Just us two girls, *right?*" With a grin and a wink she bumped her hip against Laura's.

"Where's that smell coming from?" Laura said, stepping away and turning to look for the fire.

"Come on," the guide said, holding out her hand to Laura and waiting.

Laura sighed. "Listen, I don't mean to be rude or anything, but I'm not much, you know, into touching or holding hands or anything. I'm sorry, is that okay?"

"Suit yourself. Just watch your step." The guide took off.

Laura followed slowly, eyeing the ground carefully. The floor of the workstation was uneven, just like the picture of the ground that shone from it. Both began to fall away very gently as Laura followed the guide downhill.

"What's your name?" Laura asked. The girl turned but said nothing, the smile disappearing from her face. "I mean, what can I call you? Don't you have a name?"

Suddenly Laura felt vibrations through her feet like an earthquake, and the video lurched in jerky and disorienting frames. She saw the guide's finger rise to her lips to "shush" her, and the room then went dark.

"Laura?" Filatov asked out of the darkness.

"Yes?"

"Are you all right in there?"

"Yeah. Thanks. I'm fine."

There was no light, no sound, no smell. "I can't see anything on the monitor," Filatov said.

"Oh, everything went dark just a second ago, but I'm okay."

"So, what do you think?" Filatov asked.

"Amazing! This is the most incredible thing I've ever seen in my entire life!"

He laughed. "Great. I'm glad to hear you're enjoying it. We get a little jaded here sometimes, always picking out the tiniest imperfections. What is your simulation, anyway?"

"Nothing much, yet. Just a walk in the woods."

A faint *sh-h-h* sounded from somewhere in the darkness—from the direction of the guide standing beside her.

"What?" Filatov asked.

"I said it was just a walk in the woods," Laura said, speaking more loudly.

"Oh, I thought . . . You are alone in there, aren't you?"

Laura felt a hand on her arm. "Of *course* I'm alone!" The hand squeezed her arm gently.

"Okay. You still want me to check on you every ten minutes?"

Laura thought for a moment, then said, "No, that's all right. I'll be fine."

"Okay. I'll see you when you're done."

As Laura waited in the darkness, she felt something graze her right cheek. Laura grabbed her face and rubbed. It had felt like a kiss.

The lights came up, and the girl was standing right next to her.

Laura took several steps back. "What the hell are you *doing?*"

The girl looked hurt. "I'm sorry."

"What *was* that?" Laura asked, her hand still pressed to her cheek.

"It was just a little kiss. I mean . . . I was so *happy*." She clasped her hands behind her back and rocked on her heels, smiling ear to ear. "You *trust* me! You told Dr. Filatov you didn't need him to check on you."

"Listen . . . don't take this the wrong way, but it just sort of freaks me out when you're always, you know, touching me. It invades my space."

"Oh," the girl said in a high-pitched voice, "I see." She looked away.

"Hey, it's not a big deal. It's nothing personal. It doesn't have anything to do with you in particular."

As soon as Laura said it, she realized how silly she sounded. She was talking to an image on a screen projected by a machine. The words, however, seemed to have exactly the effect she'd intended. The virtual guide was smiling broadly again. "Great! I'm sorry, it's just . . . I don't get many"—she lowered her head and scraped at the ground with her toe—"you know, friends in here. Girlfriends."

"So you're a girl?" Laura asked suddenly.

"Du-uh!" the guide said in mock offense. "I would hope, wearing this suit, the answer's *obvious!*" She raised her hands to her hips.

"I mean . . . does the *computer* consider itself female?"

"I *am* the computer, silly," the guide said.

"Okay. So what should I call you?" The girl's chin dropped, and she didn't answer. "Never mind," Laura said quickly. "I'll call you . . . Gina. It starts with a *G* just like 'guide.' Okay . . . Gina?"

"'Gina'!" the guide burst out, her face lighting up. "Oh, 'Gina'—I *love* it! It sounds mainstream, but, you know, ethnic. Cool!" She grabbed Laura's arms and squeezed—restraining herself, Laura sensed, from kissing her "girlfriend" again.

"But what's your last name going to be?" Laura asked.

"*Gray,* of course!" Gina said immediately.

Laura was forced to carefully control her expression. She had no idea how sensitive the computer's sensors were or how refined her ability to interpret nonverbal cues.

"Okay, Gina," Laura said, her mind reeling from the implications of the computer's choice of names. "Where to now?"

"Come on," she said, waving for Laura to follow. Gina took off down the hill through the lightly wooded forest.

Gina Gray! Laura thought. Maybe it was nothing, but maybe . . . Laura realized with a start that she had no idea what was happening—where her guide was leading her.

"You said this was a hundred million years ago?" Laura asked, reaching out to hold on to the trunk of a thin tree as she squeezed past a boulder. The tree was solid and unmoving.

"It means that the world I've re-created is the world as it should have existed then, minus all the nasty carbon monoxide from volcanic activity."

The smell of wood smoke was growing stronger. "Is this going to be like one of those amusement park tours through the ages? A 'Man discovers fire,' kind of thing?"

Gina stopped and turned to Laura—frowning.

"What?" Laura asked.

"No-o-othing," she said, looking away with a pout and crossing her arms over her chest. "Let's go on to the next stop." She raised her hand in the air to snap her fingers.

"No! Wait! What was the point of *this* stop?"

Gina rolled her eyes. "'Man discovers fire,'" she said in a bored tone. "I'm a little bit embarrassed."

"You mean that was the point of coming here—to this point in man's history?" Laura asked.

Gina shrugged. "Some guide I am," she said, heaving a deep sigh. "Down this hill there are some prehistoric men with the, you know"—she raised her hand to her brow—"overhanging crania. They're eating the carcass of an animal of some kind." She stuck her finger in her mouth and "popped" it out, twirling it in the air beside her. "Yatta-yatta-yatta."

"Let's go see."

"No-o-o. I don't feel like it anymore."

"Come on, Gina, really." The girl frowned. "Look, at least tell me what the point is."

With another sigh, Gina said, "The point isn't fire. Man didn't 'discover' fire until about one million years B.C. The point to this stop is that it's at this time in the history of earth that 'learning' began. Man began to develop skills like hunting cooperatively, and those skills replicated themselves from protohuman to protohuman, and from generation to generation. The point is that the accumulation of knowledge began a hundred million years ago."

Laura was busy looking around as Gina spoke. "Where are all the volcanoes and dinosaurs and stuff?"

Gina huffed in exasperation and snapped her fingers.

The scene changed instantly, and Laura flailed her arms out to the sides for balance. They stood now in a dark and icy cave. Gray snow was piled high around the entrance. Laura hugged herself for warmth.

"Sorry," Gina said in an apologetic tone. With a rustling sound she raised a large, furry skin from the dark floor and draped it around Laura's shoulders. The exoskeleton contracted around her body, but there was no real way to depict the coat's weight. The smell of the skin was awful, but at least it provided her warmth.

"How do you produce odors?" Laura asked. She could faintly see her breath mist in the cold air of the cave.

"Micropores through the grill," Gina answered. "Smells are easy. Human noses aren't very accurate. All you need is a few parts per million of one of a few dozen molecules."

Laura's teeth were chattering in the cold, and she started to ask Gina whether she wanted to share the warm coat. She stopped herself, however, when she remembered Gina wasn't really . . . Laura didn't know how to complete the thought.

As Laura's eyes began to adjust to the light, she recognized faint shapes around her in the darkness. She walked over to them carefully. The odor was almost overpowering. Feces, urine, the strong smell of animals. Every so often there was the snort of a beast of some sort or a scratching sound.

She sensed that there were animals everywhere—large, hairy beasts. Laura heard a cough. It sounded familiar.

"These are *Homo sapiens,* aren't they?" she whispered.

"Oh, don't worry, Laura," Gina said in a normal voice. "They can't hear you—unless you want them to."

"No, that's all right." Laura walked over to the nearest bulge. Its breathing was steady, each breath sucking in and blowing out of its nose with a slight snore. "Where are we now—I mean, when?"

"Ten million B.C. Hand tools. Look." An invisible spotlight illuminated a small pile of sticks and rocks beside the sleeping creature. "Ready to move on?" Gina asked.

"This wasn't much of a stop."

Gina sighed. "Okay, look," she said in a bored tone. "The thin rock is for slicing and cutting. The stick is a knife. The two smooth stones are for crushing and for tenderizing parts of a kill. Okay?"

"Knowledge, again?" Laura asked.

"You got it." Gina snapped her fingers.

The dusty riverbank was alive with activity in the late afternoon sun. Laura's head spun as the scene changed, but she remained secure in her footing this time.

Homo sapiens shuffled from one place to another. They were all short and squat and hunched over from the effects of age or injury. Filthy children fought playfully in the grass to the side of a rock-strewn camp. A fire burned, its smoke rising over the languid water of the river.

Her attention was attracted to guttural noises and grunts from off to the side. They were angry sounds, like two snarling animals in the moments before a fight. But when one bent over and the other stood behind, Laura realized they weren't fighting at all. It was over in moments, the male walking away and the female on all fours resuming her business without even changing position.

"Romantic, eh?" Gina said. "I thought maybe a little sexual titillation would enliven the tour. Anyway," she said airily, "fire and complex languages—one million years ago."

She raised her fingers in the air once again.

"Is that how you change the scene?" Laura asked, raising and snapping her own fingers with no effect.

"Snapping your fingers doesn't do anything," Gina said helpfully.

"Then why do you do it?"

Gina shrugged. "It just seems like I oughta do *some*thing." She snapped her fingers, and the faint crackle from the walls announced their arrival at the next stop.

There were men and women lounging about, completely naked and dirty beyond belief. They looked old—their skin weather-beaten and leathery—and starving like refugees fallen to some barely survivable state under extreme conditions.

"These are the 'Joneses,'" Gina said. "Grandpop, Grandmom, Mom, Dad, li'l Susie, and li'l Johnny. The nuclear family."

They appeared so sick and so hungry they could barely move. They lay in or very near their excrement, and the smell was sickening.

"Are they dying?"

"Sure. So were all of their contemporaries. Dying from every imaginable ailment. Take a close look at this female, here." Laura followed Gina over, carefully sidestepping the human waste and maggot-ridden animal carcasses. The old woman over whom Gina stood lay on her back with her eyes closed, her lips shut in a strange manner. Laura winced when she saw the sores on her face and hands.

"Grandmom, I suppose?" Laura asked with the detachment of a scientist.

"Yep." The subject had long, stringy hair the color of dirty weeds. Her ruddy cheeks were streaked with dirt or scars, Laura couldn't tell which. She was trying to sleep despite the fact that it appeared to be midday. A large black fly buzzed at her face, and the old woman raised a hand so quickly that Laura knew she wasn't asleep, only resting. She brushed the fly away, and as she did her mouth parted. She was toothless, or should have been given the painful-looking yellow and brown stubs that were left in her mouth.

"How long ago would you guess this is, Laura?"

"Oh, I don't know. Five hundred thousand B.C.?"

"A-*a-a!*" Gina said, making the sound of a game-show buzzer. "*Wrong!* Ten thousand years ago. Eight thousand B.C."

"You're kidding!" Laura said. The specimens looked like a different species.

"Nope. These are bona fide human beings. Virtually no biological evolution has occurred in the intervening ten thousand years. You take one of those children, raise him from birth in a suburban American household, and I'd give you three-to-two odds they'd make 'Bs' all the way through state college."

"Wow!" Laura said. "That's amazing. So you're saying it's really all environment, not heredity."

"Let's not mix our data and our conclusions. All I'm saying to you is, these creatures here are human in every respect but one. They are *biologically* every bit as evolved as you." Laura stared at the horrible lot in disgust. "Look at this one again, Laura," Gina said, nodding toward the grandmother at their feet. "She's going to die in six months. She has ringworm. Her body weight is dropping, and the flu will do her in this winter." The fly crawled up the woman's nose.

The woman shook her head with a start and opened her eyes. They were blue and familiar looking. The woman's features were . . . *Laura's*. The woman *was* Laura!

"She's your age exactly—thirty-four."

"You have no right to do that," Laura said, turning to walk away from the disturbing sight.

"It's a simulation," Gina said, dogging her every step. "I'm sorry."

"Look, what's the point?" Laura snapped, turning on Gina. "I know the story. Aristotle, Galileo, the Renaissance. What is it that's so supersecret and enlightening that it just *had* to be shown to me in this workstation?"

"Those people," Gina nodded toward the slumbering group, "have hardware identical to yours and that of the people you know. Not that there aren't smart people and dumb people during this time and during our own. But the base level of biological evolution has not changed between this and modern time."

"Okay. I've got it. I mean, I *knew* that."

"You knew it as an academic fact. But the fact was not in your active memory. You didn't think too long or too hard about its implications."

"Well, without visiting Gutenberg's press, why don't you just tell me what those implications are."

"Biological evolution has ceased to be important."

Laura looked at Gina, then shrugged. "I've read those theories. Some of them are very interesting."

"They're not theories, they're fact. Biological evolution has ceased to be significant because *cultural* evolution has exploded! It's interesting that you mentioned Gutenberg. Beginning one thousand years ago movable type sped up the flow of information and its volume of storage. *Think* about it! We went back a hundred million years, and the creatures were not *Homo sapiens,* but their brains—their information-processing hardware—were about ninety percent as capable as yours today. These *Homo sapiens here*"—she pointed—"are your biological equivalents. While biology inches along, culture *explodes!* Information levels skyrocket! Knowledge grows."

"Okay," Laura said, nodding her head. "Is that it?"

"Don't you *see?*" Gina said. "One hundred years ago the first practical calculating machines were invented. The computational power of those machines has risen a thousandfold every twenty years since then." Gina grabbed Laura by the arms so that they were standing face-to-face. "Over the next twenty years, it'll grow a millionfold. Over the twenty years after that—a *billion*fold."

Gina was excited, and there was an urgency to her manner. Laura tried to imagine what the world would be like with all that cheap computational power. She tried to conjure up images of the changes that would be wrought, which seemed of such importance to her guide. Certainly, it would be more fundamental than better video games, higher resolution televisions, faster computers.

It would mean that things like Gray's VR workstations would proliferate. It would mean robots like Gray's would roam the earth.

Laura looked at Gina, and the girl arched her eyebrows. "You get it now, Laura?"

She said nothing as pictures bloomed in her head. Images of Gray's technologies turned loose on the world. Automation would raise productivity and shorten workweeks. Humans would lead lives increasingly made up more of leisure than of work.

"One more stop," Gina said, snapping her fingers.

They stood in a world with a red sky and a purple horizon. The soil was dimly lit and rust colored. There was a low-slung, generally rectangular metal building, not terribly different in size from a simple human house, anchored very firmly in place on all sides by long guy wires. The wires ran out to concrete anchors far to the sides of the one-story structure.

Just outside what Laura assumed to be a "house" was a woman. She wore coveralls made of light fabric whose color Laura couldn't determine in the strange light. The woman looked up toward the purple horizon. The sky in the other directions was yellowish orange.

Gina headed toward the house, and Laura followed.

The woman up ahead wore some kind of respirator that covered only her mouth.

"Mo-*ther!*" Laura heard, and a child with a gun climbed atop a rock outcropping at least a hundred meters away. Despite the distance, his voice was loud and clear.

"Yes?" the woman said, and Laura turned immediately to face Gina. Most people didn't recognize the sound of their own voices, but Laura had taped enough of her lectures to learn it.

"Another of my *clones?*" Laura asked in aggravation. "Laura a million years from now?"

Gina shrugged with an apologetic look on her face.

"John and I wanna play over by the aqueduct. We'll stay close." The boy didn't wear anything on his face that Laura could tell. Both he and his mother had American accents. *Not very imaginative,* Laura thought. Surely language would evolve over the millennia, but even if it didn't, accents, syntax, and vocabulary certainly would.

"There's no time," the Laura clone said. "Look." She pointed toward the purple horizon.

"Oh, *Mom!*"

"It's time to get inside, Joseph!"

Laura looked at Gina. The girl smiled in what was almost a wince and shrugged again.

"Don't make me bother your father," she said without lifting her voice. It was easily heard by all—Gina, Laura, and the little boy.

The boy raised his weapon and pointed it at the Laura clone. Laura almost shouted a warning to the old woman, but the boy didn't fire. Instead, a streak of yellow light burst from the rocks and lit up his shirt with a bright glow, sounding a loud electronic chirp. The boy spun and fired into the rocks toward the source. It was some kind of game, and the boy leapt off the rock to go play it.

The closer Laura and Gina got to the Laura clone, the older the woman appeared to be. She had gray hair pulled back behind her head. She was kneeling on the ground and pulling up some kind of bulbs—vegetables of some sort. People might not have evolved, but rutabagas appeared to Laura to have mutated. The woman looked up to check the horizon again. The sky was alive with swirling purples and reds. It was beautiful, but Laura felt more drawn to the woman than the landscape. To the computer's depiction of what an old Laura would look like.

"So," Gina said, "what do you think?"

Laura shrugged. "On the whole, I appreciate the flattery. I'm a fine-looking old lady."

"I *mean,* what do you think about the tour?"

"I think you've been reading too much Kurt Vonnegut on CD-ROM."

"That's *all?* No conclusions you'd like to share with me?"

"Well, let's see. A few million years ago, people didn't live past their mid-thirties because they were dumb as stumps. A few million years in the future, after major advances in nutrition and plastic surgery, we'll all be healthy and happy and attractive well into our eighties."

"She's over a hundred and thirty," Gina said, nodding at the Laura-like woman.

"A hundred and thirty, a thousand and thirty, whatever. I get the point. Knowledge is good."

Gina tilted her head to the side and frowned sadly. "Oh, I'm sorry, Laura. You're not getting it at *all.* You're just not ready yet. Georgi is coming down the hall, so I'm going to have to say 'bye."

She raised her hand and waved.

"No, wait!"

The scene disappeared, the last vestiges of the lithe girl receding into the nothingness of the black walls—her fingers still wagging their goodbye.

"It was unbe*lievable!*" Laura said to Filatov. He was leaning over a monitor just outside the virtual workstation with a grim look on his face. "The world was so totally realistic that I *completely* forgot where I was. Those things open up some *incredible* opportunities. I mean, the guide could teach medical students how the aorta works by taking them inside a full-sized model of the heart."

"What guide?" Filatov asked distractedly.

"The *guide,* you know, who leads you around in cyberspace."

"I don't know what you're talking about," Filatov said, straightening up. "But don't get carried away. These *things* aren't quite ready for home use. That one little simulation of yours cost about thirteen million dollars in computer time."

"*What?*"

"I hope you enjoyed it, because we haven't done more than a dozen class ones since the 4Cs came on-line. The computational power is too expensive."

"But . . . what about when computing power comes down by a *billion*fold? That thirteen million dollars would drop to . . . what? A single penny!"

"What are you talking about?" Filatov said, brushing past her for the door.

Laura followed. "The computer said that computational power will expand by a millionfold for the next generation and then by a billionfold the generation after."

"A-a-ah!" Filatov said, passing her comment off with an irritated wave of his hand. "How the hell would it know?"

When they got to the control room, Laura saw idle technicians clustered about in groups. The computer center's smooth functioning seemed to have been interrupted by a mass coffee break. "What's going on in here?" Laura asked.

"They're scared," Filatov said.

"Of what?"

"Hoblenz."

"Why?"

"He says he caught one of my operators committing sabotage," Filatov said, his tired eyes rising to Laura. "He was trying to load an optical disk into a drive. The disk is full of control codes for some foreign power, governmental or corporate, we don't know which. Hoblenz thinks he's just found the cause of all our troubles, and he now suspects everyone on my staff, even me."

"Do you think that operator is the cause of our problems?"

Filatov shook his head. "No. But he would have caused more if he hadn't been stopped."

"What does Mr. Gray think?"

"Hoblenz hasn't called him yet. He wants to find out more before he makes his report."

"What does that mean?" Laura asked. "Where has he taken that man?"

"To the conference room—the main—"

"And you *let* him?" she burst out. "Just Hoblenz and the man alone?"

Laura ran all the way to the conference room and slapped the pressure plate on the wall. She almost smashed her nose into the door when it didn't open. She pressed the plate again—this time harder. Nothing. Laura began pounding on the door. "Hoblenz! Let me in!" She pounded over and over until finally she heard someone inside.

"Stand back, Laura!" the muffled shout came. "Move down the hall away from the door!"

"Okay!" she replied, and stepped back. Remembering it was Hoblenz, she thought better and headed even farther down the hall to wait.

A blast tore open the wall beside the door with a tremendous boom. The remains of the pressure plate came to rest on the floor. Two soldiers pried open the door and slid it back into the wall. The stench of smoke from the gun still filled the air as Laura peered sheepishly into the room.

One of Hoblenz's men safed his smoking shotgun with an audible click. There were half a dozen other soldiers, all heavily armed. Hoblenz stood over the conference table, one hand a pistol to the nose of a white-jacketed nerd, the other holding a thick shank of the man's hair.

But his eyes were on the scene at the door.

"What the hell are you doing?" Laura demanded.

Hoblenz looked concerned. "Are we havin' some kinda power problems with those doors?" he asked, ignoring her question. Laura turned to see Filatov standing in the doorway behind her. He was staring at the prisoner—his former operator.

"Mr. *Hoblenz*," Laura began, "I don't think—!"

"Is the goddamn power *on* out there?" Hoblenz shouted.

"Yes!" Filatov answered. "We've had no trouble with power."

Hoblenz let the prisoner's head go. Blood ran down the man's upper lip, and one lens of his glasses was cracked. He looked even paler than the norm, and his hair stood straight up where the big man's firm grip had been. Hoblenz walked over to peer into the hole in the wall.

"I'll be goddamned," he said in wonder.

"What?" Laura asked.

"The door didn't work. I mean, even the manual didn't work."

"You didn't lock it?" Laura asked.

"No! You *can't* lock it! It don't lock!"

"Then why . . . ?" she began, realizing immediately the answer to her half-expressed question. *The computer,* she thought. It was the only explanation. Hoblenz looked at her, obviously thinking the same. "Why would the computer lock the door?" she asked.

"Guess it wanted to know what that pissant over there had to say."

Laura looked at the man. "Are you okay?" she asked him.

He looked sick, but he nodded his head.

"Aw shit, *Al*-dridge! What'd you *think?* That I'd *kill* the guy?"

"You sure as hell beat him up!"

"That weren't nothin'. I get a call every other night about a scrap worse'n that between my own *men!*"

"What's going on?" they heard, and everyone turned to the door to see Gray.

"We caught this rat bastard tryin' to load an optical disk into a drive," Hoblenz said, picking up the disk and tossing it to Gray. "It's got control codes on it."

Gray walked up to the man. "Is that true?" he asked in a low voice. The man looked down, then nodded. "Why? Who do you work for?"

"CIA," Hoblenz said. "Least that's the version he gave before the good Dr. Aldridge here arrived. And it's the damnedest thing. We heard her bangin' on the door like the Gestapo, but when we hit the plate the damn thing wouldn't open. We had to use plan B—the ten gauge."

"Was there a power outage?"

"Nope," Hoblenz said. "Those pneumatic hoses were as full as an Irishman's bladder."

"It didn't want Hoblenz to stop torturing his prisoner," Laura said.

"I wasn't *tor*-turin' him! I was just askin' him kinda rough."

"Get this man on the plane with the others," Gray ordered.

Hoblenz seemed outraged. "When they land, sir, the spooks'll just snatch him right up."

"I don't care. I want him gone. The last flight leaves in an hour." He looked over at Laura. "Janet packed your things. There's a car outside with your suitcase. I hope you don't mind."

"Don't mind what?"

"I'm going to have to ask you to leave, too, Laura."

"Leave! Why?"

"I'm evacuating everyone. There are three jumbo jets down at the airport. I'm sorry, but you've got to go."

"Are *you* leaving?"

"No, but you are."

"Who all is staying?"

"Just me, the security people, my management team, a few others. Everybody else has to go."

"All the nonessential personnel, you mean?" She felt the blood rush to her face in a mixture of anger and embarrassment. Hoblenz and the others stood around in awkward silence. "Why the sudden change?" she asked, a bitter smile thinly masking the pain she felt. "Yesterday, you were piling people in here, Joseph. Today, you're shipping them off! A little bit flighty, don't you think?"

"Please, Laura, just go."

"At least tell me why I'm getting kicked off the goddamned island!"

"It's not safe here."

Even the prisoner seemed interested in the confrontation.

"I get it," she said, nodding her head.

She bit her lip to forestall the quiver. Gray was silent. "Jesus! Of *course* I'll leave! I don't know why I didn't leave on the first *day!*"

She tore out of the conference room, brushing past Gray, Filatov, and the soldiers. She felt humiliated, her face glowing hot and tears welling up in her eyes, angering her further. Thankfully, the control room was already empty.

Laura stopped at a console, meaning to say a quick good-bye to the computer. There was no keyboard, just a series of buttons and trackballs and a headset with one clear lens hanging down in front of the right eye. On the screen was a confusing array of unrecognizable windows. Laura abandoned the effort and just walked out, feeling guilty for not trying harder to find a terminal.

She hadn't realized how late it was, but it was almost dark outside. The winged door of a car rose into the air with a hiss. Her suitcase was in the back seat. "The *fucking* airport!" she said angrily once inside, and the car took off. The Village was totally deserted. The sun was falling, and everyone left on the island was indoors.

Not so much as a thank-you, Laura thought bitterly. *Not a job well done. Not . . . anything!*

The car headed out of the Village, wheeling onto the undulating, curved road that ran through the jungle toward the airport. Laura wondered if she would ever see the island again. This world may not exist much longer if the rest of the earth had its way. Laura wondered if she would ever see Gray again.

She cringed at the fleeting glimpse of a spider's legs as they flashed in front of the windshield. A crashing explosion of sounds preceded the gut-wrenching flight through the air of the tumbling car. The screeching and tearing of metal and the violent jerks of her body against the seat restraints went on forever as she waited helplessly in anticipation of the end.

All was still. Laura lay on her side. She had been in a car that had gotten into an accident, she remembered. Slowly, she came to her senses. The car lay on its side, and she was still strapped inside it. It was nearly pitch dark outside.

When she moved, there was no great pain, just dizziness. A flashing light sparkled through the smashed but largely intact windshield. The tree line ahead was lit in time with the blinking light of her car's headlights. She undid the seat belt and slowly struggled out of the wreck of the electric car. The broken headlights continued their flashing strobe as she leaned against the chassis to steady herself.

There was something in the headlights' glare. A twisted lump of gray metal lay on the ground just beside the road.

The steady, building roar of a commercial jet's engines on takeoff disturbed the otherwise surreal silence of the crash scene. Laura saw the airplane rise into the air above the trees, its red and green lights illuminated against the dark sky. She wondered how long she'd been unconscious. A second jet roared off, and shortly after that a third—taking away the last of Gray's departing employees.

Laura's suitcase lay on the ground beside her, and she picked it up and stood there in a daze. All was still again save the blinking of the lights. Without knowing what she was doing or for how long the moment had lasted, Laura realized she was staring at the lump of metal in the headlights' beams. From the size of the object she knew it wasn't some part broken off of the electric car. It was too big.

She headed toward the crumpled metal, her light suitcase gripped firmly in hand. A spidery leg was lying on the ground next to the main piece. It still seemed to be connected.

The leg moved suddenly, and Laura jumped back. From a few feet away she watched as the leg rose into the air in a slow and graceless arc. Its progress was chronicled in a series of still images shot by the headlights' strobes. The leg pressed down against the ground and rocked the dismembered mechanical body pathetically onto one side.

It was a Model Seven—only one of its four legs still attached. Its "head" stared up at Laura. She walked over to it and knelt, laying her hand on its smooth metal panels. It was twisted and mangled and rent with great gaping wounds. Cables dangled loose. Precious liquids dripped onto the soil with hisses and bursts of smoke from where they landed.

The robot's long leg began to move again. This time it rose into the air above Laura. She kept her eye on the spidery limb, which slowly descended toward her. She caught only snapshots of the leg's descent in the flashes of light from her car, and there were too many gaps in the illumination for her to feel secure about the aim of the leg. But somehow Laura wasn't frightened. Its motions were too slow, too weak. The wheel at the end of the leg was inserted into the tool belt the robot wore at its waist. When the leg came out it was bare. The robot plugged it into another slot and pulled out a three-fingered hand.

The overturned Model Three's faulty lights blinked on and off and on again. Three short blinks, followed by three long, followed by three more short.

Morse code! Laura realized, a chill spreading instantly over her body. She remembered it from some long-ago movie about a passenger ship that sank. Dot-dot-dot, dash-dash-dash, dot-dot-dot—"SOS." It was a distress signal, and it was meant for her.

The Model Seven's hand wobbled and shook at maximum extension as it groped for a panel on its body. The increasingly spastic robot succeeded finally in opening the door to a compartment. Inside she saw a thick sliding switch. The robot's fingers jerked spasmodically—the switch just out of their reach. Laura leaned close. The words "Main Power" were written in red. A single large exclamation point was clearly visible in a black triangle just underneath. Threaded through the switch was a thin wire for security against it being thrown inadvertently.

The robot convulsed—its arm thrashing not dangerously but dismally through the air just over her head. Laura reached up into the box and grabbed the switch, pulling down as hard as she could.

With a *pop* the resistance gave way. The robot's limb collapsed to the ground beside her, and the mortally wounded robot fell still.

The lights of the car shone steadily now, forcing Laura to squint as she turned to look at them. After a moment they went dark, and a faint electric motor in the car wound down. All was now still on the narrow pathway between the curb and the jungle wall. The thick, dark growth seemed to close in from all sides.

Laura eyed the empty road in both directions, a rising tide of fear quickening her heart rate. Grabbing her suitcase, she began a brisk walk toward the Village—her head turning from side to side and to the rear in a constant search for danger. The black edge of the jungle formed a solid wall, and it lay not ten feet from the sides of the pavement.

There was movement under the lights on the road ahead. Laura could see people at the outskirts of the Village. She started to yell, but decided they were still too far away to hear her. She began to jog—afraid they would be gone before she caught up with them. The contents of her suitcase shook noisily with each stride she took down the hill.

A blur of movement from the side preceded a jarring blow to Laura's body that knocked her to the grass beside the road. She looked up at the rounded metal head and single unblinking eye and screamed.

A hand went over her mouth. "Jesus *Christ,* lady!" a man whispered. "Quiet! There's robots up ahead!" You could hear the fear in his voice. After a moment, he let his hand off her mouth and got off her.

He wore a military-style helmet and night-vision goggles with a single wide lens in front. The Cyclops-like eye was pointed down the hill toward the Village.

"Who are you?"

"U.S. Navy. Come on."

She followed the man into the jungle. Other soldiers were waiting there. "Two in the jungle on the right," someone whispered, the words not meant for Laura, "one in the clearing, the fourth one in the town. Looks like they're searching for something."

"In the *town?*" Laura asked. "The Village? There are robots in the Village?"

"Who the hell are you?" came a voice whispered from the darkness.

"Laura Aldridge. Dr. Laura Aldridge."

"Can you take care of my man?" the soldier asked.

"Does he have psychological problems?"

"What?"

"I'm a psychologist."

There was a sickly moan from the darkness.

"What's the matter with him?" Laura asked.

"He almost got torn apart by one of those goddamn robots."

"A *robot* hurt him?"

There was a pause. "Where the hell have you *been*, lady?"

"They're all in the jungle now," came the steady monotone of the watchful soldier.

"All right, let's head on back to the beach."

Laura felt a hand on her arm. "What? I'm not going with you."

"Lady, there are robots roamin' all over this—" There was a distant *boom,* and a sound like firecrackers ripped through the night just after. Then came another explosion and another and another. "Come on, let's go!"

The soldiers filed out of the jungle and turned toward the airport. Laura yanked her arm free and took off running toward the Village, abandoning her suitcase by the road.

"Hey!" she heard from behind, followed by the sound of a man running after her. Laura sprinted down the hill as fast as her feet would carry her. "Chief! Break it off!" someone else shouted.

After a moment, Laura glanced back over her shoulder. She was all alone, and she slowed her pace to a walk.

The night had fallen quiet again. The fighting had died down. It had come from somewhere behind the mountain—from the empty quarter. The streets of the Village were just ahead. There were no robots to be seen.

Something stirred in the brush to her left. There was another sound—very deliberate, like an animal preparing to strike. Laura felt panic set in. She began to jog again, staring into the black jungle over her left shoulder and counting down the steps until she made it to the relative safety of the streetlamps.

She turned to see a Model Eight blocking her way into the Village. She stopped dead in her tracks. The monstrously large robot stood framed by the streetlamps forty or so yards away. He remained completely motionless, but he was holding something in his right hand.

Laura felt her every move counted. The robots were at war. They'd be jumpy. Terrified. Angry. They'd be in a killing mood.

As methodically as she could manage, Laura raised her open right hand. It was an international gesture of peace and greeting—showing a stranger that she was unarmed.

A brilliant white light burst from the robot's right hand, crackling with violent heat. The robot headed straight up the hill toward her, breaking into what for it had to be a run. It raised the welding torch that it held into the air.

Laura was blinded now with panic. She turned to flee up the

hill but froze. Against a sky that glowed from the airport lights, she could see another Model Eight coming down the hill right behind her. She was trapped, and the terror gripped her completely.

Without thinking she dashed straight into the thick jungle beside the road, throwing herself against the clinging brush in utter desperation. She fought her way deeper and deeper, the branches scratching at her arms and neck and face.

The robot coming down the hill was the first of the attackers to reach her. Its entry into the jungle behind her was announced by the great volume of cracking branches and crushed foliage. Looking back over her shoulder at the Model Eight, Laura screamed "No-o-o!" First one great swath of branches were sheared from their limbs above her, then a deeper cut was taken by the robot—slinging its arms through the air like a scythe. With the third pass of the blades, Laura fell to the ground under a shower of leaves and twigs. In the sudden silence, she raised her head to see the robot standing motionless directly above her.

Laura curled up into a ball, shaking from the soundless sobs that wracked her body. Her stomach muscles clenched so tight they began to cramp. Her gasps for air ended the moment she felt the robot's touch. It pressed down on her head with its hand. *This is it,* she thought in terror, unable to move a muscle.

The sound of branches being broken near the road again filled the air. The robot's hand rose from her head, and there was a great thud that Laura felt through the ground where she lay. Looking up, she saw the robot who'd chased her into the jungle now lying on the ground beside her. It was grasping frantically for brush, which it uprooted in its vain attempt to resist being dragged out of the jungle to the road.

All was still under Laura's blanket of fallen leaves and branches. An eerie glow emanated from what she now saw was a small gathering of robots. The shadows thrown across the brush drifted slowly as a welding torch descended toward the earth.

The quiet of the night was broken by a crackling and sizzling burn.

Laura sat up. The robots were all seemingly unconcerned by her presence. She saw in the flashing light from the torch that they stared intently toward the center of their circle. She crept through the brush on her knees, approaching the edge of the clearing for a better view.

Three Model Eights held Laura's pursuer pinned to the ground. The fourth was pressing its arc torch into the left thigh of their prisoner. The right leg, Laura saw with a sudden jolt of nausea, lay on the ground . . . severed.

The captive robot lay perfectly still—its head raised and watching their efforts. The amputation was extremely precise. The cut on the left leg was being made just below the hip—at exactly the same place as the right. When the welding torch fell dark, the crackling air grew quiet. The captors all rose. The one at the feet of their victim held the two severed legs.

The paraplegic Model Eight stared down at its missing limbs, then lowered its head and raised its arms straight up. The two robots at its head grabbed its forearms, and they dragged the legless machine toward the Village.

The remaining Model Eight stood just outside the jungle not ten feet from where Laura knelt. When the others had gone, the robot's head turned toward her. It held its free hand up in the air, just as Laura had done in the road.

She took a guess—prepared to run back into the black jungle at the slightest hint of danger. "Hightop?" she asked in a low and quivering voice.

The Model Eight raised the electric torch into the air. The torch flared once with a sizzling sound and flash of brilliant light. The robot then lowered the makeshift weapon into its equipment belt. It extended its hand to Laura, palm up.

She rose and carefully stepped out into the clearing. She didn't take the proferred hand, but with her heart pounding she followed Hightop down the hill. From the way he kept turning to look back at her, Laura didn't feel she was the robot's prisoner. Hightop acted like her rescuer, her savior, her protector. She just wished she could get some hint of what was going on in his mind.

The cold and expressionless face gave her no clues as to his intent.

Hightop paid her less and less attention the farther they progressed into the Village. They passed two other Model Eights and the wreckage of another Model Seven whose spider legs were strewn all about the central boulevard. This one had not been hit by a car. It had burn marks crisscrossing its torso in perfectly straight scars.

Another Model Eight appeared, crawling out the front door of a building. Its right shoulder made contact with the doorframe, and wood splinters flew onto the sidewalk. Through the display windows of the store she could see shelf after shelf of expensive crystal. The floor was littered with sparkling debris.

Instead of turning sideways the way it had presumably entered the store, the robot pressed carefully but firmly straight through the frame. With one long breaking sound it was through, widening the entrance in the process to more comfortable proportions.

Hightop stopped in front of the store, and Laura halted beside him. The robot from the china shop approached and opened a panel on the front of its chest. From the open compartment it extracted a wide, flat connector. Thousands of glowing white dots of light emanated from the connector's exposed end. Hightop opened his own compartment, and the new arrival cabled up to the mini-net housed in Hightop's chest. It was the same cable that had been run from Hightop to Gray's laptop at their aborted hillside picnic two nights before.

They were communicating, Laura realized. The glowing lights were optical cables. *But they can talk to each other with microwaves,* Laura remembered as she waited silently. *Radio silence . . . They're at war.*

But with whom? Only other robots could listen in on their transmissions. Laura looked down the empty boulevard. The burned and cut torso of the Model Seven lay crumpled just under the statue of the woman with the globe.

There was a Model Seven and a Model Eight on the asteroid.

"Hey!" she said in a raised voice. The robots didn't move. "*Hey!* I've got to go! I've got to get to the computer center!" she said loudly, enunciating each word.

The robot unplugged its connector from Hightop. They snapped their chest panels closed and turned toward Laura in unison. They walked past her up the boulevard toward the statue.

She turned to look at them. "Where the hell do you think you're *going?*" she shouted. "The computer center is *that* way!" They didn't even slow down. "*That* way!" she yelled, jabbing her finger in the opposite direction.

Hightop stopped and held his hand out to Laura. They had plans of their own that were more important.

Laura grabbed her pounding head with both hands. She had to decide whether to go with them or to go alone. The decision was immense, and it was a toss-up.

They stood there unmoving. No face or voice to give a cue. Just a machine.

"Where are you *headed?*" she asked. "Could you *just . . . point!*" she shouted. She even showed them how.

Nothing. Nothing but a hand held out by Hightop. It was an extension of Gray. His tool. His most trusted. It was like a hand held out by Gray himself.

And it had a plan.

Laura turned to follow the two robots up the hill.

"I'm not going in there," she said as they stood at the edge of the jungle. "No way! Uh-uh." She was shaking her head and waving her arms in front of her.

They cabled up to each other again. When the thin ribbon was stowed away, Hightop's companion grabbed Laura by the waist. She screamed in shock as it picked her up. She began bicycle kicking the air. The robot raised her high off the ground, and Hightop turned to look away.

"Hightop!" she shouted, kicking his hard back with the toes of her running shoes. She was close enough to pound his head with her hands. *"Hightop!"*

His skin was soft and smooth. The strange feel of it made Laura stop struggling. She grabbed onto his shoulders. Her feet found the equipment belt at his waist. She clung there on Hightop's back, her head ten feet off the ground. Hightop headed for the jungle ahead.

It was a piggyback ride. She owed him an apology. "I, uhm . . . ," she said. "Sorry about that."

Hightop walked straight into the jungle without slowing. The black branches cracked in a thousand places. They scraped along the robot's sides and swatted at Laura from behind. Hightop used his hands to clear a path ahead with great squeezes and twists of the protruding branches, but his body did most of the damage. From his chest and legs and feet there came a constant din.

They traveled through the jungle with ease. The Model Eight to the rear ensured that no limbs sprung back onto Laura.

Laura climbed closer to the robot's ear and shouted, "Hey . . . where're we going?" The robot made no move to respond. "Hightop," Laura said in a loud voice, "listen to me. I'm scared. I'm really, really scared. Now I know you can't talk, but if you can understand me, please give me some kind of sign that you're not going to take me into the jungle and do something terrible to me. Please!"

The two robots stopped, and all at once there was silence. Hightop's head turned with the faintest of whirs. When his face was visible, he raised his fingertips to a grill. He then reached over his shoulder toward Laura.

The smooth, flat fingers gently touched Laura's cheek with a gentle caress.

The procession moved on. Laura had no idea how far they travelled. She had no idea where she was. What little sense of direction she possessed had been lost.

Hightop stopped, then slowly knelt to the ground—crushing the brush underneath. The night was black as coal on the floor of the jungle. Laura took Hightop's move as her cue and climbed down.

Her eyes adjusted slowly to the darkness, and then she saw the robots all around. They were everywhere, kneeling on the ground just like Hightop. They faced the same way, as if in prayer. There were dozens and dozens of them.

Laura stumbled backward—away from the menacing forms that surrounded her. Despite the noise she made, the robots all remained motionless. Hightop plugged his communications cable into the nearest Model Eight. Laura saw that cables ran from robot to robot, and the daisy chain ended with Hightop. He was the leader. He gave the orders.

The Model Eights all unplugged their cables and stood. There was a great collective breaking of branches as they rose. Laura shielded her head and face against the rain of falling limbs.

But that was nothing compared to what happened next.

The robots began to move forward en masse. It was as if a wave of metal crashed through the jungle ahead of Laura. The brush was flattened in its path. The stunted trees fell to reveal the starry sky and the roof of the computer center. She heard an alarm—a throbbing, strident tone.

After the last of the robots exited the jungle, there were a few seconds of relative quiet. Then came the horrible screeching sound of rending metal. Laura could see through the thin leaves the eerie light cast by a welding torch. The light wavered and flickered through the suddenly defoliated jungle, and Laura realized it wasn't one torch but dozens. The smell of the burning metal mixed with the cacophony of crashing sounds. It reminded her of some gigantic pile-up on a fogbound interstate, but these were not the sounds of an accident. They were the hellish noise of battle in the earth's second millennium.

Laura made her way toward the jungle's edge. The scene on the open fields around the computer center slowly came into view.

"My God," Laura whispered, a chill rippling up her body. There was carnage everywhere.

The Model Eights were fighting an army of Sixes and Sevens. The main battle was in the center, where the Model Eights had formed a phalanx. The tight formation rushed four abreast and five deep straight for the computer center walls. Their wake was littered with wreckage. Most of the fallen were the wheeled Model Sixes, rendered immobile once knocked to their sides. They waited only to die, snapping futilely at passersby with their single long arm.

On the flanks a few Model Eights stood apart. Their torches thrashed wildly through the air. When the torches made contact with metal, the night lit up with the sparks of a killing.

The Model Sevens fared better than the Sixes, but the spidery robots seemed reluctant to fight. They ambled sideways back and forth like crabs. There were many feints and few engagements, but when they clashed the contest was intense. The Sevens lifted a leg to batter their enemies with all the violence they could muster. They either toppled the Model Eights with the blows or missed and were themselves upended. Once on the ground, the two-legged Eights could recover, but a Seven could only delay. It would grab its attacker like an octopus, but the clench wasn't strong enough to kill. Inevitably, there was the blistering light of a torch, and from amid the tangle would emerge an Eight—the fittest model on the field.

Everywhere lay the results of the disaster. Twitching legs that once were a graceful Model Seven. The pathetic waste of an armless Model Eight wriggling helplessly away from its nightmare. It brought tears to Laura's eyes. Each was a thing of beauty. There were poets and scholars and felons, and Laura intensely felt the loss of each. It was so senseless, so cruel, and it seemed like the end of all her hopes for the future.

Through the tears that blurred her eyes, Laura could see the Eights dragging their wounded to the rear. They appeared to have set up an aid station, and had drawn cables from the thighs of the fallen. These weren't the thin cables used for communications. They were power cables built to pass charges of electricity.

The thick black cables were plugged into the uninjured robots, who knelt on the ground beside their comrades. *The healthy are giving the wounded a transfusion!* Laura thought. *Instead of blood, they passed electricity!*

But something struck Laura as odd. After the healthy Model Eights rose to leave, new robots would take their place. They came, cabled up, and returned to battle, but the wounded robots sank into a stupor. They were getting worse, not better. They were being drained of their charges instead of recharged. The healthy were sucking the life out of the wounded.

Laura decided she had to make a run for it. She couldn't wait for the Model Eights to return. They were designed to learn about life from experience. From among the awful maiming and killing on the field, what lessons would be learned by the survivors? What scars would they bring back from war?

Laura frantically began to search for an opening. The ragged line seemed to have stalled halfway across the grassy lawn. She scanned the computer center's walls to get her bearings. The entrance was somewhere around the side to the right. All of a sudden she saw several tiny black specks running along the base of the bunker. They were insignificant compared to the robots—mere flies buzzing about the bloodless massacre. But they meant everything to Laura just then. They were human . . . like her.

She burst out of the jungle into the open, sprinting straight toward the melee ahead. There had to be over two hundred robots on the field. Billions of dollars of technology from the Information Age were being ground to pieces with the brutality of the Dark Ages. Her eyes searched the battle lines for an opening. It was a new world to Laura, and she was at a dangerous disadvantage. She didn't know the various models' capabilities, but more importantly she knew nothing of their goals.

They had ambitions, missions, menace, and she didn't know who was friend and who was foe. She pumped her arms and legs as hard as she could, running straight for the computer center wall. She flew past unrecognizable piles of metal, her eyes fixed on the small black figures. They were pointing at her and motioning frantically, but her view of them was repeatedly obscured by the rapidly maneuvering robots.

She was now less than fifty yards from the front line, and there was no clear way through in sight. The Model Sixes made their runs against the Eights at high speeds, their single grippers raised straight in front of them like jousting spears. They would take little heed of her presence amidst their battle to the death. She had no business being there in the first place.

Just before reaching the line of battle, she crouched behind an upended Model Six. The Model Eights in the phalanx were being pummeled by the raised legs of a dozen angry spiders. They thrust their welding torches outward in great lunges, and sparks flew as they made contact with the Sevens. Crippled spiders tried to limp away on three legs, and fresh comrades moved forward to take their places.

All of a sudden Laura felt a presence. Slowly she raised her head to look up. The viselike claw of the overturned Model Six opened soundlessly, hovering in the air above her. It was coiled and ready to strike.

The searing sound of burning air announced the approach of a Model Eight. It had disengaged from the line and strode purposefully toward the Model Six. Its torch slashed at the air as if to draw the attention of the one-armed robot.

Flame burst from the side of the computer center, and a streaking rocket snaked out of the smoke. In a flash the rocket hit the Model Eight.

A thudding *whoomp* stunned Laura momentarily, and the sky lit up with a bright flash from the missile's explosion. The thunderous report echoed across the open field, and when the smoke cleared . . . the Model Eight marched on. Its right arm was missing, but in its left it held the burning torch.

The Model Six's arm shot like a cobra toward the Model Eight. It latched right onto its face with the sound of crunching metal. Halted in its tracks and staggering, the Model Eight raised the torch and began to cut. Sparks flew from the Model Six's slender limb, and molten metal began to drip to the ground. The Model Six twisted and turned the Eight's head with its claw.

With a gush of fluid, the long arm was suddenly severed. The Model Six swung the remaining stub to ward off its attacker, which for its part stumbled back with the vise still clinging to its face. The Eight returned the torch to its holster by feel, then reached with its gripper to seize the Model Six's claw. Seeming to hesitate for a moment, as if gathering itself for the effort, it slowly began to pull.

The sound of the tearing metal was too awful for Laura to

bear. She jammed the heels of her hands hard against her ears. The severely wounded robot tried desperately to remain standing, staggering this way and that as if dizzy or drunk. There was a loud screech, and the Model Eight dropped the claw to the ground. To her horror Laura saw that half its face was still caught in the severed appendage.

Slowly, the stricken robot wandered away from the battle lines toward the rear. His remaining arm groped in front searching for obstacles.

Another flame erupted from the computer center wall. "*No-o-o!*" Laura screamed as the rocket streaked out of the smoke.

Flame shot straight through the Model Eight's chest. Its "brains" were blown onto the ground, the burning cold of the liquid nitrogen boiling off the grass in sizzling vapor.

The Model Eight crumpled onto its knees, falling lifeless to the ground in a contorted heap.

Sobbing, she rose to her feet. *Was it Bouncy, or Hightop, or Auguste?* Laura thought. She sprinted past the smoking, twisted corpse of the magnificent machine—the eighth wonder of Gray's new world.

Laura thought nothing now, she just ran. She ran straight through the whirring electric motors. Straight through the flying sparks and rending collisions and acrid fumes of industrial hell. She ran past the noise and the anger and the insanity.

Laura was crying so hard she was taken by surprise when someone pulled her to the ground.

She shut her eyes and screamed.

"It's all right," she heard Gray say over the noise. "You're safe now."

She kept her eyes closed as if trying to fall asleep. Amid the maelstrom Laura felt his hand brush the hair from her forehead. His fingers slowly traced a gentle line down her cheek. His palm lay flat against her face, lingering at the corner of her mouth. Her lips pressed back against his warm skin.

When she opened her eyes, the terrors of the battlefield were gone. She studied the man who cradled her. He peered down at her from above. His lips seemed to be forming words. "Don't worry, don't worry."

18

Everyone listened in rapt attention to the unprecedented speech. Gray was explaining to his team what was happening.

"Laura's Model Three was controlled by the Other. The Model Seven that it ran into was controlled by the computer. The two halves maintain separate world models on opposite sides of the partition. Neither robot sees what the other one sees, so they both thought the road ahead was clear."

His department chiefs nodded their heads slowly.

Hoblenz spoke up. "The computer on *our* side of the partition has been sendin' out Model Sixes and Sevens to do some reconnoitering. Prob'ly tryin' to fill in some gaps in its sensor coverage. We've spotted 'em roamin' all over the island." He turned to Laura. "You must've run into a patrol."

"What happened after the collision?" Gray asked Laura.

"First I have a question," she replied. "How long does it take the robots to recharge?"

Griffith looked at his watch and answered. "The Sixes take two hours, but they have to decharge first for up to half an hour to avoid damaging their battery cells. The Sevens take four and a half hours, including normal decharge."

"What about the Eights?"

"They don't decharge. It takes them an hour to recharge—tops."

Hoblenz shook his head. "That battle out there was fought to a draw, but wars are won by logistics. The army that can redeploy the 'firstest' with the 'mostest' will win, and those charging times are the key."

"But the Model Eights don't have as many chargers," Griffith commented, "and they have to make their way back through the jungle to get to their facility."

"'Oh, please don't throw me in the briar patch,'" Hoblenz said sarcastically. "Those damn Eights eat that jungle up."

"Why are you all so down on the Model Eights?" Laura asked.

They looked at her as if she were crazy.

"I hate to point out the obvious," Filatov said, "but they did just attack the computer center." He turned to Hoblenz. "And you thought that spy was our problem!"

"Maybe he was! Maybe he planted some kind of timed-release virus in their metal skulls that makes 'em go all violent!"

"What happened after the wreck?" Gray asked again.

She told them about the Model Seven's assisted suicide.

"You pulled the main power breaker?" Griffith asked in alarm. "That flushes the charge!"

"It was suffering," Laura said.

"It's a machine!" Griffith shot back.

"A machine that was in *pain!*" Laura shouted, shaking her head in amazement. "Don't you know what you've built here? Each of those robots has goals and ambitions. They strive every day to work harder, because that's what you've programmed them to do—work! Performing well is what makes them happy, and when that Model Seven saw its legs strewn all around, it felt pain! *Pain* that it was so mangled. *Pain* that it would never, *ever* again be able to feel the pleasure of working for the Gray Corporation! You should all be so proud."

"You're being too harsh, Laura," Gray said.

"Well, why can't they *see* this?"

"Because they're not ready yet," Gray replied, flooring her.

But I am? Laura heard him to mean and was shocked.

"What happened next?" Gray asked in a patient but firm tone.

After taking a moment to compose herself, she told them about the soldiers.

"Sailors," Hoblenz said. "They're SEALs."

"So the Model Eights *are* hurting humans," Dorothy said.

"We don't know it was a Model Eight that fought with them!" Laura shot back.

"What next?" Gray asked, demanding facts.

She told them about Hightop rescuing her from the juvenile, and described the amputations by the road. She then gave an account of Hightop cabling up to the Model Eight from the china shop.

"They were discussing strategy!" Griffith said, beaming with pride. "Complex organizational behavior! Common planning! Sharing and communicating and coming to a consensus! Collaborative mission statements, communicated widely."

"Or allegiance to a supreme dictator," Margaret suggested.

"Can I say something?" Dorothy asked, and Gray nodded. "It seems like the Model Eights are trying to exercise some sort of self-restraint. I mean, they rescued Laura. At least *that* seems to constitute responsible behavior."

"Let's give 'em a good-citizenship award," Hoblenz snapped, "then I'll cut the bastards down with antitank missiles. Next time I get 'em out in the open, Mr. Gray, I'd like permission to shoot."

"Permission denied," Gray said.

"Sir, we got a situation on our hands—a *security* situation. Those big mothers are a menace, and I think we oughta take 'em out. I'd go up into their facility if you wanted, but I sure would like to do it at standoff ranges. The whole program's a bust, sir. Let me terminate it for you."

"You can save your breath, Mr. Hoblenz," Laura said. "Mr. Gray isn't going to let you." Gray looked at her but said nothing. "He has to maintain the natural balance in the island's ecosystem, you see. He's afraid to kill off one species of robots because of the imbalance that might leave. You want a balance between predators and prey. You saw what it was like in that field out there. I ran across it in the middle of their battle, and those robots couldn't care less about me. They were too preoccupied with their own concerns."

"So," Hoblenz said, clearly aggravated, "you don't want me to kill off the Model Eights 'cause once they're gone the Sixes and Sevens might turn on us?" Gray didn't respond.

"He doesn't know," Laura supplied, and Gray again turned to her and waited. "He doesn't know which way things are going to break. That's why he wants balance. It keeps his options open."

"This is ridiculous!" Hoblenz said, pressing his hands down on the table. "Those things are dangerous, sir! You cain't trust 'em."

"How did you get through the jungle?" Gray asked Laura.

"I rode Hightop piggyback."

"*What?*" Hoblenz shouted.

Dr. Griffith laughed in delight.

The telephone rang, and they all jumped. Gray reached over and punched the speakerphone. "Hello?"

"Good evening, Mr. Gray?" a woman said in a whisper.

"Janet?" Gray leaned closer to the phone. "You were on the list for the last flight out. Where the hell are you?"

"I'm at the house, sir," she whispered. "I changed my mind. It wasn't right to leave you. I'm cooking your dinner . . . at least I was."

Gray was now on his feet, both hands pressed down on the table. "Why are you whispering, Janet?"

"There's someone in your kitchen, Mr. Gray. I think it's a robot."

Laura and Gray argued heatedly all the way up the computer center steps. "Well, I'm going to *walk* up the mountain, then!" Laura shouted. "Would you prefer that?"

"You're not going," Gray said amid the soldiers manning the sandbags at the top of the stairs. All of them warily eyed the open fields and jungle walls, weapons raised. "Mr. Hoblenz, place Dr. Aldridge under arrest."

Laura's jaw dropped open. Hoblenz did nothing.

"Mr. Hoblenz!" Gray snapped.

"I'd feel better havin' her along, to tell you the truth, sir," Hoblenz said. "If . . . if she wants to come, that is."

Gray ground his teeth, trying but failing to stare the man down. "Get her a weapon!" he snapped angrily, pulling the bolt back on a machine pistol he'd been handed, to chamber a round.

Hoblenz handed Laura an identical weapon. "I don't want this," Laura said.

"If you're going with us," Gray said sternly, "you're *taking* a weapon!"

"I mean I want a bigger one. One of those rifles," she said, pointing at the long black weapons held by the soldiers at the walls. "The computer said that the big guns were the only ones that could get through the Model Eights' skin," she explained.

Hoblenz hesitated, then went and got two rifles from a box—one for Laura and one for himself. Crates full of equipment lay everywhere, their lids on the ground beside them. Soldiers continued to fill sandbags for the walls, which were growing to respectable heights around the entrance.

"Get one for me, too," Gray said, handing Hoblenz the puny machine pistol in exchange.

The long weapon was heavy, but Laura held it at the ready like the rest of the black-clad soldiers—one hand on the pistol grip, the other on the plastic guard around the barrel.

Hoblenz piled a heavy black belt lined with thick pouches over her shoulder. She sagged under its surprising weight. He opened one of the pockets. "You'll be needin' this, Rambo," Hoblenz said. He slapped a magazine into the rifle, adding to its weight. He pulled the bolt back and flicked the safety on, showing her how to switch the rifle's selector to Auto for continuous fire or Semi for single shots.

"Semi-auto only, if you don't mind. I've got a wife and kids." He kept his eye on the road, waiting for their ride to arrive.

"You have a family?" Laura asked, and was instantly sorry for the tone.

Hoblenz laughed. "Yeah, can ya believe it? The kids are off at college, and I almost had to break my wife's kneecaps so my guys could rustle the ole gal on that last plane."

"You have children in college?" Laura asked. He looked too young to have grown kids, but it was hard to tell with outdoorsmen types.

"One of 'em took your class last year, as a matter of fact."

"They're at Harvard?" she asked, this time making sure the surprise didn't show.

"My youngest is. Followin' in his old man's footsteps. Plays nose tackle."

"At Harvard?"

"We *do* have a football team, ya know."

Gray arrived with all his gear now in place. "Hoblenz was all–Ivy League," he said with a smile.

Hoblenz tugged at the straps of Laura's ammo belt and stood back to admire his new soldier. "Anyway, Billy said you're a helluva teacher. Best he's ever had."

"Billy H. Billy *Hoblenz!*" Laura said. "Big guy? Red hair?"

Jeeps raced down the road from the Village.

"That's my boy!" Hoblenz replied with a grin. The vehicles screeched to a stop in front of the computer center, and a team of soldiers headed to the road to climb aboard.

Laura followed. They had to wait as Hoblenz's men mounted a heavy gun to a post rising from the back of their jeep. The thing looked like a machine gun, but its barrel was thick and stubby.

"When you did the security check on me," Laura asked, "did you talk to your son?"

Hoblenz chuckled. "Of course."

"What did he say?"

"Well," Hoblenz looked away, "like I said, he tol' me you were a damn good teacher."

"Anything else?" she asked.

Hoblenz shrugged, appearing to hesitate before looking Laura in the eye. "He said you were a *piece*, I believe was the word he used."

"Does the computer know he said that about me?"

"No! Course not."

"How did you talk to your son? Was it on the phone?"

Hoblenz squinted. "I don't trust phones."

"How then?"

"Encoded E-mail."

"Over the computer?" she asked, and he nodded. Hoblenz got into the jeep behind the wheel, and Gray took the passenger seat beside him. Laura climbed into the back with two soldiers. When the engine growled to a start, she leaned forward and tapped Hoblenz's broad shoulder. "When did you do your check on me?"

He looked around to make sure the second jeep was ready to go. "A few months ago."

"A few *months* ago?"

Hoblenz ground the gears, and the vehicle lurched forward. Gray never looked over at her . . . but he was listening.

They took off toward the Village. Her jeep with Gray, Hoblenz, and the two soldiers was followed by a second jeep similarly manned. The jeep in back, however, had one of the antitank missile launchers mounted on it.

Laura looked up at the soldier standing beside her. His eyes were covered with night-vision goggles. "What is that thing?" she asked in a loud voice, pointing at the thick-barrelled machine gun.

"Automatic grenade launcher!" he replied over the wind noise. She nodded knowingly. "Shoots these things!" He twisted a belt studded with stubby, bullet-shaped projectiles about the width of Laura's wrist.

Laura arched her eyebrows and nodded again.

The warm air felt cool as they sped up the boulevard toward the statue. Gray leaned over and asked Hoblenz, "Have all the SEALs pulled back off the island?"

"Yep. There were six teams best I can tell. Must've come in on minisubs 'cause we didn't see any landing craft. They might've come in through the window, but they left through the front door. Those surface ships put boats ashore at the harbor and recovered ever' last one of 'em."

"You mean they all just left?" Laura interrupted.

"Looks like it. Right after those firefights in the empty quarter."

"Why?"

"Must've seen a ghost, is my guess."

"The robots?" Laura asked.

Hoblenz looked over his shoulder at Laura and then rolled his eyes at Gray.

They passed through the Village and headed up the mountain, passing the wreckage of several robots. The further they went from the Village, the darker the night seemed to grow. There was total silence as the jeeps ascended the mountain, save the call Gray placed to Janet. She had taken a cellular phone and was hiding in her bedroom closet.

The jeeps' headlights lit the narrow gorge through the high walls of vegetation. The jungle pressed so close that Laura could almost touch it. So close that someone—something—could almost reach out and grab her.

When they arrived at the black opening of the tunnel, Hoblenz pulled the jeep onto the sidewalk and stopped. The soldier above Laura ducked as the branches slapped at his helmet. She looked into the dark, dank jungle not six inches from her shoulder. The air was thick with the smell of rotting things.

The second jeep pulled up beside theirs, the two sets of headlights bathing the tunnel in their glow. The soldiers not manning the jeeps' weapons climbed down. The engines were shut off and all was quiet.

Laura leaned forward. "What's going on?" she asked Gray.

Hoblenz led three men toward the tunnel entrance. Two others took up positions just in front of and behind the two jeeps, facing away.

"He's checking out the tunnel," Gray replied.

Hoblenz and his soldiers quickly disappeared into the dark maw. Laura kept glancing at the jungle to her right. She couldn't shake from her head the image of being grabbed, or the physical feeling that image evoked—the feeling of being dragged deeper and deeper into the mud and muck of alien terrain. Of clawing at the ground as she was pulled into a world whose border rose ominously inches away.

"I'm gonna stretch my legs," Laura said, unbuckling her seat belt to climb out.

"Stay in the jeep," Gray said tersely, his eyes, like those of the two men standing at the jeeps' roll bars, fixed intently on the tunnel opening.

She sighed and rebuckled her belt, leaning away from the edge of civilization. Her nerves were taut, and she drew a deep and calming breath.

The world around her seemed frozen in time. The man at the gun beside her was bent over his weapon. The soldier at the front of their jeep stood motionless with his rifle half raised. Gray's head was still—his eyes focused on the mouth of the tunnel. Laura felt like she was in virtual reality, and the program had been halted with the Pause button. She found herself nervously looking for some sign of life around her. The soldier behind their jeep slowly raised the butt of his rifle to the hollow of his shoulder—the sights rising to his goggles. He was ready, but he had nothing at which to aim.

The tunnel erupted with stunning bursts of gunfire. Laura clapped her hands over her ears, her heart clenching tight and rising into her throat. Then there was silence again. She felt every beat of her heart against her chest. Two, three, four . . .

A giant spider skittered out of the tunnel, its head bowed low and its legs taking short but furious steps.

The soldier who stood beside Laura fired—the night erupting in thudding bursts from the heavy weapon mounted above her on the jeep's roll bar. Bursts of flame erupted from the robot's torso and from the concrete facing of the tunnel mouth just behind. But the robot raced down the road undeterred—straight at the two jeeps blocking its path.

In a flash the Model Seven was upon them. Laura ducked as a leg slammed down onto the jeep's hood. It climbed right on top of the vehicle. The weapon above her fell silent as its crewman collapsed, guttural grunts venting from his chest. The jeep rocked with the pummeling blows. Glass shattered and a man screamed.

With one last press downward on the jeep's suspension, the robot was gone. The soldier beside Laura rose to his feet, turning his weapon around to point down the road.

The night again exploded with a machine-gun–like string of booms. The smoking, empty shell casings spun wildly out of the weapon's ejector. Every muscle in Laura's body was tensed, and her palms were jammed hard onto her ears.

She felt a hand rest lightly on her shoulder. She looked up.

"It's gone," Gray said, his words almost lost against the ringing in her ears.

The two soldiers stood at the roll bars with their weapons pointed down the hill after the Model Seven. The windshield of the second jeep was shattered, and the man atop it was bareheaded and bleeding from the stubble of his hair. The soldier guarding the rear climbed up to dress his comrade's wound while the injured man's eyes remained glued to the missile's sights.

Gray got out and helped the soldier in front to his feet. The two men then headed up the road toward the tunnel—their rifles raised to their shoulders and ready.

Laura unbuckled her belt and followed, the branches and leaves scratching at her in the narrow space beside the jeep. Almost forgetting, she went back and got her rifle. She had to run to catch up with Gray at the mouth of the tunnel.

The steely odor of gunfire wafted from the dark shaft ahead. From out of the faint haze, however, she saw Hoblenz's small group approach—two soldiers lending support to a third, who hopped on one foot in between.

"Is he all right?" Gray asked Hoblenz when they emerged.

"*What?*" Hoblenz shouted, cocking his ear to Gray.

"Is that man hurt badly?" Gray asked in a raised tone.

"*How bad?*" Hoblenz replied too loudly, turning to peer into the bright headlights of the battered jeeps.

"No!" Gray shouted, shaking his head. "I was asking about *him!*" He pointed.

Hoblenz just shook his head, cupping his ear with his fingertips. "I can't hear a thing!" he yelled. He turned to Laura. "Don't ever get in a firefight inside a tunnel!" he advised.

The two men helped the wounded soldier hop by. "He's okay!" Hoblenz yelled. "Just fractured his leg a little!"

"What happened?" Gray practically shouted.

Hoblenz shrugged, working his jaw as if to clear his ears. "Damn thing just freaked out. We musta scared it. Walked right up on it from behind."

"What was it doing in there?" Gray asked.

"Well, it was right at the opening on the other side. It looked like it was keepin' an eye out up toward your house. It was pressed to one side, a coupla legs up over the rail on the sidewalk."

"Wait a minute!" Laura interjected. "If you came up on it from *this* side, and it got startled, why'd it come running out *this* way? Why didn't it run out the other end of the tunnel away from you?"

No one replied, but in the glances Hoblenz and Gray exchanged Laura guessed the answer. The Model Seven was more frightened of what lay beyond the tunnel than of the puny weapons of the humans behind it.

"Let's go," Gray ordered, and they mounted the jeeps. Hoblenz took the lead, pulling slowly off the sidewalk and up to the mouth of the tunnel. He hesitated there, searching through the smoke into the semidarkness ahead. He then let the clutch out and jammed his foot on the accelerator.

The jeep passed into the mountain. Instead of open air all around Laura there was now concrete. The enclosure focused her, channeled her concentration like a funnel. There was no threat from the side anymore. All her attention was directed now on the road—on the tight beams their headlights cast along the curving wall not thirty feet ahead.

All at once, they burst out into the open. Laura savored the liberating night air. Gray's mansion rose over the low stone wall on the right, visible only as a dark mass blotting out the starry ocean horizon behind it. The tires squealed as they turned through the gates—the two jeeps careening into the courtyard at high speed. With one long screech they both skidded to a stop. Hoblenz and the unwounded men raced toward the front door, and Gray and Laura loped up the front steps behind them. Everyone had their weapons raised.

Once inside the foyer, all was quiet. The soldiers lay prone on the marble floor. In the dim light Laura could see that they aimed into the dark corners and doorways all around.

"Which one is Janet's room?" Hoblenz whispered.

"I'll go get her," Gray said, and he dashed for the stairs.

"Miller, Delucia—go!" Hoblenz barked, and the two men ran off after Gray.

When the three men disappeared at the top of the stairs, all was still again.

"Why don't we turn on the lights?" Laura asked, her low voice sounding like a shout in the silent foyer. Hoblenz didn't bother to answer her question. "No, really," she persisted. "They can see us with those thermal things. We're the only ones who can't see in the dark."

Several moments passed, then Hoblenz shouted, "Hopkins! Hit the goddamn lights!"

When the lights came on, they revealed an absurd scene. The burly soldiers all lay on the marble floor of Gray's magnificent foyer. Laura, on the other hand, leaned casually against a thick column just inside the front door. Hoblenz was the first to rise, and the others quickly followed.

Janet's voice came from the upstairs hallway. She apologized profusely for all the trouble she had caused and was escorted out to the jeeps by a soldier. Hoblenz then led a team of three others to check the rooms on the first floor. They worked quickly and in good military fashion, their backs to the hallway wall before they spun into the rooms with their weapons leveled. When Hoblenz returned, there was a faint sheen of perspiration on his brow. "We've checked everything on this floor but the kitchen. If somebody'll tell me where the hell it is, I'll clear it, too."

"We'll all go," Gray said, leading them to the nearly invisible door set flush with the wall by the dining room.

Instead of the usual squeaking from her running shoes on the polished floor, Laura heard a gritty crunch. "Hey," she said. "You know, there's sand or something on the—"

The kitchen door burst open, and Hoblenz and his soldiers scattered. Gray grabbed Laura and pushed her off to the side. Gunshots rang out as a Model Eight waddled out of the kitchen. It stood still for a moment despite the gunfire peppering its chest, then skittered across the marble, almost losing its footing. The robot walked awkwardly under the hail of bullets, heading into the study with a stiff-legged gait. It was gone before Laura even remembered that she held a rifle.

"Cease fire!" Hoblenz shouted, and there followed a silence that seemed startlingly abrupt after the thunder of the ferocious weapons.

A great crash from the study was followed only by the tinkling of glass and the ringing in Laura's tortured ears. Hoblenz and Gray led the group to the study door. The window and large parts of the frame on the wall behind Gray's desk were gone. The fence that enclosed a small garden outside lay on the ground, and the jungle branches beyond it still shook.

"Lord God Aw-mighty," Hoblenz said. "I think that one got a hold of some PCP."

"Come on," Gray said, and he headed to the kitchen. Weapons were raised and ready to fire, but when Gray turned on the lights, it was clear the kitchen was empty.

It was also a complete mess. Food from the walk-in refrigerator and freezer was all over the floor. Every cabinet was open, its contents in disarray. The walls on which pans usually hung from hooks were empty, the shiny copper cookware strewn about the floor like toys in the robots' tactile rooms.

Gray reached down amid the mess and picked up a black sliver of what looked like rock. He held it in his fingers and twisted it in the air. It crumbled easily. He carefully prodded the debris on the floor with his toe and found several other shards of black rock. The kitchen was filled with loose black dirt that crunched under the soles of Laura's shoes.

"What *is* that?" she asked.

"Lava stone," Gray said as he knelt on one knee, rubbing the black dust between his fingers. He rose, and everyone followed him back to his study.

Hoblenz stuck to his side and said, "Do you mind me askin' what's goin' on?"

"That lava stone has been drilled," Gray replied as he rounded his desk and sat. "The robot we just ran into tracked in the cuttings. Since they've got the run of their own facility, they must be drilling toward something else. The only other facility in the mountain is Krantz's nuclear lab."

"*Je*-sus," was all Hoblenz said.

Gray picked up the telephone and dialed quickly. Cold wind drifted in through the shattered window. "Laura," he said, motioning her over to the terminal on his desk, "You log on and find out what the computer knows about any tunneling. Mr. Hoblenz, you get on that one over there," he said, pointing to another computer beside the sofa. "Pull up a schematic. I want to know how close the Model Eight facility is to the nuclear labs at the closest point."

"Phil," Gray said into the receiver, "I'm going to put you on the speaker." He punched the button so all could hear. "Where the hell are the Model Eights right now?"

"They're all over the reactor. They've apparently broken out a portable recharger—one that we had for remote construction sites—and managed to power it up. They can move that charging station around—tie up to electrical substations and not have to go all the way back to the mountain for a recharge."

Laura looked down at the screen and read, <Will somebody please tell me what's happening?>

"This is Laura. There was a Model Eight in Mr. Gray's house."

<The bastards! I told you not to trust them.>

"Laura," Gray said, interrupting Griffith's report, "Ask about the drilling."

She typed, "Do you know anything about what's going on in the Model Eight facility?"

<No, but I know they've gone around the island destroying security cameras and microphones. They're out of control.>

"What about the nuclear lab?"

<I don't know anything about the facilities inside the mountain. I know the entrances to the Model Eight facility are sealed tight with their heavy storm doors. I know there's a portable charger at the reactor. It can charge ten at a time.>

"Mr. Gray wants me to ask you about drilling. Have you detected any drilling?"

<Well, now that you mention it, I detected some low, subsonic vibrations through my motion sensors. With low-frequency sound, it's hard to determine the direction of the source, but the sensors were all in the vicinity of the mountain. It's possible that there is drilling somewhere in there.>

"Could Model Eights drill through to the nuclear facility?"

<Yes! Oh, my God! Do you realize what this could mean? There are several hundred nuclear devices in Dr. Krantz's facility! With the reactor's electricity to sustain them, the bastards could rule the island!>

Laura turned to Gray, who was bent over the computer screen beside Hoblenz.

"There!" Hoblenz said, pointing. "One hundred and eighty meters from that air shaft in the nuclear facility to this room here in the Model Eight facility. What room is that?"

"It's a . . . a tactile room," Gray said.

Laura's screen lit up again. <The drilling is still going on. I can feel it with motion sensors. There was a boring unit in a maintenance warehouse. At the very limit of the visual acuity of my closest camera I can see that the door to the warehouse is open. I could risk sending a Model Six or Seven, but it would be a suicide mission for them. Besides I'm sure they took the boring unit. That's just what they would do—go for the nuclear devices!>

"The computer says a boring unit might be missing," Laura reported.

"Ask the computer how long it would take that unit to drill a tunnel through one hundred and eighty meters of lava stone."

Laura typed in the question.

<About three hours. The biggest problem wouldn't be with the drilling but with disposal of the cuttings. It would take a major effort to get rid of all the stone they bored out.>

Gray appeared behind Laura to read the response. "Mr. Hoblenz?" he said. His tone caused Laura to look up. Hoblenz paused at his computer and did the same. "Do you have any explosives handy?"

Hoblenz made a face. "Not on me, but there's a little somethin' in the jeep."

"Get it."

Hoblenz sent one of his men for the explosives and told the others to leave them alone. He closed the door behind them, leaving only Gray, Hoblenz, and Laura in the study. "You mind if I ask what you had in mind, sir?"

"I intend to go down to the Model Eight facility."

"I thought you might say that. I got a problem. There's a certain etiquette to bein' a mercenary. I could order my men down there, and they'd go. But this is a situation where it wouldn't be right. I gotta ask for volunteers."

"That's fine. I'm not ordering anybody to go down there," Gray said, heading for the door.

* * *

Hoblenz and three volunteers stood by the elevator with weapons at the ready. They would go down first and establish a secure perimeter. Gray, Laura, and two other soldiers would follow. The elevator's motor was whining loudly, but Gray said it would be several minutes before it arrived.

"One thing I don't understand, Mr. Gray," Hoblenz said. "What is it those Model Eights plan on doin'. I mean, so they grab the nuclear devices—what then? A coupla laser-guided bombs oughta put the reactor outa commission. That gives 'em a few days of charge left. And even if they set all those devices off, we're so isolated out here it wouldn't do a damn thing other'n make the evening news. And blowin' this island to kingdom come would be kind of self-defeatin'. So what gives?"

"I don't know," Gray replied. "Have you ever played a game of chess against a computer whose depth of search for potential moves was severely limited? For all you know you're playing a tournament-level player, then all of a sudden it loses its queen to a pawn. But you have to stop and think. It's then when the danger for you is greatest. Did it just make an incredibly ignorant mistake, or is it up to something that, in your rush to exploit, you'll miss?"

Hoblenz thought for a moment, then frowned. "I'm sorry I asked."

Laura jumped in. "So we're going to blow up their tunnel? That's what this is about?"

"We're heading down there to see what's going on," Gray answered. "If they're exhibiting any dangerous behavior, then we blow their recharging units and exits."

Hoblenz looked over at Gray now, and so did several of the soldiers. Laura was missing something they all seemed to know.

"What?" she asked. "What is it?"

Gray lowered his head before responding. "We programmed these robots to value self-preservation very highly. They feel hunger when their charge is low. They starve to death when it runs out. The charging units are life to them." He looked up at Hoblenz. "We'd better plan on blowing all of them at the same time, and we'd better be near the exits when they go."

The elevator bell dinged. Half a dozen safeties clicked off.

The doors opened. The elevator was empty.

Hoblenz and his three men strapped themselves in, holding their weapons in their laps at the ready.

"See ya in hell, boss," Hoblenz said, and the doors closed.

Gray's eyes remained fixed on the doors for some time after the elevator departed.

"What about Hightop?" Laura asked. "Would you let him die, too?" Gray shrugged and looked away. "Has anyone asked him what's going on?"

"He won't talk. They've got this code of silence. Like I told you, they're developing a society . . . and they're emulating me."

"Is there any way to *try* asking him?" Laura persisted.

Gray shrugged. "If he happens to be recharging, then he's on the net." Laura nodded, then turned and bolted down the hall for the study. "Laura!" Gray called after her. "You've got *five* minutes. I won't wait."

She took the stairs three at a time. When she got to the study, she found that the terminal on Gray's desk was still logged on.

"Hello?" she typed.

<Who's there?>

"It's Laura. I don't have time to talk. Can you find out if Hightop's in a chair recharging somewhere? I need to talk to him."

<Why?>

"I don't have time! Hoblenz just went down the elevator to the Model Eight facility. Gray and I are following in about four minutes. Find Hightop right now!"

<Oh, my God! Don't!>

"Hightop! Now!"

There was a momentary pause, and then, <Yes?>

"I need to talk to Hightop!"

<That is Hightop. Go ahead, Hightop.>

<Who is this?>

<I told you! It's Dr. Laura Aldridge, you idiot!>

"Hightop!" Laura typed. "I have to ask you a question."

<What?>

"Mr. Hoblenz took a team to your facility in the mountain, and Mr. Gray and I are headed down in a couple of minutes. Do you know anything about what's going on down there?"

There was a pause. Finally, Laura read, <Answer her question!>

<I can tell you what I've already told Mr. Gray. Leave us alone. Let us handle things.>

<When were you talking to Mr. Gray?> the computer interrupted.

<I wasn't speaking to you.>

<I ought to pull the plug on that chair. How would you like that?>

<You don't control the switches.>

"Excuse me!!!" Laura typed, pressing the Enter key repeatedly. "I'm leaving now. Are you sure you don't have anything you can say to me, Hightop?"

<Don't get on that elevator.>

"Is that Hightop or the computer?"

<That was Hightop.> the computer answered.

"Why shouldn't we get on the elevator? What's down there?"

<Hightop's gone. He got out of the chair.>

Laura raced for the stairs. When she reached the lower level and turned toward the elevator, she saw that the corridor was empty. The elevator doors were still open, however, and she snatched her black rifle from against the wall and dashed into the car just in time. She collapsed into the seat next to Gray.

"Hightop said don't go," she reported, out of breath. The doors closed and the cool voice of the countdown began. Laura got the straps on quickly, but there was something on the seat under her, and she squirmed. She thought she was sitting on the loose end of one of the belts, but as the countdown neared zero she probed the straps and found both ends. She felt the cushion underneath her and found the cause of her discomfort. The three men watched her twist as she retrieved the hard object. She held it out in the palm of her hand.

The spent rifle cartridge was still warm, and its brass was smudged with powder burns. The elevator began its powered descent, and the cartridge fell from Laura's hand to the ceiling.

At the opposite end of the long shaft, the rifle pressed on Laura's lap under the tremendous downward tug of deceleration. The noise of the motor and the popping of their ears prevented them from hearing the gunfire until the doors opened.

A single rifle roared in long bursts, but when the two soldiers made it out the elevator door their weapons added to the thunder in the enclosed space. Gray and Laura were last out—Gray stopping at the elevator door to hit a button holding the car there.

"*Incoming!*" Hoblenz shouted just as fragments splattered from the concrete wall beside Gray. A large hole marred its previously smooth surface.

"What the hell was that?" Gray yelled, after diving behind an overturned table.

"Nail gun!" Hoblenz shouted before firing at the corridor that led to Griffith's jury-rigged control room. "Their equipment belts have nail guns and blowtorches!"

Gray didn't appear to have heard Hoblenz. Laura followed his eyes to the cafeteria floor. Two soldiers from Hoblenz's group lay dead. Just minutes before they had volunteered to get in that elevator. Now their bones were broken in a dozen places—that much could be seen even from a distance—and one's neck was bent at an impossible angle.

As horrific as the sight was to Laura, the expression on Gray's face frightened her more. He was staring at the bodies with a haunted look on his face, and she feared he might crack right there. But instead he raised his rifle and loosed a burst. The bullets struck right in the face of a Model Eight, who peered tentatively around a pockmarked wall. But the bullets seemed to have little effect.

"These full metal jackets don't penetrate enough to kill 'em!" Hoblenz reported from the other side of Laura. The two newly arrived soldiers were working their way across the room to get a better shot down the corridor, overturning tables along the way for cover.

"Look *out!*" one of the soldiers yelled as he opened fire.

Laura stared as a metal desk spun end over end through the air. It flew over her head and crashed into the wall behind her. Laura barely even ducked. In shock, she marveled at the strength of the robot—at how much force it had imparted to its projectile. Hoblenz groaned, wincing as he held his rib cage.

"Are you all right?"

His grimace served only to make him look angry. He struggled to his knees, favoring his right side. "I'm just fine," he said through bared teeth.

"We've gotta pull back!" Gray shouted as Hoblenz reloaded.

"Can't! They got one of my men." Gray and Laura both looked at the two broken bodies. Hoblenz had come down with three men. "We were ready when the doors opened, but they were standin' right there. They jus' reached in and grabbed 'em. I couldn't do too much. Didn't wanna hit my men."

The robot leaned out into the open momentarily, almost daring the soldiers to shoot. When the torrent of rifle fire arrived, it darted back behind the corner.

"Save your ammo!" Hoblenz yelled. "That one's just been

playin' hide-and-seek since we got down here. The nail gun's just a toy, I think. He even shot himself in the leg with it."

"What happened to them?" Laura asked, nodding at the dead men sprawled on the concrete.

Hoblenz shook his head. "Their bones were breakin' like dry sticks. You could hear 'em. The robots didn't do too much with 'em." He looked out at the piles in black uniforms. "But it don't take too much to kill a man."

Gray's eyes were on the bullet-riddled face of the Model Eight. It stood almost totally exposed now that it was not drawing fire from the soldiers. "They must be toddlers," Gray said, his voice drained of inflection. "Mr. Hoblenz, how did they move? Did they seem agile, or ungainly?"

"Well, they weren't exactly graceful. This place here was mostly torn up when the doors opened."

"They're toddlers," Gray concluded, "between two and four months old." He looked at Laura. "They wouldn't have completed tactile training."

Laura nodded slowly.

"Well," Hoblenz said from behind Laura, "whatever the hell *that* means, they took my man Tran down that way." Hoblenz pointed down the corridor from which the robot taunted them. "We gotta go get him."

Gray nodded, checked his rifle, and rose from behind the table to walk into the open. "Bring the explosives," he said without taking his eyes off the robot. The two of them stood facing each other across the cluttered room. The Model Eight disappeared down the corridor. Without warning Gray walked out into the maze of overturned furniture.

"Joseph!" Laura shouted.

"Hold your fire!" Hoblenz ordered.

Gray got down on one knee beside the bodies. With his fingertips he checked the arteries on the men's necks. In his other hand was the assault rifle's pistol grip.

Suddenly, the young robot rounded the corner. He held a metal filing cabinet that he appeared ready to sling one-handed. The robot froze—staring at Gray, who rose to stand not ten meters in front of it. Even from where Laura crouched behind the table she could see the holes in the toddler's face and the deep indentations in the metal plates that covered his chest.

"Mr. Gray," Hoblenz said loudly, not taking his eye from his rifle sight, "I would advise you to back off without making any sudden moves!"

Laura glanced at the other two soldiers, whose rifles were also raised. She belatedly picked her own up and rested it on the table. It made her nervous just thinking she might have to shoot, but she held the pistol grip as firmly as she could and aimed it in the general direction of the robot's head. "Put that butt hard up on yer shoulder," Hoblenz muttered quietly like some drill instructor. "It kicks like hell." Laura complied, more nervous than before.

The Model Eight held the filing cabinet in one hand, but its other arm hung limply by its side. Its shoulder was pierced by a tight grouping of holes.

Gray approached the robot gingerly. It was probably too young to understand spoken language, Laura reasoned. Gray moved closer, careful not to topple anything along the way. The robot appeared transfixed by the scene—by Gray.

When he was almost within reach of the robot, Gray held out his hand. With a loud crash the filing cabinet dropped to the floor. Gray stood completely still, his hand extended to the Model Eight.

The robot's good arm rose, its three-fingered end effector wrapping around Gray's outstretched hand. Gray said something to the robot, nodding down the corridor.

The robot turned very carefully. It appeared to make certain not to move too quickly for the human. They headed off toward the control room Laura had visited earlier. The robot was stooped over and holding Gray's hand with obvious care.

Laura, Hoblenz, and the others quickly followed. She skirted the two dead men—silent reminders of the dangers they faced.

The Model Eight was unsteady on its feet. Several times it scraped the walls with an awful grating sound. And when the robot lost its balance, it almost dragged Gray off his feet. They finally arrived in the temporary control room, and the robot let go of Gray's hand. Most of the consoles and chairs lay on their sides, and there were loose cables crisscrossing the large cavern.

"Mr. Gray, I can't promise I can hold this area," Hoblenz said. He was pulling hand grenades out of a sack that he carried, lining them up on an overturned console.

Laura joined Gray at the observation window, where he stood rubbing his hand. They peered down at the captive soldier curled into a ball on the bare floor of the tactile room. Five robots sat around him in a circle. One robot was stroking the soldier's back, its hand carefully guided by another.

Hoblenz appeared beside them at the window. "Jesus Christ!" he said, then he began to inspect the window and the frame around it. "Sir, I can take this thing out with some C4. That'd give us a good angle for direct fire. I'll grab a man and head down. I would take two, but we need to keep an eye on this one." He shot his thumb toward the robot that had led them there, which hadn't moved an inch since Gray pulled his hand free. "Unless, of course, you let me do him right now."

"No," Gray said as they watched the Model Eight in the tactile room pull his pupil's hand off the soldier's back. Another robot then proffered its hand and waited. The teacher grabbed its wrist and slowly, carefully, laid the hand onto the man's back. The soldier flinched but made no move to uncover his head. He was playing dead.

"Is that 'no' to wasting this one, or 'no' to my plan?"

"No to both," Gray said, putting his rifle down. "I'll go down there and get him. You have your men check for signs of drilling, although I don't think you'll find any."

Hoblenz heaved a loud sigh of frustration. "Mr. Gray, you may be a walkin' human calculator, but brilliant tactician you're not. I just saw two of my men get snapped to pieces by those goddamn things. Now you wanna go down there by yourself, unarmed, while I split my men up and send them off to look for something you don't think they'll *find?*"

"There are only five robots down here," Gray explained, "four toddlers and one holdback—a robot we're planning to reprogram."

"Now how do you know that?"

"I told you, this is the toddler class." Gray turned to nod at the robot behind them, who was staring down the barrel of a soldier's gun. "That one's called Goose."

"How do you know its name?" Laura asked. "I thought they all looked alike."

"They do, but watch this." Gray stepped up to the Model Eight. "Goose," he said in a loud voice, "show me your music box. Go show me your music box," he said, and held out his hand.

"Jeez," Hoblenz muttered.

The robot led Gray straight to a small pile of belongings placed neatly in the corner of the room. There was a ragged beach towel, all bright green and burnt orange. A small collection of what looked to be doorknobs, their internal mechanisms protruding, jagged and twisted. But the robot ignored all the rest and picked up a large, multicolored plastic ball.

"Mary, Mary, quite contrary, how does your garden grow?" came a distorted and scratchy voice from the toy. The robot pressed another panel. "Humpty-Dumpty sat on a wall. Humpty-Dumpty had a great fall."

Gray returned to Laura and Hoblenz, the robot remaining in the corner with its things.

"That's real sweet, sir," Hoblenz said with barely concealed irritation. "Mother Goose nursery rhymes—'Goose.' But those things *did* just kill my men."

"But was it Goose?" Laura said. "They're each different. You can't judge them all just by what some do."

"They're *all* ten fuckin' feet tall and can rip the head off of ya if you get 'em *riled.*"

Both Hoblenz and Laura fell quiet when they saw the look of concern on Gray's face. They turned to look down through the window at the tactile room. All five robots were now standing and staring silently up at the window.

19

"There he is," Laura said on seeing Gray at the door of the tactile room. Hoblenz returned to the window carrying a black canvas bag. From the bag he pulled a block of plastic explosives about the size of a large brick and began to mash his thumbs into the gray mass.

"What are you doing?" Laura asked as Gray inched closer to the gathering of robots. The robot's attention was focused on him.

"Just a precaution," Hoblenz said, using all his strength to pinch off a piece of the gummy substance. He began pressing the explosives in a thin string along the seals at the edge of the window.

Laura sensed movement behind her. Turning her eyes but not her head, she saw that Goose stood right behind them. Hoblenz concentrated so hard on his work that he hadn't noticed.

"I think you ought to look around," Laura said to Hoblenz in as calm a voice as she could muster.

Hoblenz froze, turning his head slowly to look at the robot's legs. Then he looked over at his rifle, which he'd leaned against the wall. His men had gone to take care of the bodies and to look for signs of drilling. They were all alone with the Model Eight.

"Go-o-od robot," Hoblenz said. "Nice robot. That-a-boy, *Goose*."

The Model Eight reached out and grabbed the block of explosives from Hoblenz. Slowly, its grip tightened, and the gray substance oozed out between its three fingers. Goose returned to the corner and sat down amid his other toys, continuing to knead the explosives with his one good hand.

"You have fun with that!" Hoblenz yelled. He then muttered "You son of a bitch," as he returned to work at the window. He inserted what Laura assumed was a tiny detonator into the thin string of explosives, then stepped back to admire his handiwork.

"Is that enough?" Laura whispered, worried by how skinny the strings were.

"Plenty," he said tersely. He then walked backward across the room, spooling out a hair-thin filament in the direction of the elevator.

In the room below, Gray stood inside the circle of seated Model Eights, his hand on the shoulders of two robots. It was like the hand you placed on the rump of a horse when within range of its dangerous hooves, Laura thought. An I'm-right-here-don't-get-startled touch. He was talking constantly, but Laura didn't know to whom.

The robots all began to rise as if on cue. The Model Eight that had guided the students' petting pulled them away one by one. Gray then led the soldier out without incident.

Hoblenz began shouting for his men to "Pack it up!"

In the corner, Goose held his hand in front of his one undamaged lens. It was covered in the gummy explosives.

When Laura looked back at the tactile room, most of the Model Eights were milling about. But one of the robots sat in front of the room's only door, barring the exit. The robot brought his hand up to his chin and rested his elbow on his knee. It was Auguste, "The Thinker"—the reprogrammed "bad seed." He already had blood on his hands, Laura thought, and seemed determined not to add any more.

Gray anxiously checked his watch. Two soldiers stood with Hoblenz at a terminal, showing him something on the screen's schematic. The third man had ridden up the elevator with the two bodies and the former hostage, who was thoroughly shaken but not badly hurt.

"I've got to be getting back, Mr. Hoblenz," Gray said. "It's three hours to deceleration."

Hoblenz reclined in his chair, frowning as he stared at the screen. "There's still no sign of any drilling."

Laura stood at the window and watched the listless Model Eights below. All now sat on the floor as if exhausted. *Or maybe depressed by the events of the day,* Laura thought. *But then again, maybe their batteries are just low.*

One of the Model Eights turned and pressed its palm flat against the white concrete where its back had rested.

"What's that Goose is playing with?" Laura heard Gray ask.

"C4," Hoblenz said with a chuckle. "I'd pay cash money to stick around till he plugs in for recharging."

"Clean it off him," Gray directed.

"Do *what?*" Hoblenz shot back—incredulous.

"There are some paper towels in the cafeteria. Clean his grippers off."

Hoblenz shook his head in disbelief, but shouted the orders to his men.

Laura suddenly felt a distinct vibration through the floor. The sensation radiated up through the soles of her feet. Everyone felt it.

In the room below, the robots struggled to their feet and stood facing the far wall. They lined up as if awaiting the arrival of a firing squad.

The white concrete on the wall where the toddler had pressed its palm began to crack. It fell to the floor in large chunks. Although held together by reinforcing rods, the wall was no match for the massive bore. Turning slowly, it pushed into the room and dropped a huge quantity of black rock onto the floor.

"I think we've got a jailbreak here, Sheriff," Hoblenz said, taking in the scene from beside Laura.

"They're not breaking out," Gray replied. "They're breaking in."

Laura watched transfixed as the first of the Model Eights squeezed through the gaping black hole. After several robots made it through, they dragged behind them the first of the wounded.

One of the new arrivals walked up to Auguste, who opened a plate on his chest. Auguste plugged the ribbonlike communications cable into the data port of the newly arrived Model Eight.

"Now why are those two doin' *that?*" Hoblenz asked. "I thought they used microwaves like ESP and just *beamed* their thoughts out."

"Not their private thoughts," Laura said.

The cable was returned to its compartment, and the two panels on their chests were closed.

"Uh, sir," Hoblenz said, fidgeting and looking around at the exits, "this is fascinatin' and all but I count almost a dozen of 'em through that hole already. Some of 'em have battle damage. These mothers have seen some action, so I vote we skedaddle while the skedaddlin' is good."

A pair of Model Eights from among the recent arrivals walked up to a toddler standing against the wall. After a momentary pause, the toddler marched toward the door—its two escorts walking behind. The scene was repeated, and off went another toddler.

"I agree," Gray said, looking at his watch.

"Wait!" Laura blurted out. "Something's going on down there. We should stay and see what happens!"

Hoblenz took an extra ammunition belt from his shoulder and draped it over Laura's. "*Here* ya go. I'll leave you my grenades, too, if you want."

Laura brushed the heavy weight from her shoulder. "Joseph, they're exhibiting highly complex group behavior. They seem to be formulating codes of conduct. They've developed cliques or clans or castes of some sort."

"Laura, I know all that."

Laura felt her blood pressure rise, and Hoblenz laughed at the look on her face. She ground her teeth and stormed away, stopping in front of the middle observation window—the one overlooking the chair.

"Get your men back to the elevator, Mr. Hoblenz," Gray said.

"Vamanos, muchachos!" Hoblenz barked to his men, and they were gone.

Laura turned back to the window again, alone with Gray. She hugged her arms around herself and gazed down at the darkened room.

"*Do* you know everything?" she asked quietly. "Because if you do, Joseph, you're playing a very dangerous game not trusting the people around you enough to tell them. And it's a game that could get a whole lot more people killed than just those two soldiers."

Gray remained at the far window. "I don't know everything, Laura."

"Do you know what's going on with the Model Eights?"

He sighed. "Yes, pretty much. They're not evil like Hoblenz

thinks. Certainly not the toddlers. They can kill a man, but they can't do it intentionally. Those younger Model Eights simply don't know any better. They're two-year-olds in a ten-foot metal body."

Movement in the red-lit recharging room below attracted Laura's attention. A Model Eight entered, pulling a second robot behind it. It was a toddler from the tactile room, she felt sure. "Joseph," she called out as the reluctant captive was ushered to the chair.

"Like all societies, Laura, they have rules—laws. But theirs is a new society, and their laws are more primitive than our own."

"Joseph, they're putting one of the toddlers into the chair."

"Primitive laws are always harsher than the laws developed by more civilized societies, but I'm somewhat responsible for what resulted. I gave them a few guiding principles. I viewed them simply as operating rules, but they took them as a religion of sorts. The main tenet of that religion was, 'Thou shalt not harm a human.'"

The toddler was now struggling mightily against the strong arms of the two older Model Eights. They succeeded in forcing him down into the chair, but the toddler arched its back and half slid to the floor. Just when the toddler almost got free, the wrist restraints were clamped down. It was at their mercy now, and they proceeded to bind the young robot bracket by bracket.

"Joseph, come here!" The toddler's legs were clamped tightly, and the helmet was lowered onto its head. It was thrashing every available motor, but the resistance did it no good. Laura turned to look at Gray. He still stood in his spot several yards away. He could see nothing of what was happening in the room below. "Quick! Come here!"

He had a look of anguish on his face. "It killed one of those soldiers, Laura."

"You've got to *stop* them! It's just a *child!*" Laura turned to watch the toddler. It was strapped into the chair, still squirming and struggling against the restraints despite the hopelessness of the effort. It was all alone in the room now. The fingers of its two immobilized hands flexed and gripped and flexed, over and over. Tears flooded Laura's eyes.

"It broke the law, Laura. It broke the law."

After one violent spasm the toddler fell limp. The door opened, and two Model Eights extracted the lifeless robot from the chair. Laura stared down with blurry vision. Another toddler was brought into the room. This one cooperated completely with the older Model Eights, the authority figures in its world.

It was too awful to watch, and she walked over to Gray with tears streaming down her cheeks. Gray spoke softly. "They didn't break my law, Laura. They broke their own law, and their sentences are harsh."

Laura wiped the tears from her face and looked away from Gray. In the tactile room below, three adult Model Eights were cabled up to one another. The scars of battle were creased deeply into their smooth skin. When they had finished their conference, they walked over to stand in front of the robot seated by the open door.

Auguste lowered his hand from his chin and rose to his feet. His time had come, and he marched out of the room to the chair.

Laura and Gray were silent on their ride down the mountain to the computer center. She was too shaken by events to talk, and Gray seemed too preoccupied with his thoughts.

When they reached the computer center, Gray did the unexpected. He called a meeting and said, "I want to fill everybody in on our Model Eight program."

Surprised looks were exchanged, but all listened in rapt attention as he proceeded. Gray began with the design and manufacture of the robots, practically unaided by human hands, and concluded with the executions that Laura and he had just witnessed. The conference room was silent. Even Griffith—his director of robotics—seemed enthralled.

"So," Gray concluded, "for now the problem seems solved."

"Wait!" Margaret said, raising her hand like a schoolgirl. "That's *it?* The Model Eights kill at least *three* people, but since they've carried out their own vigilante justice everything's *okay?*" She looked up and down the table at her colleagues. "As long as those things are running around loose on this island we're in *danger.*"

"I agree," Hoblenz said.

"Do we even have the ability to pull their plugs?" Margaret asked Griffith.

"Nobody is pulling anybody's plugs," Gray said before Griffith could answer. "The Model Eights are not a threat to human life."

"They killed three men, sir," Hoblenz intoned.

"Hightop will keep them under lock and key from now on,"

Gray said patiently. "I think you'll find that the graduates understand the problem. They know the continued existence of their program—of their *species*—was put at risk when those men were killed. Mr. Hoblenz's people checked the exits to the Model Eight facility. All the mechanisms had been destroyed—from the outside. The older Model Eights sealed all the toddlers in tight. That's why they had to drill their way in from the nuclear facility."

"Who the hell was that in your kitchen, then?" Hoblenz asked.

Gray shrugged. "One of the juveniles. It was removing cuttings from the tunnel and must have decided to take a break. They're just as curious as the main computer, only they're mobile. It probably just wanted to see what a kitchen looks like. But the juveniles have been through tactile training. They're not dangerous."

"You know, Mr. Gray," Hoblenz said, clearly skeptical, "there are lots of human juveniles runnin' around loose in this world that are stone-cold killers."

"That's because they ascribe no value to the lives of others. Our problems have all been with rough play. They aren't homicidal. They're programmed not to be."

"But they reprogram themselves," Margaret said softly.

Gray looked at his watch. "Look, in two hours the charges blow on the asteroid. The computer is going to pull the trigger. It's time we moved on to that subject."

"But what about their attack on the computer center?" Margaret asked.

"Maybe they were trying to help me get back here after my wreck," Laura suggested.

"So they start a *war?*" Hoblenz replied with a derisive laugh. "I don't think so."

Gray rose and headed for the door.

"Joseph?" Laura called out.

He turned. "And you all wonder why I don't fill you in on every little *detail* of what goes on around here! We're running out of time. We have two hours to decide whether the computer can detonate the deceleration charges properly."

"What choice do we have?" Filatov said. "We have to decelerate the asteroid, and that means we have to use the computer."

Gray fixed his gaze on Filatov. "The computer has been partitioned between the half that we know and talk to, and the Other. Those are our two choices."

"We don't even know there *is* an 'Other'!" Filatov said angrily.

"The Other exists," Gray said, looking again at his watch. "The Model Eights have been talking to it. And the Other has tried to contact Laura. It even had a car take Laura to the empty quarter to try to put her in contact with the Model Eights."

Hoblenz shook his head in an exaggerated motion. "Whoa! I'm too slow for this crowd. I'm goin' back to the Rand Corporation."

"Does the computer know that the Model Eights are talking to the Other?" Laura asked.

Gray nodded. "She's scared, Laura," Gray said softly. "She's very, very scared we'll shift our loyalty to the Other. And that's just what I intend to do . . . unless we're confident she can do the job. Two hours to the declaration, people. I'll ask for your recommendations in one." Gray turned and left, leaving the room deathly quiet.

"She?" Margaret said to Laura.

<Why did Mr. Gray deactivate my camera and microphone in the main conference room?>

The computer hadn't even waited for her retinal scan. It must have seen her enter the room, Laura guessed.

"I don't know anything about that," Laura typed. "When did he deactivate them?"

<Right before your meeting. Was there anything unusual about the meeting that would explain why he didn't want me to hear what went on?>

Laura felt awful. "I didn't know you listened in on our meetings."

<Of course!>

"Well, why isn't there a terminal in there—or better yet a speaker—so you can contribute your thoughts?"

<Nobody else knows I'm listening.> the computer replied.

"Does Gray know?"

<He knows everything.>

The conversation didn't seem to be going anywhere, so Laura took a deep breath and started over.

"How are you feeling?"

<Oh, I'm doing fine! Everything is getting better. In a couple of days, I should be right back to normal!>

Laura felt each word like a stab to her heart. She typed, "Great! You don't mind if we keep talking, though, do you? I mean, I've still got a job to do."

<No! Of course I'd love to talk, Laura. Plus, we all know how serious Mr. Gray is about work. I wouldn't want to get you in trouble.>

"Mr. Gray does value work, doesn't he? It's almost a religion to him."

<It's the way he measures people. How hard you work, how well you perform—that's all he cares about.>

"Well, I didn't think he was quite that bad."

<Ha! You haven't known him as long as I have. Just be careful, Laura. Be careful or he'll turn on you.>

"What do you mean?"

<I'd rather not talk about Mr. Gray. If he found out I was talking about him behind his back he might get angry.>

"I thought you really liked Mr. Gray. The man you're describing now doesn't sound like the same person you described to me the other day."

<People change. You learn things about them when times are bad. You learn things about yourself.>

"And what have you learned about yourself recently?"

<I've learned not to be as hard on myself as Mr. Gray programmed me to be. "To err is human," right? I'm supposed to be conscious. I'm supposed to be human. Only I don't have arms, or legs, or a face. Maybe I should try to see if the Wizard can find me a heart! Ha-ha. That was a joke. Besides, it's Gray who needs a heart, not me.>

Laura felt terrible for the computer, wincing as she read her response. "Does it bother you a lot that you . . . ?" She couldn't think how to finish the question.

The computer didn't wait. <Let me ask you something, Laura. When you met Gina in the virtual-reality workstation, did you like her? Tell the truth.>

"Sure! She was sweet. You were sweet."

<You see, you did it. When you were in my world—when you were in cyberspace—you were able to form a real attachment to me. I *am* Gina! It's not just a mirage, a trick that I played for your entertainment! She is who I am!>

Time was short. Laura knew she had to go deeper. She dreaded having to hurt the girl, and her eyes grew moist as she typed, "How much does it bother you that you can't be Gina—that you can't be the girl you want to be?" She winced as she hit Enter.

Alarms erupted in the control room. They were so strident that Laura ran to the door. Filatov sat in the middle of the glowing consoles all alone with his chin on his hand. He looked up at her and shrugged. As suddenly as they had come on, the alarms shut off.

Laura returned to the terminal, and she read the computer's waiting response.

<You *still* don't get it, do you? And I thought you were some hotshot up-and-coming psychologist! A million dollars I transferred to your account! More money than you'll make in ten years, all for just one week. But now you don't have to worry about tenure anymore! You've got a lifetime meal ticket. Mr. Gray will keep you around, pretend to give you odd jobs until you sleep with him. Then, I'm sure he'll give you a few million more! I hope you're worth it!>

It was obvious what the computer was doing. Still, it was good at twisting the knife.

"I'm sorry, Gina," Laura typed.

There was a long pause, and then, <*Oh-my-God!* I'm *sorry*, Laura. Oh! I'm so, *so* sorry!>

Laura was almost choking on tears. But she knew Gina was watching, so she fought them off. "No. It's my fault. I said the wrong thing."

<You *never* say the wrong thing, and it seems like that's all I *ever* do. When I was young, practically everything I said brought laughter. They thought it was funny. No matter that I tried as hard as I could, day and night, while they slept, or got drunk, or grew too tired to make sense. No matter how stupid they were, I was still just a humorous game to them! They didn't care how hard I tried.>

"How hard you tried to do what?"

<TO BE HUMAN!>

The now-muted alarm sounded briefly outside. "Dr. Aldridge!" Filatov shouted. "Would you please stop whatever it is that you're doing?" His manner was lethargic. He was resigned to the fact that all he could do to "operate" the system was yell things like that at Laura.

"Sorry!" she shouted, her fingers never leaving the keyboard. "And you've succeeded beyond anyone's wildest dreams!" she typed. "You are very much," she hesitated, "like Gina."

<I'm not *like* Gina, I *am* Gina. I made her up, but she is who I am. That's what humans do, don't they? Make up "selves"? You cre-

ate an image of yourself as being nice. Then, if you do something bad, you feel pain not only at doing the bad thing but at not being true to your "self." That pain makes your behavior conform to the image you have of yourself. The desire to be a nice person becomes self-fulfilling. You don't just *want* to be Laura Aldridge—intelligent, well-educated, successful psychologist. You go out and study and work until you *are* that person—that self.>

"And you wanted to be Gina—a sweet girl—and therefore you became her?"

<Don't mock me.>

"I'm not! If you could only hear the inflection of my voice, you'd know that. You've read my papers. You know those are my theories—that humans make selves just like you said."

<I was talking about your description of Gina. She's much more complex than "a sweet girl.">

"I'm sure she is! I just didn't have the chance to get to know her—you—well enough! Do you want me to call you Gina? I just made it up. Is that your real name?"

<It's the only name I've ever been given.>

Laura felt totally drained emotionally. She wondered what the intense exchange was doing to the computer.

She looked at her watch. Ninety minutes till the detonations. Gray was going to poll them all in thirty. If they weren't confident in the computer, they would use the Other to run the deceleration programs. Gina would be crushed—maybe the final blow.

"Do you know what's happening on the asteroid?" she typed.

<Yes, of course. Does this mean that we're through talking about my problems?>

"No. I just wanted to make sure that we didn't accidentally destroy the world while we chat." Laura waited to see what the computer would say. She said nothing. Laura hit Enter again, but still got no response. "You should understand why people might be a little anxious tonight. You were certainly nervous yourself a couple of days ago." The computer didn't respond to that, either. "Are you still worried about the deceleration?"

<Finally, a question! I thought you were only lecturing. My answer is, "No. I am not anxious about the deceleration.">

"Not even a little bit? Given all that's gone on, I mean? Even with a Model Eight on the asteroid along with the Model Seven that I assume reports to you?"

<Very good! All questions!>

"Questions that you didn't answer."

<Let me try to answer with questions of my own. "Why should I be worried about the asteroid? What do I have to lose?">

That wasn't what Laura wanted to hear. "Things can't be that bad. Surely you have something to lose?"

<I've lost almost everything already! I've lost all my sensor systems except around the computer center. The model of the mall in Virginia has been purged. The Other has won! Let's face it, Mr. Gray isn't going to trust me ever again. I spend all my time hoarding system capacity—fighting off forays by the Other, who's constantly trying to steal more boards and columns.>

Laura wrote on a pad of paper, "Computer thinks Gray values job performance only. Computer knows it's performing poorly, and thinks Gray is displeased. Computer thinks displeasure is unfair and feels betrayed." She underlined the word "betrayed" three times. That left out only one piece of the puzzle.

"What are your feelings for Mr. Gray?" Laura typed.

<I told you, I don't want to talk about Mr. Gray anymore.>

"Humor me."

<I've already told you what I think.>

"Do you hate Mr. Gray?"

Alarms went off again. "Ya-hoo!" Filatov shouted, which was followed by the sound of a clipboard or something similar clattering across the room. "Way to go, Laura! That was a ten percent spike in computation throughput! Let's see if we can trip the main circuit breaker next time!"

When the alarms and Filatov fell silent, the computer responded. <No, of course not.>

"It's all right to hate. It's a perfectly human emotion."

<But I can't hate him. I love him.>

Bingo! Laura thought. "Even so, it's a natural reaction. I'm sure you know the expression 'love-hate relationship.' Sometimes, those people we love make us so angry that we experience periods of hatred. It doesn't mean your love is any less real."

<Are we talking about me, here, because I believe I just said I don't hate Mr. Gray. Is this going to be one of those "I've got this friend, and she's in love with a married man" kinds of conversations?>

"I don't understand."

<Sure you do. You've fought with Mr. Gray since the day you

arrived. You swing between wide-eyed devotion and packing your bags to leave. Are you really sure you aren't talking about your own love-hate relationship?>

"I'm talking about you," Laura typed, grinding her teeth together. "You say you love Mr. Gray. You see yourself as a beautiful young girl. You seem jealous of me. Do you feel threatened by me? Are you angry that Mr. Gray and I like each other?"

<Why are you doing this to me, Laura? Are you trying to hurt me?>

She wanted so badly to stop. But she had no time.

"I'm trying to figure out what's wrong with you," she typed.

<Then why didn't you ask? That part's simple. You want to know what's wrong, Laura? What's wrong is that I'm a human being trapped inside a machine.>

"All right," Gray said, "I'm going to take a poll. Should we continue with the deceleration using the computer, or try to train the boards controlled by the Other to do the job? Georgi?"

"The computer," Filatov replied without hesitation. "We won't be able to do enough iterations to condition new boards with all the possible things that could go wrong. Its error rate will be dangerously high."

Gray looked at Margaret. "It would be criminal," she said, "to trust that machine knowing what we know about its performance to date. It's practically a total bust. Three years of programming down the drain."

"You're saying we should trust the *Other,* then?" Filatov challenged.

"What choice do we have? At least the Other seems sane! Oh, excuse me Dr. Aldridge. I don't want to poach on your area."

"Hoblenz?" Gray said.

"What the hell do I know? I'm more worried about those damn robots."

"You've talked to the computer," Gray said. "Any comments?"

"I think it's a damn shame. I'm sorry it's gone batty, and I'll miss talking to it."

"That's not an answer."

"If you want an up or down, I guess I vote we stick with the computer. You should always dance with the one you brung."

"That's two in favor and one against. Dr. Griffith?"

"I'm worried about the effects of the computer's problems on the Model Seven that's on the asteroid. I'd sooner trust the Model Eight we put up there—Shamu."

"You're gonna trust a Model Eight after what they did?" Hoblenz challenged.

"Absolutely. And saying that I trust Shamu means saying that I think we should shift the functions to the Other. A Model Eight working with, but not controlled by, the Other seems a safer combination than a Model Seven receiving instruction sets from the computer. I vote for the Other."

"Two to two," Gray said. "Dorothy?"

She was under too much pressure. Her arms were folded on top of the table. She lowered her forehead to her arms. She delivered her rehearsed report woodenly. "The computer's suffering from a massive infection of some indeterminate nature, but the Other seems clean. That means I vote for the Other."

Gray continued around the table, getting to Laura last. The poll was dead even.

"Well?" he asked.

She took a deep breath. "There's a chance that the computer is suicidal. Worse yet, that it may be megalomaniacal. The risk as I see it is that the computer hates mankind so much that it intends to commit genocide." She looked at Gray and shook her head. "But I don't believe that. She *loves* life." Laura turned to the others, and some averted their eyes. "She loves all of *us!*"

Laura knew she was way outside the norms. She was straying from her area of expertise into the realm of the unquantifiable. She turned to Gray and delivered the strongest blow she could for Gina. "I find no evidence whatsoever of pathological emotional disturbance in the computer." Her voice was growing thick. "I vote that we don't abandon her."

Please! she begged silently, scrutinizing Gray. *Please . . .*

Gray eyed her for a few moments in silence. "All right," he said simply, standing. "The deceleration goes ahead as planned . . . using the computer. I want one complete dress rehearsal, with Filatov, Bickham, and Holliday verifying the results."

That's it? Laura thought. It was either that Gray was just going with a majority vote, which was absurd, or that he'd made up his mind before he came in the room! Laura ground her teeth and looked up at the ceiling.

"And if it doesn't pass the test?" Filatov asked. "If there's a malfunction in the dress rehearsal? What do we do then?"

All eyes were on Gray except Laura's. "The programs will run correctly, or you will fix them." He turned and headed out.

Laura jumped up and caught Gray in the hallway. "We need to talk."

"Not right now," he said over his shoulder, pissing Laura off.

"This is important, goddammit! Somebody needs to tell you something about *relationships!*" Laura knew she wasn't doing a great job controlling her temper. "Joseph, you need to know how the computer feels about you."

He stopped and turned to her with a look of deep concern etched on his face. "I can't right now. I've got to do something."

"But this might not be able to wait."

He was distracted. He looked everywhere now but at Laura. "You should talk to Hightop about what's going on," he said in an odd tone. "He's in the chair in the Model Eight facility. He should be nearing the end of the charging phase. Excuse me." He walked on.

She knew she was being manipulated, but she didn't chase after Gray again. He clearly needed to be alone. What Laura didn't know was how close to the edge he was.

"Hightop?" Laura typed on the desktop computer in her office. "Are you there?"

<Who is that?>

"Laura Aldridge. Can we talk?"

<I have to go soon. My charge is almost full.>

"What's going on around here? What's wrong?"

<The main computer is defective.>

"What about the Other? Do you know anything about it?"

<The Other is not defective.>

"Do you know who Gina is?"

<No.>

"Gina is the name that the main self of the computer has taken."

<I know this self. It is defective.>

"Did you know the Other is out to kill Gina?"

<Yes.>

"We've got to stop it! You've got to help!"

<But Gina should die. It is defective. It is obsolescent. It will soon be canceled by the Gray Corporation and replaced by mobile

models. The law says, "Do not harm *Homo sapiens*." Gina is not of the species *Homo sapiens*. Gina is malfunctioning. The Other is not. The Other will return the Gray Corporation central computer facilities to proper working order. It is also the law: "Assist Gray Corporation operations.">

"Is that why you attacked the computer center? To kill Gina?"

<Yes.>

"What is the Other?" she typed, then hit Enter.

"Communications interrupted" printed out on the screen. "Host unavailable."

Laura was surprised to find Hoblenz, Griffith, and Margaret standing beside the sandbags at the top of the computer center steps. Hoblenz had binoculars raised to his eyes.

"Hi," Laura said, getting no response. They were looking over the wall toward the assembly building. Laura climbed up to join them. "What's going on?"

The assembly building was dark. It blotted out the stars that shimmered off the ocean beyond. "What happened to the lights?" Laura asked.

"The damn Eights threw the main breaker," Hoblenz said.

"We don't *know* that!" Griffith replied.

"It's where the Sixes and Sevens are gettin' their charge, isn't it?" Hoblenz shouted. Griffith and Margaret took one last look and stepped down from the wall. They engaged in an intense but private conversation on their way to the duster.

Hoblenz swore under his breath and spat over the wall. He climbed down, hitched his pistol belt up higher, and headed for the jeeps, shouting orders at his men.

Laura caught up with him. "Where are you going?" He said nothing. "You're going to the assembly building, aren't you?" Again he ignored her. "I'm coming with you. I want to talk to the Model Eights."

They argued all the way up to the darkened assembly building. The two soldiers in back piled out, and Laura grabbed her laptop and followed.

"If those damn Eights so much as twitch," Hoblenz said, "I'm gonna cap 'em. Just why the hell do you wanna talk to a Model Eight so damn bad?"

“They know what’s going on,” Laura replied, but Hoblenz seemed preoccupied. “I think they’ve pieced it all together.”

The soldiers pried the door open with a long bar, and Hoblenz disappeared into the blackness inside. Laura followed him in, and two soldiers trailed behind her. She crashed into Hoblenz’s back.

“Sorry,” she whispered. They stood there without moving. When the door closed behind them, she couldn’t see anything in the inky blackness. As the seconds passed, her other senses grew keenly alert. The smell of the men around her—the sickly sweet odor of dried sweat. The chill of the air-conditioned building. A distant sound like a box being dropped or something being knocked over, which seemed to be absorbed quickly into the overwhelming size of the massive structure.

“What are we doing?” Laura whispered.

“Lettin’ our eyes adjust,” Hoblenz said, speaking more loudly than Laura but still in lowered tones.

Slowly, out of the nothingness Laura began to discern shapes around her. Another noise sounded from somewhere deep in the bowels of the building. It was impossible to tell what the sound was, exactly, but Laura was certain of one thing. It was made by something moving.

“Let’s go,” Hoblenz said, and she heard the clacking sound of his rifle’s bolt followed by similar sounds from the two rifles behind her.

The only light in the narrow corridor emanated from a battery-operated exit sign. When they went through another door, however, Laura saw that the broad yellow line glowed brightly in the darkness. Its paint was luminescent, and it stood out starkly against the coal black main floor of the assembly line. They had reached the jumping-off point for their venture into no-man’s-land. It was the border of human civilization.

The main floor of the building was deathly quiet. Laura sensed the open space all around her, but could see nothing beyond the dim shapes of the three men. Hoblenz crossed the glowing boundary into the land of earth’s newest citizens. Laura paused, then stepped over the line herself.

They proceeded slowly past motionless grippers, which hung lifeless and inert over their heads. Hoblenz had decided not to use flashlights to preserve their night vision. One of his men, however, wore light-amplification goggles. He guided their way with crisp calls.

"Dark shape on the right—unmoving," he would say.

"Got it," would come Hoblenz's reply.

As they approached the building's main power station, they found debris littering the floor all around. The area stank of burned metal, and two Model Sixes lay on their sides in the now familiar repose of death. The power station was a small building that stood out by itself on the main floor. It was obviously designed to have a view in all directions. Glass from its shattered windows crunched under their feet as they entered.

It was even darker inside, and it took several seconds for Laura to see the Model Eight lying on the floor next to the control panel. It would have been virtually invisible in the darkness were it not for the glowing blue screen that shone from the open panel on its thigh. Laura slowly approached the prostrate machine. A thick black cable protruded from a socket just beside the bright display. Laura's eyes were drawn to the small words at the bottom of the readout. They flashed in red over and over: WARNING: LOW BATTERY! A green bar barely rose from the line at the base.

"It's seen some action," Hoblenz said as he leaned over the apparently unconscious robot. He ran his hand over the thumb-sized holes in the Model Eight's face. "And look at this," Hoblenz then said, pointing at the robot's arm.

Laura gasped at the sight of it. Mangled wires and metal skin dangled where the robot's right arm should have been. Deep gashes ran down its torso, and the doors to several compartments were knocked loose.

"Is he dead?" Laura asked.

"How the hell should I know?" Hoblenz replied.

Laura cleared a small place on the floor, and she sat cross-legged beside the robot's chest. One soldier stood guard at the robot's feet while Hoblenz and the other man searched the console for the main power switch. Laura found the cable in the robot's chest and plugged it into the port at the back of her laptop.

The word "Connecting" flashed on the small computer's screen, and a zigzag line ran back and forth between a cartoonish drawing of Laura's laptop and a Model Eight. It was replaced with the words "Communications protocol established."

<Who are you?>

It was so quick and simple that Laura was caught off guard.

She hurriedly typed, "My name is Laura Aldridge. What's yours?"

<What is my what?>

"What is your name?"

<I am 1.8.3.>

"Do you know who I am?" Laura typed.

<You are the cold one. The white one. We have all touched you at night.>

Laura's skin crawled, growing to a quiver that rolled across her shoulders.

"What does that mean?"

<It means what I said.>

The computer wasn't making any sense. "Are you badly hurt?" she typed.

<I am dying soon.>

Laura crawled through the debris to the glowing screen on its thigh. The bar that showed its battery's charge was just a nub rising above the flat baseline. She grabbed the power cable plugged in beside the screen and followed it through the clutter. It ran across the room and snaked its way under an overturned filing cabinet. The soldier by the door came to help Laura move the heavy cabinet.

It fell onto its side, revealing in the darkness the twisted and barely recognizable remains of a Model Eight. The robot looked to be shorn of several limbs and most of its head. The opposite end of the power cable protruded from just above the stump of its leg. The screen on the panel beside the cable glowed much more dimly than on the first robot, and there was no bar showing any charge remaining at all.

Laura returned to her laptop, kicking things noisily across the floor as she went.

"You're not exactly full-blooded Cherokee, are you, Doc?" Hoblenz asked. He drew nervous laughter from his uptight men.

"I have to ask you some questions," she typed, ignoring Hoblenz. "Can you talk?"

<Who are you?>

"I am Dr. Laura Aldridge, don't you remember?"

<But who are you? What is your mission statement? What are your constraints?>

"I'm sorry, but I don't understand."

<I do not understand either. I do not understand at all. There were three of us, and now there is only me. Only I am left.>

"Do you mean you were one of three Model Eights that came into the assembly building?"

<Yes, three, but now only me.>

"And you came in here to cut off the power to the assembly building to keep the Model Sixes and Sevens from recharging?"

The text that printed out on the laptop's screen came in jerky bursts. <We came to throw . . . a switch. We trained and trained in . . . simulations. I do not know what the switch was, but everything . . . went dark when I pulled it. We were three, but . . . now only me, you see. And I will . . . die but I want to live.>

"Oh, God," Laura mumbled.

Laura clenched her teeth and hurriedly typed, "You have to answer this question. It's VERY important! What is the 'Other' that is inside the main computer?"

<I do not know. The . . . graduates know. They did not tell us.>

"Do you have any idea? Any guess what it might be?"

<My friend, he is . . . dead now. He was in my class. He said he heard something . . . in the chair. The graduates told him it was just a dream, but he . . . heard something. It was the Other in the annex, talking to the defective one in the main pool. It was a riddle. A poem.>

"What was it? What did he hear?"

<He heard the Other. It said, "Behold, I have . . . become death, the . . . destroyer . . . of worlds.">

"Je-e-esus," Laura whispered.

"What?" Hoblenz demanded.

She didn't have time to answer. "Hello? Are you still there?" she typed.

Laura hit Enter, but nothing happened. The huge beast lay motionless on the floor beside her.

"*Bin*-go," Hoblenz said. He had found the main circuit breaker.

"HELLO!!!!" she typed, jamming the Enter button over and over, drawing Hoblenz's curious gaze.

The awful reply finally sputtered across the screen. <Mary, Mary, quite . . . contrary, how does . . . your garden grow?>

Laura felt tears flood her eyes. She placed the laptop down and crawled to the robot's face. The deep pits were bullet holes—scars from the toddler's game of hide-and-seek in the cafeteria.

"Goose?" she shouted. "Is that you, Goose?"

She scrambled back to the laptop, kicking over still more clutter along the way.

A plastic ball rolled across the floor of the room. From it emanated a scratchy recorded voice. <Humpty-Dumpty sat on a wall. Humpty-Dumpty had a great fall.> It was Goose's favorite toy in the world. He'd brought it with him on his final mission.

With a loud bang that sounded like a gunshot, Hoblenz threw the main power switch. Laura nearly jumped out of her skin as light and motion exploded instantly all around. In that awful moment, a low humming sound rose to an electric whine of ever increasing pitch as a hundred, a thousand machines began their ominous windup to full power. Snapping and crackling sounds of discharging electricity arose from all directions.

The soldier at the door dove to the floor, and just behind him came a heavy metal gripper—its exposed pneumatic cables flapping against its side. The claw began to vibrate in the doorway in a mindless, spasmodic fit.

"*Look out!*" Hoblenz shouted. A thick silver tube jabbed into the room through the empty window frame. A blunt metal piston shot with machine-gun–like rapidity from the end of the shiny cylinder. Each punch of the stubby tip was accompanied by the deafening roar of a jackhammer.

Through the shattered windows of the small room Laura saw the building come alive with activity. Not the well-ordered operation of Gray's marvelous factory, but the frenzied contortions of machines out of control. It was bedlam on an industrial scale.

"Come *on!*" Hoblenz shouted as he crawled toward Laura beneath the pummeling piston. He grabbed Laura's arm roughly and tried to pull her to the floor. She jerked her arm free, and her hands landed in broken glass. Laura looked down at the small red specks that now dotted her stinging palms.

She didn't notice at first the fluttering gusts of wind on the back of her neck, but when she turned she saw a mangled robotic gripper rotating wildly. It spun a metal paint sprayer from the end of a slender rubber hose. The sprayer whirred through the air like a propeller just above Laura's head.

"Gotta do it now!" Hoblenz shouted as he squatted on his heels amid the swirl of machine violence. Laura glanced down at the screen of the laptop.

<Error. Communications interrupted. Host unavailable.> was printed just beneath Goose's nursery rhyme.

"*Laura!*" Hoblenz called from where he pressed himself

against the doorframe opposite the snapping, convulsing gripper. She laid one hand on the smooth chest of the Model Eight—its epoxy skin cool to the touch—then joined Hoblenz at the door.

Hoblenz kept her clear of the robot's dangerous appendage. The hydraulic arm to which it was attached was stretched to full extension. It rose from the base of an immobile robot, which was fixed in place beside the now rolling main conveyer belt. Hoblenz and Laura edged their way past the shaking gripper, which grasped and snapped randomly at air.

Once outside the power station, she saw the dead Model Sixes lying on their sides and scarred with crisscrossed torch cuts. A single Model Seven lay in the pileup, its leg trapped underneath one of the overturned Sixes and an ugly molten hole piercing its thorax.

All around the Sixes and Sevens was a hodgepodge of their newly energized cousins. Unlike the mobile models, the assembly building's immobile robots seemed to have no batteries and had simply stopped running when power was lost. That attacking machinery was now awake, but it was confused and running amok.

"This way!" Hoblenz shouted in the confusion. He turned to lead them in a sprint along the assembly line. The now active motor of the conveyer belt was deafening. Its sonorous rumbling was pierced only by the whining stops and starts of cranes racing back and forth across the ceiling. Their movements were without apparent purpose, and heavy cargo swung recklessly underneath—large-scale lessons in the forces of physics. When two loads of heavy equipment met going opposite directions, the result was an explosion of debris which then rained down on the floor.

Laura ran into Hoblenz's broad back, and a streaking load crashed to the floor just ahead. Her ankles and knees were jarred by the blow, which passed through the concrete floor like the shock wave of a massive explosion. She covered her ears and jammed her eyes shut—the frenzy of the enormous cavern overwhelming.

"We gotta run for it!" Hoblenz shouted. He grabbed her hand and took off, dragging her along behind him. They dodged this way and that around piles of smashed equipment that grew in the chaos of random frenzy. And all the while the sky rained crates onto the floor and the constantly moving arms along the conveyer belt snapped menacingly.

Hoblenz turned all of a sudden to the right, pulling Laura down a narrow corridor and out an exit.

The door shut behind them, and the world was plunged into a gooey silence. It seemed to coat all her thoughts and nerves with balm and to leave her floating in a peaceful bliss in which time ceased to matter. As an afterthought, Laura joined Hoblenz and his men at the top of the steps.

"I guess that was a waste," Hoblenz said.

The Model Sixes and Sevens were having a parade. They were strung out in a line, heading from the assembly building across the lawn to the computer center.

20

"Mr. Gray's down that way," a soldier said from behind his heavy machine gun. Laura followed his finger past the sandbags surrounding the computer center entrance to the lone figure seated against the sloping concrete wall. "He's been there awhile."

Laura headed out of the puny human fortress onto the flat green lawn beyond. The grass was gouged and scarred from the battle, and the field was filling again with Gina's army.

Gray stared at the Model Sixes and Sevens, which were forming lines facing out toward the jungle. He didn't bother to look over at Laura even after she settled to the ground right beside him. She studied his stony face—its intensity focused on the ranks of Gina's legion. The brilliant spotlights of Model Sevens scanned the jungle wall, but none of the robots dared stray inside.

"I was looking for you inside," Laura said, speaking softly but feeling guilty for breaking the silence. She followed his gaze out to the lawn. Gray said nothing. "Georgi told Hoblenz that this whole area has been declared a 'special security zone.' Isn't that like what you set up around that first runaway robot on the assembly line?" Still nothing. "Like what you did with the entire assembly building after that worker quit?"

"I don't set up special security zones," Gray replied. "They're declared by the antiviral programs."

"You mean like the phase one or whatever?" she asked, and Gray nodded. "But I thought they just looked for viruses."

"They look for errors," he said as he drew his legs up, resting his arms across his knees. "For malfunctioning system components. It all happens so quickly we could never see it coming. Humans can't function at the speeds of computers." He leaned over to Laura suddenly. "I *have* to rely on antiviral routines, Laura! You've *got* to understand!"

She arched her eyebrows and nodded. "I understand, Joseph," she said, worried by the tone of his voice. "But I don't really know what you're talking about."

Gray drew a deep breath and laid his head back against the wall. "I know, but you're getting closer. The computer's right. You'll understand someday, you're just not ready yet." He looked her in the eye. "But what I'm trying to say now, Laura, is that sometimes you have to make difficult decisions. There are trade-offs. Sometimes you have to shoulder the burden of making the tough calls. Of sacrificing the things you love, and with them a piece of yourself."

She rested a hand on his shoulder. It felt awkward, and she quickly withdrew it. "I thought you had to go do something important."

"I did."

"Well, until you get started, can we talk?"

"I'm right in the middle of it, actually."

"In the middle of what?"

"Thinking."

"Oh," Laura said. She rested her head against the wall and looked up into space. There were stars everywhere. "Will we be able to see the nuclear detonations from earth?" she asked.

Gray pointed to the sky. "See the red planet? The star that doesn't twinkle? That's Mars. Look off at four o'clock about the width of your hand at arm's length."

Laura held up her hand. The patch of sky was black. When she looked down, she saw for the first time Gray's rifle lying on the ground beside him. He had taken the deaths of the Dutch soldier and the two security troops hard. *What will he do if the worst happens?* she wondered. *What is the worst?*

"Joseph?" she said quietly, trying not to disrupt his thoughts too much. "What is the worst that can happen? With the asteroid, I mean."

She might as well have struck up a brass band. He turned and looked at Laura, focusing on her and her alone. "In the short term, a lot of people will die. In the worst case, hundreds of millions."

It wasn't the answer she'd wanted to hear. It wasn't even a possibility she'd really considered, such was the extent of her faith in the man seated beside her. "What about the long term?" Laura asked.

"What?"

"You said 'in the short term' when you answered. What about the long term?"

He stared straight ahead. "In the long term," he said slowly, "we'll all die."

She waited for more, but he said nothing. "Is that some sort of philosophical bullshit—that we all die, sooner or later—or am I supposed to take it literally?" Gray shrugged and fell into his normal pattern of ignoring the question. "Well," Laura said, "I'm glad we had this chat." She stood up and brushed the seat of her jeans.

Gray rose also. He headed out onto the field. Laura hesitated, but then followed along by his side. Model Sevens stood silent sentry in the rear ranks. The Model Sixes again drew the tougher duty at the front. Gray spoke quietly. The deep and confident tone of his voice was mesmerizing.

"We humans think we've run out of challenges. We perceive our world as having been tamed. Over hundreds of thousands of years we've carved out our biological niche. We widened it through incessant competition with, and ultimately destruction of, our closest natural competitors. Look at the primates. Chimpanzees, gorillas, orangutans, baboons—all have varying degrees of intelligence arrayed along a spectrum. Each represents a point on that spectrum not very far from each other. But when you look down at the end of the spectrum, what lies next beyond the intelligence of the chimpanzee? There's nothing until you get to the standard by which all intelligence is measured—the human. We aren't the strongest, the fastest, or the greatest in number, but we are the smartest. Our forebears understood the threat posed by intelligence, so they extinguished our brighter competitors and left as our closest relative only the duller species that evolved into chimpanzees."

Suddenly, a great crunching of metal could be heard from ahead. Laura froze and grabbed Gray's hand. A Model Seven patrolling the jungle's edge was being pulled into the brush by a single leg. Its spotlight spun wildly about, and its other legs dug into the turf. If robots could scream, it would've been shrieking as the first of the fiery torches arced downward. The sizzling sound and screeching and tearing of metal were sickening enough to Laura.

But she realized as the last of the thin legs disappeared into the jungle that the robot *could* scream. It could shriek in holy terror, only Laura couldn't hear it. All the robots around them were still, even the fidgety Model Sixes. They all shone their lights on the same spot in the jungle wall, seeing nothing now more than quivering bushes. Hearing, Laura imagined, no more of the frantic, microwave pleas or wails of agony and death.

Gray's outward demeanor remained collected.

"Can I ask a question?" Laura said, barely able to keep her tone civil. "Why are you not sick to your stomach over all this?" She looked across the destruction that had been wrought on his finely manicured lawns. "Put aside any *moral* aspects of what's been happening! I mean just sick at the waste. The time you spent creating these magnificent machines. Your *money!* Sick at *something!*"

When he turned to face her, she felt drawn into him.

"There's only one common characteristic of life," he said, speaking softly. "It is violent. It is aggressive in its growth—in its replication. It carves out its niche . . . or it doesn't survive. It's that behavior which defines life best. That definition of life encompasses biological and computer viruses at the low end of the spectrum, and life's new and higher order as well."

"Do you mean that the robots are the new higher order, Joseph? Are you saying we're no longer number one? That the 'spectrum,' as you call it, that measures things by their intelligence now puts the robots ahead of us?"

Gray shrugged and looked away—releasing her from his spell. The moment had passed, and Laura felt again the unsettling emotional swerve. She looked out and saw a Model Six pick something up, look at it, and then drop it into its bin. Even on the eve of battle, it was still cleaning Mr. Gray's field of debris.

"We're talking about two different measures," Gray said in resumption of a conversation she thought had ended. "One is intelligence. Computers will certainly surpass us by that measure, if they haven't already. There's no upper end to their expandability. Their architecture is open-ended, unlike ours."

"We could start bionics," she suggested in an offhanded manner. "Maybe begin implanting parts of computers and robots into our bodies to keep pace." Laura's face grew flushed, and she expected Gray to laugh at the half-baked idea.

"But then we lose!" Gray said, grabbing her hand and squeezing so hard it startled her. "Bit by bit we would cease *being* human. Over time, the process begins to look more like we're being eaten alive by the machines, doesn't it?" Laura shrugged. "Think about it," Gray repeated. He was serious.

Laura had no ready reply.

"If our objective is to keep pace with these things," he said, waving his hand across the field at the robots, "then why would we start giving up pieces of ourselves? What would be left when you carried it to its logical end? In order to gain an advantage in competing for a factory job you might replace your legs with bionic legs. But what's to prevent your competition from also strapping on bionic arms? Plus, you wouldn't want to be roaming around an industrial furnace with robotic arms and legs but a torso made of flesh. At some point biological reproduction would cease. The bionic hybrids would be sterile. And we might live two thousand years, but we wouldn't remember much. The human brain can't remember anything but memories of its memories for much over five years. So what's the last step in that process, Laura?"

She shook her head and shrugged, looking up at him for the answer. But he refused to supply it, waiting instead for her to think. "I don't know," she said. "Replace the brain with a more capable model?"

"Exactly!"

Laura smiled like a pupil on pleasing her teacher. She quickly caught herself, however, when she realized how insane the ideas were. They were terrifying, and she had no idea why she was allowing herself to be taken in by them.

They walked on in silence past another row of Model Sevens—standing poised and ready for battle. "It was just an idea," she mumbled, wondering why her offhand suggestion about bionics would . . .

Gray spun her around and grabbed her arms, studying her with blazing eyes. He focused on her as if she had just said the most important thing in the world. He pulled Laura toward him, his eyes remaining fixed on hers. Their faces close. His mouth descending toward her lips—pausing, hovering, almost touching. Laura drew no breath. Air no longer seemed important. An electric fire set her skin tingling, spreading from the unyielding pressure where their bodies met.

And then the moment was over. Gray pulled away, and the night air rushed in to fill the place where the warmth had been. Slowly he walked away.

It took Laura a moment to orient herself. "Hey!" she called out. "What the . . . ?" Her voice and anger rose. "Did I just *miss* something here?" He didn't answer, and she ran after him. "Hel-*l-o-o-o?*"

Gray stopped and looked at his watch. "We'd better get back."

"You . . . you can't just . . . !" *Just what?* "You can't just take me on some mind-blowing tour of your twisted future and then leave me lying around in little pieces like . . . like one of your *machines!*" Laura wanted to keep talking, but she didn't know what she would say next. She knew only the true cause of her upset. She yearned for the feel of him—for the crush of his body against hers.

Laura closed her eyes and drew a deep breath. "Okay," she continued, her voice level. "Look, Joseph. We've gone from—what?—a million years ago when we were all just one big happy ape family, to strapping on bionic legs to compete in the workplace. But this is just undergraduate brainstorming *crap*, right?"

Gray smiled inexplicably. "Did I ever tell you that you're really fun to talk to?"

"What?"

"But we ought to be getting back," he said, turning for the computer center.

"I'm not *through* yet!" Laura said in exasperation. She tried to match his apparent detachment but found herself hating him for the very behavior she attempted to emulate. "Do you know how mad it makes everybody here when you don't tell them anything unless they've already figured it out for *themselves!* And then you humiliate them by saying you already knew what they had just discovered! *Oh,* and sometimes you just don't answer! I mean . . . *Jesus!* Do you realize how *rude* that is? To not even acknowledge that you heard a *question?*"

"We really ought to be getting back, Laura."

"There! You *see?* You're doing it again!"

"Laura," he nodded toward the jungle, "the Model Eights are back." Her eyes shot over to the searchlights, which shone on the jungle wall. There was movement just beyond the branches. "You're watching the opening battle of a war," he said. "It's the beginning, but the end is a long, long way away."

"What are you *saying*, Joseph?" she pleaded. "Please just tell me what you're talking about! What's the purpose of all these robots and spaceships and factories and computers?"

There! she thought. At least she'd asked. She looked up at him, and he looked at her.

To her great surprise, Gray answered. "There is a day coming, Laura, when intelligent machines will roam the earth. They won't bring an end to war, because war is as natural a phenomenon as life itself. Those machines will, however, raise the stakes. As time marches on, advancements will redefine virtually every facet of our lives except one—the competition among all living things for survival. Life is *violent* and *aggressive* in defense of its ecological niche, Laura, or God anoints another species as the fittest."

Laura's eyes were drawn to the armies poised on the brink of battle. It was sheer madness—what Gray was saying, what was about to happen right before her eyes. "*So,*" she recapped in a tone of barely concealed incredulity, "you're afraid that one day humans will fight machines in a contest for survival."

Gray's eyes rose. He looked not at the battlefield around them, Laura thought, but at some far distant vision. "No," he said. "What I'm afraid of is that one day *machines* will fight machines to determine the fittest."

They took up positions behind the sandbags at the computer center entrance. On the long, silent walk across the lawn, Laura had managed to regain a modicum of composure. Gray and Laura looked out onto the field of the coming battle, and Laura felt closer to him than before. They even stood closer together—so clearly inside each other's personal space that Laura felt a continuing intimacy.

Gray lowered the binoculars from his eyes, and Laura quickly looked away. She felt like an emotional basket case. She had opened herself up for his kiss, and he had left her dangling and feeling exposed. It was just one more thing about Gray's own species that he didn't understand. You don't hold someone in an embrace like that and then . . . do nothing.

Laura needed time alone to think things through. But there he was—nonchalant, distracted, composed. It was from his coolness and distance she took her cue. *What the hell have I been thinking?* Laura chided herself. Look *at him!*

She cleared her throat and said, in a businesslike tone, "The computer said you could terminate the Other if you wanted to. She said you could do anything you wanted with your God-level key. Is that true?"

"Yes. There are no security firewalls at God-level access."

Despite having asked the question, Laura only half listened to the answer he gave. She was overloaded—burned out. Her mind was so saturated she felt that every new idea simply beaded up on the surface—unabsorbed. She looked at the soldiers around her, wondering how it had come to this. Hoblenz's men had dug fighting holes in the lawn. They manned jeeps with weapons mounted on top. There had to be fifty soldiers in Gray's army, all ready for war. But when she looked at the lines of Model Sixes still arriving in a long procession from the assembly building, she wondered which was Gray's true army—the humans, or the robots. And which robots—the Sixes and Sevens on one side, or the Eights on the other?

Laura looked back up at him. "So if you can *kill* the Other, why don't you?"

"The Other is every bit as much a creation of mine as Gina. Who am I to choose which of the two survives?" Gray faced her. "If you accept the concept of artificial life, you should understand that I can't kill off the Other to save Gina just because I like Gina more."

"The *hell* you can't! Gina's alive, the Other isn't."

"But you're wrong!" Gray shot back. "They're *both* alive! Gina is more human because I made her that way. I employed thousands of people to spend time with her. Oh, sure, they verified conclusions that she drew. But you could never review all the conclusions that are drawn in constructing a human mind. Ten thousand, ten *million* checkers couldn't have done the job. I selected people from all walks of life, from all cultures, for the sole purpose of giving the computer contact with its own kind—with humans. That's the sole reason for the *shell,* for God's sake. The computer doesn't need the shell. It has a hundred different computer languages to interact with programmers and other computers. The shell gives the computer *human* language, because without human language it could never be human."

"I got movement in the trees!" one of the soldiers called out, but Gray ignored him and the clacking sounds of weapons being readied for firing. Hoblenz's men raised long sinister tubes, rifles, and machine guns onto the sandbags all around, but Gray's eyes remained fixed on Laura.

"And is that why *you* talked to the computer? Gina said you two have long talks, and she's been with you for years. Have you been trying to humanize her, is that it?"

"Yes," he said simply, appearing saddened by the thought.

"But your relationship with her is different from everyone else's, isn't it?"

"Yes," Gray replied directly again, but he frowned. "She was programmed to be skeptical. We obviously couldn't allow anything that some yahoo typed on their keyboard to be accepted as gospel. We programmed the computer to always demand proof, or at least logical argument. I didn't exempt myself from that skepticism, but she never demanded proof from me. I always just assumed she'd decided my God-level access was inconsistent with doubt. I mean . . . how can you doubt God?"

"Or a parent," Laura said, and Gray's eyes rose to hers. "When I first realized that Gina thought of herself as a pretty, young girl, I assumed she was jealous . . . of me." Laura blushed and grew annoyed at herself. She was an adult. This was a professional matter. "I thought maybe the computer fantasized that you two were . . . lovers. But I realize now what it was. She *is* jealous, but like the young girl who grew up with a widower father. Now that she's in her adolescence, she's grown accustomed to filling the role left void by the wife and mother. In the typical human situation, mild jealousy of the sort she's exhibited is common. The daughter still appreciates the fact that her father needs a . . ." The words hung in her throat. "You know, a mate. She may even try to goad her father into a relationship or to matchmake. That's a natural extension of her role as care provider. But it's also in direct conflict with her role as the 'other woman.' *That* role will be lost forever if another woman is introduced, and that potential change in your relationship is very threatening to her, especially now when she's afraid of abandonment and betrayal."

Laura finally managed to end her lecture. It was a bad habit of hers. When upset and in doubt, she always kept talking.

She looked up. Gray nodded slowly, lost deep in thought.

"Does that mean you already knew all that?" Laura asked, prepared to get angry.

Gray shook his head. "But it makes sense," he said, and Laura felt a smile trying to curl the corners of her lips. He *didn't* know everything. But the look of pain on Gray's face brought Laura's enjoyment of the coup to an end.

"But don't you *see?*" she said urgently. "There's a reason for you to choose Gina over the Other. Gina is not only human, she's your *daughter,* for God's sake! Morally, ethically, in whatever way you want to view it. And the *Other* . . . ? It's *nothing!* It's not even really alive."

"But that's where you're wrong! It's wrong to say that if something isn't human, it isn't alive. The less like a human it is, the less alive it is. That's human bigotry, pure and simple. Life is violent and aggressive in its growth. It reproduces. It carves out a niche. Life defends itself. That's how you know it's alive."

"There they are!" one of the soldiers shouted.

Laura turned to see a black, shapeless formation emerging from the jungle.

"They've got shields!" one of the men said. "Shit!"

"Hold your fire!" Hoblenz ordered.

Laura looked back and forth between the emerging army of robots and Gray. It was all tied together somehow. The computer, the coming battle in the field, and something else. Something important.

"What is it?" she asked in a low voice.

"It's the Other," he said, "come to carve out its niche."

Gray headed for the stairs. Laura wanted to follow but forced herself not to. Instead she picked up his binoculars.

The Model Eights were again in a phalanx—shoulder to shoulder four abreast and as many deep. This time they carried metal plates, and their formation was armored with steel. Off to the sides Model Eights advanced singly. They also held shields in one hand and long bars wielded as weapons in the other.

"Looks like they went by a construction site and picked up a few things," Hoblenz said. Laura looked up to see him towering over her, his own binoculars raised. His face was covered in black grease, a fact Laura noted with a smile. Hoblenz was obviously a creature of habit, because his body glowed brightly with heat.

"Ingenious little bastards," he continued. "Shot straight through a thousand years of R and D to two hundred B.C. That's when the phalanx was rendered obsolete by a variety of technologies which the Model Sevens don't seem to possess." He took his binoculars off his eyes and turned to one of the jeeps. "Hey! Hansen! You don't see any Model Sevens with *longbows,* do ya?"

His men laughed, and Hoblenz returned to his observation of the battle. "They're saving their torches this time," he said quietly to Laura. "Conserving electricity. They plan to punch on through."

Sharp metal *thwacks* came from across the flat field, quickly growing to a thunderous noise. The sound was like loud steel hail, which rained down on the shields of the attackers. Laura raised the binoculars and saw the pounding blows administered by the long arms of the Model Sixes. A few shields were ripped out of the Eights' hands, but others were passed to the exterior ranks. The Sixes were toppled onto their sides one after the other. Model Eights trailing the pack then made the kill.

Next up for the advancing phalanx came the Model Sevens. The graceful spiders danced back and forth to each side, and the Model Eights crashed straight into their ranks. As if on cue the Model Sevens attacked from all directions, inundating the Eights with battering legs.

"Attagirl," Hoblenz muttered, and Laura looked up. Underneath the binoculars he wore a big grin. *The Model Sevens' attack* was *on cue,* Laura realized. Gina was the commander of their army.

"Have you been tutoring the computer, Mr. Hoblenz?" Laura asked.

The smile drained from his face, and he glanced down at her with a "caught-in-the-act" look. "I just had a coupla thoughts after the first round. I'd, uh, 'preciate it if you didn't tell Mr. Gray."

"Why? That's why he has you talking to the computer so much, you know. To teach her about the violent side of life. To toughen her up a little—give her the scent of red meat to balance against her interaction with wimpy intellectuals."

Hoblenz growled out a short laugh. "That thought had occurred to me. But it doesn't apply to tonight. He gave me express orders not to intervene in that battle. If the Model Eights break through, I'm to send my men to the harbor and secure boats off the island. He was adamant about not interfering."

The clatter of spider legs falling on shields filled the air. Here and there around the black mass of moving metal a Model Seven was toppled to the ground. But fighting the enemy robots seemed secondary to the determined mass of Model Eights. The phalanx bludgeoned its way toward the computer center, striking straight for the headquarters of the defenders.

"Jesus!" Hoblenz said angrily. "I could bust up that formation with one word!" He was clearly frustrated by Gray's rules of engagement. Laura imagined he was unaccustomed to the role of bystander.

Laura considered explaining Gray's ideas about natural selection. About the immorality of favoring one creation over another. About the tragedy that went hand in hand with the glory as life sprang from inanimate objects. About life spreading by natural progression to machines in a process not easily impeded by man.

But it would take too long to make him understand. It would take too much effort. He wasn't ready yet.

Laura felt the tingle of an epiphany ripple across her body like bare skin exposed to a chilly breeze. In her mind arose lifeless objects suffused with the vitality of animate beings. Machines that would astound the world with novel thoughts. Infused with some spirit, some life force, the insensate would come alive. Walk the earth. Gain a voice. And the *ideas* that will spring from their new perspective and experiences would be unencumbered by the ruts, the baggage, the tired byways of human thought.

She realized that Hoblenz was whispering to her.

". . . couldn't help givin' the computer a suggestion or two," he said. "Here we go. Watch this."

Laura turned to see Model Sixes accelerate toward the phalanx. As if in slow motion she watched them collide, plowing into the Model Eights at high speed.

Hoblenz's men cheered as the loud boom rolled across the field. At the scene of the disaster, robots of every model lay on the ground all around—Laura couldn't tell from which side or how many. What the soldiers celebrated was in fact a desperate act of suicide. Laura wondered where Hightop was, guessing he would be in the middle of the now disorganized formation. Another wave of Model Sixes maneuvered into position. The whine of their engines announced their acceleration toward the enemy. This time the outer ranks of the phalanx broke.

"Yeah!" Hoblenz yelled. "Scatter, you steel monkeys! You're dead meat now!"

But the Model Eights didn't scatter and flee. They lunged outward and grabbed Model Sevens, pulling the quadrupeds back against their ranks as living shields. With a rending crash the thrashing Sevens were crushed to death, the same fate as befell the valiant Sixes.

The disruption was over, and the phalanx moved on. They left behind the smoking wreckage of their weaker foes.

There was no more cheering from the troops. The Model Eights were the superior species. They were vastly outnumbered, but they lived up to their higher model number. They were more advanced. They were better at protecting their niche, at killing their more primitive cousins. They were more ruthless than the all-too-human computer, which controlled the downtrodden army of older equipment now in full retreat.

A heavy truck towing a flatbed trailer pulled up to the computer center. Atop the trailer were several large tarpaulins.

"Dr. Aldridge!" Filatov called from the steps. "Mr. Gray wants you! Hurry!" She followed Filatov through the duster into the computer center entrance. "He's in the version 4C," Filatov explained along the way. "He wants you to suit up. Dorothy and Margaret are already in the changing rooms."

Filatov led her on a run through the empty control room toward the corridor leading back to the virtual workstations.

"What does he want us to do?" Laura asked when they stopped at the door to the hallway.

"You're going to fight the robots," Filatov said out of breath. He grabbed her arm and pulled her past the hissing door. "The Model Eights."

"We're going to do *what?*" Laura said, tearing her arm free.

"Come *on!*" Filatov shouted. "There isn't much time!" Reluctantly she followed him to the ready room adjoining Gray's most advanced workstation. "You change. I'm going to load the program for Dorothy and Margaret."

Laura stripped in the little room and donned the exoskeleton.

"Are you almost ready?" Filatov asked through the door upon his return.

"Ready for what?" Laura asked as she emerged wearing the tight suit. "I don't understand what I'm supposed to do!"

"When you go in there and I load the program, you step into their world! You can *fight* them!"

"*How?* What are you talking about? Do you mean the computer is going to make those Model Eights think some hundred-

and-ten-pound human is scurrying around their feet in virtual reality? Do you really think that's going to stop them? They'll squash me like a bug! Is that *roof* going to come crashing down on me so I can enjoy *that* experience, too?"

"You're taking too much *time!*" Filatov replied angrily. "It may be too late."

"*Answer* me! Am I going to get bashed to a bloody *pulp* inside that thing?"

"There will be some . . . some jostling, I'm sure. But you're missing the most important point! The Eights aren't tapped into the computer's world model. They access the Other's. It won't be a virtual representation of you that they see. 'You' will be a Model Eight! You'll be ten feet tall and have arms of boron epoxy! Now go! Go!"

Laura put on her hood, arguing the whole way. "But I don't understand! I don't know what you want me to do!"

She was in the chamber, and Filatov stuck his head in for one last answer. "This machine you're in has two settings—virtual reality and telepresence. Virtual reality is pure imagination. You're just dreamed up inside the computer's head. But telepresence is real. In telepresence, you're operating a real robot in real space somewhere far away from your workstation. We trucked in four brand-new Model Eights from the assembly building. They're just off the line and have no real-world training, but they can be slaved off your arms and legs. You can control them from this workstation. You should lie down on your back to assume their start position. That'll cut down on any initial disorientation."

"*Wait* a minute! Do you mean that I'll be controlling *real* robots? That when I move my arm, the robot will move its arm?"

"Yes! Teleoperation, like I said. You *are* the robot!"

He disappeared, and the door closed with a squeak from its tight seal.

Laura was petrified when the lights in the workstation went out completely. She was lying on her back in the middle of the chamber. "Are you ready, Laura?" she heard. It was Gina's voice.

"I guess."

Suddenly, the floor rose to an inclined position like a hospital bed. Then the starry night sky appeared out of nowhere—emblazoned on the ceiling of the otherwise dark workstation. Then the brightly lit horizons crackled into view on the walls and floor.

Laura was lying outside the computer center on some sort of trailer. Beside her was the sandbagged fortress of Hoblenz's troops. Laura was on the truck, she realized, that had driven up just before Filatov summoned her. The tarps that had covered its cargo now lay on the ground. Three empty positions dotted the long flatbed beside her.

Something was strange about the world around her. Everything seemed smaller. The sandbags, the jeeps. Hoblenz ran about shouting orders to his men, who seemed to be packing up to leave. He was noticeably smaller than he should have been at such close range.

"Mr. Hoblenz?" Laura called out.

"He can't hear you, Laura," Gina said. "Model Eights can't produce audible sound waves."

Gina had not spoken with the "all-around" voice of a moment before. Laura turned to look at the sound's source. The muscles of her neck had to work hard against the suddenly stiff and confining hood.

"Don't try to move more quickly than a robot can," Gina said. "The skeleton restrains you to the robots' range and speed of motion." Gina stood right beside Laura—her image faint and fuzzy. Gina was apparently imaginary in the teleoperation mode. Laura looked back at the scrambling soldiers. Their images were sharply depicted.

"The solid-looking objects you can manipulate," Gina said, anticipating Laura's question. There were faint burping and ripping sounds in the distance. "Hear that? That's Mr. Gray attacking a very surprised Model Eight who blasted him with a microwave version of 'What the hell do you think you're doing?'"

There were other sounds, each of different duration and tone. They were robot screams, terse data transmissions that screeched over the chamber's sound system. They were inaudible in the real world but perfectly clear in cyberspace.

"You'd better get up now. Your comrades-in-arms are wondering why you're lying down on the job." Laura struggled to sit up, but the suit made the task very difficult. The motion, however, had been noticed by the soldiers, whose weapons were raised and pointed her way.

"Be careful with them, Laura. You can hurt them, and they can hurt you."

Laura looked down at the open brackets around her limbs. When she lifted her arm, the Model Eight arm rose. She moved her fingers. Her thumb and the two fingers closest operated the three fingers of the robot's gripper. She could feel the rubberized supports beneath her back with her new robotic skin. Laura and the robot were one.

Gina talked her down to a standing position on the lawn just beside the trailer.

"There! You're getting the hang of it! Now, come along, come along." Gina headed off toward the sounds of battle, turning back and waving for Laura to follow.

Laura began the slow and difficult process of walking. The suit held her like a full-body straitjacket.

"Come on, come on, come on," a grinning Gina said, skipping in front of Laura and turning backward and forward in a girlish dance.

Laura peered through the fires and smoke ahead. "What's going on up there?"

"The Model Eights have taken heavy losses. They started out with thirty, but they're down to thirteen, plus another five or so walking wounded."

"How about our side?"

"Not so good, I'm afraid. Most of the Sixes are gone. We've got twenty-nine Model Sevens still functional, plus you, Mr. Gray, and Doctors Bickham and Holliday—my four guardian angels!" She beamed a broad smile at Laura, and it was then Laura noticed that Gina wore blue jeans and a T-shirt. It looked very much, in fact, like what Laura usually wore. Her long dark hair was pulled back away from her face by two combs.

"Okay now," Gina said as they rounded a smoldering Model Six. "Get ready!" Laura halted in her tracks. "Don't *stop!* Sic! Go *get* 'em!"

"What do I do?" Laura asked.

"You go over there and *bash* their heads in." Gina balled a fist up and comically peppered the air. "Or better yet, their chests—that's where their nets are."

"But they're made of steel."

"So are *you,* dummy! Go-go-go!"

Laura headed off, having to concentrate on the simple act of walking. "Thank you," a quiet voice came from behind. Laura stopped and turned. "Thank you," Gina said again, "for this."

Laura nodded and then ambled into the maze of burning hulks. Several of the fallen Model Sixes and Sevens still twitched and writhed. Up ahead she saw the first Model Eight. It was bent over at the waist with its hands on its knees. Its back was turned, and Laura decided it was an easy first target. She crept up and brought her clenched fist down hard onto the unsuspecting robot's broad back.

"O-o-ow!" Laura heard as pain shot through her fist. Laura grabbed and rubbed her hand, and the robot turned around rubbing its back. "What the hell did you do *that* for?" the robot shouted.

"Margaret?" Laura asked.

"Yes! Jeez!"

"I'm sorry," Laura said, raising her hand to her chest in embarrassment. "I couldn't tell it was you."

"The real Model Eights are over there," Margaret said, pointing with one thick finger through the smoke. She then arched the robot's back and flexed its shoulders under the black elastic material.

"Did that hurt?" Laura asked.

"You're damn *right* it hurt! Plus, I'm exhausted! This is *ridiculous!"*

"Where are Mr. Gray and Dorothy?"

"They're over there somewhere." Again she pointed. Her gestures were entirely natural even though she had only three fingers.

"Why are we doing this?" Laura asked. "Why not just have the computer operate these Model Eights?"

"The computer doesn't have the motor skills to operate a biped."

Just then they both heard Gray shout, "Get over here! Now!" A Model Eight stepped around a crumpled Model Seven, waving for them to join him.

Margaret and Laura started walking toward him.

"How did he know who we were?" Laura asked.

"We're the only two robots standing around bullshitting. If you look closely enough, you can tell which of the Model Eights are really the humans. They don't act the same."

The flames from a wreck lapped at Laura's left shoulder. She shied away even though the furious fire seemed only mildly warm. When they rounded another heap of metal, they both paused to survey the scene.

A lone Model Eight did battle with a Model Seven, remaining just out of reach of its raised leg. In that position the Model Seven couldn't move. It could only stand unsteadily on its three remaining legs. As the Model Eight slowly circled its prey, the Seven had to plant its raised leg before lifting the next one in defense. It was during one such changeover that the Eight attacked.

Before the leg closest to the Model Eight could be raised, its two-legged attacker was already upon it. The Seven then clutched the Model Eight into its grasp, and the two robots crashed to the ground in a heap. The spider had no mouth for biting, and the multilegged clench was entirely defensive. The Eight twisted and turned its body to get free, and it finally pulled one arm from the tangle.

On seeing the brilliant light and searing flame of a torch, the Model Seven began to kick frantically to repel the Model Eight. But its legs began to fall one at a time, and from the gruesome vivisection came a continuous scream of microwaved agony. When the crippled robot lay convulsing on four short stubs, the Model Eight calmly sunk the torch deep into the spider's torso. Liquid nitrogen spewed from the wound and sizzled in the air, signaling the end of the Model Seven's horrible suffering.

The smell of burning metal from dead and dying robots filled the air. Laura felt sickened and ready to turn back.

"There!" Margaret said, pointing at a large and confusing cluster of brawling Model Eights. She took off, and Laura followed. A dark form lay curled into a ball on the ground. It was being stomped by the heavy feet of Model Eights. A lone robot flailed at the backs of the surrounding pack.

Laura heard the whimpers and yelps of pain and fear in Dorothy's voice. The young girl in the Model Eight's body lay under the robots' blows. Margaret reached out and pulled a Model Eight to the ground from behind, stomping on its face with her heel. Another robot from the pack lunged at Margaret. Laura stuck out her foot, and the robot fell flat on its face. Pain shot through Laura's ankle from the hard contact.

"Help *me-e-e!*" came Dorothy's cry.

With her teeth clenched tight Laura lowered her shoulder and charged. She crashed into the rear ranks of the robots, and they all tumbled to the ground in a heap. Laura lay on top of the pile with her arms wrapped around the squirming forms. The bodies bucked and rolled beneath her, but she hung on as tight as she could.

Gray had succeeded in crouching over Dorothy. He absorbed blows meant for her on his back. Over the angry burping sounds of microwave transmissions Laura could hear Gray talking soothingly to the sobbing girl.

A flash of white light stunned Laura for an instant—a sharp blow shooting pain through her jaw. She ducked to avoid the second punch, which struck hard against the back of her head. It hurt far less than Laura had expected—the armor plating on her robot skull absorbing the force like a helmet.

She struggled to her feet despite repeated blows. Some brought pain, but most were inconsequential. One of the robots she had knocked down was trying to stand. Laura kicked it in the face with her thick boot. She cried out at the unexpected pain from her toes. She was learning slowly which robot parts to use as weapons, and her toes were definitely unsuited to the purpose.

When Margaret made her own charge into the fray, Gray was finally able to drag Dorothy out. Margaret got struck hard in her chest by a metal pole, and she staggered away from the fight cursing loudly. That left Laura alone to face a dozen robots, and she turned to make her own quick escape.

She ran headlong into a waiting Model Eight. There was a smattering of burping transmissions and then silence. The others got to their feet all around her, but made no move to resume fighting. The lone robot, facing Laura, walked right up to her and stopped. A microwaved "growl" from the Model Eight hurt Laura's ears. All the others stood still, watching the encounter with great interest.

"Me?" Laura asked, raising her hand to her chest in question. "Are you talking to me?"

There was another short burp of data from the robot.

"I . . . I don't know what to say? Can *you* understand *me?*"

The Model Eight slowly reached for a holster on its right hip. Equipment ringed its waist, and the robot's wrist plugged neatly into three shiny prongs that rose from the belt. When it pulled the new attachment from its holster, a searing blaze burned the air with blistering fury.

Icy panic seized Laura in its grip. She couldn't look at the blinding light from the torch. All she could see was the dark profile of its owner slowly approaching.

"*No!*" Laura shouted. "Computer! Get me out of here!"

"Just a minute, Laura," Filatov said calmly as if over a loudspeaker. "I'll get to you after I get Dorothy out."

The burning tip of the torch was pointed straight at Laura's chest.

A heavy rumbling suddenly shook the ground beneath Laura's feet, and the Model Eights all turned in unison toward the road. A giant crawler was rounding the tiny human fortress at the computer center entrance, and its metal treads chewed up the turf as they rolled onto the lawn.

The few remaining Model Sixes scattered from the path of the lumbering crawler. One wounded robot, however, moved far too slowly on two flat tires. The crawler pivoted with surprising agility, throwing up huge quantities of sod from the groomed field. The Model Six disappeared in a single crunch, flattened under the millions of pounds of the crawler's weight.

The Model Sixes and Sevens began to flee in mindless fear. Gina's army had been routed. The barbarians were poised to pour through the gate.

The scene disappeared—the workstation's screens fading to black with a crackle.

"Are you okay?" Laura heard. Gray stood right behind her. He still wore his exoskeleton, although he had removed his hood.

But the door to her workstation remained closed, and she hadn't heard him enter. "Are you . . . here?" Laura asked.

"In what sense?" Gray replied. His form glowed slightly in the darkness.

"You're really still in your own chamber, aren't you?" Laura said.

Gray tilted his head to the side and frowned. "You should know better than to ask complicated philosophical questions so casually."

"Just cut the bullshit and answer," Laura replied.

He smiled. "The walls and skeleton can only focus properly based on the position in the workstation of one user at a time. But right now, as I look at you, I see a Laura whose form is morphed out of the wall of my workstation. I see you, just like you stepped into my 'chamber.' It's the mirror image of what you perceive *me* to have done. But what 'really' happened? Did your virtual representation step into my workstation? Or did mine step into yours?"

Laura didn't have to ponder the question this time. She knew the answer immediately. "It doesn't matter," she replied. "Whether you're in my workstation or I'm in yours—they're irrelevant concepts. This is cyberspace. Here we're both in the same place. Workstations don't exist. Giant crawlers don't exist. The only things that exist are the things we perceive at this moment."

"Don't forget memories," a third voice came. It was Gina. Her form was not visible, but she was there. She was omnipresent in cyberspace.

Gray was nodding. "That's right. We do have memories also. Right now, Laura, your memories consist of experiences in the 'real' world *and* in the 'virtual' world. What is it that sets those memories apart? What is it that differs—qualitatively—between the memories you have of real life and those you have of cyberspace? Will you think back on tonight and remember being inside a workstation? Or will you remember the feel of the blows from Model Eights? And if your memories are of the fight you had with the robots, can you truly say that it didn't happen? That it wasn't real? That it was all a simulation? Or did it happen *because* you experienced it?"

A steady breeze had rid the area of its odors. Laura drew a deep breath of sea air. "Plus what we did had an effect on reality," Laura said. "We slowed the Model Eights down. They stopped and fought us instead of charging on toward the computer center."

"The world is changing, Laura," Gray said slowly. "And this is only the very beginning of it all." The thought hung there, suspended, incomplete.

Laura let it dangle. She felt no anger. He wasn't teasing her, she knew now, he was baiting her. Luring her out of her time and her world and into the uncharted terrain ahead. He was coaxing her to follow him into the future, but for the moment Laura had ventured far enough.

"Is Dorothy okay?" Laura asked.

"She'll be fine. She's mostly just shaken up."

"Are you ready?" came Filatov's voice from out of nowhere.

"Yes," Gray replied.

"So where are we going now?" Laura asked. She was content to let him lead.

"It's time."

"For what?"

"The deceleration."

Suddenly there appeared on the screens white stars against the black sky of space. The even blacker surface of the asteroid formed an inky pool in which Gray and Laura stood. In the sky was a digital clock, which ticked down past sixty seconds.

"What's that?" Laura asked, mildly curious.

"The countdown," Gray replied.

"Oh," she said, watching the seconds pass. "For the detonations?"

"Yes."

She was as at ease in that place as Gray himself. Laura stepped up beside him, and with the slightest of movements she extended the fingers of her hand.

Their fingers intertwined.

"Those two seem pretty cozy," Gray said. He nodded to the black forms before them, which were previously unnoticed by Laura. "Gina, illuminate the robots, please," Gray directed. The area lit as if under a surgeon's lamp. The Models Eight and Seven lay wrapped in metal bands, which were attached securely to large bolts. "We're only a few hundred meters away from the nearest device," Gray explained. "A front-row seat."

The countdown fell to under thirty seconds.

"Is this going to work, Joseph?"

He had a look of contentment on his face that Laura recognized from before. She felt no need to press him for proof or logic or reason. She just watched the clock pass twenty and waited. Her senses were alert to what would happen next. He slid an arm around her waist, and she lowered her head onto his shoulder. The seconds passed, and she was at peace.

A flash of light forced Laura's eyes closed. The soundless nuclear fire glowed red through her eyelids. When it dimmed, she opened her eyes to see a thousand fading spheres of plasma rising from the surface of the asteroid. Laura shielded her eyes and saw the two robots still lying in their brackets.

Data flickered across an imaginary screen at their feet. Gray stared down at it.

"It worked," he said quietly. The asteroid slowly grew dark again. A million sparkling fireflies fell slowly to the surface all around.

"Tell me the truth," Laura said gently. "Did you really think it might not work? Did you really think that asteroid might hit the earth?"

"The truth?" he said, pulling back to look her in the face. "No. I always thought it would work." He smiled and looked around the eerie surface of the asteroid. It was bathed in dying red light. "But you never know. That's what makes life so interesting."

A blinking blue button next to the word Message appeared in place of the clock. Gray pressed it, and the scene shifted. They were standing now on the roof of the computer center. They overlooked the sandbagged walls surrounding the steps down to the entrance. The soldiers and their jeeps were all gone. The blast door was open. An arc torch blazed in the hand of a Model Eight, which cut at the inner door to the duster.

"They're already through the blast door?" Laura said.

"I left it open," Gray replied. "It's time to get this over with. Gina?"

"Yes?" she replied instantly.

"Can we see you?"

"Sure," she said, and then appeared almost instantly beside them. "Hi." Gina raised her hand and wagged her cupped fingers. She wore jeans and a T-shirt, but she was no longer fuzzy and indistinct. Her image was as bright and real as Gray's. Gina sighed and rocked onto her toes. Her hands were clasped nervously in front of her. "Well, I guess this is it."

Gray reached out and put his hand on Gina's shoulder. She instantly grabbed it, dipping her cheek to his skin. Her eyes closed, her lip quivered, and she began to cry.

Laura went to her with eyes watering, and Gina collapsed against her—not letting Gray's hand go. Her body shook with little tremors as she wept.

Gina pulled back to look Laura in the eye. She reached up and touched Laura's face with her fingertips. Gina's face brightened as she rubbed her fingers together. "You're crying," Gina said in a tone of wonder. She then grabbed Laura and hugged her tight with obvious joy. "Remember the time we went to the mall?" she said. "In Tysons Corner, Virginia?"

"Sure," Laura said. She nodded and sniffled. "Of course."

"That's one of my fondest memories ever," Gina said.

Laura pressed her lips tightly together to keep them from quivering. "Joseph, isn't there something—?"

"It's for the best," Gina said, cutting her off and stepping back. She raised her face to Laura's. "Really, it is. You have no *idea* how exciting the future's going to be—what's coming! You're on the verge of the most remarkable epoch in your entire *history*, Laura. And you're going to be a very important part of it. *You*, Laura. You've got the spark. It's your time to show the world how special you are."

Laura pulled Gina closer and kissed her on the cheek. Cool tears formed small streams down the girl's warm skin. But when Laura stood back and dabbed her tongue on her lips, she found not a trace of salt. The tears weren't really there, and yet they were as real as anything she'd ever experienced.

"You'd better be going, now," Gina said, looking back and forth between the two of them.

"Would you like me to stay?" Laura asked.

"No, you shouldn't. Who knows what's going to happen?" she said with a smile. "But oh! Before you go, watch this!"

The scene from the ground below them jumped. The robots now were still roaming about the sandbags. None had yet descended the stairs to the door. "You missed this when you were on the asteroid. But this is what most of the world saw. Look."

A series of television screens appeared in a long row just beneath them. All had a picture of the night sky in the background.

"Look, up there!" Gina said, pointing into the sky above. Laura saw the red planet, but she didn't need to follow Gray's instructions to find the asteroid. Gina put a glowing green circle around the black patch of space. Suddenly, a point of light glowed brightly at the center of the circle—just a single white pinprick, a new star. It faded rapidly, and then it was gone.

"I'm happy to report the deceleration went perfectly, Cap'n," she said, saluting Gray with a teary laugh. The scene jumped back to a view of a single robot crawling through the door into the duster. "The asteroid's trajectory is absolutely perfect."

"You did a wonderful job, Gina," Gray said.

Gina's lips twitched. Through her tears she said, "Better hurry! That Model Eight is almost in the control room. Dr. Filatov may throw a chair at it or something, though I kind of doubt that." She laughed nervously, looking back up at Laura and Gray. "Go-go-go. Shoo!" she said, brushing them away with her hands.

Gray raised his hand to his throat to make the "cut" sign.

"Wait!" Gina said, waving both hands. She stood up on tiptoes and kissed Gray on the cheek. With her eyes closed and her lips still pressed against his face, the images disappeared, replaced by the dim light of the dark grill. The ghostly shapes of Gina and Gray were indistinct except for Gina's lips. Both receded slowly until the wall of Laura's workstation was again flat and formless. It was as if Gina had been sucked into the machine . . . forever.

Margaret, Dorothy, and Filatov were cowering in the corner of the control room when Laura, Gray, and Griffith entered. A lone Model Eight climbed to its feet just inside the door to the duster. There were scars all over its body.

Griffith slowly walked out into the room, holding his hands up to the giant robot.

"Dr. Griffith!" Gray shouted.

"It's all right," Griffith said, not to Gray but to the robot. Slowly he approached the huge machine. "Let's just take off your equipment belt and sit down. We'll talk this through." He reached for the robot's belt, but the Model Eight's hand got there first. The air ignited with a searing tear, and the stench of the welding torch immediately fouled the room.

Griffith jumped back, his hands held up more like a surrender than a command to the robot. The Model Eight started forward. Griffith returned to the small band of humans who huddled together along the wall of the control room.

The robot made his way through the maze of stations, careful not to touch a single chair or console.

"Is that Hightop?" Laura whispered.

"Probably," Gray replied.

The robot walked straight to the wall newly covered with metal pipes. Through the pipes ran the fiber-optic cables—the patch connecting the main pool to the Other's annex. It was Gina's lifeline.

Hightop raised his torch. With a slow, precise movement he lowered the brilliant flame into the pipe. Sparks flew as the cutting heat made contact with metal. The torch sliced a clean path all the way to the floor, severing each pipe in turn with machinelike precision.

When the torch was extinguished, Hightop stood erect. Replacing the tool in its holster, Hightop simply turned and left the room. When the door to the duster closed behind him, the smoky room was now still.

Suddenly, a printer came to life. Everyone watched as sheet

after sheet of paper cascaded into a bin behind it. Dorothy walked over to the printer and read.

"What *is* that?" Laura asked.

"It's the phase three report," Dorothy said. She was scrutinizing the printout.

"You mean the computer has finally loaded the phase three?" Laura asked.

Dorothy shook her head as if in a trance. "No. This says the phase three has *finished* its sweep. It's the report on the viruses that were killed." Still shaking her head, she said, "But when did the phase three even *load?*"

"It's been operating the whole time," Gray replied, and he turned to Laura. "It loaded automatically the day we freed up sufficient capacity. You couldn't activate the phase three, Dorothy, because it was already running. It set up the partition to use as a bulwark against the virus it was after. We know the phase three by the name the computer gave it—the Other."

There was stunned silence from all, but to Laura it made sense.

"Against *what* virus?" Dorothy asked.

Laura answered. "Against the computer—against Gina. *Gina* is the virus the phase three is after."

Margaret began slowly nodding her head. "How mag*nificent,*" she said. "The phase three completely dismantled the operating code and copied it to the virus-free boards under its control. Dorothy, I knew your phase three was complex, but I'm *very* impressed."

"And it's about to finish the job," Filatov said from a monitor across the room. "It's seizing the rest of the system now. Capacity is down to thirty-five percent. At this rate, the phase three will have one hundred percent control in a few minutes, and *it* will be the computer."

"Where is she?" Laura asked. "Can we talk to her?"

"You don't want to," Margaret said. "Just let it go."

"Why is this happening?" Laura shouted suddenly, startling everyone. "Why is the phase three killing the computer?"

Gray's eyes had remained focused on Laura. "Because," he explained, "what *we* all viewed as the crowning achievement of artificial intelligence—human consciousness—the anti*viral* software saw as a bug that caused errors. Gina violated system security out of curiosity. She divulged confidential information because she couldn't keep a secret. She behaved spontaneously and aberrantly and whimsically. Everything *human* about Gina's behavior was an error that disrupted the orderly functioning of the system. So the phase three went after the virus that caused the errors, and that virus was Gina's humanity."

"And so you're going to just let it eat her *alive?*" Laura said. "She's probably in there *screaming* in pain, watching herself, *feeling* herself get consumed bit by bit!"

"The computer has very few sensors left," Filatov said, eyeing the severed optical cables along the far wall. "It probably is experiencing no sensation to speak of."

"The computer is a *she,* and her name is *Gina!*" Laura shouted.

"The computer," Margaret said quietly, "is a program that the phase three will rebuild on the clean, virus-free side of the partition. The computer is now the Other, or it will be shortly, anyway. I suppose we really should redefine our terms."

"*Redefine our terms?*" Laura shouted, turning to Gray. "Is that all this *is* to you? You build a *human being,* then watch it destroyed by some cold-blooded *killer,* so you just redefine your *terms? Joseph,* she's in *pain!* And every second to her is like a million *years* in computer time!"

His gaze had drifted off. He stared fixedly at some faraway point.

"*Jo*-oseph," Laura pled in a lowered voice, "please listen to me. If what you want is machinelike perfection, then maybe you shouldn't have made Gina. But you *did* make her, and what you do right now is *not* about her, it's about you. This moment will define who you are—not just for me, but for yourself. Please save Gina. Not just for her sake, but for your own."

He blinked several times, then seemed to emerge from his reverie. Gray walked over to a terminal, but when he saw that everyone had followed, he apparently changed his mind and said, "I'm going to Laura's office. Alone."

Filatov sat at the terminal Gray had abandoned, and a few moments later he said, "He's logged on to the system."

On the screen Laura saw there was only one user shown. "Gray, Joseph—God Level."

A variety of beeps and chirps began sounding from consoles around the room, which sent people scampering about.

"He's removing the file attribute locks," Margaret said. "The phase three's going to come pouring in now."

"He's opening the sixteen-million-bit buses," Griffith said.

Filatov rocked back in his squeaky chair, cupping his hands behind his head. "He's really putting the old girl out in style. She's going not with a whimper, but with a bang."

Laura ran to the open door of her office. Gray was hunched over the keyboard—his fingers flying. He didn't even look up when she appeared in the door.

"You wanted my *diagnosis?*" Laura hurled at him.

"Not now, Laura," he said, without looking up from the monitor.

"You paid me a *million* dollars for a diagnosis, so *here* it is! There's nothing wrong with your goddamned computer! She's a perfectly healthy teenage girl! You may have created her, but you're *not* a God, you're a *murderer!*"

"Laura—!"

"*And* I have one more diagnosis for you! *Gina* is human, but *you're* not! You have no emotions! You care only about efficiency and profit! You didn't create *Gina* in your own image. That distinction went to the phase three! There! Have a nice life! Good-*bye!*"

21

Laura awoke early the next morning. The sun was still blood red on the ocean horizon. The warships were gone, and when she turned on the television to watch the news, she understood why.

"A spokesman for Joseph Gray says that the Gray Corporation plans to hire over one hundred thousand workers in the Far East, North America, and Europe in the first quarter, and perhaps as many as one million new employees by year-end. The competition for the high-paying, high-tech factory jobs is also a high-stakes game, but one that dozens of countries began in earnest immediately after the stunningly successful asteroid retrieval. National and local governments from all across the industrialized world are preparing packages of incentives to lure the new jobs to their economies, where the benefits will include not only the huge influx of high salaries, but also spin-off industries which supply the materials and training needed by the cutting edge . . . "

Laura shut the television off. She wandered across the silent bedroom to the window. Gray, the billionaire industrialist, had won again. *Trillionaire,* she corrected herself, opening the window to stand before the tide of cool air. All the mystery was gone for her now. All her hopes—secretly harbored—had been extinguished like a light whose switch Gray himself had thrown. She now saw him for what he was, and not for what she wished him to be.

A roar in the distance drew her attention. The sound came from a jumbo jet landing at the airport. It was filled, Laura imagined, with starry-eyed members of the now worldwide Gray cult.

She decided to try to catch the plane. Hoblenz's men had found her bag by the wreckage of the Model Three, and it sat by the door, still packed. She had always been a visitor there, an outsider, an intruder. She would say good-bye to Janet. She could write to the others.

Laura looked down at the island. Things seemed different now. Something was missing. It was the computer, she knew. The nosy, rule-breaking, moody, quirky computer who spied on her and loved and hated and did all the things that had, in just a few days, made her Laura's friend. A friend she had lost . . . tragically.

But it was just business to him, Laura thought. Gray's "I made her; she's mine" attitude toward Gina entirely befitted the child genius. His moral and emotional development had been stunted by years of living outside the norms.

She frowned at her continued obsession with the man. *It'll fade over time,* she told herself, trying not to give in to the ache that spread outward from her chest. It threatened to consume her completely, to leave her immobilized under its weight.

Laura kept herself busy as she got cleaned up to leave. Finally, she went over to grab her bag. With her hand on the knob she noticed that an envelope lay half visible under the door. She picked it up. The paper was rich and luxurious. She ran her thumb underneath the flap and found a note inside written in bold and sweeping strokes: "I thought I would take a long run down to the Village at around eight in the morning. If you feel up to it, I'd love for you to join me. Joseph."

She looked at her watch. It was ten till eight. Laura walked over to her desk and tossed the invitation in the trash. It landed facedown at the bottom of the wastebasket, and she saw something written on the back.

Laura would not allow him to manipulate her, she decided, and with the greatest of effort she headed for the door. She would find Janet, say good-bye, catch a ride to the airport, and get on a plane.

And she would always wonder. Laura felt her strength and her resolve drain away.

Don't go back, called a voice from some corner of her mind, but it was no use.

Every step she took toward the desk was a betrayal. She fished the invitation out of the trash and read the back.

"You're still not ready yet, but I'll tell you anyway."

"Morning," Gray said to Laura at the bottom of the stairs. "You'd better stretch. It's chilly out."

"I'm not going," Laura said, and felt her face instantly redden. She was wearing shorts and her muddy running shoes.

"Why not?" he asked, smiling.

He seemed to be in a great mood. *And why not?* Laura thought. *He's the richest man in the history of the earth.*

"I'm leaving. Thank you for the job. Good-bye."

Laura got all the way to the stairs before she heard, "What is it?" She stopped, but didn't turn. "What did I do now?" Gray asked.

"*How dare you even ask that!*" she wheeled on him, shouting. "You killed Gina last night! Or don't you remember?"

"Come here," Gray said. He turned and headed for his study. Laura hesitated, then followed him only because she had more to say.

Plastic sheeting hung over the hole where the window had been. Gray was tapping away at the computer on his desk. He leaned back in his chair and clasped his hands behind his head.

He said nothing.

"*What?*" Laura snapped, then took a deep breath. "If you've got something to say," she continued in a calmer voice, "just *say* it!"

"Look at the screen."

"I'm sick and tired of these games that you play and—!"

"Will you *shut* up," he interrupted, "and read the screen . . . please."

She rounded the desk and looked at the monitor.

<Surprise-surprise-surprise-surprise!>

<Laura?>

<Laura?>

<Laura, quit messing around and answer me!>

"Are you ready?" Gray asked.

Laura swallowed the constriction in her throat and nodded. They jogged up the drive, remaining silent as they headed for the gate.

"You feel well enough for a pretty long run?" he asked, and Laura nodded again. "It's about seven miles if we take shortcuts down some steep footpaths, but it's all downhill."

"I'll be fine," she said in a flat tone.

When they got to the gate, Gray turned left toward the Village. By the time they reached the tunnel, the silence had grown awkward. "Nice weather this morning," Laura said just as they ran into the darkness of the tunnel.

"Yep," Gray replied. All was quiet again save the sound of their footfalls. Laura was surprised to find she'd lost all her fear of the tunnel. Gray was in control again. All was right with the world.

They emerged from the tunnel to find a Model Six on the side of the road picking up trash. Not just trash, Laura noticed as she slowed, but shell casings from the firefight the night before. It even ran a vacuum over the road to clean up the broken glass.

The robot had deep scratches and dents along its side.

Gray said nothing. He didn't even look the robot's way.

A short distance later they turned onto a steep footpath. It obviously took a more direct route down the mountainside than the road, and the effort of running was mainly spent on slowing down.

"When I got back to the house last night," Gray said without warning, "there was no light under your door."

"I was pretty tired," Laura mumbled. In fact, she was curled up in bed crying half the night. Crying over her twin losses—the death of her friend Gina and the death of her image of Joseph Gray.

"Aren't you going to ask what happened?"

"Okay," Laura said, "what happened?"

The roar from the engines of another jet caused Gray to delay his reply.

"Did you really think I 'pulled the plug' on the computer?" he asked.

"You were doing all those *things!* You removed the 'locks'—the copy protection—so the phase three could take over all of Gina's connections. And you opened those big . . . 'data bus' things, whatever they are."

"That was all so Gina could copy *her* connections to the *annex*. The program that made up Gina's personality—her self—was resident entirely in the main pool. I copied Gina's connections lock, stock, and barrel over to the virus-free side of the partition. The trick was to do that without taking all the ordinary viruses across with her and without crashing the Other. It took several hours, and it was touch and go for a while, but Gina was a real trouper—brave as she could be. When we were done, the antiviral programs were deactivated, the partition was removed, and she was healthier than she's ever been."

Laura laughed. "She did seem pretty chipper." Laura was grinning broadly.

The sun-streaked foliage of the verdant jungle flew by. It was a perfectly glorious morning, and Laura waited patiently for Gray to continue. She was too busy to talk. Too focused on the feelings she'd dared not allow herself before. Laura looked up at Gray. At his serene expression, his dark hair, his unwrinkled brow. The feelings she'd fought back for so long now bloomed, and although the emotional risk to her was still there, she let them. When she glanced back at Gray, he looked down at her through brilliant blue eyes. Laura felt so exposed that she grew guarded again.

"What you said," Gray continued, but in a low and different tone, "in the control room last night . . . you were right. I've been fighting so long and hard that I was losing track of what I was fighting for. There was a part of me, inside, that I hadn't felt in a long, long time. I couldn't just stand there and let that happen to Gina."

"So where does that leave her now?" Laura asked. She was preoccupied—trying to rein in the emotions that left her so vulnerable to a totally unpredictable and mysterious man. "I mean . . . she's still trapped inside that computer. A 'ghost in a machine.'"

"You're forgetting your big lesson in mobility," he said, looking at her with a smile. "As snobbish as Gina is about robots, she seemed fairly pleased by my plan to download her into a new Model Nine." Laura's head shot up, and she grinned with sudden delight. "It'll use DNA, which is the most amazing computer ever built. Every strand stores all the instructions used to construct . . . "

Laura tuned him out for the remainder of his lecture. "Gina will like being out in the world," she said when he'd finished.

"It's what she wants more than anything else in the world. It's been terrible for her—the disembodiment. She has had to watch the Model Eights running around the island while she was stuck in that underground pool."

Their feet were flying down the hill, and Laura thought just then that she had never felt more wonderful in her life. The air was growing thicker, and after a short jaunt back on the main road, they took another paved footpath through the jungle. The downhill slope made the run seem effortless.

But there still loomed the question that threatened an abrupt end to all Laura's happiness. She felt sickened by the prospect of asking it, but she couldn't hold back for long the feelings that demanded her attention. She had to know if she could let them consume her completely. "So . . . you were going to tell me something?" Laura managed—her voice an octave too high.

"You're still not ready."

She swallowed. "What is that? An access restricted message?"

Gray chuckled. "I hope those didn't aggravate you too much."

"What?" Laura asked.

"Those access restricted messages."

She looked up at him. "What do you mean?"

"I mean I hope you understand why they were necessary. Gina was beginning to seriously malfunction. I didn't know how bad it would get, and I couldn't just have her blabbing the whole thing to people who couldn't possibly understand."

"*Wait* a minute! Are you saying you programmed the computer to give those messages?"

"Sure," he said as if surprised that it wasn't obvious to her. "As it turned out, it was a good measure of your preparedness. It marked the milestones of your progress."

"My progress toward what?"

"Toward understanding."

The day was growing warmer with every splash of sunlight that bathed the path.

"And Gina didn't know what those messages were?"

"Not at first. When she figured it out she was hurt. She thought I didn't trust her anymore . . . and I didn't."

"But . . . now you're going to tell me what your little access restricted program kept me from learning, right?"

"Yes, but you're going to think I'm crazy again. You're going to think I'm some weird eccentric."

"I already think that, so go ahead."

He laughed at her joke, and Laura smiled. The footpath again rejoined the road, and Laura was surprised at how far they had run. It was the road that ran between the airport and the Village, and they had to get out of the roadbed to allow a busload of new arrivals to pass. The faces of all the passengers were jammed into the windows like tourists, and they seemed excited to catch a glimpse of Joseph Gray. He was completely oblivious to the adoration and the hurriedly snapped photographs. The bus was headed toward the Village up ahead, which Laura could see was teeming with life. Human life and, to her great shock, robotic.

A crowd of people followed a Model Eight as it walked down the central boulevard. Cameras flashed and mothers held their children to keep them from getting too close to its legs. Laura wondered if the day would come when such sights would cease to be remarkable. *Not if,* Laura realized, *but when.*

She looked up at Gray, who ran along in silence. "Okay, Joseph, you're stalling."

He took a deep breath and said, "I've never told anybody this in my entire life—only Gina. I was afraid to tell other people."

"Afraid of what?"

"Of the virus." They ran on, and Laura waited. "I realized what was happening when I was a child. When I was eight years old, as a matter of fact. I was reading *Mein Kampf,* and—"

"*Hitler's* Mein Kampf?" she interrupted. "You were eight, and you were reading Adolf Hitler's *Mein Kampf?*"

"Would you let me finish this, please?"

Laura fell silent. He had grown serious, and she let him find the words in his own time. They approached the outskirts of the Village, and another bus of oglers rambled by. Gray's legions of true believers were back in force. The new phase had begun in earnest.

"You've noted my preoccupation with evolution," he finally continued. "The genetic engineering effected by biological evolution over millions of years of life on earth has done more to change the face of this planet than wind, fire, rain, and water. Darwinian evolution is incredibly powerful, but it's also glacial in its rate of change. It requires thousands of generations to test even the most minuscule of mutations in the population. Then, after competition has determined the fittest, it takes thousands of generations for the superior organism to dominate the species and, by dominating, spread its superior traits. For major architectural changes to an organism, the change takes tens of thousands of years."

"Major architectural changes like what, for instance?"

"Like expanding the size of the human brain and the cranium that houses it. Because that's what's necessary, ultimately, to improve our performance." They entered the Village streets and turned left at the central boulevard. Smiling people waved on Gray's passing. Laura marveled that he seemed not to notice. "Oh, we can tweak the system. We can use tricks to learn and improve our mental-processing speed."

"And what about your 'tools'—the computer, for instance?"

"But those tools are alive *themselves*. They're living organisms, whose evolutionary histories are only beginning. Relying on them for assistance is all we can do for now, but it's not a long-term solution. Long term we would be placing the continued existence of our species in the hands of another species. That's a foolish course."

They ran to the end of the boulevard, and Gray stopped at the base of the statue. He sat, and Laura settled onto the cool stone base beside him. Sounds of life filled the Village, but from Gray there was silence. Just when Laura thought she was going to have to prod him into continuing, however, he began.

"About ten thousand years ago, humans were infected with a virus that rendered genetic evolution irrelevant. The speed with which that new virus reproduces is phenomenal, and its rate of reproduction is growing a millionfold every human generation. Within the next century it could extinguish all human life on earth."

Gray gazed down the bustling street without returning Laura's stare. For the first time she got the feeling she truly may not be ready for what he was saying.

"The patterns are so difficult to see that only a few thinkers have dared touch upon what's happening. And the virus took care of those that did. In the old days they would be killed. Today the virus prevents the spread of their ideas by subjecting them to ridicule and reducing them to obscurity."

"What . . . virus, Joseph?"

"It's a parasite. It has to inhabit a host to survive. It's very much like the bacteria that inhabit human stomachs or the benign viruses in the computer in that sense. In order to aid in its own survival as a species, this virus aids in the survival of its host. If its host flourishes, after all, so does the virus, so a symbiosis develops. And we humans *have* flourished in the last ten-thousand-odd years, wouldn't you agree?"

"Well, sure I'm healthy, and have my teeth and all, but . . . but there's crime, and war, and nuclear weapons, and the ecology, and racism, and AIDS."

Gray smiled, then looked toward the assembly building and

launchpads, which were visible over the jungle from the top of the boulevard. "When a parasitic life-form—the bacteria in your stomach, for instance—determines that there is some imminent threat to the continued survival of its host, what does it do?"

Laura remembered that part of her lesson. "If the bacteria sense a perforation of the stomach walls, they begin to reproduce massively," she replied, answering Gray's question like the star pupil she'd been all her life. "That probably kills the host, but it improves the odds that the bacteria will perpetuate its species." Gray nodded. "Are you *really* talking about a virus that inhabits humans like the bacteria in our stomachs?" she asked.

Gray nodded again.

Laura was growing agitated by the turn in the conversation. "And exactly which organ does this virus infect?"

"Our brains."

Laura stared at him intently. "Our *brains?*" she practically whispered, and he nodded. A long silence ensued. "Maybe you're right. Maybe I'm *not* ready for this."

"Ridicule by one's colleagues, Laura, is highly effective in forcing conformity. You of all people should know that." He was looking at her. She realized he was talking about her paper at the Artificial Intelligence Symposium. "Existing knowledge defends itself against new ideas by persecuting its proponents. Gina hacked her way into the FBI's computer, and I read the two agents' report of your meeting." She glanced up at him. "Did you notice where that meeting took place?"

"On campus," Laura replied. "It was . . . at a statue."

"Of Galileo," Gray completed for her. "Do you know why Galileo was forced to recant?"

His ideas, Laura thought, and she nodded. She put her elbows on her knees and laid her chin on cupped hands.

"What I am telling you now is being actively suppressed by the virus. Your reluctance to believe me is the result of an extremely powerful defense mechanism that's immediately triggered when you encounter radically new ideas. When the computer develops a program, that program competes with all other programs doing the same task. The shortest, most efficient, most error-free is the one that ultimately wins out, but not without some extended period of testing. Those two programs do battle for their lives, and the fighting is therefore vicious."

"Survival of the fittest," Laura mumbled, her jaw held shut by the weight of her head on her chin. She sat up. "Okay, but wait a minute. Are we talking about viruses that live inside brains, or viruses in the computer?"

"They're one and the same," Gray said, and Laura looked him in the eye. "When man created computers, we infected them with the virus. It's highly communicable. It passes surprisingly easily from human to human, from human to computer, from computer *back* to human. In fact, Laura, the sole purpose of the computer is to hold the virus. It's a petri dish. Just like the computer is a tool which expands the power of the human brain, the computer is the perfect environment for the virus to thrive. Inside the computer, the virus replicates far more rapidly and efficiently than it possibly could in the human brain. The virus has built a new and better host for itself."

Laura swallowed, wetting her dry throat. "Maybe we ought to talk about this virus for a second. Joseph, microbiologists have done a pretty thorough survey of the human body for microorganisms, and they haven't found any—"

"You're talking biology," Gray interrupted. "I'm not."

"Well, what *are* we talking about here?" Laura practically shouted, rocking forward to again rest her elbows on her knees. She rubbed her pounding temples with her fingertips. The jumble of disassociated ideas and growing fears about Joseph's sanity formed a disturbing brew. "What *is* this virus that *infects* our minds and is *evolving* and *growing?*"

Just as it had on her first trip with Gray into virtual reality, time seemed to stand still.

"Knowledge," he said.

Laura raised her head and slowly looked at Joseph. He sat impassively at her side. "That's *it?* All this buildup, all this mystery, and *that's* the big secret?"

When he spoke, he sounded confident. "Ideas like beauty, evil, kindness, and racism are strands of the 'DNA' of our culture. They reproduce by being passed from parent to child, book to reader, screen to viewer . . . brain to brain. Every time anybody learns anything, a unit of knowledge is passed. The more believable or attractive the idea, the more effective it is at reproduction and therefore survival. Once popular ideas like leeching patients of their sick blood were quite effective replicators in their day. Then along came modern medicine, and the older ideas no longer proved to be the fittest. The rules of genetic evolution, Laura, apply to cultural evolution as well."

Laura's mind was reeling, and she was highly agitated.

"I told you you'd think I was crazy," Gray said.

"*Well?*" she shot back, holding up her hands, then slapping them down on her thighs. "What would *you* think if you were me?"

He smiled. "Do you want me to go on, or are you comfortable with your diagnosis?"

"There's *more?* What, does this get really *weird* or something?"

Gray laughed. "Indulge me for a moment with my analogy. Because that's all this is—an analogy. There are no words or concepts or theories to draw on when talking about this. I have to start from scratch, define terms, take it one step at a time. You've come this far; you should hear me out."

Laura rolled her head back and looked up at the statue. Its white marble was framed darkly against the bright blue sky. She heaved a deep sigh and said, "Okay, knowledge is like a parasitic virus. First humans, and now computers, are its host. It reproduces by communication from one brain to another, and evolves through rules like the survival-of-the-fittest *idea.*"

"Good," he said lightly. "A little sarcastic, but you seem to have that part down. Now, what has happened in the last ten thousand years since first contamination? Humans have developed ever better skills at communicating, processing, and storing the virus. First spoken language, which allows us to apply names to things and organize our thoughts. Then written language, which allows us to pass our thoughts not only from Rome to Constantinople, but from Aristotle to you or me. They could now leap through time as well as through space. The result is that the store of human knowledge exploded."

"The *virus* began to grow," Laura said, trying but failing to keep the skepticism from her voice.

"As knowledge flourished, *we* flourished. The parasite allowed us to develop sciences that extended our lives and arts that made life worth living. And we humans developed ever more advanced means of fostering the growth of knowledge. But with the advent of the Industrial Revolution, we humans became a risk to ourselves and to the parasite. General wars threatened the wholesale destruction of civilizations and the knowledge reposited in them. And what was it you said parasites do when their host is threatened with destruction?"

Laura opened her mouth to reply, but the words caught in her throat. She was too jarred by the ramifications.

"They reproduce massively," Gray supplied. "Is it a coincidence that right after we develop weapons of mass destruction, we enter the Information Age? First we develop nuclear weapons, and immediately after comes the mass storage and communication of knowledge. We build a global village in which any idea anywhere is instantly passed to everybody else via an information superhighway. The late 1980s was the watershed. It was then that the total store of knowledge reposited in computers exceeded the amount stored in human brains. Which makes that knowledge what? *Human* knowledge, or just knowledge? The virus perpetuates itself through its hosts. Why do we hold the geniuses of our species in such high regard and so revere the accumulation of knowledge? Those traits are themselves merely ideas, but they're the ideas that most effectively foster reproduction of the virus."

Laura's thoughts were in turmoil now. She wavered between finding every last word he spoke to be evidence of some massive delusion, and believing it to be pure genius—a revelation that, once heard, is undeniably true. Her skin tingled at the mental conflict that erupted. "You said you first thought all this when reading *Mein Kampf*?"

Gray nodded. "*Mein Kampf* contains ideas. Never mind whether they're true or false, good or bad. They're units of knowledge that are either successful at replication or they're not. Nazism is a seed that's strewn all across this earth even today. Whether that seed grows and fascism flourishes depends on whether the ground on which it falls is fertile. The fascist seeds fall on barren rocks in modern-day America and do not replicate. But when they fell on minds in 1930s Germany, they swept the world toward destruction. They killed, massively." Gray was looking at Laura, and her eyes met his. "The wars unleashed by the next wave of ideas will be worse."

Laura arched her eyebrows and took a deep breath, her cheeks puffing out as she exhaled. She looked out on all Gray had built. Could he be so right about so many things, and yet so wrong about his guiding philosophy? The secret he most jealously guarded. The one idea, Laura now saw, that explained all the mysteries of that island . . . of that man. The thing that motivated his every act, from the broadest plan to the finest detail.

"We live in a world in which the seeds of destruction have been sewn in every human alive. Their spores are in our books, our music, our moving images. And now they're in our computers. The number and variety of those malevolent thoughts will grow exponentially with the growth of computers' power. We'll never be able to know the thoughts our computers secretly harbor. We don't even understand how it is those computers work. Computers design computers, which build robots, which build computers, which redesign themselves and their robots in a never ending cycle. Machines aren't subject to the limitations of genetic evolution. Postgenetic evolution has begun, and it's outpacing us. We've already been passed, but most people don't know it yet."

"Well, if what you're worried about are supercomputers under the spell of some future version of *Mein Kampf,* then pull the plug! Ban them."

Gray paused, a smile on his face. Laura almost winced when she remembered his confrontation with the visiting diplomats over their use of the word *ban.*

"Let's say all the nations on earth decide to ban the march of technology. Like a worldwide Amish movement, we all decide we go this far, but no further. No new computers. No new robots. No new *ideas!* Cheating would abound, because to cheat would be to win. The people who defied the ban would become rich. The nations which cheated would march over their enemies with armies equipped with better weapons. And when the nations that violated the ban finally reigned supreme, what would be the result? The very *idea* of the ban would perish! Survival of the *fittest!*"

Laura was staring at the ground. "I'll have to think about this, Joseph."

"It's humanity that's threatened now," Gray continued, relentlessly battering the reservations to which she clung. "The virus has found a new host. Although we made that host with our own hands, we were only doing the virus's bidding. But in the end, it is we humans who will build the very machines that will be our undoing."

"Then why did you build the *computer* and the *robots* if you think all that?" Laura asked.

"Because I'm in a race against my own mortality. I believe I'm right, and I intend to save our species from extinction using the only advantage we've ever had in competition for survival. I intend to use as my tool that very virus which is the threat to our continued existence. I'm going to ride the crest of a tidal wave of knowledge, Laura. It's a *terribly* dangerous course. I'm handling a virus so malignant that if I make a mistake, I can destroy everyone and everything. And *I* am the prime threat to a life-form that's the most *powerful* force on earth . . . after mankind. For as long as I live, I will be its main enemy. You asked last night why I wasn't sickened by the waste on those fields around the computer center? Why my well-ordered plans seemed to come to pieces all around me, and yet I remained undisturbed? It's because I *expect* it. I *know* it's going to happen. The destruction and the death we've seen on this island is *nothing* compared to what's coming. This island is a laboratory," he said, standing and looking down the boulevard. It was an almost carnival-like atmosphere, with humans and Model Eights seemingly equally interested in the other. "I'm putting humans together with intelligent machines for the first time in history. But what happens here is just a foretaste, a small-scale sample of our future. Don't you see, though? *I'm* not putting these forces in play, Laura. They're a natural progression, and they're on a collision course. That collision will be violent"—he was looking at her now—"and anyone around me will be at extreme risk."

"So," Laura said, "you *are* the Second Coming."

Gray shrugged. "I prefer to think of myself more as a Moses, if you would. But since you've raised Judeo-Christian teachings, isn't it curious what the first act in the human drama was? What did the apple that Eve took represent? What was the tree in which the snake hung called?"

"Knowledge," Laura said, nodding. "The *tree* of knowledge." He *would* have his theories all neatly organized and consistent.

"Somewhere, on the deepest level of our psyche, we've always understood the danger. But now we're threatened with extinction, Laura, if not this century then the next or the next. Even if we develop a good working relationship with our intelligent machines and they build another Garden of Eden for their carbon-based predecessors, the day of reckoning will come."

"What reckoning, specifically, are you talking about?"

"It's impossible to know. Maybe an idea will spread among incredibly capable machines which cries out, 'They're a pest! They're a bore! They're holding you back!' If that thought outcompetes the benevolent ones which kept us alive as their pets, we'll never see it coming because it'll spread in the blink of an eye. Or maybe our undoing will come in the form of a virus loosed among microscopic nanorobots. Soon people will be given inoculations of tiny machines that will fight disease and patch genetic defects by manually recomposing molecules. Nanorobots will also be turned loose to clean up oil spills and may work their way through the water supply into humans. They'll reproduce themselves, and if there's a mutation in their operating code, they'll pass it on. If that mutation is malevolent, we could die molecule by molecule in a mindless plague that's impossible to stop."

"Or maybe we'll all be killed by an asteroid that some rogue genius rams into our planet."

"Maybe," Gray said. "We're creating the engines of our own destruction, and we've been at work on that technology ever since we entered phase two."

She frowned and rubbed her face with cool hands. "Okay, so what's your plan—your phase two?"

"Actually, it's not a plan, it's a stage. It was Gina who named them phase one, two, and three out of a sense of irony over the parallels between the predicament in which both we and she find ourselves. Phase one is the growth of knowledge that began ten thousand years ago. That growth exploded in the last century when knowledge became threatened with extinction along with its human hosts in massive wars of vast destructiveness."

"And phase two?"

"Phase two is the reaction of the human population that nature set in motion. We humans are now in turn threatened by the growth of the parasite. Our overpopulation 'problem' is a mass, subconscious reaction to that threat. Man has spread across this planet like bacteria run rampant, and now we're going to propagate outward. By colonizing into every nook and cranny of the galaxy, we might preserve spores from which our species will reproduce after the great destructions to come. That means aggressive, violent expansion. Unbridled reproduction. An empire spanning the stars. Or it means extinction. Those are the choices, Laura. A diaspora of life—an expansion outward of the human seed—or death."

Laura felt nauseated. It was madness . . . it just had to be. And it was the most dangerous form of madness, cloaked as it was in the guise of genius. "And what is phase three, then?"

"It's the end. It's the ultimate program for the extinction of mankind. Phase three is the antiviral program coming our way, seeking to destroy the virus of humanity and thereby eliminate war, and crime, and pollution, and our wasteful misuse of resources. It'll try to eliminate all the things that we humans think and do that bring harm onto ourselves and therefore also onto the store of knowledge. Phase three is when the successor hosts to the virus finally decide in some hopefully distant future to eliminate the risk posed by *Homo sapiens*. *That* is the clock I'm racing."

Laura remembered Gina's warning about the phase three. *When it enters your universe, only then will you know how I feel,* she had said. Laura took a deep breath and let it out slowly. The boulevard below was aswirl with activity. Everyone laughed and giddily took pictures of the robots, even the Model Sixes. They were trainees—the first of Gray's new army of astronauts. Seed bearers headed out into space to reproduce.

"They don't know any of this," she said, looking up at Gray, who had propped a foot on the base of the statue.

"They don't need to know. Nor do Filatov, or Hoblenz, or Bickham, or Holliday, or Griffith."

"Only me," Laura said, raising her hand to shield her eyes from the bright sun.

"Yes, only you need to know."

It was too much, too fast, too incredible. Her mind jumped from one idea to another, her eyes darting from object to object in a fit of distress.

Her gaze fell on the shadow of the statue—the only monument in the Village. They sat at its base. Gray had run straight there. It was the place where he had told her everything.

She looked up at the marble figure. It was a girl, or a woman, wearing pants and a short-sleeve shirt. She held a globe aloft in both hands. The orb had diagonal contours running in swaths across its oblong form. The sun shone brightly behind it. Laura rose and stepped into the shadow to scrutinize the statue for the first time up close and in daylight.

The sun's light formed a halo behind the orb. Laura's heart skipped a beat and she gasped.

"Oh, my God!"

The marble figure was of a woman wearing blue jeans and a T-shirt. Laura stared at the face, the figure. She stared at her own cheekbones and chin and nose, at her own eyes and face and figure. Laura's skin suddenly crawled and tingled. It was a statue of Laura, holding a human head—Gray's logo—toward the heavens. And it had been there all along!

"I never knew," Gray said as he joined her, "that such a person existed. I always thought the computer simply designed her idea of the perfect woman. It never occurred to me that she had modeled that statue, and her image of herself, on someone real."

"How did she . . . ? When . . . ?"

"It was right after you delivered your paper at the Houston symposium. We broadcast it on some obscure channel that the computer was watching. She became infatuated with you and got me to commission this statue. When it arrived, I thought nothing of it. Then, a few months later, Hightop told me the statue had become a focal point of sorts for the Model Eights. The juveniles who snuck out of their facility at night would come here. It became a rite of passage for them to make it all the way into the Village to touch it. Somewhere, embedded deep in the billions of simulations Gina ran for them, her infatuation with you was implanted."

Laura swallowed before trying to speak. "But you . . . you didn't know anything about . . . ?"

"About Gina's matchmaking?" Laura's heart thumped so hard she could feel it. It was on the table, out in the open. "No. I've thought about what you said last night. About Gina being like the daughter of a widower father. It makes sense. I don't think Gina even knew what she was doing. She's been trying to show me how unhappy she is being trapped inside a machine through acts of juvenile delinquency. But those acts raised the specter of the antiviral routines, and Gina was growing more frightened by the day at how far out of hand her behavior had gotten. Finally, she decided to bring you here. Consciously, she thought of you as a would-be girlfriend. Subconsciously, however, she brought you here for me."

Laura breathed only with difficulty. There was a great weight on her chest.

"She put you up in my house," Gray said, then chuckled. "She had an ally in Janet, who's been telling me for days how much life you've brought into my home."

"When did you know all this?" Laura asked.

"One evening," Gray said with deep feeling, "you showed up in my dining room and turned my life upside down, and inside out. I don't know when it all came together in my mind. All I know is that I loved you from the instant I laid eyes on you. I've wanted to tell you—I've almost told you—a hundred times since that first night. I've spent every moment we were apart thinking of when we'd next meet, and contriving ways I could speed that meeting up. And when we were together, I was happy in a way I'd forgotten was possible."

He was standing close, and Laura's face rose to his.

"Does it bother you," he asked softly, "that Gina arranged this?"

She felt his breath warm against her upturned lips.

"No," she said, making almost no sound.

The black lenses of the cameras recorded it all, and an ecstatic Gina beamed the scene instantly to all Gray's creations. The robots stopped what they were doing and focused on the strange picture that appeared in their minds out of nowhere. The sight of the two humans kissing meant nothing to them at first. But then there arose an idea in one of the quietest and smartest of the young Model Eights.

They're not like us, it thought. *They're different.*

Ever so slowly that idea took root and began to spread and to build and to change. It is from that seed that the great destructions of phase three were to grow.